THE COMPLETE WORKS OF WALTER TROBISCH

ANSWERS ABOUT LOVE, SEX, SELF-ESTEEM & PERSONAL GROWTH

With an Introduction by Ingrid Trobisch

INTERVARSITY PRESS
DOWNERS GROVE, ILLINOIS 60515

InterVarsity Press is the book-publishing division of InterVarsity Christian Fellowship, a student movement active on campus at hundreds of universities, colleges and schools of nursing. For information about local and regional activities, write Public Relations Dept., InterVarsity Christian Fellowship, 6400 Schroeder Rd., P.O. Box 7895, Madison, WI 53707-7895.

Distributed in Canada through InterVarsity Press, 860 Denison St., Unit 3, Markham, Ontario L3R 4H1, Canada.

Cover photograph: H. Armstrong Roberts, Inc.

ISBN 0-87784-524-7

Printed in the United States of America

Library of Congress Cataloging in Publication Data

Trobisch, Walter.
The complete works of Walter Trobisch.

Bibliography: p.
Contents: I loved a girl—Love is a feeling to be learned—Living with unfulfilled desires—[etc.]
1. Dating (Social customs)—Religious aspects—Christianity. 2. Marriage—Religious aspects—Christianity. 3. Sex—Religious aspects—Christianigy. 4. Love. 5. Spiritual life. I. Title.
HQ801.T77 1987 306.7 87-2995
ISBN 0-87784-524-7

---

16 15 14 13 12 11 10 9 8 7 6 5 4 3 2 1
99 98 97 96 95 94 93 92 91 90 89 88 87

Acknowledgments

Acknowledgment is made to the following for permission to use copyrighted material:

I Loved a Girl *copyright © 1963, 1964 by Walter Trobisch. In the French edition copyright 1962 by Walter Trobisch. Introduction © 1965 by David R. Mace. Published by arrangement with Harper & Row, Publishers, Inc. All rights reserved.*

Love Is a Feeling to Be Learned *© 1971 by Editions Trobisch, Box 2048, D-7640, Kehl/Rhein, West Germany.*

Living with Unfulfilled Desires *© 1979 by Inter-Varsity Christian Fellowship of the United States of America. First published under the title* Mit Unerfüllten Wünschen Leben *© Editions Trobisch 1978, Box 2048, D-7640, Kehl/Rhein, West Germany.*

My Beautiful Feeling *© 1976 by Editions Trobisch, Box 2048, D-7640, Kehl/Rhein, West Germany. The authors gratefully acknowledge the help of Elisabeth Goldhor and Marie de Putron in the translation of this book from the original German,* Mein Schönes Gefühl.

My Parents Are Impossible *© by Editions Trobisch, Box 2048, D-7640, Kehl/Rhein, West Germany.*

I Married You *copyright © 1971 by Walter Trobisch. Published by arrangement with Harper & Row, Publishers, Inc. All rights reserved.*

All a Man Can Be *© 1983 by InterVarsity Christian Fellowship of the United States of America. Originally published under the title* The Misunderstood Man. *Acknowledgment is made for permission to use the following copyrighted material: From* Goethe's Faust, *Parts I and II, translated by Louis MacNeice. Copyright 1951, 1954 by Frederick Louis MacNeice; renewed 1979 by Hedli MacNeice. Reprinted by permission of Oxford University Press, Inc., New York, and Faber and Faber Ltd., London. From "Das Tagebuch"* Goethes und Rilkes "Sieben Gedichte." *Walter Trobisch's adapted translation is used by permission of Rowoht Verlag, Reinbek bei Hamburg. From "A Growing Love" in* Love Reaches Out *by Ulrich Schaffer. Copyright ©1976 by Ulrich Schaffer. Used by permission of Harper & Row, New York.*

A Baby Just Now? *© 1969: Editions Trobisch, Sixth Edition 1978; Editions Trobisch, Box 2048, D-7640, Kehl/ Rhein, West Germany. Originally published under the title* Please Help Me! Please Love Me!

My Wife Made Me a Polygamist *copyright 1971 by Editions Trobisch, Box 2048, D-7640, Kehl/Rhein, West Germany.*

Love Yourself *© 1976 by Editions Trobisch Box 2048, D-7640, Kehl/Rhein, West Germany. The poem "Loving Myself" by Ulrich Schaffer is reprinted by permission of Harper and Row, Publishers, from* Love Reaches Out, *Copyright © 1976 by Ulrich Schaffer.*

Spiritual Dryness *© 1975 by Editions Trobisch. This study was given at several conferences for African pastors and missionaries. It is based on an article published in* Das Missionarische Wort *No. 7, 1952, written by Prof. Adolf Koeberle, Germany, to whom grateful acknowledgment is made.*

Martin Luther's Quiet Time *© 1975 by Walter Trobisch.*

"Of Flight and Forgiveness" originally published in 1950. Revised edition copyright © 1987 by Ingrid Trobisch. Used by permission of Ingrid Trobisch.

"What Happened When I Wrote I Loved a Girl,*" originally published under the title "Missionary by Mail" in* The Lutheran Standard, *© 1973 by Ingrid Trobisch. Used by permission.*

"Church Discipline in the Light of Law and Gospel," Copyright: The Lutheran World Federation. Used by permission.

"God's World Strategy" originally published under the title "This Was Not Done in a Corner" in Evangelize *magazine, October 1957.*

Unless otherwise noted, biblical quotations are from the Revised Standard Version, copyright 1946, 1952, © 1971, 1973.

Acknowledgments

Introduction by Ingrid Trobisch 9

DATING AND SEX 19
I Loved a Girl 21
Love Is a Feeling to Be Learned 117
Living with Unfulfilled Desires 139
My Beautiful Feeling 255
My Parents Are Impossible 329

MARRIAGE 361
I Married You 363
My Wife Made Me a Polygamist 509
A Baby Just Now? 541
All a Man Can Be 577

PERSONAL GROWTH 651
Love Yourself 653
Spiritual Dryness 693
Martin Luther's Quiet Time 703

APPENDIXES 715
Of Flight and Forgiveness 717
What Happened When I Wrote *I Loved a Girl* 725
Church Discipline in the Light of Law and Gospel 729
God's World Strategy 737

Notes 745

Introduction

In the handwritten notes for his last book, *All a Man Can Be,* published posthumously, Walter wrote:

"It was in the plan of God that I was born in the next to the last hour of the next to the last day of the next to the last month in the year of 1923. Somehow this fact is a signal, a call, to me to have the courage in this 'temporary' world to proclaim that which is the next to the last. He who wishes to have the last word, never says it. In all that we do, we need to have the courage for this 'next to the last' as far as the direction in which we are going. But the foundation upon which we stand, from which we come, and out of which we live, can be nothing less than the Last. . . . It is a sign of being redeemed to be satisfied with that which is temporary and 'next to the last.' "

His son David wrote in the foreword of *My Journey Homeward,* "One cannot understand Walter Trobisch aright as only a theorist and systematist, and although he was a fascinating speaker, his real gift was the gift of 'Seelsorge' (soul care). He never looked upon marriage and family counseling as an end in itself. Rather, it was the 'landing strip for the Gospel' as he once called it."

An old German proverb says, "The child is the father of the man." To better understand this man, his ministry and the books he wrote, all collected in this volume, we have to go back to his roots, his childhood and his youth.

Walter Trobisch was born in Leipzig, Germany (now behind the Iron Curtain) on November 29, 1923. He was the oldest son of Martin and Gertrud Trobisch, both elementary schoolteachers. Gertrud, a professor's daughter, taught school for ten years before her marriage. She was an enthusiastic pedagogue and more than once did I hear her say, "You never teach subjects. You teach children. If a child is to learn well, there must be a joyful atmosphere in the classroom."

After Walter was born, she began to pour her pedagogical gifts into the wet cement of her own children's hearts. Walter often surprised me in the early years of our marriage by reciting long poems and singing funny songs.

"When did you ever have time to learn all those?" I would ask him.

The invariable answer: "My mother taught them to me before I started school."

She also succeeded in giving him a hopeful and optimistic outlook on life. His "basic trust," which he could later transfer from his good parents to his relationship to his heavenly Father, remained unbroken despite all the political tragedies of growing up in Nazi Germany.

Martin Trobisch was a kind and faithful father. He taught Walter how to play the piano and gave him his love for the great evangelical hymns, many of which Martin knew by heart. Martin's ancestors had escaped from Moravia during the time of the Counter Reformation and had settled in Dresden where they were protected by the Protestant emperor, Frederick the Great. Only after Walter had studied theology for five semesters did his father tell him that he had prayed since his birth that his son might become a pastor.

Both parents kept detailed journals of the physical and mental development of their three children. When Walter was two, his father followed him around during one day of their family vacation and recorded in shorthand every word his son had said during that day. His mother describes in her journal the first time Walter went to visit his grandmother without her. She told him and his younger sister to be careful when they crossed the busy street. When they returned home safely two hours later, Gertrud asked them, "Did you look both ways before you crossed the street?"

His three-year-old sister answered: "I watched for both of us. Walter was thinking about something else."

It was this ability to tune out disturbing elements which enabled him to write and put his thoughts down clearly. His greatest joy during his school years was to write compositions and study the great German poets. One of his high-school teachers invited students to his home in order to read those authors who were banned in Hitler's era.

Walter always admitted that the symbol of happiness was for him "a sheet of blank paper and a table to write on."

Shortly before his untimely death, Walter was asked by a friend what he would do if he knew he had only six months to live. Walter's answer, "I wouldn't travel at all, but stay at home and write, write, write." His first published work, written when he was thirteen, was an adventure story printed serially in a newspaper for deaf youth. To escape the meaningless and boring ceremonies of the Hitler Youth, Walter had volunteered in his early teens to work in the Leipzig School for Deaf and learn sign language. This early experience, as well as his great love for music (especially opera) gave him an unusual sensitivity to "hear" the needs of others even without words.

When he was eighteen, he graduated from the Petrusgymnasium in Leipzig. He had one week to celebrate his achievement before he was drafted into the army and sent as an infantry soldier to the Russian front. As a Christmas gift for his mother that year he had written several poems on slips of paper kept in the inner pocket of his uniform. "I cannot die yet," he penciled in German script on the margin, "not until I have posted these."

He survived the Battle of Stalingrad the winter of 1942. Severely wounded, he was thrown on the back of a truck that managed to escape through a gap in the Russian lines surrounding the defeated German army. He wrote, "It was in the turmoil of the Battle of Stalingrad with only hours to live that I made a clear decision for Christ. When I was rescued from there as one of the last survivors, I felt that God had called me in a special way to serve Him." He wrote to his parents in December 1942, "Nothing is greater in my heart than my longing for homecoming in the Kingdom of Love."

One of his gifts was the ability to relax and go to sleep almost instantly when he had the chance. When I asked his secret, he replied, "All I have to do is recall the sounds of the clickety-click of the wheels of the hospital train on that long journey through Russia, Poland and Czechoslovakia—a journey from what would have been certain captivity and death to healing and new life."

During his months of convalescence, he was faithfully discipled by a Jewish Christian friend, Wolfgang Caffier, the youth leader in his home church in Leipzig. Walter asked his friend many difficult questions. Wolfgang taught him to read a portion of Scripture daily from the Moravian Daily Texts. By the first light of dawn Walter read and memorized the text, which in turn gave him strength and guidance for the day.

While in Poland on his way to the front a second time, this time to southern Russia, he wrote in his pocket journal on July 7, 1943, "Never before did I experience the nearness of Christ as yesterday when I walked to the railroad station. He was walking beside me, clearly and earnestly. He was in me. He walked ahead of me. Yes, he even protected me from behind."

A week later he noted, "Only place to sleep is the foxhole. A peculiar frame of mind: to want to hang on to your life with every phase of your being and at the same time to rejoice over the prospect of going to heaven soon."

July 27, 1943. " 'He who stands firm until the end . . .' The temptation is great just to give up and remain lying down."

September 11, 1943, Mariopol. " 'Trust in the Lord forever, for the Lord God is an everlasting rock' (Is 26:4). Shot in the head, wound in left arm, crawl back . . . That which is loud and recognizable is temporary. That which is quiet and unrecognizable is eternal.

'You are a hiding place (Schirm) for me;
You protect me from distress.

You surround me with people who are rescued,
and shouting joyfully about it.' (Ps 32:7)

This 'shouting joyfully' *('froelich ruehmen')* will be my theme for the rest of my life."

This was the Daily Text and it gave Walter the strength to crawl through the sniper's fire behind the lines where he was rescued and put on a hospital train headed for Vienna. There he was admitted to the Catholic Hospital, *Zum gottlichen Heiland,* the same hospital where forty years later one of his grandsons was born. When the nurses, thinking Walter was an older man, cleaned him up and shaved his beard they were astonished to see the fresh face of a twenty-year-old. Here, through the kind offices of a Christian doctor, he was allowed to study theology for two semesters at the university while the injured nerves in his left arm were treated on an out-patient basis. He had six hours of Greek and two of Hebrew, besides his courses in theology. He also had time to become acquainted with the family of the Bishop of the Lutheran Church of Austria and later became engaged to his only daughter, Erika.

Walter was sent to the front once more, this time near Florence, Italy. Here he began conducting devotions for smaller groups and soon most of the company gathered for these meetings. He was wounded a third time near Bologna. After recuperating he was assigned to an officers' training school. Here he became fully aware of the demonic character of the Hitler regime. The military situation became so critical that his company was recalled to Germany and found themselves in battle near Nuremberg. Here he was captured by an American Negro—the first black man he had seen in his life. He enjoyed telling the story later to his African friends.

The tens of thousands of captives were confined in an open field surrounded by barbed wire. Walter was thankful to have in his backpack a volume of church history which he studied. Since he could prove to his American captors that he was a theological student and not a member of the Nazi Party, he was one of the first to be released in May 1945. The railroad stations were destroyed so he walked most of the three hundred miles back to his home in Leipzig. In his heart on that long road home, he sang joyfully the song of deliverance from death (Ps 32:7).

American troops held the city of Leipzig until August, when, according to the Potsdam agreement the Russians moved in. It was a time of great physical privation for this beseiged city with its half million inhabitants. Walter lived at home with his parents and younger brother. His beloved sister had died of diphtheria in a Hitler Work Camp. He continued his studies at Leipzig University for four semesters and led the active Christian youth group in his congregation. These Christians still meet to strengthen their hands in God when they have occasion. Many are lay leaders in their churches in East Germany.

A Communist-dominated youth committee of ten members was also formed for the city, and Walter was chosen to represent the forty Lutheran congregations in the city. It was a dangerous position. He was warned one day that there had been a meeting of the youth committee without him. He knew he had to flee his homeland. With only his backpack, dressed as a peasant and carrying a hoe he walked across the border to West Germany while the Russian guards were having their noon-day meal.

He went to Heidelberg, where Professor Kampenhausen, one of his teachers in Vienna, befriended him so he could continue his theological studies. In July 1948 he passed his state exams there. But the key experience of his life came in the fall of 1947 when he met Pastor Herbert Fuchs, who was to be his spiritual mentor from then on. After being a student of theology for seven semesters, Walter describes this upheaval: "As a youth evangelist, working with Pastor Fuchs in the villages of the Palitinate, I had a new deepening of my spiritual life—the decisive experience of declaring total inner bankruptcy and of the forgiveness of sin through the blood of Christ. I confessed my sins to God in the presence of a brother in Christ who gave me to the absolution in His name."

This renewal experience made him also re-examine his engagement to Erika and his whole future. Erika too had come to the same independent conclusion and their letters crossed when they each asked the other to be free.

Walter went back to Austria and to Lichtenberg to celebrate their "disengagement." When he returned to his student quarters in Heidelberg, there was the official letter from Geneva announcing that he had received a scholarship to study as an exchange student at Augustana Seminary in Rock Island, Illinois.

He described his flight to America in a little booklet published in German entitled, *Of Flight and Forgiveness.* The English translation is printed for the first time in this volume, in the appendix. An interview shortly after his arrival in the United States was entitled: "Forgiveness Stressed by German Student." "My first word as a German student in America shall be forgiveness. The biggest problem facing the world today is 'How can man live with man?' and this question can only be answered through a spirit of forgiveness which is to be found under the cross. This is why the world so desperately needs the cross today." Walter also stated that his main purpose of study in this country was "to build bridges—not to accuse [and] not to defend."

In an editorial printed in the *Augustana Observer,* Walter wrote,

> God is not a Santa Claus, not an old grandfather walking around in his bath-robe with an ever smiling face, always ready to underwrite our plans, and always glad when we say to him a gracious, Thank you.
>
> He can make the cities wasted without inhabitants, the houses without men, the land utterly desolate (Isaiah 6). If I write as a German student, then I can write only as one who experienced that the wrath of God is a reality. . . . You as students have an immense task to make this known to the people of your nation, so that the wrath of God may not one day also destroy your beautiful country. . . . Germany is a warning to the world. If this sign is heeded, then we do not suffer in vain. We suffer for you, perhaps instead of you.

I met Walter Trobisch a few weeks after his arrival in Rock Island. He asked if we could exchange addresses since I was leaving for study in France before going to the mission field in Cameroun, West Africa. Two years later we were engaged and then married in Mannheim, Germany, on June 2, 1952.

After his return from the States, Walter had served as an assistant pastor in a large congregation in Ludwigshafen. He was ordained there in 1953 upon the call of the American Lutheran Church to serve in Cameroun, West Africa. In June 1953, we arrived at Tchollire in northern Cameroun where it was our task to do pioneer work in the Rey Bouba area. From 1957-63 he was chaplain and teacher at Cameroun Christian

College at Libamba, Makak. In 1963, when we came home on furlough from Libamba, Walter concluded in a letter to our friends:

1) There is a great upheaval in Africa today in marriage and family life. No other realm of life is so troubled. Africa must suffer through this crisis.

2) The biblical message about marriage and the family is therefore one of the most promising doors through which the Gospel can enter Africa today.

3) The printed word is one of the most effective means by which the Gospel can be proclaimed to Africans who are hungry to read.

I am about to draw the practical consequences from these conclusions which also touches deeply our own marriage and family life. Since I published the correspondence with one of my students dealing with these issues,* I have had an avalanche of readers' letters from all over Africa. "You have answered François' questions in your book. Now please answer mine." I feel like Peter in Luke 5, when he caught so many fish that the nets were breaking and he had to call his helpers from the other boats.

Friedrich Heer has said, "Through marriage, the destiny of the world will be decided. Through marriage, history will be made. Here the forces of birth and life are bound together. Here, when marriages do not succeed, the forces of destruction, of hate, of murder are unleashed. God wants to bring the world home to Himself, through marriage, through those people who live in marriage."

Kierkegaard once said, "The thing is to find a truth which is true for me, to find the idea for which I can live or die." For Walter Trobisch this idea was "to release couple power." Couple power can only come into being because of the healing of both man and woman—when both become whole people. That's what these books which you will find in this collection are all about.

As far as his own family life, I would like to pay tribute to my late husband by saying that "the man and his message were one." My life

---

*"*J'ai aimé une fille*" was privately printed in 1961 and later became the internationally known book *I Loved a Girl.* See "What Happened When I Wrote *I Loved a Girl*" in the appendix for the story of how the book was published.

was enriched and stretched, trying to keep pace with Walter Trobisch. I count it the greatest honor God could give a woman—to be the mother of his five children. At the time of this writing, seven years after his sudden death of a heart attack at his beloved home in Lichtenberg, Austria, on October 13, 1979, his children are scattered throughout the globe. Our oldest daughter, Katrine, who once said of her father, "He never put me down" is now the wife of the U.S. consul in Lahore, Pakistan. Our oldest son, Daniel, a psychologist, and his family live in our home in Austria, where their goal is simply "to show people the way Home." Our second son, David, a theologian, is teaching New Testament at Heidelberg University. Stephen, our third son, is actively engaged in the world of theater and film-making and is the family consultant for the filming of his father's book *I Loved a Girl.* Ruth, our youngest daughter, is in her last semesters of medical school at the University of Vienna.

Details of our ministry together are found in three books: *On Our Way Rejoicing* (Tyndale), *Learning to Walk Alone* (Servant) and *My Journey Homeward* (Servant). Perhaps it would be fitting to close this introduction with a personal word from Walter himself. Before we left on our last journey together (a three-month missionary trip which took us around the world in the summer of 1979), Walter wrote in our Marriage Dialog Notebook the answer to this question: "If someone wants to understand me in depth, what are the ten most important things he has to know about me?" I found the following response several months after his death:

1. That I have been ready to die many times; therefore, everything in the here and now is secondary—even inconsequential—in light of the hope of eternal life.

2. That basically I am not a go-getter, fighter, or invader, but rather a withdrawn spectator, a quiet enjoyer of life, who feels uncomfortable in the limelight.

3. That I depend ultimately on God and that I can face, endure, and enjoy life only because I am *not* dependent on it.

4. That I live in constant fear of being overpowered by an anonymous, demonic force of organization, administration, bureaucracy, be it of church or state. I love and need freedom.

5. That my wife and children mean more to me than any other human beings, and that my relationship to them is secondary only to my relationship to Jesus Christ.

6. That I am happiest when I am creative and that for this, voluntarily chosen and granted solitude is at times more precious and important to me than fellowship.

7. That I enjoy helping others both inwardly and outwardly.

8. That sexuality is for me one aspect of enjoyment among others; one expression of love among others, but not basic.

9. That I love shelteredness, comfortableness, having an overview, order, and a regular schedule. That I have a far greater longing to explore the inner world than the wide outer world. The paradox is that the more I succeed in reaching the depths of the inner world (books!), the more the burden of the outer world becomes my own.

10. That I only lose perspective of things when I do not have enough sleep, and that I cannot find sleep when I lose perspective (a vicious circle).

Walter Trobisch was a warm, loving human being whose early death left a great gap for his family and friends.

Ingrid Trobisch
Easter 1987

PART I

DATING AND SEX

BOOK ONE

I LOVED A GIRL

Introduction

by David R. Mace,
Executive Director,
American Association of Marriage Counselors, Inc.

It was in 1962 that Walter Trobisch first sent me a copy of his little book *J'ai Aimé Une Fille. . .* At that time I had not yet met him, but we had corresponded. I knew that as a missionary in Cameroun, West Africa, he had been especially concerned with the sexual and marital problems of the people among whom he worked. He explained that his little book concerned the personal problems of a young African man who had sought his help; that pastors often had to deal with such problems; and that by publishing the letters he and François had exchanged he hoped it would be possible to help other young people in similar situations.

As I read through these letters I became aware that Walter Trobisch was an unusually sensitive and perceptive man who cared deeply for the people to whom he ministered; and that because of this, he was ready to reach out to these people at the level of their most intimate personal needs in a way few missionaries ever can. I realized also that in the telling of this poignant personal story through the medium of the letters exchanged he had hit upon a powerful dramatic medium for portraying the dilemmas faced by the young African of today, caught as he is between the backward pull of tribal tradition and the forward pressure of cultural change. As Cecile put it, "the new and the old bump against each other so suddenly."

It was soon clear that the story of François had an appeal that extended far beyond Africa. Published at first for the French-speaking Africans of the Cameroun, the story soon appeared in German and in English, and was widely read in Europe. People who would never have thought of studying African tribal life and customs identified with this young man's struggles and aspirations, with the way in which the book portrays the African's hopes and fears as he emerges from his sheltered past into the maddening complexity of life in the atomic age. Suddenly the distant, remote, inscrutable African became for them a very understandable human being, and his frustrations and indignations found an echo in their own hearts.

At this point the drama of François took a new turn. Readers who had made his cause their own clamored for the continuation of his story. The tragic situation in which we leave François in *I Loved a Girl* . . . is heartrending. His last words are: "It makes me suffer more than I can bear, and it will kill me. . . . I do not expect an answer, for there is none."

What happened next? Obviously, the story had to be continued. In 1964 the adventures of François were resumed in *I Love a Young Man.* For the first time we were able to meet Cecile and hear, through the correspondence with François and with the pastor and his wife, her side of the story. This took us further still into the complications young Africans face as the old tribal patterns dissolve before the impact of the modern world.

The appeal of the story now entered a third phase. Originally it had drawn the interest of African youth because they too were struggling with the problems that plagued François and Cecile. Then it had provided a revealing window through which sympathetic non-Africans could look in upon the complexities of life in the new Africa. And now Western youth discovered that this African couple struggling with the frustrations of their love were not so distant after all. Many of the problems faced by François and Cecile were very similar to their own. They recognized in the experiences of these two the joys and sorrows, triumphs and disasters that inevitably follow when "boy meets girl" the world over. Christian youth especially were able to recognize, under a sultry African sky, the familiar pattern of their own victories and their own defeats.

As the influence of François and Cecile increased, the responsibilities of Walter Trobisch rapidly expanded. Having returned to his native Germany for a secluded period of graduate study, he suddenly found himself inundated by hundreds of letters. From all over Africa, and from the Western world, too, perplexed young people wrote to the sympathetic pastor for guidance.

The friendship Walter Trobisch and I had established by mail was deepened by a face-to-face encounter when he and his wife Ingrid visited my wife and myself during one of their trips to the United States. The Trobisches are, as one would expect, remarkable people. They speak English, French and German with flawless fluency, and doubtless possess some mastery over African languages as well. Their warm sincerity and the radiance of their Christian faith are contagious, and they share a sensitivity to human needs which derives from their dynamic religious faith. Walter is not the only author in the family. Born in Africa of American parents, Ingrid has told in her charming book *On Our Way Rejoicing* the fascinating story of the pioneer missionary family to which she belongs.

When the American edition of the story of François and Cecile was first projected, Walter asked me to write an Introduction. I count it an honor to do so, for my expectation is that the book will arouse wide interest in this country, as it has already done throughout Africa and Europe.

American readers will have the advantage of reading the full story in one volume. They will find it to be deeply moving, poignantly direct, told with lyrical simplicity. It has the appeal that the love story has had since the dawn of human history. But beneath that level are significant undertones that make it an allegory of the age-old struggle of the soul for purity, integrity, for the Vision of God in a dark, confusing world of seeming injustice and unmeaning.

The drama centers around the traditional African custom of the "bride-price." To a Westerner this seems more barbaric than it actually was, for like many practices of primitive peoples it makes good sense within its cultural framework. The "bride-price" is, for all practical purposes, identical with the *mohar* of the early Hebrews, familiar to us in several of the Old Testament stories.

As Pastor Amos points out, the "bride-price" used to be paid in cattle. When a young man desired to marry a girl, the cattle were transferred from his family to that of the girl, to make up to them for the loss of their daughter. The term "compensation-gift" would more accurately describe this transaction. Significantly, the cattle were not to be disposed of by the girl's family but, for a time at least, to be held in trust. If the girl turned out to be an unsatisfactory wife, the tribal leaders could stipulate that she be returned to her family, and the cattle to the young man's family. In the event that the husband mistreated his wife, however, the tribal leaders might decree that the family could reclaim their daughter and still keep the cattle, thus punishing the badly behaving husband.

As Africans have adopted a money economy, this sensible system of safeguards has broken down sadly. In recent years, avaricious fathers have been known to sell their daughters to the highest bidders, regardless of the personal implications for the girls. Cecile's father is not a man of this sort. But he needs money badly, and the wealthy Monsieur Henri has position and prestige which, perhaps not only in African eyes, seem to offer Cecile excellent prospects of economic security; whereas the penniless François offers nothing but his love. And, as Pastor Amos plaintively reports: "Cecile's father does not understand what love is. How shall I explain that to him?" Cecile's letter to her father, which closes the book, sums up the entire problem as the daughter tries to justify to her father this completely new approach to marriage which challenges traditional practical considerations.

Other traditional African practices conflict with those of the modern world. The over-riding necessity that a man beget children, and especially sons, was the primary justification for polygamy. Indeed, polygamy was an obligation under the levirate system, which required a man to marry his brother's widow. François is the unhappy child of such an arrangement. And Cecile, in her letter to Ingrid, opens her heart and speaks of fears that every African girl has entertained: "I'm afraid that

François will divorce me if I am barren. Or that he will take a second wife."

This obligation to have children challenges, too, the Christian concept of sexual morality that these two young people are trying to accept. For Cecile there is the temptation to test her fertility before marriage. François is prey to the widespread African belief that a man must prove his manhood by using his sexual powers and especially by fathering a child—and that to restrain sex, withholding his seed, is to risk illness. Goaded by his African friends, again and again he challenges the pastor to justify the exacting demands of the Christian ethic. Western Christian youth will readily identify with him here, for though in the West the arguments are somewhat different, the predicament is the same.

The pastor's difficult task is to justify the Christian ideal of love between man and woman in a cynical world that constantly taints and degrades and exploits. Is the long, hard struggle for integrity and idealism really possible, and is it worthwhile? This is the question that the Christian is continually having to ask himself—in Africa, in Europe, in America. And it is a question that merely happens at the present time to find its focus in the area of sexual behavior. It applies equally to every aspect of the life of man where the way of Christ challenges the convenient compromises that human nature has made with primitive impulse and practical convenience. How much personal struggle and sacrifice can we be expected to undergo in quest of such lofty ideals as integrity, love, unselfishness and justice?

This question raises in turn some very practical dilemmas in the area of church discipline. The story of François sounds a challenge not only to the churches in Africa, but also to those of the Caribbean and elsewhere. Is it justifiable to impose stern discipline, including exclusion from Holy Communion, upon those guilty of sexual misdemeanors, and to be relatively indifferent to the more subtle forms of sin? How can the Church reconcile its functions of representing both a punishing and a forgiving God? If punishment is given considerable emphasis, as in some African churches, does forgiveness become too dear to be meaningful? If there is little or no emphasis on punishment, as in some American churches, does forgiveness become too cheap?

With all these questions, and with others, Pastor Trobisch manfully grapples, as the story of François and Cecile unfolds and the drama of their love is played out against the kaleidoscopic background of African cultural change. We move with them through the gamut of their widely alternating moods—gratitude and anger, faith and doubt, hope and despair. Above the stage, on one side, hovers the dark, demonic figure of Monsieur Henri; on the other that of the pastor, like a guardian angel. The stage is life itself, and the powers are good and evil. It is the eternal drama that is being played out; and the players are not just an African boy and girl, but the human race, whose representatives could just as well be any of us.

March, 1965
Madison, New Jersey

Preface

Those who may be shocked by the frankness and intimacy of these letters should know that those who wrote them did not at the time entertain any thought of their communications being published. Later, both the boy, François, and the girl, Cecile, proposed that this correspondence be put into a book because of their belief that the counsel which had helped them might also prove helpful to others.

The book made its first appearance in Africa in 1962. Since that time it has been translated into more than thirty African dialects and a number of European languages. The warm response to date would seem to indicate that François and Cecile were right.

The possibility of book publication in the United States occurred only after François' story, serialized in HIS, a student magazine, produced a vast and unexpected response.

To me and my wife this was inspiring evidence that the human heart is everywhere the same, whether it beats under a black skin or a white one.

Walter Trobisch

M. . . . , January 8

Sir,

This letter comes to you in my place. I'm too ashamed to go to see you. Besides, I don't have the money for the trip, because I'm no longer a teacher. I've been fired.

Last Friday, I loved a girl—or, as you would put it, I committed adultery—at least that's what the whites call it and the Church, too. But the girl wasn't married, nor had any bride-price been paid for her. Consequently she didn't belong to anyone and I don't understand who it is that I have wronged. I myself am unwed and I have no intention of marrying the girl. I don't even know her name. So, the way I see it, the commandment, "You shall not commit adultery" does not apply in my case. That's why I can't understand why the Church deprives me of Communion by putting me under discipline for six months.

One of my pupils told on me. And now I don't know where to turn.

Sir, you baptized me and taught me at school. You have counseled me often and know how I became a Christian. You know me even better than my own father does. I'm terribly sorry to disappoint you, but at the same time I tell you frankly, I don't feel very guilty. I'm ashamed because of all the talk about it, but I'm still a Christian.

I dare to tell you openly what I think even if you get angry. Aren't the desires of my body supposed to be satisfied? Aren't my sex organs given me to be used? Shouldn't you take advantage of that which is available? Why is it a sin to use what God has made?

Since everyone condemns me, I do not expect an answer.

I will stop now. There's nothing more to be said.

Sincerely,

Your unhappy François

B. . . . , January 19

My dear François,

I got your letter and I'm thankful you told me what happened before I heard it from someone else. Of course I'm sad. It's embarrassing for me too, because it was partly on my recommendation that you were given your job as a teacher.

But I'm not at all angry with you for being frank. Rather, I'm deeply moved by it, for then perhaps I can help you. May I answer your questions just as frankly as you have asked them?

Let us put aside for a moment the question of whether or not your case should be called adultery. You are absolutely right in saying that sex is no sin. Your desires, your thoughts when seeing a beautiful girl are not yet sin; neither is it sin if you feel attracted. You can't avoid physical desires any more than you can avoid having the birds fly around your head. But you can certainly prevent them from building nests in your hair.

Indeed, sexual desires are created by God. They are a gift of God, one of the most precious gifts you have received for your young life. But the existence of a desire does not justify its satisfaction. The presence of a power does not imply that one should be guided by it, blindly and without restraint.

What would you say about a fellow who stands in front of the window of a butcher's shop in a big city and reasons as follows: "Now that I see this meat, I'm hungrier than ever. The meat arouses my appetite. That proves it's meant for me and that I should have it. Therefore I have the right to smash the window and help myself."

You ask if that which exists should not be used. Yes, but only in its own time and place. Just imagine, for instance, that one of your friends has become a policeman. For the first time in his life he possesses a revolver. Now he says to himself: "I didn't acquire this revolver myself. It was given to me. Because it was given to me it should be used. Therefore I must shoot somebody with it—no matter whom."

No, he does not have this right. If the revolver has been given him, then he is responsible for its proper use.

The same is true about sex. It should be used, but in its proper place and time, according to God's plan. Within that plan the sexual instinct is a good thing, a powerful source of life and unity between two beings. Outside of God's plan, it quickly becomes a means of division, a source of cruelty, perversion and death.

I could say it also this way: Within God's will, sexual union fulfills its purpose only when it is an expression of love.

One phrase in your letter struck me especially. You wrote, "I loved a girl." No, my friend. You did not love that girl; you went to bed with her—these are two completely different things. You had a sexual episode, but what love is, you did not experience.

It's true you can say to a girl, "I love you," but what you really mean is something like this: "I want something. Not you, but something from you. I don't have time to wait. I want it immediately, without delay. It doesn't matter what happens afterwards. Whether we remain together, whether you become pregnant—that has nothing to do with me. For me, it's right now that counts. I will make use of you in order to satisfy my desire. You are for me only the means by which I can reach my goal. I want to have it—have it without any further ado, have it, immediately.

This is the opposite of love, for love wants *to give.* Love seeks to make the other one happy, and not himself. You acted like a pure egoist. Instead of saying: "I loved a girl," you should have said: "I loved myself and myself only. For this purpose I misused a girl."

Let me try to tell you what it really should mean if a fellow says to a girl, "I love you." It means: "You, you, you. You alone. You shall reign in my heart. You are the one whom I have longed for; without you I am incomplete. I will give everything for you and I will give up everything for you, myself as well as all that I possess. I will live for you alone, and I will work for you alone. And I will wait for you—it doesn't matter how long. I will always be patient with you. I will never force you, not even by words. I want to guard you, protect you and keep you from all evil. I want to share with you my thoughts, my heart and my body—all that I possess. I want to listen to what you have to say. There is nothing I want to undertake without your blessing. I want to remain always at your side."

Do you understand now how far removed your experience was from an experience of love? You don't even know the name of the girl. For you, she wasn't even a person, not even a number. You're not interested in her past, and certainly not in her future. You didn't even care what happened in her heart when you possessed her. And if she became pregnant—that's her affair. What does it matter to you?

No, you did not love her. True love involves responsibility—the one for the other and both before God. Where love is, you no longer say "I," but "you"; "I am responsible for you. You are responsible for me." Together then you stand before God where you do not say "you and I," but rather "we."

Only in marriage does this "we" become a full reality. Only in marriage can love really unfold and mature, because only there can it find permanence and faithfulness. True love never can and never will end. That's why you should use the great words, "I love you" very sparingly. You should save it for the girl whom you intend to marry.

Here in marriage is the right place to use your sexual powers. There they will help you to love your wife. They are one expression—one among many others—by means of which you make her understand how much you love her.

If you use your sexual powers apart from this kind of love, you are preparing yourself for an unhappy marriage.

Let me close here. This letter will give you enough to think about. Please remember that in spite of everything you can count always on my friendship and my prayers.

Hoping for another frank letter from you,

Sincerely yours,

T.

M. . . . , January 25

Dear Sir,

Your letter has reached me. Thank you very much for it. I'm grateful that you do not give me up. You criticize me severely, but you help me too. I'm very glad that I have found in you someone to whom I can write frankly, but I must admit I didn't understand everything you said to me. What surprised me the most was what you said at the end of the letter.

Sir, if I did have a true motive for my action, it was precisely that of preparing myself for a happy marriage. But now you tell me just the opposite. I ask you, sir, how can one know without first learning? How can one learn without experimenting? Didn't we do the same thing in our chemistry and physics classes?

In my mother tongue we have a proverb which says: "One must sharpen the spear before one goes hunting."

What use is it to be married if one is impotent because of not having trained sufficiently the powers of his body? Isn't there even a danger that the organs will remain underdeveloped if they are not used?

Do you understand what I mean? I hope you will find time to answer me once again.

François

B. . . . , February 3

My dear François,

Thank you again for writing so honestly. I take it as a sign of your confidence.

There's a strange comparison between love and death in the Bible which says: "Love is strong as death" (Song of Solomon 8:6). Both love and death have this in common that you cannot try them out beforehand. But just that is what makes both of these experiences so powerful. Do you think you could try out what it feels like to be dead by sleeping very deeply? Even less can you try out what it feels like to be in love by a mere sexual contact. The conditions under which love can be experienced are so much higher, so much different.

Take another comparison: If you want to try out a parachute, you will be tempted perhaps to jump down from the top of a house or a high tree. But a distance of thirty or forty feet is not enough to give the parachute a chance to open up; therefore you may very well break your neck. You have to jump out of an airplane up several thousand feet if you want the parachute to open up and carry you to safety without mishap.

The same is true with love. You cannot try it outside the "high flight" of marriage. Only then can its wonders really unfold. Only then can the sexual organs function as they are meant to function.

When one is married, the sex act takes place under completely different conditions. There is no hurry, no fear of being discovered, no fear of being betrayed or left in the lurch by the other, no fear of a pregnancy resulting from it. But above all there is enough time to open your hearts and get used to one another, to correct together lovingly the awkwardness and minor difficulties which are always there at the beginning.

It is good, François, that you want to prepare yourself for marriage. But what is most important here is not the physical functioning of the sex organs. What matters is the *psychological* adjustment—in other words, the meeting of the hearts and minds of the two partners.

If there are sexual problems in marriage, it is not necessarily because of physical difficulties. These can be revealed and corrected before marriage by medical examinations. No, a far more common source of trouble is that very lack of psychological adjustment, which I have just mentioned.

Have you ever heard an orchestra tune its instruments before a concert? First comes the oboes, the violins and the flutes. If the conductor started with trumpets and drums which make a great deal of noise, he wouldn't be able to hear the oboes and violins and flutes. It's the same in the orchestra of marriage. The adjustment of heart and mind corresponds to the tuning of woodwinds and strings; then later the drums and trumpets of sex can be sounded.

It's this delicate tuning that you must learn if you want to prepare for marriage. This is what must be trained. But you are certainly not doing that when you have sexual relations with just any girl. Instead you are making your own heart numb. The drums drown out the flutes and you deaden your own feelings. What you have to be afraid of is not the underdevelopment of the sex organs, but the underdevelopment of love.

If you prepare yourself for marriage by having intercourse without this love, then, at best, you are imitating outwardly only some of its phases. You lower the sexual act to something machine-like, something bestial, for your heart is insensitive. You miss the decisive experience, the opening up of the "I" to the "you," and you block yourself from being able to love your future wife as deeply and as fully as she will expect you to.

Did it ever occur to you that sexual adventures before marriage can awaken in you a polygamous desire, a taste for variety, which may endanger your future marriage in advance? You may acquire wrong habits which will be very difficult to get rid of. Serious sexual handicaps, such as impotence, which can threaten the happiness of your marriage, can result.

When I as a pastor am called in for counsel in a marriage crisis, I can almost trace the origin of the problems to the kind of life which the husband and wife lived before they were married. The young man who has not learned self-control before marriage will not have it during marriage; so you see that your case does have something to do with marriage. In a sense, you deprive your future wife of something, even if you do not yet know her, and you endanger your happiness together.

My dear François, I hope you will understand at least one thing. I am not trying to deprive you of a pleasure, but rather I would like to protect you so that you will not spoil one of the greatest joys of your life. If you pick the blossoms of an orange tree, you will never know the taste of its fruit. So, when I advise you not to pick flowers, I do it not to take something away from you, but to assure you of a reward even more fulfilling.

May I answer your African proverb with another: "In trying to make himself too rich, a man often makes himself poor."

With brotherly greetings,

T.

M. . . . , February 10

Dear Pastor,

While I was reading your last letter, a Bible verse came to my mind which I have heard many times but which now through our correspondence has taken on a new meaning: "There is no fear in love, but perfect love casts out fear. For fear has to do with punishment, and he who fears is not perfected in love" (I John 4:18).

Yes, that is true. I was afraid, and to tell you the truth, I had very little joy the night I was with that girl. But do you know, it was also fear which drove me to do it—the fear of becoming ill if too much semen were to accumulate in my loins. Sometimes during the night I have dreams which cause emissions. My comrades tell me that the only way to escape these troubles is to try to have intercourse with a girl. What do you think about that?

You warned me against awakening a polygamous desire within me. Is it not possible to love several women at the same time? There is no passage in the Bible which forbids polygamy.

I have revealed to you my most secret thoughts in this letter. I hope you are not too shocked. But I have no one with whom I can talk about these problems, not even my own parents. As far as medical examination goes, I would have little confidence in it. Our doctors do not always tell us the truth, because they are afraid of palavers with our families.

Thank you again for your patience.

Yours sincerely,
François

B. . . . , February 20

Dear Brother,

Let me start with your last question: No, I do not believe that one can love several women at the same time. Everything depends upon what you mean by the term "love." If "love" means to lie with a girl; if love is nothing but sex, you are right. But "perfect Love," which the Bible talks about in the verse you quoted, concerns not only the senses but the heart as well.

I'm sure you know this proverb: "In a heart where there is room for several, there is no room for one alone." This is true. Balzac once said: "To believe that it's impossible always to love the marriage partner alone is just as absurd as the supposition that a musician needs many instruments before he can produce a beautiful melody." The complete responsibility for the partner, as I've already explained, you can only assume for one woman.

You say that polygamy is not forbidden in the Bible. It would take too long to go into detail here about how the Bible treats this problem. Very briefly let me say this much. Even in the Old Testament, polygamy was not the rule, but the exception. Adam, Noah, Isaac, Joseph had only one wife as did all the prophets. Where polygamy occurs it is motivated almost always by childlessness. However the Bible is very realistic in pointing out clearly the troubles and disadvantages polygamy brings about—jealousy (Genesis 16:4), grief (Genesis 26:34), favoritism (Genesis 49:4). The Hebrew word for the second wife means "rival."

But the Bible does more than forbid. It gives us a positive definition of marriage from which we can draw our own conclusions. It says: "Therefore a man leaves his father and mother and cleaves to his wife (singular), and they *(two)* become one flesh." The expression "one flesh" can also be translated by "one living being," or better still, "one person."

In marriage man and wife are no longer two but one. It is a joining of two persons into "one flesh" in such a way that the two become one and yet remain distinct. This marriage person has two essential organs: the "head" and the "heart." The man might be said to be the head, the wife the heart. Both are equally important for the life of the marriage-person, which is not able to live without a head or a heart, nor if it has two heads or two hearts. There must be just one head and one heart.

This means that if you are a polygamist, your marriage may still be a marriage, but you and your wives are not "one person"; and you together can never be an "image" of God. This was God's purpose when He created man: "God created man in His own image. . . . In His own image created He them, man and wife" (Genesis 1:7). In polygamy there can be no marriage-person who can become the partner of God. Nor can such a marriage be a mirror where the mutual love between man and wife reflects God's "perfect love." Only monogamy can testify to God's love.

What your friends have told you is a plain lie. No one has ever fallen ill because of continence before marriage. Emissions during sleep are not a sign of illness, but a sign that your body is functioning normally. It's all a part of God's creation that the body gets rid automatically of that which it does not use. That is all. There is nothing mysterious, nothing unnatural behind it.

On the contrary, if you go to bed with just any kind of girl you run the great danger of catching a venereal disease, or of becoming impotent for psychological reasons.

Those who tell you that you must have intercourse in order to avoid falling ill, or to prove that you are normal are usually those who have thought up this excuse because they are not able to exercise control over themselves.

Please be assured, François, that none of the thoughts you share with me, nor any question you ask, will shock me. My heart goes out to the many young people today who suffer inwardly, because they must live alone with their problems. If only they could be encouraged to open their hearts to someone who could counsel with them!

I greet you as your brother in Christ. He is the perfect example of God's "perfect love," and He loves you no matter what.

Yours sincerely,

T.

M. . . . , February 28

Dear Pastor T.,

I write to you with growing joy, because I feel that I am no longer left alone, and that gives me new courage.

In your last letter you mentioned that one could catch a disease or become impotent by sleeping with just any girl. That is strange—it was precisely in order to prove that I'm not impotent, that I did what I did. I'll tell you the whole story now without hiding anything.

On that unlucky day, one of my friends invited me to visit his parents. It was towards evening. While we were on the way to his house he started to tease me. He told me that I was not really a man if I had never known a girl. When we arrived at his home, his parents were not there; only his sister was in the house. We started to talk and she served us some beer. Suddenly my friend disappeared and I was left alone with the girl.

She invited me, and when I refused she began to make fun of me. Above all, she called me a word which translated means "dishrag" and which we use in our tribal language to describe a man who is both cowardly and impotent.

Sir, perhaps you as a white man cannot imagine what such a term means to an African. To be called impotent is one of the greatest insults a man can suffer in our society. If I had not given her the proof of my powers she would have slandered my name everywhere.

To tell you the truth, I certainly did not "love" the girl in the sense which you give to that word. Deep down in my heart perhaps I even hated her. But there was nothing else that I could do, the fear of being mocked and becoming the object of gossip was stronger than any other fear.

Tell me, how can you be a man and have the reputation of being a man unless you act like a man?

Yours sincerely,

F.

B. . . . , March 6

Dear Brother,

I'm glad that at last you have told me the whole story just as it happened. So what drove you to do it was not really the worry about your health nor the noble desire to prepare yourself for marriage, as you have pretended, but simply the fear of mockery, of being made a laughingstock. That makes it easy for me to answer your last question.

You did not behave like a man; you behaved instead exactly like a dishrag. A man who is a man knows what he wants, makes a decision and then acts upon it. But to let yourself be made to act against your own will by the words of a girl proves that you were a coward. In my view, when you stop to think about it, I should think you would find what you did more humiliating than putting up with the mockery of the whole village.

Even in going to your friend's house, you did not act like a man. A man must be smart enough to foresee such traps. The conversation with your friend on the way should have made you suspicious. The alcohol weakened your powers of resistance. In such a situation the act of true courage is to flee.

No, you did not act like a man. A man does not let himself be pushed around. He is his own master.

I remember one day when our youth group went on a hike. After a long walk which made us very thirsty we came to a spring of clear, cool water. Our leader made us wait beside it for half an hour before we could drink. He did that to teach us self-control.

Not to resist temptation, but to satisfy every desire the moment you feel it will make you soft, a man without a backbone, whom serious girls will not respect. If a girl turns you down because you won't take her immediately, then she isn't the girl for you. Girls who are worthy of their name deep down in their hearts want only one thing: a real man and nothing less than a man.

If you want to prove that you are a man—not merely a male animal—then, as in driving a car, you must learn first of all how to use the brakes and the steering wheel. The gas pedal is easy enough to manipulate. The brakes are something else again. Not to let go, but rather to control is the sign of true manhood. All through marriage you will need this self-control; for example, when your wife is sick, or troubled, or when you must be separated because one or the other must be away.

Now you'll probably say: "It isn't easy to become a man." That's true, my friend, it isn't easy. In fact it's extremely difficult to master this young new power which breaks out within you. It's a battle, above all to resist the temptation to satisfy your desire alone by yourself. When this temptation comes over you, then remember this: *the sex instinct is given us as a means of communion.* To satisfy it by yourself means to abuse it, because it isolates you and makes you seek in yourself a satisfaction that is to be received in communion with another. For this reason it turns you in upon yourself while the real act of love should open you to your partner. Performing the act alone leaves an aftertaste of defeat, shame and emptiness.

Nevertheless, if you should come to the point of giving in to this, do not feel that you are perverted, abnormal and condemned, nor should you look upon it as a tragedy. The battle is really difficult only as long as you think of yourself as your own master. Everything will be easier when you realize that your body belongs to God and He has entrusted to you your sexual powers, as well as your talents, your time and your money to be used for the happiness of your fellow men.

The more you learn this sexual self-control, the greater will become your ability to love with the heart. You will learn to recognize the kind of love that is aroused by a smile or a gesture or a certain tone of voice and which reveals the heart of a girl. This is very soft music and you need practice in order to hear it. The more you tone down the drums, the more you will become aware of it.

Sexual control is like a kerosene lamp. If you do not manage the wick properly, the flame will leap too high, the glass will be darkened with smoke and the lamp will give no light. You have to adjust the wick for the lamp to give proper light.

There is no art without skill. Since love is an art, it needs skill. But every skill has to be learned and no skill can be without discipline.

It is a great help, until the time when you can use your sexual power for the happiness of the one whom God has destined for you, to find an outlet for this power in some creative activity. Write, paint or even compose music! Look for friends who stimulate and challenge you. Devote yourself to work which you enjoy, or to a hobby which demands your best. How would it be to learn a craft, or to play some musical instrument; to take a trip through your own country or beyond its borders? These will offer you excellent opportunities to transmute your desires and to use your masculine strength for a constructive purpose.

Above all, don't remain alone in this struggle. If I can, I should like to be a good friend to you in it. But don't forget that the best friend in any trouble is Jesus Christ Himself.

Now a final word about the fear of mockery. Your Lord was mocked; they even spat in His face. Why are you then afraid of being laughed at by a girl?

Jesus Christ, the man of God, is the only one who can make a man of you.

In Him,
T.

M. . . . , March 12

Dear Pastor T.,

You certainly hit me right between the eyes in your last letter. Perhaps I was too much afraid of that girl and her scorn.

On the other hand, I still think that it's necessary to know what a woman is like before you marry.

In my tribe one hears often about women who "have water"; women with whom it is impossible to carry out the sex act. It certainly cannot be a sin to find that out before marriage. Wouldn't it also be a favor to the girl? We have a proverb which says, "a woman who has water rarely bears a child." Shouldn't a man know before marriage whether a girl is able to have children, so that he will not be tempted to take a second wife later?

You said that you wanted to be a good friend to me, so I have the nerve to ask you these questions without beating around the bush.

I wait impatiently for your next letter.

Yours,
F.

B. . . . , March 18

My dear friend,

The questions you asked in your last letter are very important. Before I go on I want to thank you for asking them so clearly and bluntly. They help me to clarify my own thinking.

Yes, I know there are many people who think that the happiness of a marriage depends upon the structure of the female sex organs. But first of all, you must realize that it's not a question of bones, but of very flexible organs and tender tissues which, in the course of a marriage, adjust themselves. As far as the anatomy itself is concerned, you can learn more by reading a marriage manual than you can from a sexual experiment. If there is a physical abnormality then only a medical examination can reveal it with certainty.

The same holds true about the myth of "women with water." I've heard talk about this problem and I'm still not sure what to think about it. But one thing that strikes me though is that I've never yet met a man who has seen such a case himself. I've talked with both European and African doctors who have worked for many years in Africa and they all say that never yet have they examined a woman with such a condition.

In any case, it is absolute foolishness to lie with just any girl in order to know what women are like. There's no such thing, you know, as a typical woman, for every woman is different, not only her body, but her heart. Every person is unique. After five minutes with a girl in the bush, you know very little about her body, and absolutely nothing about her mind and heart.

The word *know* is a great word. The Hebrew word for it used in the Bible means "to know someone by name." In other words, to know someone very well, to take care of that one, to love and to respect him or her as a person. The Bible uses this word for the first time in Genesis 4:1, "Adam knew Eve, *his* wife." You can never know what *the* woman or *a* woman is like; you can only know *your* wife. That means you cannot know a woman except in marriage, in the atmosphere of faithfulness, where the sex act is one of the expressions of love.

Do you have to take a risk then? To a certain extent, yes. Marriage is a risk. Otherwise it would be a bore. But this risk is probably less than you think, so long as love is free to work its miracle. The fact that you say you're doing a favor to the girl when you try her out shows me that you have no idea what happens in her heart when she has a sexual experience. A girl cannot separate the sensations of her body from her heart and soul as a young man may do. Emotionally, she is moved much more deeply, and the impression of the first man to whom she has given herself will remain with her. She can never dismiss him from her mind completely even if she hates him later, even if she eventually marries someone she really loves. And even for the young man, the first girl whom he has possessed will always remain his to some extent. May she be his in reality.

Most of the time a girl, under the stress of emotion, is not altogether mindful of what she is risking. It is up to the man to know it for her. I hope you can see now that to respect a girl's virginity before marriage has much more to it than just being the narrow-minded idea of some old-fashioned people. Her very nature requires it. Therefore a time of great responsibility begins when you meet a girl. You must always keep in mind how dangerous it is for her to give herself too soon. You must realize what serious consequences this act can have, even though she seems ready to give in—yes, even though she be the one who takes the lead. Such awareness will make it easier for you to master your desire. Only by maintaining an attitude of chivalry are you really doing the girl "a favor."

You don't even have to consider the commandment, "You shall not commit adultery." You don't have to question whether or not you have broken it. To keep Jesus' commandment, "You shall love your neighbor as yourself," which He called the greatest of all commandments, would certainly mean to abstain from premarital relations; for you would be hurting your neighbor instead of loving her as yourself.

Sincerely,

T.

M. . . . , March 26

Dear Pastor,

What you told me in your last letter was completely new to me. It never entered my mind that in possessing a girl who invited me to do so, I was doing her a wrong. I always thought I would be pleasing her.

I've talked to some of my friends about this. But they think that it would still be permitted and even an advantage to have experiences with girls who are used to it, who are already in a sense "spoiled" and to whom you could do no harm. I'd like to know what you think about this argument.

You didn't yet answer my question about the wife who can bear no children. Shouldn't you find out for sure before marriage whether or not a woman is fertile, in order not to have the temptation later on to take another wife who would be able to bear children. For marriage without children certainly doesn't make sense.

Yours,
F.

B. . . . , March 30

My dear François,

Please forgive me that I overlooked the question in your last letter about a childless marriage. But first a word about the arguments of your friends.

If you get involved in a sexual experience with a girl who does not have marriage in mind, you don't have a true woman as your partner.

Alexandre Dumas has said: "If you have a sexual experience with a girl worthy of you, you do damage to her. If you have it with a girl unworthy of you, you do damage to yourself."

In your tribe I have heard that originally intercourse before marriage was punished, often very severely. That's why I wonder whether your ancestors too did not already know some of these truths. What do you think?

But however that might be, God's will is never without reason. God knows better than you do the conditions which make for your happiness. He does not cheat you when he wants you to have only *your* wife, when He does not want you to "know" another woman before your own wife.

It's really strange. All the young men that I know want to marry virgins. But on the other hand they want to experiment first. Who can know when he "spoils" someone else's fiancée whether his own will not be treated in the same way? Don't you see how contradictory it is?

That leads to your question about childless marriages. This problem is closely connected with promiscuity. I have often wondered why the number of sterile couples—for the man can also be sterile—is constantly growing in Africa. Doctors are in agreement that the main cause is so much intercourse before marriage. Such conduct encourages the spread of venereal diseases, which doctors tell me is the most common cause of sterility. Many girls will not become mothers and many young men will never become fathers because of their experimentation before marriage.

In connection with this I would like to tell you something that is not yet widely known in Africa. Normally the conception of a child can take place only when the ovum separates itself from the ovary of the woman. This is usually between the nineteenth and fourteenth day before her next menstrual period. The choice of a day favorable to fertilization is therefore very important. But I'd like to say again: every woman is different and you can only find out this day for your wife in the course of your marriage. Experimenting before marriage does not help you here at all.

Even with all our modern knowledge of bodily functioning and all our medical skills, children remain a gracious gift of God. The one to whom God does not grant this gift must realize that children, in and of themselves, are not the sole objects of marriage. According to the Bible, the union of husband and wife in one single being is a complete fulfillment. Also, you may have noticed how often God uses childless couples to carry out some great task for which they would not have been available if they had children.

But we can talk about that later if you should ever find yourself in this situation. For the moment it's enough if you realize this: many girls in Africa are afraid that their husbands would divorce them or take wives if they as wives do not bear children. The fear of barrenness is of itself enough to make a girl childless. That is why you should leave no doubt in the heart of your fiancée as to your love for her. She must know for sure that you love her, just as she is, completely, whether she bears you a child or not.

These are the pledges you will make to your wife before God on your wedding day:

I promise to love you and comfort you,
  honor and keep you, in sickness and in health;
and forsaking all others keep only unto you so long
  as we both shall live.

The most important decision of your life is the decision to follow Jesus Christ. The second most important decision is your choice of a marriage partner. May God guide you!

In Christ,

T.

M. . . . , April 4

My dear Pastor,

Why has no one ever told me this before? Neither with my parents, nor with our catechist, nor with our African pastor have I ever talked over these matters. The only recollection I have of this subject is a sermon against adultery by an American missionary which I heard when I was ten years old and which raised many questions in my mind. But when I asked my father about them, he beat me.

Now I am being punished as a guilty person and put "under discipline," without anyone taking the trouble to explain to me why I am guilty. When I have finished these six months in which I am barred from Communion, is everything automatically in order again? Can I be certain that God has forgiven me?

And still another question. I think I can see now that having hasty relationships with any girl who happens to be handy is of no real help in getting to know what a woman is like. But in order to marry, you have to choose first. How can you make a choice without getting acquainted with girls? Where and how can I meet girls? Where should I go? Where should I not go? What do you think about dancing? Why is it that all girls imagine that as soon as a fellow approaches them he has nothing else in mind but having sexual relations?

Finally, if you say that the physical aspect is not sufficient as a guide for the choosing, what then are the standards I should have in making my choice? How can I ever know whether a girl loves me or whether I love a girl?

Nothing but questions! Hoping that you will not lose patience with me.

Yours,

F.

B. . . . , April 15

My dear François,

You are absolutely right. You must get acquainted with girls before you can choose. But it's still a little difficult for me to give advice that can be put into practice here in Africa, The existence of love in the Christian sense—that is, the free and mutual giving between two persons—is still not widely recognized. In former times, girls were strictly guarded and often were "married" from the time they were born, sometimes even before.

The attitudes that grew out of these customs are still alive and you cannot change them quickly. But I think the time has come to take some steps in a new direction. In order to make happy marriages possible, we must create opportunities where girls and fellows can meet and be together as good comrades, without embarrassment or false shame, under conditions in which they learn to respect one another. Coeducational schools, youth groups, work camps during vacations: all these would offer such opportunities. There would be a real undertaking for the Church, not to stop with preaching against adultery, but to create conditions for a healthy relationship between the sexes by organizing youth centers in towns and villages.

You ask: "Where is it good for me to go?" It is difficult to give you any hard and fast rules. It is above all a matter of atmosphere. You must use your own judgment as to where and when you may dance. It is up to you to see the danger in public dance halls. It is up to you to avoid getting involved in situations from which you will not know how to escape.

One good rule is to say to yourself simply: "I will not go where I should not want to be seen by the one whom I respect and love more than anyone else in the world."

That girls suspect sexual intentions from the fellow comes partly from custom, partly from their unfortunate experiences. It's up to you to act differently. I'm sure that girls who are to be taken seriously also welcome the opportunity to meet you as friends. If a girl is sincere you will win her respect and confidence by your good conduct. This should be your aim: to become a young man who is chivalrous; in other words, of all your friends, to be the one who has the greatest respect and consideration for girls.

Naturally, the day will come when you have to make a choice. You must not take this decision lightly, as if it could be changed later on. In God's view marriage cannot be broken. Nothing but death can separate those of whom Jesus declares: "They are no more two but one. . . . Those whom God has joined together, let no man put asunder."

As a guide for your choice, it might be wise to ask these questions:

(1) First, the question of faith. I see from your last letter that God's forgiveness is important to you. That means you cannot imagine living your life without Jesus Christ. That's why your first question should be: "Is the girl a Christian? Can I pray with her?" Being one in faith is the foundation for becoming one in marriage.

(2) You should then ask yourself: "Do I really love her?" You must know that. But how can you know that? Here are some of the signs: If you cannot imagine living your life without her; if you feel pain when you are away from her; if she occupies your thoughts, and inspires your dreams at all times; if her happiness means more to you than your own. Similarly, there are signs that you can look for when a girl loves you: if she writes often to you, if she tries to please you, if she looks for excuses to meet you. A most significant sign is her breaking off of friendships with other young men.

(3) It is not enough to love her as a sister if she is to become your wife. You have to be *in* love with her as a woman. Ask yourself: "Do I want her to be the mother of my children?" You will find out that when you ask yourself this question many girls who please you only because of their superficial good looks are automatically eliminated from your choice. In the same way a girl should ask herself: "Am I ready to give myself to him? Do I want to become the mother of his children?" She will not want to give her children a father who is a heavy drinker, undisciplined, bad-tempered, irresponsible, selfish, stingy or lazy.

(4) Is she one who, by her conduct and attitude, by her likes and dislikes, by her character and interests as well as by her education and ability, will be able to help me in fulfilling my vocation? Is she one who can share with me the sorrows and joys of my work and who will stand by my side as a true companion when these joys and sorrows come? That's why in your case, I think you should look for a girl who has at least some education, so that you can talk over with her the problems of your work as a teacher. This is absolutely necessary. True love communicates. Love that finds no words to express itself soon dies.

There are also two or three other questions which you can ask yourself—about her health, about her social background, about her age. It's better that your wife be a little bit younger than you, but not too much. According to my doctor friends, the ideal age for a young man to marry is twenty-five and for the girl twenty-one. But this is only a guiding principle rather than a stiff rule.

Don't marry simply to please someone in your family. Never look upon a woman as a means to an end—any end. Love her for her own sake and not for the gain she will bring you.

However, these are all only some human counsels. Every marriage is a unique experience, filled with the unknown and unexpected, a dangerous but a magnificent adventure. Only with confidence in God can you dare to set out on this adventure.

In other words, God must guide you. It is at this point where your question about the choice of a wife touches your question about forgiveness. As long as you have not received His forgiveness, God cannot guide you. By transgressing His commandments we separate ourselves from Him. It's as if there were a telephone wire between God and ourselves. When we sin, the wire becomes disconnected. Only when the connection is working can we hear God's voice.

To repair this connection is not as easy as you seem to think: Six months "church discipline" and then "automatically" to obtain forgiveness? No, the grace of God is not so cheap. It requires you to admit your fault and to repent in your heart.

Church discipline shall testify to the world that the church does not approve of this or that behavior. But it can never replace repentance, and neither can it be a punishment. It is not up to the Church to punish sin. That would be to insult Jesus Christ, who took our punishment by dying for us on the cross. "He was wounded for our transgressions, he was bruised for our iniquities; upon him was the punishment that made us whole, and with his stripes we are healed" (Isaiah 53:5).

I invite you to read, slowly, and several times over, Psalm 32. One of the mysteries of the Christian life is revealed there: the relationship between our repentance and the fact that God guides us.

The Psalmist says: "When I declared not my sin, my body wasted away." And he adds: "I acknowledged my sin to Thee." God answers: "I will instruct you and teach you in the way you should go."

I already know what question you will ask in your next letter: "How can I repent?" This is indeed the key question in life, the answer to which comprises the answers to all other questions.

I cannot, however, give this answer by letter. We've now arrived at a certain boundary in our correspondence. So far I have been able to advise you by writing. But now we need to talk together as brother to brother. That is why I invite you to come and visit me.

No one can tell the Gospel to himself. We need a brother who proclaims it to us. Dietrich Bonhoeffer, one of the great theologians of our time, has expressed this truth as follows: "Christ became our brother in order to help us; now, through Him, our brother becomes for us a "Christ" with all the authority of this commission. Our brother stands before us as a symbol of the truth and grace of God. He is given to us as a help. He hears our confession of sin in the place of Christ, and he forgives us our sin in Christ's name."

I am ready and waiting for you.

Your brother in Christ,

T.

P.S. Make this experiment and come. Enclosed is a money order for your travel expenses.

E. . . . , May 2

Dear brother in Christ,

This is just to let you know that I had a good journey home. Almost too good. But I shall tell you about that later.

First of all my thanks for your spiritual help. Now I can admit what a great effort it was for me to come to you at all. I did not intend to do it. But when you sent me the money for the trip, you took away my best excuse. I had made up my mind not to say anything and to let you do the talking. I confess that I was afraid. The hearing before the church elders hardly bothered me at all. But to come to see you, that was hard for me.

Everything was so completely different from what I had expected. You never gave me the impression that I was standing before a judge. Rather, it was like sitting with a brother who was also a sinner.

The fact that you talked so frankly about your own defeats encouraged me to speak freely about my own. At first I wanted to do it like the farmer who admitted to his pastor that he had stolen a rope. Weeks later the pastor met him again. Still the farmer looked unhappy. So the pastor asked him: "Was there something tied on to the rope?" "Yes," he said, "a cow." I don't know how it happened, but all at once it was easy for me to talk also about the "cow." I never dreamed what a relief it is simply to speak out certain things. It's something that you can't know until you have "experimented."

Unfortunately the "cow" which was the reason for writing my first letter to you was not my only one. It took a great effort for me to reveal it to you. But strangely enough, you and I didn't become more dejected by speaking of these things. Instead we grew always happier. We even laughed. At the end the atmosphere was actually gay. Perhaps such a conversation is actually the happiest thing in the world. I noticed, too, that the main thing was not my fall, but rather my getting up again; not my sins, but rather the forgiveness of those sins.

You are right. It's impossible to confess your sins to yourself. In my best hours I had tried to persuade myself that God had forgiven me. But I had real assurance of it for the first time when we prayed together and then you announced it to me so personally by quoting Isaiah 43:1: "François, fear not; François, I have redeemed you; François, I have called you by your name; François, you are mine."

Sometimes it's hard for me to believe that the punishment which I have deserved is carried by Jesus and that this thought shall give me peace. Sometimes I think it would give me more peace to suffer—at least a little—for what I have done; not to earn forgiveness, but to show my repentance through action. But, as you said, this may be merely pride. I shall try to believe that Jesus has done everything.

But now you shall hear what happened to me on my return trip. My head is swimming. I'm all confused. I'm beside myself with joy. I am . . . I don't know what. . . . To be brief, I got acquainted with a girl!

"Girl" is the wrong word. I should rather say, "queen." And what does it mean to "get acquainted?" I can only say this: for the first time in my life I have seen in a girl a human being, a person.

That such a meeting can change one so completely! It's impossible to believe. I don't know myself. I cannot possibly describe her to you. I cannot tell you how beautiful she is and why she is so perfect. Words seem pale, colorless, unworthy. Every expression is an understatement. Just this much I will say: I met the girl who will be my wife. Now I would like to see your face!

I still have a question though. It puzzles me that all this happened so soon after my visit with you. Do you think it is possible that God guided me in this experience? That there is a connection between this friendship and my confession?

You assured me that God would guide me in a new way after the "telephone line" was repaired. But so quickly? Is God so close? I tremble . . .

There's much more to tell you. But I must close. I want to write again to "her."

Your dazed F.

B. . . . , May 6

My dear dazed François,

Thanks for your last letter which arrived today. Nothing could make me happier. Congratulations! If I understand you rightly, you are really in love. I thank God that He has given you this experience.

Yes, I'm quite sure that there is a connection between your new step in faith and the meeting with this girl. God does not always act so promptly. Sometimes He lets us wait a long time in order to teach us patience and in order to try our faith. If he has answered your prayers so quickly and so clearly, it must be for the purpose of encouraging you while you are taking the first faltering steps in the new life. But He is constantly at work and always close to you, whether you realize it or not. I hope that the tremor you feel in your heart will never leave you.

Now I am really curious and you must allow me to ask questions for once. Who is this girl? What's her name? Please tell me in detail how you became acquainted with this angel. Does she love you too? Have you already talked with her parents? May I perform the ceremony? Shall I start preparing a sermon?

Please answer soon!

Yours in curiosity,
T.

E. . . . , June 3

My dear father in Christ,

Four weeks have gone by since I received your letter. No, sir, do not prepare any wedding sermon. It will be years before we can get married, if ever.

I am dreadfully unhappy.

But first of all let me tell you the whole story from the beginning. Her name is Cecile. We met each other in the bus. She had a baby in her arms. Later I learned that it was her sister's baby. Her sister was ill. I took her for a married woman. She had two suitcases and a bundle of pans beside her. We did not have seats. On the curves of the road we had to lean against each other to keep our balance. We talked about everyday things. My first impression was: "Here is a girl who is different." It's hard to explain. She was more open than others and yet at the same time more reserved.

When she reached her destination she asked me to pass her suitcases and bundle through the window. But the driver started the bus before I was able to give them to her. Five minutes went by before I could persuade him to stop again.

I got out then and found myself in the middle of nowhere with the baggage of a stranger. What should I do? I walked back. After twenty minutes I found the girl with the baby, both of them crying.

There was little hope of getting another ride the same day. So she invited me to stay with her parents in her village a couple of miles away from the road.

A strange situation. We arrived, she with the baby in her arms and the bundle of pans on her head, I with her two suitcases. Everyone in the village stood there staring at us.

A cool reception at first. She explained the situation. A good meal.

A thousand times I have asked myself the questions you ask. The answer to them all seems to be "yes." She is a Christian, a student, and she is interested in teaching. I cannot imagine anyone better fitted to become the mother of my children. She is a little younger than I am, and in good health. Besides that, I could sense that she was not indifferent to me. Even if she did not say anything, her eyes said a great deal.

The idea of inviting her for the night never even entered my head. Formerly that would have been my first thought. I don't know myself anymore.

I left the next morning and told her goodbye. Her parents were polite. But they did not say anything.

Then the letters came—almost every day. Here is one of them which I already know, by heart, please send it back to me as soon as you can. From it you will see what a serious-minded girl she is. I swim in happiness, am full of plans . . .

But then comes the bill.

No, I can't find another word for it. Her father wants to sell her, as at an auction, to the highest bidder. He asks for a payment of $400 in advance since, he claims, there are already other bids for her. But I'm afraid this will be only the beginning, the down payment, the first installment. I cry when I think it is my angel for sale, the one whom I love.

What do you say now? You didn't think of this big obstacle, did you? All the pretty things you said about the love of the heart and the soul. A lot of good they'll do me now, won't they?

Of course, no one can stop us from loving each other. Within the clan system to get married simply because we are in love is incredible and cannot be tolerated. Under this system, the girl is never the wife of her husband, but the wife of the bride- price.

Four hundred dollars! For me this is altogether out of the question, an impossible amount. You have made me dream. But reality is cruel and destroys that dream. I've ceased to hope.

Or would you like me to work for you as a wash boy, until my hair is as white as the clothes I wash?

Look, I know that I am insolent and ungrateful. You have done nothing to deserve this tone I am taking with you. But I don't know any other way to give vent to my despair.

I would rather die than to just exist without really living. By that I mean, I guess you know, to exist without her. I want to cry aloud, cry out in the name of thousands of young men who are condemned to live without love, who are driven into the arms of prostitutes. I want to cry out in the name of thousands of girls who are forced into marriages with rich old men, who are often polygamous.

But who will hear my cry?

I accuse those who hold responsible positions in our country— those who dissipate with the money of the poor instead of breaking the monopoly which the rich hold on women, and abolishing this brutal and inhuman custom.

I accuse this totalitarian society, this dictatorship of the clan which uses the girl to balance the family budget and to fulfill the material wishes of her parents.

I accuse the selfish fathers who are too lazy to work and who use the money from selling their daughters to pay their debts, to buy alcohol, cars and wives.

I accuse the girls who remain passive when they come up against the curse of the bride-price instead of speaking out; who let their parents have their way and who only complain when their marriage becomes as much of a prison as though they were enclosed by stone walls or barbed wire.

I accuse the Church, which, instead of instructing me, placed me under harsh laws which I could not understand; and when I transgressed them and was more than ever in need of God's grace, deprived me of that grace. I accuse this Church which punishes instead of helping, and which takes away my job.

Why does God, the so-called protector of true marriage, show me His way without enabling me to walk in it? If the marriage of love remains the privilege of the rich, why doesn't God send me from heaven the $400 that I need? Where is His power? Is He not stronger than these little false gods—mammon and the clan? What a God!

You have awakened in me feeling of which I did not believe myself capable. You have taught me to love. You have kindled in my heart a fire of heavenly origin, without which I no longer consider myself a man. But now this fire consumes me. It makes me suffer more than I can bear, and it will kill me.

I do not expect an answer, for there is none.

Yours,

F.

To the Reader

I was speechless when I first read this letter from François. I really didn't know how I should react to it. In no case did I want to put him off with cheap cut-and-dried answers and empty promises or even ask him the somewhat malicious counter-question, whether he would have written the same letter if he were the father of marriageable daughters. I knew that behind this angry outcry of an African young man is the distress and anguish of thousands.

One must not weigh too heavily the words in such a letter and above all one must not be pushed to the defensive because of the bitterness of its tone and the injustice of its exaggerations. The first thing to do is simply to listen to this cry. That's why I decided that the best expression of my understanding and the most honest way to answer was just to be silent for the time being.

It is hard for us to realize that the same development which Western society has made in centuries, Africa is now making in decades. Originally the bride-price was a very meaningful custom which served to stabilize marriage. The goods involved were livestock and served as a recompense to the family of the girl for the loss of productive powers. In case of a divorce the cattle had to be returned. For that reason the girl's family was eager to preserve her marriage.

The introduction of money, which is paid today and spent tomorrow, to a large extent nullified the purpose of this custom. The availability of western luxury articles removed it one step further from its original purpose. Today, in many cases, you will find nothing short of a slave trade in girls. A prominent African lawyer once showed me shelves covering one wall of his office all filled with the records of lawsuits against fathers who had accepted money from different suitors for the same daughter.

The battlefield, however, on which this abrupt clash of old and new takes place is the human heart. There is no area of life which is more affected than that of marriage and the family. At this focal point all the social, religious and political problems of modern Africa appear to meet and become visible. Raising the status of women seems to be the basic condition for all further evolution in Africa. Man cannot be free as long as there is no free woman at his side. Political independence is not possible without independent and responsible couples. But there will be no independent couples as long as love is not the supporting foundation of marriage.

If this is true, then we stand with empty hands. If the key to the solution of Africa's problem lies in a deeper understanding of what love, in particular, married love, is, what do we have to offer? What does an African see in this area when he comes to Europe or America? Haven't we ourselves just begun to discover love as the supporting foundation of marriage? Even though we have no bride-price is not love menaced by other forms of materialism?

When I was this far along in my reflections I was able to put myself in François' place. The more we understand someone else, the more we learn to know ourselves. The same holds true for a continent. When we start to get the feel of Africa, we see suddenly our own country in a different light. We no longer stand there as condescending givers, as those who are advanced and mature, who know all the answers, but as those who are also in need of help.

This had just become clear to me, when I received the following letter from Cecile, which gave me new courage to fight for the marriage of François.

Y. . . . , July 2

Dear Pastor T.,

I'm writing to you because I'm very upset. I haven't heard anything from François for almost four weeks.

He's spoken and written a great deal about you. That's why I dare to turn to you now.

Ever since I've been going to school in Y. we have written to each other almost every day. But since the beginning of June, he has not answered my letters.

I'm very worried. What shall I do? Can you help me?

Cecile

B. . . . , July 10

Dear Cecile,

I'm happy that you wrote to me. From what François has written about you, I feel that I know you already, although we've never met.

François has been very close to my heart ever since he was a schoolboy. I'd like to suggest to you that we become a team in order to help him.

Perhaps you do not realize what it meant to him to get acquainted with you.

You know that he lost his job at the beginning of the year. He was really desperate when that happened, and we had a long and detailed correspondence about it. He felt that he had been abandoned by his church, and I was afraid that he would lose his faith completely.

Through a miracle, the opposite happened. His faith became deeper. He let himself be forgiven. That which God did for him was far greater than that which men did. He had the courage to become very small before God and that's why God could become very great to him. He threw himself into God's arms again.

That was a great moment. You must be thankful that you will receive a husband who has made such a decision.

On the way home he met you. Coincidence? For François it was more than that. It was for him a sign that God had not abandoned him. That God loved him in spite of everything. It strengthened his faith. It made it easier for him to trust in God, because he met you.

That's why it hit him all the harder when your father asked for $400 as the bride-price. Did you know anything about this?

When he received this news, his whole faith began to totter. He wrote me a raging letter, of which I'll send you a copy of the last part. It's a typical François-letter. You know him a little already. He has the tendency, as soon as an obstacle confronts him, to throw away everything: faith, love, God, state, church, me and even you.

This letter was written on June 3. Since then I haven't heard from François either.

Cecile, I've read this letter of his often and each time I feel anew: It's a great letter. He is so honest in his anger. François accuses everyone and everything—except himself. He acts as if he would be the first and only one who would have to pay the bride-price. But that's the way he is—our François. As long as something bothers others he doesn't let it get under his skin. But when it bothers him, he falls apart completely.

In no case should this letter remain unanswered. He's simply expressing what so many feel. I tell you honestly, that at first this letter left me speechless. I knew only too well that we Europeans are also to blame that a useful custom has become abused.

I was just thinking how I might answer in a helpful and effective way, when your letter arrived.

That's what gave me the following thought: At the moment you can help François more than I. That's why I'd like for you to answer the letter instead of me.

Let's become allies in the battle for your marriage. Show François that love is no forbidden land for Africans, as so many people think. Show him that Africans can—and may—love too.

This is not a question of money, but a question of faith. Show him that love does not accuse and denounce, but it fights.

Notice especially the paragraph in his letter in which he accuses the girls of remaining indifferent and passive before such a curse as the bride-price.

You're the only one who can answer this reproach. Show François that there are girls in Africa who are different, who dare to speak out.

I have great confidence in you, and I count on you.

Walter T.

Y. . . . , July 20

Dear Pastor T.,

Yesterday I did what you asked and answered François' letter. I had to fight with myself for a long time. At first I didn't want to do it at all. Now I have at least tried. Enclosed you will see the result.

It was a difficult letter. I am still afraid to send it.

All last night I thought about what I should do. Then I got the idea of sending it to you first so you could look it over. Please read it to your wife as well. If she thinks that it is also good to send it, then I will.

It's so hard to be completely honest and still not to wound. I am afraid already of François' answer. Perhaps I should omit the last four words. Do you think they are too strong?

Cecile

Y . . . . , July 19

Dear François,

I love a young man. His name is François. Please don't doubt that for a minute when you read this letter.

I was attracted to you from the first moment we met in the bus and then again when you helped me carry home my baggage. I felt even more drawn to you when you made no attempt that night to come to me. I felt then that you were not just interested in my body, but in myself. Not just in an hour of passion, but in a lifetime together.

It is because I love you I dare to write this frank letter to you.

Pastor Walter has quoted to me certain parts of the letter which you wrote to him on June 3. He has asked me to tell you what I think about it.

When I first read the letter, I was a little embarrassed for you. But now I can at least understand why I have heard nothing from you for so long.

François, I understand you very well. I have kept all your letters. When I read them over and over again I can begin to judge how hard my father's demand for $400 hit you. I know that you are poor. I know that you have lost your job. I can feel how much you love me . . .

Perhaps you are right in saying that the church has failed. Certainly, you are right when you say that there is a lot of injustice in our young nation. When the new and old bump against each other so suddenly, it can hardly be otherwise. What took so long to happen in Europe is happening so quickly in our country. That is why a useful custom, as the bride-price was in former times, is now being abused—at least so Pastor Walter expressed it. But it is not only the Europeans who are guilty; we also are guilty.

There is a good thing, too, about the bride-price. It shows us girls what we are worth to a man. That's just the way we are. We love the one who has to pay something for us, who has to fight for us, who has to conquer us.

I wrote you at the beginning of this letter: "I love a young man." A man does not only denounce and accuse. A man fights. Accusing God and the whole world doesn't change anything. I respect you only if you fight. And I can love you only if I respect you. That's why I ask you: fight for me. Fight with me for our marriage.

I don't want to leave you alone. I want to fight with you. You are right—many girls do let themselves be sold as goods without showing a will of their own. I do not defend them. But your Cecile wants to be different.

The more we have fought side by side, the more precious our marriage will be. That which just falls into our laps is not worth much. It doesn't bind us together.

I know that God means for us to be together. How I know it, I can't explain. But I know it. Neither can I tell you now how we will find the money, or how my father will change his mind, or how you will find another job. And yet I know, deep down in my heart, that there is a way, so that some day we shall belong to one another.

God doesn't help us by letting money fall into our laps from heaven. But He does go with us step by step through all the difficulties, if we just hold His hand. What we need is not money, but faith—trust in God.

Once more, I love you. But I love the young man François, not the dishrag François.

Your Cecile

B . . . . , July 22

Dear Cecile,

My husband read to me the letter you wrote to François as you asked him to do. You've hit the nail on the head by this letter—with the sure aim of true love.

First of all I must admit something to you. I never dreamed that a girl your age could write such a letter. Congratulations! I'm so thankful that you've done it and I hope we can get acquainted very soon.

Yes, I know how hard it is to be able to help without hurting. A doctor cannot always heal with a soothing ointment. Often he must use a knife to cut away the infection. In marriage each partner must be the doctor of the other one.

Only the one who is able to heal is also allowed to hurt. This is why love alone can dare to hurt with a good conscience. But love can do it and should do it. For real love is not something sentimental and weak, but something firm and bold.

I was impressed above all that you have already found the connection between respect and love.

In his explanation of the commandment, "You shall not commit adultery," Martin Luther writes as answer to the question, "What does this mean for us?" the following: "We are to fear and love God so that in matters of sex our words and conduct are pure and honorable, and *husband and wife love and respect each other.*"

There is a close connection between respect and love. Still, "respect" has an even deeper meaning than you might think. To respect means to appreciate, to find something worthy of love where no one else can discover it. I believe that a truly loving woman loves her husband even in his weakest hour, in his failure and defeat, even when he lets the leaves hang like a dried-up banana tree. Only the woman who respects her partner in this way really loves him.

Go ahead and send your letter. It is a good letter. God blesses courage and honesty. Don't be afraid. If François sees red, my husband will know how to calm him. Remember here too: "there is no fear in love."

Ingrid T.

E. . . . , July 27

Sir,

. . . So you have succeeded in getting me to write to you again . . .

I just received the letter from Cecile which you have read. It was very clever of you to use her. She knows me well and knows exactly where I am most easily hurt . . .

But the letter had just the opposite effect from what it should have had. She doesn't only criticize me; she even insults me.

And I thought she was an angel! Now the angel has shown her teeth. But it's all right. At least I know now where I am. That's why I'm happy that she wrote me this letter. I have no more illusions. This disappointment makes it easier for me to bear my fate.

I possessed the first girl because she said I was no man. This one I will leave because she says I am no man. You wrote me once: "True courage here means to flee." So!

What does it say in the Bible—Ephesians 5:22-24? I'll write it out for you, Mr. Pastor, so that you don't need to look it up:

Verse 22: "Wives, be subject to your husbands, as to the Lord."

Verse 23: "For the husband is the head of the wife, as Christ is the head of the church, his body, and is himself its Savior."

Verse 24: "As the church is subject to Christ, so let wives be subject in everything to their husbands."

In everything! If she contradicts me now, what would it be like when we are married? Like all African men, I want a wife who obeys me—unconditional obedience in *everything.* That's what the Bible says. Just as the Church is subject to Christ, so should wives obey their husbands. That is clear and without question.

I have been warned. Therefore I thank you.

F.

B. . . . , August 3

Dear François,

This is just the way I thought you would react.

You are very foolish, François. Let me repeat it—very, very foolish.

I read Cecile's letter before she sent it to you. At her request I even read it to my wife. We both wish that many fathers and mothers, young men and girls, would read it, not only in Africa but also in the rest of the world. It's a very unusual letter. We were moved by it.

Your Cecile is no piece of wood, François. Neither is she a baby nor a work-animal without a will of her own. She's not even a servant maid, but instead a very mature girl. I congratulate you on finding such a girl. You have no idea what a great gift it is that such a one loves you.

You wrote to me out of an angry heart after you had read the letter only once. You should never do that. Rather sleep on it for a night, so as to give yourself time to think. Read it again very slowly and quietly.

Don't you understand how hard it was for Cecile to write it? That she said these hard things only because she loves you?

Love is not blind; love sees. It sees clearly the weak points and the faults of the other one, but it loves him just the same, including his faults and weaknesses.

You asked me once how someone could know whether he is truly in love. I answered you: by the fact that he is not bothered by the faults of the other one. Of course, he does not love the faults, but he loves the other one with the faults. He feels responsible for the partner.

Now it happens to you that Cecile loves you in this way. But instead of being thankful, you are angry. Or do you think that you have no faults? Perhaps it is impossible to love a person who has no faults.

Be honest. Everything that Cecile said is true. Your trouble is that you give up too quickly.

Yes, I know that criticism hurts, especially that which is true. We are all very sensitive about it. A man is especially sensitive if he is criticized by a woman. This is true in our country as well. But I think African men are oversensitive on this point. That's because the woman is very seldom looked upon as an equal and one does not accept criticism from inferiors. Here is one reason why so many marriages are so empty and monotonous.

Before he was married, one of my friends wrote to his fiancée about what he expected from his future wife. I'll pick out only a few sentences from the long list he sent her. The first is this:

"She must challenge me to the highest degree by completely honest criticism of me." An un-African sentence, isn't it?

He continued: "When she is disappointed in me, she must not withdraw her confidence."

"She must help me untiringly to overcome my weaknesses."

"She must never pretend, but must tell me honestly when I have hurt her."

Do you understand? What he wanted was not a servant girl, but an equal partner who stands beside him before God. Only with such a partner can you become "one flesh" in the real depths of its meaning—a new, living being. Partnership includes the right to criticize.

And now, Ephesians 5. If we pick out certain verses in the Bible to prove that we are right, then we'd better be careful. Bible verses are not rubber stamps which we can use to certify what we think so that we say, "just look, even God agrees with me!"

God's Word is like a hammer that breaks rocks into pieces, or like a chisel that cuts into us, that may hurt us, in order to form us, change us. God's Word challenges us to the highest.

You quoted verses 22-24 because they just suited you. Thanks for copying them for me. But I opened my Bible just the same and read also verses 21 and 25.

Verse 21 emphasizes that submission is mutual. It says: "Be subject to one another out of reverence for Christ."

Then come the verses which you quoted which explain what that means on the part of the wife. Verse 25, however, shows what it means for the man. You left this verse out.

It reads thus: "Husbands, love your wives, as Christ loved the church and gave himself up for her."

That is a tremendous sentence. A whole lifetime is not enough to understand the depth of its meaning.

How did Christ love His Church? He served her. He worked for her and helped her. He healed her, comforted her and cleansed her, even washing her feet—and that was the duty of slaves in Jesus' time. The Church was everything to Christ, and He gave her everything, including His life.

Don't you see how God's Word becomes a chisel that cuts and hurts us? It cuts more keenly than any two-edged sword. Christ was not what we men like to be—a big chief or a sheik who wants to be served. He was the slave of His Church. I use this word because it hurts your African ears. Only as the slave of His Church was He her head. So also you are only the head of your wife in the measure in which you are her slave.

Even at that time the Church was not obedient to him. She left Him in the lurch, and still does up to the present day. You have much to criticize in the Church. So do I. There is so much that is not beautiful in her, if you think about all the tensions and quarrels that go on. But this is the Church He loved. He died for her. Through His love He made her lovable.

If the Church obeys Him, then she does not do this because she has to, but because she wants to. Without Him, she cannot live, just as a body cannot live without a head.

Don't you understand that Cecile really wants only one thing: to belong to you just as a body belongs to its head? By criticizing you she wants to reach only one goal: that you will be a head whom she gladly obeys.

That's why she is asking you to fight for her, just as Christ fought for His Church. That's your service to her.

True courage *here* is not to run away, but to become mature.

As soon as possible you should go to Y. and talk to Cecile.

T.

E. . . . , August 14

Dear Sir,

Again, what a letter! If I didn't know you so well, I should have torn it up. What can I say about it? What a nice sermon!

It's too bad you always look at things with one foot in heaven and the other off the ground. You don't help me towards any practical solution.

The only practical suggestion which you have is in the last line. But even that can't be carried out. How do you think that I could meet Cecile? If I picked her up after school, the news would be all over town right away, and there would be nasty gossip. She lives with her uncle. I wouldn't even dare to show myself there. A park with benches doesn't exist in the whole city. And I haven't a car. If I owned one I would also have money and I could get married.

You don't say a word about money. You talk only about love. But money and love are inseparable in Cameroun. Only those who have money can get married. That is why I need money. I can only get it when I am working. I was a teacher at one of our church schools. The Church dismissed me.

Besides—if Christ is the head of the Church, and the Church is His body, both are one—how is it possible that Christ forgives me and the Church does not?

Then too—I'm entirely on my own. Other young men have a father or family to support them. Here is my situation: My grandfather had three sons: Tonye, Moise, and Otto. Tonye was the oldest. He wasn't a Christian because he had two wives. Moise, the middle son, was a catechist and had only one wife. She bore him four children, two of whom were sons. Otto, the youngest, had only one wife, Martha, who bore him one son, Jacques.

Otto died and Martha became a widow. That is a terrible fate in Africa. When a wife dies, it isn't so bad for a husband. He has lost his property. A property can be replaced if necessary. But a widow is like a property that has lost its owner. She is helpless.

Martha was now a widow with her child Jacques.

Normally, Moise, as the older brother and next in line to Otto, would have had to marry Martha. But that wasn't possible. He was a Christian, and a catechist. He could have only one wife. That is the law of the Church. It is hard. The law of our customs and traditions would be more merciful. Because Moise was a catechist, he didn't dare to be merciful.

Moise did take the ten-year-old Jacques into his home and let him go to school. That was all that he could do.

So Martha was pushed on to Tonye. She became his third wife. He hated her from the beginning, and with her he hated Christianity. He neglected her, mistreated her and tormented her. She received neither clothes nor shoes; no hut in which to cook, not even a piece of soap. Nevertheless he had one child by her.

I was that child.

Tonye already had a son by his second wife, who was his favorite wife. He never recognized me as his son.

Only my mother cared for me. I was a dirty, neglected child. I had a skin disease because she had no soap to keep me clean. She could barely clothe me, and I was ashamed to go to school. I ran away and wandered round until I came to the mission station. From there on you know my story.

Do you understand now why I can expect no help from my family? As far as my father goes, I do not exist, especially now that I have become a Christian. My uncle Moise took my half-brother Jacques, and has four children of his own as well. I have only my mother. She has all she can do to live from her garden.

I cannot hope to inherit anything. Even if the favorite son of my father died, both Jacques and the two sons of Moise would come before me.

And now you say, I should go to Cecile. With empty hands? No.

F.

B. . . . , August 20

Dear François,

Thank you for writing your whole story to me. We have known each other for almost ten years. That is how long it took us to get this far. Why?

Your letter showed me what poor ambassadors for our God we missionaries really are. When you came to me ten years ago you told me that your father was not concerned about either you or your mother. That was true. But I had no idea how much suffering and pain stood behind it. I took you in at our station and didn't ask any more questions.

We always make this mistake. We don't ask any more questions. We don't want to know too much. We are afraid that the burden might crush us. We fear the responsibility.

We missionaries think always we have done enough if we travel to Africa. It's true that we see you daily at the services and in school; but there remains a great distance between us.

We're too lazy really to put ourselves in your shoes, to look at things with your eyes. Instead of this we shut our eyes and simply proclaim the Gospel as a law.

How ashamed Christ must be of His missionaries! As I read your letter, I was ashamed before Christ and within my self. We are so unkind—so lazy in our thinking. Someone who had only one wife becomes a catechist. His brother who has two wives is excluded from the Church. But in your story he actually plays the role of the Good Samaritan.

There just is no solution which applies to everybody. We cannot say: this is right for everyone, and that is wrong for everyone. Love is not lazy. We must take the trouble—the hard labor of love—to search out God's will afresh in each case.

Please forgive me for wanting to keep clear of this work and for not asking you any more questions.

Nevertheless, two things become very clear to me through your letter. One is this: You should be able to see for yourself now the problems created by polygamy.

You asked me once if it was possible for a man to love several wives at the same time. You see now that it just doesn't work. Either there is no personal relationship between the man and his wives, or he has a favorite wife. In any case, there is always want and emptiness, jealousy and hatred. Even the Bible testifies to that clearly when it describes polygamous relationships.

Just imagine now that your father's favorite son should die. What a fight would take place over the inheritance! Who would be able to unravel the tangle of the rights of the various parties? What a fight there would be, certainly with magic means too, between the brothers, half-brothers, step-brothers and cousins! We would certainly never wish to see it.

The other thing which is clear to me through your letter is this: how God has realized His plan in your life, in spite of all the mix-up of your family, in spite of the guilt of the mission. In spite of everything, He has called you to His kingdom.

God was in everything. In the suffering of your mother, in the lack of love of your father, God was there.

He brought us together. He saved you. He has taken you by the hand and has led you—in spite of your disobedience, in spite of my mistakes—led you to Cecile. What a work of God! *He* was not lazy. Even if we have all failed, He has not failed.

You say my letter was not practical enough. But I can't show you any more than God has shown me for you. Often God does not show us the final solution. He only shows us steps to take.

In Psalm 119 it says: "Thy word is a lamp unto my feet, a light unto my path." God does not promise us headlights that will show us the whole way. He promised only a lamp, and that for our feet. A lamp does not light far ahead, but only a little way.

Your first step is to find work again. I am glad that you thought of that yourself. I suggest you visit Pastor Amos and ask him to re-employ you. I will write to him too and ask him if he will talk to Cecile's father himself. Is that practical enough for you?

And once more: there is no doubt about it, you must talk to Cecile. Don't worry about how you can meet her. A woman thinks with her heart, not with her head. Also in practical things she often has an idea before a man does. Have confidence in Cecile. Love has imagination.

T.

B. . . . , August 20

Dear Cecile,

François has written to me again. At last he has come out of his hiding place. Your fine letter succeeded in bringing him out.

Now you must be ready. It is possible that he will be waiting for you after school, when it starts again. It will be good for you to plan now where you can go, so that you can talk together in peace . . .

T.

B. . . . , August 29

Dear Pastor Amos,

I am writing to you today concerning François. You know his story. I baptized him. You confirmed him. Then he became a teacher and I believe he did good work for three years.

Then he had a palaver with a girl. The case was made known among the pupils and he was denounced. Personally, I have the impression that it was a planned trap. He was dismissed because of it, and was forbidden to attend the Lord's Supper for six months.

Then I had a detailed correspondence with him. I'm enclosing copies of some of the letters, so that you have some idea about the case. Finally, it led to a serious conversation in which I was able to help and advise him, and to a confession which went very deep. I cannot tell you more, because the secrets of confession are absolute. I can only testify as his counsellor that he was serious about his repentance, that he accepted the forgiveness of Christ, and that he dared to make a new beginning.

We must stand by his side in this new beginning. You know that there are great temptations to faith after such a complete change around, especially when it is genuine. The devil seems to attack especially hard those who make a decision deep in their hearts. That is why we must both show François brotherly love in his first steps in the new life.

First, I'd like to ask you to allow him to take the Lord's Supper. As far as I can see, the sacrament is only forbidden in the New Testament to those who persist in open sin in spite of many warnings. I cannot find a single case where one who has been repentant and who has confessed his sins has been placed under church discipline.

On the contrary, as his counsellor, I would encourage François to take communion at the next occasion. After his defeat, he will understand it now perhaps for the first time and he will experience it for what it should be: the fellowship of Jesus with sinners.

When we exclude repentant sinners from the Lord's Supper, then it becomes exactly the opposite, a procession of righteous people who proclaim through their taking part that they either have not sinned, or have not been caught at it.

When the prodigal son found his way home again after his life in adultery, his father didn't let him wait for six months in a back room to see whether or not his repentance was genuine. No! He embraced him, accepted him immediately as his son, and ate with him as a sign of forgiveness.

This is now a real problem for François. He writes to me: "Christ has forgiven me, but not the Church. Are these two different things, Jesus Christ and the Church?"

So, do you not think it possible that François might be re-employed as a teacher? That would be a visible sign that not the law but the gospel rules in the Church; not punishment but forgiveness. I have a reason for asking this. François has got to know a girl. I think that they really love each other, and are meant for each other. But now the question of the bride-price has come up. This question is a very difficult one for François, for he has no family to support him. You know the situation. The father of the girl is demanding $400 immediately. According to François, this is just a first installment.

Could you not visit this family once? As an African, you would certainly get farther than I could, and you could judge everything much better.

In any case, please give me your opinion and your counsel.

Walter T.

E. . . . , September 16

Dear Pastor Walter,

We've seen each other.

It was like that first meeting with Cecile. Everything is changed again.

For weeks now I have lived with my mother in a distant little village. For hours I've sat every day in a dimly-lighted hut. My thoughts kept going round in circles—always around the walls. I would stare at the pictures cut out of magazines which I had pasted on the wall as if they could talk to me, give me advice. But always they were silent. At last I couldn't bear to look at them anymore. I was trapped in my own prison.

And now the walls have been broken apart. There is freedom everywhere, even though outwardly nothing at all has changed. I'm just as poor as I was before. Only one thing has happened: we have seen each other again.

A friend took me with him in his car. He had to be back the same evening. So I had only two or three hours.

I waited at the entrance of the school. Pupils, both boys and girls, streamed out. Cecile was not among them. Those were terrible minutes.

Finally she came, the very last one. She must have seen me and waited until all the others were gone. She didn't look at me; she just held out her hand. With outstretched arm I touched her fingertips as indifferently as possible, as if we greeted each other in that way every day.

Then she said, as if she had been waiting for me: "There are only two places we can go. We can go into the 'Red Donkey,' or we can go into the Catholic Church. It's always open."

I chose the Catholic Church because I had no money for a restaurant. We had to walk for half an hour to get there. I went ahead, and she followed me a little distance behind. No one would have guessed that we belonged together.

I would never have thought of going with her to the Catholic Church. It was really open. I asked myself why are the Protestant Churches always closed?

We entered and sat down on a bench in one of the back rows. We didn't touch each other. We didn't look at each other. Both of us looked straight ahead.

You ask what we talked about. I can't tell you. We hardly talked at all. It was all so completely different from what I had imagined. She said: "I'm glad that you came." I said: "Thank you for your letter."

I really wanted to say something completely different. I wanted to reproach her and to defend myself. But it was as if it were all blown away in her presence.

We were just silent. I don't know how long. Time flew. You understand—we weren't silent out of stubbornness. We were silent together. I could almost say, the silence welded us together.

How easily and how often I used to say to a girl, "I love you," and I wanted only to possess her and amuse myself. Now for the first time I should have said it and I couldn't. It was just as if the words were too small, too worn out, to say what the heart was thinking.

We didn't talk, and yet we did talk. Without words both of us knew we loved each other. This certainly worked itself deeper and deeper into our hearts, like a sweet pain, like a great joy.

It was the most beautiful hour of my life. No one should ever take the word "love" in his mouth without having experienced such an hour. It was as if we had known each other always, had always belonged together. It seemed to both of us as if we were one and the same person: she a part of me, I a part of her.

Suddenly I knew for sure: nothing could separate us any longer, no law or custom, no father or mother, no state or church.

Then I remembered that we were in a church. I thought, we are both standing before God, and we are making a promise to each other for life. I took her hand and for a long time our hands lay together, quietly and firmly.

Now I ask you, what is still lacking? Isn't that everything? Are we not married now? When does marriage begin? Does it really begin with the wedding? Doesn't it begin with the engagement, when we promise to each other: "I will belong to you all my life?" We have already made that promise before God. Hasn't our marriage already begun?

I can't even remember now about the farewell. It was as if I was dreaming. She asked me to come again soon, and I said that I was looking for work. Then we left the church one after the other, and went in different directions.

F.

Y. . . . , September 16

Dear François,

All night I couldn't sleep and I cried. I scolded myself because I didn't talk to you. My heart was so full. I wanted to tell you so much and I couldn't. Now you probably think that I'm indifferent to you, that I don't care.

Please understand that I couldn't speak because I was so happy that you had come. I have no one else but you.

Cecile

E. . . . , September 18

Dear Cecile,

Don't cry, Cecile, please don't cry. I understand you, understand you deeply. No, you don't need to be afraid. You need never be afraid when I am with you.

It was all my fault. I should have talked; I should have asked you something. But I couldn't either.

It all surprised me so much: how you greeted me, just as a matter of course. How you had prepared everything.

Then you sat beside me as if you were there just for me. That said more to me than all words.

You've cast a spell upon me. . . . I have hope again. Today I helped my mother in the garden instead of staring at the bamboo poles of the roof. She looked at me in amazement.

Your François

B. . . . , September 19

Dear François,

. . . So you were in the Catholic Church! I told you that Cecile would have a good idea. In Africa it is difficult indeed for a young man to meet a girl! The Church ought to be able to help with this difficulty.

I'm very thankful that you both have experienced this hour, and I can well imagine what feelings were in your hearts.

Your questions are hard to answer. You really have a gift for putting hard questions. They become harder all the time, and I must think about them longer before I can answer them.

When does marriage begin? The Bible says that marriage is a mystery. You cannot explain a mystery. You can only keep penetrating a mystery. You never get to the end of it. The beginning also is a part of the mystery.

You write: "It seemed to both of us as if we were one and the same person." When does a person begin? As far as the outside world is concerned, only from the time of its birth. But life is certainly there before that. When does life begin? Biology says: life begins at the moment of conception.

From that moment on, life is there. A new person has begun. And yet this person cannot be seen. It is in an in-between stage while the mother carries it in her womb. One can only say: a new person is on the way.

That is a picture of engagement and marriage. Your life together has truly begun. Did it really begin in that hour you were together in the church? Wasn't it there already before that? Did it start when you first met on the bus? Or sometime during those weeks of the first ardent correspondence? Who can say? It remains a mystery. From now on this new person, this new living being which you together make up, is on the way.

But this being on the way needs time. This new person must grow slowly just as a child grows in its mother's womb. This growing together slowly will take place during the time of engagement. All that you experience leads to this growth: the beautiful and the difficult; the joy of seeing one another again and the pain of the separation; the speaking and the silence; the writing of a letter and the waiting for an answer; hope and disappointment, yes, even obstacles and sufferings. All that makes the new person which you will become, grow and mature.

But this growth happens in secret. No one knows it, only you two and God—and the few persons in whom you have confided.

So your marriage has begun and still it is not to be seen. It is like the little one in its mother's womb between conception and birth. You are at the in-between stage. Your marriage is on the way.

The wedding day will be the birth-day of your marriage. That is when the new person appears to the world. Then everyone can see it. Then a festival takes place. Then it is made known to everyone.

At the time of engagement you say to one another: "We want to try and see whether we belong together." At the wedding day you say openly in front of everyone: "We have passed the test and it has turned out positively."

Naturally marriage does not come into being through the marriage certificate, any more than a child comes into being through the birth certificate. But still you must not underestimate these things. Marriage is not only a private matter. The official registration also belongs to it. Marriage exists in its fullest state when everybody can see it. At that time it is also protected legally. Luther said once: "A secret marriage is no marriage." That is why the wedding has been celebrated, through all ages and by all people, by a feast.

Please believe me when I say that I can hardly wait to experience this birth-day of your marriage with you. I will gladly do everything that I can, so that it will be soon. That is why I wrote recently to Pastor Amos. But I have not yet received an answer.

T.

O. . . . , September 20

Dear Pastor Trobisch,

Your letter surprised me in many respects. It was the mission which introduced church discipline to us in Africa, even though it isn't practiced in the European and American churches.

As long as the missionaries put it into practice themselves there were no voices raised against it. Now that we African pastors practice it, you criticize it. Actually we are only doing what you taught us to do.

Would François have come to you and confessed his sin if someone hadn't betrayed him? If he would have done that, if the affair had been known only to him and the girl, then I would say perhaps you are right.

But he was "repentant" only when he was caught. That is why we have to put him to the test in order to see if his repentance is really sincere. Refusing the Lord's Supper to him for six months is just a proving time. It is no sign that he is not forgiven.

This is also a warning to all the others in the congregation. Through such an example they receive power to withstand temptations. If I had not placed François under church discipline, then I would have led many others into temptation. I don't dare to do that. I am responsible for keeping the church pure. In I Corinthians 11:27 it says: "Whoever eats the bread or drinks the cup of the Lord in an unworthy manner will be guilty of profaning the body and blood of the Lord." The sin threatens not only the life of the individual but of the whole congregation.

That is why it is the duty of the Church to punish sin in front of the whole congregation. God also punishes sin in the Bible. David was punished after he confessed adultery with Uriah's wife: his son died. Ananias and Sapphira fell down dead because of a lie (Acts 5:1-11).

I know our African young men better than you do. It is very easy for them to confess something when by doing so they will escape punishment. Your way is very dangerous. If it is so cheap to get forgiveness that one needs only to come to you, and then everything is all right, then the temptation to sin again, rather than to fight against it and turn one's back on it, is very great.

On the other hand, punishment leads to true repentance. If we had not punished François, then probably he would not have repented of his deed.

That is why I can't give him back his job in our school right away. All the teachers and the pupils know of his case. If he hadn't been dismissed, that would have undermined the school discipline.

Originally, cases of adultery were rare in African society. They were punished very severely, at times even with death. Missionaries through their preaching have made adultery out to be the chief sin, if not the only sin. Through that they have made it attractive. On the other hand they forbid us to punish it. What shall we do?

I gladly agree to your request and will visit Cecile's family, though I already know with what arguments the father will defend himself. I would like to take François with me. Please ask him to visit me.

Pastor Amos

Y. . . . , September 22

Dear François,

Your letter comforted me very much. I am happy that you are not angry with me. I wanted to write to you before. But we had so much homework to do.

I have good news for you. My friend Bertha has an uncle who works in the Ministry of Education. She says he would like to give you a job as a teacher in one of the public schools in Y.

Please accept this offer. Then you can earn money and we can see each other every day.

Your Cecile

E. . . . , September 24

Dear Pastor,

Thank you for your letter. I had to think it over for a long time. The comparison between the time of engagement and the time of pregnancy is interesting. But when a child is conceived, it is easy to work out roughly what the date of its birth will be. I can't work out when we may be able to be married. That is what makes the waiting so difficult.

Your letter came in the same mail with one from Cecile. I'm enclosing it. What do you say about it? Is it possible for me as a Christian to teach in a public school?

Do you think it is good for us both to be in the same city? I long for it. And yet I know already I would miss Cecile's letters.

François

B. . . . , September 27

Dear François,

. . . Of course you can work in a public school as a Christian. If the Church could have given you a job, then it would have been right to take it. But Pastor Amos wrote to me that under the present circumstances it would be impossible. We must try to see his reasons. We must also understand that he has reached his decision only after much thought and prayer.

For you that means the way is free. God leads us step by step, just as He promises us only our daily bread, and not our whole livelihood.

My advice is this: accept the position in Y. Perhaps your testimony can be even more effective when you live among non- Christians. Be on the alert, and keep your eyes open.

Also, for the sake of your future marriage, it is good to see each other often. I wrote to you before that your engagement time should be a time of preparation. Your life together has begun, but at present it is still being tested. Not that you have to test Cecile, nor she you. But you both seek together to know whether you can become one in spirit before God.

For that purpose letters are often very helpful, because you can write many things which are hard to say in person. But you cannot really get to know each other just through letters. You must meet one another in different situations, in good moods and bad. You need to talk together so that you can get to know each other fully.

Being silent is part of the conversation. You have experienced that already. But it is only a part. Now you must also find words. You must find out if you can talk to each other and also if you can listen to each other. A marriage without plenty of talk is like a plant without sap. One day it will dry up.

It isn't necessary for you always to have the same opinion. But you must love each other so much that you will value each other's opinions.

One thing will become more difficult if you see each other every day and that is to draw a limit and to keep within it, withstand temptation. Imagine that you were a father of a fifteen-year-old daughter. Everything that you would not wish to be done to your daughter, you should not do to Cecile. I remind you again of all that I told you at the beginning of the year about becoming a man.

One more thing. Pastor Amos wrote to me that he will visit Cecile's father and that he would like you to go with him. On your way to Y. please stop at the pastor's house and fix a date. I will think about you especially on that day.

T.

B. . . . , September 28

Dear Pastor Amos,

Your letter, dear Brother Amos, is very matter-of-fact, almost cold. That is how I know that my last letter must have hit you very hard, and I can feel how difficult it was for you to answer me at all.

Thank you all the more for writing to me, and especially for writing so frankly and honestly.

Yes, we missionaries have made mistakes. We must regret many things we have done. I've written the same thing to François, in whose life story the mission is not without blame.

The miracle is that, in spite of our mistakes, God has built a church. To Him alone be the glory!

I would not defend myself, if it were for my sake. But it is for the sake of François and for so many others who are in his position. For their sakes we must seek to find what is the will of God. Please believe me, this was why I asked certain questions.

Is there really any human way by which we can determine the sincerity of repentance? Is it a proof of true repentance if one lets go of a certain sin for a certain time? Is it not God alone who can see into the heart?

You quote I Corinthians 11. There it says: Let a man examine himself' (v. 28). Isn't that exactly the opposite of what we practice in the African churches, where it is the pastor and elders of a congregation who examine the members? And even if that were commanded, why should not the pastors and missionaries also be examined?

Who is "worthy" at all? Am I? Are you? If only the worthy ones were permitted to go to Communion, who would dare to go? Only those who are conscious of their unworthiness are really worthy to attend.

It is this truth which François has discovered and now knows more deeply and more clearly than ever. That is why he looks for and needs the fellowship of Jesus. As men then, do we dare to stand between him and his Lord? Do we dare to withhold from him that which Christ wishes to give him?

Yes, I admit: God does punish. But in all the examples which you give it is always God who punishes, not men, not the church.

Dear Brother Amos: you have put a serious question before us pastors.

Is it not a lack of faith which stands behind church discipline?

And now one last question: do you really think that it is so simple and easy to confess your sins? That's what those who have never done it often say. For me it was the hardest step that I ever took. Also for François. He had a hard battle with himself. I can testify to that. A counsellor can feel it. It was costly grace for him—grace which cost Christ His life. And still the paradox remains: This costly grace is offered to us absolutely free.

I can understand what you write about school discipline. Certainly a school is not a church. I don't think it would be good for François to go back to the same school. But maybe there is another solution.

I have already written to François that he should look you up. Thank you very much for your readiness to go with him to Cecile's father. May God give you much wisdom for this visit. I will think about you specially on that day.

Walter T.

Y. . . . , October 17

Dear Pastor,

I have now been in Y. for two weeks. No, almost three weeks. How the time flies.

On the way here I visited Pastor Amos. He was very friendly to me: I was really surprised. Tomorrow we will go together to Cecile's father. My half-brother Jacques will come with us as the representative of our family. So it will be an official visit.

But before I go there I want to send you a few lines. Cecile has actually succeeded in finding work for me. Every morning when I enter school I am grateful to Cecile. But I am still more grateful each evening when I can see her.

Cecile is a genius; she always has ideas. Recently she has borrowed two bicycles. With these we can ride out every day into the bush after school is over until it gets dark. Then she has to go home to her uncle.

Yes, and now we are "discovering" each other, as you would express it. Each day is full of new discoveries. A girl is certainly unknown territory. Now for the first time I see how blind I was when I considered a girl as I would a toothbrush—something which one uses. And I wanted to "use" one in order to know how a "woman" is—oh!

Now I want to get to know only one girl—and that girl is called Cecile. It is as if all the others no longer exist. In her I get to know all girls, all women . . .

I let her ride ahead of me so that I can see her. She has her hair fastened up on her head, so I can see her long slender neck. I dreamt of it the other night. When we go up a hill she has to exert herself and pushes harder on the pedals. Then her beautiful neck moves in rhythm with her body. I could watch her doing this for hours.

Then we get off our bicycles and sit in the grass. There's hardly a topic that we haven't already talked about. She has her own opinion about everything. I didn't know that a girl could think, let alone have her own opinions.

As fascinating to me as what she says is the way she says it. I listen then to the sound of her voice, watch her hands and her eyes.

In those moments I would like to touch her. You told me once: "Keep your caresses for your fiancée." But Cecile now is my fiancée. How far do I dare to go? You advised me to keep within the limit. But what is the limit?

Oh, I'll tell you right away: we kiss. That far it always goes. Not right away. At first we both feel a little strange. Each time we have to get reacquainted. But while we talk, our hands look for each other. I can tell that she is waiting until I take hold of her hand, her arm. She is even pleased when I lean her head on my shoulder. She smiles a little, is very quiet, as if she just tolerates it. Then comes the kiss.

I must confide something else to you. When I kiss her, then the desire rises within me to possess her completely, I can't put it down.

If you had not reminded me of my own daughter on some future day; if Cecile had not written to me once: "I loved you even more because in that first night you didn't come to me," I don't know what might have happened by this time.

When I dedicated myself to Christ that night at your home, I thought that I was set free. You said then, "Christ is not a nothing. He is a power. Through His power you can overcome."

At first it seemed that way. But now the desire is stronger than ever.

My faith doesn't help me. Christ doesn't hear my prayers. They fall into emptiness. The desire is stronger than Christ. Why doesn't Christ help me, do something to me, so that I can be finished with this desire, this craving to possess a girl—once and for all?

The experience of love destroys my faith. Or must one who believes flee from love?

I'm afraid. Afraid of myself. Afraid of the animal which sleeps within me.

Do you understand?

Tomorrow I am going on a trip. When I return after two or three days, there must be a letter from you. Otherwise there might be a disaster.

François

B. . . . , October 18

Dear François,

It is almost midnight. But I want to answer your letter right away.

You write that Christ hasn't heard your prayer. I ask you, what did you pray for? That He would deliver you from being a man? What do you want? To be without sex? To have no more desire at all?

What you speak of is not possible. All that one does, one does either as a man or woman. Your sexuality is in your waking and sleeping. It is present with you when you work and when you pray. In your holiest feelings and in your purest prayers it is there.

If you believe in Christ, then you know that your body has become the temple of the Holy Spirit. If you pray for the mutilation of the temple, then Christ will not hear you. Christ wants to make you capable of living with your manhood.

Must the one who believes flee from love? I know there are many Christians who withdraw themselves and who turn their backs on it. They avoid the opposite sex and think by doing so that they are especially mature and redeemed Christians.

They fool themselves. He who believes does not flee.

Christ did not evade this issue. He came into this world. He was a young man. He came into touch with women's hands, women's kisses, women's tears.

He came to the bedside of a sick woman. He took a young girl by the hand. A woman touched His robe. Two women who loved Him are called by their names, Mary and Martha. He spoke with women alone, once at the well and another time writing in the sand. The sinner who kissed His feet was a woman of bad reputation. Those in the room were shocked. Yet He defended her. He moved among people in a free and natural way.

He is the one who has overcome because He lived the life of a human being. To overcome means to be on the way to mastery. He will lead you to that goal, not to flight.

You can't run away from your manhood: it belongs to you; it is a part of yourself.

Let me tell you a story:

Once upon a time there was a tiger. He was captured and put in a cage. The keeper's task was to feed him and guard him.

But the keeper wanted to make the tiger his friend. He always spoke to him in a friendly voice whenever he came to his cage. The tiger, however, always looked at him with hostility in his green, glowing eyes. He followed every movement of the keeper, ready to spring on him.

The keeper was afraid of the tiger and asked God to tame him.

One evening, when the keeper had already gone to bed, a little girl got lost in the vicinity of the tiger's cage and came too near to the iron bars. The tiger reached out with his claws. There was a blow, a scream. When the keeper arrived he found dismembered human flesh and blood.

Then the keeper knew that God had not tamed the tiger. His fear grew. He drove the tiger into a dark hole where no one could come close to him. Now the tiger roared day and night. The terrible sound disturbed the keeper so that he could no longer sleep. It reminded him of his guilt. Always in his dreams he saw the torn body of the little girl. Then he cried out in his misery. He prayed to God that the tiger might die.

God answered him, but the answer was different from what the keeper had expected. God said, "Let the tiger into your house, into the rooms where you live, even into your most beautiful room."

The keeper had no fear of death. He would rather die than go on hearing the roar of the tiger. So he obeyed. He opened the door of the cage and prayed: "Thy will be done."

The tiger came out and stood still. They looked into each other's eyes for a long time. As soon as the tiger noticed that the keeper had no fear and that he breathed quietly, he lay down at his feet.

That is the way it began. But at night the tiger would begin to roar again, and the keeper would be afraid. So he had to let the tiger come into his house and face him. Again he had to look the tiger directly in the eye. Again and again. Every morning.

He never had the tiger completely in his power "once and for all." Again and again he had to overcome him. Every day brought the same test of courage.

After some years the two became good friends. The keeper could touch the tiger, even put his hand between his jaws. But he never dared to take his eyes off the tiger. When they looked at each other they recognized each other and were glad that they belonged together and that each was necessary to the other.

François, you have to learn to live with the tiger, courageously, eye to eye. For that purpose Christ will set you free.

If you believe in Him, then you can dare to be tender to each other. There are Christians who think that God is especially pleased with them if they deny themselves this. But that is nonsense. Only he who truly believes can also really love.

How far do I dare to go? How far? As far as you can. Put your hand in the jaws of the tiger if you can.

But don't overestimate your strength and don't skip over any of the steps. You must learn to feel which caresses are right for the particular occasion. Please don't think, just because many do it so quickly and easily, that kissing is not an art.

Never take your eye off the tiger. He is awake and prowling. He follows every movement, knows every weakness.

François, I am sending you along a dangerous road. But I am glad you tell me everything. I don't want you to be evasive. Once more: He who believes does not flee.

I will give this letter tomorrow morning—no, this morning, because it was midnight long ago—to one of my friends who is going to Y., so that it will reach you quickly.

T.

O. . . . , October 23

Dear Brother Walter,

I want to tell you about our visit to Cecile's father.

But first, thank you for your letter of September 19. It did me a lot of good to hear from the mouth of a white man, even that of a missionary, that the whites are not without fault.

Your statement, that God can build the Church even in spite of us when we fail, has comforted me greatly.

As far as church discipline is concerned the question for me is always this: is there forgiveness without punishment?

Even the heathen believe that God punishes when His commandments are broken.

Then the missionaries came and said: God does not punish, rather God forgives. The result is that wherever Christianity has advanced, indiscipline breaks out. The heathen fear God, the Christians don't. They say: God doesn't punish, God forgives. So I don't risk anything if I sin.

What are we able to do then? I don't dare to act as you suggest. Perhaps I lack faith. Perhaps you Europeans have more faith than we do. Do your congregations really live more obediently than our congregations? Or do you just shut your eyes because you don't want to see sin?

For us Africans, when sin happens, it hurts not only the individual but the whole community. In this way I believe we are closer to the thinking of the Bible than you are. You didn't go into this point. This is also the vital point in the marriage palaver about Cecile. For her father, the marriage of his daughter is not only an affair between Cecile and François. It concerns the whole family. It isn't he who sets the bride-price. His brothers and above all the brothers and father of Cecile's mother set the price with him.

He has nothing personal against François. He thinks he is a decent and honest young man. But this is how Cecile's father is placed.

His first wife bore him no child. He felt however that he must have a son. He was convinced that he owed his father this debt: to pass on the life which he received from him. Otherwise his own life would not make sense.

So he took a second wife. She bore him Cecile and then shortly after that three sons.

It is true that he is certainly not one of the poorest in his village. He is a very industrious man who has a large cocoa plantation. But in spite of that, up till now he has only been able to pay half of the bride-price for Cecile's mother. The other half has to come out of the bride-price for Cecile.

Besides that he has three sons whom he wishes to send to school. The cost of tuition rises from year to year. And one day these three sons will want to marry also. But he has only one daughter for these three sons.

He is not just wanting to be rich, nor is he lazy; rather he is very conscious of his responsibility. Cecile's uncles on her mother's side also keep their eyes on him.

We talked together quietly. He feels that a woman is more obedient to her husband if he has paid something for her. Otherwise it would be easy for her to run away whenever there was a dispute, and say: "I don't belong to you, because you paid nothing for me." Also the husband, he says, remains more faithful to his wife if she has cost him something. In earlier times the bride-price was paid in cattle. If the marriage broke up, the cattle would have to be given back. So that helped to keep marriage together.

By introducing money into the country the Europeans have destroyed this custom—that's what Cecile's father thinks. Behind it is also a reproach against me, because I have let myself become like a European. He doesn't say it outright, but I know it.

For him the bride-price is an honorable African custom through which the son-in-law shows the bride's father his gratitude and proves to him at the same time that he is capable of taking care of a wife.

There is another reason for the large amount of money he asks. My guess is that he is thinking about taking a third wife. He didn't say that to me, but I suspect it. The birth of the three sons, coming so quickly after each other, has made Cecile's mother very weak. Polygamy makes it possible to avoid that situation. The Church says: polygamy is sin; but it does not tell us how to space the children.

We ask ourselves sometimes how the missionaries solve this problem. But they always keep silent on this subject.

Now you can understand how it looks from the other side. What should I say? I don't know myself how I should be able to pay for the education of my sons if I gave away my daughter without a bride-price. Cecile's father doesn't understand what love is. How shall I explain that to him?

You will probably be disappointed and think that I as an African could have done more than I did. That may be true. He certainly told me more than he would have told you. But there are also disadvantages.

Cecile's father and I—we are from the same clan. So we are distantly related. That hinders me, because I am too involved myself. In such a case perhaps you as a European could do more than I. You are neutral. You come from the outside. You could try . . .

I was very happy about François. He was modest and didn't try to push himself forward. But he will have to wait until he has more money. I don't see any other solution.

Pastor Amos

B. . . . , October 26

Dear Cecile,

François will have told you how the visit to your father turned out. I received a detailed letter about it from Pastor Amos.

Cecile, please don't lose courage. God is with us, even in the darkness. True faith begins there, where one doesn't see at all. When all else forsakes us, all human hope, all possibility of a solution, then there is only one thing left for us to do: to let ourselves fall into God's arms. God is never closer to us than in such moments. "Fear not, *only believe,"* the Bible commands. We are only fully in God's hands when we have Him alone.

"Only believe!" That is something which must be learned. You and François must learn it together now. Nothing can prepare you better for your future marriage. That is why God sends you now into this darkness, takes away all supports upon which you could lean. So that you can learn and practice together to put your confidence in God *alone.*

How can you learn it? First of all: let God speak to you and listen to Him. When you are together, then open up your Bibles and read a portion together. Talk about it—what He says to you. Allow yourselves to be comforted, counselled and guided by God.

Then fold your hands together and spread out your worries before God. He knows the way. He will take you by the hand and lead you. He has brought you together. He will hinder the attempt of people to separate you. Believe that with all your hearts.

Don't be embarrassed to pray in front of one another. You will have to overcome this feeling of embarrassment. Now is your chance to learn it. Now you will see if you can talk about everything—also about your faith. A common faith is the most solid foundation for a marriage. If you build your house on this rock, then no storm can destroy it.

I talked for a long time yesterday with Ingrid about what could be done in your case.

First of all, we suggest that you write a letter of thanks to Pastor Amos. He is a good shepherd. It is touching that the old man undertook such a long and difficult trip. We respect him greatly.

And now we have a favor to ask of you, Cecile. That is the reason I write to you, although the letter is meant for both of you.

From your letter of July 19, written to François, it was clear that God has given you the gift of writing good letters. Now we ask you: would you consider writing your father a letter? We know that is something very unusual for an African girl. Perhaps that is why it could be effective.

Two things seem hopeful to us in Pastor Amos's account. In one place he writes about your father: "He has nothing personal against François." And then: "He doesn't understand what love is."

Try, Cecile, to explain to your father what your love for François is—to give him a feeling of it. We often reproach fathers because they do not talk to their daughters. Perhaps it is rather the opposite: the daughters do not speak to their fathers. They do not tell them what they feel, what they suffer and what they hope.

Write this letter in your mother tongue. Write that you love your father, that you understand him, and that you don't want to leave him in the lurch.

Give him some practical suggestions. You will think of something. Of course François must be in accord with such suggestions. In that way you can try out something else: whether or not you can plan your finances together.

It is not enough during the time of your engagement just to see whether you understand each other, whether you can be tender to each other, whether you can believe and pray together. You must also see if you have the same attitude towards money, so that you can decide together about what you spend. A wife should know how much her husband earns, and you must be in agreement as to how you will spend your money.

Your attitude towards money is much more important than how much money you have.

And still one other thing, Cecile, which I tell you in confidence. At the beginning of the year, even before he met you, I wrote to François, "You are responsible before God for the girl."

Now I write the same thing to you. You, a girl, determine how far François can go. No young man can go further than the girl allows. Don't have any false pity. Be a queen. You love a young man. Make him a mature young man.

T.

Y. . . . , November 1

Dear Pastor and Madame,

Thank you very much for your letter. I read it to François and we were both very moved to know you can put yourselves in our situation, that you feel exactly as we feel and that you want to comfort us.

We didn't know that God cared so much about us, that faith had anything to do with engagement. Without faith, we would have to give up now. But just because we do not know what the future holds, we feel even more closely bound together.

We have tried for the first time to read the Bible together. At first it seemed very strange. But then it was wholesome. It helps us if we are not only tender to one another, but if we are doing something else together. But we haven't prayed together yet. I'm ashamed to pray aloud in front of François.

I have tried to write to my father, but it just doesn't work. I can't tell you how hard it is for me. As a European I don't think you can understand it. It is as if there is a wall which separates me from my father.

Our fathers do not like to hear their daughters speak to them. They are afraid they will lose their authority. They think we do not respect them and they are offended.

I know that you meant your suggestion well. I have begun a letter and will try to continue it. Every line is a battle. It is so hard to put into words what I feel.

But even if I write it, I know I will never have the courage to send the letter.

Cecile

Y. . . . , November 7

Dear Pastor Walter,

I am glad that your letter was here when I got back from that fruitless trip to Cecile's father.

I thought: what happens to all those who don't have anyone to whom they can write a letter, no one who answers them . . . ?

The story about the tiger is not bad. It shows me that neither those who put the tiger in a cage nor those who let him free are doing the right thing. The ones who follow the world are just as cowardly as those who are super-pious. We mustn't give up the fight. It is not the fault of the tiger if we fall. It is up to me whether the tiger is my enemy or my friend. I have understood all that.

But there is still one question unanswered. What does it mean: "to put your hand in the tiger's jaws?" Does that mean I can go to the end if I am master of myself, quiet and "don't skip any of the steps," as you say? Does this mean that we can become united bodily?

I asked you this question before. Then it was about a girl I didn't care about, I didn't wish to marry, and whom I hardly knew. Do you remember?

I said then that I wanted to prepare myself for marriage. And you answered: on the contrary! You are learning habits which will disturb your marriage later on.

I said I had to take a girl now and then in order not to be ill. You answered again: on the contrary. You risk your health by doing that.

I said I wanted to prove that I was a man. You answered the third time:

on the contrary, you are a dishrag.

You convinced me then. But you didn't go into one argument: that of true love!

What if one wishes to be united out of love? If it only concerned some girl on the streets, I grant you are right. But with one's fiancée? With the girl that you love, with whom you feel completely one, to whom you have made a promise for life? Why should one stop there just with caresses, when you can say, in the deepest sense of the word, that you belong together?

You said that you can never try out being with just any girl in this intimate way. I agree. But can't you try it out with your own fiancée? If engagement time is supposed to be a trial time, why shouldn't you try out that also? Would you say that also is "adultery," if an engaged couple should give themselves completely to each other?

I heard a pastor say once: "Marriage is a garden in which everything is allowed. Outside of the garden, everything is forbidden." Yes, and then suddenly on my wedding day, I am expected to be a perfect husband? How can you imagine that would be possible?

Please understand me rightly: I am not asking the right to spend the night with just any girl off the street. I'm talking about Cecile, whom I am going to marry.

Do we really need first a note of permission from the registrar's office or from the church in order to be united physically? Inwardly we feel already as much man and wife as we would after the wedding.

Sometimes I have the impression that Cecile waits secretly for the moment when she can belong to me completely. I have a friend who had already paid half the bride-price. But he didn't wish to sleep with his fiancée before the wedding. One day he received the money back from the girl's family. The family was afraid that he was impotent. I wonder sometimes whether Cecile suspects this when I do not take her. Perhaps she even thinks that I don't really love her?

Recently she stretched out in the grass. Just lay there. Gazing up into the sky. Completely innocent. Her dress was tight across her breasts, and her knees were uncovered. I just couldn't hold back any longer, and I took her in my arms with all my strength. But she broke away from me and ran to the place where our bicycles were standing. We didn't say a word all the way home, nor did we talk about it the next day.

How long can this continue? How long must we keep ourselves from each other? If only the end were in sight! But we have no hope that in the next four, five or even ten years someone will give us a license.

Shall we run away? Where to?

François

B. . . . , November 11

Dear François,

A Christian is one who can wait. Someone gave this to me as a word of advice. I pass it on to you. Wait for the complete union. By not waiting you will gain nothing and you will lose much. I will put what you would lose into three words: freedom, joy and beauty.

You would lose freedom.

Let me tell you about another couple I know. They too thought that they loved each other and that they felt inwardly already as man and wife. But after six months they noticed that they had made a mistake. They talked openly about their feelings and agreed mutually to break their engagement. It all happened very peacefully. No scars remained.

If they had given themselves to each other completely, that would not have been possible. I know that your feeling for Cecile is so much deeper that it could not be compared to your feeling for that girl at the beginning of the year. And that is just the reason why I advise you to wait. The deeper your feeling is for each other, the more lasting would be the wounds in case of a separation.

I have heard men who have been married for years say to their wives: "I knew before the wedding that I had made a mistake. But we had already gone so far that I didn't have the courage to break it off. Now I have to pay the price for my mistake."

I am glad to read in your letters how strong and true and overpowering is the love you are experiencing. Nevertheless feelings can deceive you. It takes a long time before you can really decide whether you sense something lasting. A recent survey in America has shown that in most of the happy marriages the partners have known each other for several years, and that they were engaged several months before their marriage.

A test is only genuine if it could turn out to be negative. The time of engagement is a time of testing only if there is the possibility of breaking the engagement. Breaking an engagement is an evil. It is painful. No one wishes it. But in comparison to a later divorce, it is certainly the lesser evil.

I will use the picture of a birth again in order to make clearer what the engagement means. If I compare marriage with a child which is ready to be born, then the time of engagement is the time before birth. A broken engagement would be then—using this picture—like a miscarriage, which is what happens when a child is not able to live. In the moment, however, that you come together, you reach a stage where a miscarriage becomes almost impossible. Then there is no turning back and a separation would be like the murder of a child.

So you would lose your freedom. But even more: You would spoil the joy which the growing, maturing and waiting brings with it. Having sexual relations now before marriage reminds me of the child who, out of sheer impatience, opened his Christmas presents on the twenty-second of December. A married woman, talking about her experience before marriage, put it once this way: "Everything went along fine for a while. But then there came an unexpected pregnancy. Plans had to be changed quickly and excuses had to be made. The wedding was celebrated hurriedly. Our married life began without romance and without dignity. It didn't pay."

A premature birth endangers the life of the child. Of course, many children survive a premature birth. But never without difficulty.

When Cecile ran away from your sudden embrace, she just reacted naturally and without long reflection. Her healthy, unspoiled instinct protected her. She felt that the time was not yet ripe, that your happiness would be put in danger through this step. Actually your harmony was also broken and you didn't speak to each other any more that day.

I do not really believe that Cecile doubts your love when you restrain yourself. It is much more possible that her love grows. Your being together is still in a hidden stage. It is right also at this stage that you have not completely revealed or unveiled yourselves to each other. On your wedding day a piece of undiscovered land should still lie before you.

Of course the sexual side of your marriage is very important. You know already that you are not impotent, and Cecile knows it too. If there were any doubts, then a doctor could confirm it. That is no reason for wounding Cecile's feelings nor for risking your happiness.

Sexual harmony cannot be tried out. Even an engaged couple cannot determine it reliably before the wedding. There are two conditions necessary and both of these can be found only after the wedding: unlimited time and being completely free from fear.

If Cecile has to say to herself: "Today between five and six P.M. I must meet François. Then it must happen. Then I must be ready. Then it must succeed—otherwise he will leave me." I can tell you now with certainty: these thoughts will check her and lame her, so that both of you will be disappointed.

Suppose you tried it out and it turned out negatively? Suppose it didn't work as you thought it should. Would you then say: we shall have to break our engagement? You don t believe that. Your love is not that superficial. It is already too deep. Why then do you want to experiment?

No one expects you to be a perfect married couple on your wedding day. There is no such thing as a perfect married couple. There is only a mutual growing towards perfection. Often it takes years before man and wife are really adjusted to each other. The unlimited time which you need for growth you will find only in marriage. All that you can do before marriage is to protect yourself from experiencing or learning things which will hinder you from growing.

You can't have your cake and eat it too. The magic and beauty of the engagement period lies in the fact that there still remains one last secret, there is still a room which will only be entered when the hour has come.

Just imagine that your father wants to surprise you with a bicycle for Christmas. He hides it carefully. But you take it secretly out of the hiding place and try it out. Then on Christmas Day you have to act as if you are surprised and joyful, but the holiday is colorless and empty.

Your wedding day and your first night will become more beautiful if you have waited. Not until that night will you understand me fully. The wedding is not only a formality. If you have testified in public, before God and men: "We belong together," then the experience will be much deeper and it will have a much fuller meaning when you give yourselves to each other completely.

We tell our children in Europe a fairy tale: A king's daughter was put under a magic spell by a witch, and she had to sleep for a hundred years until a prince would awaken her with a kiss. In order to protect the princess, the king planted a hedge of thorns which grew up all around the castle. All the princes who tried to break their way in before the one hundred years were up were caught in this hedge and died. But for the prince who could wait, the thorns yielded and the way was free.

I can only put you into the hands of your heavenly Father. He will give you something beautiful. Let me say it again: A Christian is one who can wait.

You won't be able to reach me by letter during these next few weeks. I have to make a trip to the North. But I hope to be back before Christmas.

T.

Y. . . . , November 12

Dear Madame Ingrid,

I was so surprised when François introduced me to you yesterday after the service that I couldn't say anything. I'm sorry that you had to leave so quickly and that your husband wasn't with you. How much I would like to get to know him also!

I wanted to write to you before. But now that we've seen each other it will be easier for me. Strange, but I just can't write to my father. I've already made many notes of what I want to tell him, I've begun the letter, but again and again I've had to stop. A letter just won't come out of it all.

Still, I have the feeling that you will understand me. You probably think that I am very happy, and I am. Just the same my heart is often heavy. I have doubts, and I'm afraid.

I have doubts about whether François really loves me. He never tells me that he does. He often asks me if I love him, and he can't hear my answer often enough. But he never says that he loves me. Then doubts arise in my heart. I can only love him if I can answer to his love. He seems to think it isn't necessary to tell me that he loves me, and why he loves me. How can I answer him then? He makes me so uncertain.

How can you test love?

Your husband has written to François the story about the princess. I wonder what the prince did after he had awakened the princess. Was he not very careful, very tender, so that she wouldn't be afraid? Did he not tell her how much he loved her, and why?

Just lately we had a quarrel. It was about something very trivial and ridiculous. I had a flat tire on one of our daily bicycle rides. I had a repair kit and François mended the tire. That made him bad-tempered—and me too—because of the time we had lost. When he had finished, we discovered that I had left the pump at home. I always take it off, to prevent it being stolen. Then he started to scold me, and said it just proved that girls have no intelligence. I was hurt because he was so rude, and out of stubbornness I didn't say a single word while we pushed our bicycles home. It was nothing serious at all. The next day we made it up again. But I ask myself—if we have quarrels already, what will it be like later on?

And then I'm afraid. I would like to be sure whether I can bear a child or not. I'm afraid that François will divorce me if I am barren. Or that he will take a second wife, like my father. Is there any justification for marriage if there is no child?

Then there is still another problem. Lately I received the enclosed letter from a certain Monsieur Henri. He is a brother of the uncle of my friend Bertha who helped François to get his job as a teacher in Y. This Monsieur Henri works in the Ministry of Finance and has a good position. He even wanted to pick me up in his car.

Of course I refused him. What shall I do if he invites me again? I don't want to be rude.

Please answer me!

Cecile

Y. . . . , November 9
Ministry of Finance

Dear Mademoiselle Cecile,

Your friend Bertha has told me about you. I would like to make your worthy acquaintance, and shall be honored to wait for you in my car tomorrow at five P.M. outside your school entrance.

Monsieur Henri

B. . . . , November 18

Dear Cecile,

How well I understand you, my sister! I could show you letters from the time of my engagement in which I expressed the same anxieties and doubts.

But we also do not make it easy for the men, Cecile. On the one hand we want a man to be strong, wise and unsentimental. On the other hand we want him to be full of feeling, to be tender and to need us. What man can combine the answer to both of these wishes in a single person?

I will try to write directly to François. Don't ask him about the letter if he does not show it to you himself. For you there is only one way—you must tell him frankly and honestly when something is wrong, when you are hurt. As long as you can do that, then there is no danger to your marriage.

One thing more: you cannot prove or measure the quantity of love before marriage. It is not true that marriage grows only out of love. The opposite is also true: love grows out of marriage, sometimes very slowly. In the Old Testament story of Isaac and Rebecca it says: "Then Isaac brought Rebecca into the tent, and took her, and she became his wife; and he loved her" (Genesis 24). They married without having seen each other beforehand. The falling in love came afterwards.

Most of the marriages that you see around you were begun without any great personal love experience. Often the girls weren't even asked. You know yourself that they are not all unhappy. Often love has grown after the wedding as a fruit of the marriage.

A man from India once said to a European: "You marry the girl that you love. We love the woman that we have married!" Another Indian put it even more drastically: "We put cold soup on the fire, and it becomes slowly warm. You put hot soup into a cold plate, and it becomes slowly cold." You'll have to decide yourself on which side you Africans belong.

I am writing in this way so that you will not overestimate the love experience. It is certainly important. But love will become fully mature only in the atmosphere of marriage.

It is not only good, it is even necessary that you have some disagreements. My husband even hesitates to marry a couple who have not yet had a quarrel! What counts is not that you never quarrel, but that you are able to make up after a quarrel. That is an art which can and must be learned before marriage. As long as you are able to forgive each other you don't need to be worried about the future of your marriage.

The one who is not ready to be the first to apologize after a quarrel should not marry; and the one who has no humor had also better not marry. It is wonderfully wholesome if you can laugh about yourselves after a quarrel.

When you ran away from François, it was the thorn hedge in you which reacted—the thorn hedge which protects the sleeping princess. Many girls who give themselves too early never become mature. That is why it says three times in the Old Testament book, *The Song of Solomon* "I adjure you . . . that you stir not up nor awaken love until it please." This entreaty stands as if it were written in flames above the door of marriage.

Perhaps the waiting will be easier if you don't see each other daily. Then each meeting will be more significant. There are no rules about this. You must find out what is best for the two of you.

How well I understand your wish—your heart's desire for the happiness of motherhood! But the most frequent cause of sterility is a venereal disease. That is why virgins have every chance of becoming mothers. But you can't be sure about God's will in this matter until you are married; then you receive the knowledge that you will become a mother as a gift from God. There is no other way.

But do not think that if you have a pregnancy before marriage it can be compared with the deep happiness of motherhood! True, one problem is solved: you know that you can conceive a child. But how many new problems arise. There is no home in which the little one can be born, no father who can carry the child on his arm. There will even be a dispute about whom the child belongs to as long as the father has paid no bride-price. You will have to leave school and be made fun of and criticized by your teachers and classmates. For the certainty that you gain, you must exchange feelings of shame and guilt, self-reproach and the loss of self-respect. It doesn't pay. The price is too high.

Or do you have the secret desire, through a pregnancy, to force your father to consent to the wedding? Please, please, I beg of you, don't do that! Don't lower your child to be a means by which you reach your own goal. God has another solution if you can wait.

Give all your anxieties about motherhood to God. Even if you should have no child, that is no ground for a divorce. Your husband also has no right to take a second wife if your marriage has been registered as a monogamous marriage.

A Christian marriage has meaning and purpose even if God should give no children to the couple. The Bible speaks about marriage only in a very few places. So it is all the more striking that the same verse is quoted four times: "Therefore a man leaves his father and his mother and cleaves to his wife, and they become one flesh" (Genesis 2:24; Matthew 19:15; Mark 10:7; Ephesians 5:31). Notice how in this key verse, repeated four times, there is no word about children. According to the Bible, children are an added blessing of God. But they are not the only reason for marriage. The love of the two partners for each other, the becoming-one-person of man and wife before God, is a meaning of fulfillment of marriage in itself.

It is serious about Monsieur Henri! I don't like the sound of his letter. Be sure to talk it over with François, otherwise misunderstandings may arise. In no case and under no condition accept an invitation from him!

Ingrid T.

B. . . . , November 19

Dear François,

My husband is away on a trip and can't write to you at present. So I am writing you a letter today. I should like to talk to you as if I were your sister.

God has placed a great treasure in your hands: Cecile's love. I would like to help you guard this treasure in the right way.

Love is not something which you can own, something which you can put in your pocket. Love is something you must win anew—over and over again. During the time of our engagement, Walter once wrote these lines to me:

"He who loves is no more alone. For the one whom he loves is always present. The one who loves has no wish to remain the center of his own life. He permits someone else to enter into the midst of it, and feels that is a great gain and happiness. He becomes empty like an open hand which holds nothing, but waits until something is put into it. He who loves has the courage to become someone who needs something."

What Cecile needs above all else is the assurance that you need her. How can you give her this assurance? Only in this way—that you tell her over and over again, "I love you. I need you." She can't hear it often enough. You must have the courage to "become someone who needs something."

A girl becomes afraid if a young man simply takes her love for granted and never bothers even to tell her that he loves her. Woman's love is different from mother love or sister love. Cecile's love can only blossom out to the fullest if it can be in answer to your own love.

Apostle Paul wrote to the church in Ephesus: "Husbands, love your wives, as Christ loved the Church." We love Christ because He has first loved us. Our love is an echo of His overwhelming love. It is strange that Paul never admonished the women to love their husbands . . .

I am not thinking now about physical love. You will never convince Cecile of your love by your caresses, your embraces and kisses alone. She wants to feel that your heart is seeking her heart and that you mean her herself and not just the beauty of her body.

A young man *is* his body. Your body, that's you. A girl feels herself *in* her body. Cecile senses that her inner being is not revealed just in her outward beauty. She wants to be loved for her own sake and not just for the sake of her beauty.

That's why your caresses are much less important to Cecile than is your whole way of acting. If you are polite to her, help her to get on her bicycle, open a door for her and let her go ahead of you—all that can mean more to her than a kiss. A woman who has been married for many years told me once with a sigh, "If only my husband would say 'Thank you' just once, when I have prepared an especially good meal."

Above all, it hurts a girl if you are more polite to others than you are to her. Then she notices that you treat her as if she were a piece of property.

When we met recently after church, you were very polite to me. You introduced me to Cecile, it's true. But during our whole conversation you didn't give her a chance to say a word. I had brought her a parcel of books which she could read as a preparation for marriage. As you went away, you let her carry the parcel . . .

You laugh. You laugh? That's such a little thing, you say, very unimportant. For a girl's heart, it is a big thing. For Cecile it is a very important thing.

Don't be stingy with words. Give her courage so that she can tell you what bothers her, what she misses in you. Listen to her lovingly, not just patiently. The most important thing is not that you are happy, but that you make her happy; not that you are understood, but that you understand . . .

Ingrid T.

Y. . . . , November 30

Dear Madame Ingrid,

. . . Your letter comforted me most when you wrote and said that you also have troubles, anxieties and doubts. The white people always try to give us the impression that their married lives are ideal and without problems. Then we read in the papers about the many divorces in Europe and America—and we can't understand how the two go together.

That's why your letter meant all the more to me. I feel that I can tell you everything. By the way, the letter to my father is almost finished. On many slips of paper. All the thoughts that I would like to say to him if only I could. But I can't. I just can't force myself to send the letter.

Monsieur Henri gives me no peace. Here is another of his letters. Almost every day I get such a letter with all those insignificant phrases. They sound as if he had copied them out of a cheap love novel.

Thanks for your clear advice. I have refused the invitation through my friend Bertha. I'd rather not write to him myself. I do not wish a letter from me to him even to exist.

Cecile

Y. . . . , November 19

Dear Mademoiselle Cecile,

I am very sorry that you have no time for me. But my love for you grows from day to day. You are the crown of my heart. You are as beautiful as the moonlight.

I've already sent my brother to your father in K. He is in accord. I will send your father 50,000 francs soon. Then nothing will stand in the way of our happiness.

Next week there will be a big banquet for the high government officials. I would like to invite you to it. Your uncle will also attend.

You will be happy in our marriage. You can have servants and even earn money yourself. You can live like a white person. Our social life will only be in educated circles.

But love is most beautiful during the night . . .

Monsieur Henri

Y. . . . , December 15

Dear Madame,

Two weeks of torture lie behind me. I've been waiting every day for a letter from you. But I know that you are alone with the children and that you have very little time before Christmas.

Monsieur Henri comes every day with his car to the school entrance. He follows us if we go out on our bicycles. He spies on us—where we go and what we do.

Recently I met him at my uncle's as I came home from school. Bertha's uncle was there too, the one who helped François to get his job. That's how I knew that everything was planned. Then we went to a cocktail party. Under this name the foreign embassies of the whole world introduce the so-called "civilization" to our society. My uncle, with whom I live, went too. We African girls can't refuse if our fathers command us to do something.

I didn't dance. But I couldn't avoid Monsieur Henri taking me home alone in his car. He said that he had decided to marry me. He said it just in that way. As if it would be a great favor on his part. He didn't even ask me what I thought about it.

He wanted to kiss me right away—just as one would bite into a banana. His breath smelled strongly of beer and liquor. It was repulsive.

He is twenty years older than I am, and he already has a wife and two children. He says she's uneducated, doesn't know French and refuses to live in the city. But since he has a position in the government he needs a wife in Y. whom he can present, who can receive guests and entertain them. That's why he chose me.

He made it clear that he can pay the bride-price for me. His salary must be at least twenty times as much as François earns. He will visit my father and take with him all sorts of liquor and several cases of beer. He's already bought a radio for him and a sewing machine for my mother. He asked me what my brothers would like to have as gifts. I didn't answer him. I was glad that I could get out of the car without being molested. But I wept the whole night.

Money! A capital invested in women! The rich can buy them. The poor can at best rent a girl for a few nights, the kind of girl that nobody wants much anyway.

NO! I made a big mistake. Money doesn't give us value. It lowers us. It makes us just merchandise. It makes us either prostitutes or second and third wives of a rich man. That is no honorable African custom. That is no thank-offering to the parents. It is simply the slave trade.

If my father accepts money from Monsieur Henri I am lost. I shall be married to him. I shall just be Monsieur Henri's shop sign, his sign of business. Purpose of marriage: the wife is the salesman for the husband!

Of course, I've told François everything. If your husband wasn't away on a trip, he would have already written to him. François is again completely discouraged and has shrunk into himself, but I love him just that much more.

But what is the solution?

François thinks that if my father receives both money and gifts from Monsieur Henri, then there's only one thing for us to do—to run away.

What do you think about this solution? I need the answer quickly.

"He who believes doesn't flee . . ." That's right, but isn't it also flight if one is forced into a marriage and gives up the battle —gives up love . . . ?

Cecile

December 19

Dear Pastor and Madame,

This is the first letter addressed to both of you. We are writing it together.

We ran away. The answer to Cecile's letter of December 15 didn't reach us in Y. before we left. We think that probably you would have advised us not to run away. But we hope just the same that you will understand us. We couldn't see any other way out.

We had heard the news that Cecile's father had accepted 50,000 francs from Monsieur Henri. You know what that means. From now on he has a legal right to Cecile. To run away was our only weapon.

We decided together to do it, and we want to bear all the consequences together—even the bad ones. The fact that the school vacation has just begun made it easier for us to prepare everything without arousing suspicion.

You wrote to us once that the wedding day would be the day on which the marriage is born. You wrote: "A premature birth is dangerous."

But aren't there also births which are past due? Aren't they even more dangerous? And then the doctor has to intervene and sometimes he even has to do a Caesarean section. He has to cut the child out of the mother's womb in order to save its life.

Our running away is like a Caesarean section.

We don't know what is going to happen—where we shall live, or what we shall live on.

We only know one thing: now we are man and wife.

We have left father and mother. We cleave to one another. We have become one flesh. Genesis 2:24 is fulfilled. For that we need no money, no civil wedding, no pastor. We need no tradition, no customs, no state and no church. We need no liquor, no paper and no singing.

We need only God. He will not forsake us. All others have forsaken us.

Our bride-price custom is no safeguard for marriage. It crushes marriage under its feet. It makes it possible to steal the bride by signing a check. Even the state supports the unmarried mother and the fatherless child. Those who want to marry must go empty handed. The Church advises us to wait, but it doesn't help us when we do that. It does not help us either, if we flee. No pastor would dare to receive us in his home.

You also haven't answered our last letters. We do not reproach you. We only ask that you do not reproach us, nor judge us. We would like to remain your children in the future.

Cecile is sick and lies in bed. She caught a bad cold the night we ran away. We had to go a long distance on foot. She sends special greetings to your children.

We are telling no one where we are, not even you. That is why you won't be able to write to us now. You can do only one thing—pray for us.

We believe that you will do this.

François and Cecile

To the Reader

During the course of our lives, God leads us again and again to borderlines where we must stand powerless and perplexed. For François and Cecile this borderline was called bride-price. For you and me it may have a different name. It may be called social status, racial prejudice, religious differences. Men or circumstances may cause it. The name of the borderline is not important. What counts is what we do when we come to it.

Did François and Cecile stand the test when they came to their borderline?

I must admit that I was disappointed when I returned from my trip and found the letter you have just read. I wished they would have had more patience. But with circumstances as they were, they had no other choice. In a way, their flight was a courageous step. Was there any other way for Cecile to escape marriage with Monsieur Henri? Surely marriage with him was not the will of God.

You ask why they fled into the wilderness. Why was there no one to receive and protect them? I'm afraid François is right: In Africa, it's hard to be a non-conformist. Nobody would risk a fight with the whole clan, just for the sake of two individuals. They evidently did not want me to become involved in such a fight either. To run away, as they did, is not rare in present-day Africa. Many couples are forced to choose this way, but with a more or less bad conscience.

Between the lines of their letter we can sense a faint trembling. And then as if to drown out an inner voice, they use a tone of mockery, which otherwise is foreign to them. Perhaps they feel already that they have made a mistake in thinking that through the physical union they become one flesh in the full sense of the word. Just as the baby must appear in the light of the world when it is born, so the legal act in public is essential to the consummation of marriage. Deep down in their hearts, when writing that letter, François and Cecile knew that they were guilty.

By their guilt, however, God opened my eyes to see my own. Suddenly I realized how much I had failed. I had not fought hard enough and not asked enough for divine guidance. Why hadn't I taken my trip at some other time? Why hadn't I gone to see Cecile or taken the trouble to visit her father in order to talk to him personally?

My wife wonders too how it was possible that she didn't answer Cecile's letter right away. Instead of taking François and Cecile by the hand and walking with them, my wife and I both feel as if we had only sent them radio messages from an airplane.

When we stand at the borderline ourselves we realize our own guilt. It then becomes crystal clear that we cannot exist without the reality of the cross of Jesus Christ. We can try to go around it by excusing ourselves and accusing others.

But if we face the cross as those who are unable to live without forgiveness, then the experience of such a borderline becomes an encounter with God. Maybe the only way we can prove ourselves is to humbly accept our defeat. Those who face God become those who are faced by Him and the road continues even though in a different way than we think.

That was the case too with François and Cecile. Their way led through deep valleys. The cold Cecile had caught during the flight developed into a serious pneumonia. Perhaps the inner conflict also weakened her outward resistance. In grave condition, she was taken at her own request to her home village.

François came and got me and I spent a week at her bedside which I shall not forget. For days we didn't know whether she could survive or not. Both she and François looked upon the sickness as a punishment and accepted it as such. When, almost miraculously, Cecile recovered we learned in a new way that all of us live by grace alone.

Cecile's father was deeply touched by all that happened. The possibility of losing his daughter suddenly by death changed all standards for him. Above all the letter which I want to share now at the end had an effect upon him. It points toward the future, not only for Cecile and François, but for all those who are in a similar situation.

It's the famous letter which we've already mentioned often, that Cecile wrote to her father. Not until she was desperately ill did François find the bits of paper upon which Cecile had made a rough copy of this letter. These were thoughts she had jotted down—often incomplete sentences. Much of what she had written was corrected, crossed out, then written anew and discarded once more. It was a moving testimony to the pains that the letter cost Cecile, to the struggle of a daughter's heart, to gain the love and understanding of her father.

I then put it all together, as one puts together the parts of a mosaic, copied it and sent it on to Cecile's father. There are signs that it was not written in vain.

Here is the letter:

Dear Father,

I have never written a letter to you before. It's very hard for me. But it would be even harder for me to talk to you. That's why I ask you to read these lines as if I were talking to you.

I will try to explain to you why I love François.

The picture I like best of him is the one in which he stretches out his hand. I can trust this hand. When I look at the picture, I always see him walking a little ahead of me. But then he stands still, turns around and gives me his hand to help me over the hard places. Then I come very near to him and he comforts me.

He can comfort me so wonderfully because I can answer him when he talks to me. I can take hold of his hand, because I'm not afraid when he stretches it out to me. He doesn't take advantage of his strength to make me feel inferior. And yet when I need protection, I'm sure that he is stronger than I am. I'm happy to be weak in his presence, because he doesn't make fun of me.

But he needs me too, and he's not ashamed to tell me. Even though he's strong and manly, he can also be helpless like a child. His strong hand then becomes an open, empty hand. It is then my greatest happiness to fill it.

That's what I mean when I say: I love François.

I know that you think I am a half-white when I write such things to you. You blame me for despising our African customs, because I want to marry the man I love and not one who is able to pay for me.

But the custom of bride-price is not exclusively African. They had it in Europe too, even in Israel. Wherever men became Christians this custom disappeared. I do not write to you as a Europeanized African, but as a Christian African.

As a Christian I believe that God has created me. To Him alone I owe my life. No earthly father has ever paid God anything for his daughter. Therefore no earthly father has a right to make money out of her.

As a Christian I believe that Jesus Christ has died for me. He has paid the only price that can be paid for me: His blood. Any other price is the price for a slave.

As a Christian I believe that the Holy Spirit guides me. But I cannot follow His guidance unless I can choose freely.

Because I have chosen François of my own accord, I shall be faithful to him. Do you really think that the bride-price could hinder a wife from running away from her husband?

I have a friend whose father received $1,500 for her when she was married. She said to herself, "If my body is worth that much, then I can make some profit out of it for myself. She began to give herself to other men in exchange for money. There you have it: If the bride-price is acceptable and decent, then why not prostitution?

Or do you think that François would treat me better, if he had paid something for me? If he would take better care of me for that reason then I do not want to marry him. Then I would be only a thing to him. But I am a human being.

It's not true that money makes a wife more obedient and a husband more faithful. In the best case, money is a chain which must hold together there where no love is. But you can break a chain. You can give back money or goods. Love that has chosen freely is an unbreakable bond.

Dear Papa, please don't think that we are ungrateful. We love you dearly. We know what sacrifices you have made for me, especially when you sent me to school. We know too about your financial difficulties. We don't want to leave you in the lurch.

All we ask is this: Give us a start without debts. Allow us to found our own home. Only then can we really help you—really show you how grateful we are.

François makes the suggestion that we take my three brothers into our home when they go to school in Y. Isn't that a greater proof of his love for me than if he gives you money which doesn't belong to him?

Dear Papa, give us a chance! Let us begin!

BOOK TWO

LOVE IS A FEELING TO BE LEARNED

IN INDIA, ONE TELLS THIS LEGEND ABOUT THE CREATION OF MAN AND woman:

When he had finished creating the man, the Creator realized that he had used up all the concrete elements. There was nothing solid, nothing compact or hard, left over to create the woman.

After thinking for a long time, the Creator took
the roundness of the moon, the flexibility of a clinging vine and the trembling of grass,
the slenderness of a reed and the blossoming of flowers,
the lightness of leaves and the serenity of the rays of sunshine,
the tears of clouds and the instability of the wind,
the fearfulness of a rabbit and the vanity of a peacock,
the softness of a bird's breast and the hardness of a diamond,
the sweetness of honey and the cruelty of a tiger,
the burning of fire and the coldness of snow,

the talkativeness of a magpie and the singing of a nightingale,
the falseness of a crane and the faithfulness of a mother lion.

Mixing all these non-solid elements together, the Creator created the woman and gave her to the man.

After one week, the man came back and said: "Lord, the creature that you have given to me makes my life unhappy. She talks without ceasing and torments me intolerably, so that I have no rest. She insists that I pay attention to her all the time and so my hours are wasted. She cries about every little thing and leads an idle life. I have come to give her back to you, because I can't live with her."

The Creator said: "All right." And he took her back.

After a week had passed, the man came back to the Creator and said: "Lord, my life is so empty since I gave that creature back to you. I always think of her—how she danced and sang, how she looked at me out of the corner of her eye, how she chatted with me and then snuggled close to me. She was so beautiful to look at and so soft to touch. I liked so much to hear her laugh. Please give her back to me."

The Creator said: "All right." And he gave her back.

But three days later, the man came back again and said:

"Lord, I don't know—I just can't explain it, but after all my experience with this creature, I've come to the conclusion that she causes me more trouble than pleasure. I pray thee, take her back again! I can't live with her!"

The Creator replied: "You can't live without her either!"

And he turned his back to the man and continued his work.

The man said in desperation: "What shall I do? I can't live *with* her and I can't live *without* her!"

Love is a feeling to be learned.
It is tension and fulfillment.
It is deep longing and hostility.
It is gladness and it is pain.
There is not one without the other.

Happiness is only a part of love—this is what has to be learned. Suffering belongs to love also. This is the mystery of love, its beauty and its burden.

Love is a feeling to be learned.

It caused Sylvia almost physical pain to give up her dream. But now she was sure: This was the end of it.

Before she had met him, she had had a dream image of what her future husband would be like: tall, slim, a good athlete, intelligent, full of spirit, a university graduate, a few years older than she, and, of course, a lover of music and poetry, possibly a professor of English literature or religion or a holder of a well-paid job with the government.

When she passed a florist shop and saw the dark-red roses in the window, Sylvia pictured to herself just how it would be some day when someone would bring her such roses as a declaration of his love.

Gone was the dream! He was so different. There was absolutely nothing exciting about him. When he had asked her for their first date she had prayed in her heart: "Please, Lord, not him! He's not the one I want to marry!"

She had never been interested in technical things and that was his whole field of interest, because he was a construction engineer. He also was rather dull. No, he didn't bring her roses. He didn't bring her anything. He just came and there he was.

He was so down to earth and so sober.

Not that he was without feeling. But just the expression of his feelings irritated her. She couldn't rely upon them, because they could change so quickly. One minute he was impetuous and enthusiastic and the next he was as solemn as a stick. When she longed for a tender word, he offered her a kiss instead, and in the same breath talked about football or his studies.

Everything was reason and will with him. He called her stupid and sentimental when she put more faith in her intuition than in his reasoning and thinking.

Why can't a boy be like a girl?

Sometimes she wanted to be like a porcupine, roll together and show her prickles in order to make him understand in a thorny way that moonlight did not increase her desire for contact.

In his presence, she felt the desire to withdraw into the fortress of freedom and hoist the flag of independence.

Yet Sylvia did not send him away. Not yet, she thought; maybe later on.

But later on, a half a year or so, a few things dawned on her. She began to understand that a young man who sends a book to her which interests him, may be more serious than someone who sends roses.

The book says: I want to share something with you which moves my heart at present. I want to give you a part in my life. I want to know what you think. It is important to me to know what you think.

She discovered to her astonishment one day, that she had stopped to look at a bridge. For the first time she saw the beauty of its swing, of its lines. Or she stood and watched as the beams for a skyscraper were hoisted upwards and thought: I should show this to him.

It was no longer important to her just to be understood. She herself had begun to understand. She had learned the first lesson in love: one has to give up dreams, because they stand in the way of happiness.

Love is a special way of feeling—something to be learned.

If this special way of feeling is not learned, if there is no romance in the relationship between the sexes, sex and love become the same thing. This is still true to a great extent in Africa. Sex is called love and love is called sex. "I loved a girl" means "I went to bed with a girl." If this special feeling is not learned, there is either nothing or everything. There is no in-between.

The consequences of this attitude are tremendous. The woman becomes little more than a womb, a well-equipped incubator. She is not a person, but a thing which can be traded, bought and sold, given and taken, exchanged and disposed of, an inferior being without a will of her own, obedient to masculine wishes. In any culture where there is little sexual restraint, no romance and no in-between, the result is that the girl becomes simply a thing, a matter, an object.

What Africa needs more than anything else is to learn how to love.

But, can we say that it has been learned in Western culture? What do African students experience when they come to Europe or America?

Do they find anything different here from what they have left at home? The so-called "New Morality," the much-called-for sexual liberty in the West, did not emancipate the woman but degraded her, made her lose her dignity and personality. In Europe and America too, it made out of her a thing, a toy, a tool, an object to satisfy masculine wishes.

All of us have to learn how to love, to appreciate the beauty of the in-between, the joy of the preliminary.

Sylvia said: "There was an easiness in our relationship, the easiness of something not yet final, and that is what I appreciated the most. In this easiness there was at the same time greatness and depth. It was just this easiness, this lightness, which gave our friendship promise.

"The easiness of the in-between did not mean that there was no pain of longing and no suffering of suspense. But it bound pain and suffering together with deep-felt happiness."

Did you hear? Pain and suffering! The hit-songs and movies lie to us when they try to tell us that happiness can be had without suffering. Just here is the reason for the failure of many a relationship, for the frustrations and torture, yes, even for the shallowness and shipwreck of many a marriage: to think that love can grow and live without suffering.

Love and suffering do not exclude each other. Rather they condition each other.

Sex problems may have their deepest roots in the refusal to accept suffering, in wanting to jump over the in-between stage with its tension and anxiety, thus making the word "love" an empty word.

It pays to suffer lover's grief.

Suffering is not something to be eliminated, regardless of the cost. If we live through it and accept it, suffering can become a spring of riches, of depth, growth and fulfillment—yes, of happiness.

Therefore, I say, in contradiction to the popular songs of today: It pays to suffer lover's grief.

John sat and thought.

It had happened again. His girl friend had broken off with him.

He really couldn't understand why. True, he had made mistakes. Maybe he had even taken too much for granted—too much and too soon.

He had felt all the time that she had never taken their relationship as seriously as he did. Maybe she was afraid to do so.

Though they were both of the same age, he always felt so inferior to her, so unsure of himself in her presence. Sometimes he had the impression that she was years older, while he felt like a baby with a beard.

Why can't a man be like a woman?

Anyway, he had to accept her decision. It was painful and his heart ached, but he didn't want to drown out the pain or dance it to death. He wanted to take it seriously.

So he sat and thought.

Maybe this was the purpose of suffering—to teach him how to discern between the true and the false, and above all, to teach him the art of sacrifice.

It pays to suffer lover's grief, if sacrifice is learned. The art of giving up, of letting go, is the most important art to be learned.

Not just for love's sake. I personally believe that the survival of mankind depends upon whether or not we give up the consumers' attitude and learn the art of sacrificing, not only our dreams, but also our desires which could be realized and fulfilled.

Suffering makes immature love grow into mature love. Immature, unlearned love is egotistic love. It's the kind of love that a child has—a love which claims and wants and wants immediately. It cannot endure tension and has no patience with anything which stands in the way. It demands and consumes and tries to dominate.

As John sat and thought, the idea came to him that the greatest proof of his love to his girl friend was to give her the freedom to say "no." Mature love does not try to lord it over the other one, but it lets go. It sets free.

Suffering transformed John's love to a new dimension.

It pays to suffer lover's grief, for nothing prepares us better for marriage. Marital love is love which has learned to surrender and to renounce.

In marriage, one no longer says "yours," or "mine," but "ours."

This word "our" is always connected with sacrifice, with giving up:

giving up one's partner as he goes to work;

giving up free time and independent planning in the interest of the family;

giving up things which one could have afforded while working as a single person;

sacrificing for the sake of the children;

and perhaps the hardest sacrifice of all, giving up the children themselves when they start to go their own ways.

Maybe this is the root of the generation problem. Parents who have not learned the sacrificing art of love are unable to apply it now to their own children. They are like hens who hatch out duck's eggs and then stand at the edge of the pond and cackle and squawk while the young ducklings swim away.

They are still learning and their children have to be patient with them. Mark Twain once said: "When I was sixteen, I thought my dad was hopeless. When I was twenty, I was surprised to discover that he had made progress."

However, it can be true the other way too. Sometimes a "no" from our parents comes out of deep concern to teach us sacrificing love. By obeying this parental "no," a child may learn the art of giving up which will later on be the greatest help when he has to face the reality of love, shape his own marriage, and educate his own children.

The art of giving up, of renouncing, is also the secret of happiness in a single person's life. To give up one's self is as important for a single person as it is for one who is married.

Those who learn this art will never be lonesome, even if they are single. Those who don't, will always be lonesome, even though they are married.

The task we have to face is the same, whether we are married or single: *To live a fulfilled life in spite of many unfulfilled desires.*

Love is a feeling to be learned by the single person as well. Those who do not marry do not have to give up love, but they have to learn love which gives up—just as those who are married must learn it. One could even say that the desire to be married is the condition for a happy single life.

Though the task we have to face is the same, whether we are married or single, let us not make the mistake of thinking that our present state is permanent. Let us not burden our hearts with the fear of finality.

Marriage can be a task for a limited time and then it suddenly ends with the death of one partner. Being single can also be but a passing task.

God does not like the decisions for a lifetime which we make out of resignation and disappointment. He wants us to live our life this day and to discover all the joyous possibilities of it with confidence and courage.

Evelyn sat in the bus and shut her eyes so that the other passengers would think she was asleep. But her heart sang with the rhythm of the wheels: "He loves me. I shall be his wife. He shall be my husband."

No, she would never be able to understand it. She couldn't even explain it—either to her mother or to her girl friend. She had known it in her heart from the moment they looked at each other and their eyes spoke: "I do mean you, and you alone, and you for my whole life."

How did Carl succeed? Had he outwitted her by pretending at first not to be interested? Had he been more clever than others in his methods?

No, he hadn't even had a method. His principle had not been; take the little finger carefully first and then the whole hand will follow by itself.

It was a rather insignificant event which made her understand for the first time his way of being a friend. It was during her first year at college that he had asked her for their first date on a Saturday evening, although he knew that she usually went home for the weekend to see her family and friends. When she accepted his invitation to attend a theater performance at his school with him, he thanked her expressly for giving up her trip home.

It was through this gesture on his part that she understood for the first time—he does not just want to spend a pleasant evening, nor is he just looking for an enjoyable partner for a few hours, but with his invitation, he meant *her*.

Love is a feeling to be learned and Evelyn knew deep down in her heart that it can never be learned by sex. She would never have reached the certainty she now had. For like loud drums which drown out the leading melody of flutes, sex would have deafened her ears to the low and gentle overtones so essential for choice.

Carl would not have heard the singing of the nightingale, nor seen the trembling of grass, the flexibility of a clinging vine and the serenity of the rays of sunshine; nor would he have felt the instability of the wind and the softness of a bird's breast.

They would have missed the beauty of the in-between, the pain of waiting and the joy of suspense, the suffering which made them so happy.

Evelyn knew: Sex would have kept their love from a chance to grow. It would have meant picking the blossoms in April and therefore never harvesting the apples.

For love does not grow out of sex. Love must grow into sex. For Evelyn, love meant above all, confidence and trust, fellowship and common experience, shared hopes and sorrows. It called for a reliable and lasting relationship. For her, love was inseparable from permanence.

Could it be, Evelyn thought, while the bus was bringing her closer and closer to her friend—could it be that girls who allow premarital sex, or even seek it, have repressed their deepest feelings and longings? That they are not the ones who are especially passionate, but, on the contrary, are rather impassionate, calculating and even cold?

What is an old maid? Someone unable to love. Someone who represses her feelings and doesn't say yes to herself. There are teen-age "old maids." There are also married "old maids." There are even male "old maids."

The opposite of the "old maid" is the virgin.

Virginity is not something negative, but something tremendously positive. It corresponds to the demands of the deepest nature of the girl. Virginity is preparedness for the fullness of love.

Sex may turn a girl into an old maid. Virginity turns her into a woman.

Carl felt that there was nothing which had helped his love for Evelyn to mature more than her virginity. Like a dam which helps to turn the power of water into electricity, restraint helps to turn the power of sex into love.

Two things in her virgin attitude had helped him—her attractiveness and her modesty. It is not enough to have one without the other.

Through her attractiveness she had taught him to love her so much that he was willing to pay a price, to make a sacrifice, for this love.

Through her modesty, she had directed his interest beyond her body to her soul and had helped him who was used to living in the realm of will and reason, to discover his own soul.

Maybe the girl has to be the teacher of the boy in this realm, Carl thought.

If she had been attractive without being modest, she would have directed him towards adventure, but not towards marriage.

Attractiveness alone, without modesty, would have tempted him to pay the lowest possible price to fulfill his desire.

If she had given in to his desire, she would have lost her attractiveness for him. Therefore, just because he loved her and did not want to lose her, he had secretly hoped for her resistance.

To refuse sex was a greater proof of her love than to grant it. By granting it she would have hurt their love.

Love can be hurt by sex. It can be killed by sex. Therefore, love has to be protected.

There is a verse in the Bible which has not yet received due attention in this respect. It is Genesis 2:25: "They were both naked, the man and the wife, and were not ashamed."

Naked and not ashamed.

"Naked" is not meant here in a physical sense only. It means to stand in front of each other stripped and undisguised, without pretension, without hiding anything, seeing the partner as she really is and showing myself to her as I really am—and still not to be ashamed.

Naked and not ashamed.

But this ultimate goal of mature love is promised only to those who, as the previous verse says, have left father and mother and cleave to each other, in other words, those who have been publicly and legally married. *These two*—not the ones before or outside of marriage—become one flesh.

These two—not the ones before or outside of marriage—shall succeed in the tremendously difficult task: to face each other as they really are, to live with each other—naked and yet not ashamed.

Naked and not ashamed—this is what the Bible means by the words "to know." "Adam knew Eve, his wife."

To know in this way is not possible outside of marriage. If it is tried beforehand, love is hurt or even killed.

Therefore, love has not only to be learned; it has to be protected as well.

It has to be protected by divine will. By listening to human reason we cannot protect love.

The trend in Europe today is to question divine will in the name of love.

"Did God say?" they ask, like the serpent asked Eve in the Garden of Eden.

Is it not love, they ask, to shorten the torment of waiting by permitting premarital sex?

Is it not love, they ask, to train sex by encouraging masturbation and even homosexual relations among teen-agers?

Is it not love, they ask, to furnish high-schoolers with contraceptives?

Is it not love, they ask, to allow your marriage partner to have sex with someone else providing he is in love with that person?

Is it not love, they ask, to give the unmarried girl the right to have a baby?

I remember how, during the time of Hitler, a film was shown in Germany which told the story of a doctor whose wife had an incurable disease. In detail the film showed how she was tormented by her sickness until her husband killed her with an overdose of sedatives. When he was put on trial for murder, he defended himself by saying: "I loved my wife."

Here, God's commandment: "Thou shalt not kill" was questioned in the name of love.

The film was shown in 1940 and was used by Hitler as a psychological preparation for the killing of the incurable and insane, for exterminating life which he judged unworthy of living. The end was the assassination of six million jews in the gas chambers of the concentration camps.

If we seek to set up the standards of love ourselves, we fall into the hands of the devil. When Germany questioned the commandment "Thou shalt not kill" in the name of love, she fell into the hands of the devil. When we question today the commandment "Thou shalt not commit adultery" in the name of love we fall equally into the hands of the devil.

Since we do not know what love is, love has to be protected by the One who is love Himself. There is never a contradiction between love and divine will. There is no action of love which goes against a commandment of God.

We always hurt our neighbor when we break a commandment, even if we don't see it immediately in our present situation. But God is greater than our situation. He looks beyond what I can see. He has the film of my whole life in view, and not just the snapshot of my present situation.

The life-view offers a different picture than the snapshot. Let me illustrate this by the case of François and Cecile, the young African couple whose correspondence with me is published in the book, *I Loved a Girl.*[1]

Those who have read this book will know that François and Cecile saw no other way out in their position than to elope. Thus they consummated their marriage before they were legally married.

Who of us can judge them? Humanly we can understand why they acted as they did in such a difficult situation.

Still, if you would ask them today about their action, they would both say that they regret it. Although they are happily married now, they would say that, in the last analysis, the consummation of their marriage before the wedding hurt their love more than it helped it.

So it is that when we take a snapshot out of its context, it may often seem to our human understanding as if a pre- or extra-marital surrender, a beautiful lie, or a gentle murder is the way of love. But if the film of life gets into focus, the way always looks different.

If you examine a messed-up life, you will see that the mess always started with the transgression of a divine commandment.

Jesus says: "If you love me, you will keep my commandments."

We cannot love our neighbor, unless we love Jesus. We cannot love Jesus, unless we obey Him.

Only the one who really loves is able to obey.

Only the one who obeys is really able to love.

"And his commandments are not burdensome" (I John 5:3).

They are not a burden, but a help. They are not a load, but a force. They do not incapacitate us, but make us mature. Actually it is much simpler to keep them than to transgress them. Life becomes much more difficult and complicated if we try to discover ourselves what is good and bad.

I know that there are some people who claim that it is normal among teen-agers today to practice premarital sex. There are even some statistics published which give frighteningly high numbers. To this I would like to say: Let us be careful with statistics in this field. There is no foolproof method whatsoever to arrive at scientifically reliable results concerning intimate behavior.

But even if these statistics were right, even if a high percentage practice premarital sex? So what?

Since when are Christians led by statistics? Since when are we guided by what the majority does? "We are a peculiar people" (I Peter 2:9). Are we or are we not? Christians are not shy animals who have to accept a protective coloring in order to be able to survive. On the contrary, unless we show our colors, we will not survive.

Bonhoeffer says: "Only the extraordinary is essentially Christian."

To conclude, let me tell you about my conversation with Karin, as we shall call her.

As I talked with her, Karin assured me several times that she had been involved in deep petting with her boy friend, but that they had never gone "all the way."

I did not ask her any questions. But the next day Karin came back. She wanted to know what is really meant by the expression: "going all the way."

I said, "Karin, I think what is meant is the complete physical union."

This answer did not satisfy her. She asked me to describe it exactly. So I said, "It is the insertion of the male sex organ into the vagina."

Karin hesitated a moment. Then she said thoughtfully: "If this is what is meant, then we have gone all the way."

Then she broke out, "Please do not think that I lied to you yesterday. You are the first one who has told me in a concrete way what is meant. When I had my first period, all my mother said to me was, 'Be careful and don't make anything dirty!'

"That was my whole sex education. Why do they all beat around the bush? 'Don't go all the way! Don't go too far!' But how far too far is, no one ever told me. Is embracing too far? Are kisses too far?"

Karin challenged me. She wanted a precise statement. I thought of many talks which I have had with young people who assured me, sometimes in tears that they had never intended to go all the way, but then they had been unable to stop.

So I said—and those who know a better answer may correct me—, "The point where it becomes impossible to stop is mostly lying down together and any form of undressing."

It is very hard to make general rules which would fit for everyone everywhere. But this can be a guide: the one who has the more sensitive conscience should be the helper of the other one. A slap on the fingers can be a greater proof of love than a French kiss. The respect for one another will grow and love will deepen. On the other hand, "going all the way" turns out to be a short cut and often means the end of the feeling of love you tried to express.

"Can sex hurt love?"

"Oh, yes, Karin. It certainly can."

A student couple who was expecting a child out of wedlock wrote to me: "Isn't all that matters is that it was done in love?"

I answered: "Love? Love to the baby for whom no proper home is prepared? Love to your partner whose professional career is now messed up? Love to your parents to whom you cause embarrassment and shame? Maybe you solved one problem—you released the sexual tension. But you created many new ones—wedding, home, support, profession . . . love?"

Love is hurt when it is not protected by divine will. Sex can hurt love. Therefore God protects love by con fining sex to marriage.

All girls give themselves out of "love" or what they think it is. But not all of them are married to the one to whom they gave themselves. Many a messed-up life started this way. Therefore let me repeat over and over again for those who have such incapable mothers as Karin: even a first and only intercourse can result in pregnancy.

"But," Karin said, "isn't it their own fault if the girl becomes pregnant? When I worried about that, my boy friend calmed my fears by assuring me that he would watch out.

"At first, I did not know what he meant by 'watching out.' Now, I know. He disengaged his member and shed his semen outside my body.

But, you see, that way I did not get any satisfaction out of our experience and therefore I thought that we had not gone 'all the way.' "

I was glad that Karin had opened up. This method of conception control as she described it provides a sort of satisfaction for the boy but rarely for the girl. This is why this abrupted intercourse—abrupted for the girl—may lay the foundation for a later frigidity or even cause an aversion, a feeling of disgust or loathsomeness in the girl's thinking, towards everything sexual and thus disturb marriage in a decisive way.

So love is hurt again.

Besides this fact, the method is also very unesthetic. Neither is it absolutely safe, for the moment of withdrawal can easily be misjudged.

"Is there any absolutely safe means of conception control?" Karin asked.

I don't know of any. Condoms can break. Pessaries can be inaccurately fitted. The so-called "rhythm method," the observation of the infertile days in a woman's menstrual cycle, is certainly not safe, for the periods are not always regular. Especially in premarital situations one can never be sure.

Even with the so-called "anti-baby pill," things are not so simple. First of all, the pills have to be prescribed by a medical doctor. But even if one finds a way around that, they are only effective if taken every day between two periods. Missing one day only makes them ineffective. Therefore it is useless to take them along in your purse when going to a dance so that in the case of necessity all you do is swallow a pill quickly beforehand.

Besides that, swallowing a pill daily over a long period of time can have a negative effect on a young girl's organism, for it can change the normal delicate balance of her hormones. As soon as she stops taking them, her ability to conceive may be especially great. Recently cases have become more frequent that more than one egg cell may be released at once. This may result in twin, triplet and even up to octuplet pregnancies. And on the other hand the normal release of egg cells may be inhibited for a long time following cessation of the pills so that the woman is indefinitely sterile. These adverse reactions are not common, but they are absolutely unpredictable and can have tragic consequences.

One girl said: "If I would take pills regularly, calculatingly, in anticipation of a possible sex adventure, I would feel like a prostitute."

"But wouldn't petting then solve all problems?"

When I asked Karin what she meant by petting, she explained that she didn't mean just holding hands or even kissing, but a mutual manipulation of the sex organs until orgasm is reached by both partners, a sort of masturbation together. In this way sexual pleasure can be experienced without fear of pregnancy and still without having to use contraceptives or having to count days.

It may also be easier, because one has not engaged in full intercourse, to calm one's own conscience. I know Christians who believe that they can outwit God in this way. After all, they have not gone "all the way"!

It does look like an ideal solution, but it isn't. It is barking up the wrong tree. It's a dead-end road.

Petting used as a method to avoid pregnancy is not absolutely safe either. The percentage of unwanted children produced through petting is surprisingly high. Even the smallest quantity of the male seminal fluid which gets into the vagina is sufficient to fertilize an ovum. It is also true that many couples who start out with petting are unable to stop and then end up in full sexual union in spite of themselves.

But another fact which is widely unknown is still more important.

There are two ways for girls to experience sexual pleasure: a more superficial way which in the final analysis is not satisfactory, and a deep and gratifying way. The latter, however, is normally only a marital possibility for it calls for a harmonious relationship with the same partner over a long period of time. Wives who progress from one way to the other consider the first one as something childish and immature. "For the first time I feel like a real woman!" they say as they experience the deep and gratifying way.

Through petting practices a girl gets used to the superficial way only. Later on in marriage she may have a hard time to mature to the deep and rewarding experience. Thus she makes herself and her husband unhappy.

So love is hurt again. The one who wants sex without marriage will not only be unable to learn love; he will also be unable to protect it. He is not mature and cannot mature.

Years ago a high-school student in a talk with me defended petting as something "beautiful." As a college sophomore she wrote to me recently that now she was ashamed of it and felt ill-used. Although she doesn't yet know her future husband, she says she will be ashamed in front of him too because of her past petting experiences.

In this connection, may I briefly point to something else. Many of those who got involved in heavy petting practices and then were left by their partners, slide easily into the habit of masturbation. This is not only true for boys, but for girls as well.

Masturbation is a cry for help. But according to my experience this help must be offered to the individuals in need of it in different ways. May I say this much here: If you are on this wrong track, by no means remain alone, but seek out a trustworthy person and talk over your problem with him.

Karin asked again: "Why didn't someone tell me these things?"

I said: "Karin, I often wonder too what the reason is for this strange silence. Maybe it comes out of a bad conscience. Maybe it comes from a feeling that one lacks authority in a field where one has failed himself. Will you become a better mother for your own children?"

"It's true!" she said, "I had a bad conscience when I said 'yes' to my boy friend. It was painful for my soul. I just pretended to be happy, but I really felt like sobbing and weeping."

"Karin," I said, "if you had only sobbed and wept, he probably would not have gone all the way. You would have challenged him as a man and he would have wanted to protect you. But since you pretended to be happy, he tried to make you happy. That way he injured you."

"I can't understand it," she said, "I did not want it, but he did. But when I gave in, he lost interest. For him it was the end. For me it was a beginning. Can't he understand that?"

"No, Karin, he can't."

"And why?"

"Because he is a boy and you are a girl."

"Well," she said, "it's too late now anyway. What has happened has happened. It can never be undone. My life is all messed up."

"No, Karin," I said, "You're mistaken. For God there is never a too-late. There is no life so messed up, but that He can bring it in order. He is almighty. He can even make done things undone by His forgiveness. For this is what forgiveness means: to make done things undone."

You do not need to continue to live with this pain in your soul. There is a possibility of a new beginning. If you would like to take this step toward a new beginning, may I give you a twofold advice:

First of all, you will hardly be able to succeed by yourself. You need an experienced spiritual counsellor as a helper.

Secondly, do not stop halfway, but make this new beginning a complete one. Here you have a chance to really "go all the way." In cleaning up the mess, don't stop with the sex corner, but clean up the other dark corners as well. Do not confess the transgressions of one commandment only, but bring to the light your transgressions of the other commandments as well.

It may well be that the cause of your failures and defeats in the realm of sex is compromise and disobedience in other areas of life where you disregarded the will of God.

Jesus says: "He who comes to me I will not cast out."

This promise is for you too without reservation. You can accept His offer without fear. With Jesus it pays to go "all the way."

BOOK THREE

LIVING WITH UNFULFILLED DESIRES

Introduction **143**

Chapter 1: "We love each other terrifically" **146**
"Because we love each other so terrifically, we wanted to sleep together. . . . It didn't work. . . . I didn't get a thing out of it."

Chapter 2: "A girl friend has to be kissed" **152**
"At that time, I thought that a girlfriend absolutely had to be kissed. . . . I imagined that I was a famous rock singer. . . . Tell me what I can do in order not to fall back into dreaming."

Chapter 3: "How can I find a real boyfriend?" **157**
"I've never had a real boyfriend. I pretend to others that I'm happy not to have one. . . . Please tell me . . . how I can finally find a real boyfriend."

Chapter 4: "My next girl friend will become my wife" **162**
I told several friends that my next girl friend would become my wife. . . . She's a Christian too and had asked the Lord for clear guidance. . . . Now I stand in front of a void."

Chapter 5: "Klaus and I stayed overnight in the same room" **167**
"Klaus and I slept in one of those rooms. During those two nights nothing happened at all."

Chapter 6: "Even one girl is too many" **171**
"Had I known how many complications your book would cause, . . . I never would have read it. . . . The way you talk about caressing makes me sick. . . . I wouldn't like to marry a girl who has already slept with five or six boys."

Chapter 7: "Is masturbation a sin?" **176**
"Does Jesus have anything against a friendship at the age of thirteen? . . . Is masturbation a sin? I can't help it—especially when I need love. . . . I eat and eat. Sometimes I really stuff myself."

Chapter 8: "I would like to shoot my cycle off to the moon" **183**
"I've read many times already that masturbation is not harmful, but this doesn't help me. . . . It would be the eighth wonder of the world if I would wear a skirt. . . . If I had my way, I would like to shoot my whole cycle and everything that goes with it off to the moon."

Chapter 9: "I'm a loner" **189**
"Up till now I've had to struggle with my problems . . . all by myself. . . . I'm a loner and suffer because I'm so shy around people. . . . It's only in this letter that I could express my thoughts frankly for the first time. . . . About two years ago I started to masturbate."

Chapter 10: "My father hates me" **195**
"Why are you born if you're not loved? . . . I was going to lose my father forever. . . . He was cold to me—down right cold—and it was him I loved the most. . . . Sometimes I wish I were already experiencing menopause."

Chapter 11: "In my home there's always fighting" **208**
"When I'm not with my friend, I feel something like a very strong longing. . . . There's always fighting at my home. I'd like to move out and live with my friend. . . . What is the difference between wet dreams and masturbation?"

Chapter 12: "All of a sudden we helped each other" **213**
"All of a sudden we helped each other get rid of our tension. . . . In the end we were very ashamed of ourselves. Both of us know we will ruin our friendship slowly but surely."

Chapter 13: "Is Napoleon the cause of the trouble?" **220**
"Formerly I was a biblical Christian, but for some time now I have been unfaithful. . . . There are times when I would like to break up with her because something is fishy. Then I ask myself whether the 'absolute' is the cause of the trouble or the 'Napoleon.' "

Chapter 14: "His kisses became more and more impetuous" **224**
"It was completely dark in the room. . . . All of a sudden he pulled down the zipper of my jeans. . . . I really got frightened."

Chapter 15: "She is too precious for a flirt" **231**
"Brigitta is too precious to me for just a flirt. . . . If I were made of wax I certainly would have melted."

Chapter 16: "I was always looking for my place" **234**
"My mother raised me in such a way that I was made to think my sex organs were something bad. . . . When I was thirteen I slept with a boy for the first time. . . . Somehow I was always looking for my place, for love and tenderness."

Chapter 17: "I'm twenty and I've never slept with a girl" **240**
"As a psychiatrist, my dad is of the opinion that premarital sex is necessary. . . . Under the surface, my friends think that it is a rite of manhood to seduce a girl in the shortest possible time. . . . She said to me, 'My rule is: No lower than the waistline.' "

Chapter 18. "My conflict: being a Christian or having a girl friend" **245**
"When I was eleven, I started to become a teen-ager. . . . I noticed that as a boy I was popular with girls. . . . The conflict is now within me—being a Christian or having a girl friend."

Epilogue **250**

Introduction

When answering mail from readers of my books, I was struck by the fact that again and again letters began—with a certain pride and satisfaction—"I am sixteen." After checking my files, I discovered that within one year, I had received nearly a hundred letters from sixteen-year-olds. Interestingly enough, there were about as many letters from boys as from girls.

It seems that this age group is in an especially difficult situation. Many have had experiences which formerly only someone age nineteen or twenty would have. These young people break loose from their families, yet at the same time are not able to stand on their own feet. They are no longer children, and they are not yet adults. It is this hanging in between which causes pain and suffering.

Their own families do not offer them the security they need. This is at least part of the reason why they hurt—and write.

Parents who read this book may be surprised that teen-agers are capable of such deep thoughts and feelings, and they will be shocked by the insignificant role parents play in these letters. On the other hand, I hope they also realize how much they could help their children by a tender gesture, a loving word, verbalized praise, physical touch, time spent with them—and simple, patient listening.

It is also striking how many of these young people find support and help in a living faith and fellowship with dedicated Christians.

Again and again while answering their letters, I found myself thinking: if only Frances could read the letter from Mary she could see that she is not alone with her problem. Or if John could read the letter from Frances—and vice versa—they both could learn how the same situation looks from the perspective of the other sex.

These thoughts prompted me to collect and publish some of this correspondence, especially those letters touching on problems which are most common. All correspondents gladly and willingly gave me their permission.

This book was first published in German. But this is not the only reason I chose letters from readers living in Germany, Switzerland and Austria. I also have letters from American high-school students and know from many personal talks that they have very similar problems. Their letters, however, are not as expressive. I've often wondered but still don't know why this is so. Maybe this book will challenge American readers and en courage them to put their experiences into words. This in itself may be helpful.

An explanation of the dance course mentioned in some letters is probably in order for American readers. These courses are offered by private dance schools in Europe over a period of half a year—usually one evening per week. Almost all high schoolers attend them with their classmates and meet other students from different schools. They offer instruction in ballroom dancing as well as in manners and conduct—so that students may learn to become "gentlemen" and "young ladies." It is an opportunity for teen-agers to meet and get acquainted without pairing off or being committed. In many ways it replaces the American dating practice which often leads to a premature commitment and involvement which is for many more of a burden than a joy.

I changed, of course, the names of my correspondents, but I purposely did not change their letters. These are their original letters—unshortened and unedited. In my answers, therefore, some repetition was unavoidable. Again and again, for instance, I had to point out the importance of the boy-boy and girl-girl friendships in the development of the person, the constructive role of the feeling of shame and embarrassment, as well as the necessity to learn how to cope with tension and frustration.

Since in our time frustration is considered undesirable and therefore something to be eliminated at all cost, the chance to mature through it is overlooked. Thus, energies are lost which prove indispensable for gaining, in the deep sense of the word, the ability to love.

By the age of sixteen an art can already be learned which will prove to be an essential asset later in life—married or not. As Dietrich Bonhoeffer puts it, it is the art of how to live a fulfilled life in spite of many unfulfilled desires.

1
"We Love Each Other Terrifically"

"BECAUSE WE LOVE EACH OTHER SO TERRIFICALLY, WE WANTED TO SLEEP TOGETHER. . . . IT DIDN'T WORK. . . . I DIDN'T GET A THING OUT OF IT."

DORIS P., AGE 16, HIGH-SCHOOL STUDENT

Dear Mr. Trobisch,

I've just read your book *Love Is a Feeling to Be Learned.* I liked it very much and your arguments made sense to me. There's only one thing I didn't like about it: you talked so much about Jesus, God and the Bible.

But let me first tell you about us. My boyfriend will be eighteen in June and I've just turned sixteen. We've been going steady for four and a half months. Both of us are convinced that we've never had either a girl or a boyfriend with whom we've felt so deeply understood, nor will we ever be able to be understood in this way by anyone else.

We believe that this feeling which we have for each other is love. We do not agree with you that having intercourse before marriage is not okay. On the contrary, you should know before marriage whether you fit together or not, also in the sexual realm.

I always felt, though, that a couple should go together for a long time before they sleep together. Once I felt differently, but that is past now.

Because we love each other so terrifically, we wanted to sleep together. We believe that the pill is the best means of contraception, so that is why I got a prescription for it.

Finally the moment came. We had time, were in the mood and would be undisturbed for several hours. But my boyfriend was so nervous and excited that he couldn't get an erection. He got terribly depressed, and it was only with great effort that I succeeded in cheering him up.

A week later the great moment came again. But again it didn't work. This time he didn't take it so hard. We just romped around instead and all of a sudden it worked, but it hurt so terrifically that I asked him to stop, which he did immediately. We petted and shortly before the climax I asked him to try again. We made another attempt. Again I had great pain as long as he was in me. Even afterwards a little bit. Is that normal? I didn't get a thing out of it. How come?

If you would please answer me, I would be very grateful.

Many thanks in advance,
Doris

Dear Doris,

It's good that you wrote to me. Maybe you did it out of a certain uneasy feeling that something's not quite right between you and your boyfriend.

There's a contradiction in your letter. On the one hand, you say that my arguments make sense to you. On the other hand, you act just in the opposite way. Could the negative experiences you have had not be reason enough to think about my arguments for discouraging intercourse before marriage?

You put the cart before the horse. You can only succeed in knowing each other sexually if you know each other in your hearts beforehand and trust each other completely. The physical union then becomes an expression of this mutual confidence which is, in turn, supported by the decision to stick together for life. Basically this is why you cannot try out before marriage whether you "fit together sexually"—just as you cannot try out how it feels to be dead by sleeping very deeply.

This trying out is not only impossible, it's also unnecessary. After all, the sexual organs are not made of bones, but of muscles and soft tissues which adjust to each other during the course of marriage.

What you should try out before marriage is whether you fit together in your hearts, inwardly, and this takes a lot of time—more than four and a half months. If you include the physical too soon in your relationship, the growth of this heart knowledge will be greatly hindered and sometimes even stopped.

Certainly that which you feel for each other is a type of love, but whether it's the kind of love which can bind you together for life, you cannot yet know after such a short acquaintance. I'm afraid that at your age, you cannot yet know it at all. Besides that, during the next years both of you will change decisively.

I would like to warn you and urge you not to take the pill. At your age, it can certainly cause great damage.

The pill contains artificial hormones which hinder ovulation and thereby create in your body a false state of pregnancy. This means that the normal process of development and maturing of your cycle is disturbed, and there is even a possibility that you may become infertile. Sometimes after taking the pill for a longer period of time, menstruation stops completely and then a complicated treatment will be necessary.

Did you know that several large drug firms, both in Europe and in the States, have stopped producing the pill because the lawsuits and payment of damages exceed their profits? Since these lawsuits are usually settled out of court, the public rarely hears of them. Why don't you stop abusing yourself for the benefit of the pharmaceutical industry?

Of course, what you experienced is not normal because the physical union should bring enjoyment and not torture. However, at your age and in the situation which you described, your experience was normal to a certain degree. Many young people have similar experiences. I know many young girls who would confirm your statement: "I didn't get a thing out of it!"

There is, of course, the possibility that you experienced pain because your vagina is still very small and that, physically speaking, you have not yet fully matured. However, there might be a psychological reason: you were afraid—and, even though you might deny it, unconsciously you had a bad conscience. This could also explain why your boyfriend was unable to have an erection.

Maybe you were afraid that the pill wouldn't work 100% or that you would be caught naked. It seems strange to me that you did not mention your parents at all in your letter. What do they say? Or don't they even know about it?

I could also imagine that both of you were simply afraid of failure. When you want to try something, then success becomes very important. If you would be honest and draw the logical conclusion, you would have to say, "We do not fit together," and then break up. Since you do not even consider this possibility, you see how dishonest it is to justify premarital sex with this argument.

Maybe you can understand now why I talk about God so much in the book you read. God wants these experiences to be beautiful for us so that we can enjoy the memories of them. For this reason he has reserved this innermost communion for marriage. God does not want to deprive you of something. He wants to make you richer.

With warm greetings and the hope that you understand,

W. T.

Reflection

Doris did not understand. She did not answer at all. When I wrote to her after she had been silent for six months, she was very surprised. "To be honest, I thought you had just given a routine answer," she said.

Evidently the fact that someone cared was a new experience for her. She answered my question about her parents with these words: "I have a very poor relationship with my parents. We only scream at each other. That's why you are the only one—and you are still the only one—who knows about Gerhard and myself in this respect. When I told my parents about the pill they did not approve of it, but they said, 'This is your business.' "

Doris's parents left their sixteen-year-old daughter alone with this important decision. She describes her dilemma: "First it didn't work at all. I was completely closed when we tried to have intercourse. Then it worked, and I took the pill for seven months. In the meantime I realized that the pill is not good for me. I gained twenty pounds, got broad hips and massive breasts which don't go with me at all.

"Then we talked about what other contraceptive we could use and decided to try the condom. We don't like it though, because it's not at all beautiful and it's so messy.

"After that experience I got the idea of having a diaphragm fitted, but my lady doctor said that the accident rate is too high, and she suggested that I use an IUD. She sent me to a gynecologist who plans to measure my uterus during the next menstruation in order to insert an IUD, if possible. The whole thing would cost me a hundred dollars. I'm just a poor high-school student, and Gerhard is an electrical apprentice.

"Some time ago my sister got an IUD inserted, but it gives her a lot of pain. I'm not sure whether I want to go through with it. If it doesn't work, the money is gone and we still don't have anything."

I am afraid Doris will never be satisfied if she continues on this road. She is indeed a poor high-school student, but in a much deeper sense than she realizes. The same is true of her boyfriend.

She does not know what to do and weighs the possibilities. She does not even seem to consider the simplest solution, namely, that of giving up intercourse. In this case, she would have something.

Then her personality could grow. Her ability to stand up under tension would develop. If she were to give up sex, new energies would be set free which, in turn, would enable her to love in the true sense of the word.

At the moment, the two are meeting at a purely genital level and do not learn much about each other. Even if they were to marry, which is quite unlikely, their marriage would probably become empty and insipid. After the sexual attraction dies down, little will be left. They are walking a dead-end road.

I am still in contact with Doris. She and Gerhard even visited us once. I will not give them up. I shall try to lead them away from the dead-end road, but it will be a difficult task since I have neither their parents nor her doctors on my side.

The phrase *accident rate* from the mouth of a woman doctor to a young girl who is supposed to become a mother some day, disturbs me deeply. New life, an accident! What have we come to?

One of Doris's statements gives the answer: "I only believe in God as long as I need him." This means that she does not believe in God. She has no antenna for the fact that the Creator has meant her for marriage and that only in this context is the gift of sexuality full of meaning.

If she continues to live the way she does, she is going to pay a high price—more than a hundred dollars. It is expensive to live against the laws of creation.

Doris's boyfriend tried to force physical closeness and lost more than he gained. How differently Reinhard, the next correspondent treats the girl he meets!

2
"A Girl Friend Has to Be Kissed"

"AT THAT TIME, I THOUGHT THAT A GIRL FRIEND HAD TO BE KISSED. . . .
I IMAGINED THAT I WAS A FAMOUS ROCK SINGER. . . .
TELL ME WHAT I CAN DO IN ORDER NOT TO FALL BACK INTO DREAMING."

REINHARD H., AGE 16, HIGH-SCHOOL STUDENT

Dear Mr. Trobisch,

A year ago I bought and read your book *Love Is a Feeling to Be Learned.* I do not agree with everything you say in this book. In spite of that I hope to get your confidence, and I hope you can help me. Here's my story and my problem:

A few weeks ago I became sixteen. I'm a high-school student. In April and May of this year I had my first girl friend. She was two months older, but shorter than I am. Her name is Christine. She goes to the same school as I do. We saw each other often and finally I fell in love with her and she with me.

At that time I thought that a girl friend absolutely had to be kissed. Therefore I was very happy when, after about three weeks, I kissed Christine. In the following two weeks, I kissed her three, four or five times because I was then still very shy.

One day she told me that she wanted to break up with me. It was after we had gone steady for five weeks. I was very sad and started to daydream. In my dreams I imagined that I was a famous rock singer and being famous made me popular with girls. Then Christine would come back to me.

After that I went with Anne. She was two years younger than Christine, but somehow looked more feminine. This attracted me at that time. We kissed rather often, met in the woods and I stroked her hands and face.

After five weeks it was I who did not want to continue. I thought everything was going too quickly. When she kissed me I didn't feel anything anymore.

In October I took dancing lessons with my classmates. There I met a very nice girl. Every time I could choose my partner I danced with her. When we met on a Sunday we walked arm in arm. But then at the next dancing class she told me that she just wanted to dance with me, but not get involved in a deeper relationship.

Again I started to daydream.

In school I saw Christine, my first girl friend whom I still loved. I dreamt that we were together again.

On November 9th I met with her and asked her to go with me again. She refused saying that she already had a boyfriend, but at the moment he was in the hospital.

Four days later she came to me at school and asked whether I would go with her again. We started going arm in arm, but we did not kiss because in the meantime I had come to the conclusion that a girl friend is not just someone to be kissed. She is also someone with whom you can discuss your problems and enjoy being with. Just being with her is enough to make me happy.

When I saw her today she told me her boyfriend had called her and said that he would beat her up when he got out of the hospital. That's why she said she couldn't go out with me anymore. This story doesn't sound very feasible, but I believe it because I love Christine.

Please tell me what I can do in order not to fall back into dreaming. Write me too what I can tell Christine so that she won't hurt other boys as much as she has me.

Please answer as soon as possible. Please seal the envelope well because I can't tell my parents anything about it.

Many greetings,
Reinhard

Dear Reinhard,

The most important insight that you gained is that a girl is not simply an object to be kissed, but a person with whom you can talk over serious things. In the first period of your relationship with girls you considered Christine more or less a toy and Anne probably too.

You have also learned that too much kissing can make you numb. Therefore it is wise to be very sparing with kisses. A kiss is like money. It loses value if there's too much of it around. Furthermore, a girl usually appreciates feeling kissable more than actually being kissed.

When you met Christine the second time and began your friendship again but did not kiss her, you didn't see her anymore as a toy, but as a human being. This was a great step in the direction of maturity.

You are still on the road to this goal. But I have to tell you something very sobering. As beautiful as they may seem, those feelings of love which you feel now are not yet real love. You are basically projecting your own image onto the girl and the girl is doing the same. The magic will continue only as long as the other one corresponds to this dream image. Sooner or later the magic will disappear and then the inevitable disappointment will come.

Christine has evidently had this experience before you. Perhaps this is because at your age, girls are often ahead of boys in their development. This explains why Christine seems to prefer a boy one or two years older than herself.

There is no way to avoid pain. Lover's grief is necessary and you have to learn to live with it. You cannot save yourself from it, nor Christine, nor the other boys. This coming and going of acquaintances and friendships with all its pain and all its happiness simply has to be lived through.

To a certain extent, daydreams also belong to this pain and happiness. You don't need to fight against them. The more mature you become and the more you discover yourself as you really are, the less you will have to flee into daydreaming.

The first step in finding this maturity is to turn your thoughts away from yourself and to try to think and feel as another person would think and feel. When you are more interested in the concerns and worries of someone else than you are in your own troubles, a real feeling of love is awakening within you.

Do you know what impressed me the most in your letter? That "very nice girl" you met at your dancing class, who told you clearly that she just wanted to dance with you, but not get involved in a deeper relationship. She's healthy and has the right spirit. She knows exactly what goes with her age and what does not. She knows how to keep the limits and how to live in harmony with her development.

That hurt you too. But it must hurt along with the rest. Otherwise you will not grow.

With cordial greetings,
W. T.

Reflection

As I have already said, Reinhard is much more careful in his approach to girls than was Doris's boyfriend. He is also very sensitive to that which is authentic and realizes immediately when a gesture becomes meaningless. His insight that talking can make his relationship to a girl closer than too early and too much fondling and kissing will help him to build a meaningful and lasting relationship later on.

Doris did not mention her parents at all in her first letter. Reinhard mentioned only that he cannot talk to them. This is normal to a certain degree. Young people at this age do not like to discuss such experiences with their parents. Nevertheless, as his letter shows, Reinhard needs someone outside of the family with whom he can communicate.

I was saddened by his plea for a well-sealed envelope. Do his parents really have so little respect for him that they would read his personal mail? This would be a great mistake for parents of a sixteen-year-old son.

When I read the manuscript of this book to my children who were then between fourteen and twenty-one years of age, they thought my answer to Reinhard was too authoritarian. That is why they wanted to know if Reinhard had answered and what he had said.

It was almost a year before the answer came: "I have read your letter many times. But I didn't answer because I didn't have any special reason for writing back. The truth is, I am now very happy, but it didn't seem to me that this would be reason enough to write you. As time went by, my problem became less and less of a burden for me. Although I still like one particular girl, since February I haven't had any more longing for her. I believe I've learned much about friendships. . . ."

The next correspondence, with Elke K., describes from a girl's point of view this hesitating, cautious approach to the other sex.

3
"How Can I Find a Real Boyfriend?"

"I'VE NEVER HAD A REAL BOYFRIEND. I PRETEND TO OTHERS THAT I'M HAPPY NOT TO HAVE ONE. . . . PLEASE TELL ME . . . HOW I CAN FINALLY FIND A REAL BOYFRIEND."

REINHARD H., AGE 16, HIGH-SCHOOL STUDENT

Dear Mr. Trobisch,

At the moment I'm reading your book *Love Is a Feeling to Be Learned.* It interests me and I'm learning a lot. Yet it doesn't seem to help me much personally. Please let me explain my problem.

In two months I'll be seventeen. I've never had a real boyfriend. I pretend to others that I'm happy not to have one. Although basically this is true, I realize there are times when I would very much like to have a boyfriend.

I fall in love quite often. Don't ask me how deeply. I cannot sleep for nights on end. I'm thinking constantly of him, dreaming of him and of sharing the future with him. Of course, the poor guy has no idea about it because I would never reveal my feelings to him.

Then when I wake up to reality after a few days and the dream ends, my feelings change completely. I almost start hating him. I think the reason for this is that in my dreams this boy does everything I want him to do, while in reality he doesn't even notice me. How could he when he barely knows me by sight?

After going through such an experience I feel somehow disappointed. This has already happened to me with many, many boys. Please tell me as soon as you can how to avoid repeating this mistake and how I can finally find a real boyfriend.

Many thanks in advance,
Elke

Dear Elke,

In a masterful way you have succeeded in putting into words the burden of your age group: this strange hanging in between dream and reality—this feeling of happiness and unhappiness at the same time. You have to learn to live with that which is difficult. It simply belongs to being seventeen. I would deprive your life of richness if I were to take away from you those precious sleepless nights in which your soul is growing.

Something new is awakening in you, something as yet unknown to you—namely, your longing for the other sex. This longing is a good longing and a healthy one. It makes you move toward a great goal, "sharing the future" as you call it. That goal includes wholeness and fulfillment.

Yet at the same time your soul—I could also say your personality—is not yet strong enough to fulfill this longing. It is not yet able to establish a real relationship with someone from the other sex. It is just this which is difficult, for your soul is still en route, on its way. It is taking its first hesitant steps. It is in the process of learning how to walk. There is no other way to learn except simply to endure this conflict.

If I were to offer you a cut-and-dried solution, I would hinder your personality from developing. It is necessary to let the deep pain hurt and to suffer through the discords of dreaming and reality. You grow just because of this suffering. Somehow growth is usually connected with pain.

It is good that you can dream. While you dream your soul is working, bringing together longing and experience. But it is also good that you keep your dreams to yourself. A bottle of perfume must be kept tightly closed, or the fragrance is lost.

Those who try to translate their dreams too quickly and too cheaply into words or actions, fail. They destroy the fine tissues woven by this unhappy happiness. Would the boys of your age be able to understand if you tried to tell them how you really feel? I'm afraid it would be beyond them and they might only be tempted to abuse your precious longing.

This is why you are wise to be silent about your dreams. Let them be dreams without trying to break through the wall which separates them from reality.

You want a real boyfriend. Yes, you are entitled to this wish. But just what would a real boyfriend be like? One who would stand up for you in every situation? One on whom you can absolutely rely? One who protects you? One who trusts you and in whom you can confide everything? One who sees you as unique, the only one, and who would remain faithful to you for life? Isn't this true?

You can see what I'm getting at. Such a friend cannot yet be. No boy, even if he were a year or two older than you, could give this to you now. It would be unjust to demand it from anyone.

This is why the longing—this good and precious longing—has to remain a longing at least for the time being. You have to learn to live with unfulfilled desires. This is the difficult art of your time of life. If you learn this skill now you will have gained something for your whole life.

Maybe what you are looking for could be given to you by a good girl friend with whom you could share your innermost feelings—even your feelings of hate and aggression. Your observation is correct that the feelings of hate and love are very close together. It is indifference—not hatred—which is the opposite of love. You are good to have noticed this.

You hate this boy because he causes you pain and disappointment. And this is precisely because you are not indifferent to him. But your pain is a pain of growth, Elke, and therefore something good and healing. Basically, any disillusionment is something positive because it destroys the illusion that the dream could be reality and that you could experience some thing which in truth you cannot.

Therefore, the experience of hating is as much a part of the maturing process in which you now find yourself as is the experience of disillusionment which I may have caused by giving you this answer.

Yours,
W. T.

Dear Mr. Trobisch,

I would like to thank you from the bottom of my heart for your letter. I was relieved because I had thought that my thinking and feeling were wrong, even abnormal. I believe this is because of the many magazines and films we see today. They make us live in the illusion that true love is something which is only beautiful and simple. In reality it looks very different.

I have talked a lot about these problems with my older brother. He is the one with whom I can share best at the moment. It was also he who advised me to write to you.

But now I've done something really stupid. I wrote an anonymous letter to a boy whom I have not been able to get out of my thoughts for more than a year now. "Anonymous" is not quite the right word, because in the letter I gave him a hint so that he could figure out who had written the letter. I told him a little bit about myself and then asked him to try to find my address and answer my letter. I also wrote him that I expected him to keep the whole thing a secret between the two of us.

Today I know that this was a big mistake. In the first place, he didn't answer and second, he made fun of me when talking to his friends. I know this because one of those friends told my brother.

Cordial greetings,
Elke

Reflection

Elke failed because of her half-hearted effort. She wants to take two steps at the same time. In this way, she oversteps the necessary phase of friendship between people of the same sex.

All of us go through three phases in our development. The first phase is called the *autoerotic* phase. *Autos* is the Greek word for "self." *Eros* is the Greek word for "love." In this phase we are in love with ourselves, not yet able to relate to someone else.

The autoerotic phase is followed by the *homoerotic* phase. *Homos* means "same." It is an in-between phase. On the one hand, we are able to direct our feelings to a "stranger," someone who is not "myself," and yet we are not mature enough to direct them to a representative of the other sex.

The third phase is called the *heteroerotic* phase. *Heteros* is the Greek word for "other" or "different." In this phase the person is mature enough to face the otherliness of the opposite sex, to relate to someone who is so "strange," so "different."

Elke has not yet reached this level of maturity. She would have been able to establish a healthy relationship with a girl friend, but her personality is not yet strong enough for a relationship with the opposite sex. Even though she dares to write a letter to a boy, she hides herself in it. The boy, of course, does not understand what causes such behavior and finds it funny, even ridiculous.

In this respect, the next letter is entirely different. It describes a conscious, direct approach between the sexes. Again we hear from a young man.

4
"My Next Girl Friend Will Become My Wife"

"I TOLD SEVERAL FRIENDS THAT MY NEXT GIRL FRIEND WOULD BECOME MY WIFE. . . . SHE'S A CHRISTIAN TOO AND HAD ASKED THE LORD FOR CLEAR GUIDANCE. . . . NOW I STAND IN FRONT OF A VOID."

AXEL R., AGE 17, HIGH-SCHOOL STUDENT

Honorable Sir,

I just turned seventeen. For half a year now I've tried to be a Christian, and I realize that many things have changed in my life through Jesus. But now I'm at a point where I don't know how to proceed.

On New Year's Eve I became conscious of the fact that I sensed something for a certain girl. Her name is Katrine. I didn't take this too seriously at first, but then the feeling of love grew and captivated me.

I prayed to the Lord that he would take it in his hands. I also told him that I wished Katrine would feel something for me. I tried to be together with her as often as possible, but every attempt out of my own strength to get closer to her failed.

Maybe it was a dumb thing to do, but I told several friends that my next girl friend would become my wife. Very conscious of this statement, I realized Katrine could be this girl.

One day my friend told me that Katrine had said that she also liked me. That very same night we had our first talk together.

For four months I had been praying for this moment and now it had come. I told her how I felt about her, and she said that it was on New Year's Eve that lightning had struck. She's a Christian too and had asked the Lord for clear guidance. Now, I thought, I have found the wife meant for me by God!

Since both of us had just turned seventeen, a period of two years loomed suddenly before us. We decided not to deepen our friendship during these two years although we agreed that we would marry someday. Since I still have two years left of high school before I can go to college and seminary, we decided not to go steady nor have any physical contact during these two years.

I was quite determined to follow this plan. We never saw each other except in our youth group. We didn't show our feelings to each other. I was completely convinced that Jesus had given Katrine to me as my future wife.

Then one day my heart stopped beating. I don't understand anything anymore.

I'd been away on a trip for two weeks. When I got back we took a walk together but Katrine didn't even look or smile at me. She said that it was already the second time that she had no feelings at all for me. She was close to tears because she felt guilty.

She asked me to let the whole thing rest because she wanted a husband she felt love for every day of her life, not one she loved for just three months and twenty-eight days. That's how many days have passed since our first talk.

Now I stand in front of a void. I just can't understand why this happened. Is it because we decided not to kiss for two years? Or does God have still a better wife for me? Can God guide in this way? Or must I learn to be "down"? Have I been too hard on myself and on her? Are we too young?

"You make wise plans and you do mighty things; you see everything that people do and you reward them according to their actions" (Jer. 32:19).

I'm convinced that God guides me, but I'm at my wits' end and I'm confused. I'm so unsure. I pray that you will be able to help me. I believe that you can.

Yours,
Axel

Dear Axel,

Thank you for your letter. First I will answer your questions. It's very possible that God has another wife for you. Maybe Katrine was the second best, while God still has the first best in store for you.

Yes, God can guide in such a way. Yes, you do have to learn to be "down." This is the best preparation for life. It pays to suffer lover's grief precisely for this reason. In this way you become a man.

No, you haven't been too hard on yourself. It was dumb to announce to everyone that your next girl friend would become your wife. Your relationship certainly didn't go to pieces because you laid down such strict rules. On the contrary, it probably would have broken down sooner if you had gone too far. Imagine how embarrassing that would be for you now—especially if you think that someday you will meet God's first choice for you.

Yes, you are very young. You can't yet make a decision about marriage and you shouldn't even try. Both of you will change a lot between the ages of seventeen and twenty. Your feelings also are going to change. After three or four years you might not even be able to understand what attracted you so much to each other.

I believe that you should be very grateful to Katrine because she told you honestly how she feels and didn't play around with your feelings by pretending something just to make you happy. There are some girls who like to play with boys' feelings, just because they are a little ahead of the boys in their emotional development.

In a way, Katrine's honesty is a sign of love. The German poet Goethe says: "To renounce at the right moment is a sign of friendship. Love often does damage because it considers the desires of the beloved more than his happiness."

Love for you now means to fulfill Katrine's wish and let things be. Both of you need this rest after the storm in order to find yourselves.

For one who is preparing for the ministry, it is particularly unwise to be bound too early by the chains of love. Because of the great demands placed upon her, a pastor's wife must be chosen with special care. Give yourself time for this choice.

Don't lose patience with yourself or with God. I am glad that you can bring all the decisions of your daily life to your Lord and that you count on him and his guidance in a very concrete way. God proves himself often as the one who makes "wise plans" when he cancels our human plans.

As far as I can see, God has already helped you. When he brings us to our wits' end and we feel as if we are standing in front of a complete void, then his way with us can begin.

Isn't it a beautiful and adventurous situation to stand in front of a void with unlimited possibilities ahead of you? It is just the void which contains the promise of the future.

Only the one who is broken can find the doors leading into the joy of Jesus Christ.

With kindest greetings,
W. T.

Reflection

When I read this correspondence to my sons, they found Axel's letter somehow exaggerated and unnatural. They thought Axel thinks too much and feels too little. They were also amused by his exact count of the days of his friendship with Katrine. This occurred also in Reinhard's letter when he reported in which week and how often he had kissed. Maybe this emphasis on data is an attempt on the part of the boys to render their feelings banal or trite.

Be that as it may, the important thing is that Axel relates his love experience to God. He refuses to be a boat without a rudder being steered by every wind that blows. Finding God's will in affairs of the heart is especially difficult. The experience of being overcome by such intense and awesome feeling is often taken to be God's voice or even God's action. This is why we often need someone from outside who can see it more objectively.

Axel's answer came ten months later: "At last I will answer your letter.

I'm afraid you'll be disappointed. Soon after I got your letter the situation cleared up. I was ready to give up everything and then Katrine came to me out of her own accord.

"I was prepared for anything. I liked her again immediately when she came and I sensed that she cared for me too.

"We've been going steady now for over a year and are happy. There would have been many occasions to break up again, but our third partner is Jesus. We've put our relationship into his hands and that's our greatest help. Looking back, I can only say we are very thankful to God."

Two things in his letter I think are remarkable. The first is the fact that here a girl takes a step toward a boy out of her own accord. A girl does not always need to be passive and hide her feelings. Here the word of Jesus applies: "The truth shall make you free" (Jn. 8:32).

To act out of truth, though, means that the girl puts herself "in the light" and that she does not play hide-and-seek as Elke did. Acting out of truth takes ego-strength because she also risks being turned down. She would have to be strong enough to stand up under such an experience.

Second, it is remarkable that the two of them have excluded the physical realm for the time being. This they told me in a personal talk when I visited them. They consider this time a trial period, and they do not want to miss out on any growth experiences by starting a sexual relationship. They would rather draw the physical limits too narrow than too wide.

The wisdom of this decision is illustrated in the next correspondence. Again we meet two Christians.

5
"Klaus and I Stayed Overnight in the Same Room"

"KLAUS AND I SLEPT IN ONE OF THOSE ROOMS. DURING THOSE TWO NIGHTS NOTHING HAPPENED AT ALL."

RITA G., AGE 16, HIGH-SCHOOL STUDENT

Dear Mr. Trobisch,

My name is Rita G. I'm sixteen and a high-school student. I just read your book *My Beautiful Feeling* and decided to write to you about my problem. I'm a Christian and have been active in youth work this past year in our town.

When I was fourteen, I had my first boyfriend. We went steady for a year. I put God aside during that time. When my boyfriend and I broke up, I had a very hard inner struggle to get really free from him. I didn't realize how deeply I had been emotionally involved. I was terribly disappointed and felt very bad.

Nine months ago I got acquainted with Klaus. He's nineteen and also a true believer. My mother knew about our friendship and she liked Klaus a lot. In April some fellows from our youth group, Klaus and I went skiing. We stayed overnight in a hut where there were only rooms with two beds each. Klaus and I slept in one of those rooms. During those two nights nothing happened at all. We lay beside each other encircling each other with our arms (which perhaps we shouldn't have done). I told this to my mother when she asked about it. She was very disappointed with us as were Klaus's parents.

Klaus had often come to pick me up for a date, but then it became less and less frequent. I tried to make it clear to him that my mother forgave him long ago, but he would not or could not believe it.

Two months later both of us were invited to a birthday party to be held at a hut in the mountains. We were both looking forward to it very much. But the day we were supposed to leave, Klaus came to me very depressed and said his parents wouldn't allow him to go. I was very mad at his parents after he left. Without thinking it over, I went to one of Klaus's cousins and asked him to take me along. He did. Klaus was terribly disappointed in me which I can very well understand.

After we got back home from the party I realized that Klaus didn't show up anymore at our house. When I asked him why, he told me that he couldn't forget what had happened and that the other boys made fun of him. He had decided to break up even though he said he still loved me.

Is this my fault? Why can't Klaus forgive and forget? I just can't shake myself free from him. I love him just as much as ever if not more. We haven't yet talked about everything. I don't know how he feels. Shall I try to talk to him again or should I do nothing? I have the feeling that he loves me, but he doesn't want to face it. If we meet in a group, he's just friendly and nice to me. Could you please help me?

Many thanks that you listened to me and that I could write to you,

Rita

Dear Rita,

Thanks a lot for your letter. I especially appreciated the fact that you also told me when you had failed.

You say that you are a Christian and active in youth work. Also you say that Klaus is a true believer. If you take the word *believe* seriously in its deepest meaning, then it means to recognize something as authentic and valid. It does not mean, as so many think, to take something for the truth which cannot be proven. Believing is an action which has binding consequences. One of these consequences is a certain lifestyle from which others can conclude that the action of believing has taken place in the life of this person and is taking place daily.

I'm of the opinion that staying overnight in the same room or the same tent does not belong to this lifestyle. It is a marital situation which belongs to the context of what the Bible calls "to become one flesh." According to biblical thinking this situation is exclusively related to marriage.

By putting yourself in compromising situations, you are doing something which does not correspond to being a Christian—even if "nothing" happens. By *nothing* I take it you mean the sexual union or some sexual play. Even if this does not happen, something else does happen. Strong desires are aroused which you must suppress very strongly. If you suppress these over and over again it is hard to correct later on.

I respect Klaus highly. Evidently he's not just disappointed in you, but also in himself because he's made a compromise with his standards. Looking at it from this point of view something must have happened for which he can hardly forgive himself. That's why he drew the line. I think highly of such an attitude. Also, he obeyed his parents even though it meant giving up his own wishes. He did this despite the fact that he is nineteen. Compare this to the way you disappointed your mother even though you are only sixteen.

He probably also realized that the friendship with you goes beyond the strength of both of you and brings you into situations which you cannot handle. I think he did the right thing when he broke up with you—maybe just because he likes you and wants the best for you.

Right now you can't do anything else but accept it. It's good for you to learn to live at a distance and still to be friendly toward each other. This is an art and Klaus is giving you a good example.

You have to pay a price for acting without thinking. If you want to develop a lifestyle from which others can conclude that you are a Christian, it is not possible to act without thinking. As Christians we are not only responsible for our actions but also for our reputation. Therefore it's important that we do not give impressions which can lead others to wrong conclusions.

In this age of permissiveness, anyone who knows that you spent two nights together in the same room would take it for granted that you had sex. That's why such behavior is no testimony for your Lord.

I'm glad that you admit your mistake and that you can even understand Klaus's disappointment about you. The only real mistakes in life, however, are the ones from which we do not learn.

Cordial greetings,
W. T.

Dear Mr. Trobisch,

It's quite a while [six months later] since I wrote you. The friendship with Klaus is finished. I apologized to him, he's forgiven me, but he says he can't forget. We see each other every Friday in our youth group, but this doesn't mean a thing. There are times when I become very depressed if I see him and I even think of suicide. At present I'm getting medical treatment for an ulcer caused by the nervous strain of this relationship.

Klaus has a very strict father who does not allow his children much freedom for the simple reason: "We were not allowed to do it either."

Rita

Reflection

A brief word about the last paragraph of Rita's letter is in order. It is one of the rare cases in which a father who acts, interferes, directs and stands up for his opinion is mentioned.

The only trouble is, he doesn't talk. The reason which he gives to his children is insufficient. He forces his children to obey without insight and this is not enough.

Why must the strong father always behave as a patriarch? What we need today are fatherly fathers—neither patriarchal nor marginal. Is this really so difficult?

Hans, writer of the next letter, is able to talk to his father but they do not seem to be able to get to the heart of matters. It was from Hans that I received this letter of protest.

6
"Even One Girl Is Too Many"

"HAD I KNOWN HOW MANY COMPLICATIONS YOUR BOOK WOULD CAUSE . . . I NEVER WOULD HAVE READ IT. . . . THE WAY YOU TALK ABOUT CARESSING MAKES ME SICK. . . . I WOULDN'T LIKE TO MARRY A GIRL WHO HAS ALREADY SLEPT WITH FIVE OR SIX BOYS."

HANS K., AGE 14, HIGH-SCHOOL STUDENT

Dear Sir,

Through an acquaintance I got your book *Love Is a Feeling to Be Learned.* Since the title interested me, I read it and then passed it on to several other friends my age, namely fourteen years old.

Had I known how many complications your book would cause and how base I would feel after reading it, I never would have read it.

I don't want to criticize your basic ideas or even put them down, but the hardness you used in expressing yourself I find simply irresponsible. According to your book, a girl who is not chaste is more or less a prostitute. If you sleep together before marriage, it's a great sin, and the marriage can't be saved anymore. The way you talk about caressing makes me sick.

After I'd read your book, I was very unsure. Of course, there's no question that friendships can suffer under things like that. Over and over again I wish that I'd never read the book. The others who read it say the same.

Everything goes wrong in your book. None of the contraceptives are safe. If a boy sleeps with a girl, he usually leaves her in the lurch. Why did you present everything in this book in such a pessimistic way?

I would be very thankful for a prompt answer.

With friendly greetings,
Your Hans

Dear Hans:

Many, many thanks for your letter. I think it is good that you blew your top and that you told me frankly what you think about my book.

Did you ask yourself why the book made you angry? I'll tell you why: because it made you have a bad conscience. Or maybe this bad conscience, this feeling of being on the wrong track was already there and my book only confirmed it.

If you are angry because the book made you feel base or vile, maybe it is because you had to face the truth. Maybe you did indeed act in a base or vile manner.

It hurts to admit this yourself, I know. But sometimes it can be the greater love to hurt someone even though he gets angry.

This leads to your question as to why I presented the negative consequences so realistically—not pessimistically, as you say. I did it because I have literally hundreds of letters here in my office which testify to the way people's lives have been fouled up because they transgressed God's commandments. Unfortunately, it's true that the unhappiness of many marriages begins with an unhealthy premarital conduct. If your present friendship with your girl friend suffers now under your own insecurity, that is still better than if your marriage suffers later. I have expressed myself as clearly and as hard as possible out of a sense of responsibility precisely to warn of trouble and to prevent disaster.

It could be, of course, that your experiences are different. Then please share them with me. I wish, though, that your girl friend would also tell me what she thinks about my book. As a matter of fact, I have a lot of grateful letters from girls. Some have even written: "If I had read your book one day earlier, my life would not have been fouled up."

Sad to say, but it does happen quite often that a boy leaves a girl in the lurch after he has conquered her sexually. I am glad that you, evidently, do not belong to this group and I greet you cordially.

Yours,

W.T.

Dear Sir,

First of all I want to thank you for your nice letter and at the same time correct an error. I must tell you the truth: I didn't write that first letter to you at all. It was my girl friend who wrote it. She wrote it using my name and my address because she was afraid her parents would read your answer and scold her.

This means that the first letter actually contained the thoughts of my girl friend, but you couldn't know this.

I have to admit you are right. Many boys do leave a girl in the lurch after she has given herself to them completely. But I also know a number of boys where this was not the case.

I certainly am not in favor of a girl going to bed with just any boy. I wouldn't like to marry a girl who has already slept with five or six boys.

On the other hand, I think—and I talked about it with my parents who agreed with me—that it's perfectly all right to be friends with two or three girls before marriage.

I believe though that it is only in marriage that you really get to know a girl or a woman. If you marry the first girl you meet, you are still inexperienced and then in the long run you may be disappointed because it doesn't turn out like you think it will. And then the marriage can break up. This is bad especially if there are children. Besides that you are transgressing God's commandment not to commit adultery.

Maybe my opinion is completely wrong, because it also says in the Bible that God wants to keep sexual relations for marriage. Still, I think it's better to have had two or three girls before marriage than to commit adultery once you are married.

Cordial greetings,

Hans

Dear Hans,

What I like about your letter is that you have an unusual gift at your age of being able to look ahead and to judge things from the perspective of the goal to be reached.

You already have marriage or the possible failure of marriage in view in deciding how you will act now.

Of course, everything depends on what you mean by the words "to be friends." Possibly your parents do not agree with you here. If you mean by being friends, to get closely acquainted, I would say that two or three girls are not enough. One has to get acquainted with many girls before one can really choose.

But if by being friends you mean sleeping together, then I would say that even one girl is too many. I am of this opinion precisely because of the goal. It has been proven that in those marriages where both partners have not known anyone else sexually before marriage, unfaithfulness is rarest.

If one or two would be all right, why not five or six? Your arguments become inconsistent here.

It is a fact that sexual experiences before marriage turn out to be more of a burden than a help later on. They can become a stumbling block to knowing girl friends in a deeper way and even disturb the sexual union in marriage. The fact that change has become a habit and comparison is possible has a negative effect on marriage.

Do you really think your girl friend, who wrote the first letter to me, would become a good wife if she keeps on the way she is going? By the way, her parents don't seem to be in agreement with her. Otherwise she wouldn't have been worried that they might read my answer.

It is dangerous to put your own norms above God's norms. Remember it was not human meanness which crucified the Son of God but human arrogance trying to be wiser than God.

I greet you very cordially,
W. T.

Reflection

The correspondence with Hans brings out a very important problem: the privacy of our children's mail. Hans does not say how old his girl friend is, but I would judge she is sixteen at the most.

To me there is no question that parents should respect the privacy of their children's mail at this age. It is understandable that parents want to protect their children from negative influences, but this is not the way to do it. They tempt their children to become dishonest and force them to use sneaky means to protect their privacy, as the letter of Hans's girl friend illustrates. Besides that they give their children the feeling that they do not trust them and underestimate their ability to judge. This is one of the reasons why these children may not turn to their parents when they need help. Once confidence is broken down, it is hard for parents to exercise influence on their children.

The greatest protection parents can give to their children is the inner certainty: "My parents trust me to make the right decision." In contrast to his girl friend's parents, Hans's parents seem to respect the privacy of his letters. Maybe this is why they are able to talk things over with him even though their talks seem to be rather superficial.

Another conclusion we can draw from Hans's letter is that it is by no means too early to talk with a fourteen-year-old about marriage. Certainly when he tries to form his opinions, the pressure of his peer group is at work. Here parents who themselves have a firm standpoint could create a good counterweight by daring to discuss very concrete questions, such as that of pregnancy and contraceptives. Hans does not even seem to think of these possible problems.

Hans is especially mistaken when he thinks that preparing for marriage means getting ready for the sexual act. Of one hundred hours of married life, one might be spent in sexual relations. It is the other ninety-nine hours which need preparation.

The next correspondent is even younger than Hans, only thirteen. Yet she has a boyfriend who is almost nineteen. She does not appear to even think of having sex with him. Rather, her sexual problems are centered in herself. That which Borghild is seeking and cannot find is a place of security, the experience of being sheltered.

7
"Is Masturbation a Sin?"

"DOES JESUS HAVE ANYTHING AGAINST A FRIENDSHIP AT THE AGE OF THIRTEEN? . . . IS MASTURBATION A SIN? I CAN'T HELP IT—ESPECIALLY WHEN I NEED LOVE. . . . I EAT AND EAT. SOMETIMES I REALLY STUFF MYSELF."

BORGHILD H., AGE 13 BOYFRIEND, AGE 18

Dear Mr. Trobisch,

I write to you because I'm looking for an answer.

I'm thirteen. You'll be surprised that I write to you. It's because of how old I am that I'm doing it. Too much so?

I have a boyfriend. He will be nineteen in two months. We understand each other in a really unique way. Really! We are both Christians. He's working as a medical aid. My parents, yes, my whole family including grandpa and our dog, accept him. He belongs to us. He visits us very often.

Now I believe one thing is important: We've known each other for six months. I want to ask you, does Jesus have anything against a friendship at the age of thirteen? Does he have anything against holding hands? No more?

Oh boy, now I'll just say what's on my heart. I hope you have time to read it.

They all think that I'm still too young and seem to agree with the saying: One kiss is already the first step into bed. Oh boy, that really makes me depressed!

Something else: Is masturbation a sin? I can't help it—especially when I need love. Then I tell myself quickly, "Jesus loves you more than all else." But when I say I'm a Christian it's hard to believe, isn't it? Or is it?

I hope this letter reaches you. I do hope so. I want an answer so very much! Please! Many thanks!

Yours,
Borghild

P.S. I'm going to leave this letter just as it is. If I write it over again I would leave something out.

Dear Borghild,

Thank you for your letter written from your heart. Of course you can be friends with a young man and hold hands, but inwardly you will not gain very much. Because of your age difference, it will be difficult to meet at the same level. At your age it would be more important to have a good girl friend.

I'm afraid that the tensions which go along with having a boyfriend will cost you too much strength at your age. A kiss will not necessarily lead into bed. Yet there is a bit of truth in that saying. Actually my wife and I have answered these questions in our book *My Beautiful Feeling.* It's a correspondence with a seventeen-year-old girl, who, by the way, also struggled with the problem of masturbation. In this book we tried to answer the difficult question of whether or not it is a sin. Maybe you could get hold of it and then write to us and tell us whether you could identify with any of it.

Yes, you made a very fine observation when you said that you are looking for love, or rather the feeling of being loved, when you masturbate. But precisely in this way you will not find it.

Write again!

Your W. T.

Dear Mr. Trobisch,
I'm really very grateful that you answered me. I read the book and really I have the same problems as Ilona.

Even with eating I have the same difficulties. I eat and eat. Sometimes I really stuff myself.

Even though I do this, I'm really very slim. Everyone says this about me. My mother thinks I almost worship my body. It goes like this: There are times when I'm not disciplined at all with eating. At other times I am, but then my stomach grumbles all day long. When I want to become slim, I stand in front of my mirror naked every night.

Every time I hear this same little voice as when I masturbate. It says: "But Borghild, it doesn't make any difference to God whether you are slim or not. God loves you anyway. You may eat as much as you want." And then I do precisely that which I do not want to do. Can you help me? Please do.

I cannot give up masturbation. Before it happens I have almost a joy of expectation: "Oh, finally a chance to flee out of the humdrum of daily life—to really show love to myself!"

Oh prunes! I really have a hard time expressing myself. I hope you have time. Honestly, I really don't want to bother you.

Mom says I shouldn't even think about "such things." (Please, I don't want to give my mother a bad grade!)

And now the problem with the jeans. We had a scene again today about it. She said, "At least when you go to church, don't wear those jeans."

I admit they are rather worn out. It's only this one pair of jeans that I wear every day. Okay! To please my mother I wore another pair but my good mood was destroyed. In the afternoon I was then permitted to wear the old ones again and I really felt better. That's the way it is!

Girls' clothes make me nauseated, even though I find femininity beautiful in others, yes, even attractive. I've felt really funny during the last weeks. Whenever I think now of marriage, intercourse, even friendship, it's too much. It even makes me want to vomit. I get really mad whenever I see lovers together. (In former times I wanted to get married. It was my only goal.) Do you know I really would like to break up with Manfred?

When I wrote my last letter to you it was still different. I wanted to be caressed, fondled. Twice we've said to each other, "I like you." When we said it the second time we touched briefly with our hands, but now I don't even want that anymore.

You know, I would like to be free and enjoy life. That's why marriage is suddenly so unattractive to me. Just imagine one's whole life with one and the same man.

Tell me, should I really break up with Manfred? I can barely stand to see him. I'm at my wits' end.

Mommy says she feels it wouldn't be fair to push him away just like that. I shouldn't have started with him in the first place.

At the beginning of our relationship, after one week, I already tried to break up with him because I wasn't sure our relationship was right before God. But then he was so sad that he convinced me. So we stuck together.

People raise their eyebrows when they see us together and this makes me uneasy. (On the other hand, there are nice sides to it too.)

Okay, if you have time, would you answer? Indeed, that would really be . . . , THANKS!

Yours,
Borghild

P.S. I've written everything straight from the heart. That's why I'm thankful beyond words.

Dear Borghild,

I'm also thankful that you write everything straight from your heart. Your expression *straight from the heart* has a very deep meaning. Inner conflicts and tensions can affect the heart and make you physically sick, especially if they are not expressed and the anger is swallowed up instead of being spit out. This can literally affect the heart. That's why it makes me very happy that you are able to get mad when you see lovers and that you also express your negative feelings about Manfred. To me this means that you are real. You have stopped playing a role which you think everyone expects from you, that is, that you must have a boyfriend because others in your age group might have one. You are honest about these negative feelings and you are yourself. Don't be ashamed of your feelings. Stand up for them and act accordingly.

Yes, you should really be free and enjoy life. That's just the reason why you should feel free to break up with Manfred.

Don't act against your conviction and make compromises. Stand up for what you think. Don't be swayed by the sadness of Manfred. That's his problem, not yours. He must learn to suffer grief without breaking down, and this is the only way to learn. In the final analysis you actually help him by being honest. "Love rejoices in the truth" (1 Cor. 13:6). This is what it says in the great chapter about love in the New Testament. Love is never an opponent of truth. It's an ally. Therefore sometimes love has to cause pain. Truth is always right before God. A compromise made out of pity is never right.

Truth, however, means that you live in accordance with your age. If you say, "I can't stand it anymore" and "I'm at my wits' end," then you are expressing exactly what a healthy girl of your age feels. No one can demand that you, at the age of thirteen, handle all the tensions which normally go hand in hand with a friendship. No one can expect either that at your age you be enthusiastic about marriage or that you even understand fully what it is or should be.

To have a deep friendship with a girl, though, would be just the thing for you now. It could be part of your freedom and enjoyment of life. It could set you free from turning around on your own axis and looking constantly at yourself in the mirror.

Nothing else could help you more to stop masturbating, which is only an expression of this turning around yourself.

We're happy that you have read our book about the subject and that you can identify with Ilona.

Basically, masturbation, eating too much or too little and even the bit about wearing old jeans are all symptoms of the same problem. You have not accepted yourself completely yet. Nor have you accepted yourself fully as a girl. In my book *Love Yourself,* you can see how these two are related.

But while you struggle with these symptoms, very softly another Borghild is awakening within you, coming out of her shell. It is the

Borghild who finds "femininity beautiful" and who some years from now will become a young woman, an attractive young lady gracefully gliding across the floor in a long dress.

Up until this point you still have a long way to go and you must have patience with yourself. All these things—that you feel funny, that feelings, sometimes nausea, sometimes deep longing, get hold of you and conflict with each other—belong to your time of life. It will all clear up later on, but you have to take a step at a time and not miss any of the stages. Because God has patience with you, you can also have it with yourself.

But it's just this dimension I feel your letter lacks. Here's where you are different than Ilona. She didn't run away from God but faced up to his challenge. This is the step you have not yet taken. You listen too much to other voices—your mother, your friend, people. It doesn't matter whether people raise their eyebrows about your conduct or not, but whether God does.

If you face up to God's challenge and listen to him and him alone, he will not raise his eyebrows, but let his face shine on you and open the door to freedom and enjoyment, enabling you to stand above the humdrum of everyday life.

I would so much like to give evidence of his love to you. It is my heartfelt wish that some day you will enter this door. . . .

Kindest greetings,

W. T.

Reflection

Borghild is so real! So straightforward! She is still very much in the autoerotic phase. Masturbation, admiring her body in front of the mirror, wearing only jeans—all these belong in this context. She does not yet know who she is.

Of course, my correspondence with her cannot be completely understood without reading *My Beautiful Feeling* which she read between her first and second letters. You can see how she has grown through it. "Bibliotherapy," being healed through reading, has been effective in her life.

At the same time, Borghild is just in the beginning of the homoerotic phase. Her danger is that she might jump this stage and approach the other sex too soon due to peer pressure. Her mother seems to intensify this pressure without giving her enough help. The advice she gives Borghild, not to occupy her mind with such things, is of course insufficient.

Borghild is lucky that she has a friend like Manfred who evidently does not take advantage of her longing for tenderness, for shelter and for other proofs of love.

But where is the father who could and should give all of this to his thirteen-year-old daughter? Why isn't he even mentioned?

My wife says that she can understand Borghild's mother, who seems to think: better Manfred as my daughter's friend than someone else. Borghild is well taken care of by him. She would probably not find a young man like him so easily again.

Something in Borghild struggles against this relationship and she would like to break it off. Her mother does not seem to have an antenna for Borghild's healthy resistance. Why does she not even think of suggesting that Borghild find a good girl friend? Or why does she not try herself to be a friend to her daughter?

And how does the whole thing look from Manfred's point of view? Why does he go with such a young girl? One of my sons suggested that for many boys a girl is a sort of status symbol, like having a motorbike or a car. At Manfred's age, he would simply have to have one and if he is not strong enough inwardly to relate to a girl his own age, then at least he can relate to a younger one.

The problems of Joela B., the next correspondent, are very similar. She has neither a father nor a friend. On the other hand, she has a very understanding mother who does not intrude on her privacy and who can wait patiently until she finds herself.

Joela, though, began earlier than Borghild to masturbate, possibly about the time she lost her father through divorce.

8
"I Would Like to Shoot My Cycle Off to the Moon"

"I'VE READ MANY TIMES ALREADY THAT MASTURBATION IS NOT HARMFUL, BUT THIS DOESN'T HELP ME. . . . IT WOULD BE THE EIGHTH WONDER OF THE WORLD IF I WOULD WEAR A SKIRT. . . . IF I HAD MY WAY, I WOULD LIKE TO SHOOT MY WHOLE CYCLE AND EVERYTHING THAT GOES WITH IT OFF TO THE MOON."

JOELA B., AGE 14, NO FATHER AND NO FRIEND

Dear Mr. and Mrs. Trobisch,

My name is Joela and I'm fourteen. Some time ago I read your book *I Loved a Girl.* It impressed me a lot that the young African François discussed his problem with you so frankly. I've wanted to talk over my problems with someone now for a long time.

About four or five years ago I started to masturbate. It was only recently that I learned what I was really doing. Since then I have felt terribly ashamed. Am I normal? Is this a sign of being sick? I would like to get rid of it.

I believe in God and I've brought my problem to him in prayer. But nothing has changed. Did I do something wrong?

I've read many times already that masturbation is not harmful, but this doesn't help me. I can't talk about it with my mother, even though I think she knows about it.

I don't have a father, because my parents got divorced when I was still very young. Up until I was ten I had a wonderful relationship with my mother, but lately I feel like I'm always under attack and then I get really vicious. I don't want to be this way at all. I feel best when the atmosphere at home is peaceful and harmonious. Can you help me? May I write to you? If I'm really honest, I don't have much hope that I will receive an answer.

Thank you anyway that I could unburden myself on paper.

Cordial greetings,

Your Joela

Dear Joela,

It is good that you unburdened yourself on paper. This was certainly a step in the right direction. We would like to send you our book *My Beautiful Feeling,* which will answer many of your questions. We'd also like to know whether your mother respects the privacy of your mail. We hope she does for we are sure she would like to help you too, just as we would, and this is only possible if we can write very frankly.

I had just written this sentence when I discovered that you had put your phone number on your envelope, so I called you. Now we have even talked together! I'm glad that your mother does not open your letters and that she seems to understand that it is embarrassing to talk to one's own mother about this special problem.

Even though we are sending our book to you, we would like to answer your main question very briefly. You do not need to feel ashamed. You are very normal. You are not sick. It is true, masturbation (M.) is not harmful, but this does not mean that it is wholesome. Somehow you feel this yourself. In any case, masturbation is not a mature and meaningful way to deal with your sexuality.

Although it is certainly not a disease, it is a symptom of a deeper problem. Very often this problem is loneliness. It could very well be that there is a connection with the fact that you do not have a father. For a girl, it also often has to do with the relationship to her mother. Your letter seems to confirm this. Probably you would be much less tempted to do it if everything were peaceful and harmonious at home.

But this is enough for today. Write again after you have read the book.

Yours,

Walter and Ingrid Trobisch

Dear Mr. and Mrs. Trobisch,

Please don't be offended that I didn't write for such a long time. I had such a funny feeling somehow after I got your letter. You were not anymore an anonymous answerer of letters, but—excuse the comparison—you were so near, so close. Somehow I was a little bit afraid. I cannot really describe my feeling.

Many thanks for your letter and the phone call. It really was a happy surprise for me.

On the phone you asked me to write down the practical conclusions I drew from reading the book. One thing is that I thought of giving myself a sort of reward when I do not give in to the desire of M. (Sorry to say this doesn't happen very often.) I have started to draw and paint. This is a lot of fun.

By the way I have the same problem as Ilona. Nothing captivates or fascinates me completely. You write that in this way a vacuum is created. This is exactly the way I feel. Even though I like drawing, in the long run it doesn't give me complete fulfillment. I also have a little bit of a bad conscience when I draw because I always think, "You really should be studying now."

There's one thing which I really haven't understood yet. What does wearing jeans have to do with the fact of whether or not I accept myself as a girl? How can I learn to accept myself?

As a matter of fact, I always run around in jeans. My girl friend said recently, it would be the eighth wonder of the world if I showed up wearing a skirt. I guess she's right.

You also told Ilona that she should live consciously with her cycle. I can't do that. If I had *my* way, I would like to shoot my whole cycle and everything that goes with it off to the moon. When I have my period, I can't do anything—not go swimming or any other sports. Besides that I always get terrible stomach pains. Why is it so important to live consciously with it?

Recently, M. happened quite often in comparison to summer vacation when it rarely happened. During the past week it didn't happen at all, until last night. Then I had no will to resist and the guilt feeling was there again.

Many thanks that I can write to you,
Your Joela

Dear Joela,

Thank you again for your frank letter. We see that you read our book quite thoroughly and you drew good conclusions. The idea of rewarding yourself is a good one. Maybe you should also reward yourself when you have done your homework by sketching and painting so that you don't need to have a bad conscience. How about doing it this way: for every hour of study you allow yourself fifteen minutes of painting. You also mentioned sports and swimming in passing. Maybe there are other things you really like to do. Don't you play an instrument?

One thing is for sure: nothing is more important for you right now than to take time to do the things you really enjoy. That will make studying easier too. You have seen for yourself that during summer vacation when you had lots of fun and no pressure, masturbation stopped completely.

One root cause of masturbation in your case is the lack of enthusiasm and joy. Another cause can be your lack of self- acceptance.

To accept yourself means to say yes to yourself—to the uniqueness with which God has created you. This means saying yes to your own characteristics, the age you are, how you look, your figure, your abilities and even lack of abilities in certain things. It certainly means saying yes to your sexuality.

Honestly, wouldn't you sometimes secretly prefer to be a boy? We can't help but read this between the lines of your letter. It could be that tomboyish girls or even girlish boys attract you at the moment.

This is normal at your age. It has a simple biological reason. At present you may have just about the same amount of male hormones as you have female hormones in your developing body. This will change later on and the female hormones will outnumber the others. Then you must decide whether you want to express your femininity or repress it. Repressing it will probably only intensify masturbation, but expressing it could bring you so much fulfillment that masturbation becomes unattractive.

One way to express it is by the way you dress. You feel like wearing only jeans at the moment, and this may correspond to your state of development. Besides that, from many points of view they really are more practical.

Someday you will discover that your body is created in such a way that a beautiful dress or a skirt and blouse is simply more becoming to you. And then you will be proud and glad to be a girl.

We think that those who try to eliminate the differences between the sexes do this out of fear. They are afraid of the otherliness of the opposite sex. Their egos are not strong enough to stand up under the tension created by the differences. If this ten sion is removed the relationship between the sexes becomes dull and insipid. This is one of the reasons why so many marriages become monotonous and unattractive. Often women who deny their femininity choose male partners who deny their masculinity.

But to accept your femininity means to accept your cycle. You simply can't shoot it off to the moon, because it belongs to you in the same way that your sexuality belongs to you. Maybe your stomach pains occur precisely because you wish you could get rid of your cycle, and you know that you're unable to do it.

From your letter we have the impression that when you use the word *cycle* you are thinking only of menstruation. There is much more involved to it than that. It is the whole miraculous process which happens in your body from one menstruation to the next. Different female hormones take the upper hand at different times. This can influence how you feel—the good, hopeful moods when you say you could conquer the whole world.

Ingrid has described this in detail in her book *The Joy of Being a Woman.* Maybe you are still a little young to read the whole book, but in the first and third chapters you will find a lot of things which can help you to live consciously and agreeably with and not against your cycle.

One day you will discover that as a woman you are rich—much richer than a man. Just remember that your cycle also has something to do with your ability to become a mother, the gift of bearing a child.

Write again!

Walter and Ingrid Trobisch

Reflection

It just happened that I had a speaking engagement in the vicinity of Joela's hometown, so I paid a visit to her and her mother about a year after this correspondence took place. I found myself in a comfortable home with a warm atmosphere. Everything was neat and arranged with good taste. Joela had a beautiful room of her own where she felt at home.

Her mother left me alone with Joela without asking any questions about the reason for my visit or the subject of our conversation. She has evidently stood up valiantly under the aggressive moods of her daughter without panicking.

When I talked with Joela, it became clear that she had overcome completely the immature habit of masturbation. She said that two things had helped her especially. One was our correspondence. "Simply the fact that someone knew about it without getting shocked was a big help," she said. "I wasn't alone with it anymore."

The other thing that helped her was finding a good girl friend, a little bit older than she, with whom she could talk over everything that was on her heart.

This illustrates that, at this age, masturbation is mostly a sign of loneliness. In the following correspondence with Matthias we can see the same thing.

9
"I'm a Loner"

"UP TILL NOW I'VE HAD TO STRUGGLE WITH MY PROBLEMS . . . ALL BY MYSELF. . . . I'M A LONER AND SUFFER BECAUSE I'M SO SHY AROUND PEOPLE. . . . IT'S ONLY IN THIS LETTER THAT I COULD EXPRESS MY THOUGHTS FRANKLY FOR THE FIRST TIME. . . . ABOUT TWO YEARS AGO I STARTED TO MASTURBATE."

MATTHIAS Z., AGE 16, FATHERLESS

Dear Sir,

I have read your book *Love Is a Feeling to Be Learned.* I was very touched by it. This is why I turn to you with my desperate problem.

I'm sixteen and have a mother and a sister, twenty-seven years old. My father died four days after I was born. Neither my mother nor my sister have talked to me about the facts of life and up till now I've had to struggle with my problems in this realm all by myself. There's no one I can talk to about my problems. I'm a loner and suffer because I'm so shy around people. I don't believe I could talk with anyone openly.

It's only in this letter that I could express my thoughts frankly for the first time, because I believe, that is, I hope, you understand my problem.

About two years ago I started to masturbate. I simply wanted to try it once. I don't really know why. I always feel terribly ashamed afterward but still I do it again and again. My will is simply not strong enough to stop. It was so bad that I even tried to run away. For this reason I was put in a boarding school half a year ago. Unfortunately, that didn't help either.

I really don't know what to do, because I want to become a normal human being. Actually I'm ashamed to write this letter, but I can see a possibility of overcoming this problem by your advice. Please help me!

Yours,
Matthias

Dear Matthias,

Thank you very much for your frank letter. You certainly do not need to be ashamed. As a preliminary I'm sending you a book which I wrote with my wife. Even though it deals with a girl, the advice given in it about masturbation is also valid for boys. Please read it first and then write again.

Cordial greetings,
W. T.

Dear Sir,

Many, many thanks for your words and for the book *My Beautiful Feeling*.

I've read it twice in the meantime and could identify with most of the things you say in it. I am sorry that I didn't write sooner, but I thought because of the insights gained through this book I could overcome this problem. I'm sad to say this is not the case. Yesterday I did it again for the first time. I don't know why, but it simply happened.

Now I shall try to put into practice your advice. I want to make an effort not to immediately satisfy every desire I have. Also, I shall consciously renounce certain things. Besides that I want to think seriously about the meaning of my life in order to have a clear goal.

I've succeeded already in doing it only once every two or three weeks, and I hope with your advice and the help of God I can overcome it completely.

I'm very thankful to you because you are the only one with whom I can talk openly.

Yours,
Matthias

Dear Matthias,

Now that you've read the book, I want to answer both of your letters. First of all, a word of praise that you are working on your improvement with such energy and will power. I believe, though, you misunderstood the book if you think that by following the advice given you can overcome your problems from one day to the next. It will only help if you work toward a goal. On the other hand, you have already had tremendous success in an unusually short time. This is a decisive step in the direction of self-respect and self-control. Matthias, you certainly do not have to be ashamed and in no way are you abnormal.

In spite of your progress, though, I believe you have to dig a little deeper. Many things are probably just a degree more difficult for you than for others of your age. Since your sister is eleven years older, you are practically an only child, and for such children life is simply more difficult. You have to realize this very soberly and accept it as God's will. In addition, the loss of your father has intensified your loneliness. So you described yourself very accurately when you called yourself a *loner* suffering from shyness.

Masturbation for you is, I believe, an expression of your lack of contact with people. This is why it is at this point that you have to start to work. If you succeed in overcoming this difficulty in making contact with people, masturbation will soon become superfluous.

I'm enclosing a sheet of paper with suggestions on how to improve your ability to express yourself and to respond to people. It is written in a very general way and meant for a broad spectrum of people. This is why you will be able to identify only with some of the suggestions. You have to decide for yourself what you think would be helpful for you and in a way become your own counselor.

Copy the points which strike you and then make a plan of action of the things you want to put into practice. (Send me a copy too.) "That which is not put into practice has no value" is a good saying.

The most important thing is that you enjoy working on your self and do not feel burdened by it.

This work, however, will not automatically give you life's meaning, but it could be that slowly a new meaning will become visible, giving you a new picture of your goal in life. The more you act, the more you become active.

One cannot steer a parked car.

Yours,
W. T.

Dear Mr. Trobisch,

Many thanks for your letter and the enclosed suggestion sheet. Here's my answer and my plan of action:

1. *My difficulties:* When I am with others I have a tendency to stay in the background and wait until they take the first step. I am embarrassed when I'm forced to take the first step. This makes me confused and helpless. Maybe I don't have enough self-confidence and self-esteem.

It's true that I often have a longing for physical touching, but at the same time it turns me off.

Very often I suppress my feelings, both consciously and unconsciously.

2. *The cause of my difficulties:* Maybe I have these difficulties because I was trained never to show my feelings. Rarely did I have the chance of learning how to express affection because this never happened in our family. I'm also afraid of being taken advantage of or of getting hurt if I open up to others.

3. *Changes I want to make:*

a. I shall try to observe how others express their feelings, especially appreciation and thankfulness. Also, when I see a good film or read a good book, I shall try to learn how the characters express their emotions.

b. When I'm supposed to meet someone, I'll try to overcome my own shyness by thinking of an honest compliment I can tell him when I see him.

c. If I feel like avoiding meeting someone, instead of running away

I'll take a deep breath and go straight toward him and greet him in a friendly way.

d. Instead of avoiding all physical contact with people around me, I'll try first of all to learn to accept physical touching and then to give it myself beginning with my own family and friends.

e. I'll tell myself over and over again that it is probably much more important to others what I think of them than what they think of me.

f. I shall concentrate more on others by listening to their problems rather than sharing my own with them.

g. If I'm in a group I won't just stare into space or look down at the floor in front of me, but from time to time I'll look straight into the eyes of the others.

h. I must learn also that painful and negative feelings can bring people closer to each other. Just when I think, "Why should I burden him with it?" (and I think that very often) I'll take a deep breath and share with him what's on my heart.

This is the plan of action I've worked out so far. Please check on me after a few weeks to see if I've done it.

During Christmas vacation I went skiing. I like it so much that I forget about everything around me. Now I go skiing every other weekend as long as there's snow.

Almost every evening I meet with some of my classmates. Besides that, I'm enrolled in a dancing course which they all attend too. I hope that through these social activities I can get away from masturbation.

Sometimes I'm still afraid, but only when I come home because then I feel so lonesome.

I think I haven't yet really found the meaning of my life. On the one hand, I want to serve God, but on the other hand I dream of a good job and a motorcycle like every boy does.

Many thanks for all the trouble you've taken with me.

Yours,
Matthias

Dear Matthias,

Your letter made me very happy. You've made tremendous progress.

I agree, skiing and dancing are the best therapy for you.

Having a good job and serving God are not necessarily alternatives. Actually you can serve God in every profession. The same with your motorcycle. I had a motorcycle myself for many years and it served me well in my missionary work in Germany and Africa.

Keep on going forward! God does wonders!

Yours,

W. T.

Reflection

I debated a long time whether or not I should include Matthias's plan of action in this book. But there are so many who ask the question: How can I work on myself?

I think Matthias gives us a good example. He does not sit on the pity pot and say, "Poor me! I have no father, no brothers and sisters close to me in age, and besides that I'm in boarding school. No wonder I am as I am. This is just the way it is and no one can do anything about it."

No. Matthias works. He makes a plan and puts it into action. Once he had opened up to me in his first letter, it was like the floodgates were broken. As soon as he had the feeling that he was making progress, new joy and strength overcame him.

Many adults could learn something from this sixteen-year-old. My wife said when I read this correspondence in our family circle: "I have great respect for this young man." One of my sons added, "He really means business."

But the most interesting remark came from our youngest daughter: "Such a fellow isn't detracted by the feelings of some of us girls." She meant that in a positive way. He does not dissipate his energies with superficial love affairs, but goes straight toward his goal.

Having no father is a tremendous burden. It could be that it is even more difficult for a girl than for a boy. The correspondence with Johanna illustrates this.

10
"My Father Hates Me"

"WHY ARE YOU BORN IF YOU'RE NOT LOVED? . . . I WAS GOING TO LOSE MY FATHER FOREVER. . . . HE WAS COLD TO ME—DOWNRIGHT COLD—AND IT WAS HIM I LOVED THE MOST. . . . SOMETIMES I WISH I WERE ALREADY EXPERIENCING MENOPAUSE."

JOHANNA G., AGE 16, PARENTS DIVORCED

Dear Walter,

I have no idea how old you are, but I just have to write you. I should have done it long ago. I've read your book *Love Is a Feeling to Be Learned.* I don't remember the contents completely anymore, but I do remember that I thought it was good. It helped me very much, and I wanted to buy it but I couldn't get it anywhere.

I'm desperate. I don't know how to go on. Why are you born if you're not loved? You're simply alone! Do you know what that means? To be alone, always alone! Of course I have a mother and a brother and sister who like me. But why have I never received the love of my father? I love him so much. I always have loved him so much, but he hates me—and how! It sounds really crazy to have everything (a room for myself, a school to attend, neither hunger nor thirst) and yet be so lonesome. It's awful when there's no love. Everything inside me is a dead stillness.

My parents have been divorced for eight years. My brother and I live with my mother. My sister is already married. Married!!! She's never had to suffer in the way that I must suffer. When she was my age she had already met her future husband and that helped her to get over the whole thing with my parents. I remember how, at that time, my girl friend's parents did not allow her to play with me because my parents were in the process of getting a divorce. She told me this on the street and I went home and cried for hours on end. A world of dreams had broken down within me.

I began then to understand that I was going to lose my father forever. It was so hard for me, even though I barely knew him. As long as I can remember I probably only met him ten times. He was cold to me—downright cold—and it was him I loved the most.

The day that girl friend talked to me, I ran home crying. I rushed into the kitchen blinded with tears and didn't see my sister until it was too late. She insisted that I tell her everything. Then she told me that she had her boyfriend and that it didn't make any difference to her what people said.

Then she said to me, "Someday you will meet a man who loves you and to whom it doesn't matter if your parents are divorced." I clung to her words. Lately, I've asked myself time and again, "What does God want from you, Johanna?" Why does he let me suffer so much? He must see that I am in anguish. All I know is that I can't stand it much longer. I shall become sick. I feel it already. Last year it was terrible. Again and again I broke down in school and had to vomit. The doctors couldn't find anything wrong with me.

But I knew what was wrong: I wanted to be loved and I wanted to love. I've tried so hard. I try to love everybody and to a certain degree I've succeeded. A lot of boys and girls come to me with their problems and cry their hearts out on my shoulder, just like I'm doing now on your shoulder (even though it's after 11:00 P.M. and my mother thinks I'm sleeping).

I've repressed my problem and I thought it would soon be over. But it didn't help. I have suffered and I still suffer in my heart. I hate myself for not being able to talk with anyone about it. Maybe I don't want to. I am two persons. I can live in such a way that no one realizes what I'm thinking. Yet I'm not happy.

Not long ago I became sixteen and I asked myself, "Doesn't God see you? Doesn't he look down upon you?" I can't remember what else I thought, but I knew one thing: God doesn't love me anymore, and he never will love me. He has forsaken me. I cried and cried. I often ask myself, "Why didn't God let my suicide attempt a year ago succeed?"

I'm so confused. Please excuse me, but I'm so mixed up. All this feeling that is boiling in me crushes everything else to pieces—simply everything. My youth is gone without my ever being happy.

I don't know whether you are the one who wrote the book *I Loved a Girl,* but you probably know about it. I am so glad for those people. But I also accuse God—yes, I do, even though my heart is broken and I'm ashamed of my words. What I really would like to do is to ask for forgiveness. Forgiveness from God the Almighty whom I love so much. But he is cold just like my father when I told him, "I love you." I don't know what God wants to do with me. A deep wound will remain in my heart my whole life. It comes from all those years when I was alone, as I still am.

My best girl friend, I love her, is from Brazil, and she has now returned to Brazil for good. She is gone, gone out of my life. I miss her very much. The little bit of life which she gave me broke again into a thousand pieces. She's twice as old as I am, but in spite of that we understood each other very deeply.

I don't know whether I can expect an answer from you or not. But through your book, I respect you a little bit because you say things as they are. From the depth of my heart I wish you and your house God's blessing.

Johanna

P.S. Thank you for everything that you do. I have a feeling that you are a pastor.

Dear Johanna,

I thank you for your letter. You guessed right. I am indeed a pastor. I'm in my fifties and I have five children, some younger and some older than you. I enclose a picture of our family so that you can get a better impression.

I think it is good that you wrote down your whole grief and pain because in this way you let it out. I listened to you attentively.

You certainly do have an especially difficult lot. When I was reading your letter and pondering your life's path, the following word from Psalm 68:19 came to my mind: "Praise the Lord, who carries our burdens day after day" (Good News Bible). In the German Bible it's translated: "God puts a burden on our shoulders, but he also helps us carry it."

One thing you must know for sure: God is not cold like your father, but he is warm. He loves you deeply, and you can never fall deeper than into his hands of love. This you can believe with all your heart even though you may not feel it. I would like to call out to you, "Johanna, fear not, only believe." *Only believe* means "to believe even though you don't see or feel anything."

However heavy your burden may be, you shouldn't give in to feeling sorry for yourself. Self-pity does not change a thing. Because God loves you, he knows exactly how much you can carry. The burden he puts on you comes out of his loving hand, and it is not one ounce heavier than your strength allows. I really believe that God has something very special in mind for you. I could imagine that he wants to train you as a real helper who is able (maybe more than I am) to aid others in the same situation—people who suffer because of the loss of their fathers and the divorce of their parents.

Evidently God has already given you a gift in this direction because you say that people come to you to cry on your shoulder. This is very unusual and extraordinary for someone at the age of sixteen. People seem to feel that you can understand them because your own suffering has matured you.

It is this gift which you must make use of and work on its development. Every gift is also a responsibility. Maybe this will be the special commission from God for your life—to help others. Therefore, you must learn to love your burden as the most precious thing which God has entrusted to you.

This will take many years of work. If you want to succeed in it, the most important thing now is that God becomes your Father in a very personal and concrete way. It could even be that you will be given a relationship to God much deeper than those who still have earthly fathers.

But in order for this to happen you must talk personally with your heavenly Father every day. The best time is the first thing in the morning. He wants to talk to you; and he waits for you to talk with him.

I'm en closing a little devotional booklet, Daily Texts of the Moravian Church. In it you will find a verse from the Old Testament and a corresponding verse from the New Testament for every day. Read these words every day just as if your heavenly Father were talking to you, his daughter.

Then you should reply to him by writing down in a little notebook the answers to the following four questions:

1. In which way do these words make me thankful?
2. In which way do they correct me?
3. For what and for whom do they remind me to pray?
4. What do they mean for my activities today?

You will see that if you start your day with a talk like this then the feelings of coldness and loneliness will leave you. You will feel that your heavenly Father walks right beside you during the whole day.

Very cordially,
Your W. T.

Dear Father,

May I call you that? Because you have a daughter my age, I think it is more correct than "Dear Walter." Besides that, you really have talked to me in your letter like a father.

I cannot yet believe what you wrote in the last paragraph of your letter, but perhaps I shall learn to believe it through you.

Your letter made me glad, yet there is a sadness which overwhelms me again and again because I have to think of my physical father. It is raining and I have the feeling that each drop of rain is a tear flowing out of my innermost being. I have written a poem which I want to send to you and I have written a letter to my physical father, just for myself. I shall not mail this letter to him. No, I shall never do it but I want to tell you everything I have written to him. I feel it all again so strongly and I long so much for love. It is hard for me to wait. It is like walking through hell for me.

My father,

My father, I have loved you since early childhood, but when you realized my love for you, your hatred grew and you disliked me still more. Father, I loved you anyway in spite of all the beatings and those cold, unloving words which came from your mouth. My heart was full of hope. Yes, my heart consisted only of hope, but the way you acted just ate it all up slowly—my whole love, my hope. When I think of you now, my heart remains cold while formerly it trembled with joy.

For a long time I thought I had forgotten you completely. I thought I was indifferent toward you, that I had blotted you out of my mind. But when you called once and I heard your voice very close to my ear, everything in me was torn apart again. Like in a film, I saw again everything before me.

That time when you beat up mama, when you wanted to kill her, wanted to kill me, your cold words so infinitely far away, your cold eyes—all that I saw again in front of me. And father, in spite of that, I was happy to hear your voice. Father, from that moment on I knew I would never forget you, even though you were a stranger to me from the beginning, even though you had condemned my life to torture. Father, I love you in spite of it all.

How happy I was when I saw the loving fathers of my friends. I could observe them without envy or jealousy. But afterward, when I was alone on the street, at school, shopping, sitting on my bed at night, yes, even in the midst of a crowd of people, I felt the pain, father, which you, probably without even knowing it, have caused me for my whole life. Often I cried when I was with people, whether I stood or sat or ran, I longed so much for your love. Tears streamed down by the bucketful. I had no power over my body, and I often cried for hours at a time. I found no relief for the cruel experience ate up my ego. It was much worse than torture.

Beloved father, I have thousands of questions to ask you, but why should I ask them, for you yourself do not know the answer. Everything has already happened. If you were to read this, it would probably be all the same to you. You might want to make up for it, but this is impossible, father. What you have killed once, you cannot make come to life again. It remains dead.

A thousand questions are on the tip of my tongue, but I won't ask them. I'll never tell them to anyone and they will continue to be a great burden for me—a burden, which I will have to carry, under which I often break down and then lie on the ground, prostrate, crying and weeping.

Father, I'm still very young, but I don't know how to continue to live. I'm afraid you might come back someday to kill me and mama. You see how much I want to live and how my soul cries out for life.

Father, you don't believe there is a soul. Did you not also grow up without a mother? Excuse me! I have a question on my lips. Father, you could have given me so much of that which you missed yourself as a child. Instead you have abandoned me to a life still worse, a life with the knowledge that you hate me and that you wanted to take my life.

Father, my father, whom I love and whom I have loved from the very beginning, I do not accuse you, but you should know that my life is desperate, that I am longing, longing for love which nobody can give me because it is too late.

Johanna

Reflection

I advised Johanna to send this letter to her father, but she has not done it. Maybe it was healing enough just to be able to write it and mail it to someone.

I wish all parents who think of divorce would read it, especially all fathers. The divorce of a child's parents means that someone takes an axe and splits the child right through the middle.

To me personally the letter was an admonition to think even more seriously of my role as a father and to accept my being a father consciously and joyfully.

I was able to visit Johanna briefly. I discovered that she had faithfully followed my suggestion of a daily talk with her heavenly Father. She had filled a whole notebook with the answers to the four questions I gave her and showed it to me with pride.

After a while she wrote another letter, this time on another subject, and addressed it to my wife. I include it intentionally in this book because so many sixteen-year-old girls have difficulty with their cycles. I also think it doesn't hurt for young men to get an idea of these problems. Here is Johanna's letter.

Dear Ingrid,

I'm making myself write you. I read once more the book *My Beautiful Feeling.* It made me very sad. Originally I wanted to wait to write to you until after your trip, but I cannot wait. I simply have to spit it out.

I enjoy being a girl and by no means would I want to be a boy. But slowly I'm beginning to hate my cycle. When I was eleven I had my first period. I wasn't quite sure then what it all meant, but I felt a deep joy which I never sensed again.

This joy also satisfied my longing. It was a deep inward feeling coming from inside my body. It was like a warm surge radiating my being. I shall never forget the way my eyes looked at me from the mirror. I was happy, really happy.

At the age of fourteen I began having terrible pains with my period. At fifteen I went to see a gynecologist.

He was very gentle and prescribed a hormone treatment, each day a pill and none during menstruation. This continued for three months! The pains stopped, but I made the shocking discovery that my breasts grew considerable during this time. As a matter of fact I can't stand women with big breasts. They strike me as so obtrusive, so pushy. Therefore, it was very clear to me—no pills anymore! Naturally, I hoped that my breasts would get smaller again. When this didn't happen, I was depressed for a long time and tried to stay away from my friends. I was very inhibited.

All the things I tried at that time were really crazy. I tried to sleep on my stomach all night and when I would wake up in the morning and discover I was lying on my back, I would be furious and put on a bra that was two sizes too small. I soon gave this up though, because my skin rebelled and I had open sores where the bra rubbed.

I still do this now and then. I'm really ashamed and angry at the doctor who changed me in such a way that I can't stand myself anymore. It was a year ago that all this happened.

And now I'm sitting here filled with fear when I think of my next menstruation. It causes me such maddening pains that I think they must already be like labor pains. Could that be—that some women have such strong pains, not just while giving birth, but also when they menstruate?

I had my last period just before a geography test. Can you imagine how I felt? It wasn't only that I couldn't concentrate—this was impossible anyway—but I simply couldn't sit still! This is the hardest thing for me because it makes the cramps worse. When I got back home that evening I cried a lot and was filled with hatred for the whole men's world. Why do we girls have to suffer, whether we want to or not, and boys always think that a woman's world is just a world of moods. I wished sometimes that at least once in his life every man would have a period with terrible pains so he could feel it in his own body. Then let's see whether he too wouldn't feel moody!

This all sounds so mean, I know. But what shall I do? I simply can't understand why for three years I had no trouble with menstruation and now there's such a change. I'd like to ask you whether there's something I can do to make the pains go away without having to stay in bed for a couple of days with a hot water bottle on my stomach. It's very embarrassing for me to know that all those around me realize what is the matter with me. Who would like to live with such a girl? I wouldn't! I'm very unhappy about it and sometimes I wish I were already experiencing menopause. I don't like to feel like a swollen-up dumpling, especially not in summer.

Please answer me!

Johanna

Dear Johanna,

Thank you so much for taking the courage to write me about this problem, which I also went through as well as my daughters. There are things you can do to help with the pains, just as a woman in labor can learn, not to fight against her contractions, but to "ride" with them.

I know a very kind and experienced gynecologist who is a good friend of ours. Since I'm just getting ready to leave on a long trip, I've asked him to answer your letter in detail. By the way, his book, *The Menstrual Cycle,* was published by W. B. Saunders Co. in Philadelphia in 1977 and has become a medical classic. He and his good wife have studied and recorded the cycle in hundreds of women for forty years now!

It may help you, Johanna, instead of being filled with fear about your next period, to say goodbye to your last one, knowing that it will never come again. It's like mountain-climbing—every step leads you closer to your goal. So take heart, lift up your eyes and discover the great adventure of being a woman!

With my love,
Ingrid Trobisch

Dear Johanna,

Ingrid Trobisch has asked me to answer your last letter. I am a gynecologist and am especially interested in the woman's development.

The pains which bother you so much are caused by your uterus. Your guess is right that they are a sort of labor pain. From other aspects also you can compare menstruation with birth. It is rather like a miscarriage because during your period, the uterus expels the nest, the lining of the womb which was prepared in case a pregnancy should take place.

Almost all young women have some discomfort during their periods—cramps, the urge to urinate and more frequent bowel movements. Some young ladies also suffer from severe colic and painful contractions. Unfortunately, we know very little about their causes.

That you had no cramps during the early years has something to do with the fact that at that time your ovaries did not yet really function. Probably no ovulation took place. Through the hormone therapy (the pills) the doctor who treated you put you artificially back into this infantile state. But this doesn't really help you because you don't want to remain a child all your life and from the point of view of nature you cannot stop growth.

The enlargement of your breasts has possibly been caused by the doctor's treatment, but it could also be your natural development. Maybe you are exaggerating a little bit because as a girl you feel somehow exposed because of your breasts, and also your breasts remind you of your next menstruation. Just look once at your classmates' breast measurements. Maybe you will find some of them with even larger breasts.

Here are a few practical suggestions:

1. Take an active part in physical education, at least once a week in a group and every evening do some exercises before you go to bed. It would be good if you could take an intensive course in women's rhythmic gymnastics. Ride a bicycle every day for half an hour, preferably uphill.

2. Diet. Take *no* weight-reducing pills. Eat a lot of proteins (lean meat, liver, fish, cheese, cottage cheese and other milk products). Drink a lot of warm liquids (milk, mint tea, herb tea with lemon juice and as little sugar as possible). Stay away from coffee and black tea. Eat a lot of fruit, fresh vegetables and salads. Be careful to eat few fats, sweets, chocolate, starchy foods, bread and baked goods.

3. During the days before your period go to bed early, keeping your head at a lower level than your hips and legs. Before your period begins put a warm, damp bath towel on your stomach covered with a warm water bottle while you sleep.

4. Clothing: Keep your feet, legs and pelvic region very warm before your period. Warm underclothes are very important. Don't wear shoes that are too tight, boots or tight belts. Don't ride on motorbikes.

5. Take some pain-killing medicine only if it's really necessary.

Did Mrs. Trobisch write to you about taking your waking temperature?

If you take your temperature every morning before getting up, you can see that it rises a little bit during the time of ovulation when the egg leaves the ovary. About two weeks later, shortly before menstruation, it goes down again. This is why taking your temperature can help you to prepare for your period.

That's enough for today. Write if you have questions.

With all good wishes,

Yours,
Rudolf F. Vollman

Dear Dr. Vollman,

Today I got up courage to write to you because the difficulties with my period are getting worse.

But first of all I want to thank you from the depths of my heart for your letter. I am very glad that I can come to you with these problems and that you give me such valuable advice.

During summer vacation I rode my bike a lot and was also very involved in sports. Shortly before I got my period I kept myself warm and elevated my hips with a pillow under them.

By taking my waking temperature I could tell just when menstruation would begin. This was one of the most beautiful experiences I had during the summer. I had no pains, or only very weak ones that didn't interfere with my daily activities.

But now I still have a question which is embarrassing to me because I don't know if it's a stupid question.

I hope you understand me. During the first days of my period when the bleeding is very strong, there are blood clumps or clots which then disappear the third or fourth day. When they are expelled I feel pressure from inside which is sometimes very painful. I've tried several things to make them milder, but I found it's best if I just stand still and wait until it's over. It's very uncomfortable and sometimes I almost feel like fainting. Perhaps you could write to me about this. I'm very happy that I can write to you.

Johanna

Dear Johanna,

I just received your letter and will answer it immediately.

Isn't it interesting that you can learn how your body functions by taking your waking temperature?

Menstruation is not just bleeding. On the contrary, the bleeding is actually a side effect. After ovulation, the inner lining of the uterus is prepared for a possible pregnancy. The lining grows, becomes thicker and is filled with special nutrients. If no conception has taken place, these preparations are superfluous. When the body realizes this, the temperature drops and the lining is expelled. Then you see these blood clumps which are a part of the nest. Through this process a small wound is caused inside the uterus which bleeds and you have your period. The expulsion is caused by the periodic contractions of the uterus, very similar to the labor contractions at the beginning of the birth process.

With friendly greetings,
Rudolf F. Vollman

Reflection

I learned from the correspondence between Johanna and Dr. Vollman that the advice to live consciously with and in a positive attitude toward her cycle is often given to a girl much too late. We may think that taking the waking temperature is only useful for married couples planning a family.

But sixteen is probably the right age to begin doing this—for certain girls even earlier. In any case, it helps a woman accept herself and in this way it is useful even if she does not marry. If she does, it's one of the best preparations for married life.

Living consciously with her cycle helped Johanna to accept herself as a girl. This even helped her cramps and lessened her pain, as she confirmed later on.

There is one theme from her first letter we have not yet touched. She commented on the departure of her girl friend, who went back to Brazil, with these words: "The little bit of life which she gave me broke again into a thousand pieces."

A lot of things would certainly have been easier for Johanna if her girl friend could have been with her. Over and over again I have pointed out the importance of having a friend of the same sex.

This will be the main topic in the next two letter exchanges.

11
"In My Home There's Always Fighting"

"WHEN I'M NOT WITH MY FRIEND, I FEEL SOMETHING LIKE A VERY STRONG LONGING. . . . THERE'S ALWAYS FIGHTING AT MY HOME. I'D LIKE TO MOVE OUT AND LIVE WITH MY FRIEND. . . .WHAT IS THE DIFFERENCE BETWEEN WET DREAMS AND MASTURBATION?"

ULLRICH S., AGE 16, HIGH-SCHOOL STUDENT

Dear Sir,

I'm writing to you because I have a lot of questions and believe that you can best answer them.

My problem is masturbation. I've talked to a lot of people about it, but I still hang onto it.

I'm sixteen. I've been a Christian for some years now, and I'm an active church member.

Maybe I'm in the process of solving my problem. In any case I've learned that I can't solve it all at once. Now I try to solve it step by step. If I do it only every third day, that's progress for me. But I don't yet see a real goal.

I'm practically an only child even though I have two brothers, one thirty-one and the other twenty-six. I have very little contact with them. I play the guitar and go to high school.

It would be my greatest desire to have a brother who's a little bit older or younger than I. Then I could room with him. (I have a room by myself.) I have a friend who's a Christian too. I'm with him very often. Once in a while I stay overnight with him or he with me. And this brings up my first question.

I've read your book *My Beautiful Feeling.* There you write about three phases everyone goes through during adolescence. The second phase is characterized by deep friendships between members of the same sex. What is meant by "signs of affection"? Why do they stop before sexual expression?

And how about feelings? I do feel something for my friend. When I'm not with my friend, I feel something like a very strong longing. Is this normal?

Nine months ago I had the same feeling about someone else, but then it disappeared. I'm afraid that this will happen again with my friend—that this feeling will vanish after a few months.

There's always fighting at my home. My parents fight very often. I'd like to move out and live with my friend, but this is not possible. Would it be good if we lived together? Could we become too attached to each other? By the way, he's seventeen and has a girl friend. Are my feelings toward him normal?

Recently, I read a book which said that wet dreams are quite normal. It also said that sexual tensions are natural and that through the ejaculation during sleep, tension is released—but what is the difference between wet dreams and masturbation?

Maybe the whole thing has something to do with my nickname. Two years ago we played a skit at a retreat. I had to play a character who was very stupid. Since then everyone calls me Snooky. And somehow my last two years are connected with this nickname. If someone calls me Snooky, I get the feeling that I'm not really accepted as a person. I can't stand the name.

I hope I will soon receive an answer from you.

Yours,
Ullrich

Dear Ullrich,

Thank you for your letter. Let me begin with your questions concerning the difference between wet dreams and masturbation. A wet dream is an ejaculation of seminal fluid which happens involuntarily at night during sleep. Masturbation is a conscious action which involves the will.

In our book *My Beautiful Feeling,* you read that everyone has to go through three phases during adolescence. The first phase is called the autoerotic phase in which feelings of love are still directed toward oneself. Masturbation is a physical expression of this phase. Therefore when you masturbate, it means you are still at least partially in this phase.

There is no reason to worry a lot about it as long as you are working on overcoming it. If you have to do it only every third day, that is progress for you. Gradually you will grow out of it and look on it as something childish and unsatisfactory. You should slowly be able to lengthen the intervals until it stops completely and you are strong enough to stand up under tension without having to seek release immediately.

Your guitar can be of great help to you in this respect. Play it as often as you like.

The second phase in this process of maturing is the homoerotic phase. It simply means that the ego is mature enough to build a bridge to another person, but it is not yet strong enough to establish a lasting relationship with the opposite sex.

This will be possible only in the heteroerotic phase. Then the ego is strong enough to overcome the fear of the otherliness of another person, and you are able to love someone of the other sex.

For the time being, however, until this maturity has been reached, a compromise is made during the second phase. Our love feelings turn toward someone who is different, yet still as much as possible like ourselves. In other words, we turn toward someone of the same sex. This is why during the second phase very deep friendships between two girls or between two boys take place.

This is what you now experience with your friend. You see, it's impossible to make a clear-cut separation between the first and second phase. There is a certain overlapping. Longing for your friend means that you have to a certain extent entered the second stage.

Such a deep friendship between two boys your age is not only normal, it's also healthy and good. You learn to deal with love feelings and to enjoy them without transforming them into sexual actions. If you learn how to do this now with a friend of your own sex, it will be less difficult later on to keep this limit when you enter into a relationship with a girl.

You don't need to be afraid of physical touching. There's nothing wrong with putting your arm around the shoulders of your friend. This won't cause too strong an attachment.

I'm sure what you're afraid of when you think of this is homosexuality. This danger is indeed present, but only when you indulge in sexual activities, such as mutual masturbation. Then it would indeed be possible for you to get stuck in the second stage so that you will not mature into the third stage and be able to enter into a relationship with a girl. In order not to cross over this fine borderline, I think it would be better not to move into the same room as your friend and, if you visit him, not to sleep in the same bed.

I can well understand that you sometimes feel lonesome in your room, but you should also learn to enjoy being alone. Many boys would like to have a room to themselves, but they can't. You have to learn two things in life: how to live alone with yourself and how to live together with someone else. The longing you experience when you are alone makes fellowship, being together, something precious.

Naturally, the feelings you have now will pass. You must be prepared for the fact that when you are eighteen you will think back on the feelings you have now and simply shake your head at your old problems. More and more you will feel attracted to girls. Living through these confused feelings is a painful but also a positive experience. It means that you are growing out of the homoerotic phase into the heteroerotic phase, but it does not mean that you should not enjoy what you are now experiencing and all that is given to you.

From your nickname you can learn who you do not want to be. This is also valuable. It's only in this way that you can learn who you are, Ullrich.

I greet you very cordially.

Your W. T.

Reflection

I hope that Ullrich's letter will bring relief to many who have similar feelings, but who do not want to admit it for fear of being thought homosexual. However, I also hope that my answer will help many to respect the borderline between two members of the same sex.

It could be that some of those who read this book have already made mistakes in this respect. To them I would like to recommend the next exchange of letters and assure them that even then not all is lost.

Chapter twelve deals with two girls who have crossed the borderline.

They have the same lot as Ullrich, homes where there is no harmony in the family. Martina is an unwanted child whose mother doesn't hesitate to let her know it. Gerda's mother is a businesswoman who has four children and neither the time nor patience to establish a warm relationship with her daughter.

None of us is a hundred-per-cent male or a hundred-per-cent female. In every man there's also something feminine and in every woman there's something masculine. Otherwise, the sexes could not understand each other. The question is, what is the dominant factor? In men it should be the masculine and in women the feminine factor.

This balance is reached when the young boy can identify with his father and the girl with her mother. If for one reason or the other this process of identification does not or cannot take place, the danger of homosexuality is present. Then the boy identifies with his mother, the feminine becomes the dominant factor, and he looks for a man as a partner. On the other hand, if a girl identifies with her father, the masculine becomes the dominant factor in her personality, and she will look for a woman as a partner.

I suppose that something like this must have happened with Martina and Gerda when they entered into a deep friendship with each other. When this friendship began to find sexual expression they became worried and wrote to me.

12
"All of a Sudden We Helped Each Other"

"ALL OF A SUDDEN WE HELPED EACH OTHER GET RID OF OUR TENSION. . . . IN THE END WE WERE VERY ASHAMED OF OURSELVES. BOTH OF US KNOW WE WILL RUIN OUR FRIENDSHIP SLOWLY BUT SURELY."

MARTINA S., AGE 17   GERDA D., AGE 18

Dear Mr. Trobisch,

We—Martina, seventeen and Gerda, eighteen—have read your book *My Beautiful Feeling.* We have been good friends for some months now and understand each other very well. We have a mutual problem and agree that we need a third person to help us find a way out. Separately, without talking it over with each other, we both thought of you.

Would you perhaps have time to deal with our problem? Can we be sure that you will not share it with anyone else except your wife?

Many greetings,
Martina and Gerda

Dear Martina and Gerda,

Of course you can write to me about your problem. You can also be assured that your letters will be treated confidentially and that no one else will read them. [Gerda and Martina later gave me permission to publish their letters.]

With cordial greetings,
Your W. T.

Dear Mr. Trobisch,

Gerda and I believe it would be better to write you separately. I have known Gerda now for six months and I liked her from the moment I saw her. I felt she understood me as no one else ever had before. I could tell her everything that came to my mind, and whenever I needed her she had time for me.

This had never happened before in my life. I only had a mother, and she had to go to work so she never had time for me. Besides that I was a burden to her. Because of me she couldn't work where she really wanted to work. I guess my mother would have preferred it if I had never been born. But she couldn't change things. She had been raped. She has often told me and made me feel unwanted.

That's why I was very happy when I could leave home. Here at the hotel where I'm working I found a person to love. Gerda has given me her undivided love, something I never experienced before. I trust her completely. Once I told her of something which had burdened me for almost ten years. I was afraid of her reaction, but she understood me. After that my love grew still deeper.

When I asked her whether there was anything she had not told me, instead of an answer she showed me a magazine article about masturbation. After that my love for her grew still deeper.

I was neither surprised nor shocked. When she came back to my room, I took her in my arms and told her that I loved her just as much as before and that I would try to help her.

Since then I've slept with her once in a while. It was so beautiful to lie in bed and talk together and touch each other. Is this bad? Once when we slept together in the same bed, I could feel that Gerda was aroused. She didn't want to masturbate in my presence, but the urge was so strong that she finally did it.

I didn't know what to do. I was also aroused, but I could not find release in Gerda's presence. I was too ashamed and later on Gerda told me that she also had been ashamed.

Now I come to the heart of the problem. One day—I don't know anymore when it was or how it happened—we laid together in bed and were both aroused.

All of a sudden we helped each other get rid of our tension. I really didn't know what I was doing. It was only afterward that we realized it. Then it happened again and again. We couldn't stop. In the end we were very ashamed of ourselves.

Both of us know we will ruin our friendship slowly but surely. It happens to us now almost every day.

We've already decided to pray. But we often forget or think there will be time for it later on. I tell myself again and again that it has to stop, but before I realize it has happened again.

I don't know any way out. I don't want to give up this friendship. It is too precious for me. Many thanks for helping us.

Your Martina

Dear Mr. Trobisch,

Finally I—the friend of Martina—have been able to bring myself to write to you. I wanted to do it all the time, but I just couldn't make myself. I was too ashamed to put into words the problem we have. I didn't want to face it, and above all I was afraid my parents would hear about it.

I'm glad that Martina had the courage to take the risk and write you. I believe that with your help we can solve the problem.

I come from a home where both parents are Christians and try to do God's will. What depresses me is the hectic rush at home because we run a shop. My mother, a businesswoman with four children, is overburdened and often has no patience. School did not challenge me enough, and I often had the impression that my life was unfulfilled and without joy or meaning. I lost good friends again and again. I often wept at home, and sometimes I didn't even want to live anymore.

Then I decided to leave home and work in a hotel. Here I changed my whole attitude toward life. I could be young, cheerful and have no worries. The reason for this, besides having a good job which challenged me, was my friendship with Martina, a curly- headed brunette with a lot of personality, who won my heart immediately. We had a wonderful summer and experienced a lot of happiness being together which neither of us had ever known before.

One day we told each other we loved one another. We shared with each other just what this love meant. It was so wonderful, and yet sometimes I thought, are girls allowed to express these feelings to each other and even to touch each other?

What happened then Martina has written to you. It is hard for me to put it into words. I just want to add that during the time when it started we talked a lot about sexual things and shared our thoughts and opinions. I believe we talked too much about it and that aroused our imaginations.

It is also important to mention that we have learned to pray together. This makes me happy.

My letter is rather confused, but perhaps you can understand it just the same.

Many greetings and again thank you!

Gerda

Dear Martina and Gerda,

It's good that you have written. A special word of praise goes to Martina that she overcame her feeling of shame and dared to write such an open and concrete letter.

Just let me tell you one thing in advance. The feelings of shame and embarrassment which both of you experience very strongly are your greatest and best guides. They are very healthy feelings which you should not suppress. Without doubt they tell you that you have started to move along the wrong path and that you have to stop and turn around.

It is not yet too late. Therefore, there is no need to worry. But it's very necessary that you change your behavior as soon as possible, otherwise you may get in a rut and it will be very difficult to get out of it later on. It could make marriage for you very hard if not impossible.

From our book *My Beautiful Feeling,* you know that the development of human sexuality undergoes three phases. The second phase is the homoerotic phase when deep boy-boy and girl-girl friendships grow.

Both of you are experiencing this second phase now, which in itself is healthy and good. The fact that you feel these things so strongly and intensely has something to do with your family situation. Martina has no father and Gerda doesn't mention hers. Both of you have difficult relationships with your mothers.

Evidently, you try to replace the love you were deprived of at home by each other. This in itself is not wrong. I can well understand how happy it makes you. Of course, you are allowed to express your feelings for each other.

But you crossed a boundary by indulging in sexual activities. At that point, your consciences reacted immediately and you were warned by your feelings of shame.

No damage has been done yet. But if you continue on this road you could become fixated by the attraction of the same sex and this would be hard to change later on. Through this intimate sex play with each other, this dependence on one another would finally ruin your friendship. Martina has rightly foreseen this danger.

Every repetition of sexual action in this way will increase this fixation. As I said before, you get into a rut that will be hard to get out of later on. It could become such an ingrained habit that you won't be able later on to bridge the gap to the other sex and you will become homosexual, or lesbian, as one calls it when women are involved.

Now you may be shocked. But I had to use the word which you probably are afraid to say. Once again, I don't think that you have yet reached this point. You certainly are not lesbian. Don't worry about it. But the danger is there if you keep going in the wrong direction.

My advice to you is to be hard on yourselves and consequently on each other. By no means should you sleep in the same bed anymore, possibly not even in the same room, so that you do not have to undress in front of each other. Also, for the time being I would advise you to refrain from any physical touching. There are so many other ways of expressing tenderness and love—through a gesture, a look, a smile, a word, a letter, a little gift, and certainly through prayer.

Help each other to avoid compromise. You will see that in this way your friendship will actually grow deeper and you will lose nothing.

It is good that you can pray together. It will give you the strength you need to obey God's commandments. I shall also pray for you.

Yours,

W. T.

Dear Mr. Trobisch,

Thank you very much for your letter which we had looked forward to with great eagerness because we didn't know which way to turn. It has always been clear to both of us that this was the wrong way for a friendship to go, but we could not free ourselves from it. Every time it happened, we felt great remorse and were completely desperate.

We had often wondered whether we were homosexual, but we could not resolve the question. Sometimes we didn't even dare to admit to each other we thought about it. We are grateful that you have made us conscious of it.

We made the following decision: From now on, each of us will spend the night in her own room. We have limited our caresses to a hug and stroking each other's cheeks. We believe that we can be responsible for this because this has never led us into temptation. We will refrain from kissing, because that was sometimes the cause. It is hard for us, but we want it this way.

We thank you for your patience and for your prayers.

Your Martina and Gerda

Reflection

Martina and Gerda have kept their word. They are now women of nineteen and twenty. We are still in contact with them. Both are developing into very normal young ladies. At present they work at different places. Each one has a boyfriend, and this fact gives them both an affirmation of their femininity. This in turn helps them very much to accept themselves as women, since neither Martina nor Gerda received this affirmation as a child from her father.

Girls are especially in danger when two things coincide in their lives:

a cold mother and an unexpressive father who does not show them that they are lovable as "little women." Parents often do not realize that they themselves put their children in danger when they could save them from danger so easily.

Martina and Gerda had the courage to write a letter. I am disturbed when I think of the many others—boys as well as girls—who are in a similar situation and who keep silent. Therefore, I'm especially thankful to Martina and Gerda that they gave permission to publish their letters.

What I like best about them is the fact that they themselves drew the boundary lines. They do the same thing now with their boyfriends. It seems to me that this is easier for them now, because they practiced it with each other before.

The setting of limits is also the topic of the next correspondence, this time with a boy.

13
"Is Napoleon the Cause of the Trouble?"

"FORMERLY I WAS A BIBLICAL CHRISTIAN, BUT FOR SOME TIME NOW I HAVE BEEN UNFAITHFUL. . . . THERE ARE TIMES WHEN I WOULD LIKE TO BREAK UP WITH HER BECAUSE SOMETHING IS FISHY. THEN I ASK MYSELF WHETHER THE 'ABSOLUTE' IS THE CAUSE OF THE TROUBLE OR THE 'NAPOLEON.' "

MICHAEL B., AGE 16, HIGH-SCHOOL STUDENT

Dear Mr. Trobisch,

I recently started to read your books. They are tremendous. But I have to explain something to you before I begin with the main topic of my letter.

I'm sixteen and formerly I was a biblical Christian, but for some time now I have been unfaithful.

For ten weeks and five days I have had a really nice girl friend. I like her very much and she likes me too. We often are together, and then it is not only the usual kissing, but we also talk with each other about problems, even about problems you deal with in your books. You could say that we have a fabulous friendship.

Here is my problem: As I just mentioned I like Susi very much. But there are times when I would like to break up with her because something is fishy. Then I ask myself whether the "absolute" is the cause of the trouble or the "Napoleon." (*Absolute* means my hand on her most intimate area. *Napoleon* means my hand on her breast.)

It happens very rarely because she does not permit it. She says: "Only when I'm psychologically down do I need this kind of a lift—otherwise not." That's why it doesn't happen often.

Sometimes I think of breaking up with her after I have called her. We talk sometimes for a whole hour on the telephone. That makes me disgusted.

However, I'm unable to break up with her because when she's with me again I feel very happy and forget everything. That's the way it is with me and my Susi.

Now I've burdened you with my problem and I hope that you can give me advice.

Your Michael

P.S. I am cold (Rev. 3:16).

Dear Michael,

Thanks a lot for your letter. In general, I must say that our feelings of liking and disliking are always going up and down.

Fortunately, love is not based only on feelings, but to a certain degree also on will. It is a sober act of will which decides to love a person at any price, in every situation and for a whole lifetime, without paying any attention to the ups and downs of feelings.

Both of you, however, are still too young for this decision. I don't believe that you can make it before you are twenty or twenty-one—a few years later is still better.

The conflict in your relationship with Susi is caused by the fact that you express your affection for each other in the wrong way. These intimate caresses such as you describe are simply more than your relationship can take at the moment. I think you are right when you say you have the feeling that something is fishy. You must listen to this feeling. It's a good and healthy feeling.

I think it's very dangerous to put yourself in the role of being Susi's psychotherapist when she's down. You don't help her at all this way. All this touching increases your desire for something more, and if you grant it, your desires are increased still more, and it will be hard to put the brakes on. Maybe Susi will even be tempted to be dishonest to herself and to be "down" more often than she really is, so that she can be comforted in this way.

I believe you can help her much more if you refuse this wrong kind of comfort and put your foot down. She will certainly respect you more and feel more secure in your presence. I would shorten those long telephone calls too. They do not help her.

I think you have to learn to stick up for what you feel is right. If I were you, I would ask myself whether the voice of God is speaking when again and again you feel this desire to break up. I think you would respect yourself and love yourself much more if you would be guided more by God than by Susi and do what you feel is right. Certainly you could succeed in having a "fabulous friendship" more with a boy right now than with a girl.

Your deepest problem, though, seems to be that you have lost your faith. I can't help but believe that this fact affects your relationship with Susi.

The crossing over of the boundary which you and Susi have set for yourselves seems to have the consequence that not only is something fishy between you and Susi, but also between you and God.

Here the "absolute" is the cause of the trouble—but in a different sense than you use the word. Susi has become more important to you than God. God, however, is a jealous God. He wants to be the absolute—the most important thing—in your life. Either you belong to him completely or you do not belong to him at all. St. Augustine has said: "He who loves not God above all, loves not God at all."

Maybe breaking up with Susi is the way to give God again the place in your life which belongs to him. And maybe this is also the greatest help for Susi to learn to deal with her "downs" in a constructive way. Just think about it!

I greet you very cordially,
Your W. T.

Reflection

Michael is a typical young man. He counts weeks and days and I'm quite sure that the intimate caresses are more important to him than "talking over problems."

Yet he has not lost his fine sensitivity. He feels immediately when something is fishy. Also, he knows when his personal faith has come into conflict with his actions. I have a high respect for him because he does not compromise, but recognizes the consequences of his actions. He doesn't consider himself a Christian anymore.

On the other hand, he does not have the strength to change his attitudes and free himself.

I don't know whether my answer has helped him. Was it too hard and self-righteous? Could this be the reason he never answered?

We just have to let it stand. But one thing is clear: a great deal depends on how physical touching is integrated into the relationship between boys and girls—even the fate of that relationship!

The following correspondence puts light on the same problem from the point of view of a girl.

14
"His Kisses Became More and More Impetuous"

*"IT WAS COMPLETELY DARK IN THE ROOM. . . .
ALL OF A SUDDEN HE PULLED DOWN THE ZIPPER OF
MY JEANS. . . . I REALLY GOT FRIGHTENED."*

GABI R., AGE 15 BOYFRIEND, AGE 16

Dear Sir,

I'm writing you because I do not know in whom else I can confide. After having read your book *Love Is a Feeling to Be Learned,* I thought you could help me understand my problems.

I'm fifteen and I have a sixteen-year-old boyfriend. We've known each other for more than two months now and we understand each other well. My parents have just as little against him as his have against me.

I must tell you that I have never had a boyfriend before who was older than I. With all the others so far I was just a good pal.

But it is different with my present friend. The other evening when I was alone with him at his home, we sat in his room and talked. The light was out, and it was completely dark in the room. All of a sudden he started to kiss me. He got more and more impetuous. Then he slipped his hand under my pullover. I just let it happen and even found it pleasant.

All of a sudden he pulled down the zipper of my jeans. A fellow had never tried that before. I pushed him away and told him to leave me in peace. I really got frightened. He tried to calm me down and pulled the zipper up again.

I think he wanted to start petting, but since I've never done that with a guy, I don't know what to do nor how it should be done. I don't think you can get pregnant through petting. I would like to avoid that if possible.

Please give me advice!

With friendly greetings,
Gabi

P.S. You can send your answer to my home address. No trouble.

Dear Gabi,

Thank you for your letter and the confidence you showed by sharing with me. It's good that you wrote immediately, before you went any further. I only hope my answer reaches you before it is too late. I would like to explain to you what happens during petting. I'm not doing it so you can try it out, but in order that you do not try it out because you are curious.

Usually by *petting* one means the mutual manipulation of the genital organs. For the male partner this usually results in an ejaculation which gives him some release, but is not really satisfying for him. It is even less so for the female partner.

Actually, petting is meant to be a prelude to the sexual union in marriage. If this union does not take place, tension is created with which it is difficult to cope. It really does not pay.

Normally, one cannot get pregnant by petting. Yet it is not impossible, for in one single seminal ejaculation there can be as many as 500,000,000 sperm. One of them, if it gets into the vagina, is enough to fertilize an ovum. If you think of the physical closeness and excitement, you can see why this happens more often than you might first imagine.

Furthermore, a lot of young people overestimate their power of resistance. They might intend only to pet, but then are unable to stop and end up having intercourse. Don't even try to see if you can put on the brakes in this way!

You're not a candy bar to be nibbled on. Don't put yourself in this role. Later on you will feel ashamed when you become engaged to someone who will be yours all your life.

By the way I want to praise you because you pushed him away. Your healthy feelings of embarrassment and shame instinctively caused this reaction. They are your guardian angels. Let yourself be guided by these voices within and be wary of those who ridicule these feelings of embarrassment and shame by calling them unnatural or neurotic!

You saw how your boyfriend respected it immediately when you valiantly defended your rights. Most fellows deeply long in their hearts for the girl to resist them. You don't lose anything by setting these limits. On the contrary, you rise in their respect. If someone breaks up with you because you stand up to him, don't shed any tears. He's not worthy of them.

You know, though, if I were in your place, I would put up my lines of defense much earlier rather than at the very last moment. You have described the steps exactly—being alone in a room, then darkness, kissing, laying down together, finally undressing and then the next step would have been intimate touching.

At the latest you should draw the line before you lie down together or even before this impetuous kissing. There's kissing, and then there's kissing. A kiss as a light touch on the forehead or the cheek can be an expression of deep-felt tenderness—just like a ray of sunshine coming through a window. But if it becomes "impetuous" and stormy, then I would ring the warning bells too early rather than too late.

Yes, even though I run the risk of being taken as hopelessly old-fashioned, I think you should be careful about being in a room alone with your friend. Believe me, you will have much more joy if you do something with others, and then you can talk about this shared experience. If you are alone in a room, then it should not be for too long and not in the dark.

You see it takes a little bit of intelligence if you want to avoid being trapped. Show this letter to your friend and talk it over with him! From his reaction you will see whether or not he is truly a "friend."

By the way, I'm glad I can write to your home address and that I don't need to use the address of a third person, as sometimes happens in the case of other correspondents your age. This shows me that your parents respect the privacy of your mail. I also see that what your parents think about your friend and what his parents think about you means something to you. Don't let them lose confidence in you.

If you had a sixteen-year-old daughter, you would want to trust her too, wouldn't you?

Cordially yours,
W. T.

Dear Sir,

I hope you still remember me. In my last letter I wrote about my friend. In this letter I'm going to write about my parents.

But before I do that I would like to thank you for your letter. It was an eye opener for me. I had a long talk with my friend after I got it. He also sees our friendship now in the right perspective. Of course, we still kiss each other and we think that if we are still going together next year we should perhaps think of getting engaged. We love each other more than anyone else, but in spite of this we want to wait until marriage.

But now about my new problem with my parents: We are slowly drifting apart. My big sister, who's twenty-four, left home a long time ago. She's a university student and my father has to support her. This puts a great burden on him. Often he's in a bad mood and sometimes my mother and I suffer because of it.

My father is fifty-three and my mother is fifty. If you saw our modern home and our whole way of life, you would think they were much younger.

They have very few friends. My mother doesn't like to have visitors nor go visiting—it's embarrassing for her. Neither do they belong to any groups or clubs. So in the late afternoon they just sit around and are edgy; in the evening they watch TV. They have a real TV-marriage.

Maybe this is the reason why they want to have me around all the time. I'm a high-school sophomore. When I've finished my homework or studied for a test and then want to go visit my friend, they always say, "Every day you run around. All right, but if you get bad grades, you'll have to break up. Your school work must not suffer."

But I do all I can to get good grades. I'm above average in my class and my grades are good enough. I just can't see why I must break up with my friend because of my school work.

On Monday, Tuesday and Wednesday I' m not allowed to see him and on the other days I have to come home early. If my parents had other interests and contacts with people, it would ease the situation. But how can they find them? I would like very much to help them. But how? Also, they should gradually begin to treat me as a grown-up. I would be very happy if you could send me some suggestions soon.

With friendly greetings,
Your Gabi

Dear Gabi,

I was very happy to hear from you again. I was especially happy that you accepted my advice and backtracked as far as intimacies go. Congratulations! It is not everyone who is able to do that. But I think that even eighteen is still too early for an engagement. Between eighteen and twenty-one you will still change very much—so will your friend. That's why I would discourage you from making such far-reaching decisions before that age.

Early marriages are one of the reasons why there are so many divorces. Just imagine being twenty-two and already having two children. It would be easy for you to look on them as disturbing factors in your life that keep you tied down. Maybe you would tell yourself, "This is how it will be for the next fifteen years of my life," and you could become very depressed.

If, on the other hand, you have already lived your own life, learned a profession and practiced it, then a crisis of this kind may be avoided. You would be a more mature mother for your children, and you could enjoy in a completely new way the challenge of being a homemaker with all of its creative possibilities.

Your parents probably foresee these things, and this is why they try to put on the brakes a little bit. I'm sure they are also fearful that you might sleep with your boyfriend, and you know yourself how close you were to that. I wonder if you could simply show your parents our correspondence and talk with them about it. Maybe this would increase their confidence in you, and they would give you more freedom.

You look at your parents' marriage very critically. Perhaps it would ease the situation if you would take the initiative and plan something you could do together over a weekend.

On the other hand, you cannot be your parents' marriage counselor, and you have to accept them simply as they are. One thing is certain, they need a lot of love and praise. You should use every opportunity to show them your gratefulness and love. Maybe as a Christmas present you could give them a game they could play together. Or do you know another couple in their age group who could visit them from time to time?

You seem to be a very fine girl, and I hope to make your acquaintance some day.

With very warm greetings,
Your W. T.

Reflection

What moved me the most about the correspondence with Gabi was the role of her parents. Certainly they are good, caring and loving people who want the very best for their child.

But do they have any idea what is happening in their daughter's mind? Do they realize that Gabi sees through the emptiness of their marriage? Do they know how much she suffers because she is supposed to replace their own lack of companionship?

As is the case with so many parents, they believe that raising children means watching over and controlling them. How much more helpful it would be for their daughter if they would have a good talk with her to explain their reasons for strict rules and concern. At the same time, Gabi seems to be in need of simple information, as her question concerning petting shows. Nowadays it is certainly the responsibility of parents to talk to their fifteen-year-old daughter about these things.

The greatest protection for a child is not in control, but in giving one's confidence completely to the child.

The attitude of Gabi's boyfriend impresses me. Frankly, I had not anticipated that he would react this way.

In spite of many pessimistic prognoses, I believe there are many young men today who can sensitively distinguish those things which help a relationship to develop and those which make it a dead-end road.

The following letter from a reticent young man underlines this again. For those who are able to read between the lines, it is a very precious letter.

15
"She Is Too Precious for a Flirt"

"BRIGITTA IS TOO PRECIOUS TO ME FOR JUST A FLIRT. . . . IF I WERE MADE OF WAX I CERTAINLY WOULD HAVE MELTED."

FRITZ H., AGE 17, TRADESMAN

Dear Mr. Trobisch,

For two years now I've been in love with a girl from my Christian youth group, but I still would like to wait until I'm eighteen in order to be sure that my love for her is real and God's will for me.

At the moment I'm hospitalized because I had an accident with my motorcycle. Brigitta writes me every week.

When I was still in good health, I noticed often how she looked at me. Of course I did the same. But when she visited me once in the hospital, she looked at me in such a way that if I were made of wax I certainly would have melted.

I realize more and more that when I leave the hospital the moment will have come for a frank talk.

But this is my problem: There are days when if she were with me I could just squeeze her for joy. Then again there are other times when I doubt my love for her.

It could be that this up and down of feelings is normal for my age, but I would like to have your advice because Brigitta is too precious to me for just a flirt.

I hope you understand me and can help me a little bit.

Yours,
Fritz

Dear Fritz,

Thank you for your direct question. I have to admire the fact that you were able to keep the feelings you had for a girl in your heart for two years, knowing that they weren't one-sided, yet still silently and patiently waiting for certainty.

You've probably sensed that even one word said too early and too directly can destroy the magic and that a gesture made too soon can squash something very, very fragile. Therefore, it is good that you resisted the impulse to squeeze Brigitta for joy. Not only would you have squashed her, but also with her your joy. For me there is no doubt that just because you both held back, your relationship was deepened.

Yes, it is normal that your feelings go up and down. It's not only true at your age, but at every age. This will lessen once you have talked frankly with each other.

I agree with you that the time has now come for such an open talk. I could imagine that Brigitta is even more in doubt about your feelings than about her own. Very often the girl is sure about her feelings sooner than the boy.

When you talk to her, tell her candidly the reasons for your reticence—that she is too precious, far too precious for you just to flirt with her.

God bless you and guide you both when you have your talk together.

Your W. T.

Reflection

I intentionally included the letter of Fritz between the letters of Gabi and the next correspondence in order to show the contrast in the conduct of the girls.

I do not know much about Brigitta, but it would not surprise me to learn that she had a family in which she felt sheltered and protected. Evidently, Beate, the next writer, did not have this experience. Just how this lack has affected her is expressed in this letter.

16
"I Was Always Looking for My Place"

"MY MOTHER RAISED ME IN SUCH A WAY THAT I WAS MADE TO THINK MY SEX ORGANS WERE SOMETHING BAD. . . . WHEN I WAS THIRTEEN I SLEPT WITH A BOY FOR THE FIRST TIME. . . . SOMEHOW I WAS ALWAYS LOOKING FOR MY PLACE, FOR LOVE AND TENDERNESS."

BEATE K., AGE 16, HIGH-SCHOOL STUDENT

Dear Mr. and Mrs. Trobisch,

I just finished reading your book *My Beautiful Feeling* for the second time. I'm sixteen and repeating the sophomore year at my high school.

I'm afraid this will be a long letter because at present I have some other problems besides masturbation.

My mother has been a Christian for about seven years, but unfortunately this has not affected her character very much. She loses her temper very quickly, but she can also quickly forget she has been angry. My mother raised me in such a way that I was made to think my sex organs were something bad.

When I was five or six, I played doctor with other children. As we played we discovered the difference in our genital organs. My mother wanted to take me to a psychiatrist and scolded me for doing such a thing. But this only made me more curious.

When I was thirteen I slept with a boy for the first time. I didn't like him very much, but I wanted to know whether what I had read in books about intercourse was true and whether the feeling of orgasm was really as beautiful as it was described as being.

You will probably be shocked, but I will write very frankly. Writing is easier for me than talking with someone. For a while I met this boy frequently, but mostly we just petted.

When I was fourteen, I came home from a walk one day, and when my mother opened the door she was pale as death. She said, "Come with me to your room." In my room she opened the drawer where I kept the contraceptives and similar things.

She said I was just like a prostitute, took a bamboo stick which she hadn't used since I was five years old, and punished me until I thought I wouldn't survive.

Then she sent me to church all the time and didn't let me out of her sight. My father didn't say a word about the whole thing. (I have no relationship with him. He's an excellent father for small children. But he's simply not capable of raising teen-agers.)

After that I had three other boyfriends. I petted with them more times than I can count, and once I had intercourse. The last one broke up with me three days after we had slept together. That was quite a shock for me.

On the other hand, it was good for me because it made me go to visit a young couple living in our neighborhood. From the way they lived, I could see for the first time that they were not just Christians on Sundays, but also Christians all through the week.

What I saw in their home bore fruit. I became a Christian. This was five months ago. I recognized my sins, confessed them and know that I'm forgiven.

I really don't know how to continue—where to start and where to end. Maybe it's best to write a few of my thoughts about your book. I have worked through it two or three times and have finally come to the point where I can identify with Ilona, even though the answers don't always apply in my case.

I masturbated (I'll use M.) for the first time when I was eleven or twelve, I believe.

Four months ago a new fellow came to our youth group. He was a real challenge to me, not as a boyfriend to go steady with, but as someone with whom I could always have a very good talk. During the time that I was seeing him, M. was never necessary.

One day through this friend I met a twenty-three-year-old, married man. When I was with him alone in my room, I again didn't know my limits. Petting! After that we saw each other twice. Petting! Petting!

Since then, M. happened four or five times, every time because my body wanted something, and I gave in to it. But what shall I do when my body longs for this quick release, especially just before my period?

The day before yesterday, I had the urge in the evening, though it did not come from my body but consciously from my mind. I read a tract about sex and that made me think it was okay to do it. So in the future I have to watch what I read.

My counselor knows nothing about all this. He and his wife are very good friends with whom I spend most of my free time. I have a very, very good girl friend who also became a Christian a short while ago, and I can talk to her about everything. . . .

This is where I stopped writing two days ago. In the meantime I had a long talk with my counselor. The Holy Spirit had told me that I should not be afraid to go to someone and say, "Pray for me. I'm in trouble."

I prayed with him and afterward I prayed alone for a long time. Most of my fears left me. I feel sheltered and at home with my Lord, just as if I could lie down, sit and walk in his hand. It's almost as if I'm not living anymore here on earth, but just in the Lord. I'm very, very happy.

I believe that M. is not necessary for me anymore. Somehow I was always looking for my place, for love and tenderness. Now I have finally understood and feel that only God can give this, and he does.

Many thanks!

Beate

Dear Beate,

You have described a long road in your life, and I thank you for allowing me to share it and walk along with you. You are not yet in heaven, and the feeling that you don't live here on earth anymore will not last. Your way will lead through mountains and valleys, but you are going in the right direction.

Of course your situation is different from that of Ilona. She was already seventeen with no sexual experience. Your way is much harder because your sexual feelings have been aroused much too early, and you have experienced what you cannot yet digest. This was not good for you and it was not the will of God.

You must also understand the reaction of your frightened mother. She may have her faults, but she wanted to protect you from worse things and pulled the emergency brake. Of course, it would have been better if your father had entered the picture.

On the other hand, you have a great advantage in comparison to Ilona: You have a counselor who senses when you are in need and who, at the same time, has the authority to act spiritually. He can help to replace your father who left you in the lurch. I can only advise you to trust your counselor completely and tell him everything, even when you have backslidden after your conversion. Allow him to be very strict with you and ask you direct questions.

After having gone astray for such a long time, not everything will change from one day to the other. There will still be defeats, but it is important that you confess them immediately and ask for God's forgiveness. The couple with whom you visit and your girl friend are your best helpers. Maybe even that young man who did not become a boyfriend "to go steady with," but really a friend, is also a helper.

As a further ally in your struggle you should put your intelligence to work. All you have to do is to decide never again to stay alone in a room with a man. Is that really so difficult?

There's a connection between masturbation and petting. Actually, petting is mutual masturbation. The majority of girls never discover M. Many girls are introduced to petting practices by their boyfriends. Then when the boyfriend breaks off the relationship, after having nibbled a little bit, they feel left in the lurch. Now their situation is difficult. Their sexual feelings are awakened, and so they try to find sexual pleasure without a partner, and they begin to masturbate. With some it could easily become a daily habit.

I think it is good that already you are able to discern whether you are overcome by a physical urge or whether it is a conscious, willful decision.

In any case, M. is a misuse of God's gift of sexuality. Sexuality is meant for communication, as a present to another person. If one gets stuck in M. he or she will never experience this dimension and thus deprive himself or herself of something very precious.

You've already understood a very deep mystery which many adults have not yet understood. In the final analysis, it is only God who can give you a place, who can give you love and tenderness. Praise God for this insight.

My wife and I send you our kindest greetings,

W. T.

Reflection

Since this last letter Beate has written to us often. Her letters describe her struggles, her ups and downs. Her defeats, however, are becoming more and more rare. I visited her once with her counselor. Our talk then confirmed and completed the picture of her we had formed from her letters.

Basically, the situation of Beate is the same as that of Martina and Gerda—a cold, dominating mother who gives orders and punishes rather than using the opportunity for an understanding and loving talk to guide her daughter. At the same time, they all have passive fathers who do not take a stand on the issues and who are therefore of little help to their daughters in finding their identity.

The only difference is that Beate does not seek the way out in a homosexual friendship as did Martina and Gerda. Beate believes she can replace through heterosexual activities what her parents did not give her.

This is one reason for the great misunderstanding in heterosexual friendships at this age. Usually, girls are not looking for sex but rather, as Beate has put it, "a place, love and tenderness." A boy in her peer group is not able to give this to her. He usually understands her approach as a wish for sexual activities and thinks that he is doing her a favor when he offers it to her. At first, the girl may also think she can find what she is looking for in sex. She realizes her mistake too late.

This is why those friendships which do not follow the way of Fritz and Brigitta (see chapter fifteen), but which include sex, usually end in a dead-end road. It's only a matter of time before both of them realize it. They meet on different levels and do not really find each other. Often the girl realizes this before the boy does. She may know in her heart that there is no future in their relationship, but she keeps on in order not to lose her friend.

Deep down in her heart, Beate is not looking for a boyfriend, but for a father. That's why she was most tempted by older, married men. If fathers could only understand how much they could help their daughters and protect them by consciously giving them time and attention. They could also help by showing their daughters a tenderness which does not shy away from physical expression. But many fathers are afraid of their growing daughters and withdraw in fear.

Beate is saved by her faith. Her story illustrates that true faith is not a luxury item which does not affect the basics of life, but a reality, a power which forms and changes and affects the fundamental issues of life.

In the final analysis even the best parents cannot fulfill the deepest longings of their children. Neither can a wife fulfill the longings of her husband nor a husband fulfill the deepest longings of his wife. The greatest fulfillment can only be had through a personal relationship to God. The relationship between parents and children and between husband and wife can only, in the best cases, be a mirror of this relationship to God.

If Beate has a weak father, Peter has a strong one. His letter illustrates that this fact in itself does not solve all problems.

17
"I'm Twenty and I've Never Slept with a Girl"

"AS A PSYCHIATRIST, MY DAD IS OF THE OPINION THAT PREMARITAL SEX IS NECESSARY. . . . UNDER THE SURFACE, MY FRIENDS THINK THAT IT IS A RITE OF MANHOOD TO SEDUCE A GIRL IN THE SHORTEST POSSIBLE TIME. . . . SHE SAID TO ME, 'MY RULE IS: NO LOWER THAN THE WAISTLINE.' "

PETER R., AGE 20 GIRL FRIEND, AGE 17

Dear Sir,

My girl friend gave me your book *Love Is a Feeling to Be Learned.* You have written the book in a way that has won my confidence. I would like to tell you that I agree with you in almost everything. Incidentally, I had come to similar conclusions the day before I read your book.

I'm twenty and I've never slept with a girl (that's a strange combination of facts in one sentence, but I can't think of a better way to put it). Most of my friends, if not all of them, have already slept with at least one girl. Under the surface, my friends think that it is a rite of manhood to seduce a girl in the shortest possible time.

Ten days ago I got acquainted with a girl. Even though we hardly knew each other, we soon realized that basically we had the same outlook on life, and so it happened that already after half an hour we talked very frankly about a lot of things. In the course of our talk she said to me, "My rule is: No lower than the waistline. Everything else belongs to marriage." (She said she was a dedicated Christian.)

You can imagine that this upset my plans. But she was so attractive I continued to go with her. In spite of our different views on sex, I fell in love with her.

I've made the firm resolution to refrain from sexual activities because the girl is too precious to me. We like each other very much—by the way she just turned seventeen—so we have already talked about marriage. And this after one week and four days!

I would like to know your opinion about this. I also talked to my father, who's fifty-six, about it. As a psychiatrist, my dad is of the opinion that premarital sex is necessary in order for the partners to see if they fit together sexually. From his experience with his patients, many marriages failed because the partners were sexually incompatible.

Please don't think that my father is an atheist. On the contrary! He believes that there would be fewer neurotics if people were oriented toward God and lived according to the rules of a religion.

Thank you very much for your interest in my problem and for deciphering my handwriting.

In respect,
Your Peter

Dear Peter!

You know, Peter, I believe you belong in a museum, not because you are old-fashioned—you may even be ahead of your time—but because a young man like yourself is so rare today. I can only congratulate you. You are simply tops!

I'm deeply impressed that you are able to resist not only peer pressure, but also the advice of your own father, given with the whole weight of his psychiatric experience.

The more I think about your letter, I dare to guess that there might be many young people—boys and girls alike—who think and feel as you do. But they are made to feel so insecure that they don't dare express what they really feel. There may be more of your friends who belong to this group than you really think. But they don't want to admit to others that they are dissatisfied. Their egos are too weak to swim against the stream—however, it's really a question of which direction the stream is running.

I believe that magazines which deal with this subject give a completely wrong picture. A young man who thinks as you do is simply not interesting for the news media. The media are interested in the others. Therefore, the impression that emerges is that all young people today sleep together as a matter of course and are very happy about it—both facts are untrue.

As far as your meeting with this girl is concerned, I think the most helpful thing was that you were able to talk together. This alone has deepened your relationship.

It is not wrong to talk about where to set the limits. On the other hand, the cut-and-dried rule about the waistline is silly. A young woman may be much more sensitive and aroused when touched on her breasts than on her genitals. You can conclude from this that sometimes it may be up to the young man to set narrower limits as the woman may overestimate her control.

If you do this then you would pass the test of being a man! After such a short time it is certainly too early to talk about marriage. On the other hand, you should be aware that for a young woman the idea of marriage is usually somewhere in the back ground as soon as she favors a young man.

As far as your father is concerned, you have to take into consideration that as a psychiatrist he mostly has to deal with sick people. But I don't think one can generalize this statement—saying that having intercourse together is a criteria for choosing a partner—even for healthy people. If their union is a success and they marry on this basis, they will soon see that this alone is not enough to fill their marriage with contentment that lasts a lifetime. It also often happens that people marry out of a sense of duty because they have already gone too far, even though they have a premonition that their personalities do not harmonize.

In case they have had sexual experiences with several partners, the possibility of comparing is a disadvantage when it comes to building up an exclusive and unique relationship in marriage. Research studies have shown that the divorce rate is lowest in those marriages where the partners knew no one else sexually except their spouse.

If your father had in mind the danger of a sexual neurosis, I would say that it is the result of forced repression for negative reasons, not, as in your case, a voluntary renunciation for the purpose of gaining greater maturity.

Of course, I agree with your father completely that it is psychologically healthy to be oriented toward God and to "live according to the rules of a religion." Only I see a certain contradiction between this conviction and the advice he gave you.

Did he mean by "rules of a religion" something different than the Ten Commandments of God? They are clear-cut. The expression "to become one flesh" in the Bible is exclusively related to marriage. According to biblical thinking, the state of marriage and the physical union—in this sequence—are coupled together unequivocally (Gen. 2:24).

Many claim that the Bible doesn't say anything about premarital relations. This is not true. You can read the very strict rules about premarital life in Deuteronomy 22:13-30 which in some cases even involved the death penalty.

Even in the New Testament, the alternative is unequivocal: "But if you cannot restrain your desires go ahead and marry" (1 Cor. 7:9). So it is either abstinence or marriage, but no compromise in between.

Also, the embarrassment of Joseph in view of Mary's pregnancy cannot be explained if it were not clear in the Bible that intercourse between an engaged man and woman does not correspond to the will of God (Mt. 1:18-25).

This is what I would understand by "rules of religion" in your case. But what impressed me so much in your letter was the fact that you followed these rules instinctively even though you were not conscious of them.

Continue on this road and don't allow anyone to confuse you.

I greet you cordially,
Your W. T.

Reflection

Peter's letter shows the great insecurity in our time about sexual ethics. A young man like him feels so alone that he might even doubt whether he is still "normal" if he has not yet had intercourse at the age of twenty.

I believe he belongs to a silent minority—or is it even a majority?—who live, in spite of the many sexual temptations and permissiveness of our society, in an old-fashioned, clean way following their healthy instincts. Their backbones need to be strengthened.

My children had the impression when I read the letter to them that Peter as well as his girl friend seem to think that being a Christian means to follow certain rules.

I think they are right. Neither Peter nor his girl friend know that rules and laws are not the essential issue. Being a Christian means having a personal relationship with Jesus Christ. If this relationship is established, one experiences the truth of God's promise "I will teach you the way you should go and I will lead you with my eye upon you" (Ps. 32:8). It is this personal eye contact which Peter and his girl friend have yet to experience.

This issue of a personal relationship to God and a personal relationship to a girl is the topic of the last correspondence.

18
"My Conflict: Being a Christian or Having a Girl Friend"

"WHEN I WAS ELEVEN, I STARTED TO BECOME A TEEN-AGER . . . . I NOTICED THAT AS A BOY I WAS POPULAR WITH GIRLS. . . . THE CONFLICT IS NOW WITHIN ME—BEING A CHRISTIAN OR HAVING A GIRL FRIEND."

RUDI K., AGE 16, HIGH-SCHOOL STUDENT

Dear Mr. and Mrs. Trobisch,

The reason why I'm writing you at such a late—or rather early—hour is as follows. I'm sixteen and go to high school, and I am—or at least I was—a Christian.

When I was eleven I started to become a teen-ager. By this I mean I was a little bit ahead of myself. And my lifestyle changed. When I was about twelve, I fell in love for the first time. At the end of my thirteenth year, at a retreat I became a Christian.

(Excuse my handwriting—I'm in bed.)

After that I gave up all relations with girls. This was possible for me because of a very close friendship with one of my classmates.

At the end of my fourteenth year, I went to a party again for the first time. There I realized that in spite of my being a Christian, I was accepted by my classmates, including the girls.

(I'm now a little tired. It's 11:45 P.M.)

At the end of my fifteenth year, I took dancing lessons at a dance studio. I sensed that it was very easy for me to invite a girl to dance. And when it was the "ladies' choice" I was among the first ones to be asked. In short, I noticed that as a boy I was popular with girls.

It was in the middle of the dance course that a particular girl tried to win me as her friend. I was not attracted to her very much. I also thought that as a Christian I was not supposed to start a friendship with a non-Christian girl. She was very disappointed when, in spite of the fact that she was sitting beside me, I asked another girl for the next dance. Then she tried in many different ways to be able to dance with me. I don't want to describe her methods here because I wouldn't finish until tomorrow (midnight).

My problem is this: I am relatively popular with girls, and I would like to have closer contact with one girl, but all the Christian girls I know stick together in a tight group so that a closer personal relationship with one of them is impossible.

It wouldn't be difficult to get close to a non-Christian girl, but I don't think that, as a Christian, I would have a meaningful relationship with an unbelieving girl. It seems to me that either the friendship or my being a Christian would not survive. This is my thinking.

I'm sorry to say that my Christian life has gone down into a deep valley because of this unsolved problem. My personal Bible study is sort of dead, if I do it at all. The Bible doesn't speak to me anymore. I still pray and talk to God. But I'm lacking the spiritual zest I had before I started the dance course. Since that time, I have felt like I'm going downhill spiritually.

The conflict is now within me—being a Christian or having a girl friend. To my closer friends, I'm becoming untrustworthy because sometimes I feel attracted to the Christian faith and other times I am attracted by a non-Christian girl.

12:30 AM.

Yours,
Rudi

Dear Rudi,

Thank you for your midnight letter. I see that your Christian faith means something to you and that you try to harmonize your lifestyle with your faith. This makes me very happy because there are a lot of young people who call themselves Christians but do not draw any practical consequences from this fact. I'm glad you are different.

Your best helpers are your "closer friends." You say yourself that the friendship with one of your classmates helped you the most when you tried to break with the superficial lifestyle of today's teen-agers. So this friendship pointed you into the right decision. You should cultivate and invest much time into such friendships. You will receive exactly as much confidence as you give. What happened to this friend in the meantime? With such a friend you should talk over the many small decisions you have to make when it comes to dealing with the opposite sex and examine your decisions before God.

On the other hand, I am also glad that you are not simply withdrawing but daring to stick your neck out and to meet with girls. It's also good that you are conscious of how you affect girls. Now you have to learn to deal with this in a responsible way. Evidently, God has given you an outgoing personality. This is a great gift, but you have to learn to master this gift, and you can only learn if you do not avoid being with girls.

That's why I don't think it's wrong that you took these dancing lessons, even though it led your spiritual life into a crisis. But it would be too cheap a solution to solve this crisis by withdrawal. The goal is rather to expose yourself to the head wind and in spite of it remain near to God. The only advice I would give is that you do not yet try to enter into an exclusive relationship with a girl. It is good to be acquainted with several girls at the same time and to date several without going steady with any one of them. It's only possible to make a choice if you know more than one.

However, I have the impression that you divide up the girls into Christians and non-Christians in a much too simple way. How can you know for sure? Can you look into their hearts? There may be a girl who doesn't talk much about it, but in her heart she might be in deeper fellowship with God than another one who witnesses to everyone at every occasion that she is a true believer.

Also, you have to reckon with the possibility that a girl might call herself a Christian, but this has nothing to do with her lifestyle. Recently, a sixteen-year-old girl wrote me that she prayed with her boyfriend, and afterward they went to bed together. She didn't seem to sense any contradiction.

On the other hand, there might be girls who have no idea whatsoever about Christianity, and still they have preserved a healthy instinct for what is right and a natural feeling of modesty so that they wouldn't try to lead you into temptation in any way.

You see that it is not that simple to divide them into sheep and goats. If you think of yourself in your present state, you see how difficult it would be to categorize you. I feel that as long as you keep your relationships with girls on the basis of a non-exclusive acquaintance, you don't have to be afraid. You also have to learn to deal with non-Christian girls. In later life you will be confronted again and again with non-Christians. I admit that an exclusive relationship with a girl who has no personal faith might bring you into conflict with your own faith. A mere acquaintance would not. Before you make the choice of your life partner, the question of faith will not really become decisive. Allow yourself time for this choice and accept my warm greetings.

W. T.

Dear Mr. Trobisch,

Thank you so very much for your letter. I know I should have answered it much earlier and not have waited for months. I hope you will be able to excuse my long silence.

You have not disappointed me with your answer. Step by step, I understood a little bit more of your letter. I see that grace allows one to be able to wait and to renounce certain things for one's own good.

At the moment I have good fellowship with several Christian girls, and I think I have a good relationship with each one of them. I believe that even the fact of sharing a common faith does not give one the right to start an exclusive relationship. I have made this mistake more than once before, but I know that the meaning of marriage and sexuality is much, much deeper. It is a task and a dimension which lies ahead of me still.

However, I do thank the Lord now for the space he gives me within certain limits to get to know and understand the opposite sex. I feel that when the two opposite poles are not too close together a fruitful tension and a creative energy are produced which otherwise would be lost. This, too, is a tremendous experience. . . .

You have opened a new way for me, more difficult than the old one, demanding more tenacity and strength. But in the final analysis it is the richer way, the more fulfilled way. For this I'm thankful to you.

Rudi

Epilogue

A personal letter to you:

Right now you have done something very unusual. You have read confidential letters which originally were not meant for you. I wonder whether you have really realized how much was confided in you—how much trust was invested in you?

I hope you are as thankful to these young people as I am that they granted you insight into their private mail, and in a way laid open their hearts before you.

But what will you do with this insight? What conclusions will you draw?

Maybe as you read this book, the thought came to you to seek someone to talk to outside your family. However, I would be much happier if you would try something else first.

Maybe it struck you that the parents in these letters do not play a very positive role in this book. Many of those boys and girls wrote to me precisely because they did not feel understood by their own parents. My impression is that for many the dialogue with their own parents has been destroyed or interrupted.

Have you ever had the idea that it is not only growing sons and daughters who need help, but their parents too? Have you wondered if you could help your parents as much as they could help you?

In any case, I would like to make a very practical suggestion to you: Try to get into a dialogue with your parents.

I do not mean a casual talk which happens incidentally without preparation. No, I mean a very consciously planned dialogue.

Start with the parent with whom you feel most at ease. Later on you can do it with the other parent and still later with both together. Maybe one day you could also invite your brother or sister so that a family dialogue is created. But for the beginning it might be best to start with either father or mother.

This is the way to go about it:

Ask for fifteen minutes time. Both of you sit down in comfortable chairs or on the floor. You will see that sitting on the floor gives a special feeling of fellowship and of being on the same level. Each of you needs a little notebook. You agree about a question (you will find suggestions for such questions at the end of this letter, but you could think of other questions yourself). The question should touch on something which is close to your heart.

Each of you notes the question in his or her notebook, and then you have five minutes to answer it in writing. After five minutes you exchange the notebooks and each one reads quietly what the other one has written. Then talk about it for ten minutes. Not longer. If you plan a longer time you never get around to starting in the first place.

When you talk it is important that you do not have a discussion but a dialogue. The point is not to reach an agreement or find a solution or convince the other one that you are right. The point is only to learn what the other person thinks and feels, to accept his or her opinion even if you do not agree and to accept his or her feelings even if you cannot share them.

Note: Feelings are never right or wrong. They simply exist. They just are. It takes courage to put into writing certain things which might disturb the other person, and at the same time to endure the pain without defending yourself or launching a counterattack, if you are hurt yourself. If you invest this courage the reward will be great.

To have a dialogue in this way means that you sit together and say to each other, "I trust you to such a degree that I dare to tell you the truth about myself, even if it might hurt you."

After ten minutes you get up and stop talking. Maybe at the end you agree about another question for the next day. Let things which have not yet been resolved stand as they are. They have lost their poison because they have been expressed, and therefore they can be dealt with.

Maybe you'll want to put this book on the table beside your parent's bed. It could be that they will read it. They might even decide one day to have such a dialogue with each other! Who knows what could happen!

I wish you much courage and joy for this work. It is work!

Yours,

Walter Trobisch

The following are suggested questions for your dialogue (most are taken from "Family Dialogue" by Betsy Larson in *Marriage and Family Living,* Oct. and Nov. 1977). They are intended to be basic questions which will just get you talking about feelings.

What do I like best about our family, and how does that make me feel?

How do I feel when I receive a compliment from someone in our family?

How do I feel when I receive a compliment from someone outside our family?

What is the meaning of my birthday to me? How does this make me feel?

How do I feel about having company for dinner?

How do I feel about going camping?

What is the meaning of Mom's and Dad's anniversary to me, and how does it make me feel?

What are my feelings as the new school year begins?

What are my feelings when I am asked to cut back or do without?

When do I feel closest to all of you, and how does that make me feel?

What are our (your) faults as parents, and how does that make me feel?

What are our (your) good qualities as parents, and how does that make me feel?

In what ways can your children (we) help? How does that make me feel?

What can we do to make our family life better? How does that make me feel?

How do I feel when Mom yells?

How do I feel when Dad gets mad at us?

How do I feel when Mom is sick?

How do I feel when I have to ask Dad for money? for use of the family car?

What is my best quality and how does this make me feel?

A man travels the world over in search of what he needs, and returns home to find it.—George Moore

BOOK FOUR

MY BEAUTIFUL FEELING

Prelude—a dialogue with the reader

You may well ask what motivated us to publish this rather personal correspondence. The reason is this. In our other books we simply mentioned in passing the problem of masturbation. To our great surprise we receive the majority of letters from our readers in response to these casual remarks.

Often these letters are desperate cries for help. This astonishes us since one hears and reads everywhere today that it is neither dangerous nor harmful to masturbate. Evidently this information is no help for those who have gotten started on this road. They long for a personal word. They want to be taken seriously as individuals.

To satisfy their questions, we would have to engage in a lengthy correspondence with each one of them as we have with "Ilona." We would have to consider the circumstances in which each one lives, get acquainted with the people around them, discuss their experiences in the past and in the present and—last, but not least—consider the relationship of each one with God, learn the biography of their faith. This is not possible, unfortunately, since there are too many letters which share the problem of this mute pleasure.

This is why we have decided to publish a correspondence. Consider this book, therefore, as nothing more than the first letter written in response. Just imagine that you have written to us—or you would like to write to us—and now this book comes along. We agree, it is incomplete and it may leave some very personal questions unanswered—as is the case with every first answer. Yet it is longer, deeper and more detailed than a letter could be which was addressed to you alone.

We have to run the risk that one or the other of our readers will be introduced to problems which he has never met with himself. But we believe that this risk is smaller than the risk that those who need help are left in despair.

Desperation is expressed in many letters which reach us. This desperation is not simply the result of a repressive education which has produced guilt feelings. That explanation is too simple. Our impression is rather that the more the sexual taboos are breaking down, the more masturbation becomes a problem for individuals. The rational conclusion that objectively no harm is done evidently does not quench the subjective feeling of a shameful personal defeat. In spite of all the soothing arguments in favor of masturbation, few are really happy with it.

An impersonal essay, however, is of little value for those concerned. They are unable to identify themselves with it and do not feel personally addressed. Nor do they feel that they are being taken seriously in their special situation when they read an impersonal scientific treatise.

Therefore we entrust to you a correspondence. It is a real exchange of letters, not a fictional one. Ilona is a German girl and her letters have not been changed. At the beginning of the correspondence she was a high-school senior, at the end a college freshman, majoring in English. That's why she was able to translate her own letters into English from the original German.

Our letters too remained basically as they were—even the dates and period of time between letters are authentic. In a few places we did some editing and added here and there a thought or an explanation. The books we refer to you will find in the notes. We recommend them if you want to gain more insight into the problem.

Ilona's personal data has been changed, of course, to make identification impossible.

This book deals in the first instance with one person only—the girl whom we call "Ilona." She lives in our midst. This is the way she has struggled through her problem. This is the way she has experienced help.

We hope that you will identify with Ilona's ups and downs, with her victories and defeats. We did not spare you the frustration of participating in these ups and downs, when territory that we thought had been won had to be given up again and a new start had to be made. This is the price we have to pay for publishing a true correspondence. If we had invented one, we could have offered you a more readable book with a steadily rising line. On the other hand, identification would have become very difficult for many who struggle with this problem.

You will also realize that some letters contradict each other. The reason is that Ilona went through a process of growth; in different stages of her development, different things were true and valid for her, different kinds of behavior adequate.

Therefore, it is irrelevant to quote from this book out of context in order to label it either "conservative" or "liberal." We know in advance that our comments will be too conservative for the "liberals" and too liberal for the "conservatives." But we believe we will be understood by those who leave behind their prejudices and take the trouble to empathize with Ilona and struggle along with her, letter by letter, just as we did.

Why did we choose Ilona?

First of all because she is a girl. The greatest number of letters sharing this problem reach us from females. It may also be more merciful to address young men (whose ego in general is more delicate and vulnerable than that of young women) in an indirect way by letting them read a girl's personal correspondence, in which their male problems are also pointed out especially when Ilona's boy friends appear on the scene.

Another reason we chose Ilona is her extraordinary ability to express herself. Her frankness and honesty, even when she fails, is so refreshing that we hope you will be able to love her as we do.

But the main reason for our choice was that Ilona is not a "special case" at all. Neither does she live in unusually difficult circumstances, nor is she neurotic in any sense. On the contrary, she is psychologically and physically a healthy, normal girl.

She has chosen her road herself. We have only accompanied her a certain distance. It is certainly not the road for everyone. Each human being is unique. God does not make people like houses—built one exactly like another. Neither does he build counseling relationships one exactly like another.

Walter and Ingrid Trobisch

October 2

To the editor,
". . ." Magazine

My name is Ilona. I am seventeen and a senior in high school. My great problem is that I do not live in peace with my sexuality. Again and again I satisfy my sexual desires myself, although I really don't want to do it. I can't seem to free myself from this drive and am unable to control it. Do you have any practical suggestions about how to learn this?

I am a Christian and know that God has given me my sexuality. Often I have prayed that I might be able to use this gift in the right way—in other words, to be patient and to concentrate on other things. But the desire seems always to be stronger than I. Since I give in again and again, I am worried for fear that I might do damage to myself, and maybe even to my future marriage. Half a year ago I didn't even know that girls could masturbate. I read about it in a sex manual and then, out of curiosity, I tried it.

The trouble is that I use masturbation as a compensation when I am frustrated because of a hard assignment for school or when I feel "down" for any other reason. Of course, masturbation does not help me either, but makes me feel still more frustrated and dissatisfied than ever. I keep telling myself how useless and stupid it is, but I keep doing it nevertheless. Am I sick? Am I abnormal?

I realize that sometimes I have difficulty disciplining myself in other areas too, for instance in my eating habits. Overeating can also be a way of escape for me when I don't feel like doing my homework.

Could you tell me how I can learn to master my needs and control my desires?

Many thanks that I could write to your magazine.

Ilona

October 18

Dear Ilona,

Your letter of October 2 was forwarded to my wife and me, and we were asked to reply. First of all we must say that you certainly have courage to write such a letter to a magazine. It's just your courage which gives us hope that we can have a good talk together. It may become a long talk, because there are no prefabricated answers applicable to any and every one in regard to your questions.

Before we can say very much, we have to get better acquainted with you and try to feel your life as you feel it. Therefore it would be good if you could tell us a little more about yourself, your family life—parents and brothers and sisters, if you have any. Do you belong to a youth group? Do you have a close girl friend? A boy friend? All these relationships we would have to think over together. The more concretely you can describe your situation, the better we can help you. We know very well that we are asking you to have a great deal of confidence in us, who are perfect strangers to you. It may help you to know that we have been married for twenty years and are parents of five children.

Just this much for today: You are not sick. Your letter gives us the impression that you are a normal, healthy girl.

What impresses us about you is your wide-awakeness and honesty.

Masturbation is not a sickness. It is a symptom, a sign of a deeper problem. You hint in this direction in your letter, and we congratulate you on how well you have observed yourself. The underlying problem is very often not sexual. It is just that the symptom has taken a sexual form.

Usually deep down, there is a feeling of dissatisfaction with oneself and with one's life, which one tries to overcome in a short moment of pleasure.[1] But one does not succeed. The desired satisfaction is not reached. This you have experienced yourself.

It is precisely because the desired satisfaction is not reached that a person is tempted to repeat it. In this way a vicious circle is created. The more you are dissatisfied, the greater is the temptation; the more you give in, the more you are dissatisfied. The fetters grow tighter and tighter the more you try to shake them loose. In the end you are revolving only around yourself.

To recognize this may already help you to see the direction from which help can be expected. The more you get away from your own self, the more you think of others and occupy yourself with other interests, the less you will turn around yourself, and the temptation will be reduced.

We don't think you have to worry about your future marriage. Sometimes there may be a connection between masturbation and sexual inadequacy, but only when it has become a long and very frequent habit before marriage. Maybe we can go into this later on.

This is not your case now. After only half a year, when it has supposedly happened infrequently, it has not yet become a habit. Still it is certainly not too soon to start to do something about it and to work together lest it become a habit for you.

Prayer is always helpful, if it is an expression of our fellowship with God. But there is also a kind of prayer which focuses on one point, on one single unfulfilled human desire. This is only a caricature of prayer.

If you pray this way about masturbation, it does not help. It is like driving at night. When you look straight into the headlights of the oncoming car for fear of crashing into it, it is very likely that you may do just that.

October 28/29

Dear Mr. and Mrs. T.,

First of all I want to thank you very much for your letter. Every time during the last few days that I remembered it, I was filled with joy and thought, "Now you are no longer alone with your problem."

I had expected to receive some anonymous response as usually happens when you write to a magazine. Instead I received a letter from a married couple—and that was a special surprise for me.

I had feared one thing—that the answer would repeat what one can read everywhere nowadays: "Keep on doing it and stop worrying. It won't do you any harm. It might even be beneficial to your sexual development." All I know is that such advice does not help me because it contradicts a voice within me. So my conflict would only have deepened, had you answered me in this way.

The fact that you did not okay it was the first help in your letter. The second was that you did not offer a cut-and-dried answer, but rather you offered to "work together" with me. I accept your offer and am ready to do so.

The "advance in confidence" is not hard for me because I already know you from some of your books. Especially while reading *I Loved a Girl,* I thought to myself, "It would be good if I too could talk so openly with someone about sexual questions!" Now I can even do it with you!

My relationship to my parents is difficult to describe. My father is a businessman and is seldom home. Even when he is there, we rarely talk together, just the two of us. I am sure he means well and tries to take good care of his family. When I was small, I often sat on his lap. But during the last few years he has stopped touching me at all. Sometimes I think that he is afraid of that. Don't misunderstand me: We don't quarrel with each other. I certainly can't say that we have a bad relationship. I'd rather say that I don't have any relationship with him. I feel distant from him.

As my father was often away from home, my mother took over our training almost completely. I have two brothers and one sister. Mother was rather strict with us, and we did not have as much freedom as most of our classmates. That made us feel different from others. We never played games at home. Instead my mother took an active interest in our homework and put pressure on us to study hard for school. In a way we always felt forced. When she thought that we had not studied hard enough for a test on which we received a bad mark, we got a severe scolding. On the other hand, when we achieved high grades, it was only to be expected and we were rarely praised.

This one-sided focus on school achievement caused a lot of quarrels between my mother and me. When I wanted to be together with other young people, I had to do it more or less behind her back. When I went to our young people's fellowship or to choir practice (I enjoy singing), the question was always put to me, "Can you really afford to spend your time this way, right before your important exam?"

Lately the situation has improved somewhat, and I have more time for myself and freedom to do what I want. Recently I was even allowed to attend a weekend retreat which was fun for me.

I have lots of girl friends, one of whom is especially close to me. I also get along well with my sister and share confidences with her which

I wouldn't feel free to tell my parents.

A boy friend? Well, I don't know whether I should answer yes or no. I think better no, because we've just broken up. We met at the home of another family. I was reluctant, because my first boy friend, who had taken the same dance course with me, had abandoned me, and since that time I had been afraid of another disappointment. But finally I accepted Martin's invitation for a walk. The third or fourth walk ended with embracing and kissing on a bench in the park. That was my first experience of this kind. I didn't even try to stop him because I had been longing for something like this for a long time.

Actually we had a wonderful time together and met rather often (my mother thought *too* often). We could talk to each other about everything, and of course there were always kisses and embraces too. In retrospect I realize that this physical attraction played a rather important role in our relationship. But we never went any further than that.

After the summer holidays other things became more important and I realized that my feelings for him were no longer so strong. When he sensed this and asked me about it, I felt that I must tell him the truth. I wasn't really sad about it except for his sake because he seemed quite hurt. I'm afraid that his feelings for me were stronger than my feelings for him from the very beginning. But I can't do anything about it. Or is there a way to help him?

This brings up a problem which has bothered me for some time. It's hard for me to feel at ease with boys. I attend an exclusive girls' school and so spend most of my time with girls. I am even affectionate with my best girl friend. Is that wrong?

My preoccupation with sex began only this year, actually even before I met Martin. I had decided to study the book, *Man and Woman* by Horst Wrage, and I found a reference there to female masturbation.[2] I learned that masturbation is regularly practiced by both sexes today. Supposedly it is simply a stage in healthy sexual development which is outgrown in time. Only if it is practiced too frequently would it be considered abnormal. This book said that it could cause neither physical nor psychological harm.

The feeling that results from a boy fondling his penis or a girl her clitoris was described as "a strange and pleasant stimulation, from mild to prickly."[3] Out of pure curiosity, I tried it. The beautiful feeling I experienced made me want to have it more often—and so it happened that I did it repeatedly.

However, there was also a "BUT" in the book: "But," it said, "young people should be aware of the fact that masturbation and the motives behind it could also be detrimental to normal development. This is always the case when it comes to an inner dependency upon masturbation so that one is unable to control it, in the same way that others are unable to control their desire for intercourse."[4]

"So it can be harmful after all?" I asked myself. Indeed on page 164, a possible negative effect was described: One could become conditioned to this special form of sexual stimulation; if practiced over a long period of time, it could lead to difficulties when having sexual intercourse later. That is why I asked you about the effects on marriage. Actually the book made these comments in reference to petting, but the form of stimulation is the same since petting is nothing more than mutual masturbation.

Well, the problem seemed to be solved when the friendship with Martin began. During this time, I never had the desire to do it. But then after the summer vacation it began again. I am afraid that it happens more frequently than you might think according to my first letter. I realize now that I have fallen into the exact trap against which the book warned. Gradually I have grown more and more dependent upon masturbation. I am afraid that it is already hindering my development, and that's why I wrote to the magazine.

It is always the same: After I have masturbated, I have no more desire whatsoever for a few days. But then the desire creeps in and dominates my thoughts until I am compelled once again to do it.

You mentioned the example of driving a car at night. I am aware that it starts with an idea which soon becomes a preoccupation: "Why not do it once again?" Yes, in this way I do stare into the headlights of the oncoming car. But I am unable to turn my eyes elsewhere. It is as if I am compelled to stare in this direction. My whole mind and body is captivated by this one thought and desire. So I get stuck in a rut.

How can I free myself from it? What is it that I really want to satisfy? Is it my sexual desire? Or is it something else?

I have tried everything under the sun, like trying to concentrate more on my studies. But after a few hours the compulsion is there again—and in order to get rid of it I give in. I observed that I am especially tempted after a test when I am completely exhausted and glad to be finished or—as I told you already—when I get stuck on a homework problem and become frustrated.

On the surface masturbation is something beautiful for me which I want to experience. But deep down it is a burden. Every time that I give in I feel guilty, even though no one ever forbade me to do it. It seems to me that Wrage's book should have taken care of any possible guilt feelings, but nevertheless they are there. Where do they come from?

You asked me to tell you what my absorbing interests or hobbies are. But I can't seem to think of any. Everything interests me to a certain degree, but nothing especially. This is also reflected in my school achievement record. Perhaps herein lies the root of my problem?

I guess my letter is long enough now. I hope you can understand what I am trying to say. Thank you for listening.

November 4

Dear Ilona,

We agree with you: The fact that you are not completely taken up or absorbed by any field of interest certainly might have something to do with your problem. Because of this a vacuum is created which you try to fill.

Yes, it is your sexual desire which you try to satisfy, but you do it in a very immature way. This is why you never succeed in being really satisfied. You see, sexuality is language. It is supposed to be a means of communication, addressed to another person. It wants to talk.

But instead you direct it toward yourself. In this way you hinder the process of becoming mature. The desire calls out into an empty room and only silence answers. So it calls out again and again until it becomes an expression of your being alone with yourself—not words directed to another, but mere lust directed toward oneself. It is this lack of communication[5] which you sense when asking, "Is not sexual desire something more than this?"

Your heart remains unsatisfied. It longs for a relationship. A relationship, however, is never established through masturbation. On the other hand, as long as you had a relationship with Martin, the temptation was gone. Also when you helped conduct that camp and discovered new abilities, your desire was stilled—but on a different level.

By the way, the only time when you mentioned in your letter that you had fun was at this camp. Having fun is probably the best weapon (tool) against your so-called being "stuck in a rut." You should allow yourself to have fun much more often.

Since your mother was so strict, you probably did not have enough fun in your childhood. Undoubtedly she meant well, and yet she appeared to you as someone who forced her will upon you without warmth and without giving you the feeling of being loved—which is the heart's desire of every child.

Could it be that for you masturbation became a way of solving this conflict? It gave you a chance to achieve some kind of satisfaction without needing your mother. Unconsciously perhaps in this way you wanted to prove to yourself your independence and freedom. What do you think? Are we feeling our way here in the right direction?

In any case it is a fact that for girls masturbation has something to do with the mother-relationship. The more a girl senses her mother as unfriendly, cool, distant, maybe even egocentric, the more frequent will be her temptation to masturbate.[6]

The relationship to the father is also important for the sexual development of the daughter, but it will affect more her sexual experience in marriage. Above all else a father must give his daughter the feeling that she can rely on him. By the way, he does not create this feeling by letting her do whatever she feels like doing, but rather by being strict and by giving her clear directions. Even if she rebels, the feeling remains: My father cares for me; I can rely upon him. Later on then in marriage, it will not be difficult to trust her husband, to believe that he is reliable, which is important for her sexual fulfillment.[7]

But you see, the relationship to your father is not destroyed. It has simply not yet been developed. And the relationship to your mother could certainly be improved. We feel that all these possibilities are still open in your situation. They are like marble blocks in the workshop of a sculptor, just waiting to be chiseled.

When others write to us about masturbation, they are often the only child in a family or have lost either their father or mother, or maybe both. Often they are persons without a real home, with few friends, and they may also lack the ability to make contact easily with others. Here it is much more difficult to help, although there are often unused possibilities.

You seem to us, however, to be rather an outgoing person who finds it easy to make contact with others. You have parents who love you, brothers and sisters, girl friends—and even a very close one. In addition to this you have a group of friends with whom you can have fun!

So we would say, by all means be with your friends as often as you can, go to your youth group, sing in your choir out of a full heart and do the things you really like to do. Can you play an instrument? Do you have a favorite game? How about a visit to a good play or movie? What about sports? Ballroom dancing?

And if your mother asks you whether you have time or money to do these things, then you say, "Not only can I afford to do them, I have to do them if I want to achieve my best in school." Prove to your mother that you are independent in this positive way, by this fruitful contradiction instead of masturbating.

Don't you think you could have a good talk with your mother and say, "Mom, why couldn't I sometimes be in charge of the cooking and baking? Or take over the household for a weekend?" That would be a creative way to achieve this wonderful feeling of independence.

And your father! After all you have one and he loves you! Can't you take the initiative and give him a hug and kiss when he comes home from a business trip? Would you consider it out of the way to tell him, "I like it when you stroke my hair?" or "Why don't you come and tell me good night as you did when I was small?" Maybe he needs some encouragement and waits secretly for a hint.

And then there are your brothers. They can probably help you the most to overcome your self-consciousness in the presence of guys. This self-consciousness is, by the way, very natural and normal— just as it is natural and normal to be affectionate with your girl friend. In order that you can understand these feelings better, we would like to explain this a little bit more.

All of us go through three phases in our development—one when we are in love with ourselves, another when we feel more drawn to the same sex and a third when we become capable of the difficult encounter with the other sex.

We go through the first phase before the age of five and we enter it again at the beginning of puberty.[8] The experience of "falling in love" or of "having a crush" is typical for this phase. We actually project our own image onto the other one and seek ourselves in him or her. In the moment we realize that the other one is different, we are disappointed and the crush is over just as quickly as it came.

Something like that probably happened in your relationship with Martin. You didn't really love him, but you were in love with being loved. Though you enjoyed his embraces and kisses, basically you were in love with yourself. This is why this phase is also called the autoerotic phase. *Autos* is the Greek word for "self." *Eros* is a Greek word for "love."

Masturbation is the physical expression of the autoerotic phase. When you masturbate you say: I am still immature. I am still in this first phase. (By the way, we would prefer to simply say m. from now on in our correspondence. This may be of help to you in case our correspondence falls in the hands of someone else.)

The autoerotic phase is followed by the homoerotic phase. *Homos* means "same." It refers to the time of the deep boy-to-boy and girl-to-girl friendships. This has nothing to do with homosexuality. It is healthy and necessary to pass through this phase. It is an in-between phase. On the one hand, we are able to direct our feelings to a "stranger," to someone who is not "myself," and yet we are not mature enough to direct them to a representative of the other sex. The purpose of these friendships is to learn how to handle love feelings without expressing them through sexual actions. To have such love feelings is normal. To transfer them into sexual activity is not normal.

This is why, at the moment, your girl friend is probably the most important person for you. You don't need to be afraid to hug and kiss each other. The more consciously you pass through the second phase, the sooner you will leave the first one and become better prepared for the third one.

In our day many young people jump over the second phase completely. Actually, as far as their attitude goes, they are still in the first phase, seeking and loving themselves although they enter into sexual activities which involve the other sex. Their feelings are not directed toward the other one, but they use the other one for their own satisfaction. Deep petting, which you call correctly a sort of mutual masturbation, is a typical expression of this situation. It is a heterosexual activity in an autoerotic attitude.

The danger is that a person remains somewhat in this autoerotic attitude even in marriage, and as a result he or she never reaches the maturity which is necessary for the encounter with the other sex, for entering the heteroerotic phase. (*Heteros* is the Greek word for "other," "different.")

Encounter with the other sex is difficult. It takes maturity to face the otherliness of the other one, to relate to someone who is so "strange," so different. Of course we are frightened by it, but it is a natural, normal fear. It takes maturity to overcome it. I believe that in our time the tendency to efface the differences between the sexes even in outward appearance is motivated by this fear. One feels inadequate to love someone who is different.

You participate in this fear when you are self-conscious around boys. It is a fear which corresponds with your present development. You are not yet able to overcome it, although probably because you have brothers you have it easier than girls who don't. For the present you must simply accept yourself with this self-consciousness, which is also a protection—and wait.

Somehow all three phases are to be found in you at the moment. The last one is beginning already to open up. You should now consciously enjoy the second one. You should gradually leave the first one behind. If you get dependent upon m. it means that you remain in the autoerotic phase, and this can be called a "development failure." You grow from phase to phase by learning how to endure sexual tension without transferring it immediately into pleasure. The more you learn to stand up under tension, the more energy you set free in order to become mature.

This is an art, Ilona, and it takes work to learn it. This is what we meant when we said that we have to "work together." It takes work to develop will power, endurance and perseverance which you will need in order to overcome the childish and egotistical desire for pleasure. The goal is not to repress your desire or deny it as if it would not be there. No, you should admit to yourself, "I now have this desire." And then, consciously, you renounce the satisfaction of it in order to gain a much deeper satisfaction than you would have by giving in. Do you understand the difference between repressing and renouncing?

You ask where the inexplicable feeling of guilt comes from. (Strangely enough, non-Christians have it as well as Christians.) I think one reason is that deep down every person knows somehow that sexuality is given to us for the purpose of communication and that m. does not correspond to this purpose.

The other reason for the guilt feeling comes from an inner voice which says: You did have the possibility of standing up under tension—for example, when doing your homework—but you chose the cheap way out, the way of least resistance. This gives you the feeling of a cop-out, a defeat. The guilt feeling says: You hinder yourself in your own maturing process.

Giving up instead of giving in is the harder way. Giving up is also very much out of date. On the contrary, the tendency of our time is to consume, to gain pleasure, to reduce tension and to avoid suffering. This is why our time is so immature, so autistic and egocentric and why the relationships between the sexes have become such a problem both inside of and outside of marriage.

So we ask nothing less of you than to swim against the stream. We also know that in the final analysis nothing will help you but the certainty: I am able to renounce the satisfaction of a desire if I want to. I am no longer dependent upon it. Neither am I defenseless against the feeling of being stuck in a rut. I am no longer imprisoned by my ego.

You ask whether you can help Martin. You have helped him already by not pretending to have feelings which you do not have and by not playing with him. He has to learn how to live with the pain of lover's grief; this will make him grow.

Growth is very often connected with pain, Ilona. We wish you the strength to face this pain and not to run away from it. By the way growth and pain are a part of marriage also. To illustrate this fact we are sending you our book *I Married You.* If you know the goal, you can find the way.

November 11

Dear Mr. and Mrs. T.,

Thank you so much for your letter and especially for the book. It gave me a new vision for my own future marriage. What I liked best was the description of your own difficulties. I think I'm beginning to understand what you mean by "growing through pain" and the difficulties encountered through the "otherliness of the other one."

By the way, your last letter caused a small clash between my mother and me. She had of course noticed the package with the book and also your letters, and wanted to know what it was all about. Of course I could not tell her, and the tension that resulted was almost more than I could bear. It made me realize once again how dependent on my mother I still am.

Yes, I think you are probably correct that m. is partly defiance against my mother, an escape into something which belongs to me alone. It's really interesting that you mentioned cooking and baking in your letter.

This is exactly what my mother never allowed me to do. At best I was accepted as her helper but never entrusted with any real responsibility.

Fortunately my mother did not open your letter. If she had, she would have certainly hit the ceiling and thought that I am not quite normal. (By the way, I still have difficulty with this term: Is m. normal or is it not? Please clarify.) Finally my father saved the situation, and I ended up having a good talk with both my parents. They understand now that I need to share my personal problems with someone outside of the family, and my mother suddenly remembered that she had done the same when she was my age.

My father was especially nice and even took me in his arms, all on his own accord! This assured me how much he loves me. Actually the distance between us has diminished, and there is even a positive side to it which I now see. Because he sees my everyday life through different eyes, it helps me to be more objective. Yes, he can be "strict" all right, but I like that. What do girls do who have no father?

What I have to tell you now is hard for me. For the first time since we began corresponding, m. has happened again. It was last Friday. I was so mad at myself that I repeated it three times. I did not even try to resist because I had no strength.

Yes, the difference between "repression" and "renunciation" makes sense to me. Renunciation stems from a completely different attitude. I can also understand that when I am able to renounce it and then give in anyway, guilt results.

But you would have to agree that there are also situations in which I am unable to renounce. The desire is so strong that I have no choice. If I would continue to resist, the tension would become unbearable and I would toss around all night. In such cases I think m. is necessary for release of tension.

I feel that the first reason you gave—that I don't use my sex drive for communication—is a better explanation for the guilt I feel. Your second reason—the inability to renounce—doesn't make me feel so guilty. Perhaps I am immature. Okay, I admit that. But is immaturity guilt? I feel that m. is then at least an honest expression of my immaturity. So in a way I feel guilty and not guilty at the same time. Do you follow me?

When I read your letter, I got the idea to read the tiger story again in your book *I Loved a Girl.*[9] I read it first a while ago, but I think that I understand its true meaning now for the first time.

When the keeper kept the tiger locked up because he was afraid of him, that was an act of "suppression," wasn't it? But then the tiger roared and gave no rest, and finally, in an unguarded moment, attacked. This is exactly what happens when the desire for m. possesses me.

However, when the keeper allowed the tiger to enter his most beautiful rooms and when he looked him straight in the eye without fear, the tiger became his friend and lay down at his feet.

As yet I have not succeeded in making friends with my sex drive. Therefore I am not yet able to master it and to renounce it.

But I would like to learn this, and as an attempt in that direction I have decided to give up m. until Christmas. I want to prove to myself that I am not dependent on it. I remember once that I made a similar promise to myself, and then was terribly disappointed when I broke it. But at that time I did not have your support. I want you to know how precious your support and encouragement is to me.

By the way, while reading *I Loved a Girl,* I came across the passage where you counsel François concerning m. and tell him to find new and fruitful channels for his desire. Do guys have the same difficulties with m. as girls?

No, sorry, I don't have a real hobby, and I'm not good in sports either. Formerly I enjoyed playing the flute. But because of school pressures, I gave it up. Since I finished my dance course, I have not danced either. I am a difficult case, am I not? But I am so thankful that I got to know you before it was too late. God seems to love me in spite of everything!

November 17

Dear Ilona,

We are glad that your parents understand that you want to correspond with us and that they respect your privacy. Children very rarely open up to their own parents with their intimate problems. It is wonderful that your father took you in his arms.

Yes, girls who grow up without a father or who have a cold, rather passive father certainly do find life more difficult. Very often they are looking for a substitute for the lack of fatherly tenderness in their relationship with a fellow. The young men, of course, misunderstand such a girl's need for tenderness and love, and think that all she wants is sex. This misunderstanding is often the reason for the "too-soon" sexual experiences. In any case, girls without a father are more tempted to premarital adventures. Needless to say such adventures end in disappointment every time because the girl does not find what she is looking for.

It is possible, however, to replace a father, to have a father- substitute, while it is almost impossible to replace a mother.

You ask about the word *normal.*[10] What we wanted to say is that m. is a typical behavior, which corresponds to the immature stage of the autoerotic phase. It is a typical expression of this phase but should not continue beyond it.

The word *normal* is not used here in the sense of a "required norm." Otherwise all those who do not masturbate would not be normal, and one estimates that at least forty per cent of all girls do not masturbate. They are, of course, as normal as all others.[11]

You ask about boys—whether they have the same difficulties. In general m. is more frequent among boys than among girls. The reason is that it is harder for boys to master their sex drive during the time of puberty. Mainly this is because of biological reasons and has to do with the hormones which the body begins to produce during this period of life. You see, no one is only man or only woman. Men have female hormones and women have male hormones. During puberty there is an almost equal balance of these hormones in the girl's body. Later on the female hormones get the upper hand and she becomes a young woman. But as long as the balance exists, male and female hormones could be said to "neutralize" each other. Therefore it is relatively easier for the girl to handle her sexual desires than it is for the boy during this period of development.[12]

With boys there is no such balance. The male hormones outnumber the female hormones considerably. Their sexual desire is therefore more impetuous and thus it may be more difficult for them to live in peace with it. This is why almost all boys pass through a period of masturbation, which they use as a means of releasing tension. They often discover it in connection with their so-called "wet dreams" at night, nature's way of taking care of the overproduction of semen. It has been our experience that boys get started easier with masturbating, but it is also easier for them to stop.

Why this is we don't exactly know. One reason is certainly a physical one: A boy loses something when he masturbates, a precious substance of his body. He cannot do it repeatedly because for him there is a physical borderline. To do it three times in a row, as you wrote, is hardly possible for a boy. That is why the danger of becoming dependent upon it is relatively greater for a girl.

We can well understand what you mean by "honesty": the acceptance of your own immaturity which makes you think you must still masturbate. We would like to add that this "honesty" must also include the honest wish to outgrow this stage of immaturity which does not use the sex drive as it is meant to be used.

On the other hand, we think it is an excellent idea to distinguish between necessary and unnecessary m. The word *necessary* comes from the Latin word *ne,* which means "not," and *cedere* which means "to give way." Agreed, there may still be situations for you in which "m. does not give way," does not yield and when it becomes inevitable or "necessary." But you have honestly to admit that this is not always the case. There are certainly other situations when m. could give way and when it is avoidable. Our suggestion would be, for the time being, to set yourself a preliminary goal; in other words, to avoid m. when it is avoidable.

If the pressure is unbearable and you indeed have "no choice," all right. Then, in this stage of your development, you may have to be "honestly immature" and give in. However, if actually there is no sexual pressure and if it is only a cowardly escape from a disliked activity, then it is certainly avoidable and you have no excuse to give in. If you succeed in refraining from m. when it is not really necessary and when it is avoidable because there are other ways of dealing with these feelings of frustration, we think that you will soon get the good feeling of making progress.

Only you can judge when m. is avoidable and when it is not. We are not your judges. It is very difficult to give any general rules about dealing with m. because sexual pressure is for some people stronger than for others. Some, including many girls, would say that they do not even know situations where m. would be necessary. Others may need this emergency release more often or for a longer period of time. This is why one has to deal with each person differently and in a way you have to become your own "therapist."

May we ask you, How did you yourself feel about your experience of last Friday?

Yes, Ilona, God loves you. Unconditionally and without limit. You have to cling to this fact without doubting. We are happy if our letters can become for you a small out ward sign of this love. But in the final analysis you stand alone before God in this experience of being loved, exactly as you stand alone before God in the experience of being guilty. He alone is judge. It is up to you, not up to us, to decide when and whether you have become guilty before the God who loves you.

November 24

Dear Mrs. T.,

Today I want to write to you personally because it is easier for me to write to a woman about something very intimate.

First of all, thank you for the preliminary goal you set for me. I know that it's only a step toward the ultimate goal, but having in sight a milestone that can be reached helps reduce my fear of being overcome by the compulsion to give in to m. I know now: I *may* give in, if it is really necessary. I am sure that this knowledge alone and the freedom from fear will help tremendously to diminish m's grip on me. I also realize that the crutch of this permission does not yet represent the final stage of maturity, but at least it helps me relax a bit and not be so apprehensive.

Therefore again: Thank you that for the time being I only have to work on eliminating the avoidable, unnecessary m.

In retrospect I would analyze my behavior on that Friday as follows:

I was mad at m. because it was dominating me—and I was mad at myself that I would allow myself to be so enslaved. I could have slapped my face! And I did by repeating m. I punished the tiger in myself and myself in the tiger. That's the way I see it now.

I realize that the repetition was absolutely unnecessary, and I am ashamed of it before God. In that moment, however, it was as if I were possessed. This makes me very much aware of how closely I walk along the abyss of dependency, yes, almost to the point of addiction, and how quickly I relapse into that state.

Therefore I can only be relieved and thankful that since that Friday when I did it so often, m. has not happened again. And that was already three weeks ago! Since summer vacation I haven't been able to go for such a long period of time without m. The temptation is still there, but somehow I have the strength not to give in, and I am even able to resist the temptation to tell myself that it is "necessary" when it really isn't.

After a hard test the other day, I "rewarded" myself in the afternoon. Not by m. as I would formerly have done, but by something better: I read a book which I had been burning to read for mere pleasure and entertainment. Result: The avoidable m. was avoided.

But now to my question: Recently I had a dream about m. I woke up and realized that I had to go to the toilet. I remember distinctly now that when I was thirteen or fourteen I discovered that when I held back my urine, a very pleasant sensation resulted. It is the same now. Is there a connection?

And something else: Sometimes I sort of envy boys who, to put it quite frankly, are able to play with their penis. Do you understand what I mean? To accept my own sexuality, the specifics of my gender, is for me still an unfinished task.

There is also an aching question I have about what it means to be a wife and mother. Why should one have children when they will only cause trouble later on? And frankly, the dull and monotonous routine of a housewife doesn't interest me much.

The man has both his home and children *and* his profession and outside interests. The married woman, for many years of her life, has practically no choice. She is bound to the home and her children. As you can see, the role of the woman is still very unclear to me. Or am

I too egotistic? Do I love myself too much?

"If you know the goal, you can find the way," you wrote me once. You talked about becoming a woman and you talked about marriage. You implied that m. could possibly hinder me from becoming a woman. Somehow I feel that you are right, though I can't explain why. In spite of your reassurance in your first letter, I can't help but worry that m. might already have had a negative effect on my future marriage. You did not exclude this possibility entirely. Maybe you could deal with this question again.

As your husband said in your last letter, you want me to cling to the fact that God loves me. Yes, gradually my eyes have begun to open, and I see how rich my life is. I really shouldn't need m. for consolation. I think I have to work harder on accepting my life as it is, and also on accepting myself.

Every day anew I must consciously remind myself that I am "somebody" and that I have been entrusted with special gifts and abilities. But above all I am "somebody" before God.

This morning God spoke to me through Isaiah 43:4. Even though this verse is directed towards Israel, it was as if God spoke to me in a very personal way: "You are precious in my eyes, and honored, and I love you." I think that this is a tremendous statement, and I find it very comforting.

I am enclosing a snapshot of myself so that you can "picture" me better.

November 27

Dear Ilona,

Your good letter—from woman to woman—arrived yesterday. Since I have to leave on a trip tomorrow I want to answer it right away. Otherwise you might have to wait for some time.

First of all, I'd like to congratulate you on getting along without m. for such a long time. Also that you thought in a creative way of a reward. By the way, I doubt that m. is ever "necessary" in the deepest sense of the word. It may be an in-between solution which helps release pressure and reduce tension, but I think it is much more "necessary" to learn how to stand up under pressure and how to live with tension.

There we are again on our topic of becoming mature and becoming a woman. It is just this which is "necessary"—not m. In this context it might be helpful for you if you start living consciously with your cycle.

Now to answer your questions: Yes, there is a connection between that band of muscle which holds back the urine and the sexual pleasure which a woman feels in the vagina.

This muscle is called the pubococcygeus muscle. The nerve endings in the muscle reach the vagina. If this muscle is weak and underdeveloped, it can be a reason why some women have difficulty finding sexual fulfillment in marriage. I have explained this in detail in my book *The Joy of Being a Woman.* I only wish that many girls would read this book before marriage.[13]

But before you can become a wife, you have to become a woman. You can become a woman without becoming a wife, but not the other way around. Yes, if you know the goal, you can find the way. Your first goal therefore is to become a woman, not to get married. You don't even know yet whether you will get married some day. This is an open question. But the goal of becoming a woman you must reach in any case.

The first goal is to accept yourself as a young woman and to live your gender. I agree with you that there is still something lacking at this point. It is interesting to me that in the snapshot of yourself you sent me in order for me to "picture" you better you are wearing jeans.

I have nothing against pants. I like to wear them myself and in many ways they are more practical than skirts and certainly warmer in cold weather. But if you feel more "yourself" when wearing pants, I wonder whether it could be an expression of the fact that you have not yet completely accepted yourself as a woman. Be honest—wouldn't you sometimes really prefer to be a boy?

This leads us to the "penis envy" you spoke of in your letter. Here too you are very "normal." Sigmund Freud built a whole theory about the development of female sexuality upon this envy. I certainly don't believe today that it is as important as he was led to believe it was fifty and more years ago. However, there is some truth in it. The day will come, Ilona, when you will realize that you do not have something less than a man so that you feel inferior, deprived or "castrated." On the contrary, you have something more: the possibility of a sexual experience which the man does not have.

This brings us back to the pubococcygeus muscle. Indeed there is a strange connection between this muscle and the self- acceptance of a woman. As long as your "beautiful feeling" is related to the clitoris alone, you are actually still in the area of a masculine experience of sexual pleasure. Physically speaking, the clitoris resembles the penis, though much smaller, and it would have become a penis had you been born a boy. Seeing it from this point of view, m. could be a sign that you have not yet fully accepted your gender. If m. becomes a habit, self-acceptance as a woman will become more and more difficult.

In comparison with a man, a woman's sexual feeling in the vagina is richer and more fulfilling. You must believe me, even though you cannot yet experience it. It is an experience which basically can take place only in the shelteredness of a good marriage as one of the fruits of mutual trust and love with the partner to whom one is united for life.

Personally I feel strongly that it is one of the privileges of womanhood to be able to carry and give birth to a child. My life has certainly not become poorer, but infinitely richer, through these children.

You think that the routine of a housewife is dull and monotonous. It depends on how you look at it. I feel it takes all the qualities of a superexecutive to face up to the challenge of being a wife and mother. It calls for every bit of creativity she can muster. Perhaps because I had a very satisfying career before marriage, I see it differently than a woman who has not had this experience. I can only say that never have I felt more fulfilled than when I could fulfill the needs of my husband and children.

I don't think that you love yourself too much, Ilona. Rather I don't think you love yourself enough.

I must close now in order to prepare for my trip tomorrow. If you write during my absence, my husband will answer your letter.

November 27

Dear Mr. and Mrs. T.,

Sorry. M. has happened again. I gave in again, just when I was so happy that I had seemingly overcome it. I guess I was just too sure of myself. I thought I had defeated the tiger, and I neglected to keep my eyes on him.

Since I went to bed very late last night, I decided to take a nap today after lunch. I should not have done that, because shortly before I fell asleep I already sensed that m. was hanging in the air. Then when the alarm clock rang, it indeed happened again.

And I had done so well during the last three weeks! I had really experienced the strength to overcome m., and I am sure that this strength was from God. But when the actual moment of temptation came, where was this strength?

I don't know where to go from here. I am just where I was at the beginning. I broke my promise to wait until Christmas. Can I really begin again after all that? I am afraid that I shall never be rid of m.

I am writing you this letter immediately after it happened and I shall mail it right away. I would like to do the same in the future. Forcing myself to write it to you may help me to stop. Will you permit me to use you as a "dumping place"? I shall feel unburdened when this letter is in the mail box.

I did not dare to mail this letter yesterday. I was too ashamed—and still am. What will you answer me?

You will probably ask me whether m. was avoidable or not. To be honest I must say yes. It could have been avoided had I gotten up immediately after my nap. But at that moment I simply did not want to renounce m.

I must admit that I always feel guilty afterwards, even if it was "necessary." But I don't remind myself of that beforehand. No, before it happens I don't think about feeling guilty.

Is m. a sin? Do I have to repent for m.? In which way does one repent? In your letter of November 17, you said that it is up to me to judge whether or not I am guilty when I give in to m. But I am not sure. I can't say one way or the other.

I am forcing myself now to send this letter.

November 29

Dear Ilona,

Don't be sad! I'm not at all surprised that you were not able to keep your promise. As for me, I would never have asked for such a promise from you, because the attempt to set a time limit usually fails. But it was your own idea and I didn't want to suggest otherwise. I wanted you to try.

The length of the intervals between your experiences of m. must develop more or less naturally, without chin-ups or forced effort. You should rejoice in the progress you have made instead of concentrating on your failures.

I would like to repeat, Ilona, you *may* masturbate as long as it is necessary. There is no reason why you should be afraid—afraid of m., afraid of my reaction, afraid that you will never become free from it. Fear is your greatest enemy. Remember the example of looking into the headlights of the car at night?

It is a little bit like skiing. You certainly are allowed to fall down. In fact it is a part of the learning process until the skier masters the slope. Of course no one aims to fall down and it is to be avoided if possible. But one knows: I *may* fall if it is necessary. The less the fear of falling, the less likely it is to happen.

If, in spite of everything, a good skier can't help falling down, he doesn't take it too seriously. He doesn't sit in the snow, feeling sorry for himself and becoming depressed. Rather, he gets up, brushes himself off and continues on his way. The next time he takes the slope, he will try to do it without falling down. If, however, the skier throws himself into the snow on purpose three times in a row just because he's angry and frustrated that he fell down in the first place and to prove he can't ski and will never learn, then he becomes guilty for he impedes growth.

This brings us to your difficult question concerning guilt. For the first time in your letters, you used the word *sin.* I have avoided it purposely up until now, because sin means more than guilt. It opens up a new dimension—that of man's relationship to God. A person who doesn't believe in God can still feel guilty before others and himself. But sin implies guilt before God. When you ask whether m. is a sin, you are asking whether m. disturbs the personal relationship between a person and God.

I would like to share something with you which has become clear to me, not only through our correspondence but through my reading and correspondence with others: M. seems to take a unique place when it comes to sexual behavior—unique in three respects.

First, one can talk and write about almost anything today without anyone being embarrassed or feeling uncomfortable: about adultery, extramarital or premarital sex, abortion, homosexuality and every conceivable perversion. Some may even boast about participating in such activities. But a peculiar veil of embarrassment, uneasiness and uncomfortableness is spread over the subject of masturbation.

Second, and I believe I have already mentioned this, masturbation is the only sexual behavior as far as girls are concerned (and probably also for boys) that is affected by the mother-child relationship.

Third, recent studies in America have called attention to the fact that no other sexual behavior is so closely connected with a person's religion and relationship to God.[14] The feeling of guilt that appears after the act has been done, although it wasn't present beforehand, simply cannot be explained on a rational, purely psychological basis. A voice from an outside source speaks.

"Where do I find strength in such a moment?" you ask. The strength lies in the ability to hear this voice and to recognize the tiger ready to spring when m. is "hanging in the air." This takes practice, however. The more you mature, the more you will acquire this ability; the more you acquire this ability, the more you will mature.

December 1

Dear Mr. T.,

Thank you so much for the "ski letter" and also that you wrote immediately. Your letter comforted me and was a challenge at the same time. It means that I have to decide myself whether m. is sin for me—or at least whether it is always sin for me. Yet I am still unable to do so.

In the meantime your wife's letter of November 27 arrived, crossing with my "ski accident" letter of the same day. Her letter confused me completely and made me reconsider whether or not I really want to give up m. I feel that I simply must write you immediately concerning my doubts and confusion.

In a way your wife's letter could also be an answer to my question concerning guilt. If one continues to follow a path even though he knows that it will not lead to the desired destination, one certainly becomes guilty. Of course, "If one knows the goal, one can find the way." Or to put it in my own words, "Unless one is sure of the destination, he is unable to choose the route to get there."

And this is where my problem comes: Since I read your wife's letter, I am no longer sure of my destination. Marriage does not appeal to me as such an attractive goal as your wife describes it.

My parents do love each other, but the example of marriage they have given me is rather sad. If I found marriage to be an attractive and worthwhile goal for my life, everything would be easier and I would have the strength and will power to give up m. But this is not the case, and therefore I vacillate between this distant and questionable goal and my sex drive.

Even if marriage is as beautiful as your wife describes it, the question torments me: What does that mean then if I never do get married?

If I knew for sure that I would someday marry, it would be easier to renounce m. for the present in anticipation of something better later on. But what if there is no "later on"?

Suppose I become a nun or join a community of unmarried women or for any other reason never get married: What will happen to my sexuality? How can I sacrifice something for a future which may possibly never come? Do you understand what I mean?

Your wife herself advised me not to set marriage as my exclusive and ultimate goal. That means that my renunciation may not only be temporary but permanent. The thought of "forever" simply drains me. It's not that I lack the strength to resist but that I simply lack the desire.

I tell myself, "Even though m. is only a poor substitute for the real thing, it is at least something—especially considering the possibility that I may never experience the real thing, the "fulfillment" your wife speaks about. I know good and well that the meaning of life is greater than sexuality—and still I cannot deny these thoughts. They are there and I have to face them.

If becoming a woman is supposed to be my goal, is it possible to become a woman without practicing sex? Yes, now I have it—this is indeed my basic and crucial question.

I thank you in advance for the answer you will send me. I hope it will be an answer which not only enables me to give up m. but which also makes me willing to give it up.

I must tell you frankly that I just did it again today, intentionally and rather defiantly. I am not willing to give it up, and I did not want to repress it. I am being completely honest with you.

And yet it is strange: I did it consciously, willingly and without any guilt feelings. Nevertheless I have to admit that I am not at peace with myself. It is exactly as you described it— unexplainable.

The only plausible explanation seems to be that m. for me is an expression of the fact that I have not yet fully accepted myself. Your wife is right—I have a problem with self- acceptance. This thought preoccupies my mind more and more.

However, as far as self-love is concerned, your wife's letter confused me here also. In your first letter you wrote that I should not rotate so much around my own self, and later on you challenged me to outgrow the autoerotic phase. Now your wife writes that I don't love myself enough. Do I love myself too much or too little? Is m. a symptom of one or the other? And what does your wife mean when she says that I should learn "to live consciously with my cycle"?

Sorry that this has become such a problematic letter.

December 13

Dear Ilona,

So you have fallen short of your goal! I am thankful that you have spoken so openly, but at the same time I rather dread answering your letter. You ask very difficult questions that deal with the basic fabric of life. There are no easy answers.

Just suppose for a moment that you will never marry. Does that mean you must deny your sexuality your whole life long? The answer is NO. This is impossible to do because your sexuality is you. You are your sexuality. That which you have to renounce is not your sexuality but only one form of its expression—the genital expression.

Can you still be a woman without this specific form of expression? The answer is YES. Let us go back to your example of nuns or a community of unmarried women. In their lives too their sexuality is a part of their being. Single people are able to radiate a special quality of sexuality when they have learned to be fulfilled men and women—

maybe just because they have renounced its genital expression.

Becoming mature, becoming complete men and women, is therefore the goal for unmarried people as well. *Unmarried* often has a negative connotation, implying an unfulfilled state. That's why I prefer the word *single,* which carries with it a sense of "freedom." Single people are free from being bound to someone else, free from being dependent upon a mate, free from marriage and the restrictions it brings. *Unmarried* then has the positive meaning of "unrestricted."

Married people, on the other hand, are "unfree" in the sense that they are tied down to their spouse and family. Try to look at singleness from this angle too. Maybe then you will not be so frightened of it.

The responsibility of becoming complete men and women belongs to married and single people alike. When a single woman has achieved this goal, then she can pour out her whole self—her femininity, her motherliness, her ability to devote herself to others (in other words, her sexuality)—into her work and calling. The fulfillment which she receives from doing this would cause her to burst out laughing if someone were to suggest that perhaps she should masturbate so that she would "at least have something." She has so channeled her sexuality into serving others that the renouncing of its genital expression is no effort for her but is experienced as a gift and joy.

In order for you to better understand what I mean, may I remind you of something we have already written you? Sexuality is language, it is communication, it is relationship; it reaches out its hand, it seeks to touch other's lives, it is ready to give. That is its meaning and that is what makes sexuality human.

The single person may also learn its language, although he or she will choose another vocabulary to express this language than the married person. Through m., however, sexuality misses its target. Basically that is why m. is an unworthy or inhuman expression of sexuality and precisely not "at least something." It divides a person in two, for he must play two incompatible roles simultaneously—that of the stimulus giver and stimulus receiver.[15]

M. is not language, it is silence—mute isolation. No communication, no relationship emerges from it. The person speaks to no one and gives to no one; he only takes something for himself.

There is no gain in this form of taking. The person takes something for himself which he desires and fears will be withheld from him. It is just by doing this though that he takes something *from* himself; he loses something, namely the ability to give himself to another.

Renouncing something may be difficult if you think of not getting something you want. But is it so difficult to renounce losing something, depriving yourself of something?

Once you can say to yourself: I am able to renounce, I can give up depriving myself, I no longer have to live under the compulsion of continually taking away something from myself—then you will discover a new inner joy and sense of freedom.

Ilona, I really want to help you gain this inner joy. I am wondering if we could not find another "training ground" for practicing "renouncement." The Bible calls renouncing *fasting.* A person fasts from something that is allowed, not from something that is forbidden. In renouncing the allowable, you acquire the ability to renounce the forbidden. Is there some area in your life in which you would be willing to "hold a fast"?

In your first letter you mentioned your eating habits. Overeating, as well as smoking, often may be a substitute form of masturbation. Here is the connection: You eat in order to fill a love need. But you would be happier if you ate less. The same is true with m. You try to love yourself through m., but you would love yourself more without m.

You ask whether you love yourself too much or too little? I think you do both at the same time. We must distinguish here between two different forms of self-love. One type of self-love is self-centered and egotistic. The other form of self-love is found in the person who has accepted himself, found himself, and therefore is able to let go of himself and give himself to others. The first type of self-love is innate, but the second type of self-love must be acquired. It is this type of self-love that Jesus referred to when he said, "Love your neighbor *as yourself.*"[16]

I would say that you love yourself too much when you think of the first type of self-love and not enough when you think of the second type. Both are evident through m.

When my wife wrote that "you should live in harmony with your cycle," she was trying to help you develop this second type of self-love;

the love and acceptance of your self as a woman. This is your goal. But she can explain better herself what she means by this statement. She will return home tomorrow.

For today, I'd just like to add this word: Start all over again, Ilona, and don't give up!

December 15

Dear Ilona,

I have just returned from my trip and I would like to answer your question right away. When I suggested that you learn to live more in harmony with your menstrual cycle, I meant that you should be aware of the process of ovulation.

Perhaps you have noticed that on certain days of the month you have a feeling of wetness at the vaginal opening. This is called cervical mucus and has nothing to do with menstrual bleeding since it begins usually a few days after menstruation. It is a sign that the time of ovulation is approaching and lasts mostly from four to six days. As it becomes more plentiful, it also becomes stretchy and clear in appearance, much like raw egg white. Some women also experience a sharp pain in the lower abdomen around the time of ovulation. It is also possible to pinpoint the time of ovulation by taking your waking temperature every morning. After ovulation, that is, after the ovum has left the ovary (usually 12-

14 days *before* the next menstruation) the basal body temperature rises a little and remains on this higher level until shortly before menstruation.[17]

You may realize that your mood changes after ovulation has taken place. Women are often more optimistic and "together" in the first part of the cycle, while in the second part they may become more easily discouraged and "down." You may also observe that your sexual desire is stronger perhaps just before menstruation. Then you can be inwardly prepared and the "tiger" cannot easily overcome you.

The knowledge of the cycle is indispensable for marriage and one of its best preparations. But even if you don't get married, this self-observance is a decisive help in learning self-acceptance and the right kind of self-love. This is why I believe that girls should begin in their teens "to live consciously with their cycle."

I hope you are satisfied with my husband's answers to your difficult questions. I am glad he answered them, for I know I couldn't have done it that well. You see, there is sometimes an advantage also in not being single. . . .

God wants to start anew with you—and that is why you also can start anew.

I'm praying for you, Ilona.

Easter

Dear Mr. and Mrs. T.,

Four months have passed since I wrote you last. Your last letter was a decisive help for me. Thank you for setting me straight again. My goal is again clear.

After I read your last letter, I sat down quietly and did some thinking about myself. I said to myself, "You are not a little girl anymore. And you want to become a young woman. There must be a way to achieve this goal." Now I understand why, from the very beginning, you did not address me as a child, but as an adult. You talked to the adult in me, and this helped me to regain my self-respect.

I came to the following conclusion: As long as I am dependent upon m. it is, without any doubt, a sin for me.

It was a happy coincidence that on the same afternoon I had to prepare a Christmas devotion about the following verse:

He has anointed me to preach the Good News to the poor,

He has sent me to proclaim liberty to the captives,
And recovery of sight to the blind,
To set free the oppressed,
To announce the year when the Lord will save his people.
(Luke 4:18-19, *Good News for Modern Man)*

When I tried to apply this verse to my own life, it was as if scales fell from my eyes, and it suddenly struck me how I myself am a captive. If I wish to tell others that Jesus can help us concretely in our everyday life, then I must also expect him to reach down and help me in my own specific situation and captivity. Again my goal was clear.

On the same afternoon a book fell into my hand with the title *Ten Great Freedoms.* In this book the author, Ernst Lange, commented on the commandment, "You shall not commit adultery." He said, "You don't need to indulge sexually— either by telling dirty stories, daydream ing and fantasizing, masturbating, or by abusing others for your own satisfaction. Don't deprive yourself of the joys of real love through the handling of the counterfeits of love. I, the almighty God, am the author of true happiness, and I desire only the best for you. You can afford to wait for the partner whom I shall send you."[18]

Thinking of your letter, I added in my heart, "You can afford to allow yourself time to grow into full womanhood."

On that afternoon God spoke to me as clearly as if we were standing face to face. But I did not repeat my mistake of setting an unrealistic goal again. I knew that if m. was absolutely necessary, I was allowed to do it. That reduced my fear and anxiety. Therefore, since November 27, it has not happened even once. Today, it is really Easter for me!

In the meantime, I have graduated from high school. The concentrated studies for my finals was also a help for me. Besides that, I made use of the other helps which you suggested—renunciation and self-observation.

In order to practice what it means to renounce, I decided voluntarily to give up eating sweets, except for dessert, when I was invited for dinner and felt it would be impolite to refuse. When I received sweets as a present, I gave them to someone else. It was really difficult, but it helped me to learn a basic attitude which has helped in controlling m.

Whether there is a connection between m. and my menstrual cycle,

I am unable to say for sure. I believe that the last two times m. happened, it was eight or nine days before menstruation. It is not even necessary for me to take my temperature to discern when I ovulate. I am able to tell from the other symptoms such as the cervical mucus and the midpain. I am keeping records and have started to live in harmony with my sexuality instead of fighting it.

Finally I want to tell you about my friendship with Arndt. He is twenty-three and from Amsterdam. We met during a special course and seemed to like each other from the very beginning. We had many good, open talks about spiritual problems and also about our relationship. We agreed from the beginning to keep the physical expression to a minimum.

On the last day, however, we kissed in spite of this. I guess the pain of separation was the main motive. I told him frankly that I could not fully back up this action with my feelings for him. We decided to continue our relationship in such frankness with each other and before God.

By the way, Martin suddenly appeared the other day on my doorstep and asked how I was doing. He caught me by surprise indeed. I still remember how disappointed I was when I broke up with him and he completely accepted it without even trying to object. Now I am equally surprised to see him again. How should I interpret this? How should I react now that Arndt is also in the picture? I am so unsure of myself in such matters. Maybe it is because I went to a girls' school. . . .

And now something stupid: I sometimes worry that I might lose you when m. is overcome. May I continue to write to you anyway?

May 5

Dear Ilona,

I don't think we need to say how happy we were to receive your letter. We must admit we were rather uneasy because you had not written to us for such a long time. On the other hand, we felt that we should not impose ourselves upon you and so we quietly endured this time of silence. That is why your letter made us doubly thankful, and we can sense the joy which you feel. You have taken a giant step forward, Ilona. You have found yourself. As Søren Kierkegaard says, "The way to yourself is the most difficult way of all."

No, you will not lose us. We are united with each other by more than just this problem. We have reflected a lot about your decision to sit down, meditate and then consciously assert your will as an ally in your struggle. We think that in our day, will power is made use of much too seldom and that the will is underestimated as a force in resistance.[19]

The simplest explanation for Martin's visit to you is that he is a young man. At his age neither a declaration of love or a decision to give up a girl are as deeply rooted for him as they would be for a girl. You shouldn't attach too much importance to his visit but neither should you underrate it. Our advice would be for you simply to keep in contact with him on a friendly, natural basis, but at the same time let him know that you have other fellows as friends. This includes Arndt.

What you say about your girls' school is certainly right. But there is also a positive side to it. Often the process of growth and maturity is not hindered as much as in a coeducational school when the fire of a love relationship can be experienced too early.

As you know, we lived in Africa for many years. During our years in the savannah where there were only a few scattered trees, we often wondered why the trees grew so crooked. Rarely did we see a straight tree trunk. We discovered that the reason for this is that every year during the dry season grass fires are lit in order to clear the ground. Of course this disturbed the growth of the trees year by year. You have been spared such disturbances in your life.

We are very happy to hear that you can live consciously with your cycle. You will see that this is certainly a great help in growing up straight.

June 10

Dear Mr. and Mrs. T.,

How right you were concerning Martin! Everything is just as you felt it would be. He called me up once, and then last Sunday he made a formal farewell visit. But this was meant for the whole family.

My correspondence with Arndt continues to be good. We have discovered many things we have in common. But we don't know yet where it is going to lead us. The next step we see is simply that we try to get to know each other better through corresponding and hopefully by meeting each other again one day.

One thing has confused me, however. Arndt wrote that when he thinks about me, his sexual tension increases to the point where he has to masturbate in order to find release. Well, I was a little bit shocked that he shared that with me, also considering that he touched on my problem, without knowing it of course. On the other hand I was happy that he had so much confidence in me to speak openly. How should I react? Can I, as a girl, help him with his problem? I decided not to react at all for the time being.

This brings up the topic of m. again. I have another very important question about it. (I hope that this is the last one!) First of all, I am really happy that I am not dependent anymore upon m., that I am no longer a captive. And I want to thank you again for your patience with me and your understanding.

But now to my question: At the beginning of this week, I suddenly felt such a joy about my body as I have never felt before. I think that I am succeeding more and more in accepting my sexuality, not only mentally but with my feelings too. In this state of mind the desire for m. returned. It came from a completely different source than formerly. It wasn't a surprise attack from outside but a deep longing from inside.

Is it possible that my "beautiful feeling" can also be an expression of the joy I feel about my own body? Or would I just cheat myself and become a captive again?

Yes, I was able to resist. I have learned this by now. But there is still the nagging question: Is m. always sin?

It was and is clear for me that m. is sin for me as long as I am captive to it. But if I am not any longer captive? If I am free? Do I have the liberty to grant myself this beautiful feeling—to "treat myself" to it as to a nice trip, a visit to the theater or a dinner by candlelight? To be sure, it would be rarely—only as something very special. I don't think that that would necessarily have to result in dependence and captivity.

I admit that it would still not be using the gift of sex as a form of communication or expression of deep commitment to another person. I also admit that it would be a superficial experience and remain on the surface. But does one always have to live like a frogman diving into deep water?

Please, don't get angry about these questions! But if you are, then please include this next question under your reasons to be angry. You wrote once that you also correspond with others about m. Am I being too intrusive to ask how others solve the problem? Do they also suffer from daydreams with sexual fantasies? Why doesn't God deliver me from them?

I remember a dream I had one night. I dreamt that I was a man and that I was about to marry my girl friend. Just as we went to pick up the marriage license, I saw my first boy friend whom I knew from dance school. Suddenly I was a girl again, and I leaned happily against him.

What is going on inside of me? Around this same time I had a deep longing for a boy friend or a girl friend who would really understand me. Perhaps that had some influence on my dream.

June 21

Dear Ilona,

No, we certainly are not angry or annoyed by your questions. Instead we feel rather helpless. Regardless of what we answer to your question, it could be wrong. If we say no absolutely and thus deny you the liberty of a special gratification to yourself, then we put you under the law and this we have tried to avoid from the beginning. If we say yes and give you a green light, then it's like telling you to walk on a tightrope where you risk falling down.

We have talked about your letter for a long time. To be honest, it's the first time we are not completely in agreement. Ingrid tends, for love's sake, to say no. She thinks the danger of self-deception is too great. She also cannot imagine that m. would be as "beautiful" as say, a trip, a concert or a dinner by candlelight.

As for me, I would be ready, also for love's sake, to give a more daring answer. I would trust you to discern between a harmless gratification and becoming captive to something which also could disturb your relationship to God. Ingrid feels that this would be putting too great a burden on you, and since she feels this strongly as a woman, I don't want to argue her point.

Your question concerning experiences which others have made is certainly justified. Thinking of those who have shared with us this problem, I must admit that Ingrid is right. Most of them were unable to make the distinction mentioned above. We are willing to confide to you some ways by which others have handled this problem. However, you must promise us not simply to transfer this to yourself. The main difficulty in finding a solution applicable to everyone is—and I think we have mentioned this already—that sexual pressure is simply different with different people. For some it is easier and for others it is harder to master their sex drive. Also the same person may find it easier or harder depending upon different situations and different stages of life. Those who find it harder are certainly not inferior people, let alone inferior Christians.

The only general experience which we have observed is that no one is really happy with m., even those who think of it as something harmless or even positive. Not only are most of them unhappy, but they also suffer.

We know people who became free completely through the experience of confession and absolution and through a new surrender to Christ. From that day on m. belonged for them to the past.

Others we know whom God guided patiently through a longer way of gradual overcoming. We think, for example, of a twenty-two-year-old girl, for whom m. had become a habit ever since childhood so that she was unable to fall asleep without it. She had to take it like a sleeping pill and suffered very much, repeating it sometimes even during the day.

It would not have helped her if we had tried to convince her that there was nothing wrong with it. She felt base, inferior and dirty. We worked first of all with her on the prolongation of the intervals while at the same time we tackled her problem of loneliness. When she could abstain from it every other day, she got the feeling that she was making progress. Gradually it became more and more infrequent and today she is completely free from it. But it took almost a year.

If we had promised her at the beginning that Christ would set her free from one day to the next, she probably would have come into a severe spiritual crisis. After a defeat she should have concluded: Even Christ does not help me; therefore there is no hope for me.

Of course she had to fight also with her fantasies. We advised her not to deny these thoughts and suppress them—not to put the tiger in the cellar, for then he roars at night. If you try to throw these imaginations out the front door, then they come back in again through the back door. We told her to simply admit to herself that she had these thoughts and then learn to accept herself *with* them—to say to herself: I am a person who has such ideas. This was for her the first step toward healing.

During a certain period of time it also helped her to jot the thoughts and imagined scenes down on a piece of paper so that they were not any more within her, but she could look at them objectively outside of her. She burned the notes afterwards or put them in an envelope and mailed them to us so that they were disposed of. At first this happened almost daily, but after a while it ceased completely.

Today she is not entirely free from such fantasies—no one is—but she does not feel threatened by them anymore. She has learned to smile at them—scornfully and disdainfully—and in this way they have lost their power over her.

There is one thing that the devil can't stand, Ilona, and that is humor. As long as we take our problems so deadly serious, we become an easy prey for him.

The real danger of fantasizing is that it may become a necessity in order to get "turned on." Later on in marriage one may be unable then to really encounter one's partner because his reality does not correspond with these fantasies. Also our imaginations may drive us into action against our better judgment.[20]

We are enclosing an article by Mary Stewart, an American psychologist. It might interest you because she also shares her personal experiences with fantasies.[21]

We wonder whether this article might also help Arndt. It was certainly wise not to react when he shared his problems with you. No, at your age, you definitely cannot help a fellow with this problem. It is also very difficult to help someone spiritually in depth when you are in love with that person. You could ask him if he would like to write to us, but in no case should you share your own struggles in the sexual realm with him. We think that if you simply keep silent, he will sense that he has overstepped the borderline beyond which sharing is unwholesome—at least in the present stage of your relationship.

Your dream means simply that there is still an overlapping of the homoerotic and the heteroerotic phases and that you still are in search of your own identity as a girl. Both of us doubt very much whether allowing yourself m. would help you in this search.

But now let us take another case. A young man training for a business career was a passionate cello player. When he had to prepare for his final exams, he decided to give up his daily cello playing. At the same time he started to masturbate. We told him simply to start playing his cello again and m. stopped immediately.

Another boy fought valiantly, but on rare occasions he had to give in. Because of these few times he left condemned, perverse and dirty, and he tortured himself with self-reproaches. In this case I told him, "Just do it if you have to. You are neither condemned, nor perverse nor dirty because of it." Years later he wrote to me that after I had told him that he never did it again. It had lost the attraction of things forbidden. Of course we might not have given this advice to someone else because this same advice could have been completely wrong to someone in a different situation.

Another young man, a Christian, called m. the "smaller evil" and justified it as a protection for his fiancée and their relationship to each other. We did not contradict him. In his last letter he said that this form of release became less and less necessary the more his love for his fiancée grew.

Widows, above all young widows, are in a class by themselves. It is especially hard for them to live in peace with their sexuality because it is fully awakened, and they are still attached with their whole heart to their beloved spouse. Sometimes it is a help for them to allow m. once during a cycle when the pressure is especially strong. This is usually the case just before menstruation. They do not think that this is an ideal solution, but it helps them to live without fear and in peace with themselves. For them it is not simply an autoerotic act because they think of their deceased husband. Again this is not the solution for everyone.

Recently a seventy-year-old widow wrote to us: "After the death of my husband I frequently had erotic dreams which sometimes caused such tension that I had pain. My gynecologist advised me to masturbate. I told her that for me m. would be sin or at least something which destroys my self-respect. She replied that I should think of the many women who are forced to live singly all their lives. This statement on her part made my opinion a little shaky."

We could only answer her that we know people who are neither bothered in their conscience nor in their relationship to God when they achieve release by m. as an emergency measure. We do not judge these people and accept the fact that they may have this liberty before God. Without any doubt this emergency masturbation is something different than a regular habit or an addiction-like dependency. It is also something different from what you speak of when you "allow yourself a gratification."

We also know people who simply declare that every time they give in to m. their relationship to God is destroyed, even if they do it in an emergency situation. For them the only help is a personal assurance of forgiveness and a new beginning in God's strength.

You see, Ilona, how difficult the answer to your question is. Everyone has to decide here for himself. No one is allowed to judge the other one and no one can decide for him. If you want to walk on the tightrope, you have to take the responsibility for yourself. We are not the lords of your conscience. It is the Holy Spirit who alone has to tell you in each situation whether you can have a good conscience or not.

We walk beside you with trepidation, but we let you go, prayerfully, into the freedom of maturity.

July 15

Dear Mr. and Mrs. T.,

I wish your last letter could have been the last one you had to send me. What a glorious conclusion to our correspondence! Ilona, the valiant and pious, has solved her problem! She can at last be released into the "freedom of maturity."

Oh no, she cannot!

I have just produced myself the best evidence that m. is and always will be sin for me. Yesterday afternoon it happened again—twice or even three times. No doubt you will be shocked and disappointed when I tell you that I don't even know anymore how often it happened.

Well, when I sat down this afternoon to think about it, all I could remember about yesterday was the terrific emotional rebellion I felt. Using psychological terms, you would probably call it "feelings of aggression." I've been trying to analyze them to get to the root of the problem. *Why* did I backslide?

On the surface there are several things that could account for it. Pressure from school made me realize that I had a lot of studying to do, and I was frustrated that I could not quickly grasp what I had to learn and that studying was so difficult for me.

Besides that, I felt a certain conflict of interests: My mother was outside working in the garden, and I wanted to help her because I knew it was too much for her. On the other hand, I had to study if I did not want to fall behind in my courses and receive bad marks.

Studying at the university is so new for me and so different from what I am used to. In high school I knew all the teachers, their individual methods of testing and grading, and I felt "at home" in the system. Now I find it difficult to develop a new style of studying where I am completely responsible for organizing my time and keeping up in all the different subjects.

I also think that sexual tension had been built up through looking at some film advertisements which I saw in town. "Brutish" is what I always think when I see such pictures, but nevertheless, I stop and look at them.

All of these outside pressures and inside feelings resulted in tension which I tried to release in m. For me, m. always derives from sadness, never from happiness. But so far, I have just touched the surface of the problem.

On a deeper level it had to do with Arndt. I had told him, as you advised me, to turn to you with his "personal problems" as I termed them. But he didn't do it directly. He sent the letter for you in an open envelope to me and asked me to forward it. I read it. I shouldn't have done that. I understand now what you meant when you wrote that I, as a girl at my age, cannot help a fellow with this problem. I am now enclosing Arndt's letter which I couldn't get off my mind. And in thinking about it m. tightened its grip on me.

But on the deepest level my bout with m. had something to do with my relationship to God. For quite a long time I have not read my Bible regularly and therefore my communication with God has been superficial. I have not been seeking his will for me, and I haven't been expecting him to speak to me through the Word of the Bible. God has seemed so distant and my prayers so empty.

The practical and visible expression of this inner situation was that I stopped practicing renouncing—not only sweets but other things as well. I simply have to admit that in behaving like this, I gave m. the opportunity to overpower me.

This is the first time I have really understood Genesis 4:7. The Revised Standard Version renders this rather dark verse, "If you do well, will you not be accepted? And if you do not do well, sin is crouching at the door; its desire is for you, but you must master it."

I would paraphrase it this way: "If you do well, Ilona, that is, if you are in contact with God, aren't you accepted then by God and doesn't that mean that you are able to accept yourself, and therefore master yourself and your desires? But if you do not do well, that is, if you are not in contact with God, then you open the door for sin. It is always crouching at the door, but only then you are vulnerable and feel its desire. Only then the tiger jumps and you can't master him any longer."

I just read the verse again and discovered that in the previous verse God asks Cain, "Why are you angry?"

Yes: Why was I angry?

That is the basic question. Not *that* I was angry at myself and the whole world around me. Rather *why* I was angry points toward my sin. My only answer is that I was out of touch with God.

There is no longer any doubt about it: M. is for me primarily an expression of a lack of communication with God, and therefore sin. Maybe it's different for other people. Then they will have to deal with it differently. But as far as my own life is concerned, m. is sin.

If I question this, it is the beginning of the end of my resistance. It is exactly as in the story of the Fall in Genesis 3 when the serpent tempted Eve by saying, "Did God say . . . ?"

Before it happens, I say that m. is not sin for me. Afterwards I realize: If m. were not sin for me, I would do it every time I felt like it and I would become totally dependent on it.

Without the knowledge that it is sin, when I let m. happen I am in danger and unable to put a stop to it. I can only resist when this question is settled once and for all. I keep praying for another word that makes it crystal clear that it is sin for me.

I can also conclude this from the fact that I had to do it not only once but twice and even a third time. No, there doesn't exist for me—or in any case, not any longer—the case that it is "necessary." If it were really nothing more than a necessary release from tension, then why couldn't I stop after one time? Why would I have to repeat it?

It is exactly the same when it comes to sweets. When I have vowed not to eat any sweets for a day and then I do in spite of my decision, I eat a great deal. I guess I become defiant and feel that since I've already broken my promise, I might as well really "live it up."

The same thing happens with m. I tell myself that I'll never be able to be a victorious Christian. I convince myself that I've already lost the battle, so I might as well give up. When I analyze my thoughts and feelings objectively, I realize that I create my own vulnerability.

Conclusion: When I open the door, I am overcome at once. No, I do not believe that I am capable of walking a tightrope. I would fall down immediately, as I just did.

This morning I read in Bonhoeffer's book *Living Together* the chapter on confession. I think that it would be really good for me to have such a cleansing talk with both of you just because it is harder for me to talk than to write. Therefore I would like to make the formal request for such a talk. Would it be possible to come and see you? I pray that I may be completely honest and not hold back anything out of shame.

So far you have never offered me such a talk, even though I sort of expected it. Your last letter helped me understand why: You did not want to give me the false expectation that confession would be like a magic wand solving all problems at once.

This letter contains my deepest thoughts, and it is in fact already a confession. All I have written I brought in prayer to my Lord last night. I simply cling to his word: "He who comes to me I will not cast out."

Father, thank you that I can come to you with all my guilt, not because my feelings tell me so, but because I know from your Word that you are faithful. Even when I am not faithful, you are. Thank you that you allow me to cast the burden of m. upon you and that I don't need to carry it with me all the coming days. Thank you that your grace is greater than my heart, and therefore I can ask you, "Lord, forgive me!" Thank you that you gave me the strength to write this letter.

July 24

Dear Ilona,

That was a great and profound letter! It showed us again that in the last count we are the ones who are being blessed through our correspondence with you.

We are relieved that you do not believe yourself capable of walking a tightrope. However, we are also happy that we did not forbid you outright to try. God himself has spoken to you, and that's why you must obey him and not us.

A thorough, cleansing talk is certainly a good place to begin. The time is ripe for you to take this step and we are very happy that we shall at last meet you face to face. We certainly cannot say that we have to "get acquainted" with you because we know you through your letters much better than we know many a person whom we meet every day.

We are especially glad that you want to come, even though you feel that such a talk is harder on you than writing to us. It is just for this reason that a personal confession is more helpful for many people than confessing alone to God or making a general confession in the church. However, it's not right to make a law about this and say that one can only experience forgiveness when confessing to God in the presence of a brother or sister in Christ. A confessional talk is not necessary for salvation, but it often gives assurance of salvation. You see, the important thing is not the confession of sins but the pronouncement of forgiveness.

Arndt's letter is an indication of the confidence he feels in you. Otherwise he would have sealed his letter before enclosing it. But this openness on his part doesn't help you, as you say yourself. Neither could you help him if you were to write him about your own sexual problems. We do understand, though, what he wanted to tell you. The following phrases are meant especially for you.

"Up till now no one has ever noticed my inner life. How much I would wish for this in order to be freed from m."

This is a cry for help, directed to you. We understand too, now, why from the beginning he didn't want to build your relationship upon the physical level. He is hoping that you will help him turn away from the physical to what he calls the "inner life." Somehow a boy needs a girl in order to make this change of direction.

That's why you wouldn't help him if you were to encourage a physical relationship with him out of pity or as a means of "therapy." We do not have the impression, though, that this is your intention. But we wanted at least to mention it, because some people think that intercourse is a remedy for m. On the contrary, we believe that it would hinder Arndt from becoming a man who has learned to handle his sexuality—to say nothing of other problems which would come up and bring you both in a still greater conflict with your conscience.

The questions which you asked us at one time about the sexual difficulties of a young man have now been answered by a very concrete example. You can see, as with yourself, that the lack of contact with one's parents plays an important role. Arndt's contact with his father is not even mentioned. The contact with his mother is mentioned only in a negative sense because she, as a doctor, was more occupied with her profession than with her children. We were deeply moved by his sentence: "She left me as I was. Certainly I loved her, but I could not show her my love."

Since Arndt did not ask any questions, no one spoke with him. That's why his first nocturnal emissions (wet dreams) gave him a shock—just as the first menstruation would to a girl who was not expecting it. His classmate in boarding school, who introduced him to masturbation, had an easy job, especially since Arndt never received praise from his teachers and therefore sought refuge in this comfort substitute.

His letter, by the way, can also clarify for you why it is harder for a young man to master his sexuality than it is for a girl. At a certain stage in his development, m. is less avoidable for him than for a girl. Girls often have no idea what they do to young men when they turn them on sexually.

You can also see from his letter how unsure a boy is of himself and how much more boys are afraid of girls than the other way around. During a certain period in his life Arndt felt so base and sinful that he didn't even dare approach a girl. It was a big step for him when he opened up to you.

In conclusion we would like to quote these lines from Arndt's letter, because they sound like a preparation for our talk: "When I was sitting in church after confession, I felt God very close to me, even within me. This feeling never came back again. . . . How much I would like to know again his touch and experience the magnificent consciousness of being a virgin!"

When will you come?

September 5

Dear Mr. and Mrs. T.,

Actually I had intended to call you last night to tell you how thankful I am for everything you have given me. But it is too difficult to express this on the phone, and that is why I am writing you. Thank you for taking time for me and for all the love you have given me.

The verse stands on my desk: "He that has clean hands grows stronger and stronger" (Job 17:9). It has become "my" verse; it shall guide me from now on, and I will always remember it when it seems that God is far away from me.

I had often wondered what it was like to repent. Now I know. It is something wonderful. To have such a conversation with God in front of witnesses can have a powerful effect on one's everyday life. It *is* power, in every sense of the word. God's forgiveness has been given to me—if I may put it this way—not as something self-evident that automatically follows sin but as a help which encourages one on the way. I received the deep assurance that Jesus also died for me. Everything which still needed to be straightened out with my parents and brothers and sisters has been done, and I have also asked them for forgiveness.

I am especially thankful for the fact that I was able to get to know you, Ingrid. Simply through your being, through the peace and joy that you radiate, I caught a glimpse of what it means to accept one's self, without reserve, as a woman. Now I am more sure than ever that self-acceptance is the decisive key in solving the problem of m.

I am beginning to understand what it means "to let the tiger into the living room." When I am involved in doing something now, I often remind myself that I am involved as a *woman,* with all the strength and beauty that my sex carries with it. I finally realize the difference between genital activity on the one hand and self-acceptance and involvement as a sexual being on the other.

The essay by Mary Stewart which you enclosed was a great help to me. I reread it again on the train. I was especially struck by the sentence, "I wanted God's Spirit more than I wanted physical titillation." I had to ask myself, "Ilona, which do you desire more?"

I also found helpful the author's discussion of her sexual daydreams and how she learned to entrust them to God. I can directly relate to this because when sexual desire becomes very strong (which generally occurs the week before I have my menstruation), I daydream a lot. I also want to give these fantasies to God so that I will be able to say, "I desired all things that I might enjoy life. God gave me life that I might enjoy all things."

However, I find it difficult to identify with Mary Stewart on one point. She experienced a clear turning point in her life. She said, "*Before* I got to know Christ I felt fear, loneliness, etc. . . . *Afterwards* it was totally different—and as I did not want to lose this, I changed my behavior."

But I never experienced such a turning point. Actually, I can't ever remember life *without* God. For me there have only been progressing stages, marked by milestones—such as my cleansing talk with you. But it seems to be a very gradual growth process for me, one with lots of valleys. Sometimes I am reminded of a wheel; one spot is always touching the earth (hitting a low point) before it continues on its way up and around. The only other option is, of course, for the wheel to remain motionless.

I know, however, that it is ridiculous to compare my walk with God with someone else's. God deals with each of us in a unique and personal way. I remember what you said during our conversation: "God doesn't build prefabricated houses that all look the same. There are no carbon copies in God's kingdom."

When I returned home, I found a letter awaiting me from Arndt. He is pressing me for a more decisive commitment. He says it is impossible for him to wait four years without having more assurance about the outcome of our relationship. He desires more than just a friendship and wants to come and talk things over.

I do not think that this is a good idea. It is premature—like picking a fruit before it is ripe. I need time to grow and find myself before I can make any binding decisions. I also want to finish my studies, and I will just have to explain all of this to him.

I am going to ask him not to consider me as his "girl friend" but rather as a friend. I think it is possible to have companions and friends of the opposite sex, just as we do of the same sex. Sure, this is also "walking a tightrope," but I think I can handle this one. In the meantime, you know that I have turned nineteen and I think that it's about time to grow up.

Of course, my heart still longs for a deeper relationship that gives comfort and security. But just a few days ago I found a card with the following text. The words of encouragement will help me to endure the tension and longing I feel. I will also send this verse to Arndt: "Only the things you can wait for are really important."

Postlude—a dialogue with the reader

Frankly, we would be happy if all of your questions were answered by now. We would like to think that you have found enough practical hints in this correspondence so that you can find your own way. However, if you find that a very personal question has been left unanswered, you may also write to us.

We are sure that you would still like to know one thing: How did Ilona fare after the last letter published here?

During the following two years our exchange of letters became less frequent. She became more independent and wrote that she would not need m. any more. It was too superficial for her, practically meaningless. She said that she had learned to enjoy deeper feelings and to say yes to her womanhood: "I am happy that I am still free and see so many possibilities to learn and to grow." Discipline in her schedule, she said, was one of her greatest helps. Twice she slipped again as she called it, but that did not hinder her "to keep on living undismayed and cheerful."

When we called her to ask whether she would agree to publishing our correspondence some day—a thought which naturally had never entered her mind—she asked for a day to think it over. Then she wrote,

"If God is so great that he can even use my guilt and failures to help others, I can only—gratefully and trustfully—say yes. The thought that these letters should be my property alone has burdened me already. This is why I am glad that I don't have to keep them for myself and can share them with others. At the same time the publication will be a challenge to me to stick to that which I have experienced as a help and to live that which I recognize as being true."

We ask you to join us in thanking Ilona by interceding for her.

Walter and Ingrid Trobisch

BOOK FIVE

MY PARENTS ARE IMPOSSIBLE

Preface

A girl is speaking here. Through her letters you hear the self-assured and aggressive voice of the oncoming generation of African women.

Elsie first wrote to me as a reader of my book, *I Loved a Girl* (Harper & Row, New York; Lutterworth Press, London). Of the many letters which I have received as an echo to this book, Elsie's are among the outstanding ones.

In accordance with her wishes, I shall not disclose her name or her home country in Africa. I have even changed a little the story of her life in order to make identification impossible. But be careful, she may live not too far away from you!

It has become very clear to me through the correspondence with Elsie just how important the relationship is between a daughter and her father. It has a deep meaning, not only for the individual family, but for society as a whole—yes, for the future of the African continent.

May the publication of this correspondence reveal to the reader one of Africa's greatest enemies: patriarchalism and its counterpart, the lethal silence between the generations.

Walter Trobisch

March 15

Dear Rev. T.,

Two days ago I bought your book, *I Loved a Girl.* When I started reading it, I did not want to put it down. I read and read until I was through.

I found your address at the end of the book and now I feel I must write to you.

I got very angry with the old man in your book. It's a shame the way he treated his daughter Cecile—not to allow her to marry the one she loved just because he couldn't pay the bride price. U-u-u-h!

But this is so typical of the older generation. Our fathers haven't understood yet that a new time has come. They block the way to progress.

And in your book, this Pastor Amos is also a coward. It would have been his duty—not yours—to talk to Cecile's father and explain the new ways to him. I know this kind of old-fashioned Christian very well. My father is a church elder and he is just the same. Christianity means for him keeping the old traditions. For me, Christianity means progress—the opening up of a new future for my country.

Old people are the same wherever they are. They all stick together and you bump your head against a wall when you try to change their views.

I am 24 years old and a member of the African Student Association of my country. I studied in Europe for two years, but at present I am teaching at a Secondary School.

Last year, in an effort to help our young generation, we decided to debate the "bride price" (in East Africa it is called "lobola") within the school premises and outside of them. We also distributed pamphlets against it.

The following week we made headlines in the newspapers: "Lobola custom must be abolished."

We didn't even have time to discuss the whole question with the old people. Nevertheless there was a big hubbub among them and we confused them entirely.

Tell Cecile, the girl in your book, that she should go to her father and borrow the amount of money which he is demanding from François. I'm sure he doesn't have that much on hand.

Then she should ask him to loan her at least half of it. If he is not able to give it to her, then she should ask him: "How many years have you lived and worked? How is it possible that you don't have this much money? And if you who are old don't have it, how do you expect François who is still so young to have it?"

If her father doesn't listen to her, she should do as many of the boys in my country do: they pay only part of the bride price and promise to pay the rest after the wedding. Then when the in-laws come to collect the rest, they flatly refuse.

I hate playing dirty tricks, but if people make asses of themselves then I find it necessary to do so too.

Formerly the old people tried to frighten the young couples by saying that the children would be deformed unless the lobola is paid in full. But nowadays we young people are better educated than the older ones and know that this is not true.

One thing I know for sure. The man I am going to marry will not buy me. If my father tries to sell me, I shall disobey him.

Frankly, I am having a hard time readjusting after having been abroad. I am getting quite impatient with my own country. I have the feeling that I have made progress while Africa stands still. As long as it is ruled by the stupid fools of the older generation, it will not move forward.

Well, I am getting off track. I just wanted to help Cecile. Tell me whether she could use my advice.

Sincerely,

(Miss) Elsie S. K.

P. S. I have a very personal question in the realm of sex. But before I share it I would like to know whether this letter reached you and whether you will keep our correspondence confidential.

Elsie's letter impressed me deeply. Girls like Elsie will not accept being pushed around and dominated any longer. Well educated and active, even politically active, they will make an essential contribution to Africa's future.

Elsie called my attention to one of the greatest problems which faces Africa today: the conflict between the generations. But the tone of her letter shocked me. It expresses spite, hostility, almost hatred. I am afraid that in such a spirit and with such an attitude it will be difficult to build a bridge between the generations.

I decided to answer her as follows:

March 29

Dear Miss Elsie S. K.,

Thank you very much for your most interesting letter and especially for your effort to help Cecile.

Let me answer your last question first. Your advice is useless for Cecile. She is unable and unwilling to talk to her father in such a way. Even if she does not agree with him, she still respects him. In Cameroun where she lives and where I also lived for ten years, I can't imagine any girl talking to her father in the way you suggest.

I am not going to argue with you here about the bride price. I've already pointed out its disadvantages in my book which you just read. Still there are two sides to it. It all depends upon the spirit in which the custom is handled. However, as a European, I am not in a very good position to defend an African custom in front of an African girl. All I want to say here is that you have to be careful about generalizations.

This is, I believe, the greatest mistake which you make in your letter—you generalize.

On the "progressive" African ship, the older generation is put into one box and thrown overboard as unnecessary cargo. They are "all the same" in your mind: "stupid fools," "cowards," "asses," a "wall," impossible to talk to and reason with. According to your opinion, all the traditions they hang on to hinder the progress of Africa.

Then you claim Christianity for the side of progress.

But, dear Miss Elsie, let me tell you, it is abusing Christianity to claim it for any human cause. It is abusing Christianity to make it a means towards an end, no matter what the end is, even if it is something good.

I am afraid that one day you will discover that Christianity stands in the way of something which you may judge "progressive" and then you will abandon it altogether. Christianity is then only useful to you as long as it serves your own cause.

But Christianity doesn't stand for either progress or regress. Christianity is essentially a personal relationship to Jesus Christ.

The fruit of this relationship is love. This is best summarized in the commandment: "Love your neighbor as yourself." In your case this means: Love the older generation as much as you love your own younger generation.

To be frank, dear Miss Elsie, I don't find very much of this spirit of love in your letter. Love does three things which you do not do: It does not generalize, it discerns. It does not confuse, it communicates. It does not judge, it understands.

Let me explain this briefly to you.

First of all, love does not generalize, it discerns. Not all African traditions are bad and not everything that strikes you as "progress" in the West is good.

You say that you studied in Europe. The technical accomplishments of an industrialized society impressed you as "progressive." Still not all of this "progress" is for the good. How about the greed for material wealth? The high divorce rate? The confusion in the realm of sexual behaviour? Would you like to transplant that to Africa?

You have to discern. Love discerns. Some African traditions, for example, the high appreciation of virginity in many tribes, are much closer to Christian standards than the so-called "free sex" which is advocated in Europe and America today.

Where is progress? Where is regress? The answer is that progress is where love reigns.

I could imagine that the free choice of the marriage partner for selfish reasons is indeed "regress," while the gift of lobola, given as a sign of appreciation for the girl and a token of gratefulness to her parents may be "progress."

It is the motive which is important. Therefore the borderline between progress and regress does not run between Europe and Africa, or between the older and younger generation, but it runs straight through every human heart, between selfishness and unselfishness, love and the lack of love.

Generalizations lead to prejudices ("The old are stupid"—"The young are immature"—"Blacks are lazy"—"Whites are arrogant"—"Germans are cruel"—"Arabs are tricky"—"Americans are superficial") and prejudices lead to hostility. Hostility will create more hostility, trickery more trickery, dishonesty more dishonesty. Generalizations never come out of love. Love discerns.

Secondly, love does not confuse, it communicates.

As a teacher you have to teach your students things which are new to them. You have to discern between those who learn fast and those who learn slowly. Especially with the latter group you must try to communicate patiently in order to get across what you think is of value for them. Why do you treat your children differently from their parents?

You accuse Pastor Amos in my book of being a coward because "he did not explain to Cecile's father the new ways." Are you any different?

Love communicates. As long as you do not take "time to reason with the old people" and as long as you let them have their "hubbub within them selves," you will not make progress.

Communication, however, does not only mean talking. It also means listening and understanding. This leads to my third point.

Love does not judge, it understands.

Someone has said, "Those who want to be understood should not marry. The important thing is to understand." Isn't this true too about the relationship between the generations? You complain of not being understood. Have you ever tried to understand?

The secret of marriage is that man and wife remain two different persons who have to struggle day by day to deepen their mutual understanding. Yet they become "one flesh." In the same way, the two generations will remain different—and yet they are "one flesh" in a very real sense as parents and children. Therefore the word which Jesus spoke about marriage could also apply to the generations, "What God has joined together, let no man put asunder."

Putting as you do one whole generation into one box labeled "stupid" means putting old and young asunder. Love tears off the label, rips open the box, discerns, communicates and understands.

Of course you may write to me about your personal sex problem. You can be sure that your letter will be treated confidentially. Neither shall I quote or publish anything you say unless you are in agreement.

May I also ask you a personal question today? You are so concerned and give such good advice to Cecile about talking to her father. How about your relationship with your own father? Can you talk to him and listen to him? Do you love him?

April 10

Dear Rev. Father,

Thank you so much for your letter of March 29th. I didn't expect you to take time to write such a long letter to me. It made me think quite a bit, especially since we didn't achieve much with our "attack."

You touched a sore spot with your personal question. There is simply no communication between me and my father—neither good nor bad.

I can't remember that I ever had a personal talk with him. I haven't lived at home, except during vacation, since I left for high school at the age of 12. My father has never written to me, not even when I studied abroad.

I guess you are right. We put each other into a "box" with a "label" on it.

At present my family lives about 200 miles from where I teach. I write home once a month, but I never get an answer. When I come home, we greet each other and say good-bye. But in between there is nothing, just a big yawning gap.

I am lonesome. I have nobody to talk to. When I read your book, it was as if you were talking to me. That's why I wrote to you.

I guess the fact that I studied abroad makes my lonesomeness still more acute. The young men of my age are either already married or they are not as educated as I am and therefore we have little in common.

My students have basically the same problem and they come to me with questions for which I have no answer.

The girls often complain that because of tradition they are not allowed to go out on dates, to the movies and such things. How can they know whether the man who asks to marry them is good or bad? Where can they get acquainted? Where could they go?

In the small town where I teach, the church is strictly against any meeting between boys and girls. They are not even allowed to talk to each other. Often the Sunday service begins with a warning along that line. The other day the pastor said to the girls: "If a boy has written a letter to you, return it to him and tell him not to write to you anymore."

One of my students told me that his girl friend was there and since then he has not heard from her. I am afraid that when the church does this, it scares the young people away instead of attracting them. I am sure, too, that my own father who is a church elder would be wholeheartedly in agreement with our local pastor here.

What could I do to help my students? In such a situation, what does "progress by love" mean? Sometimes I get tired of hanging between two generations and two cultures.

The letter was typed up to this point. Then in handwriting the following lines were added:

I cannot tell you how hard it is to share with you my personal problem. Because I am so ashamed of it, I have never talked about it to anyone. But I guess I have to. I see no other way out. I know I never would tell anyone who lives close to me.

The thing is, that while I was abroad, I acquired the habit of masturbation. I discovered it accidentally, but in spite of struggling against it and even praying about it, I cannot get rid of it.

Is it a sickness? Is it dangerous? Is it a sin?

It was interesting for me to learn that the "yawning gap" between the two generations as Elsie described it in her first letter reflected her own family situation too. What she had experienced at home, she had practiced in public.

Where can one start to bridge the gap between the generations if not within the family?

If such a lack of communication reigns within a Christian home—what can be expected from non-Christian homes?

It is quite possible that even Elsie's sexual problem had something to do with the lack of relationship to her own father. How strange that she gave Cecile such "good" advice, but she herself was not able to talk to her own father!

April 26

Dear Miss Elsie,

Thank you for sharing with me your problems, your own as well as those of your students. I realize how hard it must be to "hang in between." But often God places us in a difficult situation in order to challenge us and to entrust us with a task.

Just because you have lived in both cultures you have a unique position from which you can make a real contribution to the building of bridges. Therefore instead of sighing and developing self-pity, you should look at your "hanging in between" as an opportunity for service.

The question of suitable meeting places for young people is a real problem in Africa. Rarely are movies of good quality and even then there's not much chance of getting acquainted in a movie house. Then comes what you call "such things." Most parents are afraid of these places and with good reason. Soon I will have five teen-agers of my own and as their father I share certain fears with the parents of your students.

Whenever I met a young married couple on my trips through different African countries, I always asked them where they first met. Often the answer was that they had met in a home. Mostly it was not at the home of their own parents, but at the home of a married girl friend of the wife or a married boy friend of the husband. They had been invited there together with other people and had met for the first time.

Later when their acquaintance deepened, they used the same home as a meeting place. The parents of the girl, knowing the couple who owned the home, weren't suspicious and had no objections when their daughter went there.

The purpose of a worship service is, of course, not the meeting between the sexes. In this point I agree entirely with your pastor. Still, as long as society does not provide suitable opportunity for such meetings, I believe that the Christian congregation has a task to fulfill here in its place. This is not only true about Africa, but about America and Europe as well.

Wouldn't it be a worthwhile project for the young couples' group in our Christian congregations to open their homes to the young people and offer fellowship to them?

I believe that even you, as an unmarried but mature teacher, could do that. Why don't you invite a group of your students, both boys and girls, into your home once in a while? Then you can entertain them and play games with them. I am sure their parents would have no objections and you would help them to solve one of their greatest problems.

This is what I would call "progress by love" in your situation.

Concerning your problem of not being able to meet a young man "on your own level," I would like to ask you: Is education everything? Is it essential for a happy marriage?

I agree that it would certainly be a big step for an African man to marry a girl who has more education than he has. But couldn't just that be a sign of love and confidence?

It is not your education but your attitude towards your education which isolates you and makes you lonesome.

This lonesomeness is also the root of your sexual problem. Masturbation is a symptom, not a sickness. Your sickness is lonesomeness and self-pity. Masturbation is the result of it.

All efforts to fight the symptom will be in vain unless you attack the sickness at the same time. Everything that frees you from your lonesomeness and isolation will be wholesome for you and have a healing effect.

In this case, praying against it often does not help just because you are thinking about it while praying and thus the temptation grows. It is like looking into the lights of an oncoming car because you are afraid you will run into it. Unless you look elsewhere, you certainly will.

No, Elsie, it is not "dangerous," unless it becomes a mania or addiction, an everyday must. In this case it has to be treated by a psychiatrist, just as any other addiction, for example, drinking, must be treated.

As long as it happens just once in a while, more or less as an accident, it is certainly not dangerous. Most boys discover it by play and during the time of puberty it is for them a sort of emergency release. Usually they overcome this immature stage when they grow older and especially when they fall deeply in love with a girl.

For girls it is more often a means of comfort when they feel lonesome, left in the lurch or not understood. This is probably true in your case. Of course, it is a false comfort, not a real one.

Whether it is a sin depends much more upon the thoughts and imaginations that go with it rather than upon the act itself. In any case, I would say it is a mistake. It means using something in a solitary way which is meant for communication.

Could it be possible that there is a connection between this practice and your lack of communication with the older generation, especially with your father? Even with young men of your age and maybe also with your students.

Maybe the house parties which I proposed for your students are not only a help for them, but also for you. Everything that takes you away from yourself, any effort you make to help others will also help you with the problem of masturbation.

During the next five months many letters went back and forth between Elsie and myself which I cannot record here. It is important to remember this. Otherwise the development of her character, the changing of her attitudes and also the deepening of our relationship cannot be fully understood and may sound artificial.

Elsie accepted my advice about giving house parties for the students of her school and found much satisfaction in it. The parents of her students were very grateful to her and the students themselves very enthusiastic. Soon they preferred to meet in her home rather than in the street, in movie theaters or bars.

A new confidence developed between her and her students which also changed the atmosphere in the classroom. One of her unmarried colleagues who taught at the same school helped her with these parties and soon offered his home too.

Though Elsie never said anything, I read between the lines in her letters that she seemed to have a deep liking for this young teacher. The students started to call both of them "school parents."

The pastor of the town attended such a party once and was so impressed that he decided to open his home too and to ask some of the young married couples in his congregation to do the same thing.

While Elsie engaged in these activities, her problem of "m"—as we called masturbation between us—became less and less acute. The greatest help for her apparently had been to share it with someone.

One day she wrote: "I feel so close to you. Could you give me permission to call you father?"

It seemed rather strange to me to have a "daughter" of another race, thousands of miles away, whom I had never met and probably never shall meet. I was hesitant too, because I didn't want to wedge myself between her and her own father. But then I thought, maybe I can serve as a temporary bridge between her and her physical father and maybe even between her and her Heavenly Father.

So I gave her permission. This is the letter which followed:

October 7

Dear father T.,

Thank you for your good letter and especially for the permission to call you "father." Now I have a father to whom I can talk. You don't know what this means to me. Since your letter came, "m" did not happen even once. It is as if a knot unties slowly in my soul. Thank you so much, father.

Yesterday we had a student party again in my home. Two of the mothers brought cookies and helped serve tea. Mr. Richard Z., whom I mentioned already in my previous letters, was there too. Yesterday I was especially glad for his help.

First the students danced a bit. Then we played some games. Richard is an expert at that and has a lot of new ideas. Afterwards we opened the "question box."

This is also one of his ideas. He feels that many don't dare to ask personal questions in front of the other students because they are too revealing. So we told the young people they could write their questions on a piece of paper without signing their names and then put them in the question box.

Some questions, however, were really difficult. Maybe you can help us. Because they are still very insecure and embarrassed when they meet, the students want to know: How do you approach a girl? What should you talk about? Should one write letters, and if so, how?

Another group of questions concerns the boy friend-girl friend relationship. What is a "boy friend"? What is a "girl friend"? Can a girl have several boy friends and a boy have several girl friends? How about jealousy? Is it good or bad?

If you have time, father, I would be very thankful to you if you would help your "daughter" answer these questions for your "grandchildren."

What struck me most about this letter was the fact that these questions could have been asked by any youth group in Europe and America, as well as in Africa.

The cultures are approaching each other rapidly. Elsie studied in Europe and so will many of her students. Even those who don't must recognize the fact that the advance of the technical world of the West becomes inescapably Africa's history of today.

The students who ask these questions feel that this process forces them to become individuals as men and women. Therefore they want to meet each other as individuals, as persons. As individuals they want to talk and to write each other and eventually choose and marry each other. They no longer conceive of marriage as an outgrowth of the family, but the family as an outgrowth of marriage.

Only on the surface, however, is this understanding of marriage a result of the so-called "Western thinking." Deep down it is a genuine fruit of the gospel of Jesus Christ, which places each person as an individual before God.

I tried my best to answer their questions:

October 18

Dear "daughter" Elsie,

I am so glad that the "knot" is untying and that the permission to call me "father" helped you to overcome your feeling of lonesomeness to such a degree that it had a healing effect on your sexual problem.

Also your report about the student parties pleases me very much. I am thankful together with you for Richard's help. Let me answer briefly the questions of your students.

The first rule in carrying on a good conversation is to become interested in the other one, to find out about his home, family, brothers and sisters.

From there you can go on and inquire about his special fields of interest. What kind of books does he read? Which subject does he like best in school? Does he already have definite plans for the future?

The third step would be to share sorrows and problems and to seek together the answers to the deeper questions of life.

Advise your young people to talk as little as possible about their own feelings towards each other. The more they discover common interests which lead them beyond themselves, the better it is for the development of a healthy relationship. Such interests may be literature or music, politics or sports, playing Ping-Pong or chess, collecting coins or stamps. Anything which interests both of them will provide a lot to talk about—or write about.

The same advice is true also for letter writing. Not "love letters," but letters about common interests should be encouraged. The opportunities to meet are still so rare in Africa that many young people have no other way of getting acquainted with each other than by writing. Therefore as a teacher in a boarding school, instead of intercepting their letters, I think it better if you can help your students to evaluate them and answer them.

The boy friend-girl friend relationship is new to the African culture. It is interesting, however, that your students already use this vocabulary. I would divide the growth of a relationship between a boy and a girl into three stages.

The first stage is "acquaintance." It means that one knows that the other one exists. He may be a neighbor, a class mate, a colleague at work, or someone that you met on a trip. When his name is mentioned, then you can say, "I met him." That's all. "Acquaintance" does not involve a deeper personal relationship. Of course, a person can have any number of acquaintances.

Before I describe the second stage I would like to describe the third one. The third stage is "engagement," i. e., the mutual promise to marry each other. Of course you can have such a relationship with only one person. You can only have one fiancé and all other deeper friendships with the other sex should be broken off lest you endanger this unique relationship.

The boy friend-girl friend relationship is something in between the first and the third stage.

It is definitely more than a mere and unobliging acquaintance. It is a personal relationship, but still without the promise or even the prospect of marriage. Though one cannot have an unlimited number of boy friends or girl friends, I would not call this relationship an exclusive one. It must be possible to have several closer friends among the other sex in order to be able to compare and finally choose a life partner.

This leads to the painful but unavoidable experience of jealousy. It is a sign of love, but not yet of mature love. If I am jealous of someone, it shows that I am definitely, maybe passionately interested in him, so much that I would like to have him for myself alone.

Mature love, however, is so assured of the faithfulness of the other one and places so much confidence in him that it is able to share him with others and grant him freedom. Therefore I would say that jealousy is a sign that a love relationship has started, but that it is still insecure and unassured.

I hope this helps you a little. Please write again if there are more questions. And—greetings to Dick!

November 2

Dear father T.,

Thank you for your interesting answers. I read your letter at our last party and I can assure you that we had a lively discussion. Not all of them were in agreement with you. For example, some didn't like it that you consider the boy friend-girl friend relationship nonexclusive.

This issue led to more questions. They all complained that when they date they are automatically suspected of having sex. How can that be avoided?

Another question was about male aggressiveness. The girls want to know how to stop a boy without making him feel that they don't like him as a person. I guess they want to feel that they are kissable even when they do not want to be kissed. But it is a problem for boys as well, for there are also quite aggressive girls. How can one avoid the feeling of restraint as being interpreted as disinterest?

Difficult questions, aren't they? Could you answer once more?

Since you sent "greetings to Dick," I might as well tell you now. Richard and I have become quite attached to each other during the last months. The trouble is that he is from another tribe. I am afraid that my family, and especially my father, will not approve of him.

P. S. By the way, it is as if "m" has been blown away to a far distant land.

The last paragraph and especially the P. S. were very interesting to me. There is a connection between having found in me a father "to whom I can talk," the disappearance of "m" and her opening up towards a young man.

If a girl has a negative relationship to her own father, she tends to carry over her negative feelings to all men and therefore has a hard time to establish a healthy relationship to the other sex. She then feels isolated, lonesome, "unwanted," and "m" is often the result. If nobody loves me, she may think, I at least have to love myself.

Some girls, for lack of being loved by men, try then to be loved by a girl also in a physical way. This can eventually lead to a homosexual relationship, especially if they have a mother who continues to warn them that "all men are wolves."

When the father-daughter relationship became a reality in Elsie's life through our exchange of letters, she got rid of "m" and was at the same time able to open up to Richard. I therefore tried to strengthen her feeling of having a "father" by writing to her often and by answering conscientiously the questions of her students, who were, I am sure, partly also her own in disguise.

November 22

Dear Elsie,

The best way to avoid suspicion is to "double date." This means that two boys date two girls and that both couples spend the evening together. This is a mutual protection not to overstep certain limits. Bad talk cannot come up because everything that happened to the couple was witnessed by someone else besides the couple.

Girls usually prefer double dates and boys too will soon discover that as long as a relationship is not too serious, double dating is much more fun than being "alone."

May I say again that the questions which your students ask could have been asked by young people in any other part of the world. Therefore I would like to quote from a book which was written for American young people. In *Love and the Facts of Life* (Association Press, New York), Evelyn Duvall writes: "Two couples can have more fun and a livelier time than one couple alone. Four-way conversation is usually somewhat easier to maintain. The give-and-take of the two boys as well as the interaction of the two girls give a little 'extra' to the security of all four" (p. 198).

Concerning the other question, Duvall reports in the same book (p. 232) about a girl, who, when saying good-bye, took her boy friend's hands in both of hers and gave them a meaningful little squeeze "so that he would have a sense of being loved without anything too intense having happened."

Another girl struggled free from her boy friend's embrace, removed firmly his hands when they began to wander into no man's land which she considered untouchable by saying: "Oooh, please, you are too much for me."

A boy said to his girl friend: "I love you very much, so much that I want you close to me always. But when you sit on my lap like this, my feelings become almost more than I can cope with. So slide over and let's get something to eat." Duvall comments: "He was taking his share of the responsibility for their mutual relationship."

You see, each one has to develop his own style here. You should try to win the confidence of your students so that individually they will talk to you about their experiences. You should also have in your library some good books like the one quoted above.

I purposely quoted from a book written for American young people in order that your students may learn that other young people have the same problems. They should also realize that the restrictions which their traditional African education planted in their hearts are of a very great value. It is not at all necessary to put them away in order to be "modern." By the way, don't forget to impress on them, girls and boys alike, that the only absolutely safe contraceptive is the word "no."

I am so glad about what you wrote concerning Dick. How interesting that you became attracted to him as he played "father" to the students of whom you became a "mother" ! This experience would be a very healthy basis for marriage, much more solid than belonging to the same tribe. I certainly hope that your father will not make an issue of the fact that you belong to different tribes.

December 6

Dear father,

Your last letter was again appreciated by our students, especially your advice to get books on the subject of courtship and marriage for our library.

As far as my father goes, I am stuck. He cannot approve of the choice I have made. He says that all men of Dick's tribe are unfaithful to their wives and that he has heard rumors that Dick misbehaved at college.

However, I can tell that ever since I have known him, he has never shown me any nonsense. In both of our tribes there is a high appreciation of virginity and Dick fully accepts my decision on this point. In this respect I have remained "African" even when I was in Europe.

It is at another point that I come into conflict with our African tradition. We were brought up in strict obedience to our parents. Also the divine commandment says: "Thou shalt honor thy father and mother that it may be well with thee and thou mayest live long on earth."

I looked up Martin Luther's explanation to this commandment. He says,"We should so fear and love God that we do not despise our parents and superiors, nor provoke them to anger, but honor, serve, obey, love and esteem them."

Tell me, is there an exception to this commandment? Do we always have to obey our parents?

What I have to tell you now makes me very much ashamed. But since sharing helped me last time I might as well do it again. Once more I had an accident with "m." Can you explain this? It makes me desperate because I thought I had gotten over it.

December 25

Dear Elsie,

Sorry for the delay, but I didn't find time before Christmas to answer your last letter. It makes me sad to hear that your father does not accept Dick. "Honor your parents" means first of all in this case to try to understand them.

You see, your parents have always lived within their own tribe. They never had a chance to get closely acquainted with people of different tribes. For them an intertribal marriage was something unheard of.

When they sent you to high school and later on to college you grew up with boys and girls from different tribes. You saw their differences, but you also realized that they are not so terribly different after all. You met them as persons. Your parents have never had this experience.

True, there are certain difficulties in an intertribal marriage. Differences in customs and preferences could create barriers. But I don't think that they are insurmountable. They can be overcome by mutual love and understanding at least much easier than if you had different religions or belonged to different cultures.

I feel you should also understand each other's mother tongue. This is not only important for a good relationship with the in-laws, but also for the relationship between Dick and you. English will remain for both of you a foreign tongue. The innermost feelings of the heart one likes to express, however, in one's own mother tongue. It is indispensable for your marriage to be able to express such feelings.

Now you see where generalizations and prejudices lead to! As you said to me in your first letter about the old people—"they are all stupid fools"—so your father says about the men of Dick's tribe that "they are all unfaithful to their wives." Just as you didn't take time to reason with the old people, so your father doesn't take time to reason with you, but rather believes this slander about Dick.

Elsie, I see only one way out. "Honor, serve, love and esteem your parents" means in your case that you take Dick to your father so that he can meet him as a person. I am sure that if the two men have looked into each other's eyes and if your father sees how much you love Dick, things will start to change.

I enclose a letter which I have written to your father. Read it first and if you think it is all right, give it to him. I hope it will help to change his attitude.

Yes, there is an exception to the commandment of obedience to our parents. It is indicated in Acts 5:29, "We must obey God more than men." If our parents demand that we act against God's will, we must disobey them.

But we never should do that lightheartedly and never before having tried everything possible to reach an agreement. Even if we are forced to disobey our parents we should never "despise them" or "provoke them to anger" but rather avoid everything that could hurt them and show them every sign of love and esteem in spite of their opposition.

Thank you for sharing the accident. There is no reason at all for being "desperate." I believe that there is a connection between this accident and your father's opposition to your choice of Dick. This opposition made you feel your lonesomeness stronger than ever. You felt left in the lurch. You were longing for consolation.

In such a situation you must make a little speech to yourself and say, "Elsie, listen! You are discouraged now and you need comfort. But 'm' is no real consolation. Afterwards you will feel more desperate and more lonesome than before and therefore long for more consolation. So it's better not to give in. Otherwise you'll get into a vicious circle."

In such a moment you should remember that you have a Heavenly Father who is more real and closer to you than any earthly father could be. Earthly fathers are only poor substitutes, thin shadows and dim reflections of this Heavenly Father who loves you and accepts you even when the earthly fathers fail.

Why not open your Bible in such a lonesome hour and ask your Heavenly Father to talk to you in a very personal way?

I hope and pray that your Heavenly Father may also talk to your earthly father through the enclosed letter.

Christmas Day

Dear brother in Christ,

For a long time I have debated with myself whether I should write you this letter. But after nine months of correspondence with your daughter Elsie, I feel I should do it. I am asking you to see in me not only a fellow Christian, but also a fellow father. I write to you on Christmas Day when our Heavenly Father sent us his son in order to make us his children.

Elsie told me that you disapprove of her choice of Richard because he belongs to another tribe. I can imagine that you grew up with a feeling of hostility toward this tribe. But, you see, such feelings do not exist for Elsie. Members of this tribe were her classmates, became her friends. There is no barrier any more between her and them.

But, dear brother, isn't this a hopeful sign? Isn't Africa sick of tribalism? Isn't it hindering the building up of the African nations and the cooperation between these nations? Isn't it even dividing the churches in Africa?

Therefore, I feel we should be happy if these barriers break down. We as Christians should be the first ones to lay aside prejudice and hostility.

Many African young people who are considering an intertribal marriage have written to me. They all complain that they run up against a wall of non-understanding and silence on the part of their parents. I am afraid that the older generation is loading upon itself a great amount of guilt here and I must remind you of the Apostle's warning: "Fathers, do not provoke your children to anger" (Eph. 6:4).

I have advised Elsie to take Dick home with her once and to introduce him to you. Please receive him well. Forget that he belongs to another tribe and meet him as the young man whom your daughter loves.

It is my definite impression, as far as I can judge from a distance, that there is genuine love between both of them. One sign of it is that Richard respects your daughter's moral convictions and her personality as a girl. He has asked for her hand in marriage and has promised to be faithful to her his whole life. So he did not, as so many do, demand the surrender of her body without making possible the surrender of her soul.

Furthermore Elsie and Dick have gotten acquainted with each other as they worked together, both as teachers. All teachers are in a way prolonged and specialized fathers and mothers to their students. Elsie and Dick have taken this task of teaching very conscientiously. I don't know of any better preparation for marriage. At least, I am sure, they know a hundred times more about each other than those who try to gain this knowledge by premarital sex. As a father, I would be most happy if my daughter submitted her love to such a foolproof test.

Let me mention another point: As a father you are the first "man" whom your daughter meets. Unless this relationship is warmhearted and healthy, it will be difficult for her to establish a healthy relationship to other men. Girls with "cold fathers" tend to become "old maids," hostile to all men, or if they marry, often they become frigid wives who are unable to respond fully to the tenderness of their husbands.

Therefore the importance of the relationship between a daughter and her father cannot be overestimated. You hold the key to her future happiness in your hands when you take time to listen and talk to her when she is home and to correspond with her when she is away. Yes, you should even offer her once in a while a bit of physical tenderness, embrace her when she comes home or goes away, stroke her hair when she is sad or sit at her bedside when she is sick.

In this way you can protect your daughter from many errors and give her the best help in her most intimate problems. Many girls do not get into trouble because they are sexually greedy, but because they are starved for tenderness.

Don't be afraid that you will lose your authority in this way. Many fathers think that they can only keep their authority by ruling as patriarchs in remoteness and distance, but in this way they reveal their own insecurity. The real reason why so few fathers talk to their daughters is that deep down in their hearts they are afraid of them.

It's only a small step from the patriarch to the dictator and tyrant. The tyrant rules by spreading fear because he is a victim of fear himself.

Africa is sick of patriarchalism. What Africa needs are not patriarchs but fathers, true fathers who reflect by their loving-kindness and nearness to their children, the nearness and loving kindness of our Heavenly Father.

I hope and pray, dear brother, that this letter may help you to become closer to Elsie and make you more grateful to your Heavenly Father for having made you the father of such a wonderful daughter. You can be proud of her.

January 18

Dear father,

My parents have become impossible.

I followed your advice and went to my home village with Dick. But my father didn't even want to see me, let alone Dick.

I asked Mother whether I should show your letter to father, but she discouraged me. She was afraid father would think that I have accused him in Europe of being a dictator and tyrant.

My younger brother is on my side, but unfortunately he was not at home. Only my older brother was home. He wants me to marry one of his ex-schoolmates who studies at present in the United States, but I am not interested in him.

They expect him to return soon and are corresponding with him secretly. I tried my best to get those letters, but I failed. I am beginning to lose confidence in my family.

I tell you, when the fool comes from America, I am ready for him. I am going to teach him a lesson he will never forget. I shall not refuse to go with him to his house, but there I shall destroy and break everything that comes in my hands. When he reports it to the police, I shall accuse him of kidnapping me.

Father, I am rather stranded. I wish to get your advice. Do you understand my situation?

I feel like doing something that could hurt my father. If he is not willing to listen to my plea, he is going to regret it. I am going to be a castaway. I have decided to remain single for the rest of my life, unless I can marry Dick.

Tell me, is it possible for a girl to live her life without marriage? I see so many unhappy marriages in my vicinity that I am almost afraid to get married. Still I would like to become a mother. I could imagine my life without a husband, but not without a baby.

This last letter of Elsie's reminded me of the child who was bitten by a snake and said, "This is the right punishment for my father. Why didn't he give me any shoes?" Elsie wants to punish her father by remaining single, a state which—interestingly enough—she compares with being a "castaway." I don't know how serious she is, but she must know how she can hurt her father most.

He certainly has succeeded now to "provoke his child to anger." But just even her anger reveals her attachment to him. The opposite of love is not hatred, but indifference. As long as she hates him, she still is not indifferent to him.

What strikes me is that here again—as in my correspondence with Cecile in my book I Loved a Girl*—I run up against the wall which separates father and daughter. I am at a loss as to how to break it down. Neither Cecile nor Elsie could talk to their fathers. Cecile was hardly able to write to hers; Elsie could not even give him a letter from me.*

I believe that one of the deepest reasons why Elsie sees so many unhappy marriages is that girls have no personal relationship to their fathers. As married wives they do not expect such a relationship with their husbands. And they in turn are not prepared to give something which is not expected. When these fathers have daughters themselves, they establish the same non-relationship with them and thus plant in them the seeds of death for their future marriages.

What would happen to marriages in Africa—and maybe in the whole world—if girls had fatherly fathers?

Here is how I answered Elsie:

January 28

Dear "daughter" Elsie,

Your letter made me very sad.

How can these poor and helpless fathers ever change if nobody talks to them and tells them what is wrong with them? Why didn't you just run after your father and hug him when he did not want to talk to you?

You were so eager to give Cecile advice about talking to her father, but you yourself are not even able to hand over a letter to him from me! I am sorry that you didn't. Though I can understand your reasoning, I would have been so curious about his reaction. I don't think it could have made things worse.

When the "fool" comes, please talk to him quietly first. Don't make him an enemy unless you have to. This man may have some thoughts of his own and you may even be able to win him to your side. Maybe if he would plead for Dick, your father would listen and you would not have to remain single after all.

This is only a possibility, of course. More and more African girls are able to earn their livelihood as teachers, nurses or secretaries and thus become financially independent and able to exist without being married.

A single life is possible, Elsie, but it is certainly not easy. Even in Western society, in spite of the emancipation of women and all the talk about it, single women are still treated in many ways as "castaways," and in Africa this will probably still be true for a long time. Traditional African society did not provide a place for unmarried women and this attitude will not change overnight.

If you remain single voluntarily, at least you must know why. It's the motive which counts. The reasons you give are not valid because they are negative.

If you remain single in a sulky attitude, just out of stubbornness, in order to spite your father and to hurt him, you will not be able to master the problems of single life and you certainly are not being guided by God.

Girls who choose voluntarily not to marry for negative reasons become "old maids"—or prostitutes. Both have one thing in common—a negative relationship towards men.

There are positive reasons not to marry. For instance, God could guide you to remain single because as a single teacher you would have more time for your students and could be a better "mother" to them. This would be a valid reason. But you must be very sure about this special personal guidance. If God calls you to this life, you could develop to full womanhood or even "motherhood."

I know a nurse in a remote bush hospital who broke her engagement in order to give herself completely to the task of caring for her patients. She is actually "married" to this task and very happy.

This happiness, however, includes the sacrifice of two things: sex and her own children. It is not motherhood that you have to renounce—as mentioned above—but having your own children. The right of a child to have its own father is much more important than your desire to have your own baby.

However, in your case, dear Elsie, I have a big question mark in my mind as to whether it is God's will that you remain single. To me it looks as if you would flee into the single state as others flee into marriage.

In your first letter you wrote to me, "If my father tries to sell me, I shall disobey him." Why don't you disobey now? Isn't there any way to get married in your country without your parents' consent?

P.S. I would like to ask a favor of you. Our correspondence has touched so many problems which are the problems of hundreds, maybe even thousands. Would you allow me to publish our correspondence in part without mentioning your name of course?

February 16

Dear Rev. T.,

Yes, you may publish from our correspondence whatever you feel is profitable for others as long as you do not mention my name and reveal my country. I do not want to claim your letters only for myself.

Please do not think that I am not thankful for them even if I ask you today not to write to me anymore.

Yes, there is a way to be legally married in my country without the parents' consent. I would estimate that about ten percent of the married couples have eloped and been married at the magistrate court. Twenty-five percent of the women have children out of wedlock, because their parents did not approve of their choice of a partner.

However, if you marry against the will of your parents, the quarrels with the families will not end. They will not only create trouble but will also interpret all the troubles that occur to you as a punishment for your disobedience. If you need help they will refuse it.

As far as I am concerned I am not at peace to marry against the will of my father. In fact, I wouldn't be able to do it.

I am not going to be long today. It is not necessary to trouble you. I feel tired of what I have been facing and I want to speak of it no more.

You note the change of address. Please do not ask me any questions.

One thing has happened though through our correspondence: I have found a new relationship to my Heavenly Father of whom you once said, he loves me and accepts me even when the earthly father fails. I can believe this now. I have started to read my Bible regularly and I can pray as I never did before.

Please do not answer. I'll see the way out.

Good bye to you and your good family

from

Elsie

Just as the counsellor has to be ready when the other one wants to speak, so he too has to respect his desire to remain silent.

I never heard from Elsie again. Did she remain single? Did she marry Dick? Or someone else? Did she actually become an embittered "old maid"? I don't know.

But one thing I know: The silence between the generations is lethal, as lethal as the silence between Elsie and her father. It is the counterpart of patriarchalism and ranges among Africa's greatest enemies.

That lethal silence turned a girl full of energy, good will and constructive ideas, intelligent and gifted, on her way to womanhood and motherhood, into a frustrated and powerless cripple, fed up with life.

Elsie is a victim of the conflict between old and new. Her head was in the future, but her heart still lived in the past. With her thinking she protested and rebelled. With her feelings she submitted and obeyed.

But I am afraid this submission and obedience destroyed her life—just as her disobedience would have done, for by disobeying the patriarch she would have sacrificed the father.

Africa's problem today is that, as patriarchalism breaks down, the patriarchs are not as yet being replaced by fathers. The destruction of an authoritarian patriarchalism is in itself no solution unless true fatherliness takes its place.

Is it only an African problem? Is it not a world problem?

Isn't the unrest among the young people all over the world today a rebellion against the false authority of patriarchalism and at the same time an expression of deep longing for the true authority of fatherliness?

If this is the case, we are facing here not a social or political problem but in the first place a religious one. Wherever fatherliness and true authority occur on this earth, they are a gift from our Heavenly Father, a grace, a reflection of his image.

Patriarchalism is a sign that this image was lost.

It is not true that we create an image of God according to the image we have of our earthly fathers. On the contrary, He conveys his image to us and gives everything which is called "father" on this earth his imprint (Eph. 3: 14, 15).

This alone makes us fathers. More than that—it makes us men. Fatherliness is an integral part of manhood. Because Elsie's father did not mature to full manhood, he could not help her to full womanhood.

Fatherliness does not necessarily mean having children of one's own. Fatherly men can become spiritual fathers as many of my Roman Catholic colleagues have proven themselves to be and as I tried to become for Elsie—at least for a period of her life. In her last letter she addressed me again as Rev. T. I must admit that at first this hurt me a little, but I was comforted when she said, I pray to my Heavenly Father, who loves me and accepts me when the earthly father fails.

I take it as a sign that I served as a bridge and that she threw herself completely into His arms.

I know that He will be a better counsellor to her than I was. He alone can "turn the heart of the fathers to the children and the heart of the children to their fathers" as is promised in the last verse of the Old Testament opening up the way to the New.

PART II

MARRIAGE

BOOK SIX

I MARRIED YOU

Preface

This book is written not only for married persons, but also for those who are preparing for marriage, and even for unmarried persons. Nothing in this book is fiction. All the stories have really happened. All of the conversations have really taken place. The people involved are still living today. For this reason the name of the city is not mentioned nor are any descriptions given. The setting of these events is Africa, but the problems dealt with are relevant to all parts of the earth and to all cultures.

Walter Trobisch

1

THE EARTH CAME CLOSER. THE CONCRETE OF THE RUNWAY APpeared. The wheels touched, jumped a little, touched again, rolled. The motor howled. The plane slowed down, turned, taxied toward the airport building, stopped.

I had arrived.

I unfastened my seat belt, threw my winter coat over my arm, grabbed my hand baggage and struggled down the aisle toward the rear exit.

The African stewardess nodded to me with a smile.

"Good-by, sir. I hope you had a good flight."

"Thank you," I answered, and went carefully down the narrow steps of the landing ramp. I felt the heat like a blow.

Blinded by the bright sun, I joined the other passengers walking toward the airport building.

Halfway between the plane and the building a young girl was standing, looking the passengers over carefully as if she were searching for someone in particular. She wore a stewardess uniform. Suddenly, she took a step in my direction and pronounced my name.

"How did you recognize me?" I said.

"I saw your picture on the back cover of one of your books. I am Miriam. I wrote you a letter once."

Miriam? I searched my memory.

"Did I answer?"

"Yes, you did. You said that a broken engagement is a lesser evil than a divorce."

Now I recalled her letter. I put down my bags and looked at Miriam. She was small, fine-featured, had vivid brown eyes which sparkled below her intelligent forehead. Her long dark hair, almost bluish-black in color, was in a neat roll at the back of her neck.

"You wrote," I said with a smile, "that you were afraid that your feelings for your fiancé were not quite deep enough for marriage."

"And you said I should listen to my feelings. Girls feel it usually sooner than boys."

Now I remembered her case in full. She was a year older than her fiancé, had four more years of education and a better salary than he. That worried her.

"But, you see, I can't just leave him. He loves me and in a way I love him too. Sometimes I don't know how I feel."

"Well, Miriam, we can't talk here. Can we continue as I go through passport control?"

She took one handle of my heavy bag and I took the other handle in my right hand. I tucked my briefcase under my left arm and we started toward the building.

"Excuse me," she said, "but I have to talk to you. When our pastor told us that you would be here only four days, I decided to see you before the others come. I work for the airline. This is why I could come out here."

"Do you belong to Pastor Daniel's church?"

"Yes. He has also come to meet you. You'll see him after you go through customs."

While we were lining up for the passport control, I had the impression that she still wanted to talk. She had made a real effort. It had taken a lot of courage for her to address me, so I didn't want to disappoint her.

"Miriam, I wonder why you got engaged to that young man in the first place before you knew more about him?"

"In our country we can't talk to a boy and go out with him unless we are engaged. We can't have boyfriends. In your book you say one should not get engaged unless one is well acquainted with the other. But we can't get acquainted unless we are engaged."

It was my turn now to show my passport.

"Are you a tourist?" the officer asked me.

"I'm supposed to give some lectures in a church here."

"About what?"

"Marriage."

He gave me a brief glance, then stamped my passport without further comment.

Miriam and I walked over to the place where the checked baggage would be unloaded.

"If I leave him, he said he would commit suicide."

"Suicide? You think he really means that?"

"I don't know, but I'm afraid he does."

Perhaps it would be good if I could talk to him."

"That would be wonderful. He'll be in church tonight too."

"Then you must introduce him to me after the meeting."

"Thank you," she said with relief. "Thank you very much." From the relieved tone of her voice I concluded that this had been her wish all the time—to arrange a talk between her fiancé and me.

My large suitcase arrived. Miriam spoke to the customs officer in the native language. He waved us on.

The door swung open and we entered the waiting room. Pastor Daniel stepped forward, grasped both my arms in the African way of greeting, then hugged me.

"Welcome," he said. "You are very welcome indeed."

"Yes, I finally made it," I said, and put down my briefcase.

"I'm glad you're here. May I introduce you to my wife Esther?" He motioned me to a tall, intelligent-looking woman in her middle thirties who stood behind him. Esther wore a dark green dress with a black design and had a yellow scarf on her head. On her left arm she had a baby and at her right hand a little boy, about three years old.

She left him and offered me her hand in the Western way, while looking aside shyly.

"Welcome to our country," she said.

The little boy stared at me curiously. But when I bent over to greet him, he hid behind his mother's skirt, grabbing it with both hands.

"We watched you get off the plane," Daniel said. "We were in the restaurant on the first floor. You started your work exactly one minute after you arrived. Did you know Miriam before?"

"No, I didn't, but we had corresponded. She recognized me from the picture on the back of my book."

Miriam was somewhat embarrassed by this time. She excused herself because she had to go back to work and promised to be at church in the evening.

We walked out to Daniel's car on the parking lot in front of the building. It was a Volkswagen.

His wife got into the back seat with the two children. I sat with Daniel in front.

"How long is it now, since we first met, Daniel?"

"Exactly two years."

I had met Daniel only once and then it was at an international conference for church leaders. He had urged me at that time to come and talk to his congregation. I had not been able to accept his invitation until now.

We drove silently for awhile. Then I tried to tell him how I felt.

"I'm afraid about tonight, Daniel. I feel entirely unprepared. I would like to know a little bit more about the people before I talk to them."

"If you can stay only four days, we have to start tonight."

I could see that.

"Is this the first time you are in our city?" he asked.

"Yes, I'm sorry to say that it is. I've been in other African countries before, but never in your country. I know a little about your customs, but nothing about your particular problems."

"This could also be an advantage," he said with a twinkle in his eyes. "Our young people are looking forward very much to your lectures."

"And the older ones?"

"There is some resistance. They feel that talks about marriage do not belong in the church. Especially sexual matters are taboo to them. I guess it's about the same all over Africa. How is it in America and Europe?"

"Basically it's the same. Christians are embarrassed to talk about sex, and those who do talk about it are very often not Christians."

"Anyway, you should be careful, at least during your first lecture, not to talk too much about sex. And be as simple as possible. Avoid abstract nouns and simplify terms. You'll have to use short sentences, so that I can interpret them sentence by sentence."

"I shall do my best. Do you have a blackboard in church?" I said.

"This can be arranged."

By now we had reached the downtown area. Except for the people, it didn't look too much different from an American or European city—sidewalks, neon signs, tall buildings of banks and insurance companies, hotels, restaurants, travel agencies, supermarkets—and the constant rush of thick traffic.

"Is your family well?" It was Esther.

"Thank you for asking. They are fine."

"How many children do you have?"

"Five, but they are a little bit older than yours."

"Weren't they sad when you left?"

"They wanted to come along. Four of them were born in Africa. They feel this is their home."

"Is your wife going to come?"

"I hope she can join me during the weekend."

"Wonderful!"

I started to think about my wife and how much easier it would be tonight were she along. If only we could speak together. The more I thought of her, the more lonesome I felt.

"We wanted to invite you to stay in our home," Daniel explained. "But we decided instead to put you up in a hotel. It's not very quiet in our home, for we have callers all the time. Also, there may be some people who want to talk to you who would not come to the parsonage."

"I would have liked to stay with you," I answered, "but I can see your point."

"Will you have supper with us tonight?" Esther asked.

"Thanks, Esther, for the invitation, but I'm afraid I have no time. I have to change now. I'm still wearing my winter clothes."

"Well, I just wanted to know. Daniel never tells me when he brings guests home. Nor do I know when he'll be home for meals."

There was a brief strained silence in the car.

We stopped in front of a hotel. Esther stayed in the car with the children, while Daniel accompanied me inside. After I had registered, he followed me to my room. It was a neat-looking single room with bed, desk, and telephone. In front of the window was a living-room area with sofa, armchair, and a small table. The room had a good atmosphere. Here one could have talks.

"I'm sorry I can't pick you up for the meeting," Daniel said, "but I shall send one of our members to bring you to the church."

"I wish you could stay, Daniel, to give me advice on what to say tonight."

Daniel paused for a moment and closed his eyes. Then he looked straight into my face.

"God will give you something. Give us what He gives you." With that he left.

He is a good counselor, I thought. I wished I could help his people as he had helped me now.

I went to the window and gazed out. My room was on the fourth floor, so I could look over the roofs of the neighboring buildings. I had seen them from above, from the plane. Now they were closer, very close. I am under one of them, I thought. Not above, but under.

I took a shower and changed. Then I removed the notes of my first lecture from my briefcase and spread them out on the desk.

I started to read them. But they did not talk.

Suddenly, the telephone rang. It was the hotel switchboard operator. "Just a minute, there's a call for you." A woman's voice came on and asked for my name.

"I read in the paper that you will speak tonight on marriage. Is that right?"

"Yes."

"I would like to ask you a question. Is it always wrong to leave your husband?"

What a question! I thought, and then asked her, "Why do you want to leave him?"

"He won't marry me."

"I thought he was your husband."

"We are living together. He says, 'When you live with me, it's like I married you.' And yet he didn't marry me. He often promises me a wedding, but then he always postpones it. So I am married and I am not married. I am all confused. What makes marriage a marriage?"

"How long have you been living together?"

"For more than a year."

"Do you have children?"

"No, he doesn't want any."

I could just imagine the problems.

"He is very good to me," the voice said. "He pays for my education. He takes me to school in the morning and picks me up at night."

"Takes you to school? How old are you?"

"I'm twenty-two. My parents were not able to give me a good education. So I'm catching up now."

"Where do your parents live?"

"In a small village several hundred miles from here."

"Couldn't you go back to your parents and return only under the condition that a marriage is arranged?"

"That's impossible. My parents threw me out of their house when I started to live with him. They don't approve of him."

"Why not?"

"He's European."

This explained many things: that he had money, didn't want a child, and wanted "free love."

"Well, you really are in a difficult situation. Could you come and see me here in the hotel?"

"No, he wouldn't allow that. He never allows me to go out by myself."

"Why don't you bring him along?"

She laughed. "He would never come."

"Could you come to my lecture tonight?"

"I have classes tonight. Besides, he doesn't want me to go to any church."

"How do you spend your weekends?"

"I stay home. When he goes out, he locks me up in the house."

"Where does he go?"

"I don't know. He never tells me."

I was speechless. Then I heard her voice again.

"But what can I do, pastor? What can I do?"

The old question. "I don't know," I said, "I really don't."

"Can you at least pray with me?"

"Pray . . . ? Are you a Christian?"

I had hardly asked the question when I regretted it. What would it matter? The answer came.

"No. My parents are Moslem. But I was educated in a Christian school. There was no other school in the village."

Pray! I must admit that I had never prayed over the telephone, let alone with a person I had never seen.

Then I thought, Why not? Did it matter whether I saw and knew her? Did not God see and know her just as He sees and knows me? If we couldn't meet in this hotel room, why couldn't we meet in God?

So I prayed. I said that I had no solution. I asked God to show us a solution. When I said "Amen," she hung up.

The quietness of my room engulfed me. I stared at the lecture notes in front of me and felt helpless. They seemed to have no relationship to life.

Then it came to me with a start that I had forgotten to ask the girl for her name and telephone number. What a mistake! There was no chance to get in touch with her. Would she call back?

The telephone rang again. I picked up the receiver eagerly, hoping it would be she. But it was the operator.

"There's a gentleman in the lobby waiting for you."

"Tell him I'll be right there."

I thrust my notes in my briefcase and went down to meet him. A distinguished-looking man in his thirties wearing a well-tailored suit introduced himself as Maurice. He had come to take me to the church where I was to give my lecture, and led me to his car.

"Are you married?" I asked, as a way of starting conversation.

"No, not yet."

"How old are you?"

"Thirty-four."

Thirty-four and not married. What could be the reason for that? I thought. Then Maurice continued:

"I lost my father in my early childhood. I had to take care of my mother. Besides, I wanted to finish my studies first and have a decent job. I'm business manager for a construction company. Also, it's not easy to find a girl to marry."

"What makes it so difficult?"

"The getting acquainted. I don't know where to meet a girl."

"Do you have one in mind?"

"Yes, I do."

"And what does she say?"

"I don't know. I haven't talked to her yet."

"Why not?"

"The only place I can meet her is in the bus. I know which bus she takes when she goes to school in the morning. I take the same one and try to have a chat with her between two bus stops."

"How old is she?"

"I don't know. Not more than sixteen, I guess."

I gasped. Could this be possible? Here was a fine-looking, distinguished gentleman who had a good job with much responsibility, yet he was pursuing a young schoolgirl in a bus!

"Why do you choose such a young girl?"

"The older ones are either spoiled, or already married. Do you think it's a mistake?"

"Well, you must think that when you are sixty, she will be forty-two."

"Maybe I should think about that."

"Are we going directly to the church? It's quite a long way," I said.

"I made a detour," Maurice answered, "in order to introduce you to one of our greatest problems. Here is our 'red-light district.' "

We had left the downtown area. Hundreds of small mud huts with thatched roofs were on both sides of the unpaved road. There must have been thousands of people living in this area.

"What makes a woman become a prostitute?"

"Many of them are barren women who are sent away by their husbands because they don't have children."

"What makes them barren?"

"The doctors say it is mostly because of venereal diseases which they often get from their husbands who have been infected by prostitutes. It's a vicious circle. Some of them are widows who are trying to make a living in this way so that they can keep their children. If they would remarry they would lose their children to their deceased husband's family."

We drove silently for awhile before we left the district and came to the paved road again. Then we stopped in front of the church.

When we entered, the people were already singing. It was filled to the last pew, men sitting on the left side and women on the right. When Maurice led me down the center aisle, some heads turned curiously, but almost unnoticeably. Daniel was in the first pew and motioned to me to sit beside him.

He gave me a hymnbook and pointed out the stanza they were singing. I could read but not understand the words. But the tune sounded familiar, so I joined in. It felt good to be doing something together with the congregation before I had to address them.

During the last stanza Daniel closed his hymnbook and told me to go first. I mounted the few steps to the pulpit. He followed me and stood by my side so that he could translate.

While they were singing the last line, I had a chance to get an impression of the congregation I was to address. There were quite a few older people filling the front pews. The younger generation, by far in the majority, were sitting more toward the back. They sat close together, their heads with the dense black hair reminding me of a velvet carpet. No one looked up at us.

I whispered to Daniel the passage I was going to read. He opened his Bible. I opened my English Bible.

Then I began.

2

THERE IS A VERY MEANINGFUL STATEMENT ABOUT MARRIAGE IN THE Bible. It is simple and clear and yet very deep.

"It is like a deep well filled with clear drinking water. You can lower your pail into it as long as you live and it will never come up empty. You will always draw clear and fresh water.

"If we listen to this statement with an open heart, we will discover that God Himself is speaking to us. He speaks as one who wants to help us. He speaks as one who wants to direct and challenge us. But above all, He speaks as one who wants to offer us something.

"It is the only statement about marriage which is repeated four times in the Bible. The Bible does not speak very often about marriage. Therefore, it is all the more striking that this statement appears four times in very decisive places. First, it sums up the story of creation in the second chapter of Genesis. Then, Jesus quotes this statement in Matthew 19:5 and Mark 10:7, after he is asked about divorce. Finally, the Apostle Paul relates it directly to Jesus Christ in Ephesians 5:31.

"This statement was written about a time which was in many respects similar to ours. It was a time of rapid social change. . . ."

Thus far Daniel had interpreted my lecture sentence by sentence, without hesitation and almost without reflection. It was as if I heard myself speaking in another tongue. But when I used the term "rapid social change" he hesitated for the first time and went into a longer explanation. I continued and tried to describe the time of David and Solomon.

"New trade routes were opening up. Foreign cultures came into contact with each other. New ideas influenced people. Old traditions were no longer practiced. Age-old customs suddenly appeared out of date. Tribes were broken up. Taboos were destroyed. It was a time of complete moral confusion. Everything was plowed-up just as today. Therefore I believe that this statement can serve as a guide for us during these next days. I would like to read it to you now from Genesis 2:24."

Up to this point I had had no reaction from my listeners. But now they started to open their Bibles which many of them had on their laps. I waited a few moments and then read:

" 'Therefore a man leaves his father and his mother and cleaves to his wife, and they become one flesh.' "

As I read it, I was again struck by the simplicity and clarity of this verse. I felt that something was placed in my hands, something to pass on. I continued:

"This verse has three parts. It mentions three things which are essential to marriage: to leave, to cleave, and to become one flesh. Let us take up one after the other. First of all let us talk about

Leaving

"There can be no marriage without leaving. The word 'leaving' indicates that a public and legal act has to take place in order to make marriage a marriage.

"In former times, when the bride left her village for the village of her husband, it was a public procedure.

"Sometimes in Africa the whole wedding party dances, often for many miles, from the village of the bride to the village of the bridegroom. There is nothing secret about it. This public act of leaving makes marriage legal at the same time. From that day on everyone knows—these two are husband and wife, they are under 'wedlock.'

"In our day, this legal act of leaving is replaced in many countries by a public announcement before the wedding, as well as by an official marriage license. The outward form is not of primary importance, but what is important is the fact that a public and legal action takes place.

" 'Therefore a man leaves his father and his mother.' Marriage concerns more than just the two persons who are getting married. Father and mother stand for the family, who are in turn a part of the community and of the state. Marriage is never a private affair. There is no marriage without a wedding. This is why weddings are often celebrated by a great feast.

" 'Leaves his father and his mother.' When I pronounce these words, you will feel a pain in your heart. This is certainly not something joyful. Where I come from tears are often shed when a wedding takes place."

There was a nodding of heads, especially among the older women. Half out loud, one said, "It's the same here."

"You would expect that the teaching about marriage begins with something more joyful and beautiful. But the Bible is very down to earth and sober. It says, 'A man leaves his father and his mother.' Leaving is the price of happiness. There must be a clean and clear cut. Just as a newborn baby cannot grow up unless the umbilical cord is cut, just so marriage cannot grow up and develop so long as no real leaving, no clear separation from one's family, takes place.

"I say, this is hard. It is hard for the children to leave their parents. But it is just as hard for the parents to let their children go.

"Parents can be compared to hens who hatch out ducks' eggs. After they are hatched, the ducklings walk to the pond and swim away. But the hens cannot follow them. They stay on the banks of the pond and cackle."

Even before Daniel had translated the last sentence, there was some laughter in the audience. But it came mostly from the young people.

"You can't get married without leaving," I repeated. "If no real leaving takes place, the marriage will be in trouble. If the young couple have no chance to start their own home, completely separate from their families, the danger is great that the in-laws will interfere continuously.

"In Africa the custom of bride price is sometimes used as such a means of interference. Some parents who do not want to let their daughter go, raise the bride price so high that the young couple remain in debt for a long time. These debts are then used to prevent a real leaving."

There was complete silence in the church now. In that silence I could feel some resistance. I could read in their faces that they were not able to accept this. Evidently this matter of "leaving" was a bitter pill for them to swallow. So I explained:

"Now some of you may say: 'This is against our African traditions. We are taught to love our parents, not to leave them. We feel an obligation not only to the small family—or as it is sometimes called, the intimate family—which is made up of father, mother, and children. We also feel an obligation to the greater family, the extended family, which takes in all our relatives.'

"This is a very valuable tradition, which by no means should be destroyed. Yet my answer is that 'leaving' does not mean to leave in the lurch. Leaving does not mean to abandon one's parents.

"On the contrary, only if a couple are given the chance to leave and to start their own home will they be able to help their respective families later on. Only if they are independent and without debt will they be able to take responsibility for them later on and serve them. The fact that they were able to 'leave' creates a breathing spell in which the love between parents and children can grow and prosper. In my experience, the extended family can function only so long as the nuclear family is intact and healthily independent.

"Is this a Western concept of marriage? It is not. I have not come to you in order to present the Western concept of marriage. I have come to present the biblical concept of marriage. This biblical concept presents a challenge to all cultures.

"Everyone has trouble with 'leaving.' If you ask a Western marriage counselor which problem he has most frequently to deal with, he will probably answer, 'With the mother-in-law problem.' "

There was laughter again—the same kind of laughter and smiles which the mere mentioning of this word causes also in American and European audiences. I continued:

"In America and Europe it is usually the mother of the husband who interferes. She just can't believe that this young girl whom he married is able to take care of her precious son. Will she be able to wash his shirts right? Will she know how much salt he likes in his soup? Even if there is no bride price to pay, money is often used as a means to keep the young couple dependent and to force them to live in the same house or even apartment with one of their parents.

"Real leaving and real letting go—not only outwardly, but also inwardly—is difficult for everyone. In Africa I have heard it is more often the mother of the wife who causes trouble. In case of a marriage quarrel the young wife tries to run home to her mother.

"So one of my African friends has claimed that this Bible verse should stipulate expressly that a woman shall also leave her father and her mother. Why do African women run home so frequently? The answer is, because the woman has left her family, while her husband has not. In your country the man stays in his home, or close to his home, and his wife has to join him there.

"The man who wrote our verse lived in the same kind of society. There it was a matter of course that the woman had to leave and become a member of her husband's clan. The unheard-of and revolutionary message was that the man also had to leave his family. This must have hurt the ears of the male listeners at that time as much as it may hurt your ears today.

"It protects the women's rights. It aims toward partnership between husband and wife. The message is, in other words: Both have to leave, not only the wife, but also the husband. And just as both have to leave, so also must both cleave—not only the wife to the husband, but also the husband to the wife, as our Bible verse expressly states.

"This leads us to the second part:

Cleaving

"Leaving and cleaving belong together. One describes more the public and legal aspect of marriage, the other more the personal aspect. They are intertwined. You cannot really cleave unless you have left. You cannot really leave unless you have decided to cleave.

"The literal sense of the Hebrew word for 'to cleave' is to stick to, to paste, to be glued to a person. Husband and wife are glued together like two pieces of paper. If you try to separate two pieces of paper which are glued together, you tear them both. If you try to separate husband and wife who cleave together, both are hurt—and in case they have children, the children as well.

"Divorce means to take a saw and to saw apart each child, from head to toe, right through the middle."

A dead silence fell upon the audience.

"Another consequence of this being glued together is that husband and wife are closest to each other, closer than to anything else and to anyone else in the world.

"Closer than to anything else. It is more important than the husband's work or profession, more important than the wife's house cleaning and cooking, or, in case she works, than her profession.

"Closer than to anyone else. It is more important than the husband's friends or the wife's friends, more important than visitors and guests, even more important than the children.

"When I come home from a trip, I always make it a point to embrace my wife first, before embracing my children. I want to show the children also in this way that father is closest to mother and mother is closest to father.

"Very often adultery occurs in a young marriage after the first baby is born. Why? The young wife makes the mistake of becoming closer to her baby than to her husband. The baby becomes the center of her life, which makes the husband feel like an outsider."

From the men's side at least came nodding smiles, showing that they were wholeheartedly in agreement.

" 'To cleave' in this deep sense," I continued, "being glued together, is, of course, only possible between two persons. Our Bible verse was worded purposely as an attack against the polygamy of David and Solomon. It states, 'Therefore a man . . . cleaves to *his wife.'*

"This verse also strikes out against divorce which makes a successive polygamy possible, where one man does not have several wives at the same time, but one after the other.

"Perhaps we would use another word today in place of 'to cleave.' We would no doubt use the word 'to love.' But it is interesting that the Bible does not use this word here.

"Cleaving means love, but love of a special kind. It is love which has made a decision and which is no longer a groping and seeking love. Love which cleaves is mature love, love which has decided to remain faithful—faithful to one person—and to share with this one person one's whole life.

"This leads us to the third part of our verse:

Becoming One Flesh

"This expression describes the physical aspect of marriage."

I remembered that Daniel had cautioned me to be careful about using the word "sex."

"This physical aspect is as essential for marriage as the legal and personal aspect. The physical union between husband and wife is as much within God's will for marriage as is the leaving of the parents and the cleaving to each other.

"I know that some people are embarrassed to talk about the physical aspect of marriage. They feel that it is something unholy, maybe even indecent, something which has nothing to do with God. I would like to ask these people the same question which the Apostle Paul asked the church in Corinth: 'Don't you know that your body is a temple of the Holy Spirit?' And so, we can talk about it. We must talk about it, even in church. I might even ask: Where else could we talk about it, reverently and respectfully, if not in church?"

The silence continued. I realized that these thoughts were completely new for many.

"You say, 'It is against our African tradition to talk about the things of the body. These things are taboo for us.'

"But it is very strange. If I talk to parents in Africa and advise them to teach their children these functions of the body, they say, 'American and European parents may be able to do that, because these things are more natural to them. For Africans this is impossible.' However, when I talk to American and European parents, they say to me, 'Mr. Trobisch, you lived too long in Africa. The people in Africa are closer to nature. They may be able to do this, but for us it is impossible.'

"It is my experience that the embarrassment is worldwide. Parents find it difficult the world over to give their children a proper education about the physical aspects of marriage. The reason is that it has either been considered as something so holy that it cannot even be pronounced—or so unholy that one is ashamed to mention it. The Bible refutes both positions. It says, It belongs to God and therefore we *can,* we *must* talk about it. The physical union of husband and wife is as dear and as near to God as is their faithfulness and the legality of their marriage.

"Of course, 'to become one flesh' means much more than just the physical union. It means that two persons share everything they have, not only their bodies, not only their material possessions, but also their thinking and their feeling, their joy and their suffering, their hopes and their fears, their successes and their failures. 'To become one flesh' means that two persons become completely one with body, soul, and spirit and yet there remain two different persons.

"This is the innermost mystery of marriage. It is hard to understand. Maybe we can't understand it at all. We can only experience it. I once saw it demonstrated in a unique way."

I reached down into my briefcase and brought out a carving of two heads—the one of a man and the other of a woman. The heads were connected by a chain with wooden links. I held the carving up.

"This is a marriage symbol which the church in Liberia gives to the young couple as a reminder of their marriage vows. If you came close and inspected it carefully, you would see that this chain has no joint. The whole piece of art is carved out of one piece of wood and conveys the message: 'Where God joins, there is no joint.'

"I never found the innermost mystery of marriage more convincingly demonstrated than here. The two become completely one, 'one flesh,' made out of one piece of wood, and still they remain two individual persons. It is not two halves which make one whole, but two

whole persons form an entirely new whole. This is to 'become one flesh.' "

I stepped down from the pulpit and gave the marriage symbol to the people in the front row. They passed it on admiringly from hand to hand. I walked over to a big blackboard which Daniel had put up on the opposite side of the pulpit and took a piece of chalk in my hand.

"Now comes the most important message of our Bible verse. We've studied the three parts: to leave, to cleave, and to become one flesh. The message is that these three parts are inseparable from each other. If one of the parts is lacking, the marriage is not complete. Only the one who has 'left' regardless of the consequences, and only those who 'cleave' exclusively to each other, can become 'one flesh.'

"These three elements of leaving, cleaving, and becoming one flesh belong together like the three angles of a triangle."

I turned to the blackboard and drew a large triangle in this way:

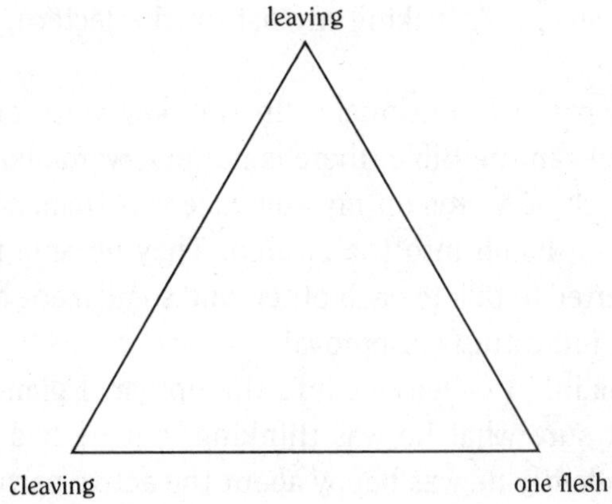

"We could also write at the upper angle, 'public and legal act' or simply 'wedding' or 'wedlock.' At the left angle we could also write 'love' or 'faithfulness.' At the right angle we could also write 'physical union' or simply the word 'sex,' if it is understood that much more is meant by this word than just the sexual fellowship of the couple."

It was the first time that I dared to use the word "sex," but the spirit in the audience was so open by now that I had no need to be afraid of unnecessarily hurting feelings. I said, pointing to the triangle:

"If you want to have a real marriage, these three things have to be in the picture. For young people who are not yet married, this is the goal they have to reach. Just as a triangle is no triangle if one of the angles is lacking, just so marriage is no marriage if one of these three elements is not there.

"But now I have to call your attention to another very important fact about our Bible verse. How does it end? What is the last thing in this verse of Genesis 2:24?"

They opened their Bibles again and hands went up quickly. "It's the word 'flesh,' " an elderly man answered.

"No," I said, "what comes after flesh?"

There was a long silence. Finally, a young man said: "A full stop."

There was laughter, but I accepted the answer.

"Yes," I said, "this full stop is of the utmost importance."

I went back into the pulpit and read the Bible verse again: "Therefore a man leaves his father and his mother and cleaves to his wife, and they become one flesh. . . ." Striking my fist on the lectern, I added: "Full stop."

After a brief pause I continued: "In this key verse about marriage, quoted four times in the Bible, there is not one word about children."

The effect of these words on my audience was tremendous. It was as if I had thrown a bomb into the church. They became restless, shook their heads, started to talk to each other, and some made a certain sound with their lips, indicating disapproval.

"Let me explain!" I called out into the uproar. I glanced at Daniel's face. I was not sure what he was thinking, but he had a very pleased expression. Evidently he was happy about the active participation of his congregation.

Full Stop

I began again:

"Don't misunderstand me. Children are a blessing of God. The Bible emphasizes this over and over again. I have five children myself and am thankful for every one of them. We have received them as a sign of God's goodness, as a very real blessing in our marriage.

"Children are a blessing to marriage, but they are an *additional* blessing to marriage. When God created Adam and Eve, He blessed them and *then* He said to them: 'Be fruitful and multiply' (Gen. 1:28). From the Hebrew text it is clear that this commandment was an additional action to the action of blessing.

"Therefore when the Bible describes the indispensable elements of marriage, it is significant that children are not expressly mentioned. Leaving, cleaving, and becoming one flesh are sufficient. Full stop. Even if there are no children the one-flesh union does not become meaningless.

"The full stop means that the child does not make marriage a marriage. A childless marriage is also a marriage in the full sense of the word.

"The full stop means: Barrenness is no reason for divorce. No man can say: 'This woman hasn't given me a child. Therefore I'm really not married to her,' and then send her away. If a marriage remains childless, this doesn't justify tearing the cleaving elements apart, nor does it question the legality of the marriage."

Daniel had translated these last statements with a special emphasis and with a certain warm concern in his voice, indicating that divorce motivated by childlessness was rather frequent in his country.

And so, although time was running short, I wanted to develop the subject further. I asked Daniel whether I could still go on for ten minutes. He said: "You have caught their ears. You can go on as long as you want." So I continued:

The Garden or the Triangle?

"There is another concept of marriage. It contradicts the biblical concept of marriage which I have just described in every point. This concept of marriage is widespread. I have found it in many parts of the world.

"The garden concept of marriage, as I like to call it, is based on a book called *Marriage East and West* by David and Vera Mace, American marriage counselors, who conducted a marriage seminar with twenty Asians in 1958 at Chiengmai, Thailand.

"This garden concept of marriage as the Maces describe it from China is based on an inaccurate biology.

"It conceives of the man as the sower of the seed and of the woman as the soil, as the garden. Man plants his seed in the woman. The woman's body nurtures the seed as the soil nurtures the grain of rice. Just as the plant grows out of the grain, so the child grows out of the man's seed. The child is the man's child, his ongoing spirit, his continuing life.

"I repeat: This is inaccurate and bad biology. Yet the consequences of this garden way of thinking are tremendous. Let me state them briefly:

"First of all: men are more important than women. The woman can never be so important as the man any more than the soil can be so important as the seed. By her very nature she is secondary, auxiliary. This explains, as nothing else can do, the discrimination between man and woman, not only in Asia, but also in America and Europe even today. Whether it is in Africa, you have to decide for yourselves.

"Second: sons are more important than daughters. It is through sons that the family line is continued. A family who has no sons and whose line dies out is like a tree cut off from its roots. Its ancestors wither and have no peace."

There was a movement among my listeners as if they were deeply involved.

"Third: The relationship between husband and wife is the same as one between a possessor and his possession, just as the sower of the seed owns the soil into which he sows. The main duty of the woman is to obey. It is also the man's privilege to choose. He chooses the garden he is going to buy. The garden has nothing to say. The standard of choice is the potential fertility of the garden.

"Fourth: Within the garden concept of thinking, a childless marriage is as useless and senseless as a barren field. If a woman fails to bear children, she fails in her destiny.

"Fifth: The garden concept explains the practice of divorce and polygamy. If a man's garden does not bear fruit, either he gives the garden back to its former possessor and asks the father of the girl to return the price he has paid for her, or he keeps the garden and acquires one or two other gardens which may bear fruit.* Polygamy is understandable only within the garden concept. Further, man can have several gardens, but a garden can have only one owner. The woman is always at a disadvantage within the garden concept.

"Sixth: I have mentioned the custom of bride price. This custom is closely related to the garden concept. Actually, it is not the price for the garden, but for the fruits which the garden is going to produce. The name is misleading. It is not the price for the bride, but for the children she is supposed to bear. That is why sometimes it is not paid in full until she gives birth to the first child, and then only if the child is a son. A widow loses her children if she marries outside of her late husband's clan which paid for these children. They do not really belong to the widowed mother. By the way, a widow is the most pitiful creature within the

*The word "polygamy" is used in this book in the sense of polygyny, the marriage of one man to more than one wife. In Africa it is used mostly in this sense because polyandry, the marriage of one woman to more than one husband, is unknown.

garden concept. She is a possession which has lost its owner.

"Seventh: This concept explains why, though both are guilty, a woman is more reproached for adultery than a man. What happens if a man commits adultery? He sows his seed in a garden which does not belong to him. He does wrong to the owner of the other garden and may have to pay him a fine if he is caught. But he is not considered as doing wrong to his own wife or violating his own marriage.

"If a wife commits adultery, however, she does the worst thing she can do to her husband. She allows foreign seed in his garden. She endangers the integrity of his family line. *She* violates her own marriage.

"Finally: There is no place whatsoever within the garden concept for the unmarried person. An unmarried girl is a garden which could bear fruit, but which is not given to a sower. This does not make sense. But the most foolish thing one can think of is a bachelor. He is a sower of seed who does not purchase a garden in which to sow his seed. Unthinkable!"

A roar of laughter followed this last statement. I saw Maurice, who had brought me to the church, beaming all over, while his friends slapped him on the shoulder.

"The biblical concept of marriage contradicts the garden concept in every single point.

"First of all, the Bible does away with the inaccurate concept of reproduction.

"It is not out of the man's seed that the child grows, but, according to the Bible and proven by modern science, husband and wife contribute equally to the creation of a new life.

"The child is not only the man's child, but belongs to both husband and wife. Just as *both* have to leave their parents and *both* have to cleave to each other and *both* have to become one flesh, so the child belongs to both husband and wife.

"The garden concept discriminates against women. The biblical concept conceives of the woman not as an inferior being, but as the equal partner of her husband, not an object but a person in her own right.

"The garden concept invites multiple marriages, for it thinks of the woman as a property which can be augmented in numbers at will. The biblical concept aims toward monogamy.

"The choice is between the garden and the triangle. Do you consider your wife a garden or a partner for whom you leave your parents, to whom you cleave and with whom you become one flesh?"

I paused. Complete silence prevailed. Many looked at my drawing of the triangle, and in their eyes I could read one great question. So I continued:

"There is one question left. Where is the place of the child in our triangle? Would someone like to answer this question?"

Many hands went up. I pointed to a woman in her late twenties who had a child on her back. She got up, came to the front, and walked over to the blackboard. Then, without hesitating, she pointed to the center of the triangle.

"Yes," I said, and I could sense a feeling of relief going through the audience. "The place of the child is in the center of the triangle. It begins in the physical union of the father and mother. It is surrounded by the love and faithfulness of both parents, and it is protected and sheltered by the legality of the marriage contract. This is the place of the child in the triangle of marriage. There alone is the atmosphere in which it can mature and be prepared for its own marriage later on."

3

WHILE THE AUDIENCE WAS SINGING THE CLOSING HYMN, I HAD A terrible feeling of defeat. They had been so silent toward the end. I couldn't resist trying to get an assuring word from Daniel.

"It was too long, wasn't it?" I whispered to him.

"I don't think so. They listened very well."

"But they were so silent at the end."

"When they are moved, our people just become more and more quiet."

But I wasn't sure whether he was just trying to be polite, so I asked him directly:

"What did you think about it? Was it very bad?"

He gave me a knowing smile as if he were familiar himself with the feelings I had, and he said:

"Well, you certainly took the bull by the horns."

"You don't think they were offended?"

"I don't think so. Many things they would not have accepted coming from me, but they will from you. And even if they are offended, what does it matter? It wasn't your message, was it? You must greet the people now."

They filed by one by one, grasping my hand with both hands as was their custom.

Miriam was the last one who shook hands with me.

"May I introduce to you my fiancé? This is Timothy."

A young man in a soldier's uniform stepped forward to greet me. He was rather dark, and although slightly shorter than Miriam, he had a strong, muscular body.

"Thank you very much for your message. I would like to talk to you."

"Why don't you come back with me to the hotel?"

I walked with Miriam and Timothy to Maurice's car.

"What did you think about the lecture?" I asked Miriam.

"I got the message all right. I think Timothy and I are having trouble with the left side of the triangle—the angle of cleaving. We don't know whether our cleaving is strong enough for the leaving."

"All right," I said, "Timothy and I can work on that in our talk together." She seemed to be happy.

Timothy and I got into Maurice's car. While we were driving back to the hotel, I said to Maurice with a smile:

"How is the sower without a garden?"

"Thinking very hard," he said. "It's so true what you said about widows—a property without a proprietor. Exactly. That's why I've always felt and still feel that I have a duty toward my widowed mother. You see, it really wasn't possible for me to leave and that's why I am not yet cleaving."

"And you had no father to buy you a garden."

"No, I had to work for my education and take care of my mother at the same time. I still feel I should continue to support her. If you say that the first condition for marriage is to leave one's mother, I'm afraid I can never get married."

"I said that 'leaving' does not mean to leave in the lurch."

"Yes, I understood that, but how could this be put into practice? If I got married I would have to take my mother into my home. How could I leave her and still have her live with me?"

"There is a difference. If you stay at home and your wife has to move into your mother's home, this usually leads to trouble. But if you move out first and start your own home, then you have actually 'left.' Then if you offer your mother shelter in your own home, there is much less danger of friction."

We stopped in front of my hotel.

"Well," Maurice said as Timothy and I got out of the car, "all I would need then would be a girl."

"I thought you had one."

"You mean the one I talk to between the two bus stops every day? I don't know. After your lecture I have doubts whether she would be the one with whom I could become 'one flesh' as you interpreted it—sharing everything."

"If you are eighteen years older, she could be your daughter. You would be tempted to treat her like that. In the best case, she would be an obedient garden, not a partner."

Maurice laughed. "I think this is why African men like to marry young girls. They prefer to have obedient gardens. The trouble is, Pastor, I don't know how to make the right approach to a girl, how to talk to her."

"Well, let's talk about that tomorrow. Will you pick me up again? And please bring your mother along."

"My mother? Why, she's in her sixties. I don't think she cares to hear about sex and love."

"Bring her along anyway."

He drove off, and I went with Timothy to my room. We sat down and began talking.

"Miriam spoke to me at the airport this afternoon," I said.

"Yes, I know. Do you think she's a nice girl?"

"She certainly is. Very beautiful too."

"Do you think it would be good for me to marry her?"

"Do you think you can get her to marry you?"

"That's just the point. I know she has her doubts about whether we fit together."

"Did she tell you why she hesitates?"

"No. We talk very little. But I can imagine what it is. I'm half an inch shorter than she is and also quite a bit darker."

"Is that a disadvantage to be darker?"

"Yes, we think it's more beautiful to be lighter."

"Well, Miriam didn't mention that."

"What did she say?"

"I wish that you would ask her yourself."

"But, Pastor, we can't talk about these things. I think Miriam wants you to tell me. That is why she has arranged this meeting."

"I know. Still, it would be better if she would tell you herself. Because in this way you could learn one thing which is indispensable for marriage. That is sharing."

He was silent.

"How old are you?"

"Twenty-two."

"Do you know how old Miriam is?"

"No, she never told me."

"How much does she earn?"

"I never asked her. I left school after I had finished the eighth grade. Then I joined the army."

"What plans do you have now?"

"What do you mean—plans?"

"Well, what are you looking forward to? What are your hopes for the future?"

"Nothing special. After a few years, I may become a sergeant. I don't know what else to say."

"But, Timothy, Miriam has a high-school education. She earns more than you do, and she's also a year older."

"Is that so?" he said thoughtfully. "But are these impediments to marriage?"

"Normally not. I could think of bigger ones."

"So you think our marriage could succeed?"

"It could succeed, but not easily. It would take a great deal of effort. It all depends upon whether you love each other enough to make this effort."

"But I love her, pastor," Timothy said emphatically. "If I can't get her, I don't know what I would do."

"Suicide?"

"I told her that once."

"This is where you made a great mistake, Timothy. It makes me doubt whether you really love her."

"Why?"

"Because you try to force her by menacing her. This isn't love. Love never forces the other one. Real love gives the other one complete freedom, even the freedom to say 'No.' If she married you in order to keep you from committing suicide, she would marry you out of fear, not out of love."

"But what can I do to make her love me?"

"Show her your love. Not by making threats, but by doing some hard work."

"Work?" Timothy seemed to be frightened. "What kind of work?"

"Work at yourself."

He looked at me without understanding.

"You see, Timothy, what worries me about your relationship to Miriam more than your difference in age and education is your lack of ambition. I am sure Miriam wants to make much more out of her life in the future. But you just told me that you may become a sergeant. Maybe. Maybe not. You lack ambition. Should you marry Miriam, this would probably cause trouble."

"But I can't change my height and age, or past education."

"You can change your ambitions, though. Change the things you can change. This would show Miriam more than anything else how much you love her."

Timothy sat in thoughtful silence. I thought he had had enough to think about.

He left, but with a sad look on his face. I am sure he hadn't expected our talk to have such an outcome. After he had gone I realized what a tiring day I had had and lay down for a few minutes' rest. I would have fallen asleep in my street clothes, but the telephone rang.

"This is the girl who called you this afternoon."

"I'm so glad you called again. I forgot to ask you for your name and address this afternoon."

"I didn't want to give you my name and address. I do not want my husband to know that I have such talks."

"Where are you calling from now?"

"From home. My husband just went out for a beer. But when he comes back, I have to hang up immediately."

"I see."

"I was at your lecture tonight. I slipped out of school, but was back before it closed. So my husband didn't notice that I was in church."

"Well, what did you think about my lecture?"

"It was interesting. Only I didn't like your triangle."

"You didn't? What's wrong with it?"

"Nothing, I suppose. I just don't like it. It has too many angles and corners and points. They sting. It's just like a man —what he would think of marriage; all straight lines and corners and everything just so. The pieces must fit exactly together. Very uncomfortable, very unattractive to me."

"Thank you."

"When I think of marriage, I think of something round and smooth and soft. Something you can put around yourself—like a warm cape."

"Maybe I should draw a circle with three sectors."

"I thought of something better. When I looked at the triangle you drew on the blackboard, I thought, It looks almost like a tent."

"A tent?"

"Yes, a tent. It has to have at least three poles, otherwise it can't stand alone. But if it stands, you can crawl into it and you feel sheltered and protected from the storm. It's very cozy in a tent when it rains. That's the way I like to think of marriage."

I had never thought of that. "Do you feel that way in your home?"

"No, I don't. My tent isn't complete. The top corner is lacking: the corner which you called the corner of leaving, the public and legal action of marriage, the wedding."

"If the top is lacking, then it must be raining into your tent."

"Yes, pastor, it's raining very hard. It isn't cozy at all. Who can help me to repair it?"

She couldn't hide the fact that she was sobbing.

"I would like to try if you will let me."

"But I left my parents and still I'm not publicly and legally married."

"Well, your leaving was a different leaving than the Bible talks about.

There was not that mutual and voluntary letting go between parents and child, which in the end binds them that much closer together. You left them out of contempt, and now they have left you in the lurch."

"But why doesn't my husband close the top of the tent?"

"Maybe it's because he knows you can't return to your parents."

"Well, at least he doesn't treat me like a garden."

"What makes you so sure of that?"

"He doesn't want children."

"Maybe he doesn't want you as a vegetable garden, but as a flower garden. Just for amusement in his free time."

"But he didn't buy me. He didn't pay a bride price."

"He pays for your education, though."

"Do you think this is another form of the bride price in order to make me dependent?"

"I can't say before I've talked to him. But it's possible."

"But I love him."

"I know you do. Otherwise you wouldn't call me."

"And he loves me too. That's why he pays for my education."

"I wish you were right. But why doesn't he close the top of the tent and legalize your marriage?"

There was sobbing again.

"Listen, can't you give me your telephone number so that I can call him?"

"Never! He's coming now." She slammed down the receiver. A tent! She must be a remarkable girl. A tent. Marriage as a tent.

I picked up my Bible and turned to the concordance at the back. More than a hundred Bible passages were listed under the word "tent." I looked up several of them, then turned to Jeremiah 10:20:

My *tent* is destroyed,
  and all my cords are broken;
my children have gone from me,
  and they are not;
there is no one to spread my *tent* again,
  and to set up my curtains.

This is her verse, I thought. "No one to spread my tent." If only I knew her name, her telephone number! All I could do now was to pray for her.

It was time for bed. As I took my pajamas out of my suitcase, a note from my wife fell into my hands. I read it: "In love and oneness with you, Deine Ingrid."

My tent, I thought, my tent. Then I fell asleep.

I woke up rather early the next morning and had a good breakfast in the hotel dining room. Daniel came soon after I was back in my room.

He had heard a lot of comments about my lecture.

"How did the older people react?"

"In general, very well. One of the oldest said to me: "When I first heard that he is going to speak about marriage in church, I thought he must be a wicked man. But now I see that marriage may have something to do with God.' "

"If I got this point across, that's already something."

"You know what I was most happy about? There was a childless couple in church. They suffer a great deal because they don't have children. But they love each other dearly and wouldn't think of divorce. They were deeply comforted that the triangle is complete without a child."

"So the garden concept is very much alive among your people too?"

"Yes, very much so. It's what our people believe right down the line. Also, that the child grows out of the seed of the man, and that sons are more precious than daughters and that the garden must be bought."

It was a pleasure to talk to Daniel. He had deep insights and I'm sure he was the best interpreter I could have wished for. Through him I felt very encouraged. He was a real brother.

"You know, Daniel," I said, "I've almost come to the conclusion that basically there are only two concepts of marriage in the world: the garden concept and the biblical concept, the triangle. Of course there may be all kinds of variations and deviations."

Daniel thought for a moment. Then he said:

"The 'leaving' is the greatest problem here in our city. Our marriages are 'leaving-sick.' Either our children leave without their parents' consent or they don't leave at all. In both cases marriages get into trouble. Our people can't see how you can leave and still remain united, or feel united and leave in spite of that."

"I don't think it can be explained. It is a paradox. The only way to illustrate it is through Christ. In his letter to the Ephesians, Paul says expressly: 'For this reason a man shall leave his father and mother. . . . I take it to mean Christ. . . .' Christ left His father and still remained one with Him. We have a hymn verse in German which translated goes like this:

" 'The Son goes out from his Father
and still he remains eternally at home.' "

"All right, but can you explain this to our people?"

"I'll try," I said. "But Daniel, may I ask you a question? What was the point last night that touched you most personally?"

He had his answer ready. "It was being closest to each other, closer than to anyone or anything else. For me it's very difficult to get my work as a pastor into balance with my marriage. I do not have enough time for my wife. My work comes first and she comes second. When she complains that she can never count on me for meals, that is very true. And even during the meal I have to get up three or four times when visitors come or the phone rings."

"I didn't know whether Esther was joking in the car yesterday or whether she was serious."

"She was very serious, Walter. And she is right. But I don't know how to change things. Also, what you said about sharing touched me very much. We don't have that. We don't take time for it."

The telephone started to ring while he was still speaking. It was the girl again.

"Where are you calling from?" I asked.

"From school. We have recess now."

"Did you talk to your husband last night about coming to see me?"

"No."

"I found something for you last night. Do you own a Bible?"

"Yes, I have one from my school days in our village."

"Then look up Jeremiah 10:20. It's the verse for you."

"I will. Good-by. The bell is ringing for classes. I just wanted to greet you."

I put down the receiver. "It's my anonymous caller," I said to Daniel. "That's the third time she's called me. She lives with a man who doesn't want to legalize their marriage. But he sends her to school and she takes it as proof that he loves her."

"This is nothing unusual in our city," Daniel said. "It's very seldom that I have a wedding in my church. People hesitate because it makes divorce more difficult. It may be that they will ask for a church wedding when they already have several children. You see, life here is not so straight-lined and clean-cut as your triangle. There are all kinds of in-between."

"Thanks for telling me. That girl did not like the triangle either. She said the corners stung her."

"They stung me all right," Daniel said, laughing.

"Well, let's get back to your problem. Couldn't we have supper together tonight after the lecture when your children are in bed? I'd like to talk with both of you."

When Maurice picked me up that night, an elderly lady was with him. She was small and thin, her hair completely covered with a white head scarf. Out of her wrinkled face, two eyes sparkled.

She greeted me and talked to me as if I understood her language. Maurice translated. "She greets you and says that she is a property without an owner."

"Did your son tell you about the lecture last night?"

She nodded, and pointing to her son, said, "Maurice is an owner without property."

"You have a very fine son."

"He takes care of me very well."

"You can be proud of him."

"But he needs a wife. I would take care of her well. She would not have to do much work. I could cook for both of them."

After Maurice had translated this last statement, I said to him: "She thinks you will bring your wife to her and she will continue to rule the household. You must explain to her very carefully what I said yesterday about 'leaving.' Especially about the kitchen. Even if your mother moved into your home, it must be absolutely clear who rules over the kitchen."

"I wish you would explain that to her," Maurice said. "It would mean more to her coming from you. It's strange, but there are certain things which we accept easier if they come from a stranger."

"I think all people have trouble with the word 'leaving.' It is simply not a human, but a divine wisdom."

We had arrived at the church. It was full again. As I stood in the pulpit beside Daniel, I had a feeling of being completely one with him concerning the message we had to say.

4

YESTERDAY WE TALKED ABOUT THE MARRIAGE TRIANGLE, TO LEAVE, to cleave, and to become one flesh which is possible only between two persons.

"Afterwards a lady called me and told me she didn't like the triangle I drew on the blackboard. 'It has too many angles and corners and points. They sting,' she said.

"I understood what she meant. Try not to think of this triangle of wedlock, love, and sex as something unmovable and stiff, but as something alive.

"For instance in a circus, I once saw three jugglers. They stood at equal distance from each other, like three points in a triangle. Each one threw balls to both of his partners and received balls from both of his partners. Each one had to give as well as receive. As long as they were able to keep up the rhythm of giving and receiving, the game went on in perfect harmony.

Interplay of Forces

"Marriage is like this skillful performance. Its life depends upon the interplay between the legal the personal and the physical aspects of the relationship." At this point I took a wooden triangle out of my briefcase and held it up for the audience to see. I grasped the bottom left angle and said:

"Marriage needs love. It receives from love its fulfillment, its joy. Love is a gift to marriage. It provides marriage with the spirit of adventure, of never-ending expectation. Love is like the blood pulsing through the veins of marriage. It makes it alive.

"And the state of being married, of wedlock, passes on this life to the sexual togetherness and provides the one-flesh union with a shelter. A woman once told me that she would rather think of the triangle as a tent. Indeed, marriage is a tent for the physical fellowship. The lovers feel protected and sheltered in it. Freed from fear, they experience great satisfaction and a sense of redeemed peace.

"This sense of redeemed peace is then passed on to love. It is the strong foundation in the ups and downs of feelings, of emotions. Within the 'tent' the experience of becoming one flesh strengthens love and makes it grow. It motivates love to faithfulness and makes it want to last.

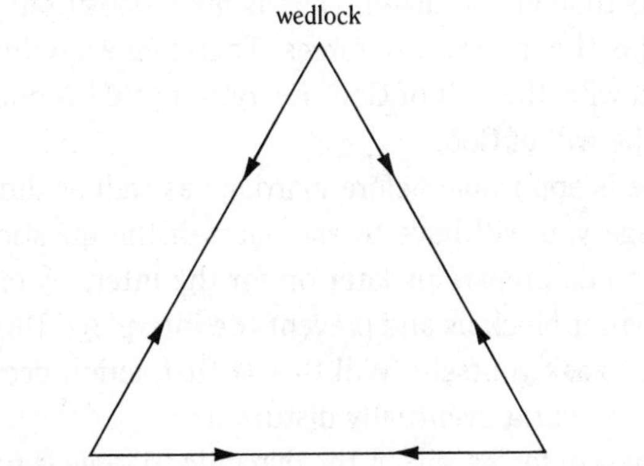

"Love does not only receive strength from the physical fellowship; it also gives the one-flesh union strength. Love longs for the physical expression, deepens it and makes it meaningful and precious. As an act of married love, the one-flesh union becomes an 'act of love' in the full sense of the word.

"Consequently, within the 'tent' the act of love not only receives, but also gives security to marriage. Through the physical surrender to each other, the lovers renew again and again their wedding vow.

"Marriage serves love through this ever-renewed affirmation. For this reason love needs marriage as much as marriage needs love. In the sad hours when love is in danger of growing cold, husband and wife cling to the fact that they are married and remind each other of their mutual promise. 'After all, I married you,' they say. Thus, marriage becomes the protector, the guardian of love.

The Will of God

"In our day there is a great confusion about sex, love, and marriage. This confusion reigns, not only in Africa, but in the East and West as well.

"In the light of this fact our key verse from the Bible appears as a very modern statement. It contains precisely the same three factors. The great question is: What is the will of God concerning sex, love, and marriage? How does God want them to be related? No one dares to answer this question.

"Nevertheless I would like to make a proposition as a guide for our actions in this time of confusion. Here is my proposition:

"God's will is the interplay of forces. Therefore everything that favors it is in accord with the will of God. Everything that hinders it is not in accord with the will of God.

"This guide is applicable before marriage as well as during marriage. Before marriage you will have to ask yourself the question: 'Will what we are going to do prepare us later on for the interplay of forces in our marriage, or will it block us and prevent the interplay?' During marriage, you will have to ask yourself: 'Will this or that action deepen the interplay of forces, or will it eventually disturb it?'

"The interplay of forces within the dynamic triangle is full of elasticity and creative freedom. In Genesis 2:24, God offers us an image which meets the personal need of every situation, every culture. For the will of God is valid not only for the Christian. It is valid for all mankind.

"The dynamic triangle, the guiding image of our Bible verse, is God's offer to everyone. I say, it is an offer, a gift. God never demands anything from us unless He gives it at the same time."

My audience sat in pondering silence. They looked at the triangle on the blackboard and at the one in my hand. I tried to read their thoughts and said:

"You may feel discouraged now. You may say: 'If marriage is such a work of art, then I am a long way from having a perfect marriage.' I know. I feel the same way. And I know Daniel does too."

Daniel nodded.

"There is no such thing as a perfect marriage. Marriage keeps us humble. The safest way to become humble about one's virtues is to get married. We always have to work on one of the angles of the triangle.

"I would say that most marital troubles point to the fact that one of the three forces is not fully integrated into the triangle. Let us try out our guiding image in diagnosing some marital sicknesses.

"Let's pretend now that you are all marriage doctors. We are going to visit a marriage hospital. Let me introduce you to some of the patients.

"The first patient is one who has had trouble with the left angle of our triangle. Love has grown cold. I call this disease

The Empty Marriage

"Let me describe how this case looks. The couple are married, legally married, and have been for quite some time. They also have had physical fellowship. But love is gone.

"The reasons for this state can be many. Maybe there was no love in the first place. Maybe they married too young and too soon, and what they thought was love lacked the quality of 'cleaving.' Or their marriage was based entirely on physical attraction, and as the years went by, this physical attraction wasn't so strong anymore. Or they neglected to put fuel on the fire of their love and became too absorbed by work in household and profession or by the children. They each followed different interests without sharing them, and pretty soon they had lost their common ground.

"It is a dangerous disease. No marriage can take it for a very long time without falling seriously ill. In the beginning this disease can be covered up quite well by the 'married look,' and the outside world is fooled. The couple still inhabit the same dwelling. But that's all.

"The disease does not stand still. As it progresses, these are the symptoms: The partners become cruel to each other in word and in deed. This cruelty on the part of both then gives way to complete in difference and a yawning emptiness in the mutual relationship.

"It is unavoidable that one day this emptiness also affects the physical fellowship. Since the three angles of the triangle are inseparable from each other, the sickness of one will infect the two others. The sex act is experienced as a duty and a burden. A tension is created between sex and marriage.

"Pretty soon the husband looks for a woman who understands him better than his wife. The wife will find a man who can comfort her better than her husband. Jealousy creeps in. Mental unfaithfulness precedes sexual unfaithfulness. Finally, adultery affects the legal foundation and affects the top angle of the triangle also.

"This disease has been described and illustrated in thousands of films and novels. In a false way, these novels and movies put the blame on marriage for the death of love.

"They would like to have us believe that only outside of marriage does love have a chance to live, that only such love is worthy of praise, interesting, attractive, and enticing.

"But the diagnosis is wrong. It is not marriage which causes the death of love, but rather the lack of love which causes the death of marriage. Love outside of marriage, however, easily becomes a destructive prairie fire which, in the end, devours the lovers.

"There is one possibility which is very rarely envisioned by these films and novels. It is the possibility of happy married love, of love as an integral part of the triangle. The true therapy lies here alone. It has to be applied, however, before love dies completely and the other two angles of the triangle are infected.

"Let us go to the next patient, the next couple. Their problem is at the top of the triangle. I call this sickness

The Stolen Marriage

"The symptoms in this case are as follows: The two think they love each other. They also have sexual intercourse with each other. But they are not yet legally married.

"This is one of the greatest temptations of our time: to consider the legal act of the wedding as a mere formality, as an unimportant piece of paper, which one can get someday, or maybe not at all. One pretends that the two angles of love and sex represent the whole of marriage.

"Some people, in all seriousness, propose trial marriages. They suggest that a couple live together for awhile in order to see whether they fit together. If then they come to the conclusion that they do not, they can separate without risking a divorce. But the whole proposition rests upon the illusion that the two angles of sex and love represent the whole. Since they do not, marriage cannot be tested in that way.

"The relationship is sick. The symptoms are as follows: broken hearts and destroyed lives, especially as far as the girl is concerned. I don't know how you feel about it, but in many cultures a girl who has lost her virginity has very little chance of getting married. In our countries, a girl who has had a child out of wedlock is at a great disadvantage. The result is that often a hurried and forced marriage takes place when the girl discovers she's expecting a baby. Many of these marriages end in divorce later on.

"We must consider also the children who grow out of these alliances. They are deprived of the shelteredness of marriage. The top of the tent is gone. It rains in. They are deprived not only of the wholeness of the marriage tent, but also of a father. It's hard to overestimate what this means in the life of a child. Certainly the top of the tent, the wedlock, is essential."

At this point, I couldn't help but think of my anonymous caller. Was she in the audience again this evening? This thought prompted me to add the following remark:

"Those who cut off the top of the tent and practice 'free-love' or 'trial marriages' usually forget to say that this makes the use of contraceptives a necessity. They pretend that this wouldn't have any effect either on the persons who apply them or on their relationship. But this is not true. Especially in premarital situations certain contraceptive methods represent a definite menace to the spontaneity and dignity of love."

Here I hesitated. I didn't know how much I should go into detail. I pointed with my finger at my notes which mentioned "early withdrawal," "heavy petting," "condoms." Daniel glanced at the words and shook his head slightly. This teamwork in the pulpit was a wonderful experience for me. I complied, of course, and continued:

"I repeat: It is a handicap for love. We can make the same observation now which we made before when we studied the case of the empty marriage. If one of the angles of the triangle gets sick, the other two are affected and infected as well. They get into a quarrel with each other.

"When love is lacking, sex and marriage fall apart. If there has been no wedding, then love and sex become hostile to each other.

"The sexual union often takes place hurriedly and secretly under undignified circumstances. Thus the experience does not make love blossom and flower, but makes it wither away.

"We have this problem very often in America and Europe. A recent German film, one of the rare good ones, illustrated very well the disease of stolen marriage. The film showed a young couple living together very happily. After the film had run about twenty minutes, the viewers realized that the couple were not married. Friends and relatives tried to convince them to marry. But they refused. At first everything went all right. Then the girl became pregnant. The love and confidence between them was not deep enough so that she dared to tell her 'husband.' She was afraid that he would leave her. She therefore decided to have an abortion secretly.

"The last scene shows her lying exhausted on the couch in their apartment after the operation. He comes home from work and understands what has happened. He sits down at the other end of a large and empty table which separates them. Silence reigns. Neither one speaks. They have nothing to say to each other anymore. Because of the missing angle of the wedding, love has no chance to prove its durability and genuineness. Sex became the death of love."

As I paused for a moment, I sensed a certain reaction among the young people. From the expression in their eyes, I concluded that this film could have been made in their city too.

"Let us go to the next patients in our marriage hospital. There is a third class of marriage diseases. They have to do with the right angle of the triangle. This angle also can fall ill. I would call this sickness

The Unfulfilled Marriage

"First of all, let me describe the situation: The couple is married, legally married, and has been for ten or twenty years already. They love each other dearly and would never think of a divorce. But in spite of this love, their physical fellowship remains unsatisfactory and unfulfilled.

"The husband says: 'My wife is cold. She does not react in the normal way. I feel that she just endures the act of love, but she never invites me. She finds no pleasure in it.'

"The wife says: 'My husband is too quick. I feel that he forces me and abuses me. He never gets enough.' Or she may say just the contrary: 'He's always tired. I am longing, but he turns his back to me and sleeps. I think he is impotent.' "

There was a roar of laughter which I had not expected. I had forgotten in that moment that impotence is a subject of great ridicule in Africa. An impotent man is considered as something less than a human being. An African man fears impotence more than death.

"The diseases of the physical aspect of marriage cause tremendous suffering to the marriage partners. Just because they love each other and would like to make each other happy, they suffer all the more. Where does this disease come from?

"In many cases the unfulfilled marriage is a direct or indirect fruit of the stolen marriage. When I say this, I'm not thinking so much of venereal disease. No, when I say that the stolen marriage often begets unfulfilled marriage, I am thinking of the superficial way of having intercourse with partners who are more or less indifferent, under time pressure and in secrecy, involving only the body but not the heart, not the whole person.

"Again we can observe how the other two angles are affected by this disease.

"When the physical fellowship becomes torture, because it always ends with the disappointment on the part of one or both partners, one or the other will soon reproach his partner for the lack of love. Monotony grows. The personal relationship changes into an impersonal mechanism. Love grows cold. As soon as this happens, the temptation is great to satisfy sexual desire outside of marriage with a more responsive or more considerate partner. Then the legal aspect of marriage is endangered. Adultery and finally divorce are the consequences. This disease, too, may lead to the death of marriage if it is not cured in time."

I gave an inward sigh of relief at this point. So far this had been the touchiest part of my lectures, but Daniel had interpreted without hesitation and the older people hadn't seemed to take offense.

I began again:

"For those who prepare themselves for marriage, the practical question comes up: From which angle do we enter into the marriage triangle?

"In general, there are three answers to this question: a traditional answer, a modern answer, and the biblical answer. Let us take them up one by one.

"The traditional answer proposes entering the triangle at the top angle. I would like to call it

The Wedding Entrance

"Until recent times this was the normal entrance, not only in Africa and Asia, but also in the West.

"The wedding is arranged by the parents and not by the couple. Sometimes the couple see each other for the first time on the wedding day or only shortly before.

"The purpose of this entrance is very clear: It is the child. For what other reason should one enter the triangle, after all, if not for posterity? The wedding entrance belongs to the garden concept."

I picked up my wooden triangle again and pointed to the top angle.

"One enters from the wedding angle and goes directly to the sex angle, or, in this case, we could call it the 'fertility angle,' because the purpose of the sexual union is seen in the narrow sense of producing children.

"The angle of love is left out or very much neglected. It could even be dangerous because it might lead to a conflict between the couple and the family. What if the young people made a different choice from that the family proposed?

"By no means do I want to maintain that all marriages which are arranged in this traditional way must necessarily become unhappy. Love can certainly grow also during marriage.

"A very popular musical play in America and Europe is called *Fiddler on the Roof.* It tells the story of a Jewish couple, Tevye, the milkman, and his wife, Golde. They are typical of the couples who entered marriage through the wedding entrance. After twenty-five years of marriage, they ask themselves the question whether they love each other. We hear the following dialogue between them:

TEVYE

Golde, I'm asking you a question—
Do you love me?

GOLDE

You're a fool.

TEVYE

I know—

But do you love me?

GOLDE

Do I love you?
For twenty-five years I've washed your clothes,
Cooked your meals, cleaned your house,
Given you children, milked the cow.
After twenty-five years, why talk about
love right now?

TEVYE

Golde, the first time I met you
Was on our wedding day.
I was scared.

GOLDE

I was shy.

TEVYE

I was nervous.

GOLDE
So was I.

TEVYE
But my father and my mother
Said we'd learn to love each other.
And now I'm asking, Golde,
Do you love me?

GOLDE
I'm your wife.

TEVYE
I know—
But do you love me?

GOLDE
Do I love him?
For twenty-five years I've lived with him.
Fought with him, starved with him.
Twenty-five years my bed is his.
If that's not love, what is?

TEVYE
Then you love me?

GOLDE
I suppose I do.

TEVYE
And I suppose I love you, too.

TEVYE and GOLDE
It doesn't change a thing,
But even so,
After twenty-five years,

*It's nice to know.**

"Americans and Europeans tend to overestimate the value of romantic love. When Africans and Asians warn us about this, we have to listen to them.

"An Indian once compared love with a bowl of soup and marriage with the hot plate of a stove and said: 'You Westerners put a hot bowl on a cold plate and it grows cold slowly. We put a cold bowl on a hot plate and it warms up slowly.'

"There is a lot of truth in this comparison. It does not deny that love is essential for marriage. But it shows also that marriage is more, infinitely more, than just love. It's not only moonlight and roses, but also dishes and diapers.

"Still, in spite of this fact, it remains doubtful whether the wedding entrance is the most promising one. The danger is very real that the power of love never joins the play of forces and thus helps to unfold the dynamism of the triangle. It is, to say the least, a great risk to arrange a wedding without the consent of the partners involved.

I once took part in a discussion group with university girl students at a large African university. The girls wanted to ask questions about marriage. To my great surprise, their most burning question was: 'How can we succeed in *not* getting married?' I asked: 'Why don't you want to get married?' The answer: 'We see so many empty marriages without love all around us that we are frightened at the thought of entering through the wedding entrance.'

"Therefore the modern answer has another proposition to make. It suggests entering from the sex angle and to use therefore

The Sex Entrance

"I would like to make one thing clear at the beginning: when I speak today about those who want to enter into the triangle from the sex entrance, I do not talk about engaged couples. Their problem is a special one and I shall deal with it tomorrow.

---

*Taken from *Fiddler on the Roof* by Joseph Stein. © 1964 by Joseph Stein. Used by permission of Crown Publishers, Inc.

"Today I speak about those who start to build their marriage with a sexual experience, because they think that love will grow out of it. Then, as a matter of course, they think that this love will change into faithfulness and from there, almost automatically, finally will lead to the wedding."

I held up my wooden triangle again and pointed first to the angle on the right, the sex angle, from there to the left, and then to the top.

"Or maybe even the other way around. They believe that the sexual surrender will oblige the other one to marry them and then with the marriage license in hand, love will somehow follow.

"Both beliefs are illusionary. Love does not grow out of sex. Love must grow into sex.

"True, within marriage, under the shelter of the tent, sex gives strength to love. But outside of the tent sex is not practiced for love's sake, but for purely egoistic reasons.

"Why does a boy try to sleep with a girl whom he hardly knows and for whom he doesn't really care? Usually there are three major motives:

"1. He is afraid that unless he has sex that he will become sick or neurotic, or both.

"2. He thinks he has to learn by doing.

"3. He wants to brag about his conquest.

"The first reason is not true, the second is not possible the third is mean, simply mean. None of them comes out of love and concern for the other one. A young man who argues like that thinks of himself only. He uses a girl as a means toward an end, as a tool to reach his own goals. He does not prepare himself for marriage.

"Why would a girl give herself to a boy whom she hardly knows and for whom she does not care?

"Again there are usually three major motives involved:

"1. She wants to be popular with the boys.

"2. Consciously or unconsciously, she wants to know whether she can become a mother.

"3. She wants to bind the boy and provide herself with a husband.

"Again all three motives come out of selfishness and not out of love.

A girl who gives herself up for one of these reasons doesn't prepare herself for marriage either.

"She may become popular, but with the wrong kind of boys. Soon she will be known as an 'easy' girl and those who choose her for this reason will certainly make poor husbands.

"She may become pregnant and thus receive the assurance that she can become a mother. But then she has degraded her baby as a means toward an end and it may also have to grow up without a father.

"To bind the boy by sexual intercourse is, in most cases, an illusion. The boy usually loses interest in a conquered fortress. Even if he would marry the girl out of obligation such a marriage has a poor prospect of success.

"A disappointed girl once told me this: 'For me it was the beginning. For him it was the end.' Instead of catching, she lost what she wanted to catch and learned from the bitter experience that sex not only does not make love grow, but that it can destroy it.

"There's a story in the Bible which could be found in any news magazine of our day. It appears in II Samuel 13. The account describes how the king's son, Amnon, seduced his half sister, Tamar. He pretended that he was sick and insisted that Tamar feed him personally. She had to bake little cakes before his very eyes. But baking cakes was not enough. She also had to put them in his mouth—and this only after both were alone in the bedroom. Tamar didn't protest at all.

"Then it happened as it had to happen: 'But when she brought [the cakes] near to him to eat, he took hold of her, and said to her, Come, lie with me' (v. 11). Tamar now tried desperately, at the last moment, to get the wedding angle into the picture. She asked Amnon to get the wedding license from the king.

"But no! 'He would not listen to her; and being stronger than she, he forced her, and lay with her' (v. 14).

"Then we find a statement of tremendous consequence. The next verse reads: 'Then Amnon hated her with very great hatred; so that the hatred with which he hated her was greater than the love with which he had loved her. And Amnon said to her: "Arise, be gone." '

"This story shows us that the marriage triangle is inseparable and indivisible. It is a living demonstration of how sexual desire can become a destroying force which changes love into aversion and hatred when the third angle is cut off and love is not upheld and protected by marriage.

"And so, the one who asks for sexual surrender as a proof of love does not act out of love. When a boy extorts this from a girl with the argument: 'If you love me, then prove it by giving yourself' there is only one adequate answer: 'Now I know that you do not love me. Otherwise you wouldn't ask for that.'

"It goes without saying that in case a girl uses the same argument and asks to be taken as a proof of love, she deserves the same answer from the boy.

"Dr. Paul Popenoe, the well-known American marriage counselor, has made a very practical suggestion in this regard. He says that a girl should slip a note to her friend which reads: 'Go slowly, my boyfriend, and see all the fine things that are in me. Or go fast, and I shall see how little there is in you.' "

There was a movement of protest among the young men in the audience, so I added: "Since we have a growing number of aggressive girls today, maybe the boys should be prepared to slip a similar note to their girlfriends.

"Let me finish today with the quotation from the letter of a girl, who together with her friend had made up her mind not to enter from the sex entrance.

"She wrote: 'Since we have made this decision there is an easiness in our relationship—the easiness of something not yet final. This is what I appreciate the most. At the same time, there is in this lightness the promise of greatness and depth.' "

5

AS I STOOD AT THE DOOR GREETING THE PEOPLE AFTER THE LECture a rather tall girl whispered as she passed by hurriedly:

"I shall call you tonight at the hotel."

"I'll be at the pastor's home. You must call there."

"All right."

"Tell me your name, so that I will know who you are when you call."

"Fatma."

Then she was gone. Perhaps she is my anonymous caller, I thought instantly. For a moment I was tempted to run after her. But then Miriam came with Timothy.

"Could we have another talk?" she asked.

"I wish you would come together."

"That's what we would like to do."

We arranged a time at five o'clock the next afternoon.

The last ones to greet me were Maurice and his mother. She held my right hand in both of hers, and while she was talking, bowed over and over again.

"She wants to thank you," Maurice explained.

"Ask her what touched her especially this evening."

The mother thought for a moment and then Maurice translated her answer:

"She says that love could enter into marriage later on. And what the woman said in the musical: 'For twenty-five years I've lived with him. . . . If that's not love, what is?' "

I looked at this little old woman with her wiry, worn-out body, looked at the wrinkled face with the lively eyes—and then I couldn't help but put my arms around her and give her a hug.

Just to think she had remembered that line! I was deeply comforted. If she had gotten the message in spite of the different languages, the different cultural backgrounds, then I could be sure that others too had understood.

Different backgrounds? So what! If a line from a modern American musical with a Jewish background, taking place in Russia, touches an almost seventy-year-old widow who grew up in the African bush—the hearts of people must be the same all over the world. The differences are on the surface. Deep down there is nothing but that naked human heart—longing, fearing, hoping—the same wherever it beats.

When I entered Pastor Daniel's house, the table was set for supper. Daniel was still in the churchyard, talking to some of his parishioners. Esther was in the kitchen together with the young girl who was helping her. Esther greeted me and asked me to take my place at the table.

"Supper will be ready in a few minutes."

"Were you in church tonight?"

"Yes, of course."

Evidently she had prepared the meal ahead of time. She must be a very efficient housewife, I thought.

After about ten minutes she put a steaming hot dish of noodles on the table. Then she brought a platter of sliced meat garnished with hard-boiled eggs and tomatoes. A large glass bowl filled with fruit salad—diced bananas, pineapple, papayas, oranges, and grapefruit—stood on the table for dessert.

"Do you prefer tea or coffee?"

"Tea, please. I'm still quite wound up. I'm afraid I couldn't sleep if I would drink coffee this evening."

We sat opposite each other. The place at the end of the table was set for Daniel.

"It must be very tiring to lecture," Esther said politely.

"It's not so much the lecturing, but the talks afterward, which take much strength."

We sat silently for a few minutes.

"Where is Daniel?"

"He's still outside talking to people."

"Doesn't he know that the meal is ready?"

"Yes, he does."

There was silence again. The food was still steaming on the table.

"Can't you call him?"

"It's no use. He won't come until he is finished."

We waited.

"I enjoyed your lecture," Esther said, probably in order to change the subject.

"It is wonderful to have your husband as an interpreter. I feel completely at one with him in spirit, so it's almost as if only one man were speaking. I have a feeling that he improves my lectures quite a bit when translating."

"He does well."

We were silent again. She picked up the hot dish and carried it back to the kitchen.

"You suffer," I said when she returned, "and you are embarrassed because of me."

She struggled with her tears, but then she got hold of herself.

"I love Daniel very much," she said. "But he is not a man of schedule. I don't mind hard work, but I want to plan my day and have order in my duties. He is a man who acts out of the spur of the moment. He is an excellent pastor. People like him very much. But I'm afraid they take advantage of him too."

"Your gifts are different, but they could be used to complement and complete each other."

"Maybe so, but we don't know how to coordinate our gifts. We don't throw the balls into each other's hands. We throw them in two different directions. They fall on the ground. No one to pick them up."

Daniel still did not come. I admired how well Esther mastered her impatience.

"Let me go out to him," I said.

She shrugged her shoulders and tried to smile, but she did not hinder me.

Daniel was standing in the yard between the parsonage and the church surrounded by a group of people having a lively discussion. I said to him:

"Daniel, I have a message for these people. Could you please interpret for me?"

He smiled in agreement.

"Ladies and gentlemen," I said, "this man to whom you have been talking is a very tired man. He is also very hungry. In his house, his wife sits and weeps, because the food is getting cold. Besides that, they have a guest. He is also very tired and hungry, because he lectured tonight in a certain church . . ."

The last words were drowned in laughter and apologies. In less than a minute they all left.

"You can do that," Daniel said as we walked to his house, "but they wouldn't accept it from me."

"Did you ever try?"

We entered the house and sat down at the table. Esther brought the hot dish in from the kitchen again. Daniel said grace. Then the telephone rang. As if stung by a bee, Daniel jumped up.

So did I. I put my hands on his shoulders and forced him back in his chair, telling Esther:

"You go and take it! Tell the caller that your husband is having his evening meal. Ask whether he could call him back later on or whether you could take a message."

She came back quickly. "It was a man. He said he just wanted to greet you. He had no special reason for calling."

We began our meal together.

"It's always the same," Esther commented. "As soon as we sit down for a meal, the telephone rings. Daniel gets up four or five times during each meal."

"You will get sick, Daniel, if you continue like this. And Esther, it's your duty to protect him."

"If only he would let me."

"Daniel, you're not the bellboy of your parish, you are the pastor."

The telephone rang again. I realized that it took all of Daniel's strength and will power not to get up. I nodded to Esther and she went to answer it.

While she was away, Daniel said:

You see now why we put you up in a hotel?"

"Yes, I understand. But you must find a solution. This is bad stewardship of your time and strength."

Esther returned. "Someone's mother is sick," she said. "But it's not serious. I could see her tomorrow morning. I took the address down."

"Really, Esther, you shouldn't have to answer the telephone either. You should train someone from your parish to take these calls at certain times."

"It's not only the telephone. The visitors and callers too are a problem. They come at any time."

"I can see no other solution. You must decide on certain hours when you are available and then post these times on the door."

Daniel said, "Africans wouldn't understand it. They would think it is very impolite. It is against their traditions."

"Listen, my brother, if you would come to Germany and I would take you to any local parish, I can promise you that the pastor there has the same problem. It's a question of whether you are obedient to your customs or to your calling. You know the story about the lighthouse keeper. It was his responsibility to keep the light burning and supplied with oil night and day. The lighthouse guided ships as they passed through a dangerous strait. The people of the nearby village would come to the lighthouse keeper and would ask him for just a little bit of oil for their lamps. He was too good-natured ever to say 'no.' So he gave away his supply of oil little by little. One day there was no oil left and the light went out. A ship went on the rocks and sunk. His good-naturedness had caused the death of many."

"You are right," Daniel said. "I just can't say 'no.' "

"It's not only your ministry which is at stake, but also your marriage."

"We have to make a new start, I know. It's the right angle of the triangle which we need to work on—the angle of sharing."

"If we could only have fifteen uninterrupted minutes together every morning!" Esther said. "But we stumble into our day without a plan and then we just wait and see what happens. I never know what he is going to do. He doesn't know what I do. We have no fixed mealtimes. It's hard on the children too."

There was a knock at the door. Both of them looked at me inquiringly.

"What is the girl in the kitchen doing?" I asked.

"She is waiting to wash the dishes when we are finished."

We heard the knock again.

"Tell her to go to the door and tell the caller to come back tomorrow—"

"But it must be before nine o'clock," Daniel interrupted.

After a few moments the girl returned.

"What did he say?"

"He agreed."

"Well," Daniel said, shaking his head, "in the long run, our people will not understand this."

"If you never challenge them, of course they won't. This quarter of an hour in the morning which Esther asks for is like the rudder of the day. Don't forget: the testimony which you give with your own married life does more than a hundred lectures on marriage!"

Daniel replied: "I tell you that we have to remind ourselves many times that we are married. If it were just for our feelings of love, our marriage would have been on the rocks long ago."

"And this in spite of the fact that we love each other," Esther interjected. "I love him very much and I know he loves me."

"It's not in spite of the fact that you love each other," I said, "it's because of this fact that you have to remind yourselves that you are married."

"Is this idea, that marriage upholds love, generally accepted in America and Europe?" Daniel inquired.

I'm always a little afraid when Africans begin asking me these questions.

"Not at all," I said honestly. "In America and Europe today the triangle is very torn apart. Marriage and love are torn apart; love and sex are torn apart; and, of course, sex and marriage."

"How do they tear love and marriage apart?"

"With the argument that 'love' justifies everything. With or without marriage, you may have sex wherever you want, whenever you want, and with whomever you want—as long as you 'love' him or her."

"And what is wrong with this thinking?"

"It is unrealistic. They do not see this world as it is. There is no such thing as unlimited freedom just like a forest or prairie fire becomes destructive, so does 'free love' become inhuman, demonic. The Soviet Union tried at one time to set love free in that country. The experiment ended in failure. Marriage means for love what the hearth means for fire."

"But how can I explain this to my people?"

"There is only one way: through God's love. God Himself is love, but He gave up His freedom and power. He humbled Himself and accepted restraint and limitations. God became incarnate. Love was made flesh."

"But that would mean that only the one who believes in the God incarnate can help people with their marriage problems."

"In the deepest sense, yes, because only he knows that God Himself is hidden in the one we love. Unless we encounter God in our partner, we fail our partner."

Daniel thought for awhile.

"And how do they tear love and sex apart in the West?"

"There are, of course, many opinions. A certain trend of thinking pleads for sex without love. These people would ridicule love as chit chat. They would say, 'Sex is for fun, not for love. For sex, love is repressive. Sex is for the happiness of the moment. It's a pleasure only if practiced without obligation and without regret.' But Daniel, my brother, I didn't come to talk to your people as a Westerner. I came as one who believes in the God incarnate."

"I know that. Otherwise I wouldn't have invited you," Daniel said warmly. "But are you saying that this message would be still less popular in America and Europe today than it is in Africa?"

"Precisely. Whoever proclaims the message of the dynamic triangle is a lonesome voice in the wilderness, regardless of the culture. The one who formulated this verse—that a man shall leave his father and mother, cleave to his wife and become one flesh with her—must have been a lonesome person too. It strikes me that no one else in the Old Testament quotes this verse. None of the prophets—until Jesus uses it."

"But isn't a certain garden concept also present in the Old Testament?" Esther asked. "There is male dominance. There is divorce as a man's right. There is polygamy and emphasis on fertility."

"I think it's a process, Esther," I replied. "I think that the message of this verse started a process which permeated the Israelitic culture. There is also a trend in the Old Testament to overcome the 'garden concept.' When Jesus quotes this verse in the New Testament, he uses it clearly against divorce and in favor of monogamy."

The telephone rang again. Daniel waved his hand to his wife with the gesture of an Arab sheik. "I'll let my garden serve me," he joked.

Esther got up obediently and went to Daniel's office, where the telephone was. She came back laughing and addressed me:

"This time it's for you."

Before I could catch myself, I jumped up just as Daniel had done earlier. Daniel roared with laughter while I stood in embarrassment, realizing that I had acted against my own advice.

"You are excused," he said graciously. "First of all, except for half of your dessert, you have finished the meal. Second, you have shown me that you are not a legalist."

I picked up the receiver.

"Is this Fatma?"

"Yes."

"Tell me, are you the one who called me already twice yesterday?"

"Yes, I'm the one."

"Then at least I now know your name."

"Is that important?"

"It's easier to pray for you."

"Do you pray for me?"

"Yes."

"Why do you do that?"

"It's the only way I can help you. Humanly, I am at my wit's end. Besides, you asked me to do it once."

Silence.

"You were in church again tonight?"

"Yes."

"Without permission again?"

"Yes."

"Did you hear that I used your idea of the tent in my lecture?"

"Yes, I did. And I looked up the Bible verse you gave me. It certainly is the verse for me: 'My tent is destroyed, and all my cords are broken.' All of them, Pastor. After hearing your lecture tonight, I know that they are all broken. It's so true, what you said."

"What do you mean?"

"About contraceptives being a threat to love."

"Well, I was wondering all the time how you solved that problem."

"We haven't. That's just it. He may think he has. But for me it isn't solved. First he told me to watch the fertile days and count them on the calendar. But this didn't work and I became pregnant. He told me to abort my child."

"And you obeyed him?"

"Yes, of course. Now he makes me swallow a pill every morning. But that means that after three weeks I have a week of bleeding. And I have no pleasure. Especially since I've been taking the pills, I feel almost numb."

"Many women who take pills say this."

"Are contraceptives bad, Pastor?"

What questions she asks! "You see, Fatma, it all depends upon whether the tent is broken down or whether it's intact, whether it's whole. If the tent is whole, husband and wife can talk together in confidence. For a certain reason they may decide not to have a baby, or to wait to have another baby. Then they will agree about the method, usually with the help of a doctor who can also supervise them medically. They will be frank with each other and tell each other how they feel. Even if a pregnancy should come sooner than they had planned, this would be no disaster. Since the tent is whole there is also a sheltered place in it for the baby. Everyone needs a place, even a baby. But if the tent is broken down, if one of the poles is missing and it rains in, then everything is different."

"I know that only too well. I'm terribly afraid of another pregnancy because then he would force me to have another abortion. It's exactly as you said, if one corner is lacking, the two others don't work. As the Bible says, 'There is no one to spread my tent.' "

"Listen, Fatma. It's no use to go on making complaints over the telephone. If you want things to change, you must bring your husband to me so that I can talk to him."

"Impossible!"

"Try it anyway."

"Should he come alone, or should we come together?"

"As he prefers."

"He's coming home now. We have to stop. Good-by, Pastor. Thank you."

When I returned to the table I told Daniel and Esther something about Fatma's problem in hopes that they would be able to help.

"He really treats her like a slave," Esther commented.

"We have to face it," Daniel added. "The matter of absolute male dominance is deeply ingrained in African culture."

"Esther and Daniel," I said, "I'm ashamed to admit it, but Fatma does not live with an African. The man with whom she lives is European. It is not a question of culture. It is a question of the human heart which the Bible calls deceitful."

They said nothing. Sensitive to the feelings of others, they were saddened because of my embarrassment.

"Tell me, Daniel, if she decides to leave him, to take a job and live alone—would this be possible?"

"Not in this city. It's as good as impossible. We still live very much in the garden concept. There's no place for a single person."

"Then he has her entirely in his power. Her parents slammed the door behind her when she left with him. Another man wouldn't marry her now because she's no longer a virgin. And living alone is impossible. She is right. There is no one to spread her tent."

"In any case, she has to leave him," Daniel said. "Maybe she could move in with some relatives or friends. But suppose she actually were married to him. Do you advise people sometimes to get a divorce?"

"Would a doctor advise his patient to die? He would fight for his patient's life as long as there is a spark of hope. In the same way I would fight for a marriage as long as there is the least sign of life in it. But there are marriages where you simply have to admit: This marriage is dead."

"I can think of marriages where love has died completely," Daniel said. "The physical union has ceased long ago. All the husband and wife have left is the top angle of your triangle. They are married. The rest is gone. They may still live in the same house, but they go different ways. Mostly they live separated lives. Still they are not yet divorced. This goes on for years. To me such a marriage is dead. Still, Jesus has said: 'What God therefore has joined together, let no man put asunder.' "

"But the question is: 'Did God join them together in the first place?' "

"Would you remarry divorcées then without hesitation?"

"Not without hesitation. With much hesitation. But under certain conditions I would. In any case, I would remarry only the guilty party."

"I don't follow you."

"If someone claims that he is entirely innocent when his marriage has failed and that the fault is one hundred per cent his partner's, then I know that his second marriage will be a failure too."

"But there are people who really are innocent. Take the case of the husband who becomes a drunkard."

"Yes, but beneath this surface innocence there is a deeper level of guilt. On this deeper level, man stands not before his partner, but before God. This deeper level of guilt often has to do with the way in which the marriage came into being. I would hesitate to remarry anyone before he is ready to face this deeper level."

"Is Fatma innocent?"

"Of course, her parents are very much at fault. And then this man, too. Yet, before God, she is not innocent."

"How do you think you can help her?"

"I don't think I can help her at all until she realizes this."

I had been talking with Daniel alone about this question. Esther had sat down in an armchair to drink her tea. When we looked at her, we saw she was asleep.

"My garden went to sleep," Daniel joked.

"She's not your garden, Daniel. She's your roommate in your tent—your tent mate, if you want to put it that way. You need some sleep yourself. Could you take me back to my hotel?"

When I picked up my key at the hotel desk, the clerk handed me a letter. It was from my wife. I went up to my room, sat down and read:

"How I miss you and being able to talk things over with you. The whole past year has been one separation after another. I actually believe that we have not had one single quiet week together at home this year. Either we were trying to meet some deadline or getting ready for some trip. We had so little time to just live.

"This afternoon I saw the windows of a house high on the mountain flame in gold as the setting sun touched them. The reflection almost blinded me.

"I thought, this is the way it is when we are quiet and let Christ be reflected through the windows of our soul. And I thought, This is the way it is when I can be completely one with you in body, mind, and soul. There is a certain transfiguration. Because I have tasted this joy, I long for it. It gives me the strength to overcome all the demands of our daily living.

"This experience of complete oneness was withheld between your last trip and this new one. My heart grew heavier and heavier, so that I could hardly bear it. That's why it was so hard to let you go this time.

"So when you are working, please know that all these hopes and desires which cannot be separated from my heart and soul are also in this work. They are a kind of burnt offering which makes the time more fruitful, not only for you, but also for your wife.

"This is not a letter of complaint. It is simply sharing a fact. For me this sharing means that I can go forward with a lighter heart.

"Thanks for always listening. Now I can go forward again. I can hardly wait to join you Saturday."

What had I said in my lecture? "There is no such thing as a perfect marriage. Marriage keeps us humble. The safest way to become humble about one's virtues is to get married."

I was still fast asleep when a ringing sound wakened me. As I struggled out of bed to turn off the alarm, I realized that the ringing was from the telephone.

I turned on the light. It was 2:00 a.m. I picked up the receiver. The night clerk apologized for waking me up.

"There's a couple here in the lobby. They insist on seeing you."

Wondering if it could possibly be Fatma and her "husband," I asked the clerk to wait five minutes before sending them up. I would receive them as soon as I was dressed.

I have seen many beautiful African girls, but never anyone like Fatma. She was tall and slender and wore a national gown which went down to her ankles. She walked with grace, but with a certain restraint. Everything was neat and clean about her. She had selected her necklace, earrings, and bracelet, which set off her fine-featured face, with distinctive taste. Her large brown eyes had an air of sadness about them.

The man who was with her wore his working pants, partly torn and spotted with oil. His T-shirt was not tucked in at the waist. He was unshaved and had dirty fingernails. He was blond.

After Fatma had introduced her companion, she was full of apology because of the impossible time of their visit. She said they had argued until 1:30 when he finally gave in and was ready to come and see me together with her.

"If we hadn't come right away, he might have changed his mind."

"It doesn't matter, Fatma. I'm very glad you came, both of you." I addressed myself to him: "I'm especially glad that you came with her, sir. It shows me your concern for Fatma, Mr.—"

"Call him John," Fatma said. "It's not his real name, but it's the English equivalent of it."

John had slumped down in the armchair and sat there with outstretched legs, his arms folded across his chest. He was hostile and I wasn't surprised. Of course, he was afraid of me and naturally suspected that I was on Fatma's side. It was a difficult situation, for I had to admit to myself that I was on her side.

"You must be terribly afraid of me." No reaction. "Probably you think that Fatma has accused you. But she never did." No answer. "She told me that you take good care of her. She is very thankful to you, especially that you send her to school. I see also that you enable her to dress nicely."

He shrugged his shoulders.

Fatma said: "You are very good to me, John. I don't know what I would do without you. I am thankful to you. I love you very much. But I can't understand why we don't get married."

"The old story," he said with a sigh, and without looking up. "Why do we need that paper? There are hundreds of couples in my country who live without that paper and who are happy. There are others who have it and who are unhappy. It's not the paper that makes you happy."

"But I am ashamed when I meet one of my friends. What shall I tell them? Am I married or not?"

"Your friends! I'm not interested in your friends."

"But they are a part of me. If you love me, then you must love me with my friends. For me, it's not the paper, but the wedding feast which is important. I would like to have a real feast and invite three or four hundred people."

He threw up his arms in horror. "Three hundred people!" he exclaimed. "I tell you, *if* we get married, then it will be a very small wedding. Just the two of us and the witnesses in the City Hall. That's all!"

"But then in our country, everyone would think I was ashamed of you, that I am hiding something. I want to show the people that I am proud of you. I couldn't stand the shame of a small wedding."

There was silence.

"My impression is, John," I said carefully, "that you have taken a step, but that you are not yet fully aware of all the consequences."

"What step have I taken?" he asked in a snippy way, but I was glad that he had at least started to talk to me.

"Of taking Fatma into your house. You see, if you choose a girl in this country as your wife, or would-be wife, you do not choose just this individual person, isolated from everything else. You choose her with her education, her tastes, her likes and dislikes, her habits and customs, in short, with her culture. From this short conversation which we have had, I conclude that you might love her as an individual, her beauty and character, but you don't love her with her culture."

"I love her," he said in a stubborn, defensive tone.

"Yes, I understand. But real love means to love her with her background, her culture. A big wedding feast belongs to this culture. If you marry a girl from this country, then you must accept this fact. More than that—you must not only accept it ungrudgingly, you must even like it."

He was silent again. My impression was that these thoughts were new to him.

"You see," I continued, "marriage is a burden, a responsibility, even under normal circumstances. This additional burden of cultural differences is often the straw that breaks the camel's back. What makes these marriages break down is the fact that the partners do not fully accept each other's different cultures. This may start with tiny things, such as the likes and dislikes of certain foods or the way of preparing them—and it may end with a different outlook on life as a whole."

"Do all these marriages fail?" Fatma wanted to know.

"No," I said. "But if they succeed, it is usually because both have lived for a long time in the culture where they plan to make their home.

"Unfortunately, this is very rarely the case. If an African student marries an American or European girl, whom he meets in her country and who has never been in Africa before, their marriage almost always fails. In spite of her goodwill and sincere desire, she is unable to make the adjustment."

"She takes a step bigger than her pants allow," John joked, and then laughed at his own joke. I was glad that he seemed more relaxed now and so I dared to say:

"There's a possibility that both of you are in the process of making the same mistake."

"We love each other," John insisted. He looked to me like a little boy afraid that someone would take away his toy.

"Yes, but marriage is more than love. 'It's not only moonlight and roses, but also dishes and diapers.' "

"Diapers!" John turned up his nose in distaste.

"You don't like children?"

He shook his head.

"How about you, Fatma?"

"I love them very much and I want to have many."

"Another point where you disagree," I observed, "and a rather important one. What are your plans, John? Do you plan to stay in this country?"

"I have a job with the government, but my contract expires in a year."

"And then?"

"I don't know. I may go someplace else—like South America or Japan."

Fatma gasped.

"I take it that you want to take Fatma along."

"What makes you think that?"

"Because you said that you belong to the husbands who are happy without a paper. If one is really happy, one doesn't want to give up one's happiness."

He shrugged his shoulders. Then Fatma exploded.

"You never told me that your contract expired. I always thought that you wanted to stay in my country all your life."

John suddenly got up.

"Good-by. We have to go now. It's getting late—or rather, early."

"Just one word," I replied, taking his hand and looking him straight in the eye. "Please, John, for Fatma's sake, make up your mind. If you want to take her along, then tell her so, so that she can make a decision. If you don't, and plan to separate after your contract expires, then tell her, so that she can make up her mind whether she wants to stay with you. I'm not telling either one of you what to do, but I plead with you, stop playing hide-and-seek and make up your mind."

"Thank you very much," he said coolly.

"Do you have far to go?" I said in order to release the tension.

"No, just across the river."

Then he left the room. Fatma trailed after him without looking at me.

I went back to bed, but I couldn't really go back to sleep. My thoughts wouldn't settle down. The people kept walking through my mind: Fatma and John, Miriam and Timothy, Maurice and his mother, Daniel and Esther and my wife.

I got up and ordered an early breakfast in my room. Then I read my wife's letter again. Why couldn't she have written a more encouraging letter? "How I miss you and being able to talk things over. . . ." Hadn't we done that all the time? After all, our separation isn't long this time. Is that really so difficult?

I made an attempt to read, but my thoughts returned to my wife.

Why does she write such a letter? She wants me to comfort her, I thought. Why am I so disappointed? I feel that she doesn't understand me, my work with all these problems I can't solve, with all these people I can't help.

Since I don't feel understood, I can't comfort her, I thought. Since she is not comforted, she can't understand me. A vicious circle.

"Thanks for always listening. . . ." Was I? Was I really? At least she was talking. Wasn't she doing what Fatma and John could not do—not even Timothy and Miriam—nor Daniel and Esther either? Yes. The thought helped me. We still were talking in our tent, even if it were sagging.

I opened my Bible and read the 27th Psalm. I drank it in—every word of it—like a fresh, cool drink of water.

"Though a host encamp against me, my heart shall not fear; . . . for . . . he will conceal me under the cover of his tent."

These words had never touched me before. They had never had any special meaning for me. Suddenly they talked, talked with a thundering voice.

His tent, I thought. It's not our tent, it's God's tent. We are in His tent. His tent is not sagging.

After breakfast the telephone rang. It was Fatma again.

"From where are you calling?"

"From home."

"Why aren't you at school?"

"He said I should sleep this morning. He was very considerate—more than he has ever been before."

"Did he lock the house again?"

"Yes, he is very jealous. Isn't jealousy also a sign of love?"

"Of a certain kind of love. A very possessive kind, not very mature. Mature love has confidence and grants the partner freedom."

"Do you think he has no confidence in me?"

"What do you think?"

She evaded the answer and changed the subject.

"The reason I'm calling is I would like to know what you think of him."

"He came so unkempt and I wondered if he had even washed his hands. Doesn't his appearance bother you sometimes?"

"Yes, but I think that love must be able to overcome this. And I love him and he loves me."

She is clinging to a straw, I thought. Hadn't the talk early this morning opened her eyes?

"Yes, Fatma, maybe. But you are thinking of different things when you say to each other, 'I love you.' He thinks of sex, while you think of marriage. That's the difference. You aren't putting up a tent. You have one pole in the ground, or you think you have—your love. But then he puts one pole on the right of it and you one pole on the left of it. It will never hold up a tent."

"What do you think his plans are?"

"He doesn't want to make up his mind. This is what makes the situation so difficult for you."

"Do you think he will leave me after his contract has expired?"

It was evident that she hadn't caught on to his remarks. Unbelievable! The least I can do for her, I thought, is to let the light in so that she can see.

"There is nothing that can force him to marry you, nothing that can hinder him from leaving you."

Silence.

"And to be frank, I almost wish he would leave you. You wouldn't become happy with him."

I felt, as I was speaking, that these words were cutting her like a knife.

"But if he leaves me. . . there is nothing. There is an abyss. Where shall I go?"

Into God's tent, I thought. If only I could lead her to it. If only I could heal after cutting.

She didn't hide her crying now. Her voice drowned in sobs.

"Good-by, Pastor," she said.

"Fatma," I called, "read Psalm 27. There is a message in it for you."

I wasn't sure whether she had hung up before I could say that.

Miriam and Timothy came late that afternoon. It was almost 5:30. They explained that Timothy had been unable to leave sooner.

"Well," I said, "then we have to get right to the point, for Maurice is coming soon to pick me up. What worries me the most about your relationship is the fact that you are evidently not able to talk together. Timothy didn't even know how old you were, Miriam, nor how much education you have had, nor how much you earn. Actually, I knew more about you than Timothy did. How do you explain that?"

"We had a short talk before we came here," Miriam said, "and we too want to get right to the point."

It was interesting that she did the answering.

"We have entered our triangle from the sex entrance," she continued. There was a brief silence. I realized that it took a lot of courage for her to say that. I liked her honesty. "I told you that in our culture we can't meet unless we are engaged. But then about four weeks after our engagement we became intimate."

"What does this have to do with your inability to talk together?"

"Very much. It soon became the main thing, the main reason for our dates. We knew that when we met we would end up uniting. We thought just of this one thing. Everything else became secondary."

"But now, Timothy and Miriam, you must explain something to me so that I can better understand. You say that in your culture, you can't meet unless you are engaged. Does it also belong to your culture to become intimate during the time of engagement?"

"Well," Timothy said with a smile, and somewhat embarrassed, "you see, we belong to the younger generation. We young people of today are more modern. We stand for progress. We don't consider the old traditions binding anymore."

"That's just what I wanted to hear," I said. "As long as your customs meet with your own desires, you are 'African' and you don't hesitate to get engaged, without even knowing each other. But if your customs do not comply with your desires, suddenly you become 'modern' and 'progressive' and throw your customs overboard.

"In German we say it is like someone who wants to drill a hole in a board of varying thickness, but he always chooses the place where it is thinnest. Am I too hard on you?"

"Please be hard," Miriam said. "I wished our parents would have talked so hard to us. But they never talk. They just suspect."

"All right, then let me be hard. First you say, 'In our society it is impossible for young people of different sexes to meet. We can't even talk together, unless we are engaged.' Then all of a sudden you find it possible to sleep together in spite of all the social restrictions. Why should it be so hard to talk together and so easy to sleep together?"

They looked down at the floor. Finally Miriam said:

"It isn't easy. The only place we could find was in a car."

"It was the only place," Timothy said. "Her family is very strict, and mine too."

"Yet you found a place in spite of their strictness," I said. "If you really wanted to, you could also have found a place to talk even without being engaged."

"But Pastor," Timothy said, "I don't regret it. It's not true what you said yesterday that sex without marriage destroys love and makes it change into hatred. At least in our case it isn't true. It deepened our love. It was beautiful."

I looked at Miriam. She grasped Timothy's hand as if she didn't want to hurt him. Then she said softly:

"Maybe it was for you, but for me it wasn't."

"It wasn't?" Timothy seemed very surprised. "What exactly wasn't?"

"Everything. The place. The hurry. The secrecy. The fear of being discovered. A car isn't exactly a tent in which you feel sheltered."

Timothy drew a heavy sigh. A world broke down for him.

Miriam continued: "Too, in spite of the precautions we took, I was always worried about getting pregnant. This isn't beautiful."

"I told you to take pills."

"Go to a doctor as an unmarried girl and ask for a prescription? I'm not that modern."

"I offered to withdraw early, but you didn't like it."

"I asked you to buy condoms, but you were embarrassed to ask for them in a drugstore."

"Yes, because it's usually ladies who work in drugstores and wait on you. Besides, condoms are used mostly with prostitutes and I don't consider you a prostitute, Miriam."

"I'm not blaming you, Timothy," Miriam said with all the tenderness she could put in her voice as she grasped his hand more firmly. "I'm just trying to say it wasn't so very beautiful."

"But why didn't you ever tell me that?"

"I thought you needed it and that you would be disappointed and start to doubt whether I love you."

Timothy sighed again. They were silent for a few moments.

I hadn't interrupted them on purpose. I was glad that they had started to talk frankly to each other and to share honestly their feelings. So I said:

"Why don't you go now and continue to talk, but alone, just between yourselves. I believe you have to come to your own decision. But it might well be that these more or less frustrating experiences have something to do with the uncertainty you feel about your love."

"How can we know whether we love each other?" they both asked with one voice.

The telephone rang and the operator announced Maurice.

"I'm going to answer this question tonight in my lecture," I promised. Timothy and Miriam had just left when Maurice walked into my room. Again I was struck by his appearance. He walked in the same way that he spoke—decisively and yet without trying to make an impression. When I spoke with him, I was aware of his intelligence, yet he never tried to be brilliant. Still there was a certain contradiction in his personality. On the one hand were the manly gestures, and on the other hand, a certain helpless air; his grown-up way of expressing himself, accompanied by a boyish smile.

"Where did you leave your mother?"

"She's waiting in the car. I told her I wanted to ask you a question. She said she could not understand our conversation anyway. You remember my question: 'How does one approach a girl?' "

"Maurice, is that so difficult? Just be what you are. Don't try to make yourself interesting. Don't pretend to be someone you're not, but show that you are interested in her. Ask her about her hobbies, her likes and dislikes, her favorite books or subjects of study, her family. Try to find some common interest and then talk about that."

"As if that would be so easy."

"Tell me, Maurice, you're thirty-four years old. Didn't you ever have a girl?"

"Yes, I did, and I wanted to marry her."

"Why didn't you?"

"I sent her to the doctor for a medical checkup. He found out that she wasn't a virgin."

"And you left her for this reason?"

"Yes."

"What became of her?"

"I don't know. Do you think I did wrong?"

"Maurice, the night before yesterday you showed me the 'red-light district.' What if your girl is living now among those prostitutes? You may have pushed her into the very same fate from which you tried to save your mother."

Maurice said nothing.

"What makes me so mad is that double moral standard: Girls must remain virgins. Men must have sex. It's so illogical, so unjust."

"But don't you think one must have some experience before marriage? You can't enter marriage completely inexperienced."

"Everyone enters marriage inexperienced, Maurice. You see, each person is different and therefore each couple is doubly different. Consequently, these premarital experiences become a burden rather than a help for your marriage. The choice is only between two things: either you enter into marriage with no experience or with the wrong kind of experience. But excuse me, I think we have to leave now. The lecture begins at six-thirty."

As we were walking down the stairs, Maurice asked:

"Why do you think it is so hard to convince young people that by experimenting before marriage, they have the wrong kind of experience?"

"Because they can know this only after they have had the right kind."

"So you don't think it's because of a strong sex drive?"

"I don't think it's primarily a sexual problem at all. They need someone whom they can trust to such an extent that they will believe he or she is telling the truth, even if they are not yet able to experience it. They need to accept a truth which they cannot yet prove by way of experimentation. Only when they have this degree of confidence can they be sure that they are not being cheated, but rather helped toward a rewarding goal."

We reached the car. Maurice's mother greeted me with great friendliness and politeness.

"Ask her what she thinks about the triangle," I said to Maurice as we were driving to the church.

Shilah, Maurice's mother, made a long speech. He smiled as she spoke and then summed it up for me:

"She doesn't think of a triangle at all. She thinks of a three-legged stool. Such a stool can never wobble so long as it has three legs, even though the legs are of different length or the ground is uneven. But if you take one leg off, then you'll fall to the ground."

"You have a remarkable mother, Maurice. Tell her I like her comparison very much and ask her whether she could think of polygamy also as a three-legged stool."

He translated and she answered.

"She says that a polygamous marriage always wobbles. It makes you fall to the ground. She would never have become the second wife of a married man—rather she would die."

6

AS WE APPROACHED THE CHURCH, WE SAW PEOPLE COMING FROM that direction.

"The church is full," Maurice commented. "Those who didn't find a place are leaving already."

He was right. Not only were the pews crowded, but people were standing in the aisles. We had difficulty getting through. Chairs were placed even in the front of the church, around the altar. Some elderly, very dignified men were seated there.

Again fear gripped my heart. I knew some of the problems now. But by far not all of them. It was impossible to judge how my words would affect their lives, cut into them, cause hope or despair. It was an overwhelming responsibility.

One of the older men led in prayer. This comforted me. He wouldn't have done that, I thought, had the older people been offended.

When Daniel took his place beside me in the pulpit, I felt strengthened. I became calm, reminding myself that it was not my message I had come to deliver but God's.

The first person I spotted in the audience was Fatma. She was seated in one of the back pews on the women's side. Her face, with the bright and hungry eyes, stood out from all the others. "Please give me a word for her," I prayed silently.

There were quite a few newcomers who had not been in church the two previous evenings. So I decided to sum up briefly what I had said before:

"There are three things which belong essentially to a marriage: to leave one's parents, to cleave to each other, and to become one flesh. In other words, there is a legal, a personal, and a physical aspect of marriage. They are inseparable. If you do separate them, the whole thing falls apart.

"One of you just told me that marriage is like a three-legged stool. If one of the legs is lacking, the stool won't hold you up when you sit on it."

I saw faces brighten up. This was a good image. Shilah was right.

"Last night we discussed the question: Should we approach marriage first from the legal, the personal, or the physical side? What is the best way?

"We talked about two answers to this question, the traditional answer and the modern answer. The traditional answer was to start with the legal aspect, with the wedding. Here the great danger is that the personal aspect, the aspect of love, is then left out of the picture. This is why young people in your midst rebel today against this traditional answer, for they are just in the process of discovering the beauty of this personal aspect.

"The modern answer was to start with the physical aspect, with sex. The danger is that then the legal aspect is left out and it never comes to a wedding. This is why the older people among you rebel against this modern answer. They are afraid that family life will deteriorate altogether.

"Today we shall hear the biblical answer to our question. In order to find this answer we have to consider the first word of our key Bible verse, Genesis 2:24:

Therefore

" '*Therefore* a man leaves his father and his mother and cleaves to his wife, and they become one flesh.'

"In order to understand this word 'therefore' we must recall the story which comes before it. It is a well-known and often ridiculed story. It tells about the incomprehensible kindness of God which He wanted to show to man when He made him a 'helpmeet,' a 'helper fit for him,' a partner equal to him, completing him:

" 'So the Lord God caused a deep sleep to fall upon the man, and while he slept took one of his ribs and closed up its place with flesh; and the rib which the Lord God had taken from the man he made into a woman and brought her to the man.'

"This story is the most wonderful and unique description of the reality of love.

"Why do the two sexes long for each other without ceasing? How can it be explained that they are magnetically attracted to each other? The answer is: They are made out of the same piece—just like the Liberian carving I showed you the other night. They are parts of a whole and want to restore this whole again, want to complete each other, want to become 'one flesh.'

"The power which drives them toward each other is the power of love.

"*Therefore,* truly, for love's sake, the two shall leave their parents, cleave to each other and become one.

The Love Entrance

"When we ask ourselves the question, at which angle do we enter the marriage triangle, the Bible would answer, at the angle of cleaving."

I took my wooden triangle in my hand and pointed to the left angle: "It is this angle of cleaving which is the best door to use to enter the triangle. Love has to precede marriage and sex. It is not marriage which leads to love, but love which leads to marriage. It is not sex which creates love, but love which seeks, among other things, also the physical expression.

"The entrance at the angle of love is the most promising as far as the development and unfolding of the dynamism of the triangle is concerned. Therefore it corresponds with God's will.

"There is another reason why God wants us to enter through the door of love. The public and legal act of the wedding as well as the sex act create irrevocable facts, while love does not.

"An engaged couple may one day feel that they made a decision too soon, that the time was not yet ripe and that their engagement was a mistake. They then have the possibility of breaking their engagement without causing an incurable wound to the partner. For love's sake they can let each other go."

At this point I could not help but think of Miriam and Timothy and look for their faces in the audience. I spotted them sitting together in the very last pew. Miriam was the only girl sitting on the men's side of the church. After all, I thought, they can shun their traditions if they want to.

"So long as the other two angles are not involved, the angle of love is like a revolving door—a door through which you can enter, but in case of necessity, through which you can also leave.

"The wedding act is not like a revolving door. It's like a door which shuts and there is no handle inside. Of course, it can be forced open. But this is much more difficult. We could say that a divorce is more difficult and has more consequences than a broken engagement, regrettable as this may be.

"The same is true about the sex act. It also creates an irrevocable fact.

"According to biblical thinking, two human beings who have shared the sexual act are never the same afterward. They can no longer act toward each other as if they had not had this experience. It makes out of those involved in it a couple bound to each other. It creates a one-flesh bond with all its implications.

"According to the Bible, this is the case regardless of whether the couple is serious or not, regardless of whether they intend to get married or not; yes, says the Apostle Paul, it is true even in the case of prostitution. In I Corinthians 6: 16 we read: 'Do you not know that he who joins himself to a prostitute becomes one body with her?'

"After the sex act they are a couple in spite of themselves.

"Robert Grimm says: 'The flesh has an indelible stamp imprinted upon it. I cannot divorce myself from my own body.' "*

There was a movement at the back of the church. Someone wanted to leave, but since the door was blocked by late-comers, this created quite a disturbance.

---

*See Robert Grimm, *Love and Sexuality* (London: Hodder & Stoughton; U.S. edition, New York: Association Press), pp. 52, 56, 66.

I recognized the person who left. It was Fatma.

From then on, I was ill at ease. I told myself maybe it was because we had started late and she had to be back at school before John came to pick her up. But somehow this explanation didn't satisfy me. I had the feeling that something was wrong. For the moment, though, I had no choice. I must continue:

"I repeat: You may also succeed if you enter through one of the other doors, but it is risky. If you want to retreat, you will hurt your partner and yourself.

"This leads us to a very practical question. I know many young couples who say: 'We would like to enter through the door of love. But how can we know that our love is deep enough to lead us to a lifelong cleaving, to complete faithfulness? How can we be sure that our love is mature enough to take the wedding vows and promise to stay together all our lives until death separates us? If sex is no test of love, what is the test then?'

"May I give you my answer:

Six Tests of Love*

First: *The sharing test* "Real love wants to share, to give, to reach out. It thinks of the other one, not of himself. When you read something, how often do you have the thought, I would like to share this with my friend? When you plan something, do you think of what you would like to do or what the other one would enjoy?

"As Hermann Oeser, a German author, has put it: 'Those who want to become happy should not marry. The important thing is to make the other one happy. Those who want to be understood should not marry. The important thing is to understand one's partner.'

"The first test question then is this: Are we able to share together? Do I want to become happy or make happy?

Second: *The strength test* "I got a letter once from a worried lover. He had read somewhere that one loses weight if one is truly in love. In

*Some of these tests I have taken from the fine book written by Evelyn Duvall, *Love and the Facts of Life* (New York: Association Press, 1963).

spite of all his feelings of love, he didn't lose weight and that worried him.

"It is true that the love experience can also affect you physically. But in the long run, real love should not take away your strength; instead, it should give you new energy and strength. It should fill you with joy and make you creative, willing to accomplish even more.

"Second test question: Does our love give us new strength and fill us with creative energy or does it take away our strength and energy?

Third: *The respect test* "There is no real love without respect, without being able to look up to the other one.

"A girl may admire a boy when she watches him play soccer and score all the goals. But if she asks herself the question: 'Do I want this boy to be the father of my children?' very often the answer will be in the negative.

"A boy may admire a girl when he sees her dancing. But if he asks himself the question: 'Do I want this girl to be the mother of my children?' she may look very different to him.

"Third test question: Do we really have enough respect for each other? Am I proud of my partner?

Fourth: *The habit test* "Once a European girl who was engaged came to me and was very worried: 'I love my fiancé very much,' she said, 'but I just can't stand the way he eats an apple.' "

There was understanding laughter in the audience.

"Love accepts the other one *with* his habits. Don't marry on the installment plan, thinking that these things will change later on. Very likely they will not. You must accept the other one as he is now, including his habits and shortcomings.

"Fourth test question: Do we only love each other or do we also like each other?

Fifth test: *The quarrel test* "When a couple come to me and want to get married, I always ask them if they have once had a real quarrel—not just a casual difference of opinion, but a real fight.

"Many times they will say: 'Oh, no! Pastor, we love each other.'

"Then I tell them: 'Quarrel first and then I will marry you.'

"The point is, of course, not the quarreling, but the ability to be reconciled to each other. This ability must be trained and tested before marriage. Not sex, but rather this quarrel test, is a 'required' premarital experience.

"Fifth test question: Are we able to forgive each other and to give in to each other?

Sixth: *The time test* "A young couple came to me to be married. 'How long have you known each other?' I asked. 'Already three, almost four weeks,' was the answer.

"This is too short. One year, I would say, is the minimum. Two years may be safer. It is good to see each other, not only on holidays and in Sunday clothes, but also at work, in daily living, unshaved and in a T-shirt, or with hair that needs to be washed and set, in situations of stress or danger.

"There is an old saying: 'Never get married until you have summered and wintered with your partner.'

"In case you are in doubt about your feeling of love, time will tell.

"Last test question: Has our love summered and wintered? Do we know each other long enough?

"And may I make a final statement with all clarity: Sex is no test of love."

Here I was interrupted. Daniel told me many people asked if I would write down the six tests on the blackboard. I agreed. I wrote in English on the left side—Daniel wrote on the right.

It took quite a long time. Many took notes. Daniel discovered to his dismay that some who had no paper along used the pages of the hymn book to take down the tests of love.

Then I wrote under the six tests with large capital letters:

SEX IS NO TEST OF LOVE

I don't know how Daniel translated it, but I thought, We have made some progress since the day before yesterday in that we could write the word "sex" on a blackboard placed in front of the altar!

I explained:

"If a couple want to use the sex act in order to know whether they love each other, one has to ask them: 'Do you love each other so little?' If both of them think: 'Tonight we must have sex—otherwise my partner will think that I don't love him or that he does not love me,' the fear of a possible failure is sufficient to prevent the success of the experiment.

"Sex is no test of love, for it is precisely the very thing that one wants to test which is destroyed by the testing.

"Try to observe yourself when you go to sleep. Either you observe yourself, then you don't fall asleep. Or you fall asleep, and then you haven't observed yourself.

"The same is true about sex as a test of love. Either you test, then you don't love. Or you love, then you don't test.

"For its own sake, love needs to wait with its physical expression until it can be included in the dynamism of the triangle.

"This waiting is usually harder for the young man than for the girl. Therefore, the girl has to help the young man here, who, because of his natural impetuousness, is more tempted to aim short of the goal.

"The first help she can give him is to learn how to say 'no' without wounding, how to refuse without breaking off. This is an art. She will soon discover, however, that a simple and definite 'no' is more helpful and effective than long explanations and excuses. If he loves her, the young man will respect her the more because of it. She will have to teach him, too, that an honest compliment may be more meaningful to her than a passionate embrace.

"Another help she can give him is through her ability to blush. One says that formerly girls blushed when they were embarrassed. Today they are embarrassed when they blush. But this blushing, this natural reaction of shame, is nothing to be ashamed of. It is a defense and a protection at the same time. Girls should consider their natural feeling of shame and modesty in certain situations as a gift and put it into the service of love."

It was now completely quiet in the church. I knew that this natural feeling of shame and modesty is still much more prevalent in African society than in Western society. Scenes in movies showing long and elaborate kissing are repugnant to Africans. The audience gets restless when they appear on the screen and some refuse to look at them. Still these movies are shown all over Africa and those who see them start to distrust their own feelings. This is why I owed them a word of reassurance.

Daniel and I were still standing in front of the first pews. I checked with him on the time. He said I could go on for another ten or fifteen minutes. So I decided to close by dealing with the special situation of engaged couples:

"Let's imagine now that we have a couple who did not enter into the triangle through the sex entrance, but through the love entrance. Their situation is different and we have to discern very carefully these two approaches.

"They have known each other for a long time. They do not need to test their love by sex. They have learned how to share. They both have more energy and strength because of their love. Their mutual respect has deepened. They have accepted the habits of each other and really like each other. They have quarreled and gone through stormy times. They know they can forgive each other.

"They are now at the point where they can make the promise to each other: 'We want to cleave together for life.' This means they become engaged. They have entered the triangle through the door of love—love resolved to cleave. But now they have to make a crucial decision: 'Which of the two other angles shall we reach first? Shall we first get married and then sleep together or first sleep together and then get married?' "

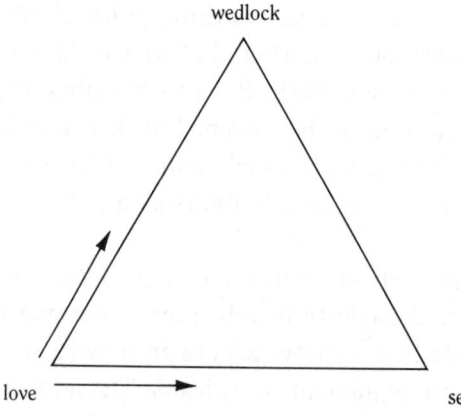

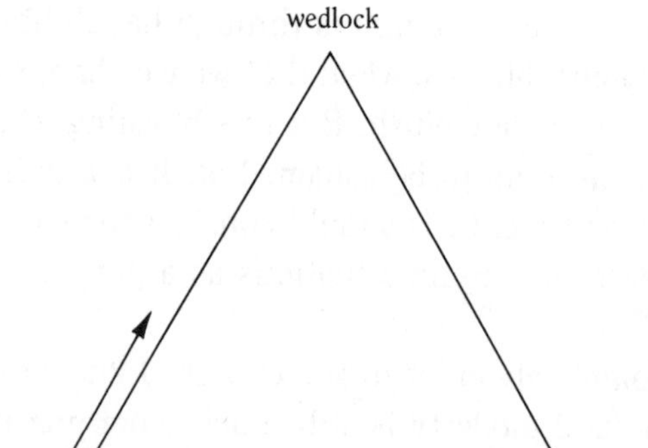

I paused, looked at the young people, and said: "What do you think?"

It was as if I had pulled a cork out of a bottle. Everyone started to talk at once. After some effort Daniel was able to quiet them down. I repeated:

"This situation is entirely different from the one we had yesterday when we discussed the 'sex entrance.' This couple do not consider sex as the first step without any commitment to each other. They have committed themselves and this after a long and careful examination. They really have no egoistical motives but have accepted responsibility for each other.

"Now they ask: 'Why can't we express this love also in a physical way? Why must we first get an official license to go to bed together? Is it really that piece of paper which brings marriage into being?'

"Of course it isn't—any more than a birth certificate brings a baby into being. Still, it's more than just a piece paper. It protects human life legally.

"The same is true about the marriage license. It protects marriage legally. We have seen that the legal aspect is as essential for the unfolding of the play of forces within the marriage triangle as is the personal and the physical aspect.

"Those engaged couples who want to take a right turn and start their marriage before the wedding overlook one fact: the unpredictability of human life. How can they be so sure that they will get married?

"What if one of them dies before the wedding? Car accident? Heart attack? Is he then a widower or not? Is she a widow? Can they inherit from each other? Is she a Miss or a Mrs.? And in case she is pregnant—what is the family name of the child? These questions show that a marriage license is more than a piece of paper. So long as they are not yet ready to take the legal step, they are not ready to take full responsibility for each other. Responsibility calls for legality.

"Does this mean they suppress all signs of affection? Walk first to the altar and then expect the great revelation?

"No, certainly not. This would block the unfolding of the play of forces just as much as the disregard of the legal aspect. The secret is that the lovers grow and make progress in both directions at the same time without skipping any of the steps."

I turned to the blackboard and drew parallel lines in this way:

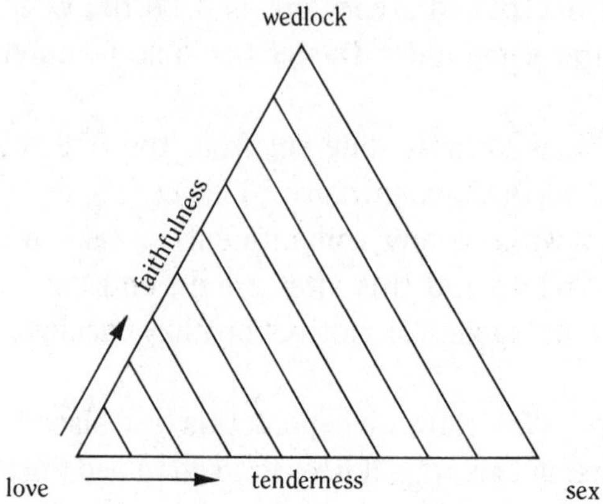

"Each step in the direction of faithfulness and wedlock should go hand in hand with the deepening of tenderness and intimacy, until finally, coming from the entrance of love, the two other angles—wedlock and sexual union—are reached at the same time.

"Only from the perspective of the goal can this question be answered. The point is that each step toward intimacy must be balanced by the same measure of responsibility and faithfulness."

I turned to Daniel, who stood beside me, and asked him in a voice that all could hear:

"How about your young people? Do they usually reach the two angles at the same time?"

There was loud laughter even among the older people. Daniel smiled knowingly and waited until it was quiet again. Then he became serious. I sat down in the first bench beside Maurice, who whispered in my ear the interpretation of what Daniel was saying:

"What usually happens here is this: The young man says to the girl, 'I love you,' and what he means is just an inch in the direction of faithfulness. But the girl is so happy about it that she, in turn, allows him to go three inches in the direction of intimacy."

Again an outburst of laughter.

"Then the boy thinks, This worked fine, so he adds another inch toward faithfulness. The girl replies by giving him four more inches in the direction of intimacy. Before they know it, they end up at the sex angle, without being able to carry the full responsibility for this step. Instead of parallel lines you then have slanted lines."

Then Daniel rubbed out my parallel lines and replaced them with slanting lines:

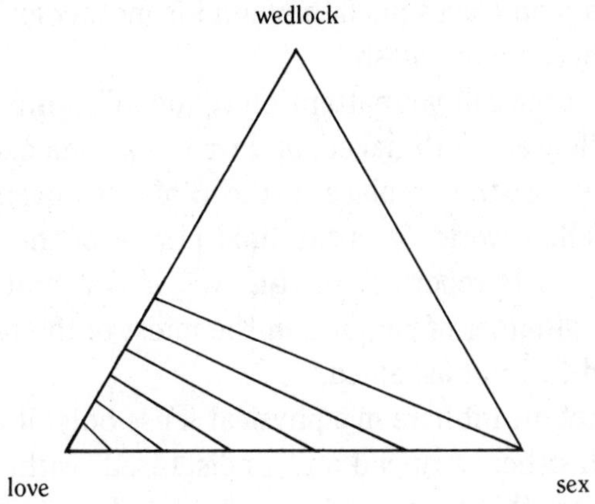

I marveled at Daniel's way of illustrating the situation so simply. He motioned to me, and I again took my place at his side to finish the lecture.

"As you see," I said, pointing to the slanting lines of the triangle, "there is now a vacuum, an empty space in the triangle. This is the situation of many of our engaged couples in America and Europe, too. They think they love each other. But then they go too far too soon. An emptiness creeps into their relationship. They become less and less sure of their love. So they intensify their intimacies in the hope of intensifying their love. The more they do it, the less they are sure of their love.

"On the other hand, they don't dare to break their engagement because they have already gone too far. So they get married, but they carry this emptiness into their marriage and thereby lay the foundation for many troubles and problems later on.

"To keep the parallel lines from slanting is a difficult job. It takes more than human wisdom and strength. It needs divine wisdom and strength. It needs the help of the master artist of marriage who is God Himself.

"He knows why He relates the three elements of marriage—leaving, cleaving, one flesh—so closely together that they become inseparable. We have to trust Him and know that by doing so He does not want to take something away from us, but He wants to give us something—to help us create a work of art. This confidence and trust in Him will give us strength to obey His divine will:

" 'Therefore a man leaves his father and his mother and cleaves to his wife, and they become one flesh.'

"In closing, let me call your attention to the following verse: 'And the man and the wife were both naked, and were not ashamed' (Gen. 2:25).

"This verse has a strange place in the Bible. It hovers between paradise and the fallen world. It is the final phrase of the creation story, just before the fall is reported. In this way it is a hint that marriage reflects a feeble glimmer of paradise in the midst of the fallen world.

" 'Naked, and . . . not ashamed.'

" 'Naked' is not meant here in a physical sense only. It means to stand in front of each other, stripped and undisguised, without pretension, without hiding anything, seeing the partner as he or she really is and showing myself to him or her as I really am—and still not to be ashamed.

" 'Naked, and . . . not ashamed.'

"But this ultimate goal of mature love is promised only to those who, as the previous verse says, have left father and mother and cleave to each other; in other words, those who have been publicly and legally married.

"These two—not the ones before or outside of marriage—become one flesh. It is very meaningful that the Bible uses the term 'becoming one flesh' only in the context of marriage.

"These two—not the ones before or outside of marriage—shall succeed in the tremendously difficult task of facing each other as they really are, of living with each other—naked and yet not ashamed.

"Maybe there has to be a sense of shame before marriage in order for there to be within marriage the grace of not being ashamed.

" 'Naked, and . . . not ashamed.' This is what the Bible means by the word 'to know.' 'Adam knew Eve his wife' (Gen. 4:1).

"Husband and wife can 'know' each other only within the tent.

" 'Therefore a man leaves his father and his mother and cleaves to his wife, and they become one flesh.' "

7

AS SOON AS I HAD FINISHED, I HURRIED TO THE DOOR. MY HEART was not at rest because of Fatma. I didn't even wait for the closing hymn. The last thing I heard was Daniel announcing something in the native language. I took it that he was saying there would be no meeting on Saturday night, but that I would preach on Sunday and it was hoped that my wife could be present at that time too.

I asked some of the young people, who I knew understood English, about Fatma. They could tell me only that they had seen her leave hurriedly.

My apprehension grew.

"Did someone accompany her?"

"No, she left alone."

Maurice took me home in his car, but by a different route.

"Where are you going?" I asked.

"I'm taking my mother home first. Then I would like to invite you to have your evening meal with me in our finest restaurant."

"Wouldn't your mother like to come with us?"

"Oh, no, she wouldn't feel at ease in a restaurant. She belongs to the generation that prefers the 'three-legged stool.' "

Shilah was tired and didn't talk. We let her off at her home and returned to the city, where Maurice stopped in front of a very modern building.

As soon as we were seated and had given our orders, Maurice began shooting questions at me:

"Did you know you contradicted yourself tonight?"

"Did I?"

"Yes, first you said that according to the Apostle Paul the sex act creates a one-flesh bond even if one has intercourse with a prostitute. Then you said the Bible uses the term 'one flesh' only in context with marriage."

Maurice had a triumphant grin.

"You are right," I said. "I Corinthians 6: 16 is indeed, according to the Greek text, the only place where this expression is not used in context with marriage. But I think this is in order to demonstrate the absurdity of becoming one flesh outside of marriage. It is absurd to become one flesh with a prostitute. Paul wants to say: 'Outside of marriage, this act is entirely out of context.' "

Maurice thought for awhile as the soup was being served. Then he said:

"Yes, but are they now one flesh or are they not one flesh? You see, first you said that they became one flesh through the sexual union, even if they were not serious or did not intend to marry, in other words, without even wanting to build a tent—and then you said that they can fully become one flesh only within the tent, within marriage."

"Oh, Maurice. You are too intelligent for me. You put your finger exactly on the weakest point of my lecture."

"If a man can become one flesh with a prostitute, then everyone who sleeps just once with a prostitute would be married to her."

"I said, the act forms the couple. I didn't say they are married."

"And what's the difference?"

"That's precisely the question."

Maurice looked puzzled. We were silent for several moments.

"You see, Maurice, what you touch on here is indeed an unanswered question. But there are two things which are clear to me. First: the sexual union is a very consequential action even if it involves a prostitute. Second: to become one flesh involves much more than just the sexual union even with your own wife. We have to grope for the right way somewhere between these two truths."

Maurice sighed. Two truths—it's much easier to have everything straight, right down the line.

"So they are an unwed couple," Maurice suggested.

"Put it the other way around: they are coupled unweds. That way it sounds more absurd."

"Where would prostitution fit into your triangle?"

"It is the complete isolation of the right angle. Sex alone, separate from love and marriage."

"And yet they enter the tent? Become one?"

"How can I describe this absurdity with an image? It is as if they enter the tent and then discover that it has no top. They open the door to a house, lock it behind them, and then see that it has neither walls nor a roof. They go in and still they end up being outside."

We were interrupted as the waiter brought the next course. After he left Maurice said:

"You stung my conscience this afternoon when you blamed me for not marrying that girl who was no longer a virgin. Would you say that as a general rule, one could marry nonvirgins, without qualifying this statement?"

"No, of course not. It all depends upon the girl, her character, the circumstances under which it happened, her attitude toward this fact. But when I see these girls, many of them thirteen, fourteen years old, I can't help but feel sorry for them. No one has given them any sex education. The only thing they were taught is that because they are girls, they must obey all men. Then a man came and they obeyed. They were not trained to resist . . . You see, Maurice, virginity is not just a mark of the body, a question of having the hymen or not. To me it is much more a question of the heart, of the ability to love. It is not something which a girl loses, but which she gives."

"I don't follow you."

"Every girl has a unique gift—the ability to give herself completely once to a man. This gift is like capital in the bank. But many girls spend it in small coins. Every day they draw a little bit out of their capital, and in flirtations, here and there, throw it to the wind. Technically speaking, such a girl may still be a virgin, but she has lost her ability to love through a lot of necking and petting experiences. On the other hand, there may be a girl of whom some man took advantage because she was inexperienced. Technically speaking, she lost her virginity, but as far as her heart is concerned, I would call her a virgin."

"I would like to tell you something," Maurice replied. He paused. "Whether you believe it or not, Walter, I am still inexperienced. I am still a virgin."

"Thank you for telling me, Maurice. I believe you."

Then he asked: "Do you understand now, Walter, why it was especially hard for me to think of marrying a girl who was not a virgin?"

"No."

"Even as a Christian?"

"Just because you are a Christian. Who else would do it, if not a Christian? I don't see otherwise how you could pray honestly the Lord's Prayer: 'Forgive us our trespasses, as we forgive those who trespass against us.' "

"But forgiveness must be mutual."

"She goofed in this respect. You goofed in others. What's the difference? I can't think of any better glue for cleaving to each other than mutual forgiveness. Just that is the uniqueness of life with God. He is always ready to begin anew with us. Therefore, we can always begin anew with others. And I tell you, there is not a single day in marriage when you don't have to begin anew in some respect with your wife. And she with you."

We finished our meal in silence. But this silence was part of our conversation, not the end of it. On the way back to the hotel I asked Maurice whether he would consider marrying a widow.

I couldn't have asked him anything more alien to his thinking. Had his hands not been on the steering wheel, he probably would have thrown them up in the air.

"What makes you say that?"

"I feel a strong sympathy for young widows in Africa. No one takes care of them. They have no pension, no social security. They are not all prostitutes. Some try to make an honest living. I wish they could have a husband like you. Take a young widow with children. You would make a good father at your age. I can just see your mother's face if you would bring five grandchildren home to her at one time!"

Maurice had to take a deep breath.

"You must be joking," he said.

"No," I assured him, "I'm not."

"You really think that a widow of approximately my age could be a better partner for me than a young girl?"

"She could be a partner, not a daughter."

"And if I had my own children with her, wouldn't that be difficult?"

"Yes, but it would be much less difficult than bringing up children without a father, and for the children, much less difficult than having a mother who could be the daughter of their father."

"Then I could marry a divorcée too?"

"Depending upon the circumstances, yes. Either we believe in forgiveness or we don't."

We reached the hotel and entered the lobby. I asked the clerk for my key.

"Walter," Maurice said, "you turn everything upside down in me."

"I don't want you to become an old maid."

Maurice laughed and gave me a spontaneous hug.

The clerk, who had overheard our last words, looked at us in amazement. "There was a gentleman calling for you several times," he said.

"Did he leave his number for me to call back?"

"No, sir. He said he would call again."

At this moment, the operator came out of her booth and said that the man was calling again.

"Put it through, please. I will take it in my room."

I hurriedly said good-night to Maurice. As I was waiting for the elevator, he returned and gave me his card. "In case you need me, you can call me any time. I am free tomorrow."

I picked up the telephone as soon as I got to my room.

"This is John."

"I'm very glad you called me. How are you? Have you thought over our talk last night?"

"Sir, I want to tell you something," he said in a cold, harsh voice. "The dirt on my hands is honest dirt. It got there through hard work. I am proud of it. My work is harder than chatting with girls in hotels. And the way I dress is my business, not yours. Also, Fatma is my business. I know how to take care of her. I told you that story about leaving the country in order to see your reactions. I know what I want to do. You can't interfere in my affairs. And if you don't send Fatma home immediately, I will call the police."

"She is not here."

"I don't believe you."

"I assure you she is not here."

"I don't believe one word of what you say. She wasn't in the house when I came home from work. She sneaked out through the window. I know that she went to church."

"Please listen, John. I'm very sorry that I hurt you. I apologize for that remark about your hands. But the important thing now is to find Fatma."

"I know she went to church."

"Yes, she was in church. But she left early. I thought she probably had to meet you."

"It's now eleven o'clock. If she's not home by midnight, I'm going to call the police and accuse you if something has happened to her."

"Please tell me, John . . ."

But he had hung up. I tried to breathe calmly. I had made a horrible mistake. The remarks about his hands had been unnecessary. Every negative remark about someone is a prayer to the devil, I thought, and is fulfilled immediately.

How did he know about it, though? Was it possible that Fatma had told him? But he had said he didn't see her all day. Or had he lied to me?

And where was Fatma? It is dangerous for a girl to go out alone at night. Anything could have happened to her. If only I had the slightest idea where she lived! Where could she have gone?

I went to bed with a feeling of helplessness and powerlessness. If I had had the slightest idea where to search for her, I would not have hesitated to go out again. Indeed I wondered what counselors who are unable to pray would do in such a situation.

I don't know how long I had been asleep when I suddenly woke. It was as if I had heard a voice in my room. John's voice. Then I remembered I had dreamed of him, reliving his visit in my dream: he was about to leave and I asked him whether he had far to go. "No, just across the river," he had said. It was now close to 3:00 a.m.

An anxious thought flashed through my mind.

I went to the telephone and picked up the receiver. A sleepy voice answered. It was the night clerk.

"Tell me, is there a river in this city?"

"Yes, sir."

"A big one?"

"A little bit big."

"How far is it from here?"

"It's a little bit far."

"How long does it take to walk there?"

"A little bit long."

This could mean anything between fifteen minutes and two hours.

"I didn't see any river when I went to the church where I lectured."

"That's because you don't have to cross the bridge to get there."

"Tell me, if someone is here at the hotel and says, 'I live just across the river,' does he have to go over that bridge?"

"Yes, sir."

"And when he goes from Christ Church and wants to get on the other side of the river, does he have to cross the same bridge?"

"Yes, sir."

"Is there only one bridge?"

"There is only one bridge, sir."

"Are there taxis available now?"

"It is difficult. I wouldn't suggest that you take a taxi alone now."

"Then please dial this number."

I heard the ringing sound for a long time. Then Maurice answered.

"This is Walter, Maurice. You told me I could call you any time. I need you right now."

"I'm at your disposition."

"How long does it take for you to get to the hotel?"

"Fifteen minutes."

"Try to make it in ten."

I got dressed, went down and waited for Maurice in front of the hotel. The streets were entirely empty of people and traffic. Finally, the light of Maurice's car appeared. He stopped and I climbed in.

"Do you know where the bridge is?"

He laughed.

"Please don't ask me any questions. Just take me to the bridge, but before you drive onto the bridge, pull over to the side and stop."

We drove silently. I was glad Maurice didn't ask any questions. Then I saw the bridge. It was long and narrow with a stone balustrade on either side. There was a small walk for pedestrians on the right side.

Maurice stopped as we approached, but in a spot where we could see out over the whole bridge. There were no street lights, but there was moonlight and we could easily see the other side.

There she was. There was Fatma, leaning over the balustrade and staring down at the rushing waters.

"Do you see that girl there?"

"Yes."

"I can't tell you her story now. But I know she is desperate and might commit suicide. Is there a police station close by?"

"There is one on the other side of the bridge."

"All right. Drive now onto the bridge. Go past her about twenty feet, so that she'll think we're driving on. Then stop and I will jump out and try to catch her before she jumps."

"And if she jumps?"

"Then go as fast as you can to the police and give the alarm."

"Okay."

"If you see me talking to her quietly, then turn around and park a little distance away, so that you can't hear us, but you must see us."

"Why?"

"There may be a lawsuit. I need a witness for everything I do with this girl. Let's go now."

"Shall we have a word of prayer?"

"Please."

There was no time to lose. Maurice prayed for a few moments, his folded hands resting on the wheel. I looked at those faithful hands and knew they were more than human hands.

Fatma didn't move as we approached her. She remained standing with her back turned toward us, leaning on her elbows, her eyes fixed on the water.

Maurice passed her slowly, then stopped. I threw open the door, jumped out and ran toward her as fast as I could. She whirled around, frightened. Before she had a chance to react further, I grabbed her by the arm.

"Fatma, foolish girl, what are you doing?" I cried.

She looked at me for a second, then, struggling free, turned to resume her position. She didn't say a word as she continued to stare at the moving water.

Maurice drove on a short distance, turned around, and parked on the other side, about a hundred yards away. He turned off the headlights. There was no one else on the bridge, just the three of us.

The quietness was interrupted only by the sound of the gurgling water below us.

I stood beside Fatma, leaning with my elbows on the stone balustrade and looking down into the water just as she was doing.

After a short pause, I asked her in a voice as calm and relaxed as possible: "Do you know where you will get when you jump down there?"

She did not reply and I waited. Minutes passed.

"I don't care," she said finally. "The main thing is that it is finished."

"It isn't finished. That's precisely where you make the mistake."

"When I am dead, it will be finished."

"You will not be dead and it won't be finished."

"But the burden will be gone."

"On the contrary. You will take your burdens along with you into eternity. And the burden of having committed suicide in addition to all the others. It solves nothing, absolutely nothing."

"What does it matter? All I know is I can't go on living like this. I can't carry the burden any longer."

"I didn't ask you to. I want you to live without the burden."

"Pastor, you don't know what you are saying. You don't even know half of my burden. I lied to you. I lied to everybody. It's much worse than you think. You would be shocked if you knew the truth about me, the whole truth."

"I promise you, I shall not be shocked."

Without moving, she looked down at the dark water. Then she said:

"If I don't take my own life, I might take someone else's. Death is what I deserve."

"I agree."

"You agree?"

"Yes, whether I know everything about you or not—you deserve death. So do I. Everybody does. The only difference is that some know it and some don't. I'm glad you do."

"Why don't you let me die, then?"

"Because you are too late. Someone else has already died your death."

"It's too late to change my life, but not yet too late to die."

"The other way around, Fatma: It's not yet too late to change your life, but much too late to die."

"Too late to die?" She turned her head and looked at me. "I don't understand."

"Let me tell you a story. Have you ever heard of Barabbas?"

"You mean the murderer who was a fellow prisoner of Jesus?"

"Yes, that's the one. It was the Jewish custom to release a prisoner at the time of the passover. Pilate asked the Jews whom he should release—Jesus or Barabbas."

"I remember, and they chose Barabbas."

"Right! Now just imagine—Barabbas was free and was walking through the streets of Jerusalem on that Good Friday. He saw the crowds of people streaming out to Golgotha and followed them. When he arrived there, whom did he see?"

"Jesus on the cross."

"You learned your lesson well at that village school."

"I heard the story often, but it never meant anything to me."

"Now listen, Barabbas recognized his fellow prisoner. Suddenly it dawned on him: If Jesus were not hanging there . . . Can you finish the sentence, Fatma?"

"Then I would be in his place," she said.

"Yes, Fatma, you would. And I would. Both of us would."

We were silent again and watched the water swirling by.

"Continue the story," she said after awhile, again without looking at me.

"Imagine Barabbas would have thought, 'It's unjust that He dies. After all, I am the murderer, not He. I have deserved death, not He. All I can do now is to kill myself.' What would you think about that?"

"He would have been foolish."

"Exactly, just as foolish as you would be if you jumped down there. You are too late, Fatma. The death you have deserved Jesus has already died. Since his death, every suicide is too late. It's unnecessary. You are free. Free like Barabbas."

"Free?" She turned around and looked me fully in the face, leaning with her back toward the balustrade. The apathy was gone. In her eyes was desperation. "Free? I am free?" A short, bitter laugh. "I am locked in, pastor. The door fell shut behind me. The door without a handle."

"Is that why you left the church so early?"

"Yes, you took away from me the last straw of hope."

I shut my eyes. What had I done? What kind of a messenger had I been?

"I entered the tent. And when I was inside, I found it had no top. It was raining in. But still I couldn't get out. Then I had this horrible feeling of being locked in. I wanted to get out. Any place. To jump! Any place!"

I stood in front of her with my eyes shut. I shuddered. "Fatma, I . . ."

"What does it matter whether I am married or not? 'Afterward they are a couple,' you said, 'in spite of themselves.' I am coupled in spite of myself."

She started to shout, forgetting herself in wrath and desperation.

"I am marked. The flesh has an indelible imprint upon it, you said. I am marked, marked, marked. Not just with John. With at least six others before. My door is six times shut, Pastor. Or maybe six doors and no one to break the locks.

"One flesh, yes, one flesh," Fatma continued. "But not with everything 'I am and I have' but just with this poor, dirty, damned body. 'You can't divorce yourself from your own body,' you said. All right, I can't. I am not married and still I'm not divorceable."

The law kills, I thought. The law kills. If she would have jumped from that bridge, it would have been my fault, not John's. You, Who woke me up tonight, give me the right word now. On this bridge between heaven and earth, between two banks of a river, between death and life, give me Your word.

"Fatma, the church was full of young people. They had not yet built their tents. I had to warn them, to save them from the same fate as yours. This was not the message for you."

"And what is my message?" She had turned around again and was leaning over the balustrade.

"That God can break the door open from the outside—regardless of whether there is one, or six, or a hundred."

"Divorcing me from my own body?"

" 'With men it is impossible, but not with God; for all things are possible with God.' "

"And how could He do the impossible for me?"

"I haven't told you the end of the story yet. Barabbas realized that if Jesus were not hanging there, he would be. Barabbas didn't stop there. He turned around. With the cross behind him and the world in front of him, he said: 'Because He has died for me, I will at least live for Him.' "

Fatma said nothing. I waited. Then John 8:11 came to me for her:

"Jesus said to the adulteress: 'Neither do I condemn you; go, and do not sin again.' "

"Go where?"

"Did you read Psalm 27 as I told you on the telephone?"

"Yes, and I found my verse."

"Can you say it?"

" 'My father and my mother have forsaken me.' For me everything is turned around. It's not like you said in your lecture, not I who have left father and mother. They have forsaken me."

"I wasn't thinking of that verse for you. But if you quote it, then you must also listen to how the verse ends: 'For my father and mother have forsaken me, *but the Lord will take me up.' "*

"And where is the Lord?"

"Right now I am His mouthpiece and in His name let me tell you the verse which deeply comforted me yesterday and which I thought of as the verse for you:

'For he will hide me in his shelter
  in the day of trouble;
he will conceal me under the cover of his tent,
  he will set me high upon a rock.' (Psalm 27:5)

"No," she replied, "Jeremiah is better for me: 'My tent is destroyed, and all my cords are broken; my children have gone from me, and they are not. . . .' Remember, I aborted them. I killed them. 'There is no one to spread my tent again, and to set up my curtains.' "

"But there is, Fatma. God Himself is your tent."

"You mean, I can have a tent—even living alone, single, unmarried?"

"Yes, a complete, waterproof tent, with a top and everything, a shelter where you can hide in the day of trouble."

She turned again to the balustrade, but she did not look down into the river. Her eyes followed the river to the horizon. The clear, dark African sky gave way to a tender gray—the first sign of a new day.

"I can't enter God's tent with all my sins. I forgot Him, left Him out of my life."

"He did not forget you, but He does forget your sins."

"How can you say that without knowing them?"

"I can, absolutely, even without knowing them."

"And when God forgets them?"

"It is as if they had not happened."

"I can't believe that. Not yet. Give me time to think. Help me to build my tent."

"I will."

"I can't go home now. I am afraid . . ."

"Then I suggest we go to Pastor Daniel's house first."

I gave Maurice a sign. He started up the motor of his car and drove to where we were standing. I made Fatma sit beside him and sat in the back.

"Sorry to keep you waiting," I said.

"Never mind. I was busy," was Maurice's reply.

"I could feel it, Maurice. Your work was not in vain."

Maurice drove silently, casting only a shy glance from time to time at the distraught passenger sitting beside him.

When we came to Pastor Daniel's house, we found a little sign on the door, written evidently by Esther, which read: "Please, dear friend, if at all possible, call between eight and nine in the morning or between five and six at night." It was now between five and six in the morning. Once more I had to act against the advice which I had given Daniel.

We knocked for a long time. It wasn't until Maurice knocked at the bedroom shutter that we got an answer.

"Who is it?"

"Some early callers, so undisciplined that they cannot keep your office hours."

"Walter!"

Daniel opened the door after quickly wrapping himself in his toga. "Are you up already?"

"Night shift," said Maurice.

Daniel looked from me to Fatma and from Fatma to Maurice. Indeed we were a strange-looking party.

"Come in."

I explained briefly the situation. Then we discussed who should call John. Fatma refused. Daniel volunteered, but Fatma was afraid that John would then know where she was. She pleaded with Daniel not to tell him.

"I doubt whether I'm the right one either in this case," I said. "At least I don't want to talk to him until Fatma has made up her mind. He is very angry with me. . . . Fatma, did you ever talk to him about our telephone conversations?"

"Never!"

"But he knew that I had remarked about his dirty hands."

"He taped our telephone calls."

"All of them?"

"Yes."

"Also the one when you called here at the parsonage?"

"Yes, I discovered yesterday afternoon that he had a tape recorder connected to the telephone. I was afraid he would beat me when he came home. I escaped through a window and went to church before he got home from work. But then when I heard you speaking about the door with no handle inside, I felt even more locked in than at home and I lost all hope. I couldn't go to John, neither to my parents, nor to you."

Then Maurice volunteered to call John. There was no answer.

Esther came into the room, carrying her just-wakened baby. I introduced her to Fatma.

"Here is a very tired girl. She has to make a crucial decision. But she needs quietness in order to do this. First of all, though, she needs something to eat and then some sleep."

"She can have our guest room," Esther said.

"When she has rested, I wish you could have a good talk with her, Esther," I said.

Daniel smiled understandingly and Esther agreed.

"When is your wife coming?" she asked me.

"At four p.m. That is, if the plane is on time."

"Good. Esther and I will pick you up at the hotel at three-thirty. If you like, we'll also have supper together—the four of us—at the airport restaurant."

I agreed, and took my leave with Maurice.

At first Maurice was very silent as he drove me back to my hotel. Then he asked:

"Did it ever happen to you before that your telephone calls were taped?"

"No, Maurice, I never even thought of this possibility."

"But he may have needed that criticism about his outward appearance. Maybe it was good for him."

"Maurice, if I didn't believe that God could use even our mistakes, I'd have to quit this work immediately. The same is true of the remarks I made about the door without an inside handle. It was right—and still for Fatma at that moment, it was wrong."

"Still God used it with Fatma," Maurice replied.

"This is what we call 'grace,' Maurice. God plays billiards. We may push the ball in the wrong direction, yet God bounces it back and it ends up where it should—at the goal."

We reached the hotel. Maurice, in his typical African politeness, accompanied me to the lobby. He didn't say anything. I had the feeling he was preoccupied. There in the lobby was John. He looked haggard and bleary-eyed. But he wore a suit.

We greeted each other and I told him what had happened. I gave him time to think. I could see that he was struggling with himself. Finally he said:

"I want to tell you one thing. Fatma is free to do what she wants to do. She can stay with me or leave."

"Thank you, John. I am glad to hear you say that."

I promised to keep him informed about Fatma. He said good-by coolly, but at least he departed in peace.

As I watched him leave the hotel, I couldn't help but feel sorry for him. What might be his story? Maybe he had had trouble in Europe. Maybe a fight with his boss or a broken engagement. Maybe a child out of wedlock or a divorce. Or maybe he wasn't even divorced and thought that distance would solve the problem. But distance never solves any problem, even if camouflaged by missionary zeal.

I turned to Maurice who was still deep in his thoughts and thanked him again for his help. We said good-night—or good-morning. When I went for my key at the desk, I asked the telephone operator not to put through any calls nor to allow, any visitors until noon, for I had to get some sleep.

"But please be very polite and explain that I got up at three this morning. Most people who call have troubles."

"What is your work, sir?"

"Trying to help people with their troubles."

I had the feeling that she wanted to say something more, but the clerks at the desk were listening attentively. So she promised to do her best and took her place at the switchboard.

I went up to my room and fell asleep immediately.

8

IT WAS NOON SHARP WHEN THE TELEPHONE WOKE ME UP.

"I'm sorry to wake you, sir, but there's a call for you."

"That's all right. Were there many calls?"

"Yes, there were. And a couple who say they are Timothy and Miriam have been waiting here in the lobby since ten o'clock. They want to talk to you."

"Please tell them to wait until I have had a quick lunch. Then I will see them."

"Yes, sir. And one thing more. May I have a talk with you too?"

"Of course. Do you want to come up here?"

"It's against the hotel regulations for the personnel to enter the rooms of our guests. We would have to talk by phone."

"When are you off work?"

"At eleven p.m."

"All right, could you call me this evening before you leave?" Then she put the call through.

It was Esther. She reported that Fatma had rested and that she had had a good talk with her. Fatma had not yet made up her mind what to do. She was still struggling.

"I told her she could stay with us for the time being."

"That's fine, Esther. Thank you. It reminds me of other suicide cases. A solution could have been found had they just waited a day longer. Staying with you is, of course, no final solution. It doesn't meet Fatma's deepest need. There's one thing, though, that I can't understand, Esther. I've read so much about the 'extended family' in Africa. But when it comes to an emergency like this, there doesn't seem to be a soul to help."

"The extended family still functions in the villages, but not in the city."

"But Fatma said she wanted to invite between three and four hundred people to her wedding."

"There is a difference whether you invite people to a wedding or whether you need them for help."

"True, but she called them 'friends.' Wouldn't there be one single real friend among them? This is what I can't understand."

"I shall try to talk to Fatma about it. I know this city quite well—it is no easy problem. But what did you mean when you said that having her stay with us is not yet meeting Fatma's deepest need? What is her deepest need? Do you think it is marriage?"

"No, not necessarily."

"Is it sex? Could it be that she is so wound up that she can't live without sex?"

"I don't think so. She's rather bored and disappointed as far as sex goes."

"What is she looking for, then?"

"A place."

"But I offered her a place in our home."

Typical, I thought. It's so hard for married people to understand the problems of those who are not married.

"Your offer is very good, Esther. For the time being it is the best thing I could wish for Fatma. But this is not what I mean by 'place.' She needs a place where she belongs, which is her own, where her name is on the door and where she has her own furniture. A place where she is at home and where she can become a place—a place for others. I think she has been looking for such a place during her whole life, but she has never found it. She thought she would, when she let herself be taken in by men. All she found was a bed, but not a place. The lack of a place is one of the main motives for suicide."

Esther thought for awhile. Then she spoke: "In other words, unless someone marries her, she will never become happy."

She hadn't caught on yet.

"Not necessarily," I said patiently. "There are married couples who never become a place. And there are single people who have a place, who are a place. When you visit them you feel that you come into a place."

"And God? Where does God enter into all of this? Wouldn't you say that Fatma's deepest need is God?"

"Yes, Mrs. Pastor's wife."

"But you said that her deepest need is a place."

"It's the same. God is the only place there is. Those who find a place, find God. And those who find God, have found a place—regardless of where they are and regardless of whether they are married or single."

"I have to think that over. I think what we need just as much as marriage guidance is single life guidance," Esther said.

"Yes, I wholeheartedly agree. What's Fatma doing now?"

"She's writing. I don't know what. I didn't ask her."

"Good."

"What if she wants to go back to John?"

"Just let her go."

"And if she asks me to go along to pick up her things?"

"Then you go along, of course."

"But I . . ."

"And try to have a good talk with John at the same time. He needs help too. You are the logical person to help him. The door is shut for me in his case. I failed him."

"But Pastor Walter, I have never done anything like that. I have no training."

"Just use your feminine intuition. Even if you had a lot of training, it wouldn't help you much without that. Counseling is an art, not a science."

"But I am a complete zero."

"So am I. We are both zeros, Esther. No one knows that better than I do after last night. But this is just when God can use us. He's the One in front of the zero. That's all that counts."

"Well, thank you, brother zero."

"Thank you, sister zero. And God bless you when you go to John's."

I hung up before she had a chance to reply.

After I had finished a quick lunch, Timothy and Miriam entered my room. There was a different air about them. They seemed to be more sure of themselves. Timothy was the first one to speak after they sat down together on the sofa. They had evidently planned it that way.

"We talked together," he said.

"Where?"

"In my brother's home."

"So there are places where you can talk after all."

"Yes, there are," he said with a smile. "We talked and we came to the conclusion that Miriam was not quite right yesterday when she said we had entered the triangle through the sex entrance. The truth is that we entered through the love entrance as well. We sort of switched back and forth between them. You see, we are a special case, an in-between case."

"I guess ninety-nine per cent of us are special in-between cases."

"At the beginning of our relationship I think there was love, genuine love. So, as you would say, we did enter through the love door. But then once we were inside, we went to the sex door. Pretty soon we almost forgot how we had come in. How shall I put it? We became one flesh, but not completely. We shared our bodies without sharing our minds. As soon as we realized this, we tried to switch back to love. But we couldn't find the door again."

"I was afraid to say 'no,' " Miriam finally said. "I thought that to love means never to say 'no.' And I was ashamed to blush."

"You are able to blush, Miriam," I interjected. "I saw that yesterday when you talked about the things not so beautiful."

"I shall respect your 'no's' and your blushings," Timothy said with a new assuring tone in his voice.

"All right," I said, "this is the diagnosis. What's the therapy?"

"We have two questions," Timothy answered. Again it was clear that they had carefully prepared the talk. "The first question is: Do you think that because of our differences in age, education, and character our marriage would fail in any case?"

"I wouldn't say that. Not in any case. In fact, I think it could be a real testimony if your marriage would succeed."

"How do you mean that?"

"It would be evident to everyone that yours is not a 'garden marriage' where the husband dominates his wife and respects her only as the bearer of his children. Miriam will never play the role of a garden. Either she marries as a partner or she doesn't marry. The people around you will notice that. This is what I mean by 'testimony.' "

I paused.

"But—" said Timothy.

"But what?"

"Well, you said that you did not think our marriage would fail in *any* case and that it *could* be a testimony, if it *would* succeed. So there must be a 'but.' "

I had to laugh. "True, if Miriam doesn't have enough tact and discretion and plays instead the card of her superiority and if you do not have enough self-denial and humility to accept her being ahead of you occasionally, then your marriage will be in danger. This can become the straw that breaks the camel's back. At least it will take very special effort."

"But do you think we could make it?" Timothy asked anxiously, while Miriam touched his hand.

"To be aware of the danger and to look it straight in the eye means that you have already half overcome it. However, it takes more than that to perform the extraordinary."

"But we are just very common people. There's nothing extraordinary about us."

"You are not extraordinary, but God may want to do something extraordinary with you."

"Do you mean that as Christians we could dare it?" Miriam concluded.

"I mean that the quality of the life you live with God will be decisive."

They were silent.

"This leads us to our second question." It was Timothy who picked up the conversation again. "Is it possible to start all over again?"

"What do you mean?"

"Starting from scratch, as if we had never entered the triangle. Approaching the love door slowly and then proceeding from there in both directions without skipping any steps."

"He means," Miriam added in her frank and direct way, "could we refrain from sex from now on until we are married, in spite of the fact that we went too far already?"

"It certainly will not be easy, for once you have started, the temptations will be greater. But I don't think it's impossible. With human strength alone it cannot be done. It takes special grace—an extraordinary power. I have seen others do it, though."

"And what was the outcome?"

"Usually it deepened their relationship. As soon as sex was out, they were able to get acquainted on a deeper level. But they helped each other, of course."

"How can we help each other?" Miriam wanted to know.

"Avoid certain situations. Give up your car rides alone at night, for example. Go out with other couples. Be honest. Don't pretend some thing is beautiful if it isn't."

"Won't this lead to tensions?"

"It certainly will. So what? Many sexual problems in our day arise because people think they, at all costs, have to avoid pain, renunciation, and tension. I believe that tension is something positive. It belongs to growing up and becoming mature. One day you will have to learn to stand up under tension—and a good time to learn it is before marriage."

"Does the tension keep on even within marriage?"

"Yes, it does. Those who have not learned to stand up under it before marriage will face a crisis during marriage. There is tension between all three angles of the triangle: between sex and love, between love and wedlock, and between wedlock and sex. It's like with a tent. It will be waterproof only as long as the canvas is tightened between the poles. As soon as the tension is gone, the tent sags."

Timothy and Miriam said nothing more. They said good-by and left hand in hand.

Daniel came to pick me up to go out to the airport. When we passed the desk, the telephone operator lifted up her head from the switchboard and greeted me with her eyes. I nodded to her. Suddenly, I remembered that I had made no room reservation for Ingrid.

We asked the clerk whether I could change to a double room. He explained that everything was filled up for the weekend.

"If only you had asked yesterday, or even this morning," he said.

"I really feel ashamed, Daniel. Here I've been so busy the whole week talking about marriage and sharing that I completely forgot to arrange for a room which I could share with my wife."

The clerk suggested a single room for her on the same floor, just across the hall from my room, and we settled for that.

"It will look as if we are not on good terms with each other," I said. Daniel comforted me: "It does have the advantage that you can have talks separately. It was good that we had an extra guest room today when Esther talked with Fatma."

Esther was waiting for us in the car. I asked her who had watched the children when she was talking with Fatma and also during her long telephone conversation with me at noon.

"My husband did," she said proudly.

Daniel sighed audibly.

"Are you suffering, brother?"

"Terribly! If she goes on like this I don't know where it will end," he joked. Then he changed his tone of voice. "Seriously though, Walter, Esther is a different person since she has taken part in the work. I have a new wife."

"Who's watching the children now?" I asked.

"Fatma offered to take care of them so I could go with Daniel and you to the airport."

While we were driving to the airport, Daniel wanted to know whether I had given lessons in counseling to the telephone operator of the hotel.

"I tried to reach you this morning shortly after nine and the operator told me in a soft, kind voice: 'Sir, I know you must be a very troubled man. But please don't give up hope. The doctor is sleeping now. I'm not supposed to wake him up before noon. But I'm sure he will help you if you call again at that time.' "

We laughed wholeheartedly, all three of us.

"I just told her to be polite," I said. "But who would have thought that you would be the first 'client'? There were many calls today. I can't understand why no one has thought of starting a counseling service by telephone in this city."

In the meantime, we had arrived at the airport and learned that Ingrid's plane would be half an hour late. While we were waiting Daniel and Esther had a comment about my lecture the evening before.

"Last night we discussed the triangle with the slanted lines," Daniel began, "and the empty space created in that way, the 'vacuum in the relationship' as you said. But we know many engaged couples to whom this description does not apply. Their situation is different. They have known each other already for a long time. They are certain about their love. They have proved their faithfulness again and again. They've struggled together through many a crisis. Step by step they have grown in their expressions of love and at the same time in mutual responsibility. But due to some outward circumstances they are not yet able to get married. Maybe they don't have a place to live or they are both still in training, students, for example. Actually, there is no vacuum created, but only a very small space in between which separates them from the wedding and full physical union. Their case would look something like this."

Daniel took a card out of his jacket and drew a triangle on it with parallel lines where only the last one was slightly slanted:

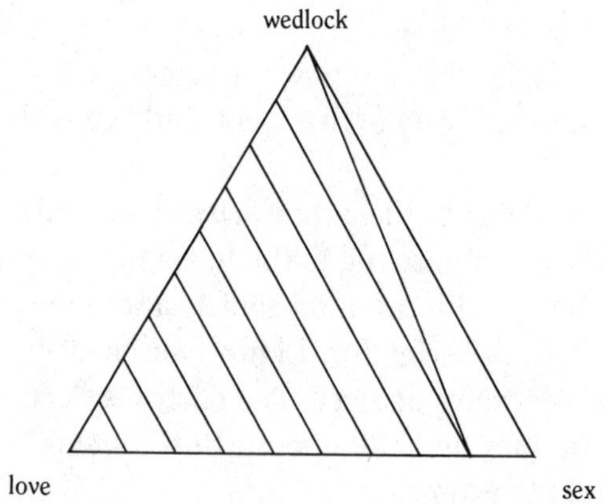

He explained further: "These couples say, 'It is not our fault that we have to begin our marriage before the wedding. We are forced to do so by outward circumstances. We know it's not ideal, but it seems for us to be the lesser evil. We take this risk which is better than the danger of repressing our natural desires, of becoming tense and nervous, and maybe even of losing each other.' Frankly, Walter, when I hear them talk, I must admit they do have a point. By waiting for such a long time they may disturb the dynamic play of forces more than by giving themselves to each other before the wedding."

"This is really the most difficult as well as the most widely disputed case," I replied. "No one on the outside has a right to judge or even condemn them."

"But don't some people claim that premarital sex makes marriages happier?" Esther wanted to know.

"Personally," I replied, "I know of no couple who have ever claimed that their marriage would have failed had they not consummated it before the wedding. I know some couples who would say that premarital sex has not done any damage to their marriage. But I know far more couples who, upon looking back, view it in a different light, although they began their marriage before the wedding with the best of arguments."

"We read your book, *I Loved a Girl.* Are François and Cecile among the latter?" Daniel asked.

"I believe so. They both thought that the high bride price for Cecile which François couldn't pay justified their crossing the 'small in-between space' in the triangle. Today I think they wished they had waited."

"But what would you say to such a couple?"

"Well, first of all, I would check with them all their reasons for not getting married. Sometimes the real motive is only false pride. They are too proud to start their wedded life with just a table and a bed. Why not? It may even be good to rough it a little in the beginning. I would tell them, if you start at the bottom, then you can only go upward."

"So you would even encourage them to begin in a small rented room with a hot plate as a kitchen stove?"

"I think that postponing the wedding just because one does not have a new bedroom suite is foolish."

"The trouble here is," Daniel explained, "many of our church members don't get married because they cannot afford the white man's clothes—a dark suit for the bridegroom and a satin wedding dress for the bride. Others delay because they think they have to give the traditional wedding feast which is expensive."

"This makes me even more convinced that we should encourage simple weddings!" I exclaimed. "An engaged couple who have tested their love and faithfulness for an ample period of time should be encouraged by their family to celebrate their wedding as soon as possible."

"And what if that isn't possible?" Daniel insisted.

"Then you must call their attention to the fact that although they may solve one problem through their physical surrender—that of releasing their sexual tension—there are many new problems coming up."

"And what are the main problems for such a couple?" Esther asked as we waited.

"The couple have to be reminded that there is no point of return. The revolving door is stationary from that day on. Also, if the couple have no place of their own, mutual adjustment is difficult. It is the girl who suffers more from the feeling of not being sheltered than the young man, and this may hinder her from reaching full sexual satisfaction."

"And how about contraceptives?" Esther asked.

"Often they haven't even thought of this when making their decision. They soon recognize that there is no ideal solution to this problem and that a compromise has to be made with every method. It's not so easy to come together without living together."

Ingrid's plane had arrived at last. The first passengers appeared.

Then I saw my wife. Upright and queenly she moved slowly down the steps. She was wearing a light brown suit with a green scarf tucked in at the neckline. Her favorite colors, I thought.

As I watched her striding with measured steps the distance between the plane and the building, swinging slightly her long arms which betrayed her Swedish descent, I felt proud to be married to this fashionable lady. Daniel was silent.

Ingrid's face was fresh and radiant as she waved to us. Unbelievable that the same person had written such a depressing letter a few days ago, I thought.

I took a look at her hand baggage and hoped secretly that she had remembered what I had forgotten: gifts for Daniel and Esther.

After we had all exchanged affectionate greetings, we went to the airport restaurant. We sat down, the four of us, around a table and ordered a meal. As we waited, Ingrid distributed gifts for everyone: a blouse for Esther, a tie for Daniel, a large calendar with colored pictures of the Austrian Alps for their home, small toys for the children.

The surprise gifts broke the ice fast. Before long we were conversing like old friends. I appreciated the ease with which Ingrid made contact.

They wanted to know if Americans had the same problems as Africans, if they needed the marriage triangle as much as they did.

Daniel said he had read about the "swinging" clubs in the States where total sexual freedom reigns. Husband and wife go there together, pair off with whomever they want, without getting emotionally involved, and then leave again as husband and wife. But the managers of these clubs have noticed that a couple can't keep it up for very long. Something in them seems to rebel.

"Yes," Ingrid said, "they think it's an escape from what they call 'monotonous monogamy,' but the result is usually more emptiness and loneliness. Americans need the triangle as much as Africans do. We have to show that monogamy can be an exciting adventure, integrating both sex and love into marriage. There's nothing more boring than adultery, nothing more empty than divorce."

Esther had a vision. "It would be great if we could once proclaim this message together, all four of us, an African and a European-American couple as a team."

"Yes, it would be a tremendous help if Africans could hear this message out of an African mouth," I agreed.

"But it would be still more striking for Americans and Europeans to hear this message out of an African mouth," Ingrid added.

"I think so too," I answered, adding, with a knowing glance toward Esther, "providing you are honest zeros—neither pumped up, wanting to be a little bit more than just zero, nor shrunken up, wanting to be a little bit less. The shrunken zeros want to appear humble in the eyes of others. You see, inferiority feelings often cover up hidden pride."

"Don't you dare give my wife counseling lessons again," Daniel protested laughingly. He turned to Ingrid: "Your husband made my wife a pastor and me a children's nurse. I tell you it's enough to have one pastor in our family."

"They have the same problem as we do, Ingrid," I explained,"never an undisturbed moment, many interruptions, and the constant conflict between their marriage and their work. He has time to listen to everyone's troubles, but not to those of his wife. It sounds familiar, doesn't it?"

Ingrid thought for a moment. Then she said: "There's only one solution. You need a hiding place. Some place out of town where no one can find you and which nobody knows about. There you should go together once a week for a whole day or at least half a day."

Esther's face lit up. "I know where we could go," she said.

"Where?" Daniel wanted to know.

"I'll tell you when we are alone," she said with a roguish smile. "No body else is supposed to know it."

"Walter sometimes goes to a Catholic monastery when he wants to work undisturbed," Ingrid said.

"Yes, that's true," I said, "and then I always envy the priests for not being married."

Esther wanted to know whether I was serious.

"Sure he is," Daniel replied in my stead. "I think every married man has moments when he wishes he were single."

Daniel motioned to the waiter for the bill. He insisted on paying it himself. We were careful not to refuse his African hospitality, although I knew that, with his small salary, this was a real sacrifice.

As we drove from the airport to the hotel, the two ladies sat in the back seat. Esther thanked Ingrid again for the good advice concerning the hiding place.

"I read a book once," Daniel said to me while Ingrid and Esther talked together, "in which the author advises the counselor not to give advice."

"That's also an advice, isn't it?"

"Yes, but he says that to give advice means to direct people. One should not do that."

"You can't avoid it, Daniel. Not to direct is also a way of directing-perhaps the most clever way. I agree with Paul Tournier who claims that no one can be really morally neutral, and that although we say nothing openly, our secret reflections and judgments do not escape the other one's intuition.*

"Even if you say nothing, he will imagine what you are thinking and he will spend a lot of time thinking about what he thinks you are thinking. This way he may come to entirely wrong conclusions. I believe it's more honest and less dangerous to share frankly with the other person your opinion—and then, of course, give him the freedom to accept it or not."

"But, Walter, the author said that if you give advice you are like one who is sitting on the safe bank of a river talking to someone who is in the water. Instead, you should jump in and swim with him."

"On the contrary," I replied, "if you don't give any advice, you stay out of the water. But if you give advice, it's like jumping in. If the other one accepts and follows your advice, you are responsible. You are linked together. You swim right along with him."

We arrived at the hotel and said good-by to Esther and Daniel.

"Please call me up when you get home," I said to Daniel, "and tell me how Fatma is."

I was glad that there was no lecture this evening. I still was tired from last night.

When we were alone in my room, I took Ingrid in my arms. Tears came to her eyes. "It's all too much," she said.

"How did you leave the children?" I asked.

"They're all fine. I took the boys back to their boarding school on Thursday. Here's a letter from David for you."

I read the sprawling lines of my twelve-year-old son: "Last night I had a strange dream. I dreamt that I went with you and Mommy to Africa. You asked me what my motto was. I thought awhile and then the words of the song came to me: *Gehe mit dem Herrn allewege* ['Go with the Lord all the way']."

This giving up of our children causes us to discover them in a new way, I thought, and maybe even aids their inner growth.

"But wasn't it hard on little Ruthy when you left? She's only eight,"

*Cf. Paul Tournier, *A Place for You* (New York: Harper & Row, 1968), p. 85.

I said to Ingrid.

"She was all excited about staying with our neighbors while I'm on this trip. She had put your old sea captain's cap on her stuffed elephant so she wouldn't be lonely for you. And do you know the last thing she said to me? 'Mommy, don't be sad because you're not going to see me. You know the days will go by fast!' I often think they are braver than their mother. Tell me, how did your lectures go?"

"Ask the people who heard them, not me."

"Esther already told me about them in the car. I wasn't surprised. I knew even before I started out on this trip that God was using you."

We sat down together on the sofa where Miriam and Timothy had been just a few hours before.

"Your complaining letters don't make it easier for me, you know."

"I didn't mean to complain. I just wanted to share the facts."

"But when you share these facts, I feel accused. It's as if you were saying that it's my fault that I leave you alone. That I don't love you enough."

"That's not what I wanted to . . ."

"Don't you understand that I need a different kind of letter when I do this work?"

"Yes, I know it so well, but I can't write you other letters unless I am first able to share how I really feel. When I am so helpless, I don't know what else to do. I have no one to talk to about my innermost feelings when you are away. If I can't write them to you, I don't know what would happen."

Ingrid didn't try to hold back her tears anymore. She put her head on my lap and sobbed quietly. Gone was the queenly lady. All that was left was the sensitive child.

The telephone rang. I reached for the receiver while my left hand kept stroking her hair. It was Daniel.

"I just wanted to congratulate you on your wife," he said. "You know, she strikes me as an angel. I never had this impression about anyone else. First I thought, she isn't real. But she is. She radiates something."

"Yes," I said, while Ingrid continued to weep, her head buried in my lap.

"When she enters a room, the room becomes different. Esther too is completely taken by her."

"Thank you. Sometimes I wonder how a clumsy, bearish fellow as I am could have found such a wife."

Ingrid lifted up her head, but I pressed it down tenderly.

"But how is Fatma?"

"She's fine. When we came home we found her playing with the children and then she ate supper with them. She seems to be at peace with herself. It looks as though she has made up her mind, but I refrained from giving her any advice."

"Don't worry," I said, "she knows anyway what you want her to do."

"She said she's written a letter to you, but it isn't finished yet. She wants to give it to you tomorrow after the service. But Walter, the reason for my calling is that the church is filling up again. People are streaming in. You must come and give us a lecture tonight too."

"Didn't you announce that there would be no meeting tonight?"

"Yes, I did. But the people have come anyway. Maybe I didn't make it clear enough. There are many newcomers. I can't just send them home. You have to come, Walter."

"I just can't, Daniel."

"Are you trying to teach me how to say 'no'?"

"Couldn't Ingrid come instead of me?"

Ingrid raised her head with a start and sat up straight.

"Just let me ask her."

Ingrid shook her head violently.

"She okayed it," I said. "Pick her up in fifteen minutes."

Ingrid grabbed the receiver out of my hand, but I had already pressed down the hook and thus cut off the call.

"But I don't have anything prepared," Ingrid said. I knew her too well to be worried about that and concluded from the tone of her voice that her defense was breaking down.

"Just let them ask questions," I suggested. "I'm sure they will have hundreds once you have won their confidence, and that's not hard for you. But hurry up and change. They will pick you up soon."

She looked around the room. "Is that supposed to be a double bed?"

"Ingrid, I'm sorry. They didn't have a double room free for tonight.

So I had to take another single room for you. It's just across the hall from this one."

She didn't say anything, but I could see the struggle she had in accepting this fact.

"It might even be better this way," I said, "just in case someone wants to have a private talk with you after the meeting."

"All right," she said, "it doesn't matter." Then she went to her room to get ready. But again I knew her too well. The tone of her voice indicated that to her it mattered very much.

After Ingrid had left I tried to work on my sermon. My text was Ephesians 5:21-33.

"Husbands, love your wives, as Christ loved the church," was the key verse. How did Christ love the church? He served her, I thought. He did not come to be served, but to serve. He made himself subject to her, gave himself up for her.

This cast a new light for me on the verse which all husbands hail and all wives abhor: "Wives, be subject to your husbands." It dawned on me that then the submission of the wife is only a submission in response to the submission of her husband. "Be subject to one another."

Yes, but how? Who has ever achieved this balance? It seems to be a daily assignment.

The telephone rang again. It was the operator, but this time she was calling in her own right.

"You gave me permission to call you, sir!"

"Yes I did. What's your problem?"

"My husband drinks."

"Why?"

"I don't know."

"You should know. There must be a hole somewhere in his life."

"A hole?"

"Yes, a drunkard always tries to fill a hole, an empty container. There must be a deficiency somewhere, an emptiness in his life."

"I have no idea."

"Do you have children?"

"Yes, one child."

"How old is your child?"

"Almost four."

"Doesn't your husband want another child?"

"Yes, but if he drinks, I have to work and then I can't afford another one."

"Why don't you make a bargain with him?"

"A bargain?"

"Yes, real hard bargaining belongs to marriage too."

"All right. What should we bargain about?"

"He stops drinking and you agree to have another baby."

"Thank you, sir. I won't forget our talk."

"And now I want to give you another number to call."

"Yes, please."

"Four thirteen."

"One digit is lacking. Every telephone number in this city has four digits."

"It's a number for you to call when you need it."

"For me?"

"Yes, do you have a Bible?"

"I can find one."

"Then call Philippians four thirteen in case of need: 'I can do all things in him who strengthens me.' " There was silence.

I hung up. Again I had given advice, I thought. I am an impossible counselor, a poor husband, and a pastor without a sermon. I sat in front of my blank sheet of paper and couldn't write a line. It was the same feeling I had had on the first evening here.

When Ingrid came back from the church, I still hadn't written one word of my sermon. I could just as well have gone with her.

"How did it go?" I asked her.

"Very well, considering the circumstances. After Daniel introduced me as your wife and the mother of our three sons and two daughters, he encouraged them to ask questions about anything they wanted. He told them not to be ashamed to call things by name which God was not ashamed to create. That did it. The questions broke loose like a flood. We could have gone on for hours."

"What were they all about?"

"Mostly about women and their biological functions. When I explained the ovarian cycle and the changes it brings in a woman's body as well as in her emotions, one man stood up and asked: 'Is this why my wife is never the same two days in a row?'

"Another wanted to know what to do when his wife is pregnant and craves strange things, which sometimes cost a lot of money. Should he just laugh at her, or should he try to get the things for her?"

"I know already what you answered. You told them the story about the apples when we were in Cameroun and you were pregnant with Kathy. And you described how your model husband made a special trip to the airport to meet the plane from Europe in order to buy two pounds of expensive apples . . ."

"Yes, and . . ."

"And that your heart melts with love for me every time you think of those apples and . . ."

"And how thankful I am to have such an understanding husband!"

"I can imagine what you said. It's a good thing I wasn't present. What else did they ask you?"

"They wanted to know where twins come from, what causes a miscarriage, whether a man can sleep with his wife when she's pregnant, why so many mothers die in childbirth—they were all good questions."

"Oh, sister, I'm glad you were there and not I. Could you answer them all?"

"Fortunately I had my teaching charts along. I used the one with the enlarged picture of the female reproductive organs in order to explain how a baby is conceived."

"You mean you hung it up?"

"Of course. Daniel had a little stand and we hung it on that, right in front of the altar where all the people could see it."

"You know, Ingrid, before I gave my first lecture, Daniel warned me about using the word 'sex.' And now you hang the uterus in front of the altar. They've come a long way, I'd say."

"They didn't seem to mind at all. Daniel had to call on Esther, though, to help him interpret when we talked about the female organs. She told me afterward how she had said it in their mother tongue. The uterus she called 'the house of the baby,' the ovaries she called 'the storehouse of the eggs,' and the vagina she explained as being 'the road for birth.'

"After I had explained about conception and the growth of a baby in the womb, one of the older men stood up. In his hand he had a closed envelope. He said he had a question which burned like fire in his heart. 'If I give you this closed envelope,' he said, 'and there's a letter inside it, can you tell me what the letter says while the envelope is still closed?' I had to admit I couldn't. 'All right then,' he said. 'How can you know what it looks like inside a woman's body, in a woman's stomach?' That was the term he used."

"Did you have the feeling that they believed you, that they accepted what you said?"

"For the most part, yes. But they had a hard time when I talked about breastfeeding. They are thoroughly convinced that if a breastfeeding mother has intercourse with her husband, her milk will be spoiled and the baby will get sick, perhaps even die. And since they breastfeed their babies at least until they start to walk, intercourse is forbidden for one year, sometimes two years after the birth of a child."

"Yes, I know. I find this belief wherever I go in Africa."

"It never dawned on me to what degree a false biological conception can have ethical consequences. If a couple don't dare to have intercourse for two years after the baby, they must become polygamous."

"Or the husband goes to a prostitute and catches a disease. Then the vicious circle starts," I added.

"I think it's here where missions have failed. Instead of moralizing, we should have given information."

"Ingrid," I said, putting my hands on her shoulders and looking into her eyes, "I'm so thankful for you. You are a good team partner. I wonder if you would help me to preach tomorrow."

"You mean in the pulpit? Never!"

"You can stand down below if you want. But it would be wonderful if you could tell the story of Mother Gerda as a part of my sermon."

"I shall see. By the way, I read something wonderful in the plane which I would like so much to share with you."

"Ingrid, please understand, not now! I haven't done anything on my sermon yet."

Ingrid hesitated, but only for a second. Then she said: "All right. I'm sorry you have no time. I have to go anyway. There's a girl waiting to talk to me. Her name is Miriam. She says she's engaged. She was very interested when I explained the symptoms of ovulation and wants to ask me some more questions about it. It's good she's starting now to get acquainted with her cycle, because after the wedding it's actually too late to start determining her fertile and infertile days."

"I'm so glad you are doing that, Ingrid. I couldn't. That's why I need you as a co-worker."

"When do we have to get up tomorrow?"

"Seven o'clock at the latest. The service starts at nine and I'd like to go over my message with you first. We have to pack too. Our plane leaves at noon sharp. We won't have time to come back to the hotel after the service, but will have to go directly from the church to the airport."

I kissed her good-night and she left.

9

THE NEXT MORNING I GOT UP AT SIX AND PACKED MY TWO SUITCASES. Shortly before seven, I called Ingrid's room to see whether she was awake. She said she would open the door. I entered her room and sat down at her bedside. She had her eyes shut, but I saw that her cheeks were wet with tears.

"Didn't you sleep well?"

She shook her head, but didn't say anything.

"But Ingrid, what's wrong? We were so happy last night. You had such a great evening. Then I kissed you good-night . . ."

"No, you didn't."

"Yes, I did."

"That's not what I call a kiss—just a little peck. I had so hoped you would come over to my room afterward."

"Ingrid, don't be foolish. I knew you were having a talk with Miriam and I didn't want to disturb you. Besides, I had work to do on my sermon."

"There you have it: Your sermon is more important than anything else."

"But I have to preach on marriage today."

I wonder what you'll have to say. You don't understand a woman. You don't know what marriage is. If you only knew how hard it is to be married to you. Sometimes I think we haven't made any progress at all in these eighteen years."

Now it was I who was silent.

Ingrid continued: "When you said you had no time to listen to what I wanted to read to you, I felt as if you had slapped me."

She paused. When I said nothing, she went on: "I got the message from you: 'Don't bother me!' All night I struggled with the temptation to believe that almost anything or anyone else is more important in your life than I am. And still I couldn't overcome my desire just to be alone with you."

"But Ingrid, listen. You're not thankful at all. We've been led in a wonderful way up to this point. This morning there's a church full of people who are awaiting a message on marriage from us. We can travel together, work together. Remember how we started our married life?"

"Yes, in a little attic room with a slanted wall, where there was barely room for both of us to stand up straight. Our kitchen was an electric plate on the washstand. Last night I kept wishing we were back in that room together instead of living in two fancy hotel rooms."

"You really are ungrateful."

"No, I'm just a woman. That's what you don't understand. You can write and talk about marriage all you want, but sometimes I think you haven't even understood the ground rules. For you, I'm just a team partner, a co-worker, a showpiece—but not your wife."

I got up from her bedside, went to the window and looked out, my back turned to her.

Without turning around I said: "But Ingrid, after all, we are married. We are together—"

"Yes," she interrupted, "we are together, but always *unterwegs,* en route, never in a relaxed atmosphere and almost never together in the shelteredness of our home."

"Everything entails a sacrifice," I said.

"All I know," Ingrid replied, "is that if fruit comes from your ministry, then it is because it has cost tears and travail."

"But you say this with bitterness."

"I'm sorry, but my feelings are numb. I don't have the strength to rejoice."

I kept looking out of the window. I discovered the steeple of the church. The bell would be ringing now. Pretty soon we would be picked up for the service. It was impossible for me to preach now, I thought. I have no message. Always when I am happiest, she does that, she tears down everything.

"Now you are wishing you were a Catholic priest," Ingrid said.

I whirled around. "Yes I do," I said without trying to hide the scorn in my voice.

"Monogamy can be an exciting adventure," Ingrid retorted, and I knew she was aware that it would hurt me.

"You know," I said, "if you were Esther, I would know exactly what to tell you. But because you're my wife, I am helpless."

"And if you were Daniel, I would know what to tell you too, but because . . ." Instead of continuing, the trace of a smile crossed her face.

I sat down at her bedside again. The minutes passed. No one to spread my tent, I thought. It had been a week of victories: Maurice, Miriam, Daniel, Fatma. And now I stood here as the defeated one. Who would help me to spread my own tent?

At last the quietness was interrupted by the ringing of the telephone. "The gentleman who always picks you up is here."

Maurice was on the line. "Shall I come up to help you with your baggage?"

"Maurice, listen, we aren't ready yet. Ingrid is still in bed."

"Is she sick?"

"No, that is, yes. In a way."

"What's the matter?"

"Our tent broke down."

"You mean you . . ."

"Yes, we have a marriage crisis."

"You're joking. Is it possible for a marriage counselor also to have a marriage crisis?"

"That's just like asking, Is it possible for a doctor to fall ill?"

"What can I do?"

"Just wait. Could you order coffee and rolls for us and have them sent up to my wife's room? I'll call you back as soon as possible."

I hung up. I knew that Maurice would pray. God had heard his prayers for me once before.

Ingrid was calm now. I bent over her and took her head in my arms.

"I want to share my ministry with you, but it actually makes it harder, not easier. If only I didn't have to preach on 'Husbands, love your wives, as Christ loved the church'!"

Ingrid tried to smile. "What did you mean when you said 'Our tent broke down'?"

"One of the girls who came to the lectures, Fatma is her name, saw my triangle. She said it reminded her of a tent."

"A tent!" Ingrid said thoughtfully. "What a good idea. That's a picture every woman can understand. It almost reconciles me to your very angular triangle with all its sharp corners."

"I knew you would like it."

"Remember when we were camping once, just the two of us, and at night a storm came up and our tent broke down?"

"Yes, I remember. The tent poles were broken and we had to spend the night covered just by the canvas while the storm raged around us."

"Exactly. The tent broke down, but we were still covered, even if it was a broken tent."

"And now? Aren't we still covered even now? Aren't we still married?"

Instead of answering, Ingrid said: "You see, Walter, this is what I wanted you to do last night—to come into my room and cover me with the blanket."

I sighed with relief and yet I was burdened at the same time. "Well, Ingrid, I could have done that, easily and gladly. But you see, this is precisely what makes me feel insecure and fearful—that you make everything depend upon one little gesture—our marriage, our work, our message, our ministry."

"It isn't a little gesture to me. It's full of meaning. It would have made me feel sheltered and secure in your love."

The maid brought Ingrid's breakfast tray.

"Who's this Maurice you were talking to?" Ingrid asked as we drank our coffee.

"He works for a construction company. He's neither a psychologist nor a theologian. Besides that, he's still a bachelor. Shall I call him to come up and be our arbitrator? He's very wise."

"It's all right with me," Ingrid said to my surprise.

It was quite a step for both of us—to come here all the way from Europe in order to help Africans with their marriage problems and then to ask an African to help us. But it was good for us. To be helped is the best, if not the only way, to learn how to help others.

Maurice came at once. He looked at us curiously as he entered the room. He probably had expected a different scene. It didn't exactly look like a serious crisis. Ingrid and I were sitting together on the couch and I was holding her hand.

He took a chair and said nothing. It was clear that he did not know what to say.

"Last night," I began, "I committed all the errors which I advise other husbands not to commit. I talked only about my work. I told my wife to give a message in church and to prepare another one for this morning. I forgot to kiss her good-night properly."

"And he didn't even say that he loves me."

"That's right. I didn't say that I love her and I didn't cover her with a blanket."

"The last thing he told me yesterday evening," Ingrid added, "was that I had to get up at seven and have all the baggage ready before church."

Ingrid finally succeeded in smiling. "And he had no time to listen when I wanted to read him something."

"She's right. Instead, I prepared a sermon about how husbands should love their wives."

"You see," she explained, "it irritated me that he had time for every one else, but not for me; that everyone else had access to him, even the telephone operator."

Maurice was puzzled. Then he picked up the word "operator" and said to Ingrid, though as kindly as possible:

"I talked with the operator while I was waiting downstairs. Your husband told her last night that marriage is sometimes real hard bargaining. Why don't you make a bargain with Walter? He listens to you while you read to him that which you wanted to share and then it's his turn to say what he wants."

Without further comment, Ingrid picked up the little booklet on her night table. It was printed by a Catholic brotherhood in Switzerland and in it was an essay on tenderness by a German author, Karl Krolow. She read the paragraph she had underlined:

"Tenderness is the pianissimo of the heart, softer than a pulse beat during sleep. For tenderness never sleeps. It is wide awake, attentive in the light of noonday and diving into the black waters of midnight. It is restless and beautiful and we can gladly entrust our innermost feelings to it. . . ."*

I looked at my wife and loved her. So this was what she wanted to share! Now I understood her.

"Walter's turn to say what he wants from his wife." Maurice was doing a good job as umpire.

I was ready: "I want her to give her message this morning in church about Mother Gerda."

Ingrid agreed. "I have no strength now to build up our tent again," she said, "but I can crawl into His tent and He will give me the shelter I need."

"It's nine o'clock," Maurice said. "The service is starting. We have no time to wait for Ingrid. We can barely make it before it is time for you to preach."

"Why don't you take me to the church, Maurice, and then return and pick up Ingrid and our baggage. I will preach until she comes and then turn it over to her."

As we drove, Maurice said that he still had a question, but he would ask it after the service on our way to the airport.

When we entered the church the congregation was already singing the pulpit hymn. The pews were packed again, but a different atmos-

---

**Zärtlichkeit* ["Tenderness"], *Ferment Jahrbuch,* 1969, Pallottiner Verlag, Gossau, Switzerland.

phere reigned than during the evening lectures. People sat stiff and upright, their faces almost solemn. This was their worship service. They were ready to stand before God, to be addressed by Him in a special way.

We had to go to the pulpit immediately. What a difference compared with the first night, I thought as I looked over the velvet carpet of black hair. I felt a bond between the congregation and me as if we were one big family. There was an openness and receptiveness, something in the air as if hundreds of empty hands were being held up, waiting to be filled.

I was poorer than ever before. Yet I felt that I had something—I was the bearer of a message and at the same time, the message bore me up.

I decided to choose only verses 25 to 32 of Ephesians 5 and read Paul's message:

"Husbands, love your wives, as Christ loved the church and gave himself up for her, that he might sanctify her, having cleansed her by the washing of water with the word, that he might present the church to himself in splendor, without spot or wrinkle or any such thing, that she might be holy and without blemish. Even so husbands should love their wives as their own bodies. He who loves his wife loves himself. For no man ever hates his own flesh, but nourishes and cherishes it, as Christ does the church, because we are members of his body! 'For this reason a man shall leave his father and mother and be joined to his wife, and the two shall become one.' This is a great mystery, and I take it to mean Christ and the church."

Daniel read it too in the national language and then interpreted my sermon sentence by sentence, quietly and effortlessly. It was again as if we were speaking out of one mouth.

"During the last four days we have studied the triangle of marriage: leaving, cleaving, becoming one flesh.

"In the text I just read, the Apostle Paul adds a new dimension to this triangle. He says: 'This is a great mystery.'

"This statement is found in an in-between place in this text. It refers to the previous verse and points to the following one at the same time.

"Paul says: When a man leaves father and mother—this is a great mystery. When a man cleaves to his wife—this is a great mystery. When the two become one—this is a great mystery.

"Indeed it is. All of us have been touched this week. We have been touched by the depth of this mystery. We have been touched by the power of God's Word. The Bible verse we studied has been like a hammer which breaks rocks into pieces in our midst. But it has equipped all of us with new hope."

Fatma, Miriam, and Esther were sitting together on the women's side. I couldn't help but glance at them for a moment. There was a trace of joy on all three faces: new vision and new depth on Esther's; assurance and resolve on Miriam's; the touch of healing on Fatma's.

"Indeed," I continued, "this is a great mystery. But then Paul continues: 'I take it to mean Christ and the church.'

"Paul says: A man leaves his father and mother—I speak about Christ. A man cleaves to his wife—I speak about Christ. The two become one—I speak about Christ."

I unfolded my wooden triangle again.

"In other words: The deepest mystery of our triangle is Jesus Christ himself. When I gave you the triangle—leaving, cleaving, one flesh—as a guide for marriage, I gave you nothing else, no one else as a guide except Jesus Christ himself.

"A man leaves his father—I talk about Christ.

"Because he loves us, Christ left his father at Christmas. He became man. A child in the manger. Did not count equality with God a thing to be grasped. Emptied himself. Humbled himself. Was obedient even unto death, even death on a cross.

" A man leaves his mother—I talk about Christ.

"Because he loves us, Christ left his mother on Good Friday. When he was on the cross he gave his mother another son. He said to her: 'Woman, behold your son' and to John 'Behold your mother.'

"A man cleaves to his wife—I talk about Christ.

"Because he loves us, Christ cleaves to us, the Church, his bride, cleaves to us faithfully, inseparably.

"The Bible conceives of the alliance between Christ and the Church as a marriage. 'For the marriage of the Lamb has come, and his Bride made herself ready' (Rev. 19:7). 'I saw the holy city . . . prepared as a a bride adorned for her husband' (Rev. 21:2).

"It is not always a marriage without a crisis. The Church is sometimes a difficult wife. We are ungrateful, disobedient, unfaithful to Christ. We refuse to be subject to him.

"Once he had to say to the Church in Sardis: 'Because you are lukewarm, and neither cold nor hot, I will spew you out of my mouth' (Rev. 3:16).

"True love does not shy away from hard words.

"But Christ never walks out on his wife completely, even if she deserved it over and over. He never goes farther away than the door. 'Behold, I stand at the door and knock.'

" 'Husbands, love your wives, as Christ loved the church. . . .'

"He is always ready with his forgiveness. He sanctified her. He cleansed her. He washed her. Just as a slave washes the feet of his master. He made her appear in splendor. Without spot. Without wrinkle. Without blemish. There can never be a divorce between Christ and his Church. He gave himself up for her. For this unsubmissive, difficult wife, he gave himself up.

" 'Husbands, love your wives, as Christ loved the church.'

"And since Paul refers to Christ when he states: 'The two shall become one,' we can also say: 'Wives, love your husbands, as Christ loved the church.' For if they are one in Christ, what is true about one is true about the other.

"The two become one—I talk about Christ.

"Because he loves us, he becomes one with us, just as the head and body are one.

"He shares everything with us.

"Whatever is ours becomes his. Our poverty becomes his poverty. Our fear becomes his fear. Our suffering becomes his suffering. Our guilt becomes his guilt. Our punishment becomes his punishment. Our death becomes his death.

"Whatever is his becomes ours. His riches become our riches. His peace becomes our peace. His joy becomes our joy. His forgiveness becomes our forgiveness. His innocence becomes our innocence. His life becomes our life.

"And he becomes one flesh with us in a very concrete sense, becomes physically part of us, in Holy Communion.

"The triangle of marriage points to Jesus Christ, reveals what he has done for us. I have talked to you about marriage all week. But in a deeper sense I have talked to you about Christ all week. And I would like to say to you, as Paul did in I Corinthians 2:2: 'For I decided to know nothing among you except Jesus Christ and him crucified.' "

Daniel's voice became warmer and warmer. I could feel how he put himself completely into every word that he translated. It was as if he anticipated everything I was going to say, as if he took the words out of my mouth even before I had pronounced them. With all his heart he wanted his congregation to grasp this message.

"You may forget many things which my wife and I said about marriage," I continued, "but one thing please do not forget:

"That Christ left his father for you, because he loves you, loves you personally.

"That Christ left his mother for you, because he loves you, loves every one of you.

"That Christ wants to cleave to you, because he loves you, loves you in spite of your not cleaving to him.

"That Christ wants to become one with you, one flesh, in a very intimate and personal way, because he loves you, loves you eternally."

The church was completely silent. Suddenly, something unexpected happened. A man in one of the front pews stood up and started to sing aloud. Before I knew it, the whole congregation joined in and sang from the depths of their hearts.

I looked at Daniel. "Do they want me to quit?"

"No," he whispered, "this means that they are glad about your message. They must express their joy. At the same time they want to give you some rest so that you can continue with new power."

Truly I had never preached to such a considerate church audience.

"What do they sing?" I asked Daniel.

"They are praising the love of God," he answered.

After they had finished, I began again, praying in my heart for a special word to meet Fatma's need.

"One of you has seen the picture of a tent in the triangle of marriage. This has given me a new insight into the mystery of marriage.

"After this earth has passed away and every tear has been wiped from our eyes, the Bible describes the new creation. Then God and His people will dwell together as closely as a married couple under the shelter of a tent: 'Behold, the tent of God is with men. He will dwell with them' (Rev. 21:3).

"But before this hour comes, Christ is God's tent among us, a tent with the three poles: leaving, cleaving, one flesh. Therefore, the message of our tent is not only a message for married people. In Christ, all those who are unmarried are included under the cover of God's tent as well. For Christ left his father and mother for them too; he cleaves to them too; he becomes one with them too.

"In Christ their life receives purpose and fulfillment, freedom and joy. In Christ they find their place, their tent.

"Since Jesus Christ came into this world, there is no one without a tent."

At this moment the main door at the back of the church was opened and Ingrid and Maurice entered. The people turned their heads to look at them. I took advantage of the pause and said:

"Would you like me to call on my wife to tell you a story?"

They were very much in agreement.

"Ingrid, please tell us the story of Mother Gerda as an example of a marriage under the cover of God's tent."

Daniel motioned to Esther to translate for Ingrid. The two women stood in the front of the church in the center aisle, while Daniel and I remained standing in the pulpit.

I sensed immediately that Ingrid was again herself. There was no sign on her face of the sleepless night and the tears. Her eyes sought contact with the audience and found it. She had passed through the valley, and this seemed to give her special authority at this moment.

"The pastor who performed the wedding ceremony for my husband

and me had seven children," she began. "After thirty years of marriage, his wife became very sick. She had a brain tumor. This meant that sometimes she could not think clearly. A strange desire would cause her to run away from home. So her husband had to watch over her day and night.

"As her sickness grew worse, she could walk and talk only with great difficulty. Her husband had to help her with everything. He had to feed her, wash her, dress her.

"This went on for fifteen years."

An audible expression of amazement and compassion went through the church. Ingrid continued:

"Whenever his friends suggested that he put his wife into a home or hospital for incurable patients, the pastor always refused. 'She is my wife and the mother of our seven children,' he would say. 'I cannot give her into a home or hospital.'

"Shortly before her death, I visited her. She could talk a little bit on that day. And this is what she said to me: 'Ingrid, whenever you and Walter talk about marriage I want you to tell the people that my husband loves me today just as he loved me when I was a bride.' "

To these last words the audience responded with deep silence. Ingrid and Esther then sat down in the front pew. After a few moments I continued from the pulpit:

"This is love which reflects the love of Christ to his church.

"It is like looking into a mirror. When we look at Christ's love, we can see a picture of how God wants husband and wife to live together.

"When husband and wife live together according to God's will, their marriage becomes like a mirror, a reflection, of Christ's love.

"Martin Luther says: 'Marriage compels us to believe.' Amen."

I went down from the pulpit and sat beside my wife. Daniel concluded the service with the Lord's Prayer, a hymn, and the benediction.

We had time only to shake hands with the people as we left the church. Then we had to hurry to the airport.

Maurice offered to take us in his car, but Daniel insisted that we ride with Esther and him. This would give us half an hour with Esther and Daniel alone. It was decided that Maurice take Timothy, Miriam, and Fatma. To my surprise, Daniel's three-year-old son, who had been in church with his mother, wanted to ride with Fatma. They had become inseparable friends.

I had already climbed with Ingrid into the back seat of Daniel's car when Fatma knocked at the side window. I opened it and she handed me a thick, sealed envelope.

"Please read it before we separate," she said, then turned and went to Maurice's car.

It was addressed to both of us. So I handed it to Ingrid to read first.

"How was the sermon I missed?" she asked Daniel while opening the envelope. Evidently she didn't think the letter contained anything important.

"To me," Daniel replied as he started the car, "the sermon meant that any marriage counseling which excludes the spiritual dimension is inadequate because it does not grasp the true nature of marriage." Then he added: "It's too bad you can't stay longer."

"I'm sorry too, Daniel," I said. "We wish we could stay longer. But we have ten days of teaching together at our next stop, and the first lecture begins already this evening. There'll be about fifty key couples attending, and we'll have classes in the morning and afternoon too. The four days here were squeezed in after I got your good letter inviting us to come. Nor could we leave earlier because of our children. To have our children suffer because of our work in Family Life Seminars would really be a paradox."

"We understand," Esther said. "Please thank your children that they let you go."

"We'll do that," I answered. Then I realized that Ingrid wasn't following our conversation. I saw from her face that she was deeply moved by what she was reading. Silently, she handed me the first page. From then on we didn't speak anymore until we reached the airport. Fatma was exposing all her past life before us and in the presence of God.

The letter began: "During the past days I have seen my life for the first time in the light of God's eyes. I see now that all I did was wrong, completely wrong. I forgot God. I went my own way. The most important thing in my life was not God, but myself. That's why my whole life is a mess."

A detailed description of her life story followed. It was as I had thought: she was constantly searching for a place without ever finding one.

When her father refused to let her marry her first suitor, she eloped with him far away from her home village. Her father tried to get her to return home, but she stubbornly refused. The legal status of her relationship to this man was not quite clear. She put it this way: "I got married to him by myself without God."

After she had lived with him for some months she discovered that he already had a child with another woman. In the meantime, she was pregnant and did not dare to leave him.

The next paragraph was an example of what a hell marriage can be. Nothing was omitted—distrust, quarrels, beatings, unfaithfulness. "I started to smoke pot, drink, and go to witch doctors and fortunetellers."

Finally she left the man, but he kept her son. She chased from village to village, town to town, always looking for a place, until she ended up in this city. She couldn't even remember all the men she had lived with before John took her in.

The letter ended: I do not blame these men. I take all the blame on myself. Consciously I transgressed all of God's commandments. I disobeyed my parents and deceived them. I am an adulteress and a murderess. I killed my baby and wanted to kill myself. I know that I have deserved God's punishment.

"But I ask God for forgiveness. I cannot set myself free in my own strength. But I trust that Christ died for me too so that I can live for him. I want to make a new start.

"Please help me to build my tent."

We had just finished Fatma's letter when we arrived at the airport. Maurice had gotten there before we did. Miriam had already gone into the terminal because she was on duty. Fatma was standing between Maurice and Timothy, turning her head in embarrassment when she saw us.

Daniel parked beside Maurice's car. Ingrid stepped out and gave Fatma a warm, sisterly hug. Then Fatma broke down, put her head on Ingrid's shoulder, and cried without restraint.

"How much time do we have?" I asked Daniel.

"It's already eleven. In about half an hour they will call your flight."

"All right. Let's continue our teamwork, Daniel, even in the last hour of our stay. Here are our tickets. Could Maurice and Timothy check our big suitcases? And could you and Esther take our hand baggage and give it to us at the gate?"

While the others went to the counter with our baggage, Ingrid and I took Fatma between us and went to the waiting room. It was full of people and very noisy. We found three armchairs in a row.

"Are you shocked, Pastor?" Fatma asked.

"No, I am happy."

"Happy?"

"Yes, because there is great joy in heaven over one sinner who repents."

Fatma seemed relieved that we did not condemn her. "Do you think I can be forgiven?" she asked.

"Yes," I answered. "But first you must realize that you didn't write the letter to us but to God. We are only your witnesses."

"Yes, I know that."

"Are you willing to accept our word of forgiveness as God's word of forgiveness?"

"Yes, I am."

"Then please read the last paragraph of your letter again." I handed her the envelope and she unfolded the letter on her lap.

"I want to start a little before the last paragraph," she said.

She read in a half-loud voice, pronouncing every word distinctly: ". . . I transgressed all of God's commandments. I disobeyed my parents and deceived them. I am an adulteress and a murderess. I killed my baby . . ."

Her voice choked. She sobbed and her whole body shook. "Do you understand that I killed a life?" she cried. "Abortion is murder, regardless of what they say. How can I ever make that good again?"

Ingrid put her left arm around Fatma's shoulder and said: "Fatma, there are things we can never make right again. We can only place them under the cross."

At that Fatma was calmed and could continue to read: "I . . . wanted to kill myself. I know that I have deserved God's punishment. But I ask God for forgiveness. I cannot set myself free in my own strength. But

I trust that Christ died for me too so that I can live for him. I want to make a new start. Please help me to build my tent."

Fatma put the letter back in the envelope. She placed it on her lap, covering it with her folded hands. She closed her eyes and bowed her head slightly. I knew that she was praying.

It was a strange situation. People were rushing by. Some were watching us, not knowing what to think. The loudspeaker announced constantly arriving and departing planes.

But we forgot all those around us. We were in God's presence. He's not only in churches. He's at airports as well.

I put my left hand over Fatma's folded hands and Ingrid put her right hand on top, leaving her left arm protectingly around Fatma's shoulders.

I said: "Lord, I thank you that you have forgiven me my sins and that I can now pass on what I have received."

Then I placed my right hand on Fatma's head and said: "Thus says the Lord: Fatma, fear not. Fatma, I have redeemed you. Fatma, I have called you by name. Fatma, you are mine. Though your sins are like scarlet, they shall be as white as snow; though they are red like crimson, they shall become like wool. Take heart, Fatma; your sins are forgiven. Go, and do not sin again. Everyone who commits sin is a slave to sin. If the Son makes you free, you will be free indeed."*

Ingrid added: "I want to give you Jeremiah 3:14 in a very personal form, Fatma: Return, O faithless child, says the Lord, for I married you."

Without moving, Fatma sat with closed eyes. Her body was trembling slightly. Then she said:

"I'm in God's tent now, am I not?"

"Yes, this is your place. As Ingrid said, God married you."

"I shall get my things from John's house tonight," she said.

"Take Esther along."

"I will. I shall stay with her for the next few weeks. She told me what you said about a place. Daniel will try to find one for me."

Our flight was being called over the loudspeaker.

"Just two more things, Fatma," I said. "First, you are free now, absolutely free. The past is effaced from God's memory. If you continue to

---

*Is. 43:1, 1:18; Mt. 9:2; Jn. 8:11, 34, 36.

burden yourself with your forgiven sins, you commit a new one."

"I understand."

"Second, the grace of God is like a growing light which falls into a dark room. But this is a process which goes on and on. It may well be that during the next days you will discover still more dark things in your life which you could not see today. Do not be depressed and desperate if you do. It means simply that your life is exposed to the light of God."

"Thank you."

Daniel came rushing toward us: "You have to come right away. Here are your boarding cards, people are already getting on the plane and you haven't even gone through the passport control yet."

"But they just called our flight."

"That was the second call. You didn't hear the first one."

We got up and followed Daniel as quickly as possible. Fatma stood with Ingrid as I gave the official our passports to be stamped.

"How do you feel, Fatma?" Ingrid asked.

She thought for a moment and then she said: "Strange, I'm alone and still I don't feel lonesome."

"That's just the point. I believe that only those should marry who are able to live alone. God wants you to prove yourself."

I gave Ingrid her passport and we dashed to the gate where Miriam was checking the boarding cards.

Esther and Daniel gave us our hand baggage. Now we had no hands free, so our friends hugged us warmly.

"God used you both," Daniel said.

"In spite of ourselves," I answered.

As I turned to say good-by to Maurice, I remembered that he still wanted to ask me a question.

"Please write your question to me," I said.

"I've done that already," he answered, thrusting an envelope into my jacket pocket.

We passed through the gate, leaving the others behind. Miriam was the only one allowed to accompany us to the plane.

In her usual directness, she asked: "Do you remember my first letter to you when I wrote you that I was afraid that my feelings for Timothy were not quite deep enough for marriage? And you told me I should listen to my feelings, because girls usually feel it sooner than boys. Now what I'm wondering is, when things work out, is it also the girl who feels it before the young man?"

"What do you think, Miriam?"

She didn't reply immediately. When we were halfway up the landing stairs, she called out:

"I'm sure she does!"

I could only wave at her in approval. We were the last ones to enter the plane. The stewardess was already closing the door as we took our places beside each other and fastened our seatbelts. Before long the plane started to move and taxied out to the runway.

Ingrid put her hand over mine.

"I'm sorry and ashamed about this morning," she said. "Sometimes I just have the feeling I can't quite keep in stride with you. Do you understand?"

"It was a good way to keep us humble," I replied. "I think God lets us go through these valleys in order that we understand the problems of other couples better."

The plane was now racing for the takeoff. The concrete of the runway disappeared. The earth moved away. The plane headed into the open sky.

We were on our way again—*unterwegs,* en route.

"Why don't you open Maurice's letter?" Ingrid asked.

"What do you think is in it—another confession?"

"I have a feeling it's something else."

"What makes you think so? Feminine intuition?"

"Yes."

"Tell me before I open it."

"Didn't you notice how happy Maurice was when it was decided that Fatma ride with him to the airport?"

"You mean . . . ?"

"Open it and see."

I hadn't even thought of that. I tore the envelope open and read:

"Is God also a matchmaker? When I prayed in the car on the bridge while you were talking to Fatma, a voice came to me as clear as a bell: 'This girl with whom Walter is talking will be your wife.'

"It was crazy. I had never seen her before, had no idea who she was, what she looked like. I could only see her figure vaguely in the darkness.

"Could this voice be God's voice? Please send me a telegram Yes or No from your next stop."

"You and your feminine intuition!" I said to my wife with envy.

"That wasn't hard," she said.

"Poor Maurice," I muttered."He wanted so much to marry a virgin. And he ends up with Fatma."

Ingrid contradicted me: "But she is a virgin, Walter. She's cleansed—as the bride of Christ. 'Without spot. Without wrinkle. Without blemish.' "

Indeed, Ingrid was right.

I called the stewardess and asked her whether the pilot was still in radio contact with the tower.

"Yes," she said, "but not for private messages."

I have a very important message to an employee of your airline." She promised to try. I gave her Miriam's name and said: "Here's the message. Just three words: 'Tell Maurice Yes.' "

Silently we sat together. Then Ingrid turned her head and looked at me.

"What's on your mind?" I asked her.

"I'm glad I married you," she said with a smile.

"So am I."

BOOK SEVEN

MY WIFE MADE ME A POLYGAMIST

Foreword

Originally this book was meant as a textbook for teaching family-life seminars in Africa. However, the high divorce rate indicates that the problem of "successive polygamy" as well as that of the "triangle marriage" is also a vital one in so-called monogamous societies of America and Europe—and wherever western influence spreads. Therefore this book is made available now to a wider reading public.

As far as Africa is concerned, recent publications by church leaders and missionaries show a growing insight into the fact that the disciplinarian approach to the problem of polygamy has failed. The counseling approach to husbands and wives living in polygamous marriage as proposed in this book is new. We are still here in the experimental stage. Therefore I welcome constructive criticism, especially from those who live in polygamous marriages—be it an African or western type—and from those who care for such people.

Walter Trobisch

ON ONE OF MY TRIPS I WORSHIPPED IN AN AFRICAN CHURCH WHERE nobody knew me. After the service I talked to two boys who had also attended.

"How many brothers and sisters do you have?" I asked the first one.

"Three."

"Are they all from the same stomach?"[1]

"Yes, my father is a Christian."

"How about you?" I addressed the other boy.

He hesitated. In his mind he was adding up the number of children. I knew immediately that he came from a polygamous family.

"We are nine," he finally said.

"Is your father a Christian?"

"No," was the typical answer, "he is a polygamist."

"Are you baptized?"

---

[1]Literal translation from the African language meaning that they have the same mother.

"Yes, and my brothers and sisters too," he added proudly.

"And their mothers?"

"They are all three baptized, but only the first wife takes communion."

"Take me to your father."

The boy led me to a compound with many individual houses. It breathed an atmosphere of cleanliness, order and wealth. Each wife had her own house and her own kitchen. The father, a middle-aged, good-looking man, tall, fat and impressive, received me without embarrassment and with apparent joy.

I found Omodo to be a well-educated man, wide awake and intelligent, with a sharp wit and a rare sense of humor. In the following dialog I will attempt to restate the gist of our long conversation. From the outset he made no apologies about being a polygamist.

"Welcome to the hut of a poor sinner." The words were accompanied by hearty laughter.

"It looks like a rich sinner," I retorted.

"The saints very seldom come to this place," he said. "They don't want to be contaminated with sin."

"But they are not afraid to receive your wives and children. I just met them in church."

"I know. I give everyone a coin for the collection plate. I guess I finance half of the church's budget. They are glad to take my money, but they don't want me."

I sat in thoughtful silence. After a while he continued.

"I feel sorry for the pastor. By refusing to accept all the polygamous men in town as church members he has made his flock poor and they shall always be dependent upon subsidies from America. He has created a church of women whom he tells every Sunday that polygamy[2] is wrong."

"Wasn't your first wife heartbroken when you took a second one?"

Omodo looked at me almost with pity.

"It was her happiest day," he said.

---

[2]Polygamy is used in this book in the sense of polygyny (the marriage of one man with more than one wife). In Africa it is used mostly in this sense because polyandry (the marriage of one woman with more than one husband) is unknown.

"Tell me how it happened."

"Well, one day after she had come home from the garden and had fetched wood and water, she was preparing the evening meal while I sat in front of my house and watched her. Suddenly she turned to me and mocked me. She called me a poor man, because I only had one wife. She pointed to our neighbor's wife who could care for her children while the other wife prepared the food."

"Poor man!" Omodo repeated. "I can take a lot, but not that. And I had to admit she was right. She needed help. She had already picked out a second wife for me. They get along fine."

I glanced around the courtyard and saw a beautiful young woman, about 19 or 20, come out of one of the huts.

"It was a sacrifice for me," Omodo commented. "Her father demanded a very high *lobola* (bride-wealth)."

"Do you mean that the wife who caused you to become a polygamist is the only one of your family who receives communion?"

"Yes, according to the church my wives are considered obedient to God's will regarding marriage because each of them has only one husband. I, the husband and father, am the only sinner in our family. The Lord's Supper is given to sinners, but I am excluded from it. Can you understand that, Pastor?"

I was confused.

"And you see," Omodo continued, "they are all praying for me that I might be saved from sin, but they don't agree from which sin I must be saved."

"What do you mean?"

"Well, the pastor prays that I may not continue to commit the sin of polygamy. My wives pray that I may not commit the sin of divorce. I wonder whose prayers are heard first."

"So your wives are afraid that you will become a Christian?"

"They are afraid that I will become a church member. Let's put it that way. For me there is a difference. You see they can only have intimate relations with me as long as I do not belong to the church. The moment I become a church member, their marriage relations with me become sinful."

"Wouldn't you like to become a church member?"

"Pastor, don't lead me into temptation. How can I become a church member if it means to disobey Christ? Christ forbade divorce, but not polygamy. The church forbids polygamy, but demands divorce. How can I become a church member if I want to be a Christian? For me there is only one way—to be a Christian without the church."

"Have you ever talked to your pastor about that?"

"He does not dare to talk to me because he knows as well as I do that some of his elders have a second wife secretly. The only difference between them and me is that I am honest and they are hypocrites."

"Did a missionary ever talk to you?"

"Yes, once. I told him that Europe and America have a successive form of polygamy—divorce—while we have a simultaneous polygamy. Ours is more honest, more humane. That did it. He never came back."

I decided to remain silent and asked Omodo to accompany me back to the village. He gladly obliged. Evidently he enjoyed being seen with a pastor.

"But tell me, why did you take a third wife?" I asked him while we were walking.

"I did not take her. I inherited her and her children from my late brother. Actually my older brother would have been next in line. But he is a church elder and not allowed to sin by giving security to a widow."

I looked in his eyes. "Do you want to become a Christian?"

"I *am* a Christian," he said without smiling.

My silent response to Omodo did not mean that I agreed with everything he said. But I wanted him to feel that I accepted him as he was, not that I judged him without knowing his situation. Therefore, instead of arguing, I decided to listen. My experience has been that if I listen long enough, most people point themselves toward the help they need.

Listening is harder than speaking. It is much more tiresome. Listening to Omodo and making a real effort to understand him before judging him demanded concentration, empathy and the willingness to see things within a framework different from my own.

But when Omodo, without smiling, made his confession of faith at the end of our conversation, I knew that a bond was established between us. It was as if he extended an invitation to me to continue our talk.

I regret that I was not able to see Omodo again. But I have thought much about him and others in similar situations. While I was talking to Omodo, a word which Jesus had said to the Pharisees kept coming to my mind: "You blind guides, straining out a gnat and swallowing a camel!" (Mt. 23:24).

It is always healthy to see one's self with someone else's eyes. So the first question I asked myself was, "Where is Omodo right?"

Basically, he makes two accusations: First, that the policies practiced by churches and missions in Africa in dealing with the problem of polygamy are illogical, contradictory and arbitrary, and second, that the church's and mission's stand against polygamy is contradictory to the Bible.

There can be no doubt that Omodo is right in his first accusation. Most of today's African church leaders and many missionaries would admit that.

Rev. Judah B. M. Kiwovele, President of the Southern Synod of the Evangelical Lutheran Church in Tanzania says: "The answers given by leaders of the Church and missions as defenders of monogamy do not satisfy. . . . There is a request to reconsider both missionary methods and Church structure."[3]

The picture is indeed confusing. Some churches demand that a polygamous man separate from all his wives; others demand that he separate from all but one. But there is disagreement about which one. Some say that he must keep his first wife; others allow him to choose for the sake of the smaller children. None of the churches has come forth with a satisfactory answer to what should happen to the wives who are sent away—who, after all, were married and had their husband's promise of lifelong responsibility for them and their children. (This is the meaning of "lobola" which Omodo mentions.)

Some churches permit these wives to stay with their husband under the condition that he has no sexual relations with them. Evidently they see the "sinfulness" of polygamy mainly in the performance of the sex act.

---

[3]*African Theological Journal,* February 1969.

Strangely enough, as far as church membership goes, most churches take issue only with the man, not—as Omodo rightly observed —with the women. Usually all of the wives are baptized, although sometimes it is only the first wife who is permitted to take Holy Communion. But no one has been able to explain just which interpretation of the sacraments justifies this practice.

Some churches do not even allow polygamist husbands to enter catechumen class. Others allow them to do so, but do not baptize them. Again others baptize them, but exclude them from the Lord's Supper. A few, for example, the Lutheran Church of Liberia, allow polygamist husbands full church membership. But even they do it only under two conditions: that he "entered into polygamous union in ignorance of the Christian Gospel and Law" and that he not "hold office in the Church or congregation or be engaged as a Christian worker."[4]

In short, the contradictions are so evident that it is no use to even argue this point with Omodo. The policies are not only contradictory in themselves, but, worst of all, the churches contradict their teachings by their practice. Rev. Kiwovele says: "If salvation were based on monogamous marriages . . . the salvation looks as though it were earned meritoriously, by fulfilling certain conditions rather than given by the grace of God through repentance of sins and faith in Jesus as Saviour of mankind." Rev. Adejunmobi from the Baptist Church in Nigeria adds: "What the Independent African Churches question is the making of a right marriage a passport to salvation, or at least to church membership."

This contradiction between doctrine and practice did not escape Omodo either, when he observed, in a slighted manner, "I, the husband and father, am the only sinner in our family. The Lord's Supper is given to sinners, but I am excluded from it."

There's no point in arguing with Omodo here. He is right. The African churches face a problem here which simply has not yet been solved. The picture on the African scene is one of uttermost helplessness. One must admit too that the disciplinary approach—I could also call it the "church-membership approach"—has entirely failed.

[4]Minutes of the Third Biennial Convention, Zorzor, Liberia, January 1951.

Rev. Joseph Conrad Wold, a Lutheran missionary in Liberia, says:

> Missionaries become hair-splitting legalists like the Pharisees, willing to cross seas and mountains to make a single convert, and then lay on them burdens that they themselves are not called upon to bear. For the pagan the distinction is apt to be, not between those who follow Christ and those who do not, but between those who practice polygamy and those who do not. The missionaries have tried to reject polygamy by rejecting polygamists . . .
>
> The grace of God will not be bound in the cultural box of Western social patterns. If uncircumcised Gentiles can receive the Holy Spirit and be baptized (Acts 10:44), then, by the grace of God, polygamists can become Christians without being forced to thrust a wife into adultery or break a serious and honorable promise to a wife's father and family . . . If man is lost, let it be because he refused to accept Christ as risen Lord and Saviour, and not because he loved both his wives too much to disgrace and ruin them, or was too upright to lie, or live in deceit.[5]

How I wish that my friend Omodo—"too upright to lie or to live in deceit"—could read these lines! It would at least show him that he is not alone, that there are people who start to understand him.

I am grateful that, in Christ, we have the freedom to accept defeat. In him we are redeemed from the love of self-defense out of hurt pride. Accepting defeat and humiliation is certainly a better testimony to our crucified Saviour than futile arguments in order to "save face." I am sure that Omodo was greatly surprised that I accepted defeat. At the same time we both started to feel that we had something in common, that we started to broadcast at the same wavelength.

Omodo, however, did not just attack church policy. He did much more. He played the church against the Bible, against Jesus Christ himself: "How can I become a church member if it means to disobey Christ? Christ forbade divorce, but not polygamy. The church forbids polygamy, but demands divorce."

In other words, Omodo accuses the church of having misinterpreted

---

[5]*God's Impatience in Liberia* (Grand Rapids, Mich.: William B. Eerdmans, 1967), pp. 179ff.

the Bible and of having disobeyed her Lord. Is he right here too? The answer is much more difficult than the answer to his attack on church policies. For here the answer has to be *Yes*—and *No.*

At first glance he seems to be right. For the Old Testament writers, polygamy was indeed a legally recognized form of marriage and home life. Nowhere is it considered "permanent adultery," as I once heard a missionary say. Adultery is never permanent. It is a momentary relationship in secrecy with no responsibility involved.

In contrast "a polygamous marriage," says Rev. Gerhard Jasper, Tutor at the Lutheran Theological College, Makumira, Tanzania, "is, for the Old Testament, a marriage in the fullest sense of the word with all the protection which the law and the elders of Israel could give to it. An Israelite who had two wives was by no means considered one who had fallen in his faith or in the necessary obedience in faith. He was not placed into the category of a second-class Israelite who was under discipline and first had to repent before he would be admitted to full congregational membership."[6]

The difficulty is, however, that in the Old Testament polygamy receives a different rating depending upon which way of life it is compared with. Therefore the answer to Omodo's criticism has to be Yes and No.

Compared with the way of life of Israel's neighbors in Canaan, polygamy was still the better solution. There Israel witnessed a morass of lax sexual behavior. The worship of the Canaanitic gods of fertility involved intercourse with temple harlots and, since practically the line between cultic and secular harlotry was hard to draw, prostitution as such.

Therefore all extramarital relationships were as rigidly condemned in Israel as in many African tribal societies in the precolonial era. Adultery deserved capital punishment (Deut. 22:21; Lev. 20:10) and, to make this point clear, the term "adultery" included, in Israel, also premarital relations, since the whole conception of life was seen in view of the future marriage (Deut. 22:21).

Contrasted with such sexual licentiousness, polygamy was tolerated in Israel as by far the smaller evil. Sometimes grudgingly—one even has the impression that some of the writers of the Old Testament were

[6]African Theological Journal, February 1969, p. 41.

embarrassed to report it— but it was tolerated.

However, it must be stated that marriage in Israel was generally monogamous. Adam, Isaac, Noah and the prophets Hosea and Isaiah should be mentioned as examples. Contrasted with monogamy the polygamous way of life fell under sharp criticism.

With relentless realism the Old Testament does not tire of pointing out the negative aspects of polygamy.

Abraham's polygamy is reported as a criticism. No blessing rested upon it. It constituted a poor, human makeshift solution, a sign of lack of faith, leading to contempt, jealousy, quarrelling in the home and estrangement between husband and wife (Gen. 16 and 21).

Esau's two wives "made life bitter" (Gen. 26:35) and Jacob had nothing but trouble with the two sisters he married within one week. There was rivalry and hatred in his home (Gen. 29:30-31), envy and wrestling between the two wives (Gen. 30:1, 8) and finally anger between him and even his favorite wife Rachel who was unhappy and desperate (Gen. 30:2).

Then the jealousy continued among the children. The story of Joseph, the son of Jacob's favorite wife Rachel (Gen. 37), cannot be understood without the warning message against polygamy which it contains. His brothers cannot "speak peaceably" to Joseph; they conspire to kill him and finally sell him into slavery.

In the story of Abimelech, polygamy actually leads to murder. In a war of succession, he kills his 69 brothers with the help of his maternal uncles (Judg. 9:5). The same is reported about King David. The features of the Jacob story repeat themselves—favoritism and injustice. His sons kill each other since their adulterous father has lost all authority to settle the question of heritage (2 Sam. 14). When finally through last minute intrigues, Solomon (the son of David's favorite wife, Bathsheba) became king (1 Kings 1), his kingdom too was ruined through polygamy for "his wives turned away his heart after other gods" (1 Kings 11:4).

This is a very dark picture indeed. For Africans, however, it is not hard to believe. It confirms the scepticism expressed by many African proverbs and stories. This is the daily pageant of polygamous family life: heritage quarrels, succession feuds, tribal wars, endless intrigues, murder or at least the constant fear of being killed by magic power used in the interest of the adversary. (In Africa there is a direct link between black magic and polygamy.)

Therefore, Omodo is not right when he indiscriminately claims the Old Testament for the case of polygamy. Confronted with the sexual morass of Israel's neighbors, it may have been the smaller evil for the time being until deeper spiritual insights could grow. Compared to monogamy, the Bible has little to say in defense of polygamy. It falls intolerably short of God's will for marriage.

The Old Testament leaves no doubt about God's will here. In the creation story as recorded in Genesis 2 the Bible sets forth, powerfully and with indisputable clarity, monogamy as God's original and final will. This story breathes the spirit of monogamy in every word, line, illustration and comparison.

God plans Adam's wife as "a helper fit for him" (Gen. 2:18). This Hebrew expression means an equal partner, a correcting opposite—not a subordinate servant. Such equality is only possible in a monogamous union, for polygamy enhances the subordination of women.

The story of the creation of this helper out of one of Adam's ribs is only understandable as an illustration of monogamy: Since they are taken from the same material, the two parts fit together exactly again. The creation story conceives of the "one flesh union" in the first place as an anatomical completion, involving thus an exclusive relationship. This comparison is unthinkable within the context of a polygamous image of marriage. A third part would have no place in it.

This exclusive relationship extends then to all the other realms of life—material, emotional and spiritual—proposing marital love as an exclusive relationship, possible only between one man and one wife.

Though the word "love" is not mentioned, the whole story is actually an unmatched description of the reality of love, of monogamous love.

The idea is this: Because they are taken from the same material, the two equal parts are drawn together again with irresistible power, a power which can grow only between one husband and one wife, a power stronger than all family ties.

"Therefore (because of this power of love) *a man leaves his father and his mother and cleaves to his wife, and they become one flesh"* (Gen. 2:24).

With these words of inexhaustible depth and divine wisdom, the biblical witness who speaks in Genesis 2 sums up the creation story, proclaiming a message which he believes valid for all times and all cultures. In his time this message contained an anti-polygamous spearhead, pointedly addressed to the corrupt government circles of Israel, corrupt through polygamy in the places of King David and King Solomon. It was proclaimed with the intention of bringing forth change in Israel.

And it did. It started a process, a movement.[7] It permeated the thinking of the nation. The Old Testament testifies to this process. More and more, monogamy emerges as the ideal form of marriage. During the time of the New Testament the message of Genesis 2:24 had brought forth change to such a degree that simultaneous polygamy seemingly was no longer a burning issue.

However, it was still practiced during the time of Jesus. His silence about this fact is, therefore, surprising. Could it mean that he was in favor of the counseling approach and rejected the disciplinarian approach?

In any case, the silence of the New Testament about polygamy is complete. The passage stipulating that a bishop or elder should be "husband of one wife" (1 Tim. 3:1; Titus 1:5) may not even refer to polygamy, but rather to advice against remarriage of a widowed church leader.

During the time of the New Testament, the issue had evidently changed from the issue of simultaneous polygamy to that of successive polygamy through easy divorce.

When Jesus was confronted with the question of divorce, he stood up against this successive form of polygamy by referring to the creation story: "Have you not read that he who made them from the beginning made them male and female, and said, 'For this reason a man shall leave his father and mother and be joined to his wife, and the two shall become one'? So they are no longer two but one. What therefore God has joined together let no one put asunder" (Mt. 19:4-6).

---

[7]This process of changing an institution by a message can be compared with the process by which the institution of slavery was overcome. Paul sent the slave Onesimus back to his master at the same time as he proclaimed a message incompatible with slavery. This message finally caused its downfall. But it took centuries.

Then the Apostle Paul, comparing the love between husband and wife to love between Christ and the church, quoted Genesis 2:24, adding to it: "This is a great mystery, and I take it to mean Christ and the church" (Eph. 5:32). As a husband leaves his father and mother in order to cleave to his wife and become one flesh with her, Christ left his father, when he was born man (Phil. 2:7), his mother, when he died at the cross (John 19:26), and cleaves to his bride, the church, and becomes one with her as the one head to the one body (Eph. 1:22-23) in an exclusive relation ship: "Husbands, love your wives, as Christ loved the church and gave himself up for her" (Eph. 5:25).

Thus the message of Genesis 2:24 became a key verse, the only verse about marriage quoted four times in the Bible. It started a dynamic process. This process is reflected in the Bible and is still going on in our day.

We are just now beginning to understand the full implications of this message. If monogamy means reflecting the love of Christ to his church, then monogamy is not a western concept of marriage pertaining only to one culture. It is a biblical concept, presenting a challenge to all cultures.

Certainly such togetherness as is proposed in Genesis 2:24 cannot grow in a polygamous home. Neither does the mere fact of being married to one spouse bring monogamy into realization in the deep sense in which the Apostle describes it. The exclusiveness as well as the full equality of the relationship between husband and wife is still highly disputed in the west and far from being realized. Sometimes it is my impression that the outwardly monogamous society of the west with its sex adoration, "free love," concubinage, prostitution, adultery and divorce may be further away from the biblical ideal and closer to the sexual morass of the Canaanitic fertility cults than the potentially polygamous society of Africa.

We are on our way together, Africans and westerners alike, involved in the same process. But it is not enough merely to work out a biblical ideal to refute Omodo's second accusation. It is not enough to admit, with Omodo, that the traditional approach of the church and missions is grossly inhumane and contradictory. Saying that one approach is wrong is not yet saying which approach is right. It is easy to tear down, but hard to build up. If the disciplinarian approach has failed, what is the alternative? To me there is only one: *We have to approach the problem through counseling.* By this method we help each other face the challenges of God's Word.

Two things have to be kept in mind.

First, both the polygamist and the monogamist participate in the same process. This should make the monogamist humble and help him avoid the "downward slant" in his attitude. But above all it should give him patience and make him careful not to ask more from the other one than he can put into practice, depending upon what stage of the process he is in.

Second, there are different motives leading to polygamy. For Abraham and Elkanah (1 Sam. 1) it was barrenness; for Lamech (Gen. 4:23) it was pride; for Gideon (Judg. 8:30) it was prestige; for Boaz, who married Ruth, the widow of one of his cousins (Ruth 4), it was the levirate marriage; for David and Solomon it was power and sexual lust.

The Bible discerns the motives. The disciplinary approach deals with polygamy as an object and tries to find a general approach. Therefore it has failed. The counseling approach deals with the polygamist. It is personal. It tries to match the answer to the motive.

Omodo's motive for taking a second wife was entirely different than his motive for taking a third. When talking to him again one would have to discern carefully his motives.

Omodo's First Wife

Omodo's first wife was overburdened with work and wanted help. Therefore, she asked Omodo to become a polygamist. It is strange that missions and churches in Africa have almost entirely overlooked the female motive for polygamy. There is a justification for it. The African wife is overburdened. It is usually the man's work to clear the field of brush and trees, but she has to do all the other work—hoeing, planting, cultivating and harvesting.

To help here with this problem would not be easy and would take time. What is actually needed is momentous—to change the concept of marriage from a concept of inequality and subordination to a concept of partnership. The idea that garden work is women's work is not necessarily a correlate to a patriachal system. On the South Pacific Island of New Caledonia I found a patriarchal society with virtually no polygamy. The main reason was that the men helped their wives in the fields.

If I could have gone back to Omodo, I would have taken my wife along and asked her to tell him what she would think of me if I would let her work all day in the garden, get wood and water, care for the children and prepare the food, while I sat idly in the shade under the eaves of my hut and watched her work all day.

She would have explained to him what the Bible means, when the wife is called "a helper fit for him" (Gen. 2:18): an equal, a corresponding opposite, a partner. My wife might have told Omodo that he does not have three wives, but actually no wife at all. He is married to three female slaves. Consequently he is not a real husband, but just a married male. Only a real husband makes a wife a real wife. Since Omodo claimed that he was a Christian, he could not refuse this biblical challenge.

In the meantime, while my wife talked to Omodo, I would have talked to Omodo's first wife and told her precisely the same: Only a real wife makes a husband a real husband. She had not asked enough from her husband. She had behaved like an overburdened slave, trying to solve her problem by getting a second slave. Instead she should have asked her husband to help her. She should have behaved like a partner and expected partnership.

Neither Omodo nor his wife would have understood us immediately. It would have taken many talks, visit after visit, during weeks, months, maybe years. The disciplinary approach is the lazy approach. To count the number of wives and then to excommunicate the "guilty" man takes neither effort nor love. The counseling approach demands the hard work of love and patience.

After a while we would have talked to Omodo and his wife together, if at all possible. For this is the most effective way of marriage counseling—as a couple to couples. Unfortunately pastor's wives are usually not trained for this work and many pastors may not yet even have seen the possibilities here.

The only way to teach a marriage of partners is by example. One day we were discussing partnership in the marriage course I taught at Cameroun Christian College. The students were telling me that African women are just not yet mature enough to be treated as equal partners. While we were discussing this, it began to rain, pouring down on the metal roof. We watched through the window of the classroom as an African teacher's wife jumped from her bicycle and sought refuge under the roof of the school building. After a little while a car drove up. Out stepped her husband, handed her the car keys (he must have taught her how to drive) and off she drove with the car, while he rode the bicycle, following her.

This settled the argument. It is the husband who makes his wife a partner, in monogamy as well.

Of course, one would have to investigate the concrete situation of Omodo and his wife in order not to demand too much at a time. They may desire to change, but not be able to do so immediately, especially if their gardens are so far apart that they cannot be taken care of by one person. However, this should not hinder at least challenging them toward this goal.

Omodo's Second Wife

It is interesting that barrenness of his first wife was not Omodo's motive for taking a second wife, as it was for Abraham and Elkanah and as it is very frequently in Africa today. Omodo's first wife had children and even sons.

Neither was his motive to space the births of his children. Polygamy in Africa has served as a method of "birth control," at least as seen from the point of view of the individual wife and mother. If these motives would have been involved, other advice would have to be given.[8]

Omodo said he took a second wife to give his first wife a helper: "It was her happiest day. . . . It was a great sacrifice for me."

When I saw the second wife, I had doubts. She was beautiful, but very young and fragile. She did not look as if she could do hard garden work, nor as if she had had much experience in the kitchen, let alone with children. Could it be that consciously or unconsciously there was a secondary motive involved here? That Omodo considered his first wife

[8]In this case, the advice given in the book *Please Help Me! Please Love Me!* would apply also to Omodo.

as "dark bread," while the second was to satisfy his appetite for sweets? I call this the "candy-motive," a motive which was certainly also involved in Jacob's marriage to Rachel.

I can well imagine the story of Omodo's "Rachel." She probably was given into marriage to Omodo at a very young age without her own consent. African fathers who are poor sometimes marry their young daughters to 60-year-old polygamists, because they are rich and can pay more. This is one of the dangers of the bride-wealth system.

The counseling approach would involve talking to Omodo's second wife and listening to her side of the story. It is significant that especially in the story of Jacob the Bible presents polygamy very pointedly also from the female aspect.

Young and attractive as Omodo's second wife was, it was hard to imagine that the affection was mutual. The age difference between her and old, fat Omodo must have been between 20 and 30 years. It is very likely therefore that she had a younger lover alongside.

Those who advise polygamy as an antidote against adultery see only part of the problem. Once an inclusive sex-partnership is accepted, the step toward adultery is easy to take. Women married to polygamous men often live individually in adultery because their husbands, staying usually with one wife for a week at a time or with the favorite wife only, are not able to satisfy them sexually. Again the story of Jacob hints toward this problem, when it reports that Leah had to "buy" her husband for one night from Rachel (Gen. 30:16).

It seems to me that the best way to solve the problem of Omodo's second wife would be to help her marry the man she loves. If she knew a man and wanted marriage, it would again involve hard work.

First, I would have to talk to Omodo, ask him to see her as a person with her own needs and inquire about his real motive in marrying her.

Then, I would have to talk to his first wife again and ask her how she feels now about this "helper." Does she feel jealous in her heart? Why did she choose her in the first place? Furthermore, why did she use the mocking technique ("poor man!") with her husband? Had she been hurt by something and taken revenge without really meaning it, while Omodo quickly jumped at the chance? All this would have to be carefully explored.

Next, I would talk to the young suitor of the second wife. Is he qualified? Is he fully aware of what he is doing? Would he accept a girl who is no longer a virgin? How about his own relationships to other girls?

Let us assume that these questions were satisfactorily answered and the second wife and young suitor decided to marry. This would involve talks with the family of Omodo's second wife and with the family of her future husband. Then the three families would have to talk and talk over the thorny question of bride-wealth. It would be quite a *palaver!* Omodo would have to be refunded and a new price settled for his former second wife, taking into account that she is now a divorced woman.

Is she? Yes. If polygamy is recognized as a legal form of marriage, polygamists cannot become monogamists without divorce. There is no solution to this dilemma. It can be justified only if both parties agree and if the divorced wife is cared for. If this is not the case or not possible, "It would be sheer brutality on the part of the Christian Church to confront men with the choice of baptism and institutional polygamy."[9]

But the talks we had up to this point would have enabled me to talk to Omodo meaningfully about sin. Not about the "sinfulness" of polygamy! That would be as of little avail as talking to a soldier about the sinfulness of war or to a slave about the sinfulness of slavery.

However, I could talk to him and his wives now about their concrete sins in their polygamous state—in the same way as I would talk to any monogamous couple with whom I wanted to talk spiritually about their sins in their monogamous state.

So I would try to help Omodo to become honest about the "candy-motive," to see the selfishness of it and admit his lack of concern for his first overburdened wife and also of the second one, forced into marriage with him for his egotistic pleasure.

To Omodo's first wife I would have talked about her "happiest day," encouraging her to share the negative feelings against her husband which she was hiding in her heart and making her see the mistake of her mocking approach, by which she tore down his self-esteem as a man.

With the second wife I would have had a very serious talk about her

[9]Karl Barth, *Church Dogmatics,* 111/4, p. 203.

adultery and also asked her why she had not become pregnant. Possibly she had used medicine to cause an abortion, a deed which deeply troubles the conscience of African women.

In this way the topic of our conversations would have switched from the topic of polygamy to the topic of "salvation given by the grace of God through repentance of sins and faith in Jesus as Saviour of mankind."

After Omodo had had a personal experience of forgiveness, I would have baptized him, even though we were still working on a solution for his second and third wife. I would have expected such a solution as a fruit of his baptism and not as a condition for it. As Pater Eugen Hillmann, a Roman Catholic missionary among the Masai people in Tanzania puts it: "A non-baptized person should not be expected to have actually attained the Christian ideal of marriage *before* he has had any possibility of participating in the sacramental life of the church."[10]

Omodo's Third Wife

The situation of Omodo's third wife is entirely different from the second. This fact illustrates again how important it is to discern the motives.

Her husband, Omodo's brother, had died. A widow is the most pitiful person in Africa. She is a property which has lost its proprietor. According to African custom, the brother of her late husband is responsible for her and her children—the same custom which in Israel was called the "levirate marriage." If she were to marry a man from another family, she would lose her children. The bride-wealth given for her by her late husband's clan included also the children. So she has to choose either to give up her children or become the second or third wife of an already married brother of her late husband. Remaining unmarried is almost impossible in traditional African society unless she wants to turn to prostitution.

Complicating Omodo's situation was the fact that his late brother's wife had become blind. There are no pensions for widows, no homes for the aged and blind in the traditional African society.

Therefore Omodo is right when he claims that marrying her was an

[10] Theodor Bovet, *A Handbook to Marriage* (Doubleday, New York, 1958).

act of unselfish mercy and when he observes with critical irony, "Actually my older brother would have been next in line. But he is a church elder and not allowed to sin by giving security to a widow." To marry a blind woman and accept the responsibility for her children was certainly a sacrifice.

However, I would have talked to her, too, and asked how she felt about her situation. I have seen courageous widows in Africa who have stayed alone and who have supported their children through their own hard work, without going into prostitution. But they were rare exceptions and they lived in an urbanized situation or were employed by the church or the mission. For a *blind* widow even this possibility is out.

If she wanted to stay with Omodo, I would not have demanded him, not even after his baptism, to divorce her—unless her congregation was prepared to take full responsibility for her and her children.

Would then the "walls break" and the church be "flooded with polygamists"? I do not believe so, especially since polygamy is on the retreat in Africa anyway, mostly for economic reasons. Then too, the young generation of Africans look for a monogamous marriage of partnership. At least this "flooding" is not the experience of the Lutheran Church in Liberia. This church adopted the policy of baptizing polygamists in 1951. Dr. Roland Payne, the African President of the Church, reports that these cases have certainly been the exceptions.

If the motives are carefully discerned and the counseling approach dealing with each polygamist brother individually is used, there is no danger. This approach, however, would demand an army of trained counselors. In order to emphasize this, I would like my African co-worker, Jean Banyolak, to put it in his own words.

I will close this book with the sermon I preached at the marriage of Jean and Ernestine Banyolak in Europe. This sermon contains a direct answer for Omodo, who still lives in the "garden concept of marriage" as it is called in the sermon.

It brings forth the biblical meaning of monogamy. It is my deep conviction that the most urgent need today is not the negative approach of fighting against polygamy in Africa or the "sex morass" in the west, but rather the positive approach of interpreting what monogamy, lived in Jesus Christ, really means.

Africa Needs Marriage Counselors

by Jean Banyolak, Cameroun

Why are marriage counselors necessary at all? Haven't centuries passed during which people married and families lived without the aid of a marriage counselor?

Of course, there have always been marriage counselors, but in a different form. According to the custom of my village, after a quarrel between husband and wife, the wife leaves the house of her husband and returns to her parents. Then the husband follows her to her home village and the wife's family gives their judgment about the matter. In this family court the parents of the wife have the supreme authority. If the case is not very serious, they counsel the quarrelling couple and tell them how they should act from now on in order not to have palavers. In this case, we could say that the marriage counselors for this couple in difficulty are the members of the wife's family.

Or the young couple might live in the home of the husband's parents (though less often now than formerly). In this case, the husband's parents think they have the right to interfere in all the problems and decisions which the young couple have. Their parental counsel, based on their patriarchal authority, is often respected and acted upon. If, for example, the young wife makes a mistake, then the husband goes to his own mother and asks her to teach his wife how she should act toward him. The husband's mother then teaches the young wife how to please her husband so that all goes well. On the other hand, the husband's father counsels his son on how to treat a woman. In this second case, we see that the young couple's marriage counselors are the husband's parents.

In my country one could say that, generally speaking, the marriage counselor of the new generation is the older generation. Obviously this was taken for granted in former times. It was the natural thing because for hundreds of years the same rhythm of life was carried on without great changes. Thus, through experience the older generation knew exactly what to do in all domains of life.

However, since the beginning of the industrial revolution, the structure of the family has changed. The fathers of the family leave their homes early in the morning to go to work and are only at home during their hours of leisure. The children become independent at a very young age and live on their own salaries far from their families. The wives and mothers of the family are no longer content just to do their household tasks at home, but also look for a paying job.

The result is that many decisions, which were made formerly by the family as a whole or by the clan, are made today by the individual or the young couple. But they are not prepared to make them. They have no rules, no standards, no guide. The customs and traditions which formerly served as guides are not sufficient in this new situation. This is why the older generation feels itself incapable to guide the new.

It is no wonder then that one hears cries for help. The request for guidance by personal counsel becomes urgent. The marriage counselor becomes a necessity. This is true for all societies where the industrial revolution has already taken place. The many offices in America and in Europe, organized by the church and by the state, offering marriage guidance, are proof of this fact.

For us in Africa, the need for marriage guidance is perhaps even more important since the industrial revolution has advanced so rapidly.

The development which has taken place in western society over a period of centuries has taken place in Africa during a single generation or even in a decade. For this reason the problems of the individual and the couple are even more touchy; the conflict between that which is old and that which is new becomes even more intense and the confusion greater.

Therefore, Africa needs marriage counselors.

Wedding Sermon for an African Couple
(preached to a European congregation)

Jean Banyolak, a teacher from Cameroun and former student of Pastor Trobisch, came to Germany in 1964 to receive an education as a marriage counsellor. In 1965, his fiancée, Ernestine Bout, followed him. The church wedding was celebrated on Easter Monday, 1965, at Gengenbach in the Black Forest, Germany, as a part of the morning worship service.

The following message is a translation of the wedding sermon preached in German by Pastor Trobisch who married the couple. The reader should not forget that the listeners to this sermon were almost exclusively Europeans. In an indirect way, this sermon answers also some of the questions which were left open by the case of Omodo.

Be subject to one another out of reverence for Christ. Wives, be subject to your husbands, as to the Lord. For the husband is the head of the wife as Christ is the head of the church, his body, and is himself its Saviour. As the church is subject to Christ, so let wives also be subject in everything to their husbands. Husbands, love your wives, as Christ loved the church and gave himself up for her, that he might sanctify her, having cleansed her by the washing of water with the word, that he might present the church to himself in splendour, without spot or wrinkle or any such thing, that she might be holy and without blemish. Even so husbands

> should love their wives as their own bodies. He who loves his wife loves himself. For no man ever hates his own flesh, but nourishes and cherishes it, as Christ does the church, because we are members of his body. "For this reason a man shall leave his father and mother and be joined to his wife, and the two shall become one." This is a great mystery, and I take it to mean Christ and the church; however, let each one of you love his wife as himself, and let the wife see that she respects her husband. (Eph. 5:21-33)

This text contains one phrase to which all men in the whole world would gladly agree: "Wives, be subject to your husbands."

The reaction of an African husband is apt to be something like this: "Wonderful! This is exactly what I think! Wives should be subject in everything to their husbands. Did you hear? In everything! I believe with all my heart that the Bible is right. It confirms my conviction that men are made to rule and women to obey. They are inferior beings, belonging to the second class. It's great that even God agrees with me!"

We find this discrimination against women not only in Africa. It can be traced to almost all cultures of the earth. It permeates the history of mankind."Educate a woman and you put a knife into the hands of a monkey," the Brahmins said in India. Originally, the wedding ring which we wear today was in the Germanic culture a ring which the bride had around her neck. A chain was connected to it, and thus the husband, riding high on his horse, led his young wife home after the wedding ceremony. As late as 1897 the German theologian Bettex wrote: "Continuous activity of the brain nerves has a negative effect on the female organism. Therefore the hope that a woman can be educated scientifically and politically is utopian." Even today Europeans usually feel disappointed when "only" a girl is born.

Where does this downward outlook toward women come from? Is it because a man is stronger, more intelligent and resourceful? Or because he has seized the money and the power?

To me, only one explanation seems plausible. It is the explanation which Dr. and Mrs. David Mace offer in their book *Marriage East and West.* They say that the discrimination against women is due to a false biological concept of the process of procreation. Before science defeated this concept, it seemed obvious and logical.

The old concept of procreation was this: The husband is the bearer of the seed of life; the wife is the soil—the garden. Just as a plant grows out of a seed of grain, so does the child grow out of the man's seed. The body of the mother is just nourishing soil. But the man sows the seed and the substance of man grows into the child.

Most African languages use this vocabulary when describing the process of propagation. It was universal thinking until 1759 when the anatomist Kaspar Friedrich Wolff, in a thesis for his medical degree at Halle University, proved for the first time that both parents contribute something to the substance of the offspring. Not until 1944 was the union of the parent cells, sperm and egg, actually observed for the first time by the microscope.

This explains why the "garden concept of marriage," as I call it, could reign for such a long time. It is still prevalent in Africa. The ethical consequences of this false biological concept are tremendous.

First of all, the conclusion is that the child is the man's child. The woman simply carries his child. If the child is a son, it continues the man's life, living on in his family, thus giving the man's life meaning and purpose. Consequently sons are more appreciated than daughters. When one asks an African father how many children he has, he will very likely be told only the number of sons. When a European father states that he has three children, one may often discover that he actually has three daughters.

The next conclusion is this: Men are more important than women just as the bearer of the seed is more important than the soil. The woman's function is inferior to the man's function. By her very nature the woman is secondary and auxiliary. Perhaps this is the root of the discrimination between man and woman.

This garden concept is reflected in the African custom of bride-wealth. The man acquires for himself a garden—or rather what grows in the garden. The bride-wealth is a refund for the reproductive powers which the wife's clan loses. In other words, it is given for the children which the wife is going to bear. If she bears a child before the bride-wealth is given in full to her family, then this child, according to the rule of many African tribes, still belongs to her father and not yet to her husband, because her father is still the legal owner of the garden.

The garden concept also affects the choice of the marriage partner. Naturally a garden cannot make a choice. In the traditional society the girl had very little to say about the choice of her future husband. The father gave his garden to whom he desired, most likely to the one who offered the best exchange. The main criterion for the young suitor's choice was the fertility of the soil he was going to acquire. This is why, still today, virgins are usually preferred because it is believed that virgin soil is more productive.

Naturally in this garden concept a child constitutes the only purpose of marriage, if not of life. A childless marriage is meaningless. In this case there are two possibilities: successive or simultaneous polygamy. Either the husband divorces the wife—returns the garden to its owner and demands the refund of the bride-wealth in order to acquire another garden—or the husband adds a second garden along with the first and hopes that the second will bear fruit.

Polygamy is the logical result of the garden concept. It is a man's concept. A man can own several gardens. Each garden, however, can only belong to one man.

This is the situation we have to face now in Africa. I hope you can imagine to a small degree at least what it means to proclaim in Africa today a text like, "Therefore a man leaves his father and his mother and cleaves to his wife, and they become one flesh" (Gen. 2:24). Like a hammer crushing rocks, it defeats the garden concept in every single point.

Jean Banyolak, our bridegroom, was an upperclassman at Cameroun Christian College, where we used Dr. Theodor Bovet's *A Handbook to Marriage*[11] as a text in our marriage class. In this book Dr. Bovet makes the following statement: "One of the most fundamental rules of married life is that husband and wife shall never again employ the expression 'my family' or 'your family.' These bonds should have been dissolved by the marriage, leaving only 'our family.' "

In Europe I did not have any difficulty with these words. But when we read them in Cameroun, the students took offense. There was a real uproar in class. The wife should leave—that was understandable. In a patriarchal society, that goes without saying, just as it did in Israel. But that the *man* should leave? Leave his father instead of continuing his life? No! Never! This was unacceptable. The students interpreted this demand as an offense against their ancestors, as ungratefulness to those who had given them the gift of life.

And yet this word "leave" may be the most necessary word for Africa today.

[11]Doubleday, New York, 1958.

It may cause the one great basic revolution which is necessary in order to make all the small revolutions succeed. It may upset the whole economic system. If a man leaves his father and his mother—not leave them in the lurch, but leave them in order to establish his own home, his own family—instead of joining his family to the clan, he becomes economically independent. His economic resources can thus be used in the interest of the nation, instead of in the interest of his tribe. Therefore the word "leave" might reach deeply into politics.

Why are there so many difficulties in the young African states today? No longer is it white colonialist exploitation which hinders independence; it is the exploitation of the couple by the clan. Obedience to the commandment "leave!" may cause the downfall of tribalism, Africa's greatest enemy today. There can be no independent nations if there are no independent couples.

"And cleaves to his wife." This is the second blow to the garden concept. Again, the *man* cleaves to the wife, not the other way around only. The joining becomes mutual. And what is still just as important and revolutionary, a man cleaves to the *wife,* not to his clan. He gives his children to his wife, not to his clan. Being joined together, cleaving together, means that husband and wife become closest to each other, closer than to anyone else.

Within the garden concept a woman views herself as the daughter of her mother in the first place, as the mother of her children in the second place, and only in the third place as the wife of her husband. Husband and wife become parallel for the purpose of procreation, but they are not really united. The wife confides in her sisters, but not in her husband. The husband confides in his brothers, but not in his wife.

When I suggested to my African students that a husband should tell his wife how much money he earns, they hit the ceiling. Impossible, they said, how can you trust a woman? But do you know that eighty percent of German husbands do not tell their wives how much they earn either?

The marriage of trust and love will start another very necessary revolution in Africa. A man who marries a girl because he loves her is closer to her than to his clan. There is a real war going on in Africa today—a war of the clan against the marriage of love. The clan is Africa's fetish. The marriage of love will overthrow this idol and overcome eventually the narrow-minded clan-egotism.

On the other hand, the marriage of love will create the nuclear families which alone are able to serve the extended family. It will prove that to leave the parents does not mean to abandon the parents. It will prove that a couple which has a chance to really *leave,* to exist independently without being indebted, will be able to really help their parents. The health of the extended family depends upon the health of the nuclear family. The marriage of love will change the extended family from a group which seeks its own interest to a group which contributes constructively to society as a whole.

Jean and Ernestine Banyolak, who sit here among us, have left their parents 4000 miles away. It is a tremendous step for an African couple to marry in a foreign country. But if they are getting married today because they love each other and intend to remain closest to each other—they start a revolution. Let us pray for them in this respect.

"And they become one flesh." One. Not parallel, but one! This is the third blow to the garden concept. They become united as one single body, one flesh. It is not the substance of the man which grows into the child as the garden concept concludes. The man and woman both contribute to the child. In stating that "they become one flesh" the Bible is scientifically correct—3000 years before the microscope could establish this truth. The child belongs to both of them. There is absolute equality. Both have to leave, both have to cleave. Both become one flesh.

However, such equality is possible only between two partners. Three can never become one, especially since the expression "one flesh" touches not only the physical realm, but also life as a whole. They are to share equally all that they are and have. The biblical concept of equality excludes polygamy.

It is not difficult to imagine that with this changed concept of marriage a great need arises in Africa today. Many Africans are saying: "We would like to have such a marriage. But how do we go about it? How does one live with an equal partner?" Many complain: "Our women are just not yet ready for this kind of equality."

In many cases they are right. Therefore let us pray for the bride in our midst—that she may become a real partner to her husband and that through her testimony she may become a contributor to the African society. There can be no doubt: The future of the African woman decides the future of the African continent.

But now comes the most surprising thing in our text—the final death blow to the garden concept. It is the period, the full stop after this verse 24. "And they become one flesh." Period. Full stop.

In this verse about marriage, quoted four times in the Bible, there is not one word about children.

There must be no misunderstanding: The Bible is not hostile to children. On the contrary, according to the Bible, children are a blessing of God. But they are an *additional* blessing of God.

The message of the period, of the full stop, is simply this: It is not the child which makes marriage, as marriage has meaning even when it is childless. That man and wife become "one flesh" is meaning enough. Children originate from the one-flesh union. But they do not constitute it. The fellowship of love between husband and wife is the fulfillment of marriage in itself.

The consequences of this full stop for Africa cannot be overemphasized. Its message is like a stick of dynamite thrown into African society. If the child is not the *only* meaning of marriage, the whole garden concept is blown up. It affects virtually all African marriage customs.

The bride-wealth system will lose its meaning, for it is a compensation for the fertile garden, not for the childless woman. Childlessness will no longer be a reason for divorce. Neither simultaneous nor successive polygamy can be justified any longer because of childlessness. The standards for the choice of a marriage partner will change from fertility to personality. The girl will be married for her own sake and not for what she is going to produce. This full stop, this period, makes out of the woman a human being.

But then our African brethren will ask: "What is the deepest meaning of marriage? If it means something more than just the production of children, what is it?"

There is only one answer to this question: It is the freely given mutual love between husband and wife. Thus far the church has confronted the African society with a negative message on marriage by saying: Those who have more than one wife cannot become church members. But it has failed to proclaim a positive message on marriage. It has failed to interpret to Africa the meaning of monogamous married love.

At this point, however, we stand with empty hands in front of our African friends. I was often ashamed in front of my former student, Jean Banyolak, when he came to Germany. What would he see when he was invited into our families? What would he witness when he went through the streets of our cities at night? What would he conclude when he went to a movie or read a magazine?

We Europeans are just as poor as the Africans when it comes to this positive testimony. The monogamous union of love is not a western concept. It is a divine concept. Therefore there is only one way to make clear to Africans and Europeans alike what married love really is. It is the way which the Apostle Paul chose when he wrote his letter to the Ephesians. He pointed to the love of the Son of God: "Husbands, love your wives, as Christ loved the church and gave himself up for her" (Eph. 5:25).

How did Christ love the church? He served her! He did not come to be served, but to serve. He lowered himself to become the lowliest servant, giving himself up for her when dying at the cross.

Now the circle closes. What then does it mean, "Wives, be subject to your husbands, as to the Lord?" The last four words make all the difference. It is not a forced submission to a superior ruler. According to the Bible this patriarchal subordination is a result of sin—"and he shall rule over you" (Gen. 3:16). "As to the Lord" is a different submission. It is a voluntary submission *in response* to the submission of her husband.

Why do we submit ourselves to Christ? Because he rules over us like a patriarch? No. We submit to him out of gratefulness, because he submitted himself to us first. We love him, because he loved us first. We serve him, because he served us first.

In the same way, a wife submits to her husband out of gratefulness because he submitted to her first. "Be subject to one another out of reverence for Christ."

In Christ, the wife becomes again the equal "helper fit for him" she was meant to be. In Christ, the husband becomes the equal helper fit for her that he was meant to be. In Christ, both become fully human. Their marriage will reflect the love of Jesus Christ. This mystery is great. It is the deepest meaning of married love.

BOOK EIGHT

A BABY JUST NOW?

Foreword

When Joseph first wrote to me and complained about his "disobedient" wife, I did not know that our correspondence would end up in such a lengthy discussion about the problems connected with family planning. While we were searching for the answer, we became more and more aware of the relationship between marital happiness and the success in spacing one's children, preventing or favouring conception—as God guides.

Joseph is an African. But his problems are basically the same as in any other part of the world. Perhaps they are more sharply focused because certain African customs and traditions may make it harder for Joseph to find solutions than for others who belong to another culture. But just for this reason our correspondence may prove helpful to many.

As you will see, the idea of publishing part of our correspondence occurred to both of us while we were writing. Still the advice I have given to Joseph is, in the first place, meant for him alone in his specific situation. Please don't make the mistake of generalizing it and misunderstanding my suggestions as a general law valid for everyone.

This book does not attempt to give the answer for everyone everywhere. But one thing it does want to teach: The seeking of God's will by both husband and wife together is vitally important to family planning. It is the basic condition for any answer to this great human problem.

Walter Trobisch

January 7

Sir,

I have heard about your work and therefore I take the liberty to write to you and to place my case before you. Here is my problem: I am 24 years old. Three years ago I was married to a 15-year-old person. But now this person does not want to obey me anymore.

I am a teacher and have ten years of schooling. My wife stopped after her sixth year. I purposely did not choose someone who had reached a higher level of education than I had. I intended to train my wife for life: to drill her for cleanliness as a housewife and to raise her for marriage as a spouse. In short, she should become exactly as I wanted her to be.

At the beginning of our marriage it worked somehow. But during the last year she did not satisfy me anymore. Regardless of what I command her to do, she never does it. If I tell her something, she refuses. If I insist, we start to quarrel even to the point of fighting.

Sometimes we make peace and try to start anew. But it lasts only for one day. Then we fall back into quarrelling. My wife gets angry very easily. Sometimes she even throws our household out of the window. The only thing she seems to enjoy is jealousy.

I might also mention that God blessed us with a child who is already one year and one month old.

I have confidence in you and hope that whatever you tell me will serve as a remedy to our sick marriage.

Joseph

January 28

Dear Mr. Joseph,

Thank you very much for your letter and also for your confidence. I wish I could pay you a visit. Then it would be easier for me to find the root of your trouble. I am afraid it will be hard for me to help by letter-writing alone, but I shall try my best.

Your wife was too young when you married her. This is certainly one of the reasons for your difficulties. At 15, a girl is still a child. When she is 18, she is a young woman. The change she goes through between 15 and 18 is tremendous. For a girl these are the most important years of maturing. Not only does her body change, but also her spirit, her character and her emotions. At 18, a girl is an entirely different person than she was at 15, especially if she has become a mother in the meantime, as is the case with your wife.

May I speak frankly? I am afraid that when you married her you did not look for a wife, but more or less for a daughter, perhaps even a maid. You did not plan so much to become a husband to her as you did to become a father or even an employer.

The verbs you use when describing your relationship to her are very revealing: "to train," "to drill," "to raise." Do you know that one could use these verbs also for an animal?

You planned to educate her as you educate your students in class, to dominate her as a superior dominates someone in an inferior position. Instead of a marriage partner you were looking for a servant.

It is hard for me to judge from this distance, but my impression is that your wife rebels against being treated like a servant. She wants to be treated as an equal partner.

God loves your wife as much as he loves you. Both of you are equal in his eyes. God has a plan for you as well as for your wife. He has given unique gifts to your wife and he wants her to make use of them. He wants her talents and skills to unfold just as a flower unfolds from a bud. It is your task to help her become what God wants her to be, not what you want her to be.

Her jealousy shows that she loves you, but that she cannot fully trust you. This may be a reflection of the fact that you do not trust her either. As soon as she feels that you have confidence in her, she may be more cooperative.

Marriage is like the echo in the forest. What you call out will come back to you.

If you say that she does not satisfy you, you must ask yourself: "Do I satisfy her?" If you complain that she does not have confidence in you, you must ask yourself: "Do I have confidence in her?" If you criticize her for not obeying and serving you, you must ask yourself: "Do I obey and serve her?"

If you feel she hinders you from becoming what God wants you to be, then you must ask yourself: "Do I give her a chance to become what God wants her to be?"

There is one expression in your letter which I did not understand. You say that your wife "throws the household out of the window." Do you mean that she literally throws the dishes out into the street?

Let me share this last thought with you. I was struck by the fact that your quarrelling started about the time your child was born, approximately one year ago. How long is the period of lactation in your tribe when you abstain from sex relations with your wife?

You see it is not God's will for a married couple to abstain from physical union for too long a time.

Sharing and meeting each other's sexual needs is so important that the apostle Paul advises against prolonged abstinence: "Do not refuse one another except perhaps by agreement for a season, that you may devote yourselves to prayer; but then come together again, lest Satan tempt you through lack of self- control."

My question is this: Could it be that your quarrelling is a result of such a temptation and that there is a sexual problem behind it?

Feel free not to answer this question if it embarrasses you too much. I just have to ask this question because its answer may help me to find the "remedy for your sick marriage."

February 15

Dear Pastor T.,

I can't express the joy caused by your letter. It is as if you had lived right among us. Since your letter came, the troubled sea of our marriage has already calmed down. I do not know how to thank you, for I am sure that you have already found the reason our marriage is sick.

It is just as you assumed. In my tribe we abstain from sex relations for two years after the birth of a baby. This is because of certain superstitions of our ancestors. They say that sex relations with a woman who has a small child will endanger the life of her baby.

This custom is embodied in us and we are afraid we will lose the baby if we have intercourse with the mother as long as she breastfeeds it. She does that until the baby starts to walk.

They also say that boys die easier than girls—and our child is a boy. My father-in-law emphasized that fact to me after our boy was born. Therefore for fear that we cause his death we abstained from intercourse for several months.

But it was hard, especially for me. In former times when polygamy still reigned in our society, I guess it must have been easier to follow this custom. But I despise polygamy as do most young men of my generation. It is something which belongs to the past. In any case, even if I wanted to take a second wife, it would be impossible for me because of financial reasons.

My wife knows that many husbands commit adultery in such a situation. As a church elder and as a teacher at a church school I would not even think of going to a prostitute. Still my wife suspects it and this makes her distrustful and jealous.

To whom could I have turned to solve my problem? One day I met a friend who advised me to use a method which I felt was vulgar. He told me that it is the sperm inside the woman's body which kills the baby, because it mixes with the milk. But if I would withdraw and shed the sperm outside of my wife's body, intercourse would not be dangerous for our baby.

Something in me rebelled against this, but since I felt that my wife and I were gradually drifting apart as long as we abstained from sex relations, I tried it. That's the way we do it at present. It has given me some release, but it has not helped our marriage.

There are many things which I do not understand. It seems to me that my wife is not satisfied if I ejaculate outside of her body. Could it be that the sperm has another quality or effect when it is not used for the purpose of procreation? Is it possible that only sperm inside my wife's body contributes to sexual harmony?

I would be very grateful to you if you could clarify my thinking on these questions.

P. S. "Throwing the household out of the window" is an expression in our language for gossiping and slander. My wife started to tell our secrets to the other women in the village, and that makes me feel terribly embarrassed. But sometimes in an outbreak of anger she actually breaks plates and cups and throws them on the earth and toward the wall.

February 27

Dear Joseph,

I am so glad that my question did not hurt you, but rather caused you to give me a full picture of the situation. I can well understand now why your wife rebels.

You are really in a dilemma. On one hand you do not want to become polygamous and on the other hand you want to follow a custom which presupposes a polygamous society.

The reasoning behind this custom is not entirely wrong though. Since there was neither fresh nor powdered milk available in your tribe, babies had to be breastfed, usually for about two years. If the mother got pregnant before that and could not nurse her baby, the baby could easily have died.

It is also true that girls are more resistant to disease than boys. That explains the statement of your father-in-law.

This high rate of infant mortality in former times, however, was not caused by intercourse. The sperm does not mix with the milk. This is a biological impossibility. Those babies probably died because of an inadequate diet when their mothers' milk supply dried up due to another pregnancy.

Your ancestors observed correctly that couples who had intercourse before their baby was weaned were more apt to lose it. Their conclusion was that abstaining from intercourse gives the baby a better chance to survive. I know some other tribes where this period of abstention lasts for three years. But then—as you say—husband and wife drift apart gradually. A period of abstention of six weeks before and after the birth is all right, but in no case is it advisable to abstain from marital relations for two or even three years.

You are right: It must have been easier when a man had more than one wife. From this point of view one could say that polygamy was the traditional African way of "conception control." It helped the women to space their children.

You rule out polygamy for yourself for emotional and financial reasons—and I am the last one who wants to contradict you. In addition to the reasons which you give, let me briefly mention here that the Bible points out very soberly and realistically the disadvantages of polygamy. Genesis 26 says that it makes life bitter (v. 35), Genesis 29 that it causes rivalry (v. 30) and hatred (v. 31), Genesis 30 that it leads to envy (v. 1), anger (v. 2) and wrestling and fighting (v. 8). Genesis 37 stresses the effect of polygamy on the children: favoritism and injustice (v. 3), hostility (v. 4), jealousy (v. 4) and finally murder (v. 18).

I do not know of a single passage in the Bible where polygamy is not mentioned under a negative aspect.

Also I am glad that you reject prostitution as well. I believe that prostitution is the main reason for so many childless marriages in Africa. Men who sleep with prostitutes can easily catch a venereal disease, infect their wives and cause them to become sterile.

In fact, many of the so-called "prostitutes" in African towns are such sterile women, who were abandoned by their husbands because they could not bear children. If they have a venereal disease, they pass it on to their customers who in turn may make their own wives barren. Then the men leave these wives because of their barrenness and many of the women have no other choice except to earn their living through prostitution.

It is really a vicious circle. I once heard an African judge say, "Whoever sleeps with a prostitute commits a criminal act against his own people. It is comparable to high treason." I don't think he exaggerated.

Yes, indeed: To whom could you have turned? Formerly you would have consulted with the elders of your tribe, but now you are in a different situation unknown to them. I am afraid that your church also just left you with a negative message, saying that polygamy is wrong and prostitution is sinful. What you needed was positive advice on how to space your children in a monogamous marriage.

The method which your friend advised is called "coitus interruptus" or more commonly "being careful." It consists in the withdrawal of the penis from the vagina before ejaculation occurs.

Let me simply quote what the Medical Hand book of the International Planned Parenthood Federation says about the disadvantages of this method:

> Various emotional disturbances in the form of anxiety in both the male and the female partner are said to be produced by the prolonged and continued use of this method. The female is constantly in fear that the male will not withdraw in time, and the male must be in a continued state of vigilance in order to gauge the right moment for separation. Thus one of the desirable features of intercourse, complete freedom from anxiety, is lost, and replaced by unavoidable tension. This may possibly result in impotence in the male, frigidity in the female, or a state of nervous tension in either.[1]

Now you know why you quarrel and also why your wife "throws the household out of the window" by word of mouth or by action. Both of you are in a permanent state of nervous tension.

The name "interrupted intercourse" is misleading. Actually intercourse is not interrupted in order to be continued later on, but it is broken off. Since it takes much longer for a woman to reach her climax, usually only the male partner experiences a sort of satisfaction, while the female partner remains tense and unsatisfied. It is not the lack of sperm which leaves her unsatisfied, but the lack of time, connected with fear and worry.

The inability to relax due to congestion may actually cause her abdominal pain and in the long run she may develop a loathsome and disgusting feeling against everything sexual.

Consciously or unconsciously she blames you for it and develops a negative attitude against you. She does not feel loved but exploited. Through her "disobedience" she protests against this exploitation. By breaking cups and plates she tries to find release from tension.

But, Joseph, this means that her disobedience is basically a cry for help. She tries to call your attention to her need. What she really wants to say is: "Please help me! Please love me!"

I would strongly advise you to choose another method for preventing conception, especially since "coitus abruptus," as I prefer to call it, is not a safe method either. Not only can the moment of withdrawal be easily missed, but it is also possible that sperm may be present in the small amount of pre-ejaculation moisture at the tip of the erect penis. Therefore any movement of the penis in the vagina automatically causes this moisture and the sperm to be deposited on the vaginal wall. Pregnancies have even occurred following movements of the penis against the moist part of the vulva without actual penetration or ejaculation.

In your case I would advise you to turn to "Natural Family Planning" (NFP), which means to live in harmony with the biological laws according to which you were created.

March 20

Dear Pastor T.,

The last paragraphs of your letter of February 27th leave me dumbfounded. I am quite sure that you are right in the analysis of our problem. So is my wife. I let Jeannette read your letter and while she was reading it, she sometimes giggled with laughter. That's the way she always does when something strikes her.

We agree that the method of birth control which we have been using is responsible for lots of our trouble.

Your diagnosis is good, but I do not understand your alternative. I simply do not know what you mean by "Natural Family Planning." What are those laws according to which we were created? Since, as a teacher, I have more education than the average man in my country, I guess I am not alone in this ignorance. Our district pastor does not know what it is either. Sex education was not a part of the highly praised western education which we received.

There is a Protestant mission station not far from here. I know the missionary families quite well. Some get a child almost every year and seem to have no feeding problem. Others get them in regular intervals of two years. How do they manage that? What kind of magic do they have? Why do they never talk to us Africans about the methods of birth control which they use?

April 4

Dear Joseph,

You stung my missionary conscience. I believe that you are right in your criticism.

I agree, it is unkind and merciless if missionaries discourage polygamy, but keep silent about other methods of conception control. No, my dear friend, they do not have any "magic." They solve their feeding problem with the help of powdered milk and if they want advice for spacing their children, their missionary doctor will provide them with everything they need.

Thank you for not hiding your ignorance. It was an eye-opener to me. What a tremendous task of giving out information lies before us! When will schools in Africa start to include sex education in their schedules?

But before I start explaining what I meant by Natural Family Planning let's get our terms straight. You will notice that I did not use the expression "birth control" in our correspondence. That was intentional, because the term "birth control" conceives of birth as the beginning of life. Consequently a willful abortion could also then be justified as a means of " birth control."

I prefer to use the term "conception control" because it sees the fecundation of the female ovum by the male seed as the beginning of life. Every destruction of this new life—in other words, every intentional abortion—is murder.

Natural Family Planning means simply to abstain from intercourse during the fertile days in a woman's menstrual cycle.

A woman can only conceive during the time when the egg cell or ovum separates from the ovary. This process is called ovulation. If the ovum is not met by a male sperm shortly after ovulation, no fertilization takes place and the woman experiences a slight bleeding about two weeks later, as if the womb were shedding "tears of disappointment." We say then a woman has "her period" or "her days" or "she menstruates."

You can control conception by adjusting intercourse to the natural rhythm of a woman's body. This explains the name, "Natural Family Planning." If a couple abstains from intercourse during the time of ovulation, which is her fertile time, no conception can take place.

I suggest this method to you because I feel that it would ease the tenseness of your wife and give her a better chance to find satisfaction by experiencing an orgasm.

By the way, do you know what made me most happy about your last letter? The fact that you shared it with your wife! This means that you have stopped treating her as a "daughter" and started to recognize her as an adult and as a partner. Tell her that she may write to me too, if she cares to.

April 28

Dear Pastor T.,

Thank you for your letter. Could you give me permission to copy some paragraphs and pass it on to friends who have similar problems? I know quite a few who would be very grateful for this help.

However, if I do this then my students could also get a hold of it and I am afraid that they would abuse this knowledge, applying it to premarital relations. How could I avoid this?

Some months ago we had to send a girl away from school because she was pregnant. When I questioned her, she claimed that she was sure that intercourse had occurred on her "safe days," which she said were the days halfway between two periods. She thought she could only conceive immediately before or following her period.

So you see, our students have some kind of knowledge of these things, but very often it is incorrect. I am sorry that at that time I was unable to correct her error.

My question is, if I had already known what you explained to me in your last letter, should I have told her? Wouldn't I have led her into temptation? And could she have been sure that the days which you describe are absolutely safe?

My wife also has a question. I enclose her note:

Good morning, Pastor. This is Jeannette writing. I read your letters to Joseph. I would also like to ask you a question.

I am very interested in your suggestion that we have no intercourse when the ovum is leaving the ovary. But my question is: How can I know? Do I feel this? Are there signs to help me recognize when ovulation takes place?

July 6

Dear Joseph and Jeannette,

You did not put enough stamps on your last letter and it went by surface mail. Because of this I am very sorry that I was not able to answer your important question sooner.

Let us take "ladies first." Thank you, Jeannette, for your note. Yes, there are symptoms to help you recognize your time of ovulation. Perhaps you have noticed that just after your menstrual bleeding has finished, there are a few days of dryness at the vaginal opening. When this dryness changes to a feeling of wetness you will know that your fertile time is beginning. Then for two or three days you will notice a transparent, stretchy fluid, very similar to raw egg-white at the mouth of the vagina. This is the symptom or sign that ovulation is taking place. This fluid is called "cervical mucus" and your body produces it in order to help your husband's semen enter into the womb and meet the ovum.

If you want to have a baby, then you would have to unite during the days when you see this cervical mucus. If you do not want to have a baby just yet, then you should not have intercourse during these days plus three days after the slippery egg-white mucus has stopped completely. It is necessary to wait for three days in order to be sure that the ovum is no longer living. Otherwise conception could still take place.

After that, the infertile time of your cycle begins and you are not able to conceive until the fertile time of your next cycle. Some women in your country describe this fertile-type of mucus as being similar to the soup of gumbo which you cook—stretchy and quite clear. You can examine the mucus on two leaves, or with your fingers, testing it to see if it will stretch. Some women think when they see this symptom that they are sick. On the contrary, this is a sign of good health.

Now back to Joseph's questions. I am glad you raised the problem of premarital relations. The premarital situation and the marital situation are different. Usually when methods of conception control are discussed, the two situations are not kept apart properly. What is applicable in a marital situation is not applicable in the same way in a premarital situation.

This is especially true about Natural Family Planning. For premarital intercourse it is almost useless as a safeguard against an unwanted pregnancy. The boy would have to believe the girl when she says that she is "safe." How can he be sure that she tells him the truth as in the case of your student? And even if she does know the truth, what guarantee does he have that she has interpreted this symptom correctly?

Girls who give themselves easily before marriage are usually not very trustworthy, disciplined, conscientious and—by the way—not very intelligent either. Natural Family Planning needs a high measure of discipline, conscientiousness and intelligence. Girls who use NFP and live consciously in harmony with their cycle are automatically trained in these qualities. This is, in turn, their best protection against indulging in premarital sex.

Does knowledge lead into temptation? Yes, it does, if it is abused. I do not think that there is any means to prevent the abuse of knowledge. If we refuse to give true knowledge, false knowledge will spread. The case of your girl student illustrates this in a striking way.

Those who want to have premarital relations will have them anyway, whether or not we give out information. But by giving correct information we may save some of these young people from disasters and from destroying their lives.

So much depends upon the atmosphere in which such knowledge is conveyed. When talking to unmarried teenagers, you must emphasize that there is no "absolutely safe" method of conception control, except for one. This is the word "No." If your students feel that you stand behind your words with your action and your own conduct of life, they will readily accept your advice. Reliable and trustworthy information may prevent them from experimenting themselves with disastrous results. Once they are married and away from you, they will remember you gratefully.

September 20

Dear Pastor T.,

During vacation I went to my home village. This is why it has taken me until now to answer your letter of July 6th.

Again when I read it, I thought of so many others who need such information. The idea is quite widespread here that it is the third day after her period when a woman can conceive. But I have no time to copy your letter so often. Could you help me to mimeograph it or even print it?

This is only to tell you how thankful we were for your explanation. Still, I have to confess to you, dear Pastor T., that we are not too happy. We tried now for half a year to watch symptoms, but it often happens that on the infertile days, when we could unite, we are hindered by some outward disturbance.

On the other hand, during the fertile days, when we shouldn't come together, we would like to and also circumstances would allow it. It's really tricky.

This brings up another handicap. As a European it will be hard for you to understand this. For us Africans it's very hard to talk about these things. I simply cannot bring it across my lips to ask Jeannette about her mucus symptoms nor is she able to tell me. So I am never sure whether she forgot to watch for this sign of fertility.

True, my wife is less jealous, but we still have problems with this method.

What has helped us most is to share your letters. The fact that she knows that I know how she feels and cares about it has made our marriage more peaceful.

I heard that a mother can't conceive as long as she breastfeeds her baby. Is that true?

I read in a magazine that millions of American women take the so-called "anti-baby pills." What do the pills do? Kill the baby? What do you think about them? Can it be sinful to prevent conception? What is God's will about family planning?

October 6

Dear Joseph,

I am glad that we are in contact again and that you share your experiences with me so frankly.

What you have heard is right. Normally a woman does not menstruate as long as she breast feeds her child completely. This is because she has no ovulation and consequently she cannot conceive. Many doctors believe that it is the stimulus of the sucking of the baby which prevents ovulation. However, it is not true that a woman cannot become pregnant as long as she is nursing a baby, although it is extremely unusual before the first menstrual period if she is completely nursing her baby. The average nursing mother will not have a period for several months after giving birth. When she does begin to have menstrual periods, in most cases at least one and often several of these will be without ovulation. That is why it is very important for a breastfeeding mother to notice the return of the mucus sign which means she can conceive again.

You ask about God's will about family planning. It is, above all, a matter of conscience. It is the motive which counts before God, not the method or the means.

If a couple does not want to have children because of selfish reasons (for example, material greed, love of luxury or simply laziness), then any kind of conception control is sinful.

If, on the other hand, a new pregnancy would endanger the mother's or the baby's life, it would be sinful not to use conception control. A father whose income is small and who already has five or six children whom he wants to give a fairly good education may want to limit the number of his children for this reason. He may do so with a good conscience before God, because his motive is unselfish.

The important thing is that father and mother together make such a decision. Together they have to examine their consciences before God as to their motive. Together they are responsible to God. This is what we call "responsible parenthood."

Now a word about the so-called "anti-baby pill." The name "anti-baby pill" is awkward. No baby is killed. What the pill does is hinder ovulation. As long as a woman takes these pills, no ovum is released from the ovary. Consequently, fertilization cannot take place.

That means that a couple can have intercourse on any day between the periods without restriction. Whether this makes marriages happier is a disputed question. Some couples feel that it takes the spice out of their relations and makes them monotonous when they could have them every day. The increased sexual demands are too great for a number of marriage partners, who then suffer from frigidity or impotence. Especially the wife may complain of becoming "depersonalized." She may feel that she has degenerated into a sexual object instead of being an equal partner in married love. Somehow intervals make intimate relations more attractive and the happiness of loving is refreshed and intensified.

But as far as effectiveness goes, the pill is as effective as Natural Family Planning. However, there is one important hitch to this effectiveness: between the menstrual periods one pill must be taken every day for 21 days. Otherwise the effectiveness cannot be guaranteed.

Consequently—and this is what you have to tell your teenage girls—it is useless for a girl to take one pill along with her when going on a date and then swallow it quickly just in case.

Again we have to distinguish between marital and premarital use of this method. In premarital situations the pill cannot be considered an effective method. The boy who has dated an unmarried girl would have to believe her if she claims to have taken her pills every day. Effectiveness depends upon whether she tells the truth or not.

As I said before, "easy" girls are not usually very conscientious and the conscientious girls with high moral standards would most likely agree with the American girl who said: "If I would take pills regularly, calculatingly, in anticipation of a possible sex adventure, I would feel like a prostitute."

More and more doctors caution young girls especially from taking pills, because it can have a negative effect on a girl's organism and change the normal delicate balance of her hormones. In any case, pills must be prescribed by a medical doctor and medical supervision is imperative, especially since we still have very little knowledge about the after-effects in later years. Because I assumed that such supervision is difficult in your village, I did not advise you to use this method. The pills are also quite expensive.

In many cases as soon as a woman stops taking the pills, her ability to conceive is especially great and many unwanted pregnancies occur during the first months after she stops.

Or on the contrary, the normal release of egg cells may be hindered when a woman quits taking the pills and she may be sterile for a longer time.

If you decide to use this method I would advise you, as the husband, to keep the pills and give one to your wife every day. In this way you also take a share of the responsibility and you cannot blame Jeannette for being forgetful in case of an unintended pregnancy.

You have to decide. But in order to decide you have to talk. I know that it is difficult, but I am afraid you will have to learn. It is impossible to live a marriage without talking to each other. Sharing is the secret of marriage.

October 18

Dear Pastor T.,

When your last letter arrived I was not at home. But Jeannette was so eager to read it that she opened it, though it was addressed to me. Was that right?

You said that the secret of marriage is sharing. Does this mean that husband and wife are allowed to open each other's mail? I must say that I did not like it.

So for the first time since we started to correspond with you, we again had a little disagreement. On the other hand, I must say that sharing your letters has helped us a great deal to talk to each other even about sexual matters. I think you are right when you say that Jeannette's "disobedience" was just a way of saying that she wanted to be listened to, understood and cared for.

Jeannette refuses absolutely to take pills. She says it would give her the feeling of being poisoned even if she knows that they contain no poison. She has an instinctive horror of such pills.

Most of us Africans are much more open to watching natural symptoms than to using artificial means.

On the other hand, Jeannette and I are not yet friends with the idea of periodical abstention. So our basic problem is not yet solved. We do not want another baby just yet. Powdered milk is too expensive for us and not available here in the village anyway. We are afraid to use fresh milk because our children die if they drink it. I know that the children of the missionaries don't get sick from it, but ours do.

The other day we heard about a woman who already has eight children. She went to a dispensary about 50 miles from here. There a nurse put something into her body which looked like a little snake. She said that this would prevent conception and not do any harm. Have you ever heard about such a thing?

November 1

Dear Joseph and Jeannette,

Opening each other's mail is a delicate problem. I shall address my letters from now on to both of you. I should have done that already with my last letter because it was definitely meant for both of you.

Sharing does not mean sneaking. Normally, I would say, each one should open his own mail, even if it is only for the joy of opening a letter. But it should be a matter of course that one shares gladly one's own mail with the marriage partner, talks about it and decides together what to answer. You have already experienced how much sharing the mail helps towards peace and understanding.

Sharing is especially important in order to avoid mistrust and jealousy when correspondence takes place with the opposite sex.

A pastor's mail is definitely an exception. He may receive confidential letters which he is not allowed to share with anyone, not even with his wife. This puts the marriage of a pastor to an especially hard test. If he has a wife who does not understand this, she can wreck his ministry—and his marriage at the same time.

I have made an agreement with my wife—who also receives confidential letters—that we never open each other's mail. Normally we share it. But if one of us does not feel free to share a letter, the other one does not ask any questions about it. This is only possible, of course, if full and complete confidence reigns between husband and wife.

I am happy that you both have read my last letter and talked about it. Joseph, please do not try to persuade Jeannette to take pills she does not want to. If she has an aversion against them, just this alone would greatly hinder her achieving sexual fulfillment. A woman who feels "poisoned" does not enjoy sex.

However, I disagree with you entirely about fresh milk. The missionaries boil their milk before drinking it. This is the reason why their children do not get sick. Your children would not either. On the contrary, they would thrive.

May I say frankly, if you only want to wait to have another baby because you refuse to boil your milk, this is not reason enough to practice conception control.

The thing that was inserted in the woman you mentioned was an "intrauterine device" (I. U. D.). This is no "snake," but a plastic spiral or sling which is placed inside the uterus, or womb, to avoid the implantation of the fertilized ovum.

This brings up a theological question connected with this method. The question is: "When does life begin?" If we claim that life begins in the moment when the sperm unites with the ovum, it would mean that the I. U. D.'s produce a preclinical abortion. I know many people whose conscience does not allow them to use this method for this reason.

From the medical point of view the tender tissues of the uterus are in danger of infection through the presence of the I. U. D., a foreign body in the womb. Certain side effects such as bleeding, pain, and sometimes perforation of the uterus cannot be entirely avoided.

There is also the possibility that an I. U. D. is spontaneously expelled especially during a menstrual period. If the woman doesn't notice this, then conception usually follows.

In passing, let me mention a few other devices here. Sooner or later you may be asked about them and I want you to be informed.

In some countries, a three-month injection has been given to women to prevent pregnancy. This is very dangerous and can cause permanent damage to a woman's reproductive system.

Another method consists of covering the mouth of the uterus in order to prevent semen from entering. The device used for this purpose is called a diaphragm. A doctor's advice is necessary for fitting it. Even then, a diaphragm does not offer much security except in combination with a sperm-killing ointment. If it is not inserted properly, it is useless.

Flooding the vagina with water after coitus—the so-called "douches"—cannot be effective, since sperms can reach the cervix within 90 seconds of ejaculation.

Joseph, I feel like almost apologizing to you for writing you all this. I certainly didn't think, when you wrote me the first time, that our correspondence would end up in such a lengthy discussion of contraceptive methods. But if you think of using a mechanical device at all, I would think of something rather harmless, the condom.

I mean the rubber sheath which completely covers the male organ like the finger of a glove. The seminal fluid is caught in it and cannot enter the vagina.

However, during the time of the fertile days it is not very reliable to prevent conception, while during the infertile days you would not need it.

November 16

Dear Pastor T.,

Before I tell you what I think about condoms, I would like to ask some general questions about "conception control."

Jeannette took your letter to one of her friends who is the mother of fourteen children. She came back home with a whole bag of questions which we were unable to answer.

Jeannette's friend claims that the Bible does not say anything about contraceptives. She says that God gave Adam and Eve the commandment, "Be fruitful and multiply and fill the earth." Therefore the use of any contraceptives, even observing the infertile days, would be against

God's will. It would be sinful to have intercourse if you did not intend to produce offspring. One should not interfere with the course of nature, but rather leave everything entirely in God's hand and trust him and believe him.

We did not know how to answer her. She is a very pious woman and really believes in the Bible.

When you have answered, I shall tell you my story about the rubber sheath.

November 28

Dear Joseph and Jeannette,

Now you turn tables!

Remember, it was not I who advised you to wait with another child! You had made this decision without me, long before you wrote to me the first time. However, the method which you had used to space your children had disturbed the harmony of your marriage. This was the reason why we discussed other methods which would be less disturbing.

I think it is good that you bring up the basic question: Is conception control in harmony at all with the will of God? What does the Bible say about it?

The Bible does not make any direct statement about conception control. In this, your wife's friend is right. Neither is any specific method mentioned in the Bible. This is the more surprising since certain methods were already known and practiced during the times when the Bible was written.

The Bible stresses again and again that children are a blessing of God and a source of joy: "Children are an heritage of the Lord, and the fruit of the womb is his reward" (Ps. 127:3).

According to divine will, sexual union and procreation are closely related to each other. The fact that there is no ideal method of conception control is a silent testimony to this truth. Every method has its disadvantages and disturbs the fellowship of the lovers in one way or the other. To ignore entirely the deep connection between the sex act and offspring—as it is done in prostitution for instance—is certainly sinful.

However, the Bible does not consider procreation as the only purpose of the sex act. Your wife's friend is mistaken here. Both the Old and the New Testament testify that sexual union is a legitimate expression of marital love, even if the production of children is neither achieved nor intended. Barrenness is never recognized in the Bible as a reason for divorce. A marriage remains a marriage even without children. The love between husband and wife as expressed by sexual union has the promise of fulfillment in itself.

Therefore the Bible can speak about this love without mentioning children. In Proverbs 31, you find a twenty-five-verse description of a good housewife. Only one of these twenty-five verses mentions children. This shows that in Israel a woman was much more than just a means to produce offspring or a sort of breeding machine.

In Genesis 29, you can read about the love of Jacob and Rachel and in I Samuel 18 and 19 about David's love to Michal without there being a question of children. The same is true about the Song of Solomon.

In Genesis 2:18, God says to Adam, "It is not good that the man should be alone; I will make a helper fit for him." This means that according to the Bible, the woman is not essentially a womb, a sort of well-equipped incubator, but an equivalent to man as his suitable, corresponding partner complementing him and forming with him a new entity.

The Bible praises this entity, this total fellowship of body, mind and soul with the phrase, "they become one flesh" (Gen. 2:24).

Children are not mentioned. The emphasis is on the dignity of the woman, not on procreation. This is especially true in the New Testament where Jesus gave a new dignity to the wife by forbidding divorce. There is no commandment about procreation in the New Testament. Parenthood is a free gift of God's goodness, but childlessness is no shame.

When the apostle Paul talks about the physical fellowship between husband and wife in I Corinthians 7:3, the question of children doesn't even enter in. When he explains the relationship between husband and wife in marriage in Ephesians 5, children aren't mentioned either.[2]

To sum it up, according to the biblical testimony as a whole, the fellowship of love in marriage has its own dignity—apart from the question of children.

If this is true, then it is a logical conclusion that man has to make a decision about the question of children. It is not an automatic, mechanical process. To "leave nature to its course," is not at all the same as "leaving it entirely in God's hand." This is not biblical thinking! According to the Bible, nature belongs to this world which has fallen out of God's hand. Therefore not "to interfere with nature" can be against God's will. Uncontrolled fertility can be destructive and a way to worship and serve "the creature rather than the Creator" (Rom. 1: 25).Therefore it is biblical for the Philippine Independent Church to state: "The irresponsible procreation of children can be sinful."

If the mother of fourteen children who talked to Jeannette has a sense of humor, you can tell her that when God commanded man to "fill the earth" he did not mean that she should do it all by herself.

Seriously though, since you say she "really believes in the Bible," you should challenge her to quote the verse in full. That which she has quoted to Jeannette is just the first half of the blessing which God gave to Adam and Eve. The full verse reads as follows:

"And God blessed them, and said to them: Be fruitful and multiply, and fill the earth and subdue it; and have dominion over the fish of the sea and over the birds of the air and over every living thing that moves upon the earth" (Gen. 1:28).

What I have dominion over, I am responsible for. If I am put in the driver's seat and given dominion over a car, I am responsible for steering it. A statesman who has dominion over a nation is responsible for the course it takes. A director who has dominion over a factory is responsible for its output. If man is given dominion over "every living being" it means that as father and mother, he is responsible for the use of his procreative powers.

Therefore I prefer to speak about "responsible parenthood" rather than about "conception control" or even "birth control."

In view of the fact that the population of the earth will have reached the number of 6.3 milliards by the year 2000, some have raised the question whether the commandment "fill the earth" is not already fulfilled. Is not the task of subduing the earth endangered by overfilling it?

In any case, the task of man is not multiplication, but dominion; not nature, but culture.

Therefore man is responsible for the way in which the commandment "Be fruitful and multiply" is carried out. It is an abuse to interpret this commandment as an invitation to irresponsible procreation and to find in it an excuse for not making a decision.

If you want to give Jeannette's friend a Bible verse as the basis for responsible parenthood, then give her I Timothy 5:8: "If any one does not provide for his relatives, and especially for his own family, he has disowned the faith and is worse than an unbeliever."

December 12

Dear Pastor T.,

I must have asked you a very difficult question in order for you to write such a long letter! Please be assured that it is worth the effort. The whole neighbourhood is already participating in our conversation and your letters go from hand to hand.

If I understand you correctly, you draw your conclusions for "responsible parenthood" from the biblical concept of marriage in general. You say that because procreation is not the only purpose of the sex act, man has freedom and the obligation of making a decision about offspring. But you arrive there only by way of conclusion.

Therefore Jeannette's friend, the Bible-believing woman with fourteen children, was not at all convinced. She still claims that there is no commandment in the Bible to use contraceptives and neither is there any advice about which means or methods to use.

The basic question as I see it is now: "Are we permitted to do something which God has not expressly commanded?"

The woman also quoted the story of Onan in Genesis 38:9, 10 and maintained that God punished Onan by death because he prevented the procreation of offspring by spilling his seed on the ground.

She concluded that the practice of any means of contraception is sinful. I have never read this passage from this point of view. I always thought that it talked about masturbation. Is the woman's interpretation right?

I am not clear about these things. This brings up the story about the condom. Just because I am not clear, I probably made a mistake the other day in class.

One of my students had brought such a rubber sheath along into the classroom. He claimed that he had found it under a tree and asked me innocently what it was.

Of course, he just wanted to embarrass me, and all the students—boys and girls—giggled. Therefore I didn't give him any answer but punished him severely. I am not sure whether this was the right reaction.

I was wondering all the time why you had never mentioned condoms in our correspondence. Frankly, I cannot imagine myself going into a pharmacy and asking for them, especially if a woman waits on me. This could spoil my reputation as a teacher and my testimony as a Christian. In our country condoms are thought of as items to be used with prostitutes only as a prevention against venereal disease.

Well, I am afraid you will have to write another long letter. Thanks in advance . . .

December 28

Dear Joseph and Jeannette,

I am sorry that I wasn't able to answer sooner. Now that Christmas is over, I have more time to think about your important questions.

Are we permitted to do something which God has not expressly commanded?

I suppose you wash yourself with soap and water every morning and you brush your teeth. I am sure you will not find any Bible verse where this is "expressly commanded" and still you are entirely in accordance with the will of God by doing it. How do you know? By way of conclusion!

We confess in our Creed, "I believe in God the Father Almighty, Maker of heaven and earth." This means that our physical life is entrusted to us by God. We are responsible for our body, which is a "temple of God" (I Cor. 3:16). Being responsible for our body means to be responsible for its health. This includes cleanliness.

What would you say if someone would argue: "Since there is no commandment in the Bible which tells us to wash ourselves, we should just 'let nature take its course' and trust in God that he will take the dirt away"? Or: "Since the Bible does not recommend any specific brand of toothpaste, it is sinful to use any at all"?

Once a bus driver had an accident because he didn't put on brakes when going down hill. Several passengers were killed. Could he have excused himself by saying, "I am not permitted to put on brakes, because it is not expressly commanded in the Bible"?

The Bible commands, "Love your neighbour as yourself" (Lk. 10:27). This means that we are responsible for our neighbour's life. Observing the traffic rules is one way to protect this life. Therefore the driver sinned by not putting on the brakes, even though there is nothing written in the Bible about automobile brakes and their use.

I admit, you arrive at this only by way of conclusion. But why did God give us our brains, if not to draw conclusions?

Let's take the example of Kenya. In 1969, its population was about 9 million. The annual rate of increase is 3 per cent. This means that Kenya's population doubles every 23 years. In 92 years it would be multiplied by 16 and reach 144 million in less than a century.[3]

Similar numbers can be given about most of the other African countries. Africa is expected to have the fastest growth rate in the world. Its population is going to double every generation. The danger is that this may wreck all the progress Africa achieves. "Family planning does not solve all problems, but without it, solution of many of them in Africa as elsewhere is impossible."[4]

Now a brief word about the case of Onan in Genesis 38. First of all, this passage does not refer to masturbation.[5] Onan did not masturbate, but used the same method as you did first—the "coitus abruptus."

Nonetheless he was not punished for using conception control, but for his sinful and egoistic motive. He was supposed to give a child to Tamar, his late brother's wife. But this child would not have belonged to him and would not have borne his name. "Onan knew that the offspring would not be his." Therefore—he spilled the semen on the ground, "lest he should give offspring to his brother." When God slew him, he punished Onan's selfishness. This passage has nothing whatsoever to say about God's will concerning responsible parenthood.

As I said before, it is the motive which counts in God's eyes. If your motive is unselfish, you have the liberty of choosing the method which serves your marriage best.

Why didn't I mention condoms? Well, I thought you knew about them and had your reasons for not using them. You see, Joseph, the difficulty in corresponding with you is that you have so many wrong ideas. For example you say: "sperm kills the baby," "pills are poison," "milk makes babies sick," "condoms are only for use with prostitutes." Strong emotions are connected with these ideas. I may succeed in convincing you in your head that these ideas are untrue, but that still doesn't change the feelings they cause in your heart.

Your reaction concerning condoms is what I expected. You certainly made a blunder in your classroom. Brother, you missed a unique chance to teach your students a lesson in sex education and at the same time to win their confidence! I am afraid they will hesitate to ask you any questions again for fear of being punished.

The basic rule in sex education is: Answer every question that a child asks immediately, honestly and naturally, regardless of when, where and why the question is asked.

My own children often ask these questions at the dinner table, usually when we have guests. If I would hush them or show any embarrassment, I would give them the impression that sexual matters are sinful, and just in this way make them interesting and attractive. That's why I think by refusing to answer your students, you lead them much more into temptation than by giving them a true and simple explanation.

What a chance to point out to them the difference when contraceptives are used in marital or extramarital situations! The safety risks and apparent inconveniences of physical and psychological nature are certainly much greater in extramarital and especially also in premarital situations.

You will find that young people are very open to this truth if you confront them with facts. From counseling, my impression is that the condom is used relatively seldom by unmarried young people. A medical doctor in charge of the public health program of a large American city confirmed this. One of the reasons is probably that the condom can only be put on when the male organ is in a state of erection. Thus the love play has to be interrupted and this disturbs the spontaneity which characterizes young romance.

For me this is just one more evidence that according to divine will, sex should be an expression of marital love. For in marriage both partners can prepare to cope with these difficulties much more easily.

Here, Joseph, you have to use your own imagination and reasoning. You—and especially your good wife.

January 2

Dear Pastor T.,

For more than a year now you have not heard from me. I am sure that you were worried and I apologize very much that I have not answered your last letter. There were two reasons for my silence. The first is that for some time now, Jeannette and I have been quite happy in our marriage and we did not have any special problems. The second is that about six months ago we moved away from our village, because I was appointed to teach at a school in a larger town. You may have written to me, but the mail probably was not forwarded.

When I say, we have been quite happy, I really mean it. Shortly after we received your last letter we agreed to use NFP. Jeannette made a real effort to watch the symptoms as you explained them in your letter of July 6th. I put a small calendar up in our room. On it she marked an X each month on the day when her period started and M on the days when she felt the wetness from her vagina and mucus. This way I could check too, without her having to tell me.

During the days of "wetness" we abstained from having intercourse and then waited after the mucus had ceased for three more days to be sure that the fertile time was past.

Of course Jeannette did not reach her climax all the time. But as soon as she was sure that she could succeed and that I tried to help her to reach full satisfaction, she changed her attitude entirely and became "obedient," but not as a maid or a slave as I had expected when I first wrote you. It was a different kind of obedience. How can I describe it?

I got the impression that she almost seemed to like it when I gave her "orders." Sometimes she even asked me of her own accord whether

I wanted something or did even more than I asked of her. It was an obedience not out of forced submission but out of willful cooperation.

But now, as you imagine because I write to you again, we have different problems. There are two of them.

The first is money. We never had a money problem as long as we lived in the village. But now we do.

In the village we had a garden and Jeannette fed our family from what she raised. She could sell some of her vegetables at the market and with that money she bought meat, oil, salt and sugar. We also had some chickens and a few goats. I never gave her cash and she never asked for it.

Here in town we have no garden. Neither can we keep animals. Jeannette has to buy every bit of food that we use. There is a large supermarket not far from here and in this store are thousands of cartons and cans with every imaginable kind of food product.

When Jeannette goes into this store it doesn't take her more than ten minutes to spend all the money which I have given her for the whole month. She buys many things which we do not need. Often she buys more food than we can eat, so that it spoils after a few days.

This often leads to new quarrels between us. What can I do to make her buy the right things and to prevent her from spending more money than she can afford? How can you teach a wife to keep her budget?

But there's a second problem too. Please don't laugh at me now! After our long correspondence, it is hard for me to share it. We now have the opposite problem from what I first wrote about.

When we moved to this town our child was already two years old. That's why we decided about six months ago that we would like to have another baby, especially since powdered milk is available here.

Now we want another baby very badly, but it doesn't come! Every time Jeannette has her period she cries, because this means that she is not pregnant. What can we do? She has already had a medical examination, but the doctor could find nothing wrong. What is the reason for infertility?

P. S. from Jeannette: My husband let me read this letter. I think he exaggerated a little bit. Ten minutes are not enough for me to spend all our money in the supermarket. I need at least thirty.

January 27

Dear Joseph and Jeannette,

I was very happy to hear from you again after such a long time. I took your silence as a good sign that you were happy and therefore I didn't worry too much.

Jeannette seems to have developed into an artist of love. Congratulations! I am now convinced all the more that we should publish parts of our correspondence. I wish that many women would read your last letter. Or still better, that many husbands would read it to their wives.

As I said before, every method of contraception involves some handicap to the fellowship of love. If this is true within marriage, it is even more true outside of marriage. The advocates of "free sex" are usually strangely silent about this fact.

In his book on marriage, Dr. Bovet closes the discussion about contraceptives with the following paragraph:

"I must end with a solemn word of warning. We must often be thankful for contraceptives, but the great danger in using these technical things lies in the failure to realize the inherent problem—in other words, using them quite arbitrarily and ignoring the profound association God has once and for all established between sexual union and procreation. "

This leads to your questions about infertility. But first let me say a word about your budget problem.

The humorous P. S. of Jeannette shows me that you have also started to share the letters you write. Since you know how to share your problems you are not any more overcome by them. Sharing problems means to divide them into halves.

Sharing money means also to divide it up. You must first of all get away from the idea that you, Joseph, earn the money and that Jeannette spends it. In marriage you have become one flesh. This means that all the money belongs to both of you and you are both equally responsible for the way it is spent.

Therefore Jeannette has to know exactly how much you earn and you must agree on a family budget which you divide up together each month. Some couples pray before they do this.

First you take out your tithe for God. The rest you may divide up into four main parts: clothing, housing, food and emergencies.

The amount for food is taken care of by Jeannette. But you have to be patient with her and not blame her for making mistakes. She has never learned how to handle cash, so you have to teach her. Maybe you should go along a few times when she goes shopping and help her decide what to buy and what not to buy. Jeannette is an intelligent woman. I am sure that after two or three months she will be an expert shopper.

It is also very important that you include in your budget a certain amount of spending money for each of you. Yes, Joseph, you read right. Jeannette, too, should have some pocket money of her own for which she doesn't need to give an account.

Money certainly shouldn't play a major part in our lives. But we have to be realists and recognize the fact that it plays a very important minor part. Hidden feelings of hostility and rivalry in marriage often show up through the medium of money problems. Therefore it is right to deal with them consciously.

In your first letter to me you used the expression "the person I married." The word "person" had a somewhat degrading meaning in your statement. But the real meaning of "person" is very deep. To treat someone as a "person" means to recognize in him the image of God. If you really want to be married to a "person," show this, among many other things, by giving Jeannette her own spending money.

But you can show it too, by allowing her to become again a mother. I am so glad that you are thinking of having another baby. I thought already last year that if you were only willing to boil your milk, you could have had another child long ago. But it was not up to me to make this decision. It was up to you and your wife—before God.

If you now have to wait longer than you planned, it should remind you anew of the fact that children are a gift of God. They are an answer to prayer, a special blessing which God can refuse or give, just as he pleases. He is the Creator, not we.

However, just as God can use a doctor's advice to heal someone from sickness, so also can he use medical help to remove the causes of infertility. There are many causes. J. G. C. Blacker of the United Nations Economic Commission for Africa says: "Infertility is due to physiological causes, possibly the high instance of indigenous malaria, possibly forms of malnutrition and above all probably to high incidences of venereal diseases."

It's good that Jeannette had a medical checkup. But it would not hurt if you would have one too, Joseph. Many ignore the fact that the husband can also be the cause of a childless marriage. It is foolish for husbands to refuse to be examined while they blame their wives for barrenness.

However, in your case, it is very unlikely that there is a medical reason, since you already have a child which was born normally and since you have remained faithful to each other. Therefore let me give you some hints.

You can use Natural Family Planning not to prevent, but to favor conception. You could make it a point to come together on the fertile days when the ovum is released from the ovary. Some doctors give this advice: abstain from intercourse a few days before the fertile days begin and then have intercourse three or four nights in a row in order to give the male semen the maximum power.

Though female orgasm is not absolutely necessary to conception, it seems to favour it.

Still, dear Joseph and Jeannette, all this is only human talking. God may make use of our human wisdom, techniques and tools— or he may not. This is entirely up to him. If he does not want to use them and give you another child of your own, you always have, of course, the possibility of adopting an orphan and in this way, of providing a home for a child who otherwise would have none. Still an adopted child is not the same as your own child. If God does not give you another child of your own, you will have to accept it and love each other just the same.

You made a very profound statement in your last letter, Joseph. You said that Jeannette has become obedient "not out of forced submission, but out of willful cooperation." I have never heard anyone else put in such clear and simple words what the apostle Paul must have meant when he wrote: "Wives, be subject to your husbands, as to the Lord" (Eph. 5:22). But he also admonished the husbands to love their wives "as Christ loved the church," in other words, unconditionally, including their shortcomings.[6]

Therefore, if the Lord does not want to give you another child of your own, you will have to accept it in the same attitude as Elkanah did.

He had a wife called Hannah, but the Lord had "closed her womb." Her rival provoked her sorely and irritated her. Hannah wept and would not eat. Then Elkanah comforted her with the following words:

"Hannah, why do you weep? And why do you not eat? And why is your heart sad? Am I not more to you than ten sons?" (I Sam. 1:8).

Elkanah acted that way because "he loved Hannah" (v. 5).

BOOK NINE

ALL A MAN CAN BE & WHAT A WOMAN SHOULD KNOW

ONE
The Suffering Man *586*

The Insecure Man *587*

The Inadequate Man *589*

The Inferior Man *591*

The Fearful Man *593*

The Superfluous Man *594*

The Frustrated Man *596*

The Vulnerable Man *599*

TWO
The Man Reacts *602*

The Almighty Patriarch *603*

The Unapproachable Chief *605*

The Silent Buddha *606*

The Frozen Iceberg *608*

The Man's Man *609*

The Tired Man *610*

The Unfaithful Man *612*

THREE
The Free Man *618*

The Guided Man *621*

The Laughing Man *624*

The Talking Man *626*

The Motherly Man *629*

The Fatherly Man *634*

The Sheltered Man *637*

The Loving Man *641*

Foreword

"Man is suffering, but woman don't know it." I once saw these words painted on a small bus in Accra, Ghana. Perhaps this is the essence of what Walter wants to say in this book. He talked more about it to his friends and me than about any other book which came from his pen.

The unfinished manuscript lay on his desk at the time of his sudden death, October 13, 1979. The first two parts were written in his generous longhand with notes on the margin to be included in his second draft. The final section, "The Free Man," was found only in skeleton form—like the bare bones of a tree in winter which give us only the form of how beautiful the tree would be in spring, summer and fall.

The last part of the book is the answer to the first two. After we read of how a man suffers and how he reacts to his hurt, we read of the man set free to be a man—the redeemed man. He is healed of his wounds, made whole. He has accepted himself, his strengths as well as his weaknesses because he knows he has been accepted by the heavenly Father.

I've often asked young people whether they know a freed man, a redeemed man. Most of them shake their heads sadly and say, "I know none." I asked the same question of an older woman who said: "I don't know any either—only those who are on the way to becoming redeemed men. Walter was one of them."

Walter had the courage for the provisional, for the temporary. I found this sentence in his notes for an epilog to this book: "It belongs to being redeemed—to be satisfied with the provisional, the temporary. Even if one never reaches the goal, it is good to be going in the right direction . . . It is not my intention to give the last word on men in this book. Those who are only satisfied if they can write the last word will never write anything."

It is in this spirit that we share the next to the last of Walter Trobisch. May it help men to better understand and accept themselves. May it help wives to better understand their husbands.

Ingrid Trobisch

Acknowledgment

Acknowledgment is due the very important work of Walter's best friend, Pastor Wolfgang Caffier, who helped me to decipher the marginal notes and to put together the pieces. My son David also edited the first draft, making "all the words stand up straight," and removing repetition. I am deeply grateful to the staff of InterVarsity Press for bringing this unborn child to birth.

Ingrid Trobisch

The Typical Man: A Lament

Kurt Tucholsky

The typical man
man
man—
He's the misunderstood man.
He has a car, a job, a home and a position.
He has a bank account for food, gas and tuition.
He also has his opinion, contra or pro,
And even has a wife,
but this he may not know.
He calls her "Mommy" or "Baby"
with a smile and happy pat.
He's a man and that is that.
He's the self-sufficient man
who feels that a woman will never
quite understand him—ever.

The typical man
man
man—
He's the misunderstood man.
His wife lies beside him as he snores in his bed
wishing he'd be just a little gentle instead.
But he thinks: Is she not my wife?
Does she want more out of life?
He has no need to be needed.
He feels completely completed.
He bought her a dress and a hat.
He is a man—and that is that.
He's the self-sufficient man
who feels that a woman will never
quite understand him—ever.

The typical man
man
man—
He's the misunderstood man.
He does not try to court his wife.
There are more important things in life.
It's up to her, whatever his mood,
to do his laundry and cook his food.
The main thing is she obeys his will.
If not, he could have another still.
And should she doubt his loyalty, then he gets tough:
"I am a man and that's enough."
He's the self-sufficient man
who feels that a woman will never
quite understand him—ever.

The typical man
man
man—
He's the misunderstood man.
That's the man who meets his ends,
but whom no one understands.
He has no need to be needed.
He feels completely completed.
He feels he's whole and not just half.
He is a man—and that's enough.
So being a man makes him feel good,
Except he never feels quite understood.

Adapted translation by Walter Trobisch

Prolog

I first heard Kurt Tucholsky's poem in 1976, forty-five years after it was written, being performed by a cabaret singer. In the tone of her voice the singer expressed all her hostility toward men, thus winning the sure sympathy of the women who were listening. She flung the staccato words "man, man, man" like a drumbeat into the auditorium. Drums! Loud and hard, without concern for sacrifice, without the luxury of violins and flutes and soft, intertwining melodies—*that is what a man is.*

Alas!

Of course, the figure in Tucholsky's lament is a caricature and makes its point by exaggeration. But is there not, as with every exaggeration, a kernel of truth that can only be expressed this way?

It is debatable whether this kernel of truth holds only for the German man or whether it applies to men everywhere and is just more pronounced in the German variety. The path of my life has led me to countries all over the world, and I must confess that I find there is a kernel here that is true for men in general, including me.

Be that as it may, as they read this poem, men involuntarily ask themselves why they feel so misunderstood. If they are truly so self-sufficient and contented, then what torments them so that "a woman will never quite understand"?

In the following pages I would like to offer my thoughts on this question. I could have written a long book: there is certainly enough material, and a long book is easier to write than a short one. But would it be read? I suspect that it is hard to get most men to read a long book. And I want my book to be read by as many men as possible.

Years ago my wife wrote a book with the title *The Joy of Being a Woman.* Since then I have felt tempted to write a sequel: *The Pain of Being a Man.* Of course the title is intended humorously. We men do not really have it that bad. But it is interesting, just the same. Much is said and written about the stress and distress borne by women. Their joy, therefore, in being a woman must be strengthened. We men, on the other hand, are usually portrayed as strong and heroic or brutal and oppressive. We must play the role of the strong sex, and, therefore, we need someone to understand us in our weakness. This is exactly what I want to try to do.

I will refer to poets, psychologists and doctors in this book. In the third chapter I will consult the book that has been called the most honest, the truest and the most realistic book in world literature—the Bible. It tells of suffering and defensive men. It also tells of the possibility of living as a freed man, a redeemed man.

You will notice that the book is divided into three main parts: what a man feels, how he reacts to these feelings and how he can be freed to become all God intends. Notice too that the seven subsections of each part are parallel. For example, an insecure man often reacts as an almighty patriarch whereas God intends to solve his insecurity by guiding him with his sure hand.

Once you have read the book, leave it where your wife is sure to find it. It will do her good too. It will be even better if you talk it over together—better for both of you, better for your understanding of one another.

For all men who read this book, my wish is that in the end you will share my conviction that we need not be condemned to a life of being misunderstood but that we can reach toward all God desires us to be.

One

The Suffering Man

The Insecure Man

Did you ever hear the story about the lawyer who asked one of his fellow attorneys to represent him in a court case? He had worked out his defense, and all his friend had to do was read it at the trial. In the margin at the fourth point he had scribbled, "Raise your voice and pound on the stand when you read this. It's the weakest argument."

Some men do pound their fists on the table to emphasize their points. But mostly they save themselves this effort and instead pound on their accomplishments. In Tucholsky's poem at the beginning of this book, the typical man pounds on his business achievements, on his civic position, on the fact that he has more than done his duty to his wife. Yes, he even bought her a hat. But all these arguments are just as weak as the fourth point of the lawyer's defense. That's why a man has to pound his fist on the table.

I don't know whether anyone has made a study of all the monuments in the world. Most of those that I have seen depict men. It is mostly men who have been the pioneers, the inventors, the artists, the military heroes, explorers and conquerors. This is a man's role in the theater of the world. This is why he pounds his fist, for in a way he has to be his own monument.

But deep inside, he is really tired of always having to structure, to invent, to conquer. He would rather possess. He would rather have something that stands still, a piece of land that no one will take from him. That is what he would like to have in his marriage too. He is tired of disputing every inch of ground which he has won. He would even like to have God as his partner here because wasn't it through him that he was "joined together" with his wife?

Instead, the roles are reversed. He, the man, the proud conqueror, the monumental figure, has to admit when it comes down to the bare facts that he is dependent upon the woman. He has been on the receiving end since the beginning of his life—and it is the woman who is the giver.

All over the world it is the same story. The one who is on the receiving end always feels inferior, put down in face of the one who gives. The history of world missions shows how developed and not-yet-developed countries are burdened by this. The inferiority complex of those on the receiving end is the main problem in any kind of aid.

This is also true of the help the man receives from the woman in his childhood as well as in his marriage. A child gets security from his mother. She is there for her child and dedicates herself to him. A man would like to have this same security when he is grown. Could it be that *Playboy* magazines and posters of women with naked round breasts, which many men find attractive, are geared to an unconscious and unsatisfied thirst in their lives as infants? Many men find their desire unmanly and even unworthy and can't understand why it has such power over them.

But not only as a child does a man receive more than he gives. His love life is that way too. He would like to think of himself as the Great Lover and as the one who gives. Biologically speaking it looks that way, for he gives his wife seminal fluid. But in reality—in the depths of his being—he feels he is the one who is taking something, the one who is receiving. His wife gives him her body, and he experiences the height of pleasure, climax and then deep relaxation.

Even our language betrays this. A young man thinks he can go out and "get" a girlfriend. He wants to go "steady" with her. A mature man, it is true, "takes" a wife, but he also knows that it is she who "gives herself."

It is this split between our dreams and our real role which gives us men a feeling of uncertainty. That in turn keeps us from living at peace with ourselves. Just as we tend to overlook our wives and their needs, so we pass by ourselves. A woman seeks a man who needs her, who longs for her gifts, who even enjoys being on the receiving end. The one who puts himself in the role of the Great Giver and who, because he is a man, thinks that he is all-sufficient, is only manifesting to the world, with every step he takes, his own inadequacy.

The Inadequate Man

It's all very good, all that a man has to brag about—how hard he works, how he provides for his family, how well he can fix things, yes, even all the committees and organizations he gives his time and money to. But deep down it is never quite enough. His wife affirms him and stands loyally behind him. She even admires him, and yet he feels inadequate. For whatever else she says or does,just by her very being, she is always reminding him of his inadequacy as a man. This is what bothers him and what she can't comprehend.

If he can meet her in a condescending, fatherly manner, calling her his "baby" or his "dear child," then he feels safe. And as a maid, as the one who does his washing and sews on his buttons, she does not make him feel insecure. She also fits into his pattern if she is the source of his pleasure—the one who satisfies his sexual wishes. He can even handle thinking of her as a marriage "object" which he "possesses" like a piece of furniture he has bought. But as a real woman, as a person, she simply doesn't fit into his thinking. She gets in his way, lies diagonally across his path, and he doesn't know what to do with her. "He may also have a wife," as Tucholsky says, "but this he does not know."

"A little tenderness would heal her inner core." But a man doesn't quite believe it. He knows from experience that a huge dose of tenderness is not enough. Yes, when he thinks that he has given her all the tenderness that he can give and his store is depleted, that's just when she's looking for more. At the least expected moment, when he's really feeling good about himself, that's just when she starts to cry—and for no reason at all. It's as if something deep within her is always crying for comfort, and it dawns on him that he will never be able to satisfy completely her deepest longings.

A young doctor came with his wife to talk about their marriage. "We've been married for a year now. I have tried every way that I know to satisfy my wife. But," he sighed, "no matter what I do, I always feel I am inadequate."

The longing of lovers—when they are truly lovers and not just partners joined for the purpose of reaching certain goals—goes far beyond satisfying certain sexual desires, establishing a happy family or even reaching certain comfortable standards of life. It encompasses the basic longings. It goes beyond our own person, our own ego. As the poet Manfred Hausmann has put it: "It's a question of an experiment made magic, . . . trying to reach that which is beyond reality. This is an experiment doomed to failure and yet it's always attempted again and again with the courage and persistence of despair."

The desire to grow beyond ourselves as individuals, seen in the union of man and woman, is placed in our hearts by God himself. In the second chapter of Genesis we read that God made woman out of one of the ribs of the first man. Adam was jubilant when he recognized Eve and said, "This at last is bone of my bones and flesh of my flesh." But she is part of him as a woman and not as a second man, not as a buddy, a comrade or even as a friend. The woman is a part of the man, and yet she has her own identity. She is related to him, and yet she is completely different. She is his closest confidant, and yet she is a stranger to him. And the great longing of man and woman which God has placed in them goes in the direction of completing one another.

A wife suffers greatly when her husband seems to find his greatest satisfaction in goals that are so much less than hers. A husband suffers greatly because he feels inadequate to reach the total oneness which is the great yearning of his wife. And so he resigns, he gives up the struggle and takes refuge among other men—in his factory, on the football field, at the office, maybe even in the army. As Schiller says, "On the battlefield, a man is still worth something. There his heart is still weighed."

When his heart is put on the scale by the woman, it is always found too light. And that is why he feels like a schoolboy with a note on his report card reading, "Unsatisfactory."

The whole world acclaims his victories and his superiority. But when he has to face his wife, the man feels inferior.

The Inferior Man

Even if men might call me crazy or declare war on me, I maintain that every man, if he's really honest, feels inferior to a woman deep down in his heart.

In Africa they tell the story about the chief who called all his men to come to his palaver hut in the center of the village. It was his fear, he said to them, that there were no longer any real men in his village. He had the impression that his men were being ruled too much by their wives. To find out if this were true, he asked all the men who felt that their wives bossed them around to leave the hut through the door on the right. Those who felt that they were in charge at home should leave through the door on the left. Lo and behold, all the chief's men left through the door on the right—except one.

So the chief called his men together again and gave a speech of praise to the lone wolf. "At least we have one *real* man in our village," he said. "Could you please share with us your secret?"

The man looked rather sheepish and at last, he said, "Chief, when I left home this morning, my wife said to me: 'Husband, never follow the crowd!' "

Where does this feeling of being subject to the woman, of being inferior to her, come from? I think it goes together with the fact that a woman has a gift which the man may have too, but in a much lesser degree. I'm talking about the gift of intuition. She seems to know things from the inside, intuitively, without thinking or mulling it over a long time. It's her heart which determines her decisions. While a man says, "This is what I think," she is apt to say, "This is what I feel." She is superior because she does not need to think things over. Of course, this is relative. There are men who are gifted with intuition just as there are women who have little of it. I have observed too that often the more emancipated a woman is, the poorer she may become in this gift. But on the whole, I think we are safe in saying that intuition is more a gift of women than of men.

When we have an important decision to make in our marriage, I take a piece of paper and draw a line in the middle from top to bottom. Then on the right side I write down all the reasons for the decision and on the left side, all the reasons against it. After hours and sometimes days of turning it over in my mind, I still don't know what we should do. Then one day my wife comes into my study with that certain shining look in her eyes and she says, "You know what we should do? We should accept that invitation," or, "How about doing it this way?" In the almost thirty years of our marriage I have never yet found her to be fundamentally wrong.

It is experiences like this which give a man the feeling of inferiority. In spite of long thought about a problem, he does not reach the quick conclusion which his wife does seemingly without thinking. He cannot trust his intellect in the same way that his wife can trust her feelings. Because he doesn't trust his own feelings, he is suspicious of the intellect of his wife. And this distrust makes him even more unsure of himself.

Even on a physical level a man feels he cannot compete. A man often gets less attention paid to his appearance than a woman. When you meet a couple on the street or look at a wedding picture in the window of a photography studio, a woman always looks first at the other woman. And the man? Naturally, he looks first at the woman. There is certainly something true in the expression "the fair sex."

Maybe this feeling of inferiority can also be explained by what he experiences sexually and how he experiences it. At least at the beginning of a marriage, a husband usually reaches a climax and achieves sexual pleasure much easier and more quickly than his wife. And just this taking, "free of charge," gives us men the feeling of being cheap. We must admit too that it's possible for us to gain sexual satisfaction without inwardly participating, without personal dedication and even without the investment of our feelings. At the same time we turn physically to a woman, we can still remain turned inwardly toward ourselves.

Zoologists tell us that in the animal world, sexual pleasure is only recognizable in the male of the species. In contrast to his wife, a man feels he is at a lower level, yes, even animallike, and that in turn makes him feel inferior. This feeling can make us unhappy although we are simultaneously experiencing sexual pleasure. We suspect too that while we can separate sexual pleasure and love, this is foreign to the deepest feeling of a woman. While the man can satisfy his sexual desire in intercourse without love, for the woman this is usually impossible.

On the other hand, in spite of the great love in his heart, a man may be incapable of uniting physically with his wife. However, it is always possible for a woman to unite with her husband physically even when she feels no love. We husbands have to reach that stage in love where the wife who loves has been from the beginning. She is miles ahead of us, and we come limping behind her. I am convinced that this difference is the main reason why a man feels inferior to a woman.

The Fearful Man

Every man has had a negative experience with a woman at one time in his life. That was before his birth when he was the prisoner of a woman. For nine months before *she* gave birth to him he was contained within her body. Passive and defenseless he was born and delivered up into the hands of the woman who gave him birth.

Perhaps an unborn child doesn't feel like he's imprisoned. And yet unconsciously the man, more it seems than a woman, carries this memory within himself so much that it is often reflected in his dreams. I think many men live in constant, if subtle, fear that they might end up being such prisoners again. Of course a healthy relationship with a mother who does not smother but is willing to let go can offset this fear. Otherwise it may become the root of many conflicts later in marriage.

A husband comes home from work and his wife holds up a list of things that need to be done. The faucet is dripping here and a screw is loose there. The kitchen drain is stopped up and the basement fuse is burned out. He gets the feeling that his wife would like to take complete possession of him and boss him around. Fear swells up in his heart, the fear that he's in danger of losing his freedom. So he reacts negatively, even with hostility.

His wife is completely baffled by this reaction. She has no idea that her harmless request has awakened his old fear—the original fear of men toward women, the anxiety that someone is going to take possession of him, overcome him and even do violence to him. She almost becomes to him an impersonal force vying for control of his life.

A German theologian and psychoanalyst, Rudolf Affemann, says the same thing. "The woman is more of a unity (body and soul) than the man; therefore, it is her desire not only to love him completely, but also to possess him for herself alone. This desire makes a man feel very uncomfortable. He already has the deep-rooted fear within him (though he might not admit it) that the woman will rob him of his independence. Perhaps this is the fear which is an echo of his unconscious consciousness that she already possessed him completely at one time, namely in those months before birth."

A deep-rooted fear that he doesn't want to admit, an unconscious consciousness—these paradoxical expressions show how he is torn apart. They expose the inner conflicts under which the man suffers and which, because he can not solve the problem, frustrate him.

But before I say more about the man who feels frustrated, I would like to consider the man who suffers because he feels superfluous, a feeling that is only strengthened by his frustration.

The Superfluous Man

Strangely enough, a man gets the feeling that he is superfluous at the moment in which a new dimension is added to his manhood, namely, when he becomes a father.

The first major crisis in marriage often happens at the birth of the first child. It is the child who becomes the center of the mother's life. So the father can't help but feel superfluous, unnecessary and even like a pain in the neck.

When the first joy of his wife's announcement that she is going to have a child has faded away, then he realizes suddenly that he is only a helpless spectator, standing by during the whole process. All during his wife's pregnancy he can never quite get rid of this feeling. No matter how much he loves his wife and cares for her welfare and even shares her hopes and joyful expectancy, he still is unable to carry that unborn child.

Then comes the hour of birth. He spends it perhaps anxiously in the waiting room, left alone, sent out of the delivery room. A man never feels more superfluous, more cowardly, more castrated. It is another man or woman who is there to receive his child into the world. A nurse is taking care of his wife. He has no role to play. He is often not even allowed to be a spectator in this theater of life.

This waiting-room experience is so painful for him because it underlines a fact that he can't deny: he can never give birth to a child. After he has begotten the child, he is no longer needed. He has fulfilled his biological function. Now they can get along without him.

Just as he cannot give birth to his child, neither can he give his child its first nourishment. He has to stand on the sidelines and watch while his wife breast-feeds the baby. Again he feels superfluous.

He also feels superfluous when he faces his teen-ager. As his children go through puberty, they need him in a difficult double role. On the one hand they need him as their ideal, their mentor, the one with whom they can identify, on whom they lean and toward whom they struggle. But on the other hand he is their opposite, almost an adversary against whom they have to revolt, from whom they have to separate to find their own way of life, to become individuals. (The word *individual* means that which cannot be divided.)

It is a very difficult double role. The father must be like the strong pole or stake to which a young tree is bound when it is planted. The purpose of the stake is to keep the little tree growing in the right direction, so it will not be swayed to one side or grow crooked. The stake also protects the little tree from strong winds which otherwise might break it off. But the time comes when being tied to the stake is like being bound by chains. The cords rub deep into the tender bark of the tree and actually hinder its growth. The cords must be cut. The tree has to grow alone without the father stake. When that happens, the stake stands beside it feeling unneeded and superfluous.

This process is natural and necessary if the young tree is to grow properly. And when a father sees that his teen-agers can get along without him, he suffers. This suffering is compounded because the protest of the young tree is misunderstood. It is not directed against the stake, the father pole. Rather it is a protest against the cords being tied too tightly or for too long.

The father's role is made even more difficult today because the authority of fathers is ridiculed and the purpose of the stake is put down. How often do we see in our society that the father stake breaks down, so that the children can neither wind around it nor climb up on it? Neither can they do battle with it so they can grow stronger. The father is not respected. He is even despised. Because he is not feared and respected, he doesn't dare to give any advice. He sinks down into meaninglessness.

Thus the father feels almost mortally wounded as a man. This time of breaking away seems to cause him greater suffering than his wife. Even in this situation she is more able to exercise her motherly functions of feeding and clothing and caring for the physical needs of her children than he as a man is able to exercise his fatherly functions. She who has a greater bond with the physical has other reserves from which to nourish her self-esteem.

It is no wonder then that the man who feels superfluous also feels frustrated.

The Frustrated Man

The word *frustrated* comes from the Latin word *frustra* which means "in vain." In other words, one who is frustrated is one who feels that all he does is in vain. In spite of putting his whole strength into a project, he does not reach his goal, and he feels that everything he begins fails. A sense of inner helplessness overcomes him when he looks at the challenges which face him.

This feeling of frustration can be strongest sexually. Nothing hits him harder, is more crushing or painful to his inner feelings, than feeling himself a failure in the sexual realm.

He feels like a bull when his sexual urge is so strong that he can barely keep it restrained. Instead of being happy about this "strength," he rather feels ashamed. It makes him impatient, desirous, unreasonable, even brutal. The fact that sexual longing can overcome him without any deep feeling or inner participation, without tenderness and love and the atmosphere that goes with it, makes him feel base and animallike.

It is even more frustrating for a man if he has an experience of impotence—the other end of the scale—so that instead of feeling like a bull, he feels like a dishrag. Probably nothing in a man's life is more humiliating or shaming for him, nothing makes him feel less like a man, than when, in spite of his great desire and deep-felt longing, he cannot fulfill the expectations which he and his wife have in their sexual union.

I am now coming to a very difficult subject, but I don't dare jump over it or ignore it if I want to put a man's sufferings into words and help his wife to understand him. We're talking about the peculiar and complicated relationship which a man has with his penis.

Again I will take refuge in the words of a poet. It is the gift as well as the task of the poet to put that which is almost inexpressible in human life into words. Johann Wolfgang Goethe wrote a long narrative poem entitled *Das Tagebuch (The Journal)* in 1810. But Goethe kept the manuscript a secret so that it was only published after his death.

The Journal tells the story of a married man who is on his way home after a long journey. It was his habit to write down the events of the day in his journal every evening "in order to give joy to his beloved." Unexpectedly, on the last day of his journey, one of the wagon wheels of his stagecoach breaks down and he is forced to stay overnight in a little village inn. While he is seated at the table in his room, writing in his journal, the maid, a young woman of great beauty, enters and serves him his evening meal. As he watches her skillfully setting the table and serving him, he finds himself suddenly overtaken by sexual longing. So he invites her to come back to his room when her work is finished. The girl, who has never slept with a man and who tells him that she is shy and reserved and has a very modest reputation in the village, decides, nonetheless, to return at midnight.

As he waits for her to come back, he finds to his consternation that his longing dies down. Whether it is because he enjoyed the anticipation more than the prospect of the event itself, whether unconsciously he is thinking of his wife and his faithfulness to her, or whether it is the purity of the girl which arouses guilt in him, when she does slip into his room at midnight and he feels her expectations as a duty, he cannot unite with her. He finds himself impotent.

In the meantime, the girl falls asleep in his arms, seemingly completely happy. "For her, it seems all she wanted was a sweet word, a kiss. That's all her heart was after." He lies awake beside her, angry at himself and putting himself down.

Then suddenly, as he remembers the first time he saw his wife and memories of his wedding and honeymoon fill his thoughts, he finds that he is no longer impotent. Now he would be able to have intercourse with the girl, but he deliberately chooses not to. They separate the next morning. He gets in the stagecoach, which has been repaired, and "comforted in heart," he lets himself be carried to the one he loves the most, his wife.

The poem ends with the lines:

 There are two levers in the world
which keep the earth's gears going:
 The lever of duty is the one,
but how much greater the lever of love.

In the course of the poem Goethe did something very bold. He gave the masculine genital organ a poetic name, since there was no other word that pleased him. He used the Latin word *Iste* which really means "This" in the sense of a pronoun. It enabled him as the one speaking to have a certain distance from "Iste," so he could talk with "This" in the familiar "Thou" form in German.

Goethe was unique in the use of this word, thus enabling him to express in words the strange and peculiar relationship of a man to his penis. In contrast to the woman who feels at one with her sexual organs—they are a part of her—the man stands opposite his, as if it were another person, a stranger. The woman *is* her organ. The man *has* his.

In Goethe's poem the word *Iste* is presented sometimes as the master and sometimes as the servant. But regardless in which role Iste appears, whether as master or servant, the man can't depend completely on either one. In either role Iste is self-willed. Iste is his own man and is not subservient to the will of his owner. And there we have the problem.

As master, Iste masters the man, and usually at the most embarrassing moments. Then in the right moment Iste can leave the man in the lurch. As love's servant, it is true, Iste does serve him. But often when the servant is needed, it may be that he refuses to obey.

And just that is the great suffering of the man. It is "not being able to count on" Iste. The man who likes so much to plan ahead, to figure out, to calculate, who likes to conquer and to have at his disposal, who gets his security in the feeling of certainty that he can manage everything: here he must remain dependent upon a self-willed servant and a moody master.

I don't know if a woman can ever completely understand this frustration. She cannot be left in the lurch by her sexual organ in the same way that the man can. Maybe she has no feeling (this is her great suffering), but still the sexual union can take place. Her inner readiness and the natural lubrication of the vagina which results from this readiness are not in the same measure a prerequisite of intercourse as is a man's erection. That's why we don't speak of impotence (inability to perform) when we talk of the woman, but of frigidity (inability to feel).

In the strict sense of the word, a man can be impotent—and that is what is so uncanny—in spite of deep feelings. Yes, it can even happen just because of his great longing.

"A woman will never quite understand him—ever." If Tucholsky is right when he says this, then a man is defenseless when he has to face deep injury and hurt.

The Vulnerable Man

Dr. Paul Popenoe, one of America's pioneer marriage counselors, often said, "Men are hard, but brittle. Women are soft, but tough." Perhaps this is true physically as well as emotionally.

When we lived in a very difficult tropical climate, I was ill more often than my wife. Especially during that time of life when she was either an expectant or nursing mother, she seemed to have unlimited powers of resistance to illness, which I, just then, in my feeling of masculine superfluity, did not have. It seemed too that when a missionary couple had to go home because of health reasons, it was mostly because of the husband.

Dr. Popenoe's statement would certainly be true in the emotional realm. I believe that a man can be more easily hurt inwardly and mortally wounded in his heart than can a woman. Suicide rates for men are higher than for women. A woman seems to have greater powers of resistance too in coping with grief. After all I have said in this book, I have no doubt, and perhaps you will agree that the ego of a man is more fragile than that of a woman.

But how can we adequately explain a man's deep vulnerability? Shouldn't he be man enough, have the courage simply to be the one he really is? Why does he have such a hard time accepting himself as one who feels insecure and inadequate, helpless and fearful, unnecessary and frustrated? It is manly to face reality fearlessly and courageously, to call things by their name.

The problem is this: reality doesn't mesh with the image the world has of "The Man." The world's picture is a dream image, a cliché which can't stand up to reality. We all like clichés. Films with their heroes and heroines, villains, poor young girls, chauffeurs, detectives—they usually bring their producers money. The films which get away from these standard roles find fewer viewers. And yet there are some courageous producers who are not afraid to create such films. We need to become the courageous directors of our own lives.

A man is so vulnerable because he has to play a role which he is not able to play. Imagine that a well-known tenor who sings in a regional opera has to change his role and sing bass because his colleague has suddenly become ill. As a tenor he is used to getting hearty applause. And he feels sure of himself as a tenor because he has trained for this role and has spent long hours rehearsing it. He has mastered it. But now he stands on the stage and is supposed to sing bass. He's uncertain of himself and there's no applause,just polite coughing and murmuring.

His pride is deeply wounded, and he swears he will never again take a role which doesn't fit him, even if the director should get down on his knees and beg.

The role which we men cannot play comfortably is that of being the strong sex. We strain and strain at it and still our performance is not very credible. We may have illusions about ourselves in our early years, but later in our marriages we find that we cannot earn much applause for our efforts. The real woman sees through such pretensions and would like to ask her husband to be just a kind human being and not some sort of superman. Not as Tucholsky says in his poem, to be "a man—and that's enough," but to be a person who knows his weaknesses, can stand up to them and is willing to share them with his wife.

Are we afraid to do this? Do we think that our wives would no longer love us if they could see us as we really are? What kind of love is that which is not centered on the real you but rather on a dream image which the partner thinks you are? Dr. Affemann has said it well when he writes, "To love is a continuing process of facing disillusionment and disappointment in the other one. This task has to be faced anew every day. Only in this way will the relationship of love be close to reality. True happiness is not built on false images, but on truth." Most women I know would much rather face this task than put up with a man who pretends to be satisfied with himself while playing a false role.

Love sees the other one as he is and accepts him that way. Love means too that I can let myself be seen by my partner as I am and be accepted that way. Because of our vanity this may seem impossible, but it would be a way of healing the vulnerability of the man if he would deliver himself up just the way he is to the love of his wife.

But what does he do? He defends himself because he's afraid of being hurt. Because he feels so threatened, the suffering man now becomes the man who reacts and his last resort is adultery, unfaithfulness.

Two

The Man Reacts

When one who is weak defends himself, he usually does it by pretending to be strong. The peacock, a delicate and vulnerable bird, displays its tail feathers to scare away opponents. The strength a man pretends to have is nothing more than the self-protective action of one who is unsure of himself and who is frightened. It's his way of defending himself when he is threatened.

There are two kinds of defense: a counterattack or a retreat into an impervious fortress. Men use both kinds. Even in the second defense they succeed masterfully in maintaining their manly image, even when they flee.

The Almighty Patriarch

A patriarch defends himself through counterattack.

I have already mentioned the deep-rooted fear which a man has, but which he doesn't readily admit, that his wife could in some way rob him of his freedom. Because he is afraid of being possessed, he declares his wife to be his own private possession with him alone controlling the rights over her. He tries to reduce her to a thing so he is not threatened.

At the same time, this meets his urge to possess that which he has already conquered. He does not want to fight for ground that he has already won, to see his territory always put in question. Some even quote a Bible passage as the pious justification of a man's desire to possess once and for all that which he has won: "What therefore God has joined together, let not man put asunder" (Mt 19:6).

My wife and I were fortunate to live for several years in a region in Africa where we were not only the first Christians but also the first whites. There we could experience African society in its natural state. It helped me to understand in a new way many of my own unconscious but basic ideas.

In Africa the relationship of a man to his wife was often similar to that of a gardener to his garden. A garden's value depends on the seed the gardener sows in it and the fruit that grows out of it. If the garden bears no fruit, then there is no reason the gardener should not get rid of it and buy a new one. Let us carry this idea into marriage. If a wife has no children, then her husband can divorce her or take a second wife.

Divorce, polygamy and the choice of a partner therefore are the exclusive privilege of the man. Yes, he may even commit adultery (sowing his seed in foreign gardens), and he wouldn't hurt his own garden by doing that. On the other hand, his own garden would become guilty if it allowed foreign seed to be sown in it. This pattern of thinking has created the double moral code which makes women more guilty than men if they commit sexual sins.

The patriarch is also the ruling father. That is why he has to be the superior one, the strong one—at least the stronger one. This often takes grotesque forms. In one of her books, Christa Meves, a well-known German psychologist and a Christian, calls these bogus patriarchs "ones who play God," "slave holders," "women keepers," people who reduce women to the status of temple prostitutes. Through this wrong picture of women, this distorted image, one can better understand the women's liberation movement.

Who would dream that a man does all this because he is afraid, because he has his back against the wall? It is just a defense mechanism, a camouflage, a mask behind which a man hides his weaknesses and uncertainty. Does a patriarch pretend to be the almighty one, the omnipotent one, to cover up his insufficiency, his impotence, in the broad as well as the narrow sense of the word?

Sad to say, this defensive action against an imaginary enemy takes place in many Christian marriages because a Bible verse is not quoted in its entirety and is taken out of context. "Wives, be subject to your husbands" (Eph 5:22). I am always a little suspicious when I see this is one of the few Bible verses that most men know by heart. Out of it they draw the conclusion that the subjection of the wife is one of the main characteristics of a Christian marriage. I will come back to this later. At this point suffice it to say that this interpretation is wrong.

The man who has to use a Bible verse to secure his advantage and as a camouflage must be very unsure of himself! He is living in permanent anxiety that someone is going to tear the mask away from his face. But he has more than one weapon at his disposal: he can also keep his distance and not allow anyone to get close to him.

The Unapproachable Chief

In Africa we lived in the territory of six-foot six-inch Chief Rey Bouba. He rarely left his palace. Most of his subjects had never seen him. It was difficult to get past all his guards and have an audience with him. And those who did could only approach him with bowed heads and their eyes on the ground.

When we visited him, we had to cross an open courtyard covered with white gravel, so that we were blinded by the bright sunlight. In the semidarkness of his throne room he was encased in white cloths which covered both his body and his head. All we could see was the slit for his eyes.

A man enjoys being inaccessible, untouchable.

Once Chief Rey Bouba was sick and thought he was going to die. He sent for me and asked me to give him a penicillin shot. I can still see him whimpering in front of me, as with great delight I punctured the soap bubble of his unapproachableness.

To be unapproachable is just another defensive weapon of the Chief. It enables him to escape in honor when he feels inadequate.

I found this unapproachableness in Africa especially among fathers in relation to their daughters. This is true elsewhere as well. Just read Johanna's letter to her father in chapter ten of my book *Living with Unfulfilled Desires.* Here was a girl completely cut off from a father she longed to express love to. But he could not receive it or express any to her. And often a woman finds the same pattern of unapproachability in her husband who has simply copied the example he has seen in his own father.

The Chief is not ready to talk. That is the complaint of countless wives. First they get married so they won't be alone, and then they want to get divorced for the very same reason. As Louis Evely, a French priest, has said, "Some women become widows on their wedding day."

Husbands will complain to me, "My wife always wants to talk things over." But we receive letters from wives, unhappy in their marriages, that often read like this: "I've been married for eight years. I'm really not unhappy as a wife and homemaker, and yet I'm in deep trouble. I often have a great desire just to talk to my husband, to experience things with him. But I sometimes think I won't even be able to talk to myself, I'm so out of practice. My husband does take me along at times to lectures and conferences, and we hear a lot of good thoughts. But we don't discuss them afterward and digest them at home, or even put them into practice. He can talk to others and carry on deep conversations. Sometimes that makes me mad, but I don't dare vent my wrath for fear that he will explode. That's when the tears start coming, and then he turns his resentments into complete silence."

Thus the unapproachable Chief often becomes the silent Buddha.

The Silent Buddha

The reason men don't talk is the same reason they retreat into a shell where they can't be touched: they feel threatened, and to ward off attack they retreat into a fortress of silence, so that the blows miss their goal.

The more a wife tries to aggravate her husband—often the only way to get a reaction out of him at all—the more he withdraws and hovers like a silent Buddha above everything.

He already feels nagged and criticized by her simple request for time to have a talk. He doesn't think that his weak ego can take it.

Counselors of all kinds confirm the fact that more women than men come to them seeking help. From my point of view, one explanation is that because a man's ego is weak, he is afraid his self-image will be destroyed if he reveals that he needs help and must seek counsel. His manly desire to do everything himself would be spoiled if he has to go to someone looking for help.

Have you heard of the man who came home radiant after visiting his psychiatrist despite having postponed the visit a long time? He had wanted to get treatment for his inferiority complex. The doctor had healed him on the spot, he reported to his wife.

"How did he do that?" she asked.

"He simply told me that I don't have an inferiority complex. I *am* inferior."

If a man feels confirmed in his own diagnosis, then that's already as good as therapy for him. When he knows why he's sick, he already feels better. But that's not enough for his wife. She wants the therapy as well as the diagnosis. She would like to have her tears wiped away when she cries.

A man's retreat into silence also goes along with what I have already mentioned about his lack of intuition compared to his wife. To cover up the sense of helplessness, yes, even of inferiority, which he feels when he has to make a decision, he becomes silent. This reaction, or lack of action, can make his wife angry. It is true she doesn't want to be ruled by her husband, but she would like him to take the lead. She wants to be guided, but how can he do this if he won't talk? He is afraid of making a wrong decision which would expose his helplessness. To accept justified criticism, to admit his mistakes, this is more than his weak ego can take. If he doesn't say anything, then at least he can't say anything wrong.

The Frozen Iceberg

Naturally a man's uncertainty in making decisions is intertwined with his uncertainty in the realm of feelings. If he can't reach a conclusion with his great intellect and logic, then he certainly can't rely on his feelings either—at least not in the same measure as women who have only to dip into their reservoirs of intuition. He simply has no confidence in his feelings because he usually lacks a certainty of instinct.

When he sees that he can't help his wife, that he can't give her what she needs, he retreats. He simply says that a true man does not rely on his feelings, as if not having feelings would be a virtue. Feelings are unmanly, he would say, effeminate, not part of being a real man.

It's not clear whether this role of the unfeeling man is exaggerated and put on, or whether the uncovering of his poverty of feeling simply adds to it. They probably both work together, augmenting each other.

We must differentiate between the inability to have feelings and the inability to show feelings. Just as I am convinced that there is no really frigid woman, so I am convinced that there is no really unfeeling man. If a woman is cold, it's probably because she's had to put her feelings in the deepfreeze to keep from hurting so much. And the same is no doubt true for the man.

That's why I don't speak about the man who has no feelings but about the unfeeling man. He can't feel his feelings anymore. Because he doesn't want them to show, he's locked them up in the basement. He's out of touch with his feelings. They are beyond his reach. Even if he wanted to, he couldn't put his hands on them.

The more a man tries to control his feelings, the more they control him. But on the outside we see the cold man who sleeps soundly, snoring away, while his wife cries softly beside him, longing for tenderness. He can't be tender because he thinks a real man is not supposed to be tender. And so he draws the conclusion that Christian Morgenstern, a German poet, expresses: "You can't be something which you're not supposed to be."

Maybe when he showed his real feelings once, he was deeply

wounded. He may have heard in his childhood, "A boy doesn't cry." And so he learned, "When I show feelings, then I will be wounded. Therefore, I will show no feelings." But this unfeeling iceberg is not the real man. It's just the way he reacts. His coldness is his defense mechanism—his safe shelter into which he can withdraw and achieve a certain invulnerability.

The Man's Man

Hardly realizing it, in my description of how a man reacts to his inner pain and suffering, I have moved from his forms of defense to how he beats his retreat.

Today it is the woman who has come forth to counterattack. She no longer lets herself be possessed. She puts her right to possess along with that of her husband. But this leaves only one escape route for the man.

Dr. Rudolf Affemann describes this phenomenon thus: "When the wife confronts her husband with her total rights of possession, then he can only flee to the rear. Either he stays at home and tries to flee inwardly (his professional interests, his study-den, his newspaper, television, hobbies) or he chooses to flee in activities outside his home."

To this flight outside his home belong the men's club, the soccer, baseball and football games, yes, even the sauna. He escapes back to his own sex. Here he feels like someone. He feels adequate as a man. He is among his own. He is no longer overdemanded, threatened by that which is strange to him. Here he can leave all his fears and anxieties behind. Here he feels understood.

In reality this is a sign that he has gotten stuck in the homoerotical stage of development (see our book *My Beautiful Feeling,* pp. 31-33) in which the ego is not yet strong enough to stand up under the complete differences of the opposite sex. It is more comfortable with the known aspects of same-sex friends. Marriage thrives on polarity, and it is only out of these opposite magnetic poles that it can keep on growing until the parting of death. If a man enters matrimony without being mature enough to stand up under this tension, then he is constantly tempted to fall back into the homoerotical phase, to flee to the sameness of his own sex, so that he may even look for a male sex partner. There's no doubt in my mind that the growing rate of homosexuality in our times has one of its decisive roots in this fact.

Men with fragile egos are too weak to stand up against the strangeness of what is different, what is foreign to their thinking, even uncanny. They do not go forth to learn to face fear, but they retreat to avoid fear. They do not dare to love. They even try to fool themselves and others that being together with other men all the time is very masculine. They can even appear to onlookers as the"strong ones" by using a raw form of voice and speech as they tell certain kinds of jokes among themselves, especially in the locker room and men's sauna. Here, surrounded by so much naked and anonymous manliness, a man feels secure and warm. He doesn't even realize it himself and certainly never would admit it, but this escape is in reality an expression of his weakness. It's a warding off of fear, fleeing to a place where there are no tensions.

As I write this, I think again of those words of Goethe's Faust as he took his walk on Easter Sunday.

Old winter, his strength almost gone,
Withdraws into the rugged hills
And from them, fleeing, sends back weak
Sleet showers that speckle the green plain.
(Randall Jarrell, trans. [New York: Farrar, Straus & Giroux, 1976], p. 47.)

Helplessly, out of his helplessness, he sends showers of cold feelings over the greening meadows of feminine feelings. May this little literary association make the bridge now to the sexual sphere.

The Tired Man

There are two shields of defense against the frustration men suffer when they know they can't rely on their sexual strength— tiredness and unfaithfulness.

"You are always so tired," is the reproach so often heard from wives.

"Do you feel like it tonight, or should I take a sleeping pill?" the wife asks her husband in the American comedy *Mary, Mary* by Jean Kerr. It was meant to be funny, but the mingled response of the theater audience showed how true it was.

I mentioned earlier that a man is torn between two extremes—he feels either like a bull or a dishrag. He feels like the first when he makes use of his sexual powers without participating emotionally. He feels like a dishrag when despite the longing of his heart he is unable to have an erection and thus be physically united with his wife. In both cases he loses his self-respect and self-esteem.

As his shield of defense, he pleads tiredness. It's not difficult here to find good and plausible reasons for being tired: his job, his overdemanding profession, his countless other duties in the community, his failing health.

It's not difficult to understand his fleeing into tiredness. There is hardly anything else that a man is more afraid of than impotence. There is nothing which shames him more. Nothing makes him feel less like a man—even the guilt of infidelity. That's why if he is not completely sure of himself, he'd rather not even try. He prefers to say he is tired than risk the agony of failure.

He feels like a failure too if he is unable to bring his wife to complete sexual fulfillment. To do this he knows he must be one with her in his heart and have the emotional strength to express deep tenderness. But he fears failure. So to keep from getting hurt, he renounces their physical union and pleads tiredness— even though he is full of desire.

This does not mean that he is necessarily pretending to be emotionally tired or even using it as a cheap excuse. Emotional tiredness is not the same as emotional laziness. We must simply keep in mind that a man has a harder time finding his feelings. It takes longer for him to bring them out of his basement. Feelings cost him more strength. It takes him more time to get started, especially when he comes home at night after a hard day's work which he has only survived by repressing all his feelings. After keeping them harnessed all day, he simply doesn't have the energy to automatically release them again. He really is tired—both physically and emotionally.

Keeping in mind the biological fact that during sexual union the man is actually expending energy and giving of his substance, it is not surprising when after a day full of hard work he prefers to avoid further exertion. In addition, a French study has shown that the male sex hormone, testosterone, is at its lowest level in the bloodstream at 11:00 P.M. and at its highest level at 8:00 A.M. The effects of this would be most pronounced in a man who is a lark who likes to go to bed early and get up early. If his wife is an owl who has just the opposite rhythm, certain tensions between them come into focus.

Though more research is needed, it is possible too that a man not only has a daily rhythm but also a monthly rhythm or cycle—times in which he has more and times in which he has less sexual desire. If this is true, then a woman on the pill who is sexually more available than before can be overdemanding sexually on her husband. This can be a secondary cause for impotence.

Certainly a man who is tired does not feel very manly. But it would seem more honorable to be tired than to be a sexual failure.

By being "tired" he has chosen the smaller evil. He longs for affirmation as a man. He would find it hard to live without the certainty of his potency. If he does not find this affirmation with his own wife, then he will look for it from another. Instead of facing up to shame, he would rather run away into guilt.

The Unfaithful Man

Now I hesitate again.

When I began writing about the frustrated man, I was afraid I might offend some readers by describing an occurrence which might be shocking. On the other hand, I was afraid that I might lose other readers by trying elegantly to avoid the issue. Again the poet of love from Weimar, Goethe, comes to my rescue.

I would like to describe the unfaithfulness of the husband as his last resort—his last means of escape. Some of you may throw up your hands and say: Whoever describes adultery as a last resort—a way of escape—is defending it and is trying to arouse sympathy for the unfaithful husband instead of feeling for the wife he has run away from, has left behind. Other readers might say just the opposite: After you've made a laughingstock of us men, now you are starting to shake your finger in reproach.

This book was not written to make men look ridiculous—neither to condemn them nor to justify them. It was written in order to understand them. I wanted to help men who feel misunderstood and to help them understand themselves. It is also my hope that some of those wives who sigh in resignation or who are shocked by what I say will begin to understand. Changing begins when one understands. The diagnosis is the first step to healing.

To write about infidelity in marriage is to write about a fact. As far back as the Kinsey report in 1953, we could read that half of all American men who had reached the age of forty had had extramarital experiences. Three-fourths of all the men questioned in the Kinsey study admitted their wish for such experiences. I imagine that in the three decades since that study was made, these figures have risen even higher. When I was talking recently with a group of young people, one of the students said, "Out of one hundred men, at least one hundred fifteen of them are unfaithful." The truth probably lies somewhere between Kinsey's statistics and this rather contemptuous statement. Be that as it may, to write about the unfaithfulness of the husband as if it were abnormal would be pure hypocrisy.

I believe men tend to be unfaithful not because of weak character but because it is their last resort in the struggle to escape shame and pain. But now I ask, of the seventy-five per cent to one hundred fifteen per cent who may long for infidelity or even practice it openly without feeling guilty, do they do this only because they are afraid they might become impotent? If adultery is openly shown in so many magazines, books, films, television programs, plays and radio shows where it may either be glorified or made light of and where *faithfulness* is like a word from bygone days, then there must be a deeper reason.

Let's go back once more to Goethe's *The Journal.* You recall the man tells how he was forced to interrupt his homeward journey because of a broken wheel. He has found a place to stay overnight in a village inn. With love that is longing and full of desire, he thinks of his wife, who is waiting for him at home. At that moment a maid enters his room bringing him his evening meal:

She goes and she comes; I speak, she answers.
With every word she seems more desirable.
And how easily she slices the chicken for me,
Skillfully and more skillfully moving her hand and arm.
. . . It's all I can take, I'm lost, I'm crazy.
With a desirous look I take in her tall form.
She bends over to me; I put my arms around her.

At the beginning the man certainly didn't have anything like this in his mind. But as the Germans say, *Gelegenheit macht Diebe.* "An open door may tempt a saint." "Opportunity makes a thief," and it also makes love. The adventure comes closer, prickling, enticing. The man is no longer capable of thinking reasonably and so he grasps.

What has happened here? We won't be able to understand it unless we look at the beginning of the poem. The traveler has just experienced a disappointment. His carriage had to be repaired and his long-awaited homecoming delayed. He was sentenced to boredom, passivity. "What can I do to make the time go faster but to grumble and murmur?"

The entrance of the attractive young woman into his room, her evident willingness, lets him know with lightning speed: here I can make up for my disappointment through a successful experience. Here I can overcome my boring passivity with a thrilling, quickly passing activity. The break in faithfulness will make up for the break in the wagon wheel.

With penetrating clarity one of the roots of masculine infidelity is laid bare here. Adultery is the escape of the disappointed man. His disappointment in this case has nothing to do with his marriage. In his genial manner Goethe puts into words what psychoanalysis has affirmed in the meantime. Many men who pretend that their strong sexual desires push them to extramarital sexual activity actually are suffering without realizing it because their ambitions and hopes in other realms have been unfulfilled.

For those who are disappointed in their marriages, this is the route of escape, now more than ever. They do not see themselves as strong husbands, but as uncertain and incapable, as helpless and superfluous, frustrated and vulnerable. Because of all this suffering they feel completely misunderstood. So they try to overcome their disappointment by reacting: by being the almighty patriarch, the unapproachable chief, the silent Buddha or the frozen iceberg. And when being a man's man fails as well as their escape into tiredness, when none of these things help, then the last resort is adultery.

The other root of infidelity, which Goethe's *Journal* makes very visible, is the desire for *Geborgenheit,* that wonderful German word which means more than shelter, refuge and security all in one. *Geborgenheit* is the foundation on which marriage stands. It comes from the word *bergen* which means "to rescue," "to bring into a safe place." *Burg,* the German word for fortress, stronghold, castle, means therefore the secure place where you have nothing to fear. In a marriage which is alive, each marriage partner feels secure, has no fear, is at rest with the other because each is convinced that his or her spouse wants only the best for the other. Does a husband give his wife this *Geborgenheit?* Does a husband find this feeling of shelter when he is with his wife? Where it is lacking, it can be his fault. It can also be her fault, but mostly both partners are guilty in not providing it.

In *The Journal,* the husband cannot be with his wife, and so he does not have this longed-for feeling of shelter. This is the same situation a traveling salesman has to face, a convention visitor, a soldier, yes, even a patient convalescing in a health sanatorium.

The man who feels unsheltered will be tempted to commit infidelity. Meeting another partner, regardless in which form this may happen, will be a substitute for this shelter. It is his last hope for security. So he looks for the warm, sheltering arms of understanding sympathy and affirmation.

There is still a third motive for adultery. We don't find it in Goethe's *Journal* but in another verse he has written. I would like to quote again from the first part of *Faust* where Faust is taking a walk on Easter Sunday.

Out of the stuffiness of the garret,
Out of the squash of the narrow streets,
Out of the churches' reverend night—
One and all have been raised to light. . . .
Already I hear the hum of the village,

Here is the plain man's real heaven—
Great and small in a riot of fun;
Here I'm a man—and dare to be one.
(Louis Macneice, trans. [New York: Oxford, 1951], p. 36.)

Everything which should give him the feeling of being sheltered—the coziness of his home, the security of a place to work, yes, even his church—this person now feels, perceives, as a musty prison, as a place where he's strangled, pressed down. He can't quite breathe. Goethe was certainly not thinking of marriage when he wrote this verse, but don't we find similarity to marriage in this picture?

A marriage which from all appearances is standing on the firm ground of shelteredness might not give this feeling at all but rather just the opposite. It's more like a torturing cord which strangles the persons in it. The one who feels bound up cannot blossom, cannot grow and develop. Rather he feels hindered by the squeezing narrowness of his marriage. There is a special kind of freedom which husband and wife mutually give to each other because they belong unconditionally to each other and are consecrated to each other, which makes them wonderfully free. Dr. Theodore Bovet of Switzerland has often said, "Without freedom, there is no genuine love." If this freedom is denied one to the other, then in its place there is distrust, suspicion, and everything is carefully calculated instead. Then all the man can do is to try to break loose from the "musty rooms" and look outside, beyond the gates of marriage for an encounter where he can finally say, "Here I am a person—here I can dare to be myself!"

In his adventure of adultery the man is looking for some kind of festive splendor which has been lost in his monotonous, everyday marriage—an "Easter Sunday walk," a "resurrection" which will stir him emotionally, intellectually and arouse at the same time his masculine power of potency. He is tired of eating dark bread at home all the time. He would like to enjoy cheesecake or a cream puff once in a while.

Adultery is the last resort of the suffering and reacting man. Do you feel understood by this interpretation?

But let me say one more thing to you. You are chasing after an illusion.

There was once a very gifted king in Bavaria, Ludwig the Second. He was a lonely and misunderstood man. He did not find the happiness marriage could have brought him with a loving wife. He tried to escape from reality into a world of his dreams. So he built himself a fairy tale castle in the midst of a wonderful landscape. He decorated his dream castle with art treasures from all over the world. Whenever he sat at his desk he could look at the beautiful tapestries and paintings of lovely life-size, feminine forms. But they only decorated the walls. They were without life and without warmth. It was only a dream.

It took seventeen years to build the fairy tale castle Neuschwanstein. For one hundred thirty-eight days, the king lived in this beautiful splendor. Then he disappeared mysteriously and was found in a mountain lake.

He who searches for unfaithfulness, the adventure of adultery, is like the king who tried to flee into the fairy tale castle. Meeting a partner outside of marriage can be so wonderfully beautiful in the imagination. But the one who tries it is living under an illusion. In marriage one discovers his partner as she really is, and there one finds the true balance between the dream picture of the emotions and the real person. Reality is denied in the adventure of adultery. One remains intentionally blind so the fire of passion will not go out, so the charm and appeal to the senses of the dream person will not dim. One lives only in the dreams that are painted on the walls of one's consciousness. It is a joy that is mixed with anxiety, the fear that these dreams will one day be uncovered as sweet illusions.

A man might experience an affirmation of his potency when he looks at the beautiful naked forms painted on the wall or when he leafs through a pornographic magazine. But in the deceptive phantom of infidelity he will look in vain for the healing of his disappointments, for true shelter and freedom. Indeed, on top of all the burdens he is already carrying and under which he is suffering will come the additional burden of leading a double life, one for his wife and one for his mistress. Adultery must always show two faces. He dare not forget to put on the right mask at the right place.

Unfaithfulness as a way of escape is a dead end. One can only feel sorry for the man who is trying to find his happiness and healing by resorting to it.

And yet there is true help for the one who suffers in himself and in his marriage. There is a way out, and we will talk about it in the last section.

Three

The Free Man

I intentionally did not entitle the third part of this book "The Ideal Man" or "The Man Who Is Human" or even "The Man As He Should Be." If I had done that, I might have put on already overburdened men even more demands that would have increased their frustration. By laying before them higher ideals, I might have made men feel more like failures, tempting them to give up completely. The result might be discouragement, even despair.

What I have described in the foregoing pages is the psychological reality of how a man suffers and how he reacts when he hurts. But no man will be helped if I just offer a few psychological tips. That would be too easy an answer.

Instead, a man must be set free, released, redeemed. How does this occur? Through faith.

Faith is the act of jumping. I jump because I am pushed by logic and pulled by One who longs to catch me. It takes great courage to make this leap. It means springing over a deep abyss in confidence that there is One awaiting me on the other side.

All that I say in the rest of this book, I say out of my experience as one who has been caught. If you have not had this experience, it may be difficult for you to understand. But I hope I will not lose those readers, nor that they will be discouraged from reading further. Instead I want to invite and challenge you to take this leap. I would like to show you why it pays and how a whole new possibility of life is opened up to you if you dare to jump.

When I talk about this leap of faith, I am not talking about church membership or belonging to a religious fellowship. I am not talking about "churchianity" but about meeting God.

For the man who does not yet believe, the church is often like a wall separating him from God. For the man who goes to church only out of habit or tradition, the danger is that he may use this as a sort of bumper zone which protects him from having a personal confrontation with God on a first-name basis.

I have had this confrontation and I invite you to have it too. That's what I mean when I write the words *redeemed, set free.* It means being taken into a new reality. Let me illustrate.

There was a boy who walked by a pond every day on his way to school. During the winter the pond was frozen. His father had forbidden him to ever go out on the ice. But the boy did not obey. One day he ventured out on the frozen pond and fell through the ice. An old postman just happened to be walking by. He saw the boy drowning, hurried to him, grabbed his hand and pulled him out. He saved his life.

The boy had to stay in bed a long time. His father neither scolded nor punished him. When the boy was well again, his father took him by the hand and led him to the cemetery where he showed him the grave of the old mailman. He had saved the boy, but had to pay for it with his life.

The boy now knew: My life no longer belongs to me. I have received it anew and am alive because someone else gave his life for me.

This is what I mean when I talk about being caught. It is a passive experience. It may seem like the leap of faith is an activity, an action. It is, when you look at it from the point of view of the one who has jumped. But the one who is caught knows that he is caught even before he leaps.

So may the man who does not yet believe hear this personal question: Why should I not take this leap?

And the one who already believes should ask himself: Have I really dipped out all the rich possibilities that are mine since I have been caught?

The Guided Man

In the previous pages I described how men react to their inner uncertainty by playing the almighty patriarch. Now is the time to show the other side of the picture and to spell out the characteristics of the free man, the man who has leaped and who has been caught.

First, he can lead others. Why? Because he himself is led. He has learned the secret of being guided. He is set free from the fear of failure because he no longer depends on his own strength but on the strength of his Lord.

With some men one can sense from the first encounter that they have learned the art of being guided by God. Others who call themselves Christians do not seem to have antennae for receiving his guidance.

Recently my wife was riding in a car with a friend in Washington, D.C., who was diligently looking for an address but who couldn't find it. Bill was an intelligent man, a capable man. He was the head of his department at the university where he teaches. But he wouldn't stop and ask for directions. Ingrid finally asked him, "Bill, why is it so hard for a man to ask directions? Women don't seem to have a problem with that."

His answer: "I never ask directions because I don't want to admit that I'm lost!"

There are records in military history of valiant cavalrymen plunging into the valley of death because they refused to ask if there wasn't some way around.

A redeemed man is one who is not afraid to ask for directions. In this way he leads. Only those who are led can lead.

How then can we be guided? Let me make a few suggestions.

First, guidance comes through the Scripture and listening prayer. King David said to his son Solomon as he was about to die: "I am about to go the way of all the earth. Be strong, and show yourself a man, and keep the charge of the LORD your God, walking in his ways and keeping his statutes, his commandments, his ordinances, and his testimonies, as it is written in the law of Moses, that you may prosper in all that you do and wherever you turn" (1 Kings 2:2-3). Our decisions must be weighed on the scale of his Word. Are they in accordance with the Ten Commandments? And then if instead of praying we become silent and listen, we will hear plainly the voice of the Good Shepherd, "This is the way. Follow me."

Second, guidance is often only clear when you take a concrete step in a certain direction. You can't steer a parked car. You have to put it into gear. A redeemed man has the courage to take this first step, and then he can hear a still, small voice which says, "Keep going; this is the right direction." Or he hears the voice saying, "Stop! You're going in the wrong direction."

In 1 Kings 19 we read the story of Elijah who was so afraid and depressed that he wanted to die, even after having a great victory for the Lord. God then speaks to him —not in a strong wind, not in an earthquake, not even through a fire, but through a sound of gentle stillness, a still, small voice. Outwardly, it could hardly be recognized, but inwardly, out of a quiet, receptive state, Elijah picks up the voice of his master and receives precise instructions.

Third, once this inner antenna has picked up the radio message there is only one thing left to do: obey without looking either to the right or the left, without being afraid of contrary winds. "He who observes the wind will not sow; and he who regards the clouds will not reap" (Eccles 11:4).

In his last book, written shortly before his death, Dr. Theodore Bovet of Switzerland said this about guidance: "When we listen to all the different inner voices, which often have to do with our whole life history, then we learn gradually to liken them to the needle of a compass or even better to the directions given by a radio tower to a landing airplane. We learn to listen quietly to the voice which says: 'Keep your hands off. This is not for you,' or 'Here's an open door, a real opportunity. This is a road your feet can travel.' "

Fourth, the art of being guided means also that you are ready to be corrected. My best friend told me once, "I'm even happy when I see that I'm wrong about something because that way I'm always learning something new." It's a very humbling experience, before God and before man, to have to admit, "I am wrong here. I have made a mistake." Accepting the humiliation of being corrected is a very painful learning process for us men. If we are on the wrong path, however, we should cut our losses instead of trying to cover them up and be overwhelmed by them.

This being corrected comes when we are in eye contact with God. His promise in Psalm 32:8 is "I will counsel you with my eye upon you." If we remain in eye contact with our Lord, he shows us the next step, but not the whole road.

I was reminded of this "eye contact" one day when working in the home of my oldest daughter. I had spread my papers out over the coffee table trying to make order in them when my little granddaughter came to "help" me. She was fascinated with the colored plastic folders and the papers each one contained, but before she touched them, she looked at me with questioning eyes. She was not yet two, but her sense of obedience was keen. "May I do this or must I leave it alone?" was what she asked me with her wide awake eyes. I looked into them, nodding my permission. For a long time her little hands were occupied with making order.

Fifth, the experience of being guided includes also outward circumstances. Getting all the information together as well as the legal implications are a part of making a guided decision. I do not believe that a man can be "guided" and then deliberately do what is contrary to the law of the land in which he is living, provided that law is in harmony with God's law.

Sixth, we must not be afraid to make a decision. I have known many people who began to take the will of God seriously even in the smallest decisions. But soon they were living in constant fear of doing something that was not guided. They tried to press God's guidance into a single channel, and yet feared they would not find it.

A seminary student had a call to a small rural congregation and at the same time a call to work as a missionary overseas. He couldn't make a decision, so he went to the famous theologian Professor Schlatter in Tübingen and asked him which call was God's will. The professor's answer was short but clear: "Both."

We have a wrong view of God if we think guidance is bound to one track only. In the city of God there are many streets, all of which can be used. Often, of two possibilities both are God's will. Yes, I dare to say now and then we are allowed to decide simply according to what pleases us and causes us joy.

Lastly, the guided man also knows that God can write straight on crooked lines. He can even make something good out of our mistakes. His creative will is at work whether we are standing tall or have fallen flat.

Two people married too young without thinking through their decision. After a few years they realized they were incompatible and wanted to separate. But then they both had a personal encounter with God and made a new beginning together in faith. They discovered each other in a new light. Their love was resurrected and deepened in a way they had never before experienced. God made something much more beautiful out of their relationship than they had ever dreamed.

Knowing that God can make something good out of our wrong decisions takes away anxiety from the guided man and gives him courage to make decisions.

The strong, guided man is not tossed by the winds. He knows how to set his sails for the goal ahead and his sureness invites confidence. He is able to structure the unstructuredness of others while also knowing and accepting his own limits. He does not grieve over what is not given him, but dips out the possibilities and opportunities that are his. For this he needs humor.

The Laughing Man

A man who has been set free to be a man, who has been redeemed, can be recognized by another special quality. He can laugh about himself. He doesn't need to prove himself by bragging about his accomplishments, like the man who feels inadequate. He is understated. He does not need to put all his certificates and degrees on the wall. He does not need to hide behind the mask of inaccessibility like the unapproachable chief.

Those who have dared to be caught by God expose their life to him. God's forgiveness helps heal the past. His nearness carries us now. His hands hold the future. This security gives the redeemed man a contagious, playful serenity.

Instead of hurting others through sardonic humor or biting remarks, he encourages wholesome fun so members of his family and his co-workers don't take themselves too seriously. And if he hears a good joke about himself that hits the nail on the head, then he can laugh as heartily as his friends.

He can even laugh with his wife about sexual difficulties they may be having. Sexual demands lose their power to harm if a couple can have a playful conversation about them. A sexual relationship with no humor is like the animals'. God must love to hear the laughter of a couple behind closed doors.

If I am called to counsel a couple who are upset and who are constantly getting on each other's nerves, and I can get them to laugh about something together, then I know that the victory is already half won. Their marriage is in no immediate danger. I've often seen how just looking at wedding pictures can send a couple into gales of laughter. Memories long forgotten are recalled, and things that were painful at the time now seem so funny.

Humor helps us to live with situations which are unpleasant but which we cannot change.

My mother, who was a teacher with her whole heart and gifted in handling children, always said, "He who wants to learn must be happy." The atmosphere in a classroom often determines the success pupils will have. A relaxed atmosphere at the family table or in the congregation at church should also be highly appreciated. When I'm speaking some place and I can get my audience to laugh a couple of times, then I know that they will be more ready to swallow the hard words I will also have to speak. Those who take people too seriously, who think they are merely beings in need of moral or pedagogical change will not last long.

Loving little jokes help to affirm each other. As the proverb says, "The one who teases also loves."

In our family we have nicknames for each other, and for special occasions we would make up funny songs to celebrate each one. When our youngest daughter was small, she was delighted when I made up a song using her nickname. We had to sing it at our family table over and over again to her. It made her feel accepted. It affirmed her individuality.

"Humor is a friendly chuckle about the peculiarities of everything human," says Guardini. "It helps us to be merciful, for after a good laugh, then everything is easier to take."

Humor means that while you recognize the worth and importance of all, just as they are, you also keep an eye open for the peculiarities that they might develop.

The redeemed man is one who not only can laugh about his inadequacies but who can also talk about them.

The Talking Man

There is only one way out for the man who feels misunderstood and helpless, yes, even inferior, and who because of these feelings tries to hide behind the wall of silence. The way out is to talk, to communicate. The man who is ready to say what's on his mind and heart is redeemed from being the silent Buddha. He is ready to step out in front of his walls of silence instead of hiding behind them with his hurt feelings.

Because he is not afraid of his feelings, he can talk about them. He knows that truth always brings freedom. "The truth will make you free," Jesus said (Jn 8:32).

The redeemed man is also not afraid to face the feelings of others. He can accept his wife with her sometimes unreasonable longings and desires. If she is honest in expressing her true feelings, he can say, "I understand," without feeling either threatened or attacked. He knows that feelings are neither right nor wrong; they just are.

Because he has the courage to talk about his feelings, he discovers that many of his anxieties disappear. It is fear-reducing to put into words what troubles him. I think of the honesty of the psalmist when he says to his Lord: "I am in distress . . . Set me free" (Ps 69:17-18) or in Psalm 32:3, 5: "When I kept silent, my bones wasted away through my groaning all day long. . . . Then I acknowledged my sin to you and did not cover up my iniquity . . . and you forgave the guilt of my sin" (NIV).

Man can talk because God has chosen him as his partner in talking. God takes his words seriously and thus makes man capable of dialog. We read in Hebrews 1:1-2, "In many and various ways, God *spoke* of old to our fathers by the prophets; but in these last days *he has spoken* to us by a Son." The redeemed man, the man set free to be a man, does not need to cover up his fears and let them grow under the surface until they come up again multiplied, which can lead to stomach ulcers or to heart attacks.

A redeemed man can take criticism and can talk it over. I remember as a young pastor in Germany, I was part of a team doing evangelistic work. After each series of meetings in a village, we had a time as a team to evaluate what had been done. Each one was allowed to tell the other team members what their gifts were, what dangers they faced and where they might have overstepped their limits. I found this honest sharing of criticism as well as praise most helpful in my personal growth. Criticism does hurt. Especially criticism that is true. We are all very sensitive about this. And I believe men are especially sensitive if they are criticized by women.

Before I was married I wrote to my fiancée a long list of what I expected from my future wife, and she wrote what she expected from her husband. The first sentence I wrote her was, "She must challenge me to the highest through absolute honest criticism of me." Then it continued, "When she is disappointed in me, she must never withdraw her confidence. . . . She must never pretend, but must tell me honestly when I have hurt her." I did not want a servant girl but an equal partner who stood by my side before God. Only with such a partner can a man become "one flesh"—a new, living being. Partnership includes the right to criticize.

Some men have difficulty accepting honest compliments and praise. I have often been comforted by the words of Paul in 1 Corinthians 4:5: "Judge nothing before the appointed time; wait till the Lord comes. He will bring to light what is hidden in darkness and will expose the motives of men's hearts. At that time each will receive *his praise from God"* (NIV). A redeemed man doesn't put himself down but can accept that God's creation of his uniqueness is good.

A redeemed man is also ready to listen in other ways. A theology student told me the other day that he was being kidded because he followed some good suggestions of his young wife. His answer to the teasing? "A smart man listens when his wife has a good idea."

A successful engineer, when asked the secret of his success in producing household machines, said: "I've always listened to my wife. She may not be always one hundred per cent right, but she's never wrong."

Such words begin to show the cycle of talking and listening and talking that is dialog. This is intimately tied to the sexual and emotional well-being of a marriage. Many men try to discover the secret of their wives' bodies, what turns them on, what makes them more ready at some times than others for the sexual embrace. It's not merely a matter of following steps 1, 2 and 3 like in a military manual or the handbook for some machine to get her to warm up. The greatest erogenous zone of a woman's body is her heart. And nothing touches her heart more than loving and affirming words that tell her she is loved. Biting, cynical remarks tear holes in the warm mantle of shelteredness which a husband's faithful love gives her. Icy winds then blow through these holes, and inwardly she becomes so cold that she cannot respond physically, emotionally, spiritually.

Marriage is not something static like a body at rest. It is not an achievement which is finished. It is dynamic, a process between two people, a relationship which is constantly being changed, which either grows or dies. Fuel has to be put on the fire, and that takes work. Healthy marriages take work too and dialog is part of that work.

Some years ago, after my wife and I had conducted a number of marriage seminars, we felt burned out. We were invited to participate in a Marriage Encounter weekend with twenty other couples of every age group. The newlyweds in our group found it hard to believe that those who had been married over thirty years still felt they had work to do on their own marriages. Three couples led the group. None of them were professional marriage counselors. They worked for a bank, a supermarket and a fire department. At the beginning of each session one of the couples shared in a personal but carefully prepared way the problems they had in their own marriage and how they had been helped through dialog. Two or three questions were then dictated to us. The women were sent to their rooms to write down the answers to the questions while the men went outside or into the library to do the same.

Twenty minutes later a bell sounded which meant that the husbands should join their wives in their private rooms. The notebooks were exchanged. Each one read what his or her partner had written, and then they discussed the answers for about twenty minutes. We heard the gong again and the whole group assembled in the living room. We began again with another of the leading couples telling of their experiences, giving us new questions and having us write down our answers.

The whole process was strenuous, often painful, but wonderfully healing. At the end of the weekend we discovered we had talked together longer and more in depth than we had been able to do all year. Without our even realizing it, our dialog had become superficial.

We found that writing down the answers to the questions was more helpful than merely talking. You have to endure without flinching what you see written on the page in front of you. You can't change it through a look or an inflection of the voice or even break it off when you see the other one is being hurt. Some of the questions we had to answer were: Why do I want to go on living? Why do I want to go on living with you? What are the things you have to put up with in me? What are the things I have to put up with in you? What is my main weakness and what is my main strength—as a man/woman, father/mother, Christian? How do I feel when I think about your death?

The man who has courage to dialog, to talk over these things, is a man who has been set free from his fortress of silence. And because he has been set free through Jesus Christ to talk, he is also set free to express his feelings.

The Motherly Man

We have already looked at how we men tend to hide or deny our feelings because we think they are unmanly. The redeemed man is set free from this in a remarkable way. He is free to be motherly, to portray the tenderness of God.

The Kiga tribe in East Africa gives God the name of Biheko which means "a God who carries everyone on his back." In this tribe, only mothers and older sisters carry children on their backs while fathers never do. To portray Biheko, one of their artists made a wooden carving portraying a man who carries on his back a child with an adult face and in his arms a weaker child. This carving is a symbol of the God who takes care of human beings with the tender care of a mother. We see this God in Isaiah 46:3-4, "Hearken to me, O house of Jacob, all the remnant of the house of Israel, who have been borne by me from your birth, carried from the womb; even to your old age I am He, and to gray hairs I will carry you."

We are often not able to be in touch with our feelings because we think we must express everything objectively, without any feeling. But this is a sign that our spiritual lives are poverty stricken. We cannot mirror, cannot radiate the tenderness of God because we have not experienced it ourselves.

Yes, God is tender! The whole creation speaks of the tenderness of the Creator. The loveliness of the hills, the gentle flow of the streams, the light breeze blowing on our cheeks, the playfulness of the clouds—in all these there is a never-ending tenderness.

God is tender. As we read in Isaiah 25:8, he "will wipe away tears from all faces." And Revelation 21:4, "He will wipe every tear from their eyes, and death shall be no more, neither shall there be mourning nor crying nor pain."

What an unfathomable and yet fathomable tenderness lies in the fact that God became a child in Jesus. He became a person who could not only express his feelings of loving care, but he could also be the recipient of such feelings. He put all his love into a single glance when he looked upon the rich young ruler: "Jesus looked at him and loved him" (Mk 10:21 NIV). In modern language we would call it nonverbal communication.

Jesus was also not afraid to show his anger. In Mark 3:5 we read, "He looked around at [the Pharisees] with anger, grieved at their hardness of heart." He openly showed he was deeply upset about Lazarus's death: "When Jesus saw [Mary] weeping, and the Jews who came with her also weeping, he was deeply moved in spirit and troubled. . . . Jesus wept" (Jn 11:33, 35). He also cried over Jerusalem. "When he drew near and saw the city he wept over it" (Lk 19:41).

This Jesus who feels deeply is our example. But he is more than our model. For he lives in the redeemed man, conforming him to his image. The power of Christ within, not a man's own powers, sets him free not only to feel again his own feelings but also to feel the feelings of others. He can stand by their side as Christ would and with motherly tenderness dry away their tears with his big crumpled handkerchief.

Neither was Jesus afraid of physical touch. He held children close to him. He washed the feet of his disciples. John rested on his breast. He touched sick people and took the hands of the dead.

And he let himself be touched! A woman was allowed to wash his feet with her tears and to dry them with her hair. "Standing behind him at his feet, weeping, she began to wet his feet with her tears, and wiped them with the hair of her head, and kissed his feet, and anointed them with the ointment" (Lk 7:38). Later he reproached his host Simon, "You gave me no kiss" (Lk 7:45). Jesus didn't even refuse the kiss of Judas.

God wants to be loved as a father and a mother are loved by their children, as a friend by a friend, as a man by his wife and a wife by her husband, as a sick person by a caring nurse and as a guest by his host. God finds great joy when we express our feelings toward him.

But before a man can feel his own feelings and express them, he often has to go back to the past and deal with that hurting child within himself, that frightened child, that hating child. Jesus loves all those wounded children in our hearts. He is the only one who is the same yesterday, today and forever, who can walk into our pasts, the time even before we were born, and place his healing and comforting hand on all those deeply sensitive spots that we try to cover up with the armor of our invulnerability. This wonderful healing of memories is the key to the man who has the courage to be motherly—the courage to express his deepest longings. This is the key to the redeemed man who, because the past hurts have been exposed to the Light and healed, no longer needs to retreat into his fortress, but stands there naked, vulnerable, ready to risk being wounded again. His fear is gone.

Is not this the deepest reason for our inability and our unwillingness to express feelings? Is it not the fear to expose ourselves to hurt? To show who we really are? We don't want anyone to see through us. We are not led by a spirit of love and confidence, but by a spirit of fear (2 Tim 1:7). This spirit of cowardliness leads us to great poverty. Then the things which we try to cover up in our hearts form the picture we have of ourselves. We become what we try to hide. Only what we can express and put into words will lead us out of the blocked-up feelings. Only what we share can be worked through.

We need spiritual help to overcome fear of people. This can only come through a living relationship with God: "If God is for us, who is against us? . . . It is God who justifies; who is to condemn?" (Rom 8:31, 33-34). Could it be that we are afraid to share our feelings with others because we have not shared them with God? We are not ready to be transparent before others because we have not been transparent before God? Yet he knows us already. "He knew all men" (Jn 2:25). He only waits for us to speak.

This inability to express feelings turns into guilt when we are so reserved that it destroys our fellowship with others, when we reproach others and even look down on them. We are not able to forgive or forget and therefore cannot radiate God's love and tenderness. "A happy heart makes the face cheerful" (Prov 15:13 NIV). Such a heart comes not from within ourselves but from a secure, open relationship with our God.

What are some characteristics of a man with such a relationship? The redeemed man is not ashamed to mourn, to grieve. All change can be a kind of loss—switching jobs, friends moving away, family problems, children beginning to leave the nest, losing his life partner. He needs to openly express his feelings of sadness and pain—of anger too.

All his life he has learned how to be a breadwinner, but does he know how to nurture the inner mind and heart of those entrusted to his care? He must give to his wife, his children and friends the room, the strength and the courage which they need to express their feelings.

Someone has suggested that women have fewer problems with aging than men since women are encouraged to express their feelings openly. Fear of aging stunts our growth. I think of the ninety-year-old German farmer who said, "The best lies yet ahead of us." Or as Robert Browning has written:

> Grow old along with me!
> The best is yet to be,
> The last of life, for which the first was made:
>
> Our times are in his hand
> Who saith "A Whole I planned,"
> Youth shows but half; trust God:
> See all, nor be afraid.

One of the secrets of the motherly man is the ability to put himself in the place of others. A Native American proverb says, "Don't judge a man until you have walked for a moon in his moccasins." Hebrews 13:3 encourages us similarly, "Remember those who are in prison, as though in prison with them." Jesus lived this truth for us as none other. "For we have not a high priest who is unable to sympathize with our weaknesses, but one who in every respect has been tempted as we are, yet without sin" (Heb 4:15). When he who is God became man, he "emptied himself, taking the form of a servant, being born in the likeness of men" (Phil 2:7). Jesus could feel what people felt because he did not remain aloof, a God untouched by human pain. He became one of us.

What about us? Paul says, "Have this mind among yourselves, which is yours in Christ Jesus" (Phil 2:5).

A freed man is also a good host. He anticipates the needs of his guests, provides for them, and puts their needs before his own. "Do not neglect to show hospitality to strangers, for thereby some have entertained angels unawares" (Heb 13:2).

Finally, motherliness in a freed man means giving affirmation. When I asked the wife of a redeemed man, a man whose very being radiates Christ, what she appreciated the most about him, she answered without hesitation, "He affirms those he meets." I believe when Jesus asked us to "clothe the naked" (and that certainly is a motherly task), he also meant to clothe those who feel stripped of their self-worth and self-esteem. Love is encouragement and kindness. "You can do it!" "I'm on your side." "I believe in you." Love is also the challenge, "Now do it!"

A redeemed, motherly man holds his wife securely in his arms, even when he does not know why she is crying. He spreads a blanket over her and sees that she is not cold. He stoops over to his child and takes him on his lap. The child is safe and can grow strong to meet the storms of life. Motherliness and fatherliness, both are attributes of God. The closer we come to him and perhaps the more mature we are, the more these attributes become one.

The Fatherly Man

Men who feel superfluous at home are tempted in their pain to withdraw and flee to another place where they will find recognition. Recently I asked a young wife about her father. "I barely knew him," she said. "He left it to my mother to bring up nine children and told her, 'If I do nothing, then at least I do nothing wrong.' " Another young man said, "My father cannot show me his love, probably because he hurts so much himself."

A man who is set free to be a man, a redeemed man, can overcome his pain because of the affirmation and strength he has received from his heavenly Father. He can then give to others the fatherly love which he has experienced.

He is ready to share with his children, taking each one of them seriously and accepting their individuality. He also knows the secret of sharing his work with them. I recall that when we came home on furlough from our work in Africa, I was asked to give a missionary message in various congregations. My oldest son, Daniel, was my escort. Though only seven at the time, he felt very much a part of the team and would ask me, "Father, where are we going to preach next Sunday?" Solemnly he would take his place beside me at the front of the church and pray with me for the success of the message.

Later on when Ingrid and I were called to teach Family Life Seminars throughout the world, we tried when at all possible to have one of our children with us. Not only was it a special reward for all the sacrifices they had made in letting their parents go, but it was the only way they could know just what we had been doing in our teaching and counseling ministry. We felt that every cent we put into their travel costs was one of the best investments we could make.

But when does being a father begin? The chief of the Chaggas, a proud and industrious tribe living on the slopes of Mount Kilimanjaro, told his men, "Take good care of the pregnant woman. She is the most important person in our tribe." This wise African chief had long ago discovered what modern-day psychologists and psychiatrists are learning—that the acceptance of a child and the resulting self-image and self-esteem of that child begin long before birth. When a father knows that he is essential to the future well-being of his child, then he need never feel superfluous, especially when his child is unborn.

It is the strong, decisive, responsible, planning man who starts nurturing his wife so that she can become a good mother. He understands her in her cycle. His heart is filled with awe and wonder when he reflects that new life can come from the act of love. And that this new life is dependent on him, his protecting hand and loving care. He helps his wife in choosing a doctor who will not relieve him or rob him of his responsibility to coach his own baby's birth and will allow him to go to prenatal checkups. He stays at his wife's side at the birth of their child. He provides a safe environment and strong encouragement during the nursing period, taking an active interest in the child's daily development and growth. He is wide awake, anticipating the pitfalls and dangers that his children may face. Because of that, they can place their confidence in him. On the other hand, if a child disappoints him, his world does not crumble. He does not receive his identity from his children, but from the Father from whom every family in heaven and on earth is named.

Such a father is the hero for his four, five, six, seven-year-old child and older. When puberty comes, the child develops a strong desire toward independence, and even though he may find and seek outside heroes, the deep underlying knowledge is there: father is the best example to follow. By daring to take an active part in nurturing the whole family he has become the best example of a father. He has taught fatherliness to his sons and given his daughters the best guide for choosing a husband.

The fatherly man is patient. He has learned the secret of waiting. In the story of the prodigal son, the father let his son go—but he waited. Every day he waited. He gave his son freely of all for which he had worked, knowing that the son might waste it. The son didn't have to wait until the father died. He took his share of the inheritance and spent it on loose living. The son didn't even think what it might have cost his father—blood, sweat and tears. The son thought only, "It's my right!"

The father was relaxed about letting his son go. He knew that his son was no longer his problem but God's problem. He had given him his very best. I'm sure the father suffered pangs of not being needed, of being superfluous, but he stood up under this pain.

A few years ago I planted three birch trees in our front yard, thinking they would grow without help. At the first windstorm, one tree broke off, so I put up two poles for the others and fastened them securely to the poles. One of the poles was too strong. It was more like a fence post. Because it could not give at all, the top of the little tree bound to it broke off at the level of the post, so that today there is only a stump where there should have been a tree. But there was just the right amount of elasticity in the pole to which the third tree was bound, so that both could bend with the wind. The day came when the cords were untied and the tree stood proudly alone. It is developing evenly on all sides, and its growth is a joy to behold.

A son wrote to his father, "I'm moving out. I'm leaving home and leaving you. I, your son, am not 'at home' any more with you. I'm leaving home for good. The prodigal son didn't receive any good advice, any commandments, any rules of what to do and what not to do. For me the time has come to leave father and mother." The young man left home and went to live with his girlfriend.

The father wrote back, "The son who goes away from home is not a lost son, not a prodigal son. For his father, he was never a prodigal son. This may be what the son thought as he took care of pigs in a faraway land. And it's not true that his father didn't give him any rules of behavior. Neither for the one who tells the story, Jesus, nor for those who listened was there any doubt that the way of living de scribed in Luke 15:13 was not according to the will of the Father. Why did the son turn around if he had not been going in the wrong direction? There must have been a discussion which took place beforehand, which is not recounted in Luke 15."

It is the great ministry of the fatherly man not to give up, but to persevere. He has to offer resistance, so that his sons and daughters can grow up straight. He is a father, not only to his own physical children, but to the children of others who have no father who cares for them. It is not true that one must have wife and children in order to be fatherly. There are young men, not yet married, who are fatherly. There are priests, called to a celibate life, who are fathers for the family of God.

Where else can a man learn to be a father if not from the heavenly Father? "As a father has compassion on his children, so the LORD has compassion on those who fear him; for he knows how we are formed, he remembers that we are dust" (Ps 103:13 NIV).

The world is looking for redeemed men who have the courage to be fathers.

The Sheltered Man

In contrast to the frustrated man who would like to run away from his responsibilities stands the redeemed man who feels safe and secure. He can be a shelter to others because he himself is sheltered. He is not afraid even if at times he should lose or suffer defeat. He simply gets up again and keeps on keeping on. He is a man that has accepted himself not only with his strengths but also with his weaknesses. His secret: he knows he has been accepted by the heavenly Father. He has a roof over his head. He knows where his home is. He has a place where he can put his feet under the table. He can say with the psalmist, "You prepare a table before me in the presence of my enemies" (Ps 23:5 NIV). He can say, "Thou art my refuge, a strong tower against the enemy. Let me dwell in thy tent for ever! Oh to be safe under the shelter of thy wings!" (Ps 61:3- 4).

This is the longing of all mankind—to have security, to know where one's place is. God created man and then he created a place for him, the

Garden of Eden. When man lost God, he lost at the same time his place. Since then, the longing for a place where he belongs, where he feels at home, is in the heart of every human being. Those who have not found a place, the uprooted, the eternal Gypsies will find a place nowhere, not even in marriage. On the other hand, those who have found a place, married or unmarried, will be able to become a place where others feel at home, thus filling one of the deepest needs of our time. In light of this, Jesus' promise "to prepare a place" for us is filled with new meaning (Jn 14:2). Those who have found him have found their place.

Perhaps the best symbol of the man who feels sheltered, safe and secure, is that of the tree described in Psalm 1. "He is like a tree planted by streams of water, that yields its fruit in its season, and its leaf does not wither. In all that he does, he prospers" (v. 3). In meditating on this verse and after observing a magnificent tree in all its autumn glory, I wrote these words down in my journal, "A tree rests. A tree stands firm because the roots are deep down. A tree drinks constantly. A tree supports, gives shelter, warmth, security. A tree bears fruit. A tree is not in a hurry. It waits for the right time."

The redeemed man, symbolized by this tree, is a whole man. He is whole first of all because he *belongs* to a family, the family of God. God, his Father, makes him one of his sons.

He is a whole man because he feels *worthy*. Christ died to give him birth and therefore he can take as his own the worthiness of Christ.

He is a whole man because he feels *competent*. This competence comes from the Holy Spirit. "God did not give us a spirit of timidity but a spirit of power and love and self-control" (2 Tim 1:7).

In front of our little mountain home in Austria stood an old bent and crooked fruit tree which belonged to one of our wonderful farmer neighbors. It had had to bear the brunt of the strong northwest wind, but it was a paradise for our children. They could climb it easily even before they started school. From this vantage point they could look down on the adults who might be around. A summer visitor looking carefully at the rugged tree asked Matthias, our neighbor, what kind of fruit could possibly grow on such a tree. Matthias answered with a twinkle in his eye, "Children." This tree is a symbol of the man who radiates security, who creates the room where others can be happy and prosper. Not like the father whose son said, "When Dad comes home, a dark shadow enters the house with him."

The man who is sheltered, who is safe and secure, is not afraid to lose his freedom by giving his time and strength to his family. He counts it sweet fortune to be a servant of love. He may have been hurt in many battles himself, but as Thornton Wilder says, "In love's service, only the wounded soldiers can serve."

On our mantelpiece we have a wooden sculpture depicting the Holy Family. Mary is seated holding the baby Jesus. Joseph stands behind her spreading out his warm cloak as if to protect her. One of our friends, Ruth Heil, who admired the sculpture, wrote the following about it in a letter to us. What better description could there be of the safe and secure man?

> How wonderful to see the baby enclosed in the mother's arms and then the mother in turn protected and surrounded by the father's mantle of love. The father's protection is at the same time offering shelter and freedom, protected and yet wide open, a refuge in storms and yet challenging. This open cloak which shelters mother and child from the cold winds outside is held also by the guiding hand which lets the child go free. Because the child has been sheltered, he can also handle the responsibility of freedom. This cloak of protection, does it not also give the woman the freedom which she needs to move about and develop freely? Christ is the One who covers us and yet he does not strangle us in narrowness. He creates the place, the home, and leaves the door wide open so that we can go in and out.
>
> The mother and child are a unity in themselves. Just the two of them alone would be beautiful. But what would become of them if the wide cloak of the protector were not around them?
>
> And the man alone with his arms outstretched? It's as if he's saying, "May I not give you protection?" One is completed through the other. The child through the mother; the wife through her husband; and surrounding them all is the wide, invisible mantle of our heavenly Father, who enables them to develop and grow in the shade of his unending refuge which heals all of the torn places in our human mantles.

These torn places are often visible in the way that husband and wife express their sexuality. What freedom for a man to learn to take into account how he feels physically and put this into words, so that his wife knows that when he says he's tired, he is tired! He doesn't have to accept unconditionally all of her wishes and try to fulfill them when he knows it will lead to disappointment for her. Neither does she remain passive and silent when she is not ready to unite. A wife is not frigid because on some days she may not feel like having intercourse. And neither is he impotent if he has no desire for intercourse or may at times have the desire but not be able to have an erection.

What freedom when a couple is released from their need "to perform" and learns to enjoy the pleasures of relaxed, easy sex! They can then forget about being spectators, let go completely and enjoy their sensations. Physical love is the most intimate sphere in the life of a married couple. Every man is different. Every woman is different. Therefore, every couple is doubly different, and a part of the fun of sexual love is the originality of each couple.

When God created man in his own image, he created them as man and woman. He made Eve from the rib of her husband and brought her to him. Is there any better way to explain the great desire of husband and wife to become one flesh than that they came from one body?

"You are all around me on every side; you protect me with your power" (Ps 139:5 TEV). Because the redeemed man has experienced the love of God in his own life, he can give it to others. He knows that to love is a great risk, and he may be hurt, but he is willing to take this risk.

Ingrid and I know what the risk of loving means. We were separated by continents when we were engaged: she as a missionary teacher in Cameroun and I as a pastor in a large congregation in West Germany. Let me share what she wrote to me from her lonely station.

> I want to tell you why I love you. When I picture you in my mind, I can see you stretching out your hand to me. I trust your hand for it is the hand of a safe and secure man. It is true, you walk a little ahead of me, but when you realize I'm getting out of breath and can't quite keep up, you stand still. You turn around and give me your hand to help me over the hard places. Then I come very near to you and you talk to me and comfort me. You don't make fun of my thoughts,

neither are you threatened by them if they challenge you to try a new path.

When I am weak and need protection, I know that you are stronger than I, and so I take hold of your hand because I know that you will never use your strength to make me feel inferior.

But you need me too and you are not ashamed to show it. Even though you are strong and manly, you can also be helpless as a child. Your strong hand can then become an open, empty hand. And I know no greater happiness than to fill it.

The Loving Man

He who loves is no longer alone. The one he loves is constantly present with him. He renounces the right to remain at the center of his own life. He permits someone else to enter into the midst of it and senses that to be sweet fortune. He gives himself up and lets himself go. He becomes empty like an open hand which holds nothing, but waits until something will be put into it. He who loves has the courage to become one who needs something.

I asked several of my good friends how they would describe the loving man. How does he show his love? Here are some of the answers:

Dieter Endres said, "The loving man is one who does not let the personality of his wife become stunted. At his side, she can blossom because he doesn't put her down. He helps her in a practical way to develop the gifts which God has given her to be used for his honor and for a blessing to the family, community and congregation."

Susanne, his wife, said simply, "He is the one who loves me, his wife."

A fatherly friend and counselor, Klaus Hess, said, "The loving man is not one who is seeking to be loved, but his great happiness is to give love. Then his wife can respond. That which you would like to receive, you must give. To win a whole heart means to give a whole life. Marriage, that close relationship to one woman, is a man's training ground. There he is allowed to practice and learn that which gives him authority for all other areas of his life and profession."

When I asked his wife, Amalia, she replied without a moment's hesitation: "For me, the loving man is the one who includes his wife in his work. He holds out to the end, through thick and thin, whether it's easy or hard, and gives unity with his wife top priority. Pain is often necessary to reach this unity. We must not try to avoid or run away from pain because marriage grows through crisis."

Herta Kosche said, "The loving man is the one who creates an atmosphere of shelter where we as a family can breathe deeply and be at rest. We have no fear. He does not bully his wife, nor wound her dignity."

One of Ingrid's sisters responded, "The loving man is the one for whom it is more important that I am happy than that he is happy."

Another friend said, "He's the man who likes his work, for if he doesn't like what he does, then he doesn't like who he is, and he can't love me."

In *A Growing Love,* our friend and poet Ulrich Schaffer writes,

love never comes to stay
it can't be stored for the future
and past love does not answer to present needs

love grows out of our experience with God
love grows out of our acceptance of ourselves
love grows out of our acceptance of each other.
(New York: Harper & Row, 1977, p. 96.)

The title of a novel by Christian author Manfred Hausman, entitled *Liebende Leben von der Uergebung* (A Life of Loving out of Forgiveness), became a motto for Ingrid and me. For how can one live either singly or together without the grace of forgiveness? Our lives can be full of the goodness of the Lord if we are not afraid to admit and confess our own guilt. The banner of the forgiving love of the Crucified One stands over us to make us compassionate.

My Ethiopian friend Getahun put it this way at a marriage seminar he and his wife, Linda, were leading:

> In Ephesians 5:21-33, the man has a far more difficult job than his wife. She is told to submit to him in verses 22 and 24 and to see that

> she respects him in verse 33. But for the loving husband there is a far greater program. He too must submit, verse 21, but then he must also be the head of his wife as Christ is the head of the church, in other words, her manager, verse 23; he must love his wife and be ready to die for her, verse 25. He must sanctify her, make her clean, wash her, see that she is radiant, that she has no stain, no wrinkle. He must love his wife as his own body, for "he who loves his wife loves himself," verse 28. He must never hate his wife, but nurture and care for her. He must leave everything else and cleave to his wife, verse 31.

As Getahun explained this, step by step, he was brave enough to admit that in Paul's fourteen-point program for husbands in Ephesians 5, he, after ten years of marriage, still had a long way to go. "Perhaps I have succeeded in the first two points," he said. "We men have a very big job."

Where does this leave the man? With a burden of being a loving man that is impossible to carry because only God can love completely? No. Rather it is the opposite. The man is not expected to love perfectly. God does that. This is a great relief. We can rest in him to fulfill the woman.

We are not, however, completely relieved of responsibility. While we cannot love totally, we can love truly. To the degree God has put love in our hearts for another, we can express that love in grace and truth. In this, being a loving man is not impossible. He can show her that she is loved through a kind word, help with an errand, a hand on the shoulder, rearranging a schedule to be with her.

The loving man is, therefore, the loved man, loved by the One who is love. He does not love out of his own strength. This is foremost in his mind and heart. Life is secondary in light of the hope of eternal life. Ultimately the man depends on God and can face, endure and enjoy life only because he is not dependent on this life. His wife and children mean more to him than any other human relationship and are second only to his relationship to Jesus Christ. He loves because he was first loved.

Epilog

It belongs to being redeemed—to be satisfied with the provisional, the temporary. Even if one never reaches the goal, it is good to be going in the right direction.

I was born in the next to the last hour of the next to the last day of the next to the last month of the year. This has been a paradigm for my life and a challenge to have the courage to accept incompleteness in this imperfect world.

Thus it is not my intention to give the last word on men in this book. Those who are only satisfied if they can write the last word will never write anything. In all of life—particularly where our ultimate goal is concerned—we must have the courage to accept incompleteness. For the basis on which we stand, from which we originate and out of which we live, we must have nothing but the ultimate completeness, the final reality.

Christ is the final reality. Everything else has only a shadow existence. His love penetrates us and radiates through us.

Walter Trobisch

Afterword

My dear departed husband,

More than three years have passed since you left us and were catapulted from one moment to the next to your heavenly home. This manuscript was on your desk—unfinished. While the first two parts on the suffering man and how he reacts were quite complete in your handwriting, the last section on the redeemed man, the freed man, was only there in outline form with a few key words and sentences under each subtitle. Your friends and your children helped me put the fragments together. I then tried to make it a unity, using your own words and stories. I listened to that still, small voice and then wrote it down, trying to keep out of the way. It was my prayer that this would be your book, your message to both men and women. If it is true, as C. S. Lewis says, that in our grief we often take on some of the characteristics of the one we mourn, then perhaps it is "Walter in me" which speaks.

The last section on the loving man was the most difficult one. In your notes were only three sentences:

"The loving man is the submissive man," and you wrote the reference to Ephesians 5:21: "Be subject to one another out of reverence for Christ."

"The loving man *cleaves* to his wife." In German the word *hangen* could mean "to be attached to" or "to hang on to." You wrote, "The man is not independent, but dependent." "For this reason a man shall leave his father and mother and *be joined to* his wife."

I remember when I first knew that I could love you. We had ridden through the Palitinate in southern Germany on your motorcycle. It was a cold winter day in February 1950 with rain and sleet beating in our faces. When we reached the parsonage where we were to stay overnight, the pastor's wife gave us hot tea and made us take a warm foot bath. Then I was told to rest on the sofa until the evening meal. You found a blanket, covered me and tucked it under my feet. (Do you know that your sons do the same thing today?) That blanket was a sign of your love, and under it I felt safe and secure.

Today I want to thank you that in all the years of our marriage you helped me establish the boundaries of my daily life. When I shared with you the long list of things I wanted to do in one day, you gently said, "It is too much. Let's decide all the things you do *not* need to do today."

One of my friends described her husband as her chief "caller forth." I could certainly say the same about you. Often I would draw back and not want to take responsibility for a new task, like that marriage seminar in Indonesia two months before your death. You gave me a blessing and said, "You can do it, Ingrid." In every new venture that we felt was guided, you encouraged me. It wasn't always comfortable and I was often ready to give up. But it was good "survival training" for the time after your death. Since then I have often felt your hand on my shoulder saying: "Just one step at a time. Keep on keeping on. His strength is made perfect in our weakness." I remember too the many times we were separated in our marriage and how you said that you trusted me to make the right decisions and to act on my own in emergency situations.

I was never happier than when you said that you needed me, because often I felt that I was in your way. This was especially true when you were working on a manuscript. You were then the pregnant one. I could only stand by and wait patiently—sometimes not so patiently—for the baby to be born. After such a time you once wrote to me these words, "I sense how very much I need you as a woman, as a person, as nearness. I look forward to our being together again, and we will begin right away our dialog in depth. I need you so very much, above all, your trust, your patience, your presence."

I also thank you for being such a good father, not only for our own children, but for so many others who found healing in their heavenly Father because you stood as a bridge to help them find him. I know how you suffered too as a father. It was not easy for you to see your children cut the cords which bound them to the "father" pole and learn to stand up straight on their own. I just want to tell you that this pain which you endured has brought fruit. I want to thank you too for helping to heal that "fatherless" child in my own heart. Growing up without a father in my teen-age years left wounds which your patience helped to heal.

We had one great problem though. In spite of all these outward and inward signs, I sometimes found it hard to believe that you really loved me. When we were married in June 1952 in the Christus-Kirche in Mannheim, our chairs were far apart, a symbol of all that we would have to bridge in our marriage—two different mother tongues, traditions and geography. We both knew that neither of us was the "dream picture" that each had imagined as a partner. You even said laughingly but honestly that you would have liked a petite, dark-haired wife, and look what you got—a tall, red-headed Swedish-American! We knew beyond a doubt, though, that God had led us together and because you said yes to me, I could answer with my yes to you.

How often did it happen in our life together, that just when I was ready to answer your love, you turned and left and I could see only your back? Your self-discipline seemed to take over. I have never met a man who accomplished as much as you did in your fifty-five years on this earth. Your sense of duty was great—whether it was to answer the daily pile of mail on your desk, to finish your current manuscript, to help people in their spiritual lives and with their personal problems or to organize Family Life Seminars throughout the world. It seemed to me then that everything else was more important to you than our marriage.

I looked at your back as you turned to your work and my heart would weep. You did say that you loved me, but so often I could not accept it because I had not yet accepted myself completely.

Over the years I learned too that it is hard for any man on this earth to come into those dark recesses of a woman's heart and fill all her needs. Only One can do that. It is, no doubt, the greatest anxiety that a woman has—to be unloved. If I could tell my sons only one thing about the loving man it would be this: he is the one who can give his wife the assurance that she is loved. He does not forget to tell her in some way every day that she is number one in his life. And she must hear and accept what he is saying, both in word and deed.

How often we said in our seminars, "You can never change your partner; you can only change yourself"! Remember when our niece wrote after years of struggle in her marriage, "Since I have accepted my husband as he is, instead of how I would like him to be, we have peace"? It was so much fun to go to our first Marriage Encounter back in 1975 after we had conducted a number of seminars for other couples. My love for you was very great as you dared to share out of the depth of your heart. I have the notebook in my hands where you answered the dialog questions we were given. In the same notebook I found the letter you wrote to me after our last training seminar in Ottmaring, Germany, when each person wrote a love letter to his or her partner which was then mailed a few days later. You ended your letter with these words:

> My wish is only that also my admiration and joy, the warmth that I feel in my heart for you should reach you, lay hold of you and make you certain deep within of my love. I know that often I have not taken the trouble to tell you this, or I have not done it intensively enough and I ask you to forgive me and not to give up on me. I promise you that I will not give up on you either and that I will be faithful to you until death do us part and that I will fill up your cup with never-ending patience. Because it is only out of your filled cup that I can fill my empty sheets of paper with living words.

Each morning when we were at home, you would come into our bedroom with a tea tray. You were an early riser, a lark, and sometimes you had already written for two hours at your desk before it was even light. Deliberately and lovingly you then prepared a pot of tea and brought it to our room. After sharing it together we would read the Daily Texts according to the Moravian Church and plan our day together. Each morning as you did this loving service, I would think of how Jesus did the same for his disciples as we read in John 21. They had fished the whole night but without success. When it was morning, Jesus stood on the shore. He gave them explicit directions as to where they should cast their net. They were obedient and caught one hundred fifty-three fish. When they had pulled their net to shore and had got out on land, they saw a charcoal fire, with fish lying on it, and bread. Jesus had prepared a fire and breakfast for his tired, hungry and cold disciples.

And you did the same for me. When the door opened and I saw you with the tray, I could sense the presence of Jesus with you. We often discussed this and chose this text to be engraved on the family tombstone, "Just as day was breaking, Jesus stood on the beach" (Jn 21:4).

Then came your last morning, October 13, 1979. You had arisen early as usual, gone for your morning run, shaved and bathed. The door opened to our room and there you stood with the tea tray. It was your last deed on this earth—to fill my empty cup.

Ingrid

Selected Bibliography

Affemann, R. *Geschlechtlichkeit und Geschlechtserziehung in der modernen Welt* [Sexuality and Sex Education in the Modern World]. Gütersloh: Gerd Mohn Verlag, 1979.

Bovet, Th. *Mensch sein* [Being Human]. Tübingen: Katzmann Verlag, 1979.

Illies, J. *Kulturbiologie des Menschen* [Human Cultural Biology]. Munich: R. Piper & Co. Verlag, 1978.

Meves, C. and Illies, J. *Lieben—was ist das?* [Loving—What's That?]. Freiburg: Herden-Verlag, 1970.

Schaffer, U. *A Growing Love.* New York: Harper & Row, 1977.

Tucholsky, K. *Ausgewählte Werke in zwei Bänden* [Selected Works in Two Volumes]. Reinbek bei Hamburg: Fritz Raddatz, Rowolth Verlag, 1965.

Unseld, S. "Das Tagebuch" Goethes und Rilkes "Sieben Gedichte," [Goethe's "The Journal" and Rilke's "Seven Poems"], Insel Library Volume 1000. Frankfurt: Insel Verlag, 1978.

PART III

PERSONAL GROWTH

BOOK TEN

LOVE YOURSELF

1 Do I Love Myself? *657*

2 The Consequences of the Lack of Self-Love *673*

3 Depression & Helps in Overcoming It *680*

loving myself

when i love you more
than i love myself
i am really loving you less

loving myself less than you
i make it harder
for you to love me

your love for me
is so very dependent
on the love i have for myself

and my love for you
will be stronger
if you love yourself the way you love me

—Ulrich Schaffer

1
Do I Love Myself?

THE GIRL ENTERED OUR HOTEL ROOM. IT WAS THE DAY AFTER MY wife and I had given a lecture at one of the universities in northern Europe. The hotel room was the only place we had for counseling.

She was a beautiful Scandinavian girl. Long blond hair fell over her shoulders. Gracefully she sat down in the armchair offered to her and looked at us with deep and vivid blue eyes. Her long arms allowed her to fold her hands over her knees. We noticed her fine, slender fingers, revealing a very tender, precious personality.

"I Am a Beautiful Girl"

As we discussed her problems, we came back again and again to one basic issue which seemed to be the root of all the others. It was the problem which we had least expected when she entered the room: She could not love herself. In fact, she hated herself to such a degree that she was only one step away from putting an end to her life.

To point out to her the apparent gifts she had—her success as a student, the favorable impression she had made upon us by her outward appearance—seemed to be of no avail. She refused to acknowledge anything good about herself. She was afraid that any self-appreciation she might express would mean giving in to the temptation of pride, and to be proud meant to be rejected by God. She had grown up in a tight-laced religious family and had learned that self-depreciation was Christian and self-rejection the only way to find acceptance by God.

We asked her to stand up and take a look in the mirror. She turned her head away. With gentle force I held her head so that she had to look into her own eyes. She cringed as if she were experiencing physical pain.

It took a long time before she was able to whisper, though unconvinced, the sentence I asked her to repeat, "I am a beautiful girl."

Nobody Loves Himself

It is an established fact that nobody is born with the ability to love himself.

The German psychotherapist Dr. Guido Groeger summarizes the findings of modern psychology by saying,

> The opinion seems to be widespread that everyone loves himself and that all that is necessary would be to constantly remind people to love others.
>
> It is up to the theologian to decide how to interpret the word of the Lord, "Love your neighbor as yourself"—whether as a commandment and a statement or as a double commandment.
>
> In any case the psychologist has to underline the fact that there is in man no inborn self-love. Self-love is either acquired or it is nonexistent. The one who does not acquire it or who acquires it insufficiently either is not able to love others at all or to love them only insufficiently. The same would be true for such a person also in his relationship to God.
>
> It is true that the foundation for this ability to accept oneself is laid in early childhood. But it is also true that an adult needs the assurance of being affirmed and accepted sometimes to a greater and sometimes to a lesser degree, depending upon the different situations of his life.

> Because this affirmation is often withheld—especially in Christian circles-a type of Christian is created who loves out of duty and who in this way tortures not only others, but also himself.
>
> Often the choice of a profession is motivated by such a deficiency of love. One hopes to satisfy one's own needs by satisfying the needs of others. But this is a miscalculation.[1]

On the other hand the Catholic philosopher, Romano Guardini, in his essay, "The Acceptance of Oneself," writes, "The act of self-acceptance is the root of all things. I must agree to be the person who I am. Agree to have the qualifications which I have. Agree to live within the limitations set for me. . . . The clarity and the courageousness of this acceptance is the foundation of all existence."[2]

If both statements are true, if on the one hand self-acceptance is the foundation of all existence and if on the other hand nobody is born with the ability to accept and love oneself, we face a real challenge. A tremendous task is laid before us, and each one has to ask himself—

> Have I accepted myself fully and completely?
>
> With my gifts? With my limits? With my dangers?
>
> Have I accepted my lot? My gender? My sexuality? My age?
>
> Do I say yes to my marriage? To my children? To my parents? To my being single?
>
> Do I say yes to my economic situation? To my state of health? To the way I look?
>
> In short, do I love myself?

In our day the words love and acceptance have become interchangeable, and thus far I have used them synonymously, for I believe that this is helpful. Since the word *love* is often abused and has become trite and meaningless, I have used the word *acceptance* to prevent us from viewing love as merely romantic, sentimental or sexual. To love means to accept the other as he really is.

Precisely this was one of the problems of our student visitor in that hotel room. She could not get along with anyone, neither with her fellow students, nor with her professors, nor with her neighbors, nor with her own family. She was full of hostility and criticism.

When we asked her for an explanation she blamed it all on herself. She said that she loved herself too much, thought only of herself and called herself an egoist. For this reason she could not accept others and really love them.

We had to contradict her. We claimed that just the opposite was true. It was difficult for her to love others because she did not love herself enough. It is impossible for us to accept the other one as he is if we have not accepted ourselves as we are.

Love Yourself

This sheds a new light on the command which Jesus emphasized as ranking in importance next to loving God: "You shall love your neighbor as yourself" (Mt. 22:39; Mk. 12:31; Lk. 10:27).

In the Bible we first find this command in Leviticus 19:18. Besides the verses mentioned above, this command is found in three other crucial places in the New Testament, each of which succinctly summarizes the passage in which it is found. Galatians 5:14 summarizes the "whole law" in one word, "You shall love your neighbor as yourself." Likewise James 2:8 gives this command as a fulfillment of the "royal law," and Romans 13:9 gives it as the summation of "all the commandments." The command to love your neighbor is never given without the command to love yourself.

Usually it is assumed that everyone loves himself. Everyone is an egoist. And we are taught that this is wrong; instead of loving ourselves, we should love our neighbor. However, this is not what the verses state. They do not say, "Love your neighbor *instead* of yourself," but "Love your neighbor *as* yourself." Self-love is thus the prerequisite and criterion for our conduct toward our neighbor. It is the measuring stick for loving others which Jesus gives us.[3]

We find that the Bible confirms what modern psychology has recently discovered: Without self-love there can be no love for others. Jesus equates these two loves, and binds them together, making them inseparable.

The question now is how Jesus could assume that in his listeners this self-love, which Dr. Groeger says must be acquired, is naturally present. Part of the answer may lie in the fact that the people of Jesus' time were more composed and less neurotic than modern man. They found it easier to acquire self-acceptance and to like themselves. Therefore, Jesus could assume that his hearers had learned to accept themselves to a degree people today have yet to learn. What was presumed as a natural characteristic in their time is something which is difficult for modern man to acquire.

Could it be that the difficulty in loving ourselves is also one of the negative side-effects of our so-called civilization?

When I write this I have to think of many of my African friends. It seems so much easier for them to accept themselves than for us Westerners. I am reminded of one of my best friends, an African man who is rather short. A well-meaning person once suggested to him that he wear shoes with higher heels in order to appear taller.

This was almost an offense to my friend. Hadn't God made him short? Why should he seek to change what God had created? He had accepted himself as he was and loved himself with his height. I am sure this complete self-acceptance is one of the reasons that he can be such a good friend to me.

In the passage describing the friendship between David and Jonathan, we find the thought-provoking sentence, "Jonathan loved him as his own soul" (1 Sam 18:1). This was not meant as a criticism that Jonathan should cease loving his own soul and instead transfer all his love to David. Jonathan did love his own heart. He did not say, "I'm afraid of myself and I'm worthless." Rather Jonathan loved himself and that enabled him to have a deep friendship.

I ask myself: Do I love my own soul? Do I sometimes talk to my soul as David did in Psalm 103? "Hello, soul, listen! Can you hear me? Bless the Lord, O my soul, and forget not all his benefits."

Does all that I have discussed thus far have anything to do with marriage? It certainly does. It has everything to do with it. Everything!

In his famous passage about marriage, Ephesians 5:21-33, the Apostle Paul refers no less than three times to self-love. In verse 28 we read, "Even so husbands should love their wives as their own bodies. He who loves his wife loves himself." And verse 29 says, "For no man ever hates his own flesh, but nourishes it and cherishes it. . . ." Finally, verse 33 states, "Let each one of you love his wife as himself. . . ."

I must admit that I had preached many times about this text before this straightforward statement, which sounds so odd to our ears, really struck me: "Whoever loves his wife, loves himself." This certainly cannot mean that whoever loves his wife is egocentric. On the contrary, whoever loves his wife proves that he has acquired self-acceptance and thus has learned to love himself. It is interesting that Paul explicitly mentions the physical dimension of self-acceptance. "Even so husbands should love their wives as their own bodies. . . . For no man ever hates his own flesh. . . ."

Just as Jonathan and David's deep friendship causes me to ask myself, "Do I love my own soul?" in the same way I should ask myself, "Do I love my own body?" Do I really love myself, body and soul?

Self-Love and Selfishness

I can well imagine that many who have followed my thoughts to this point have become quite nervous and uncomfortable. Does this not contradict what we, as good Christians, have been brought up to believe? Is it not written, "He who loves his life loses it" (Jn. 12:25). "If any one comes to me and does not hate . . . even his own life, he cannot be my disciple" (Lk. 14:26). "If any man would come after me, let him deny himself. . . ." (Mt. 16:24).

Indeed we are so ingrained with the idea of self-denial, self-sacrifice and the fear of being egotistical that the admonition to love one's self seems almost a blasphemy. What then is the distinction between self-love and selfishness, between self-acceptance and egoism?

One difficulty lies in the fact that the word *self-love* has a double meaning. It can mean self-acceptance as well as self-centeredness. Along the same line, Josef Piper, in his essay "Zucht und Mass," stresses, "There are two opposing ways in which a man can love himself: selflessly or selfishly. Only the first is self-preserving, while the second is self-destroying."

An example of self-love in the negative sense is illustrated by the Greek myth about Narcissus. He was a youth who, while gazing at his reflection in a well, fell in love with himself. Totally engrossed with his own image, he tumbled into the water and drowned. From this myth, the word *narcissism* is derived. Another Greek term for "self" and "love" denoting the same idea is *auto-eroticism*.

Self-love used in the positive sense of self-acceptance is the exact opposite of narcissism or auto-eroticism. It is actually a prerequisite for a step in the direction of selflessness. We cannot give what we do not possess. Only when we have accepted ourselves can we become truly self-less and free from ourselves. If, however, we have not found ourselves and discovered our own identity, then we must continually search for ourselves. The word *self-centered* aptly describes us when we revolve only around ourselves.

To put it bluntly, *whoever does not love himself is an egoist.* He must become an egoist necessarily because he is not sure of his identity and is therefore always trying to find himself. Like Narcissus, being engrossed with himself, he becomes self-centered.

Hermann Hesse, in his novel *Steppenwolf,* which won the Nobel Prize for Literature in 1946, describes the intricate relationship between the lack of self-love (which he calls self-hate) and self-centeredness (which he calls "sheer egoism") or the inability to love others. He says about Harry Haller, the hero of the novel:

> As for others and the world around him he never ceased in his heroic and earnest endeavour to love them, to be just to them, to do them no harm, for the love of his neighbour was as strongly forced upon him as the hatred of himself, and so his whole life was an example that the love of one's neighbour is not possible without love of oneself, and that self-hate is really the same thing as sheer egoism, and in the long run breeds the same cruel isolation and despair.[4]

This throws light on modern man's striving to escape isolation and despair by trying to find himself. In his search, Haller employs various means such as drinking, overeating, "tripping" and experimenting with sex. These are all expressions of a lack of self-acceptance. Those who are searching attempt to find self-fulfillment easily through drugs, alcohol, food and sex. These result, however, in a still deeper dissatisfaction and an endless striving. Modern man's perpetual search is so self-centered precisely because he neither loves nor accepts himself.

Self-acceptance excludes self-centeredness. For love "does not demand its own way" (1 Cor. 13:5 Living Bible). Love has found its own way. We can give only that which we have, lose only that which we possess and "hate" only that which we love. The word *hate* as used in Luke 14:26 is not meant in the emotional sense. It is rather the ability to free ourselves from the bondage of our own personal desires and needs. Self-love is necessary before we can be freed from ourselves.

Self-acceptance means "I love me," and it enables me to turn my attention outwards. Auto-eroticism means "I love I" and means that I am unable to look beyond myself. Self-love must be acquired. Auto-eroticism is inborn.

All of us experience the auto-erotical phase before we are five years old and again at the onset of puberty. If we remain in this self-centered phase, however, we will never acquire true self-love.

The "crush" is an emotional expression of the auto-erotical phase. The adolescent often has an idol with whom he is in love and on whom he projects his own identity. He loves the image of himself which he sees in the other person, as Narcissus loved his reflection in the well. The dream is shattered the moment the idol is viewed from a realistic stance and is no longer congruent with the adolescent's projected image.

Masturbation is a physical manifestation of the auto-erotical phase. It is an immature sexual expression coinciding with the stage of puberty and thus ought not to cause anxiety. Physically speaking, masturbation is not harmful to one's health. Nevertheless, this is not a legitimate argument which can be used to minimize the harm caused if practiced beyond this state.

Of greater concern is the effect which masturbation might have on the development of one's personality. If a person over twenty still finds it necessary to masturbate, this may be an indication that he has remained in the auto-erotical phase and has not yet acquired self-love. The development of his personality is hindered because he is trying to play simultaneously the roles of giver and taker. He who has fully accepted himself does not need to masturbate. He can "let go of himself" in every sense of the word. He is mature enough to love.

I am reminded of a couple whom all their friends would describe as very unselfish. This couple's home is open to all kinds of people in need. They are always ready to help and to serve others.

I knew them even before they knew each other. They both came from very unloving homes with strict, demanding parents, where words of praise were scarce or nonexistent. As a result they both developed a poor self-image and struggled with masturbation as a sort of comfort and substitute for the lack of being loved. For the young man, masturbation became an almost daily habit.

As soon as they fell in love with each other, this habit came to an abrupt end, and they could both return from this dead-end road. Not because they released their sex drives by petting or premarital intercourse, but because they opened each other's eyes to see the positive sides in one another. They helped each other to love themselves. There is no doubt in my mind that this healthy self-love which they developed was the secret of their unselfishness.

Jesus and Self-Acceptance

The relationship between self-love and selflessness, between self-acceptance and self-denial, is best illustrated by Jesus Christ. Jesus wholly knew himself and he was completely in harmony with himself. With absolute authority he could say, "Before Abraham was, I am" (Jn. 8:58). And with the God who himself said, "I am who I am" (Ex. 3:14), Jesus declared, "I and the Father are one" (Jn. 10:30).

It is interesting to note that in the New Testament statements regarding Christ's identity precede statements concerning his self-denial. For example, before Jesus washed his disciples' feet, there is a majestic declaration of his total self- acceptance: "Jesus knew that the Father had given all things into his hands, and that he had come from God and was going to God" (Jn. 13:3).

Self-acceptance and selflessness are interrelated. Jesus knew who he was and accepted his identity and purpose. Self-acceptance was an intrinsic part of his life, enabling him to turn his attention outwards and to love truly the people with whom he came into contact. It was unnecessary for him forcefully to establish his equality with God, or to search gropingly for his own identity. Rather he "emptied himself, taking the form of a servant. . . . And being found in human form he humbled himself and became obedient unto death, even death on a cross" (Phil. 2:7-8). Here too Jesus' self-denial is preceded by a statement of his identity: "though he was in the form of God" (Phil. 2:6). In short, since Jesus loved himself, he was selfless and able to love others "as he loved himself."

"That's easy enough for Jesus," we might say, "but who are we?" Paul deals with this objection by saying simply, "Your attitude should be the kind that was shown us by Jesus Christ" (Phil. 2:5 Living Bible).

If Jesus Christ is our life this means that the acceptance of ourselves is indeed "the foundation of all existence" as Guardini would say. Discipleship is not possible without it. The obedience of self-denial presupposes the obedience of self-acceptance.

Learning to Love Ourselves

If it is true that self-love is the foundation of our love for others and if it is true that it is not innate but acquired, then we must face the pressing question, How can we learn to accept ourselves, to love ourselves?

Essentially, there is only one answer to this question: We must learn to let ourselves be loved. With this statement I would like to point out that it is not enough that love is offered to us. Another step is also necessary: We must learn to receive it. We must learn to accept acceptance.

The other day I observed a woman who received a compliment about a nice dress she was wearing. She shrugged the compliment off by saying, "Oh, this is just an old thing I've had hanging in my closet for years." Even if this was true—very likely it was not—it was clear to me that she had not learned the art of receiving recognition, of accepting acceptance.

The counter-example is that of a woman we know who keeps a notebook of enjoyable experiences in her life. Here she also puts down in writing compliments she has received from members of her family or friends. Just one example: One day her four-year-old told her, "You are the best Mommy in the world." Whenever she feels down or depressed, she just opens this book to lift herself up.

It seems to me that because of a misconception of Christian modesty and humility we are inclined to ward off any expressions of praise. Yes, we even tend to mistrust those who praise us and doubt the motives behind their affirmation. For this reason we discourage those who laud us until they give up expressing love to us. In this way we deprive ourselves of the experience of being loved, which is so necessary if we want to learn to love ourselves.

Martin Buber said, "Man comes to himself only via the 'you.' " Michelangelo wrote to the woman he loved, "When I am yours, then I am at last completely myself." As far as marriage is concerned, it would be entirely justified to alter Paul's statement in Ephesians 5:28 by saying, "He who is loved by his wife, learns to love himself."

The first chance we have in life to experience being loved is when we are nursed at our mother's breasts. Here our physical and emotional needs are wholly and unconditionally met. A baby just sucks and sucks and sucks, and no demands are made of him. Those deprived of this experience as infants may, later on in life, find it relatively harder to build a foundation for self-love and self-acceptance.

Unfortunately breastfeeding has been on the decline for many years, even to the extent of doctors advising mothers against it. This could explain the increasing number of people today who seek oral satisfaction through smoking and drinking.

The chain smoker is certainly not the "he-man" he attempts to portray. Neither is the woman with a cigarette hanging from her lips e-*man*-cipated. On the contrary, an addiction to nicotine and alcohol may indicate a futile attempt to provide a substitute for the mother's breast which was denied in infancy. It may express a longing for being loved which the individual hopes will enable him to love himself.

However, as Dr. Groeger has pointed out, to be accepted and loved is important not only in infancy and childhood, but throughout one's life. We need it as adults too. We all know how encouraged we are by a word of recognition or affirmation in our daily work. No one is able to work without it every now and then. It is as necessary as bread for our daily life—perhaps for men even more than for women.

Why? I don't know. But it is a fact that the male ego is weaker than the female ego. Maybe it is because the man was at the receiving end from the very beginning—as a suckling. Maybe it is because it is easier for women to attract attention simply because they *are* more beautiful.

Recently I observed teen-agers at a summer camp. I saw how easily the girls attracted others because of their beautiful figures, hair styles and make-up. The 16-year-old boys with their pimply faces, drab jeans and T-shirts were not such a pretty sight. I felt how much these boys longed for recognition and admiration. I believe few women realize how much a man is dependent upon a woman's praise, even more than the other way around.

These differences though are relative. All of us need the "daily bread" of praise, and it is precisely this "daily bread" which we withhold from each other. We are quick to criticize and slow to praise. Often we express only negative remarks and in this way destroy the self-confidence of those around us. Church circles are no exception.

Such a negative atmosphere fosters the development of the person whom Dr. Groeger defines as one who "loves out of duty," whose love does not spring from joy but is forced or, as Hermann Hesse puts it, comes out of an "heroic and earnest endeavour."

Have we not been in this situation ourselves from time to time? We don't feel like loving, but we tell ourselves, "I should love, I should love, I should love!" It is like doing spiritual chin-ups in an effort to please others and God. But we all know how it is with chin-ups. For a limited time we can pull ourselves up, but then inevitably the moment comes when we run out of strength and have to give up. It is like a car which runs out of gas. You can push it a little way, but you won't get very far, especially not uphill.

When I was in Africa, one of my fellow missionaries constructed a windmill. He planned to draw water out of a deep well by means of wind power. The idea was great. But when there was no wind we had no water. A man on a bicycle had to produce the power. You can guess just how long it was before he was tired.

A person who loves out of duty is like the man on the bicycle. He tries to produce love by his own effort. He receives no power from outside. He cannot love, because he is neither loved nor praised. And on the other hand, he is not loved and praised, because he does not love.

A Vicious Circle

What I have described thus far is actually a vicious circle:

We are unable to love others because we have not learned to love ourselves.

We cannot learn to love ourselves because we are not loved by others or are unable to accept their love.

We are not loved by others because we are unable to love them or we love them only "out of duty."

We are unable to love them because we have not learned to love ourselves.

And so the vicious circle starts again from the beginning.

And what if no "wind from outside" ever hits us? What happens to the person who has never known what it is to be loved? What happens to the child who grows up never having experienced the warmth and security of a loving home, of parents who care and spend time with him? And if he gets only reproof and criticism at school and again at work, what then? If it is true that a man comes to himself only via the "you," what happens then to someone who has never related to a "you"?

Is such a person destined to a life of loneliness and a vain search for self-acceptance? Is there no power able to break this vicious circle?

The Breakthrough from Outside

Psychologists and philosophers can ably describe and explain this vicious circle, but they cannot help us to break it. It cannot be broken from inside. There must be an outside source.

In Romans 15:7, the Apostle Paul points to this outside source: "Accept one another, therefore, *as Christ has accepted us* for the glory of God" (NEB).

Jesus Christ is the power from outside breaking the vicious circle. Now we get ground under our feet. Jesus Christ is the only one who accepts us as we are, fully, unconditionally, and therefore he makes it possible for us to accept ourselves as well as one another.

Take baptism as an example. There are certainly many weighty and justified questions which can be asked concerning the practice of infant baptism. This message, however, is conveyed clearly through it: God has accepted me unconditionally before I could do anything to earn his love.

Martin Luther, who was deprived of warmth and love as a child, wrestled his whole life long with self-acceptance. To help himself when in the throes of deep doubts, he scrawled in large print on his desk, "I have been baptized."

Through Christ, God has taken the initiative in love. He spoke the first word. He took the first step. Therefore we can love: "We love, because he first loved us" (1 Jn. 4:19).

The question is, How much does this fact mean to me personally? Does it mean enough so that I can stop blaming my childhood or my past circumstances or other people for my inability to love? Can I stop sitting on the pity pot and allow God's love to transform me?

The parents of a distinguished family phoned us. Their son was hospitalized after an unsuccessful suicide attempt.

"I am going to do it again" was the first thing he told us when my wife and I visited him.

"Why?"

"I am an error, a mistake. I am not supposed to exist." We did not understand.

Slowly the full story emerged. He had overheard a nasty conversation of his parents and learned that he was an unwanted child. His mother had forgotten to take the pill, and in anger his father had reminded her of it and blamed her for it.

This experience had crushed him. What was the meaning, the purpose, of his life, if he was not supposed to live in the first place? If his parents did not want him, who did?

God? Does God want all children to be born who are born? Even if their parents did not want them to be born? These questions had been too hard for him. So he had rung the alarm bell.

"God wants you," we assured him.

"How do you know?" He looked at us with eyes that expressed doubt and hope at the same time.

"Jesus was himself an unwanted child," I answered, "an embarrassment to his parents, unexpected and unplanned. No human action was involved in his coming into being—let alone a human desire. Actually he remained an unwanted person all his life—until they tried to kick him out of this world by crucifying him."

"And still," my wife added, "there has never been a child more wanted, more loved by God and never a person who became a greater blessing to more people than Jesus."

The face of the boy expressed unbelieving amazement. "I—a blessing?"

"Yes, a special blessing," we confirmed him.

Never had we understood in a deeper way the invasion of God into the vicious circle. The totally unaccepted one accepts the totally unaccepted. The unwanted God wants those who are unwanted. The unloved God loves those who are unloved. The Incarnation defines the true humanity of man. Therefore there is acceptance for everyone.

We prayed together with the boy and witnessed his acceptance of God's acceptance.

Love Is More than Acceptance

So far I have used the words *love* and *acceptance* interchangeably. But here it should be added that love is more than mere acceptance.

Christ accepts us as we are: "Him who comes to me I will not cast out" (Jn. 6:37). But when he accepts us, we cannot remain as we are. Acceptance is nothing but the first step of love. Then it exposes us to a process of growth. Being accepted by the love of Christ means being transformed.

In his fourth thesis which he nailed on the church door in Wittenberg, Luther stated, "God's love does not love that which is worthy of being loved, but it creates that which is worthy of being loved." God's love does not allow us to remain as we are. It is more than mere acceptance. It works and forms, it carves out the image which God has intended. This is a lifelong process and sometimes a painful one since growth is connected with pain. God says, "I accept you as you are, but now the work of love begins. I need your cooperation—your self-love."

Someone asked me in confusion, "Is this not a contradiction? On one hand I should accept myself as I am—'agree to be the person who I am.' On the other hand I should work on myself and change and grow?"

My answer: God's love does not exempt us from the obligation of working on ourselves, but it makes this work possible, promising and hopeful. To let God accept me and to accept myself does not mean to sit back passively and say, "This is just the way I am—I can't do anything about it." It means rather to allow God's chisel of love to work on me. Self-acceptance is merely the necessary first step in a process of growth.

Dr. Theodor Bovet writes, "If I love myself in the right way, then it is impossible for me to remain standing still. On the contrary, I want to change so that I can become that which God desires me to become. In the same way we should love also our neighbor."[5]

Some readers have reacted critically to my book *I Loved a Girl,* saying that I did not accept François, the young man with whom I was corresponding, because I tried to change him. Actually, I did accept him, as the first letters show. But then I challenged him to change his ways precisely because I loved him. Love is more than acceptance. We want to see our neighbor become all that God created him to be.

2
The Consequences of the Lack of Self-Love

IF WE LOVE OURSELVES IN THE WRONG WAY, THEN IT IS IMPOSSIBLE to grow and develop into the people God wants us to be. Many problems result from the lack of self-love. I have already discussed the search for self-identity through drinking, eating, "tripping" and experimenting with sex. But other problems too can result from the lack of self-love.

The Auto-erotical Choice of Profession and Partner

The choice of entering into people-oriented professions may be motivated by the need to be needed. It often stems from an unconscious attempt to make up for a deficiency of love. By placing himself in a position where he is needed by others, the unloved person attempts to fulfill his own needs and bolster his own self- concept.

However, as Dr. Groeger points out, this is a miscalculation. Such a helper cannot really help, for he needs the needy one more than the needy one needs him. He may need him to such a degree that the more he tries to help the more he becomes entangled with himself and is therefore unable to really understand the other one.

The choice of a life partner can also be an attempt to make up for a deficiency of love. Such a choice will always result in a very difficult marriage. He who cannot love himself will confront his spouse with insatiable demands and long for the love of the other one without being either able or willing to give something in return. Cruel as it may sound, marriage is no sanatorium for love cripples. A deficiency of self-love cannot be restored just by getting married.

Hostility toward the Body

If I am unable to accept myself, I am unable to accept my body. Hostility toward the body is always a symptom of lack of self-love. He who does not love himself does not love his body either.

In his book *A Place for You,* Dr. Paul Tournier gives two examples of such a negative attitude toward the body. They remind me of our experience with the Scandinavian student related at the beginning of this book:

> A pretty woman confides in me that her first act when she goes into a hotel bedroom is to turn all mirrors with their faces to the wall. Another tells me that she has never been able to look at herself naked without a feeling of shame. "This body of mine," she adds, "is my enemy."[6]

These women were unable to accept their own bodies because they were unable to accept themselves.

Such hatred for one's body will, of course, have a negative effect on marriage. As I have already mentioned, the Apostle Paul in Ephesians 5 specifically emphasizes the physical dimension of self-acceptance. Marriage problems in the sexual realm are usually connected with the fact that at least one of the partners has difficulty in accepting his body.

Could that be the reason why so many Christians fail to achieve sexual harmony in marriage? Many Christians seem to have the feeling that their physical relationship, if not "worldly" or even sinful, is somehow less good in God's eyes than their spiritual fellowship, that the body is less pleasing to God than the soul. It is not surprising that such an unhealthy attitude toward the body affects their physical harmony.

You will find in circles where the sinfulness of man is constantly stressed, and as a consequence healthy self-love is downgraded as sinful pride, that a deep-seated disrespect or even hatred of the body is the result. It is hard to imagine adherents of such a theology ever joining a gymnastic club, let alone taking dancing lessons, though this could be a decisive help in developing a positive self-image of the body and overcoming this particular neurosis.

As Dr. Tournier writes,

> Gymnastics, especially the dance, singing, and all the arts of bodily self-expression, have great therapeutic value. It is not a matter of accepting willy-nilly that one has a body, but of rediscovering its value, of using it as a genuine manifestation of one's person, and of becoming aware once more of its spiritual significance. The body is the place of love. The sex act is not merely the expression of one's feelings, but the sublime gift of oneself, a true spiritual testament.[7]

An additional aid for the woman, single or married, who wishes to learn to love her body and herself is to live consciously in harmony with her menstrual cycle. The cycle is as unique and individual as one's fingerprint. This is why the intimate knowledge of its individual characteristics can help a woman tremendously in finding her own identity.[8]

Abortion and Hostility toward Children

When we travel from country to country we are struck by the increasing hostility toward children throughout the world. Interestingly this is not so prevalent in some of the countries behind the Iron Curtain, let alone in the Third World, but especially in the so-called "Christian West."

I remember when we came from Africa to Germany with five children of kindergarten and grade school age, it was next to impossible for us to find a place to live, for the children a place to play, and for all of us a place where we could spend our vacations together. In Finland we met young couples with two children who would like to have had a third child (and there is certainly no overpopulation in Finland!), but they were afraid of being ostracized by society. In America too we have met mothers who were ashamed because they had become pregnant a third time.

It seems to me that there is a direct relationship between the lack of self-acceptance, the hostility toward the body and the hostility toward children. Bringing forth children is a part of the physical dimension of life. He who does not have a positive relationship to his body will find it difficult to reach a positive relationship to the child, who is a fruit of his body.

I wonder whether one of the deepest roots of the abortion problem does not lie here. Could it be that this also is the result of non-self-acceptance which expresses itself in a hostile act against the unborn fruit of the body? Can an expectant mother who wishes to abort her child really love herself? Otherwise how could she act so egotistically?

Overeating and Undereating

It is strange, but it seems to me that while a man requires relatively more personal recognition, a woman finds it relatively more difficult to develop a positive relationship to her own body. In our many interviews with women who possess a poor self-image, my wife and I have discovered two symptoms which occur repeatedly: Either these women eat too much or they eat too little. Both overeating and undernourishing one's self are expressions of the same disease—lack of self-love.

Through the lack of self-love an empty hole is created. Overeating—or getting drunk—is the futile attempt to fill up this empty hole. On the other hand, undereating, denying the body what it needs, may cover up an attempt to punish and deny the unloved self. Yes, it may be a way of saying, "I'd like to get rid of myself, be free of myself."

But true freedom of one's self, true "self-lessness" cannot be achieved so cheaply. It can only be accomplished through the longer and more costly process of learning self-acceptance.

The ultimate expression of the wish to be free of one's self, by-passing the route of self-acceptance, is suicide. Suicide is the ultimate expression of hostility toward the body and of non-self-acceptance.

Fear

Whoever takes this final drastic step and attempts suicide demonstrates that he fears life more than death. Fear too is a result of a lack of self-love.

"Love seeketh not her own," writes Paul in 1 Corinthians 13:5 (AV).

But he who does not know what love is and cannot love himself must always "seek" himself, constantly pursued by the fear that perhaps he will never discover that for which he is searching. Consequently, the self-centered person tends to be apprehensive. He revolves around his own axis, losing sight of all else but himself and his own interests. In such a person, fear takes root. The egoist feels insecure, unprotected and at the mercy of a cruel, unloving world. He clings to himself defensively, afraid that to do otherwise would ensure personal defeat and destruction.

Precisely because fear and self-centeredness are so closely bound together, we are susceptible to a specific variety of fear which is especially widespread today, namely the fear of failure. It is a natural by-product of modern man's idolatry of accomplishment. From early childhood we are indoctrinated with the philosophy that performance determines worth. When a machine ceases to be productive, it is discarded. Likewise if a person fails to per form at the level expected of him, he is considered useless. Our society has no room for "failures" and so nonachievers become ostracized.

An outcast, however, cannot love himself. He whom society judges worthless cannot acquire the feeling of self-respect and self- worth which a person needs in order to be able to live. Therefore, the fear of failure becomes greater than the fear of death.

Once more we encounter the connection between lack of self-love and of suicide. The potential suicide feels trapped between his fear of failure and his own self-centeredness. Thus he concludes that the only way to get rid of his fear is to get rid of himself.

But suicide is not the answer. The answer is to learn how to live with fear.

In this respect a word of Jesus has become very helpful to me: "In the world you have tribulation; but be of good cheer, I have overcome the world" (Jn. 16:33). The Greek word for "tribulation" conveys precisely the idea of "being pressured," "being trapped." The German translation uses the word *Angst.* It is the same word we find in "anxiety" and "anguish." It comes from *Enge* and means "strait," "narrowness," being in a tight spot, in a bottle neck, zeroed in. All these expressions describe ably the experience of fear.

For me the greatest help of this verse is that it ends the myth that as a Christian I have to be fearless. Jesus states it soberly, realistically, matter-of-factly: "In the world you have such tribulation. In the world you have fear."

The first help in learning how to handle fear is to stop fighting it. My own experience during the Second World War was a tremendous school in learning how to live with fear. Sometimes I had to live for days and weeks in the fear of being killed any minute, almost any second. Every time the roar of the Russian artillery was heard, I knew that within the next few seconds it would be decided whether I would live or die. It was an uninterrupted exercise of living with fear.

I remember that the first help for me was that I stopped fighting fear and learned to admit to myself, "Walter, you are afraid." In that moment the tight grip of fear loosened, and fear became bearable. Yes, it even became a positive force challenging my faith.

Faith did not free me from fear, but fear forced me to believe. Every time I heard the roar of the enemy fire, I threw myself down into the ditch or foxhole where I was. In an act of surrender to the One who has overcome the world, I said, "You have me completely." I can only express it in a paradoxical way: I learned not to be afraid of fear.

At this point it is important to notice that Jesus did not say, "I have overcome tribulation. I have overcome fear." But, "I have overcome the world." This gives us another decisive help in dealing with fear. We cannot attack fear directly, but only indirectly according to the rule of the "Knight's move" in chess. The Knight is not allowed to attack his opponent straight-on, but only "around the corner." In the same way we can only deal with fear "around the corner" in an act of surrender to the One who has overcome the world—including our own merciless, achievement-oriented society.

Herein lies our hope and consolation: This One who overcame the world had fear himself. He lived through such agonies that "his sweat became like great drops of blood" (Lk. 22:44). Through the power of his fears Christ gives us strength to live with fear, not to be afraid of it, yes, to "cheer up" in the midst of fear and tribulation. "Cheer up, for I have overcome the world" (Jn. 16:33 Living Bible). In Christ we can cheerfully have fear.

With the word *cheerful,* however, I touch another sore spot. Maybe the lack of cheerfulness is the most common manifestation of the lack of self-love found today. Therefore the final part of this book shall be dedicated to this problem.

3
Depression & Helps in Overcoming It

DEPRESSION TOO IN THE FINAL ANALYSIS IS, I BELIEVE, A RESULT of the lack of self-love.

It is astounding how many depressed people there are. It is still more astounding how many depressed Christians there are. I am not speaking here of superficial Christians who lack vital faith and spiritual depth. No, I am thinking of many sincere believers who live in a personal relationship to Jesus Christ and who in spite of it have to struggle again and again with deep depressions.

At the root of every depression is the feeling of having lost something. Outward circumstances can be the cause: the loss of material goods, the loss of health, the loss of a beloved one, the loss of confidence, the loss of self-respect in becoming guilty, the loss of an ability perhaps as a result of aging. We react to these experiences of loss with sadness, self-pity, mourning, disappointment, envy, shame and self-depreciation. All these feelings flow together like little brooks in the stream of a general feeling of depression.

Today especially three kinds of depression are on the increase. First, there is a depression stemming from exhaustion. Especially executives, top-achievers and overconscientious housewives suffer from it. They experience the loss of being able to achieve perfection. Their feeling of self-competence and "the sky's the limit" slowly fades away and throws them into depression out of complete exhaustion.

Another specific depression is induced by moving to a different residence. Even rearranging furniture and redecorating can result in a feeling of loss. One feels uprooted and is acutely aware that one's home, the four walls one knew so well, are missing.

There is even a depression stemming from the loss of a task or of a certain burden we have to carry. Depression stemming from retirement is one version of it. Strangely enough it strikes not so long as we are burdened by a certain task, but in the moment the burden is lifted. When the job has been completed, when the battle has been won, when the exam has been passed, when the tension has been relieved and the conflict solved—then this kind of depression hits us out of the blue sky. The loss of a challenge, of work or of a struggle precipitates us into an aching void.

There is also a depression stemming from no apparent outside cause, but which assails a person from within. It can manifest itself in either restless, nervous energy or passive inertia, which make any constructive action impossible. Such a "depression from inside" is usually accompanied by tormenting self-accusations and exaggerated guilt feelings. Although no tangible source can be found, ideas of being deprived, poor, small and inferior persist and lead to a complete loss of any feeling of self-worth.

This explains why the depressed person is so vulnerable and oversensitive when confronted with criticism. He cleaves and clings to other people and longs desperately for recognition and the assurance of being loved, in order to be able to love himself.

The deepest root of depression is the feeling that I have lost myself and have given up hope of ever finding myself again. There is nothing in me worth loving. I grope into a void when I try to love myself.

This means that self-acceptance and depression are closely interrelated. The above description of various forms of depression vividly depicts a self-centeredness which we recognize as a natural consequence of a lack of self-love. Therefore, the best protection against depression is for us to learn to love ourselves, and at the same time victory over depression enables us to acquire self-acceptance.

Depression in the Bible

In overcoming depression, it is encouraging to know that the Bible, that tremendously human book, understands us with these feelings.

There is the well-known story of King Saul who was often plagued by deep depression and depended upon David, the shepherd boy, to help soothe him by playing on his lyre: "Now the Spirit of the LORD departed from Saul, and an evil spirit from the LORD tormented him. . . . Whenever the evil spirit from God was upon Saul, David took the lyre and played it with his hand; so Saul was refreshed, and was well, and the evil spirit departed from him" (1 Sam. 16:14, 23).

From this story, we can gain a helpful hint in counteracting depression. Music conveys harmony and order and thus can heal a mind in disorder and disharmony.

The Bible offers us another example in the story of Nebuchadnezzar. Having disregarded a dream sent by God to warn him against illusions of grandeur and to admonish him to repent, Nebuchadnezzar fell into a deep depression and lived as a wild animal: "He was driven from among men, and ate grass like an ox, and his body was wet with the dew of heaven till his hair grew as long as eagles' feathers, and his nails were like birds' claws" (Dan. 4:33).

Nebuchadnezzar, however, relates how he overcame this depression and gives us another helpful hint—namely the act of praise and thanksgiving: "At the end of the days I, Nebuchadnezzar, lifted my eyes to heaven, and my reason returned to me, and I blessed the Most High, and praised and honored him who lives for ever" (Dan. 4:34).

Another example from the Old Testament is the story about Elijah in 1 Kings 19. Interestingly enough depression struck him after a spiritual highlight experience, after a great battle of the Lord had been won. In a state of great physical exhaustion, he "sat down under a broom tree; and he asked that he might die, saying: 'It is enough; O LORD, take away my life; for I am no better than my fathers' " (1 Kings 19:4).

Again we can learn a lot from the way the Lord dealt with his depression. No reprimand, no appeal to the will, but instead loving care, rest, food—and touch: "And he lay down and slept under a broom tree; and behold, an angel touched him, and said to him, 'Arise and eat.' And he looked, and behold, there was at his head a cake baked on hot stones and a jar of water. And he ate and drank, and lay down again" (v. 5).

In the New Testament, the outstanding figure is the Apostle Paul. He was certainly, by nature, subject to depressions. Romano Guardini in his book *The Image of Jesus in the New Testament* vividly portrays this side of the apostle. Through his description, I must say, Paul became more human to me. Guardini writes about Paul, "He seemed to be a man who attracted that which was difficult, against whom fate seemed to be pitted, a harassed man. . . . He had to suffer much, continuously and in all situations."

Paul was a rabbinical student, a discipline which served to nurture his perfectionistic tendencies. The same depression which assails all top-achievers when they are faced with the reality of their own human limitations and failings is certainly contained at least in the undertones of the following sentences: "I do not understand my own actions. For I do not do what I want, but I do the very thing I hate. . . . For I know that nothing good dwells within me, that is, in my flesh. I can will what is right, but I cannot do it. For I do not do the good I want, but the evil I do not want is what I do" (Rom. 7:15, 18-19).

One cannot help but ask the question: What evil might this man have done to cause him to talk like this? Walter Uhsadel, professor of theology at Tübingen University, comments on this: "The inner vulnerability of depressed persons causes them to be more aware of their failings and to suffer more under the burden of this knowledge than other people."[9]

Focusing on the last few chapters of 2 Corinthians, Uhsadel points out another typical symptom of a depressed person which Paul demonstrates as he vacillates between boasting and self-devaluation. Simultaneously, we can sense Paul's deep longing for recognition, appreciation and love as expressed in 2 Corinthians 12: 11: "I have been a fool! You forced me to it, for I ought to have been commended by you. For I am not at all inferior to these superlative apostles, even though I am nothing."

I am aware that one must be careful not to "psychologize" Scripture. But I believe it was precisely Paul's sensitive nature which God used to clarify man's character and his relationship to God.

The book of the Bible, however, where I feel most understood is the Psalms. The one who prayed Psalm 31, for instance, certainly knew what depression was:

Be gracious to me, O LORD, for I am in distress;
  my eye is wasted from grief,
  my soul and my body also.
For my life is spent with sorrow,
  and my years with sighing;
my strength fails because of my misery,
  and my bones waste away. (vv. 9-10)

This feeling: I am spent, consumed, "eaten up." I am becoming less and less; I am vanishing away. Time crawls slowly along without an end or purpose. We can visualize them—this crowd of sighing Christians.

What psychosomatic medicine has discovered today the psalmist experienced long ago. Body and soul are a unity. Grief of the soul means grief of the body. The psalmist's depression assaults even his bones.

I am the scorn of all my adversaries,
  a horror to my neighbors,
an object of dread to my acquaintances;
  those who see me in the street flee from me. . . .
Yea, I hear the whispering of many—
  terror on every side!—
as they scheme together against me,
  as they plot to take my life. (vv. 11, 13)

This feeling: I am threatened, trapped. I have only enemies. Everyone is against me; nobody understands me. Nobody accepts me. Nobody loves me. I have no more strength to defend myself, no more ambition to seek friendship. I am hopelessly alone.

I have passed out of mind like one who is dead;
  I have become like a broken vessel. (v. 12)

This feeling: I cannot contain myself, hold myself together. I am being poured out; everything is flowing out of me and I am losing, losing, losing.

Helps in Overcoming Depression

The Bible clearly shows that God realizes we have these feelings and that he understands us when we do. Maybe from this fact we can derive already a help in dealing with depressions: We do not need to be ashamed of them. They are no flaw in our make-up or a discredit to the name "Christian."

On the other hand, however, we should not sit on the pity pot and mope the whole day. At one time when my wife was rather depressed, she asked one of our teen-age sons, "What shall I do?" After a few minutes' reflection, he answered, "Above all, Mommy, do something! Don't just do nothing!" It was precisely the right word for her at that moment.

In a way each person is his own best doctor when it comes to curing depression.

I know a lady who often suffers from depression with no apparent outward cause. When she is in this state it prohibits her from thinking clearly and acting objectively, so she has made for herself what she calls a "depression emergency kit." Like a doctor's prescription, she has written down instructions to herself telling her what to do in case of a depression.

First of all, she has a little box of cards with special Bible verses containing promises and assurance. She picks out a card and reads it aloud. Next, she makes herself a good cup of tea which she sips slowly while listening to a favorite record. She also has on hand an absorbing book which she has been burning to read but which she has saved for this occasion. Afterward she calls up a friend and combines the visit to her with a walk in the fresh air.

Do we sense that we must have at least a bit of self-love if we would choose this method of attacking depression?

I mentioned already the unhappy childhood and strict religious upbringing which caused Martin Luther great difficulties in learning to love himself. To love himself meant for him only the sinful streak in man tending toward egoism. From what we have learned thus far concerning the interaction between the lack of self-love and depression, it is no wonder that Martin Luther was a man sorely afflicted by depression. Precisely because of his own experiences he is able to give us sound advice. I would like to share some of his suggestions with you, adding comments of my own:[10]

1. *Avoid being alone.* Luther states that isolation is poison for the depressed person, for through this the devil attempts to keep him in his power. "Talk among yourselves, so that I know I am surrounded by people," requested Luther in one of his "table talks." It was supposedly at a moment when he felt himself down.

2. *Seek out people or situations which generate joy.* Joy is always pleasing to God, even though it may not always be of a religious origin. Enjoying a good play or movie is just as legitimate as taking a long walk in the woods.

3. *Sing and make music.* Here Luther emphasizes the active involvement necessary for a person to make music of his own rather than simply listening to it. He once advised an aristocrat who was despondent, "When you are sad and feeling discouraged, just tell yourself, 'Up! up! I must play a song on the organ in praise of my Lord.' For the Scriptures assure us that God delights in song and playing musical instruments. So play upon the keys and give yourself to song until the gloomy thoughts are passed, just as David did. If the devil continues to pester you, reprimand him saying, 'Be gone, Satan, I have to sing and play now for my Lord Jesus.' " Again, Luther refers not only to religious music here but to music in general. God is really the listener, and we give him joy by our playing, a joy that returns to lighten our own heavy hearts.

4. *Dismiss heavy thoughts.* Luther warns us of the danger of becoming engrossed by gloomy or despairing thoughts which tend to keep us awake at night or assail us the first thing in the morning. He advises us either to laugh at the devil or to scorn him, but by no means to give in to him on this matter: "But the very best thing would be to refuse to fight with the devil. Despise the depressive thoughts! Act as if you would not feel them! Think of something else and say: 'All right, devil, don't bother me. I have no time now to occupy myself with your thoughts. I must ride horseback, go places, eat, drink and do this or that. Now I must be cheerful. Come again some other day.' "[11]

5. *Rely upon the promises of Scripture.* They encourage our mind to think positively, just as the lady with the depression emergency kit realized. Especially helpful are the verses known by heart because they

have helped us in a specific situation. They are like rods and staffs comforting us when walking through the valley of the shadow of death, to put it in the words of Psalm 23.

6. *Seek consolation from others.* In a state of depression, we often make a mountain out of a molehill. A friend, however, sees things in the right perspective and recognizes the positive side to which we are momentarily blind. Just as it is impossible to lift ourselves out of a swamp by grasping our own hair, in the same way we need the assistance of others to rescue us from the grip of despair. We should ask ourselves, in turn, are we the sort of people who are able to offer help to others just as God sent help to Elijah—touch, in the form of a warm assuring embrace, a good meal, rest in a quiet, orderly room. Yes, even a bouquet of flowers can put away a depression.

7. *Praise and thanksgiving.* These are powerful weapons against depression. We are reminded again of Nebuchadnezzar, who, when he raised his eyes to heaven and praised God, overcame the depression which had seized him. It helps to make a list of the things one is thankful for and then praise God for them audibly.

8. *Think of other depressed people.* This is rather a surprising suggestion from Luther, but it makes sense to me. It shakes the person out of his self-centered sorrow in which he maintains that no one else in the world has suffered as much as he.

9. *Exercise patience with yourself.* The word *exercise* is important here and can also suggest the idea of practicing or training. Sometimes we must resign ourselves to the fact that life contains valleys and deserts that simply must be endured. Just as any other skill has to be learned, we must learn how to persevere during such times of personal stress.[12] I would like to add a suggestion from my own experience. Physical exercises of any form—jogging, swimming, dancing or gardening—are all excellent devices for practicing patience with yourself. Any sweat-producing activity (and the sauna should certainly not be forgotten) that enables the entire skin surface to "weep" results in an amazingly quick recovery from depression.

10. *Believe in the blessing of depression.* There can also be a positive, fruitful side to depression. This final suggestion of Luther contains an important insight which I would like to discuss in conclusion.

The Gift of Depression

The German word for depression is *Schwermut. Schwer* can mean "heavy" as well as "difficult." *Mut* is the word for "courage." So the word *Schwermut* contains a positive message. It means the courage to be heavy-hearted, the courage to live with what is difficult.

There is a courage involved in being depressed. There is such a thing as the gift of depression—a gift which enables us to be "heavy," to live with what is difficult. Once I heard an experienced psychiatrist say, "All people of worth and value have depressions." Indeed, shallow, superficial people seldom have depressions. It requires a certain inner substance and depth of mind to be depressed. Young children, whose mental and emotional development have not yet reached this stage, cannot experience actual depression.

Suicide can be an indication of a person's inability to be depressed.[13] It may be much easier for those lacking depth in their personality to cut the thread of life. In reference to this fact, the philosopher Landsberg made a comment which becomes increasingly meaningful the more one contemplates it: "Often a man kills himself because he is unable to despair." Suicide appears here to be a result of the inability to know true despair and endure depression. The suicide lacks the courage to be depressed. Luther's surprising suggestion, "Believe in the blessing of depression," belongs in this context.

It seems to me that creative people such as artists and musicians tend to be more susceptible to depressions, perhaps because this "courage to be heavy" is a prerequisite for fruitfulness. It is no coincidence that the poet Rainer Maria Rilke, who searched for the secret of creativity with a passion exceeding that of his contemporaries, writes in a letter from Rome in May 1904:

> We know little, but that we must hold to what is difficult is a certainty that will not forsake us; it is good to be solitary, for solitude is difficult; that something is difficult must be a reason the more for us to do it.[14]

Note that Rilke associates the acceptance of what is difficult with the acceptance of solitude.

In another letter of August 12th of the same year, Rilke points out that depression—just like self-love—in working upon us transforms us and produces change. When we read his lines we are again reminded of Luther's advice to have patience with ourselves:

> So you must not be frightened if a sadness rises up before you larger than any you have ever seen; if a restiveness, like light and cloud-shadows, passes over your hands and over all you do. You must think that something is happening with you, that life has not forgotten you, that it holds you in its hand; it will not let you fall. Why do you want to shut out of your life any agitation, any pain, any melancholy, since you really do not know what these states are working upon you? Why do you want to persecute yourself with the question whence all this may be coming and whither it is bound since you know that you are in the midst of transitions and wished for nothing so much as to change? If there is anything morbid in your processes, just remember that sickness is the means by which an organism frees itself of foreign matter; so one must just help it to be sick, to have its whole sickness and break out with it, for that is its progress. In you, dear sir, so much is now happening; you must be patient as a sick man and confident as a convalescent; for perhaps you are both.[15]

The poet Owlglass reports the following conversation between two friends, one of whom was suffering from a deep depression. The first asks, "Why are you so depressed, my friend?" The other one replies, "I wish I could fly away and leave all my burdens behind me. I am so full of them and so heavy-hearted because of them. Why can't I be lighthearted?" His wise friend responds with the counter-question, "Why are you not empty-hearted?"

Given the choice, which would we rather be—lighthearted and empty or heavy-hearted and full? I believe it is possible to love ourselves with a full heart, even if it is heavy, while hardly could we love ourselves with an empty heart.

Some readers certainly must have been puzzled when I dealt with the depression of King Saul. Here the Bible uses a very strange expression. It describes depression as an "evil spirit from God" (1 Sam. 16:23). An evil spirit from God?

Yes, this is authentic biblical thinking: Depression can be a part of God's plan. In the story of Saul, depression was an instrument which

God used to bring David into the king's palace. To believe in the blessing of depression means to recognize that God uses even depression to fulfill his plans.

No doubt there is a God-related depression, a "godly grief," as the Apostle Paul calls it, because it "produces repentance that leads to salvation and brings no regret" (2 Cor. 7:10). Or as the Living Bible translates this passage, "For God sometimes uses sorrow in our lives to help us turn away from sin and seek eternal life."

However, such a "turn" as a fruit of depression does not happen by itself. It needs the work of faith to consciously relate depression to God and receive it out of his hands. Otherwise such a turn may not take place and depression becomes a "worldly grief producing death" (2 Cor. 7:10).

This is what actually happened to Saul. He did not succeed in relating the evil spirit to God and change his life, but he became more and more entangled in his depressive moods, until finally even music did not help him anymore and he brought David into danger: "And on the morrow an evil spirit from God rushed upon Saul, and he raved within his house, while David was playing the lyre, as he did day by day. Saul had his spear in his hand; and Saul cast the spear, for he thought, 'I will pin David to the wall' " (1 Sam. 18:10-11). Depression can lead to sin when we do not relate it to God. It can become "worldly grief" producing death.

The counterpart to Saul is the depression of Jesus in the garden of Gethsemane, when he told his disciples, "My soul is very sorrowful, even to death" (Mt. 26:38). But in his prayer he succeeded in relating his depression to God and in opening himself to resources which did not come from himself: " 'Father, if thou art willing, remove this cup from me; nevertheless not my will, but thine, be done.' And there appeared to him an angel from heaven, strengthening him" (Lk. 22:42-43).

There is a depression in the midst of which we encounter God, in which we are held by God. This experience gives us the courage to love ourselves *with* our depressions and be cheerful even with a heavy heart. It reflects a depth of faith which the Apostle Paul expressed with the paradoxical statement: "As servants of God we commend ourselves in every way: . . . as *sorrowful,* yet always *rejoicing*" (2 Cor. 6:4, 10).

I wish so much that the girl whom I mentioned in the beginning and who could not believe and accept that she was beautiful, would read this book. Maybe it would help her to work on herself and undergo the painful-joyful learning process of self-love.

On that day when my wife and I talked with her we had too little time to do more than get her started. However, we did not let her go without taking action: We laid our hands on her and blessed her in Christ's name.

In our ministry we have experienced again and again the effectiveness of this action in the counseling process. For only Christ-centered counseling is really client-centered counseling.

We do not know where this beautiful girl is now. But we remember the words which were given to us for her. They were the same as the ones quoted above by the Apostle Paul. We blessed her that she might prove herself a servant of God—sorrowful, but always rejoicing.

BOOK ELEVEN

SPIRITUAL DRYNESS

Symptoms

It can be safely said that joy is the most elementary and most natural expression of a life lived in close fellowship with the living God. "Rejoice in the Lord always; again I will say, Rejoice" (Phil. 4:4). In Psalm 84:2, the psalmist cries out, "My heart and flesh sing for joy to the living God."

However, all of us know that there are days or even weeks and months when we cannot echo honestly what the psalmist says. Our heart does not "sing for joy," let alone our flesh. In fact, any joyful feeling seems far away and all our efforts to bring about such a feeling fail.

The "living God" seems dead. We read the Bible, but its words do not speak to us. Our devotional life becomes an empty habit. We have no desire to pray. The sacraments leave us indifferent. Christian virtues strike us as dull and unattractive. Our conscience be comes insensitive and blunt.

Verses like: "How sweet are thy words to my taste, sweeter than honey to my mouth!" (Ps. 119:103) strike us almost as mockery. On the contrary, we are tempted to say God's Word tastes insipid or even bitter. We could say with David, "My years are spent with sighing" (Ps. 31:10).

Such periods of spiritual dryness cause a tremendous amount of suffering in the life of a Christian. He tortures himself with the question: Why am I not able to love God as I did before? He endures deep conflicts, especially when he has to act as if he loved God, while inwardly everything is dead in him. If at least he could be silent during such periods! But the world around him needs and expects his love. The sick and the dying want to be comforted. Hurt and lonely people want to be understood. His family, students, congregation and fellow Christians want to be ministered to and strengthened. Nobody really knows what desperation is who has never faced another human being craving help when inside he feels completely empty and dry.

The so-called "dialectical theology" would probably say that the problem of "spiritual dryness" is entirely unimportant. It does not matter whether we feel joyful in our encounter with God. In fact, our "feeling" is entirely irrelevant to faith. What counts is that we believe in God's Word and its promises even if we do not feel anything of his power. The lack of feeling even challenges the greatness of our faith.

This argument is not altogether wrong. It may well be that when everything is dead in me, I can only cling to the fact of God's promise that I am and remain his child whether I feel like it or not.

Nevertheless, we should not conclude that this state of faith without feeling should always remain and that this is the normal situation for a Christian. Such dryness and barrenness is not normal, and we should endeavor to overcome it.

But to overcome spiritual dryness we have to first understand the causes. I would venture to give five possible reasons.

Causes

1. Sin

Sometimes a definite transgression of God's commandments, a conscious action against his will, which a person refuses to admit and to uncover puts him into a state of dryness: "When I declared not my sin, . . . my strength was dried up as by the heat of summer" (Ps. 32:3-4).

However, my experience in counseling has taught me that people who suffer from spiritual dryness are often very conscientious, sincere Christians who long for the nearness of the Lord and who are most careful to follow his will. Their problem is that in spite of this longing and carefulness and without being conscious of guilt, they feel remote from God and cannot help themselves.

2. Undernourishment and inertia

It is a spiritual law: "The one who gives out much must also take in much." The transgression of this law leads to spiritual dryness. The question which comes up here is the order of our daily devotional life and personal Bible study. It is not enough for a Christian to study the Bible only for a special purpose—in order to prepare a sermon, a Bible study or a message for a specific occasion. The daily quiet time where he allows his Heavenly Father to address him personally is as important for his spiritual health as his daily meals are for his physical health. If he gives out continuously without taking in, he will run dry.

However, in the spiritual realm, undernourishment can be caused not only by not taking in enough, but also by not passing on enough. The one who takes in much must also give out much—otherwise he may lose what he has.

Jesus once said: "To him who has [the passing on] will more be given, and he will have abundance; but from him who has not [the passing on] even what he has will be taken away" (Mt. 13:12).

Spiritual dryness may well be the result of an undernourishment which is caused by not feeding others. Many Christians are not inactive because they ran "dry," but they ran "dry" because they are inactive. Their inertia is not the effect of their dryness, but rather its cause.

3. Overfeeding and overstrain

I have observed that we are often afflicted with spiritual dryness after religious highlight experiences. After a retreat or Bible camp—especially if it was fruitful—or after the church festival days, Christmas, Easter, Pentecost, when we have been blessed by the richness of God's Word, we may suddenly fall into utmost poverty.

Therefore, we have to recognize that there is not only the possibility of a spiritual undernourishment, but of a spiritual overfeeding as well.

There are Christians who are able to take in an unlimited amount of spiritual food. They may belong to three different weekly Bible study groups or prayer circles and seem not to suffer any harm.

However, we have to realize that there are other Christians, just as sincere, whose soul condition is more sensitive and whose capacity to take in spiritual food is therefore limited. Overfeeding may damage their spiritual life and put them into a state of uttermost dryness.

There is also the possibility of spiritual overstrain. After a heavy week of teaching Christianity courses, leading Bible studies and devotions and preaching sermons, professors, Christian leaders and pastors may feel dead in their hearts on weekends.

Such spiritual overstrain can even affect a person over a longer period of time. A forced religious education in childhood—an overfeeding with joyless, "waterless," routine family devotions—may result in an adult dried-up state of indifference concerning spiritual matters. The mere sound of a reed organ (children of such families sometimes call an organ the "psalm pump") may cause antagonistic feelings.

4. Disregard of our body

Another cause of spiritual dryness is hinted at in Psalm 31:9: "Be gracious to me, O Lord, for I am in distress; my eye is wasted from grief, my soul and my body also." Just as joy affects heart and flesh (Ps. 84:2), distress affects soul and body.

It is an accepted fact today that body and soul are a unity and that a sick mind can be the cause for a sick body. "When I kept silence, my bones waxed old [RSV translation "my body wasted away"]. . . . My moisture is turned into the drought of summer" (Ps. 32:34 KJV). Here illness of the soul causes physical illness and "drought."

However, we have to learn that it can also work the other way around: Disregard of our physical life may affect our psychological health and cause spiritual "drought."

We Christians usually tend to overemphasize the spiritual side of life and underestimate the importance of biological facts—body chemistry, atmospheric pressure, weather, water and air pollution. We tear body and soul apart. What is said about husband and wife in marriage may well have its meaning also for body and soul: "What God has joined together, let no one put asunder" (Mt. 19:6).

It is true, a good pianist may be able to play on an old instrument. But even the best pianist cannot give full expression to the music he would like to play if the piano is out of tune.

Disregard of the physical aspect of life may cause spiritual dryness.

5. Loss of balance

Our conversion to Jesus Christ does not relieve us from observing the order of the creation of which we are a part. God's creation is built upon the balance between work and rest. "The seventh day God rested from all his work which he had done in creation" (Gen. 2:3).

In this respect, our lives are often hopelessly out of balance. We are overworked and are even proud of it. But if we neglect this rhythm between work and rest and despise the balance which God has put into his creation, we pay for it by the loss of our creative spiritual forces and again the condition of spiritual dryness results.

Therapy

Help for those who suffer from spiritual dryness has to be determined according to the cause.

1. Forgiveness

Confession and renewed assurance of forgiveness is the only help if a definite sin has been committed and is recognized as cause. However, as mentioned above, seldom should sin be automatically assumed. A gentle feeler in this direction may not hurt, but the counselor should be careful not to make the mistake of Job's friends who insisted that sin must be the cause of sickness. It can even be harmful for a person paralyzed by dryness to be exposed to moral imperatives.

2. Discipline and responsibility

If undernourishment is the cause, practical help for a new discipline in personal devotional life is indispensable. The more practical, the better.

We depend too much on secondhand sermons and devotions. Learning from others is good and necessary, but it *alone* is not enough. What we need to learn is to live more by firsthand experience—to dig out our spiritual food ourselves through personal Bible study.

Many need to be challenged by someone else in order to submit to a certain order of life. Order is not legalism. Legalism kills; order revives our spiritual life. Once a person has committed himself to a certain order and discipline, he feels almost momentarily refreshed. There is no life without order—also no spiritual life.

In this respect it is good to make a decision about the best time for daily devotions. Although the morning hour is ideal, it is not always possible. The recommendation of a Bible reading guide and suggestions for prayer may be helpful. Also the advice which Martin Luther gave to his barber Peter Beskendorf may be in order here:

> If the Holy Spirit should come . . . and begin to preach in your heart, . . . note what he proclaims and *write it down,* so will you behold wondrous things. . . .

Such "wondrous things" may mean being willing to take on a certain responsibility in God's kingdom. The fulfillment of a task, even if it may be very small, will have healing effects on an undernourishment which is caused by inertia.

3. Religious fasting

The cause of spiritual overfeeding demands the greatest courage of the counselor. In this case it could make things worse to tell such a person to pray more, study the Bible longer and attend more church meetings. This would be the same as advising a diabetic to eat more sweets and sugar.

It is probably much more helpful to prescribe to such a person a period of spiritual fasting, to advise him to limit his devotional life to a minimum, to pray only shortly, to abstain from the reading of religious books and to step back from congregational activities for a while—until the appetite for spiritual food is aroused again.

As I said, it certainly takes courage to give such advice and the one who does it will be exposed to severe criticism by dear, pious people who need habits—even if they are empty—in order to feel "secure" and who give in this way proof of their deep-seated insecurity.

4. Diet and exercise

Sleep and rest is the first answer in cases where a neglect of the physical aspect of our life is indicated. Also the diet is important. Does it, for example, include enough vitamins? More fruits and vegetables should be recommended and hiking and swimming encouraged. Then too, clean skin and air, good digestion and sunshine may sometimes do more good to our spiritual health than soul massage or hell-fire and brimstone sermons.

5. Playful serenity

A new balance of life may be more difficult to achieve than many think. It may demand a complete rearrangement of one's work and schedule and a change in the general style of life. Yet, spiritually, it may be very important. Do I take time out to relax, to celebrate, to play games? Do I sometimes do something without a purpose, allow myself to be completely absorbed by a hobby?

A playful serenity achieved in this way may be a greater testimony for our Lord than pious seriousness. At the same time such serenity may revive in us new creative forces and open the gates to new spiritual depths.

"This Illness Is Not unto Death" (John 11:4)

One final point has to be made: We should not consider spiritual dryness as only a calamity.

First of all, it should deeply comfort us that the Bible knows about such suffering and understands us as the above-quoted passages show. People in the Bible who walked close to God have had the same experience as we have: "My tongue cleaves to my jaws; thou dost lay me in the dust of death" (Ps. 22:15).

In fact, all those who have lived an intensive religious life—I think of Luther, Pascal, Kierkegaard—had to struggle through periods of spiritual dryness sometimes to the point of desperation. Often the intensity of such suffering may be in direct relationship to the intensity of a person's life with God, just as deep valleys show up only in the face of high mountains.

Therefore, we do not need to be ashamed of "dryness"; we can give up our attempts to hide it behind an ever-ready "Christian" smile, pretending to be joyful when we are not.

I have always been deeply comforted by the thought that suffering because God seems far away is only possible because at other times I have experienced his nearness. If we look at it in this way, then the suffering because of spiritual dryness may be a sign that the Holy Spirit is present in us, and it may contain the promise of new spiritual health.

We should therefore learn to consider spiritual dryness not only as a sickness, but rather as a wholesome fever, a symptom of recovery. We can think of those who suffer from it as the ones who are already sick among those who are not yet sick. It may be God's way of knocking at the door to announce that he wants to enter into our life anew.

Someone may ask: Why does God have to come to us again and again? Is he not always there—always near to us? Did he not say: "Behold, I am with you always"? He did. He is with us and yet he has to come. This is the mystery of our Christian life.

Seen from God's point of view, he is always equally near to us, closer than our own skin, whether or not we feel him. His relationship to us is an uninterrupted line.

Looking at it from our side, our relationship to God is often an interrupted line. Sometimes we feel closer to him, sometimes farther away. As day and night, heat and frost, summer and winter reign in God's creation, our spiritual life too is submitted to change and has its dry and rainy seasons.

Again and again we have to struggle through the empty stretches between the dashes of the interrupted line. Again and again God wants to come. Every desert contains the promise of a new advent:

"He turns a desert into pools of water, a parched land into springs of water. And there he lets the hungry dwell, and they establish a city to live in; they sow fields and plant vineyards, and get a fruitful yield" (Ps. 107:35-37).

BOOK TWELVE

MARTIN LUTHER'S QUIET TIME

MARTIN LUTHER HAD A BARBER. HIS NAME WAS PETER BESKENDORF. One day Master Peter must have taken the liberty of asking his world-famous customer and doctor of theology, "Dr. Luther, how do you pray?"

And Martin Luther answered. It was not beneath him to write a long letter to his barber—a letter of forty printed pages! It was published in the spring of 1535 under the title *A Simple Way to Pray, for a Good Friend.*

It is a precious letter. Not only does it give us deep insight into Martin Luther's personal spiritual life, but at the same time it is a classic example of counseling—competent spiritual counseling. Listen to this opening paragraph:

Dear Master Peter,

I give you the best I have. I tell you how I pray myself. May our Lord God grant you and everyone to do it better.

This is Luther talking to his barber! This is counseling. Luther puts his counselee up and himself down. Humbly he stands under him and therefore "under-stands" him. He places himself in Peter's world, and this enables him to pick up Master Peter where he is.

> A good clever barber must have his thoughts, mind and eyes concentrated upon the razor and the beard and not forget where he is in his stroke and shave. If he keeps talking or looking around or thinking of something else, he is likely to cut a man's mouth or nose—or even his throat. So anything that is to be done well ought to occupy the whole man with all his faculties and members. As the saying goes: he who thinks of many things thinks of nothing and accomplishes no good. How much more must prayer possess the heart exclusively and completely if it is to be a good prayer!

Today we call this "empathy"—feeling how someone else feels his life. Here we have a good example of how this can be done in a letter. Do we in our day really appreciate the possibilities of counseling by personal correspondence?

At the same time, this paragraph contains deep comfort for all of us. Luther had the same difficulty in his prayer life as we have—lack of concentration. Here is the first help he offers:

> It is a good thing to let prayer be the first business in the morning and the last in the evening. Guard yourself against such false and deceitful thoughts that keep whispering: Wait a while. In an hour or so I will pray. I must first finish this or that. Thinking such thoughts we get away from prayer into other things that will hold us and involve us till the prayer of the day comes to naught.

Luther knew that prayer can come to naught. He knew what it means to live through days of spiritual dryness. Again and again he shares without pretense his own struggle of being distracted by "foreign business and thoughts" and his often-experienced listlessness in praying. He says,

> We have to watch out so that we may not get weaned from prayer by fooling ourselves that a certain job is more urgent, which it really isn't—and finally we get sluggish, lazy, cold and weary. But the devil is neither sluggish nor lazy around us.

We feel "under-stood" as Master Peter must have felt "understood." Who of us does not know periods when our quiet time has become an empty, meaningless duty, dreaded and even hated, but in any case boring. And boredom is the deadly enemy of the Holy Spirit.

What suggestions does Luther offer to help us escape from the kingdom of satanic coldness in order to experience anew the atmosphere of the Holy Spirit with its warmth and joy?

Luther believes in a period of "warming up." The expressions "to warm up the heart" until it "comes to itself," "feels like it," "gets in the mood" occur several times in his letter. Actually the whole letter is nothing but detailed and practical instruction on how to "warm up the heart" *before* the Bible study starts, and it ends with the statement, "the one who is trained [in this warming-up practice] will well be able to use a chapter of Scripture as a lighter [*Feuerzeug*—the same word used in modern German for a pocket lighter] to kindle a fire in his heart."

For such a "warming-up prayer," the bodily posture seems to be important to Luther. Evidently he does not believe in sitting down. "Kneel down or stand up with folded hands and eyes towards the sky." Then he warns, "Watch out that you don't take too much upon yourself, lest your spirit get tired. A good prayer need not be long or drawn out, but rather it should be frequent and ardent."

And its content? Your personal needs and concerns? Oh no! Luther answers: Start with the commandments! Luther prays the Ten Commandments! Not that he rattles them off one by one. As a former Catholic priest, he has a lot to say against "heaping up empty phrases" (Mt. 6:7), against chattering, babbling and prattling. He calls it *zerklappern,* which means literally "to rattle something to pieces."

To avoid this danger Luther takes just one commandment at a time, "in order that my mind becomes as uncluttered as possible for prayer." To formulate a free prayer in his own words, he shares with Master Peter his personal method:

> Out of each commandment I make a garland of four twisted strands. That is, I take each commandment first as a teaching, which is what it actually is, and I reflect upon what our Lord God so earnestly requires of me here. Secondly, I make out of it a reason for thanksgiving. Thirdly, a confession and fourthly, a prayer petition.

Then Luther takes the trouble—and the time—to go through all ten commandments and to write out for his barber such a "garland of four twisted strands" as an example for each commandment. What a counselor!

For example, Luther writes the following about the seventh commandment, "You shall not steal":

> First I learn here that I shall not take my neighbor's property nor possess it against his will, neither secretly nor openly; that I shall not be unfaithful or false in my bargaining, my service and work lest what I gain should belong to me only as a thief; but I shall earn my food with the sweat of my brow and shall eat my own bread with all those who are faithful. At the same time I shall help my neighbor so that his property is not taken away from him through such actions as mentioned above. . . .
>
> Secondly, I thank God for his faithfulness and goodness in that He has given me and all the world such a good teaching and through it protection and shelter. For unless He protects us, not one penny nor one bite of bread would remain in the house.
>
> Thirdly, I confess my sin and ungratefulness, there where I have wronged someone and cheated him or where during my life, I was unfaithful in keeping my word.
>
> Fourthly, I ask that God may give grace so that I and all the world might learn His commandment and think about it and improve. I pray that there may be less stealing, robbing, exploiting, embezzling and injustice. I also pray that such evils may soon end when the day of judgment comes. This is the goal to which the prayers of all Christians and of all creation are directed (Rom. 8:22).

This is praying according to Martin Luther. We see that it is not just petitioning, reciting and speaking. It is learning, meditating, searching and thus acquiring the perspective of eternity.

What next? When you are through with the commandments, Luther says, take the Lord's Prayer and do the same thing. Take one petition at a time—and maybe one is enough for a day—and twist the four strands for your garland. Again he describes to Master Peter how he does it petition by petition.

In this context, Luther calls the Lord's Prayer the "greatest martyr on earth, tortured and abused by everyone." But when he prays it in his garland-way, he says, "I suck on it like a nursing baby and I drink and eat it like an aged man and can never become satisfied."

And when he has "time and leisure," after the Lord's prayer, Luther continues by taking up the Apostles' Creed, statement by statement, praying it in the same way.

Concerning the "first article about creation," Luther writes:

I believe in God, the Father Almighty, Creator of Heaven and Earth. First of all, if you allow it to happen, a great light shines here into your heart and teaches you in a few words something which could never be expressed in all languages, nor described in many books, namely: what you are, where you come from, where heaven and earth come from. You are God's creature, God's making and work. This means by yourself and in yourself you are nothing—you can do nothing, know nothing and are not able to do anything. For what were you a thousand years ago? What was heaven and earth six thousand years ago? Absolutely nothing, just as that which will never be created is nothing. Therefore, everything you are, everything you know and everything you are able to do is God's work, His creation, as you confess it here with your mouth. This is why you have nothing to boast about before God, except that you are nothing and that He is your creator and He is able to annihilate you at any time. Reason in itself does not arrive at such insight. Many learned people have tried to understand what heaven and earth, man and creature are. They have found nothing. Here however it says: The creed teaches that God has created everything out of nothing. Here is the paradise of the soul where it may go for a walk in God's creation. But it would take too long to write more about this.

Secondly, one should give thanks here that through God's goodness we have been created out of nothing and we are kept alive daily out of nothing as a delicate creature which has body, soul, reason, five senses etc. . . . And He has made us lords over the earth, fish, the birds, the animals. This refers to Genesis 1, 2 and 3.

Thirdly, one should confess and be sorry about our unbelief and ungratefulness, because we have not thought about them nor really recognized them. So we have actually done worse than the animals who have no reason.

> Fourthly, we should pray for the right and certain faith so that in the future we can seriously believe in the dear God and hold Him up as our Creator, as this article teaches.

It is obvious that Luther finds the Creed a helpful touchstone for meditation and for worship. These thoughts he shares with his barber may serve well as a model for our own.

At one point, however, Luther interrupts his explanation and shares with his counselee the following experience:

> It often happens that I lose myself in such rich thoughts [literally, "that my thoughts go for a walk"] in one petition of the Lord's Prayer and then I let all other six petitions go. When such rich good thoughts come, one should let the other prayers go and give room to these thoughts, listen to them in silence and by no means suppress them. For here the Holy Spirit himself is preaching and one word of His sermon is better than thousands of our own prayers. Therefore I have often learned more in one prayer than I could have obtained from much reading and thinking.

Thus we see that to Luther praying does not mean just talking. It also means being silent and listening. To him prayer is not a one-way road. It works both ways. Not only is he talking to God, but God is talking to him—and the latter is the most important part of prayer.

This is exactly what we should expect to happen in our Bible study—that God talks to us. Bible study is prayer. Therefore what Luther says about prayer can be applied to our Bible study and provide us with a tremendously helpful method for making a Bible passage meaningful to our personal life. The suggestion is to proceed verse by verse and make out of each verse a garland of four twisted strands.

By changing the order a bit and putting that which God requires at the end, many Christians are enriched in their quiet time by asking themselves these four questions about a text:

1. What am I grateful for? (Thanksgiving)
2. What do I regret? (Confession)
3. What should I ask for? (Prayer concerns)
4. What shall I do? (Action)

Again let us heed Luther's warning:

> Don't take too much upon yourself lest the spirit should get

> tired. . . . It is sufficient to grasp one part of a Bible verse or even half a part from which you can strike a spark in your heart. . . . for [and this is one of the deepest insights Luther shares with his barber] the soul, if it is directed towards one single thing, may it be bad or good, and if it is really serious about it, can think more in one moment than the tongue can speak in ten hours and the pen can write in ten days. Such a dexterous, exquisite and mighty instrument is the soul or spirit.

Therefore the quantity of Bible verses one reads is not decisive. It may be more fruitful to take a passage of a few verses and shake each verse like the branches of a tree until some fruit falls down. This will change Bible study from a boring duty to an exciting adventure.

It is advisable to apply each question strictly to the text at first. What is in this *text* which makes me thankful? What is in this *text* which corrects me, challenges me to change and leads me to repentance? Which prayer concerns does the *text*—not my own wishes-offer me? What is in this *text* which causes me to take action?

An answer will not be found every time to all these questions. Often the answers are interlocked. That which calls me to repentance may become my main prayer concern for the day and even may call me to an action of restitution or apology.

On the other hand, while the text should be a feeder for our thoughts, it should not be a restriction or boundary line for them. In thinking through these questions again, we can extend them into the experiences of our daily life, thinking also of the small things which make us thankful—a day of sunshine, a friendly greeting, a beautiful flower or a good letter which we have received. We may think of something which we should not have said. People may come to our minds for whom we should pray especially on this day. In answering the fourth question, we can plan the schedule of the day ahead of us and thus discover a very practical answer to the problem with which so many Christians struggle in vain—the problem of how to find God's guidance.

From Luther's testimony in this letter, it is evident that he believed firmly that God would speak to him through his thoughts, when the "heart is warmed up" and "has come to itself in the atmosphere of the commandments, the Lord's Prayer and the Apostles' Creed." "The Spirit will and must grant this and will go on teaching in your heart if it is conformed to God's Word and freed from foreign concerns and thoughts."

However, he gives a practical advice to his friend which should not be forgotten. He tells Master Peter to have his quiet time with pen and paper at hand to note down what God tells him:

> I repeat again what I said above when I talked to you about the Lord's Prayer: If the Holy Spirit should come when these thoughts are in your mind and begin to preach to your heart, *giving you rich and enlightened thoughts,* then give Him the honor, let your preconceived ideas go, be quiet and listen to Him who can talk better than you; and note what He proclaims and *write it down,* so will you experience miracles as David says: "Open my eyes that I may behold wondrous things out of thy law." (Ps. 119:18)

Indeed, those who get used to the discipline of having their quiet time with a notebook are not likely ever to give it up. What makes our devotional life so unattractive and boring is the fact that each day, every one of us has just about the same kind of general, vague pious thoughts. This causes monotony. Our thoughts remain distant and abstract and do not come to grips with our concrete daily life. The writing down, as Luther suggests, is a form of the incarnation of God's Word. It becomes tangible, visible and concrete. It forces us to be precise, definite and particular. Monotony is replaced by variety and surprise. Taking notes enables us also to check whether we have carried out what we planned in the morning. A Chinese proverb says, "The palest ink is stronger than the strongest memory."

Writing down what God has told us is also a great help in sharing when meeting with our prayer partner—also for decision-making in marriage. My wife and I agree on the same text for daily Bible study. This is especially helpful in periods when we are separated. When we meet again we can read to each other what we have written down in our quiet times—and experience "wondrous things."

It may take a little practice. Just as in preparing for a sports event, a warming-up is necessary in order to do one's best, so also is a "warming-up training" of the heart indispensable for our spiritual life. Martin Luther uses precisely these terms. It takes training and practice to discern our own ideas from God's thoughts. When you open the faucet in a new building, brownish liquid may come out at first. But if you have patience and let it run long enough, clear water will appear.

We can experience the same thing in our quiet time. If our praying changes from talking into being silent and our being silent changes into listening, the voice of the Good Shepherd will come through unequivocally, unambiguously and plainly.

The Spirit will and must grant this, if your heart is conformed to God's Word.

APPENDIXES

Besides his books, Walter Trobisch wrote a huge volume of letters to people in need around the world, and he wrote extensively in his personal journal. He also wrote any number of articles for magazines and journals. The four collected here are representative of this last category of writing and indicate the range of ministry he had.

Appendix One
Of Flight and Forgiveness*

There are experiences which help one to discover his own life. In a way they draw back a cover, and hidden things become visible. Our life is then like a discovery trip.

So it was with my flight to America. The beginning was very dramatic. I had received a scholarship for foreign study through the Church World Service and waited in Westphalia in central Germany for my papers. As they did not come after a long period of waiting, I decided to go in person to the passport office in Stuttgart in southern Germany. I left my baggage, all packed for this world journey, in Westphalia with the intention of picking it up on my way back to Bremen, the seaport in northern Germany.

In Stuttgart, however, it was decided very suddenly that the trip should be made by plane and not by ship. I had only a few hours to reach the airport at Frankfurt. There was no time to pick up the heavy suitcases and no alternative but to fly to America with the few things that

*Written in Germany in 1950.

I had packed in my briefcase. That consisted of a shaving kit, two shirts, three pairs of socks and a necktie.

And now began the discovery of my life. First, the take-off. As our plane raised itself from the runway and the moonlight outlined sharply its silver surface, I said to myself: One must always take off in such a way. Up out of the midst of confusion. Up out of the knowing-nothing-further. Up out of the battle for existence. Up out of the activity. Up out of the unsolved problems. That is real life!

Then the flight: To be over it all in this way—to contemplate the cloud carpet from above which always blocks the heavens when we gaze at them from below. One must be able to live as if in a flight—so daring—so released—so entirely unsupported—yet carried in such a way—so restful—in such pure air—straight as an arrow—clearly piloted—so entirely in God's hand. That is living in the true sense of the word!

Finally the landing. The lights of the airport flashed past as the plane swung in. One must be able to land in this way. So effortlessly—as if from another world—not out of the muck into the muck—not out of hurry into hurry—not from the same level, but from above—over all until we are at the place where God lets us see a gleam, a calling human heart, an open door, a landing spot.

There I had discovered anew my life—in this way to take-off, to fly, and to land—that is life!

But this life costs a price: Leave your baggage behind! God had shown me outwardly what he would say to me inwardly. If you wish to live thus, then you do not dare to drag so much around with you any longer: no longer so many worries, no longer so many plans, no longer so many hesitations, no longer so many responsibility complexes, no longer so many preferences and loves. But above all, no longer so much guilt.

Guilt—a Heavy Burden

I believe that guilt is some of our heaviest baggage. It weighs us down even more than bad luck, sorrows or worries, because there's always the sting of self-reproach connected with it, because it's something that we could help. It comes over us suddenly and then accuses us, mostly indirectly, on the quiet. Then it is as if a thousand doors lock. When all self-defense bounds are broken as matchsticks, then guilt looms up in front of us as a large, dark shadow. So much that would have been possible now is no longer possible. There is something which doesn't go away. When we are guilty, it's as if we had killed someone.

There is only one way to get rid of this baggage. To go and ask for forgiveness. We are ready, indeed, to take it to God if necessary. No one sees it then, and it isn't so humiliating for that reason. The disgrace before God isn't so hard on the nerves, because we care more for the respect of people than of God. But to go and confess what we have done before people? In front of them, to whom we have become guilty? To climb down from the pedestal of human decency and beg? That slays us. That goes too far. That's why we bring it at best down to the "if" form. "If I should have hurt you, then. . . ." "If you should have misunderstood me, then. . . ." "If you should have been offended by me, then. . . ." Very seldom does one say, "I have . . ." or "I am guilty. I beg your pardon!"

Now suppose it is turned around, and someone who is guilty toward you comes to you, and it is up to you to forgive. It may sound surprising, but it is my experience, that there is something which is often even heavier for us to carry than our own guilt, and that is our inability really to forgive from the heart. It, above all, hinders us in flight.

Moreover, everything is at stake through it—not only our relationship to our fellow men, but also our relationship to God. Jesus brings forgiveness in very close coherence with our prayer life. "Whenever you stand praying, forgive, if you have anything against anyone: so that your Father also who is in heaven may forgive you your trespasses" (Mk 11:25). Only what we give to the side will be distributed to us from above. Jesus has made it clear in the Lord's Prayer according to the Greek New Testament. "Forgive us our trespasses as we *have forgiven* those who trespass against us." *Our readiness to forgive is also the condition for God's readiness to forgive. He who has no peace with his neighbor also has no peace with God.*

Therefore the call should affect us in all our hate and bitterness, in our pride and our prejudices: For the sake of our prayers, which will be hindered, and for the sake of the grace of God which will be blocked, above all, for the sake of the "flight," *forgive!*

Why is it really so hard? It seems so simple, so easy, as if it belongs to the rule of decency: "Of course I forgive you."

But how is it truly in our hearts when we say this with such a generous gesture? Be absolutely honest! Aren't we quite proud of ourselves and our readiness to forgive? Deep in the heart, isn't there even triumph over the other who has missed the mark? Or is it already spiteful joy? Doesn't it tickle our ego if we are vindicated through the failing of another? Wouldn't we be flattered if it were to be made known before a jury?

Even if we should overcome the great word, "I forgive you," and say it calmly, still there's a temptation, if it is not yet unconquerable bitterness, to hold this reservation in the heart: "Forgive, yes, but forget—never!"

Free Sailing

Because I know my own heart, I doubt if man in general is capable of getting rid of this baggage, unless he has learned it from God himself, who instructs us in it once and for all.

Once a fellow wanted to convince me that God is not almighty, because he is not able to make what has happened "unhappened." I was then a young Christian, and was confused at first. In the course of the years, however, God showed me that that is exactly his particular work; the heart of all his dealings from the first to the last chapter of the Bible. God can make what has happened "unhappened" through his forgiveness. This is a forceful sign of his almightiness. It has taken place at the Cross. I have experienced it myself. It has wiped out my past, and made possible a whole new beginning. After that, only he who stands under the cross of Christ really can forgive. Only there is life! Only there is flight! Where there is no forgiveness there is no life. Jesus is the Life, because he is the Forgiveness. He is the Forgiveness in person. To you who would bring new life to this dying world God's commandment calls out: "Forgive! Forgive in this learned-from-God, past-effacing manner."

But what about the other one? What about when he doesn't see his own guilt? When he balks? When he is entirely indifferent whether he has guilt or not? When he doesn't wish my forgiveness at all? Isn't there any way to remove this tension? What can I possibly do?

It's been my experience in all the quarrels that I have had, or that have come to me, that it's never true one party is guilty a hundred per cent and the other zero per cent. The proportion is at least ninety-eight to two.

It is good to admit this two per cent. It's the great opportunity to get close to the other. Don't wait until he comes to you, but go to him and confess your own two per cent. This is so dumbfounding that it can overcome him at once.

Taking on the Guilt of Others

But this is not yet enough. Going on from there we must take at least ten per cent of the guilt of the other on our own head. No one can do this in his own strength. Now we see the second thing to be learned from God's forgiveness. We forgive, at best, one who is guilty. Christ goes farther. He, being not guilty, takes the guilt of others on himself. He carries voluntarily, as if it were his own, the entire guilt of the world on his outstretched arms nailed to the cross. Thus is God's forgiveness!

Why do we struggle so to take upon ourselves the guilt of only one other person when Jesus carries the guilt of us all! Only this extraordinary, this taking-on-myself guilt of another, is Christlike forgiveness. As Bonhoeffer says, "Only the extraordinary is essentially Christian."

Imagine what such an attitude would mean for the tensions in which we find ourselves, whether at work or at home. We are no longer trying to convince the one with whom we have quarreled—even if he is guilty seven times seventy—that we are in the right. Nothing is accomplished by that. "He who would again be in the right," says Herman Oeser, "has only counterfeit love." In this sense, maintaining that we are right is the worst thing we can do. But if we are ready to take upon ourselves a part of the guilt of someone else, that one will be helped. Instead of our triumphing over him, he will be changed. Instead of our blaming him, he will be won—won for him, who alone is the forgiveness and from whom this manner of forgiveness can be learned.

Forgiveness is the missionary attitude to life. When we forgive, a part of the nature of Christ glows out from us. God wins the world through his forgiveness which blots out the past and takes upon itself the guilt of others. The command of God rings out once more to you who would enroll in the army of those who have begun to win the world for God: Forgive!

Worldwide Significance

Yes, forgiveness does have something to do with the whole world. Forgiveness brings us in contact with the electric network of God and connects us to his power stream. It brings unexpected consequences and radiates into the whole world.

My trip to America was an example of this. I had experienced the forgiveness of God in a new way after studying theology for seven semesters. Then, as if an answer, the promise of a scholarship for my foreign study came true. I recalled the words of Carl Zuckmayer: "The times do not change, but when a man becomes changed, the whole world will be new." The message, which God had laid on my heart for America, was soon clear to me. It was the message of the world-renewing power of forgiveness.

Even in my first days in America, there was an opportunity to express this to the reporter who would interview the German visitor for the student paper. I begged plainly for forgiveness. I can still see today the heading of the article in the paper: "Forgiveness Stressed by German Student."

In response to this, the paper received at first some benevolent, but triumphant letters from those who had not grasped the full meaning of the message. Soon however there were other voices heard, this time surprisingly from former soldiers, who now in their turn asked for pardon. I even received some things which had been confiscated in Germany to be given back to the refugees. The message of the little word *forgive* opened all doors. There were many invitations to speak, so that at the end of my stay in America, much of my life was spent in planes and sleeping cars.

I also met a pastor who told me that he, as an American, felt guided to share this same message in Germany. This is what he reported in 1949:

> Upon my arrival in Germany, I was at a loss as to the approach I should use. I soon realized that many in Europe did not understand our policies nor our method in victory.
>
> One day while in the city of Worms, God gave me His approach.

I was standing on a pile of rubble. As far as my eyes could see in every direction, I saw nothing but waste and destruction. The thought came to me: "Many innocent people have lost their homes, schools, factories, churches, loved ones; yea, even their health and normal bodies. Someone is to blame." I realized that many had no more to do with the war than I had, and many wanted it far less. There, God by His Spirit poured into my soul the approach I was to use. That evening in another city, before I addressed the audience, I first of all asked the German people to forgive me and my people for what we had done to their cities, homes, etc. There were tears in many eyes. After the meeting, a good number of people grasped my hand and said: "When you return to your people, will you ask them to forgive us also?" Wherever I have had occasion to relate my experiences in Germany, I have included the above. Always it has the same effect.

Certainly another war will never solve the problems of this world. We have fought two, and everyone will admit that we are worse off than we were before. What is needed among the people is forgiveness, love, and understanding. Forgiveness brings reconciliation—reconciliation brings peace and harmony.

In this way forgiveness has circumvented the world. It builds world-spanning bridges. It has revolutionary power.

I believe that the greatest revolution is yet to come. Until now all revolutions have begun with the assertion, "The other is guilty!" One time it was another class, then another race. It is always the others who are guilty—the communists, the capitalists, the Nazis, the Jews. The greatest revolution will start with the statement, "I am guilty."

The world cries after this greatest revolution. It cannot be brought about through pacts, programs and conferences. What the world needs is forgiveness. This is the revolution of love.

We don't need to make pious wishes. This can happen. For:

If any one is in Christ,
he is a new creation:
the old has passed away,
behold, the new has come. (2 Cor 5:17)

Appendix Two
What Happened When I Wrote *I Loved a Girl*

My idea in writing *I Loved a Girl* was not at all to offer a sex essay to the whole world. It was to break the custom of the bride price (a payment to the father to permit marrying the girl) which was causing problems for my students. I had in mind to mimeograph about 100 copies for them.

So I sent the manuscript to a friend in Germany for him to mimeograph. He responded by saying he had an old stack of paper lying around "that I can't use anymore, so I would like to make this paper a gift to you if you pay for the printing." It was only for this reason that this thing became a book. I didn't have any idea that it was of any value to anyone except me and my students.

When my friend asked me, "How many copies do you want?" I thought, well, if we're going to print it anyway, we should make enough to last for my whole life. So I said, "Print a thousand copies." And he said, "You know, the paper is enough for 3000." So we made 3000. I didn't even tell my wife—what would she think!

When the 3000 copies arrived I wasn't in Cameroun. The man who received the shipment was from the Dutch Bible Society. He opened one of the packages because he was curious about what was in it. Then he began to sell *I Loved a Girl* along with his Bibles in his tiny store.

When I came back about six weeks later I wrote him, "Could you please send me 100 copies for my students?"—because after all, this is why I had written the book. He wrote back: "There is not one copy left; even my own copy they have bought."

My Dutch friend added, "We need more copies, and we already have requests for translations—and we need an English edition." So translations have been made until today I think we have them in more than 70 languages. The last request came from Eskimos in Greenland. Maybe because it's so cold up there they wanted a hot story.

The book has also been received behind the Iron Curtain. The Communists have accepted this ethic which relates sexual intercourse exclusively to marriage. They accept this book for this message and swallow the whole religious connotation with it. Attacks on it come mostly, at least in Germany, from the Christian side, the side of the new morality.

Another surprising thing was the response by readers. Africans drew three conclusions from the book: (1) Walter Trobisch must be a man who reads letters; (2) he takes them seriously; (3) why couldn't he answer me too?

So from the first moment when the book was published, a great number of letters poured in. Some wrote a letter for the first time. But mostly for the first time they expressed their own intimate problems. I could spot this because some of them copied whole paragraphs from the book—it gave them some of the vocabulary to express these things.

We have received about 9000 letters, counting the Africans only. About 50% of them come from non-Christians who have never been in touch with any church or any Christian message. This correspondence often ends up in requests for Bibles or spiritual help—often from Muslims, whom the church has always had a hard time to reach.

They get interested for the first time because they think they may get an answer to their personal problems. For a person who has been brought up in a collective society it is a great experience to be taken seriously as an individual. It's sort of the experience which the dumb man had with Jesus (Mark 7:33): "Taking him aside from the multitude *privately.*"

The first letter usually says, "Dear Mr. Trobisch, I read your address in the book. Does this letter reach you?" He really can't imagine that a man living far away would get this letter and even answer. "And then may I ask you my problem, if it reaches you?"

I write back, "Okay, write your problem."

They register this answer like the hour of their conversion. It is touching to see: "It was on Wednesday afternoon when the sun was almost down when your letter was brought to me"—a letter with his name on it, you see.

I don't think we have really taken into account the tremendous possibilities of counseling by mail and doing missionary work by mail, personally. It's very important. I could not mimeograph a stereotyped answer and mail it out. They want their own personal name. Some say, "When you publish another book, would you please instead of *François* put *my* name in the book, because this is my case."

What are all those letters about? Well, many marriage problems; a lot about birth control and bride price and choice of partner. Formerly in the African society individuals had no decisions to make; everything was by custom. Now suddenly they are thrown into the big towns where they live as individuals and have to make decisions, and they are not equipped.

Once a boy wrote me, "I love two girls the same way. . . . I don't know whom to marry. Would you please tell me whom I should marry? But please send the answer back air mail because in four weeks is the wedding day."

Most of the letters respond to one page in the book. It's where François says, "My telephone wire with God is interrupted. I would like to repair the telephone." In other words, the majority of letters are simply a confession of sin, and raise the question of forgiveness. Cultures may be entirely different, but underneath is the same human heart, longing for forgiveness. Putting it from the other side, the gospel is a universal message for all cultures.

Once I had a phone call in Mannheim, Germany. I thought it was either an American or a British girl. "I'm Japanese," she said. "May I see you?"

She came to our home, put down her briefcase, and pulled out 200 pages in Japanese script. "Mr. Trobisch," she said, "here is your book in Japanese. I have translated it."

One of her questions was that she didn't have the word for *love.* She had studied six years in the United States so she wasn't quite sure of her Japanese anymore. "We have different words for love in Japanese," she said, "nature love, animal love, mother love, father love—it just doesn't fit."

We went to the University of Heidelberg and asked if they could direct us to a Japanese couple. It was a funny situation. We rang the doorbell and I introduced myself as Pastor Trobisch and Miss So-and-So, and we would like to know what love is! But the ladies discussed this and they found the solution.

The next morning the girl came out for breakfast and I saw she had been crying. I didn't know what was the matter. I said, "Didn't you solve all the problems?"

"Yes, but I read the book again. And I came again to the story of François with the telephone wire, and you see, Pastor Trobisch, this experience I have never had. What if I, the translator of your book—my name is in the book—the people will come to me? I'm just a hypocrite." She had spent six years in a Lutheran college in the States and nobody had had the courage to say the aggressive upsetting word to her.

"Well," I said, "if you didn't have this experience, you must have it."

"Tomorrow morning my train is leaving for Frankfurt."

"Oh," I said, "you must have the experience today."

"Does it go so fast?" she asked.

"Sure." So we started to repair her telephone wires. And she had the experience of forgiveness.

When I brought her to the train in the morning, we chatted, just small talk, until the train started up. Then she said, "Now I'll tell you the truth. I didn't come at all because of your book. I came because of my telephone wire." She had gone through the whole trouble of translating the book into Japanese to have an excuse to come to see me.

Appendix Three
Church Discipline in the Light of Law and Gospel

The Question

An African pastor who is on an exchange scholarship in America attends a Communion service on Good Friday and notices with surprise that the whole congregation, numbering almost a thousand, takes Communion without exception. In answer to the question as to whether each of the communicants had been previously examined as to his "worthiness," he is told, "No, of course not!" The question which arises in his mind is therefore quite justified. How is it possible that the missionaries, who were sent out by the very congregation in whose service he participated, could have introduced such a totally different practice in his home church in Africa?

Two Misunderstandings

This divergence in practice can be traced to two misunderstandings which (to overstate the case somewhat) may be formulated in this way:

1. *The gospel as cheap grace.* This misunderstanding looks upon God as a benevolent grandfather who closes his eyes when his grandchildren make mistakes. Forgiving sin is his job, the very purpose of his existence. He has so much forgiveness that he has difficulty disposing of it all, for which reason he offers it for nothing. Everyone can have as much of it as he wants, without humiliation, without remorse, without change, without forsaking his sins, without restitution. No one has to take his sin seriously, for God himself doesn't take it seriously. The Lord's Supper becomes a matter of lavishing the grace of God on persons who are impenitent.

> Cheap grace is the justification of sin without the justification of the sinner . . . is the preaching of forgiveness without requiring repentance, baptism without Church discipline, Communion without confession, absolution without contrition. Cheap grace is grace without discipleship, grace without the Cross, grace without Jesus Christ, living and incarnate. (D. Bonhoeffer, *The Cost of Discipleship,* p. 37f.)

The gospel misunderstood as cheap grace sows spiritual death in the form of superficiality and indifference, something to which the Christians of Europe and America are especially prone.

2. *The Law as dead legalism.* This misunderstanding looks upon God as a policeman, someone who is zealous for the very letter of the Law, as a kind of heavenly prosecuting attorney. The church becomes God's bailiff or deputy. Her chief task is to see to it that sin does not take place, and to punish it when, despite all her efforts, it does take place. The best means of doing this is exclusion from the Lord's Supper. The greatest sin is adultery. The elders of the congregation become detectives, and the church council can even consider withdrawing the baptismal certificate of good conduct. And the Lord's Supper becomes a procession of the righteous and worthy who, by means of their participation, publicly boast that they have not committed adultery during the last four weeks, or at least the fact that they have not been caught at it. Dead legalism is judging the sinner and not the sin, is confession of sin without communion, is discipleship without grace, the cross without grace, Christ without grace.

> The pious fellowship permits no one to be a sinner. So everybody must conceal his sin from himself and from the fellowship. (D. Bon-

hoeffer, *Life Together,* p. 110)

The Law misunderstood as dead legalism sows spiritual death in the form of Pharisaism and hypocrisy, something to which the Christians of Africa are especially prone.

The Biblical Way

1. *Voluntary confession (Jn. 20:23; Mt. 16:19; Mt. 18:18; Mt. 9:8; Jas. 5:16; Lk. 23:41-43; Lk. 15:21; Ps. 32:3-5; 1 Jn. 1:9; Mk. 1:5; Acts 19:18).*

> Of Confession they teach that Private Absolution ought to be retained in the Churches. (*Augsburg Confession,* Art. XI)

Luther, who throughout his life always had a father confessor, says in his 8th Invocavit sermon:

> I will let no man take private confession from me and would not give it up for all the treasures of the world, since I know what comfort and strength it has given me. No one knows what private confession can do for him except he who has struggled much with the devil. Yea, the devil would have slain me long ago if confession had not sustained me. (Luther, Sermons in Lent, 1522, *Weimar Ed.,* 10, III, 61f.)
>
> For which reason, when I admonish to go to confession I am admonishing to be a Christian. (Luther, *Large Catechism* [On Confession]; cf. *Small Catechism,* Part V [On Confession])

"Forward to Luther!" The Lutheran way is that of voluntary confession before God in the presence of a brother in Christ who, as a witness of one's remorse, addresses to one the word of forgiveness. When we forget this we fall into the two extremes of cheap grace and dead legalism.

This way prevents a misunderstanding of the gospel as cheap grace. Grace is costly. It demands humiliation. The presence of the brother forces one to take sin seriously and thereby helps one to take God seriously. He who is not prepared to humble himself in the presence of another is not prepared to humble himself before God, either. Personal confession is the test of whether one takes remorse seriously. Here grace is experienced *in* discipleship, forgiveness is imparted *by means of* the cross. Confession is confrontation with the living, incarnate Christ—in the person of the brother.

At the same time the misunderstanding of the Law as dead legalism is prevented. Here it's not a matter of discovery by the police, but the voluntary return of the prodigal son. It is the voluntary character of confession which distinguishes evangelical confession from the formalism of the Catholic confessional. This formalism is simply being substituted in Africa by the pseudo-evangelical formalism of church discipline. We do not become evangelical simply by substituting one formalism for another! In truly evangelical confession the emphasis does not lie on the Law and sins—for which reason the attempt to distinguish between "greater" and "lesser" sins cannot be maintained, a distinction which is also Catholic. The emphasis lies entirely upon the personal word of forgiveness spoken by the brother in the name of Christ. Church discipline without remorse does not change the heart. But true confession *is* conversion, because it takes the will of God seriously, in a genuinely evangelical way *(Prov. 28:13).*

> In confession the Christian begins to forsake his sins. Their dominion is broken. From now on the Christian wins victory after victory. (Bonhoeffer, *Life Together,* p. 115)

There is no place in the New Testament where one can find punishment and church discipline mentioned with respect to a sin voluntarily confessed.

> I meet the whole congregation in the one brother to whom I confess my sins and who forgives my sins. (Ibid., p. 113)

It is true, one does find voluntary, spontaneous restitution *(Lk. 19:18; Acts 19:19).* But this is only as the result of forgiveness, not as punishment for sin and certainly not as the condition laid down for the reception of grace. In this sense one can say that costly grace is not only not cheap, it is absolutely *free!*

In Jesus' Parable of the Prodigal Son *(Lk. 15:11-32),* the father does not condemn the son who has just returned to live for six months in a back room, until it can be determined whether or not his remorse is genuine! Upon the confession of his son *(v. 21)* he forgives him immediately and entirely. He clothes him, presents him with gifts, and *eats* with him! Those who frown upon such evangelical practice and who, for pedagogical reasons, shake their finger disapprovingly find their counterpart in the elder son *(vv. 25-32).*

In 1 Corinthians 11:29 we do not find "unworthy" as an attribute of the communicants, but we find "unworthily" as an adverb modifying the verb "to eat." "Unworthily" means to gulp down the Lord's Supper like an ordinary meal, to take no notice of the fact that the Lord is offering himself in this Supper in a special manner. "Worthily" means to know oneself to be *un*worthy to meet the Lord. "They alone are unworthy who will not admit themselves sinners" (Luther, *Large Catechism,* Sacrament of the Altar). Exclusion of a repentant sinner from Communion is unbiblical.

2. *Admonition and conviction. (Mt. 18:15-22.)* Here it is a question not of a secret sin touching only the person of the sinner himself, but of a public transgression which causes offense, one that is already known to several persons. The first thing which a Christian owes his brother in such a case is a private fraternal admonition and *not* the informing of others, not even the pastor or the church council. The secrecy of such a conversation must be kept with the same conscientiousness with which the secrecy of confession is kept. In case the person should not heed such admonition, two or three witnesses (and this does not necessarily include the pastor!) should be taken along to add effectiveness to what is said. Only when this, too, is of no avail should the case be brought before the congregation. Should the person concerned heed such admonition, even if only in the last stage, he has been won over, and has been set free and redeemed. And discipline is not applied *(v. 15).* The goal of such admonition and conviction is to bring the brother to a recognition and confession of his sin. It is to win over, and not to judge or punish. It is missionary activity *(2 Sam. 12:7, 13).*

3. *Exclusion. (Mt. 18:17b; 2 Thess. 3:6, 14; 1 Cor. 5:5, 11-13.)* This is an exception in the New Testament and only the last and most extreme means that a congregation has, *after* every admonition has been to no avail *(Tit. 3:10).* This is never applied to the penitent, but exclusively to the impenitent, those without remorse, those who are hardening themselves, those whose sin has become known publicly and whose continuance in sin results more in their excluding themselves than in their being excluded.

The immediate purpose of exclusion is to testify before the impenitent and the world to the totally different character of the church of Christ and to demonstrate the seriousness of sin.

The hoped-for result, however, is not the expulsion of the errant, impenitent brother, but his being won again by this extreme means. Like admonition and conviction, exclusion is missionary activity *(2 Thess. 3:15; 2 Tim. 2:25ff).*

If one compares Matthew 18:17 with Matthew 9:10, 11 and Matthew 11:19, where Jesus eats (!) with publicans (!), one must come to the conclusion that our congregations must reconsider their practice of excommunication. "And whether one member suffer, all the members suffer with it" *(1 Cor. 12:26).* Would it not be a great testimony if, because of the adultery of *one* member, the whole congregation were to refrain from celebrating the Lord's Supper for a month? In this case church discipline would experience its most profound purpose; it would become the expression of solidarity under the burden of sin; it would become a vital experience within the Body of Christ. "This idea of the struggle against the demonic powers which the church carries on *along with* sinners can be found in several passages in the New Testament where it is a question of excommunication" (M. Thurian, *La Confession,* p. 46f; *Evangelische Beichte,* p. 16, *1 Tim. 1:20*).

Borderline Cases

There are borderline cases in which one could entertain the possibility of excluding a *penitent* sinner from the Lord's Supper.

1. If the sin has become public in character and if it should therefore appear expedient for congregational or general reasons. Exclusion from the Lord's Supper for a certain period in such a case would be understood as a pedagogical measure and as a warning to others *(1 Tim. 5:20).*

BUT—would not a weak brother be deprived of the Lord's Supper just at a time when he might need it most?

2. If the person concerned sought to keep his sin secret and only because of its becoming known did he show remorse and desire forgiveness. The period of exclusion from the Lord's Supper would be understood in such a case as a test of genuine remorse.

BUT—can one really deduce a proof of genuine remorse from the fact that a person has refrained from committing a certain sin for a certain period of time? In practice, it turns out that the period "under discipline" is spent like one serves a prison sentence, and then admission to the Lord's Supper is again demanded, like a right into which one has again entered possession. The idea of reform or change is usually lost sight of.

3. If the fruitlessness of forgiveness is demonstrated by means of repeated relapse.

BUT—does this not contradict the essence of grace expressed in Isaiah 53:5 and Matthew 18:21? Can human reason presume to judge the fruitfulness or fruitlessness of grace *(Mt. 7:3-5)?*

Behind these three borderline cases lies a pedagogical understanding of excommunication which runs the danger of falling into Catholicism again, i.e., the danger of placing human conditions upon God's unconditional grace and thus of denying the Lutheran principle of *sola gratia.* This danger would be avoided if in these three borderline cases the person concerned were voluntarily to abstain from Communion, without this having been forced upon him as a condition for forgiveness, out of love to the Lord whom he had grieved and out of respect to the congregation, precisely *because he desired* the Lord's Supper. Everything, of course, depends upon the motive.

It is a question whether the love of Christ should not make us more imaginative and enable us to think of other ways of giving expression to remorse. 1 Timothy 5:20, for instance, *does not* mention the Lord's Supper as a means. There was the case, for example, of an African husband who had confessed to adultery and who agreed, *after* receiving absolution, to gather a bundle of wood for his wife each evening for a month. He did this not to merit the grace of God, but in order to make visible and to put into practice the forgiveness he had received absolutely free. This humble and (as far as the customs of his country are concerned) humiliating act was a greater testimony for his wife and his congregation, and a greater help to himself as well, than his exclusion from the Lord's table. One cannot set up general rules for such borderline cases, but pastoral counseling must find the right way in each case.

Some Pointed Questions

To the African churches:

Why are you so interested in church discipline? Is it not because by appeal to legal measures, you hope to cover up a certain lack of inner spiritual authority *(Mt. 23:24).*

To the European and American churches:

Where does your numerical superiority over the African churches come from? Does it not arise from taking the law far too lightly? Do you not try to justify theologically your own laxity and lukewarmness by charging the African churches with legalism *(Rev. 3:16)?*

To the African pastors:

In administering church discipline do you stand under that self-judgment which alone empowers one to administer discipline and without which church discipline becomes dead formalism? Do you misuse the discipline of the church to undergird externally your personal authority? Does this not become a necessity for you because you lack the spiritual authority which is the basis for being able to hear confession and give absolution? Are you not lacking this spiritual authority simply because you do not allow yourselves to be counseled and helped spiritually *(1 Cor. 9:27)?*

To the missionary:

All these questions are also addressed to you. But in addition: Why do you insist on church discipline in Africa when it is not insisted upon in your home churches? Have you not become guilty, not only of hypocrisy *(Mt. 23:4)* but also of arrogance? Have you not adopted the argument that the Africans in their "younger" churches cannot actually understand the depth of the message of St. Paul and the Reformation? For this reason have you then not tried to translate the paradoxes of the gospel into simple pedagogical common sense *(Mt. 23:13)?*

To the theological schools and mission seminaries:

Do you give practical enough guidance to your students with respect to the cure of souls, without which, even with the best of theological education on the part of the pastor, no living congregation can be built up *(Mk. 16:18; Jn. 20:23; Acts 20:31)?*

To the laymen:

Do you practice the Lutheran doctrine of the priesthood of all believers? Do you take upon yourselves the responsibility for the mutual cure of souls? Or are you in reality non-Lutheran and unbiblical in turning over this whole area to the pastors *(Gen. 4:9; Jas. 5:16, 19-20)?*

Appendix Four
God's World Strategy

A king and a queen listen to a prisoner. What a strange setting for world missions! Festus, High Commissioner of the Roman Colonial Empire, has brought the prisoner to the courtroom in chains. What a strange setting for a missionary! The military tribunes and the prominent men of the city are standing around King Agrippa and Queen Bernice, who are sitting in great pomp before the prisoner—cold, suspicious, neutral, curious, bored. What a strange setting for a missionary message!

The prisoner speaks. He starts in calm and friendly accents. Then becoming personal, he gives the story of his life. His expressions become more and more fervent, his gestures more vivid and enthusiastic. His heart gets involved, and he involves their hearts. His voice becomes impassioned as he gives his personal testimony: Christ met him on the Damascus road, Christ saved him, and Christ sent him to turn the Gentiles from darkness to light and from the power of Satan to God!

The High Commissioner interrupts him: "Paul, you are mad!"

"I am *not* mad, most excellent Festus," Paul replies. "I am speaking the sober truth. The King knows about these things, for this was not done in a corner!"

Not in a corner! When we talk about missions, we first have to make a vital decision: Do we want corner missions or world missions?

We are so fond of the corner. Jesus sent His disciples as sheep among the wolves. But when *we* become sheep of His flock, we prefer to move around among our fellow sheep. We like to warm ourselves by the hearthfire of our own piety, with our fellow church members gathered around.

The first disciples went out into cold weather. They aimed at nothing less than the whole world. They gave their testimony before hostile kings and governors, and the people said to them: "These men have turned the world upside down."

If we really mean what we say when we talk about world missions, we must leave the corner and let our view embrace the whole world.

God's strategy for reaching the world is the strategy of the running Word. This has not happened in a corner. Paul asked the Thessalonians to pray that the Word of the Lord might *run.* They prayed and the Word ran. It did not stay inside Palestine. It jumped over borders, sprang from town to town, crossed the sea, arrived in Europe, climbed over the Alps from Italy to Germany, spread to England, France, Scandinavia, Russia, sped on to Africa and Asia, reached America.

Glorious history of the running Word! This was not done in a corner. Today, too, this Word will run. It will take you into its current, make you a part of this triumphant process, will run right into your heart and through your heart into eternity.

The Word runs. It cannot run in a corner. It needs the world in order to have room to run. How can we become a part of this movement of the running Word? I should like to suggest three things.

If we want to become useful tools in God's world strategy, we must first of all learn to fight at the decisive point of the battle. Strategy does not mean to fight at every place, but to fight at the decisive point, where it pays to fight. May God open our eyes to discern those points!

During the last war, when Hitler decreed that all the disabled, crippled, and mentally incurable children in Germany should be killed in order to conserve food, one man stood up against him. It was Pastor Bodelschwing, who had a home for hundreds of such children at Bethel. When Hitler's secret police came and demanded to have those children, Bodelschwing answered: "You can have them, but you will first have to shoot me down." The killers left. Nothing happened either to Bodelschwing or to his crippled children. There at the doors of Bethel the power of evil was broken. And from then on Hitler's power declined. That was fighting at the decisive point. *That* was strategy. That was world missions. That was not done in a corner.

Right after the war, even before the official American policy toward Germany became friendly, a stream of hundreds and thousands of food and clothing parcels went from America to that defeated and poverty-stricken land. And every single one who sent such a package became a tool in Christ's world strategy! I can assure you that this was not done in a corner. Even now you can find the traces of that stream of love in many a German family that was thus touched for the first time by the love of Jesus. *That* was fighting in the decisive moment, at the decisive point.

Last Christmas I was in the Russian Zone of Germany. One of my friends presented his little boy to me and said, "This is Henry." But Henry isn't a German name," I protested. "Isn't it Heinrich?" "No," he said, "it is Henry. Henry is the first name of the man in America who sent us all the clothing we are wearing now. So we named our son after him, and Uncle Henry is his godfather, too." That is world strategy.

Of course the enemy has his strategy, too. Many African students who are now studying in Paris once studied in mission schools in their own land. But at the University of Paris they are lost among thousands of other students. There the Communists find them, help them, and finally get them to come to some university behind the Iron Curtain. That is the way they train their ambassadors for Africa. That is the world strategy of the enemy.

Every student from Africa or Asia who studies in Europe or America will become a leader of some kind in his home country. We send hundreds of missionaries overseas and spend thousands of dollars in that way, while the most influential people of the lands in which our workers are located may be right here in our own country and even in our own town. To reach them would be fighting at the decisive point. *That* would be world strategy. One cannot call it obedience to the Great Commission when a student from Africa studies for years in the United States, and then goes back without as much as having seen a Protestant church from the inside.

About twenty years ago an African student from the Gold Coast came to America and studied at Lincoln University. In his autobiography he relates the following experience:

"On one of my lecture tours I was traveling from Philadelphia to Washington, and the bus stopped at Baltimore for the passengers to refresh themselves. I was parched with thirst, so I went into the lunch room at the terminal and asked the white waiter if I could have a drink of water. He frowned and looked down his nose at me as if I were something unclean. 'The place for you, my man, is the spittoon outside,' he declared, and dismissed me from his sight. I was so shocked that I could not move. I just stood and stared at him, for I could not bring myself to believe that anyone could refuse a man a drink of water just because his skin happened to be of a different color."

The African student who reports this experience in his recently published autobiography is Kwame Nkrumah, today prime minister of the new state of Ghana, formerly the Gold Coast. *His* word, too, will run all over Africa. That glass of water that the waiter refused him marked a lost battle in Christ's world strategy. Hence we find illustrated here another important principle, namely this: *If we want to become a part of God's world strategy, we have to realize the world-wide effects of our actions.*

The world has become so small that every little incident immediately has far-reaching effects. No longer can anything be done in a corner. The world today is like a washbasin. If you splash with your fist on one side, the water runs over all around. Every drop of water is affected. If trouble starts at one spot in the world, it involves all the continents and nations. When a member of a Russian sport team stole some hats in a London department store last year, it involved London, Moscow, Washington, and the United Nations. When a G.I. shoots a Japanese woman, it involves the foreign policy of the United States. When President Eisenhower has an upset stomach, it affects the stock-market exchange in Paris. And when an American waiter refuses a glass of water to an African student, it involves the African continent.

We must wake up to the fact that there are no longer any isolated actions possible in this world of ours, so that in a much greater measure than before every individual becomes a strategic figure on one of two battlefields—either God's or the devil's.

As I was riding on an African train last year, one of my fellow travelers asked me: "Are those people in America who still cling to racial segregation and discrimination Christians?" He knew the answer, of course. He knew that some of them are Christians. His conclusion was clear: If that is true, then Christianity has no message for us.

If we want to be a part of world missions today, and if we start to think strategically, we have to awaken the people of America to the fact that our failure to settle the race problem in this country may result in the loss of the African continent for Christ.

The devil makes mighty use of our modern means of communication. One can find radios today in the backward villages of the African bush. I have met Africans who had detailed information about even small incidents that occurred in the southern states before I read about them in *TIME* magazine.

Since that is true, every church that opens her doors to members of all races becomes a part in Christ's world strategy and has a special part in world missions. Every family that invites a colored student for lunch takes a step of worldwide consequence. Such things are not done in a corner. When church history is written, men may find that the racial issue was *the* test of Christianity in the twentieth century.

To those who want to go to Africa as missionaries I should like to sound a warning. There are still missionaries in Africa who receive the Africans on the back porch rather than have them come into the house, and who let them sit on the floor rather than offer them a chair. Missionaries like that do more harm than good. So if you are not ready to eat at the same table with an African, or share your guest room with him, if necessary, you had better stay at home.

And this brings us to a third principle. *If we want to have a part in world missions today, it means that we ourselves, in our personal lives, must consciously become strategic outposts in the battle for God's kingdom.*

But perhaps someone will ask: If world missions involve such big things as continents, nations, and races, how can *I* with my small private life have any significant part in it? Let me mention a few ways that are open to you.

The first and most important thing is that you must be a truly saved person. World missions have the world as their goal, but they start at the most hidden and secret point in the world—your heart.

The *world* takes no account of numbers short of millions and billions. But the greatest number in the kingdom of God is the number one. When *one* person has fully surrendered his whole heart to Christ, world missions start. Therefore your first task is to care for your own soul.

I am impressed to see how carefully the people of Minneapolis take care of their lawns. But just think what would happen if they would give even half as much attention to their souls!

Soul care is your first step toward world missions. In order to become a strategic outpost, however, you should learn to consider your salvation not as an end in itself, but as the beginning of growth into new spiritual realms—an obligation.

You should begin, therefore, to consider your immediate surroundings as the mission field that God has assigned to you—your family, your neighbors, and your fellow church members. You should not take anyone for granted. An African pastor who is studying here at a Lutheran seminary told me the other day: "I am glad I was a Christian when I came to this country, for I am afraid I would not have become one here." So your mission field is right at your door, wherever you are.

Then, too, if you would become a strategic outpost by your personal life, your home must become an oasis of quietness, where there is no haste and hurry, where people can come and find someone who has time to listen.

The greatest number in God's kingdom is "one." The next greatest are "two" and "three." Jesus says, "Where two or three are gathered together in my name, there am I in the midst of them." If your home becomes such a place, you are a strategic outpost of the world mission field.

Can it be right for a man to spend almost every evening away from his family? Most of our Christian homes are just motels where people gas up, get some food and sleep, and then go again. Do you think a needy soul would seek out such a family motel as a place to unburden his heart? Christ cannot use such homes for his strategy. He wants our homes to be oases of quietness and restfulness, where fellowship in a deep sense is possible.

Your television set, therefore, does not belong in your living room, for that is where you receive and talk with people. When one of my fellow missionaries arrived home from a term of service on the foreign field, the light could not be turned on in the living room because his little brother had to watch a ball game!

Quietness does not cost a cent. There is plenty of it. You can have as much of it as you want. You only need the power of Christ to swim against the stream.

If you want to become a strategic outpost by your personal life, you also have to undertake the thankless task of making people think.

Shortly before he left his home in order to meet a speaking engagement, one of my fellow missionaries was called by the program chairman. She gave him the following instructions: "Don't talk longer than twelve minutes. Don't preach at us, but tell us all about your field and your work!" In other words: "Don't make us think! Give us a little missionary booster shot! Entertain us, but do not confront us with the real problems!"

If you want to become a strategic Christian, you have to rouse people out of this comfortable, sinful thoughtlessness. Otherwise they are not even able to pray intelligently.

You need, moreover, to be a very sober and realistic Christian. Our love for missions is based too much on sudden emotion and unreasonable optimistic hopes. That is why we so easily become cold.

The sober truth is this: Although mission work has made progress on the various fields, if we take the world as a whole, Christianity seems to be losing rather than gaining. In the last fifty years the population of the world has increased by 800 million people. Whatever progress Christianity may have made, it has not grown by 800 million. We need to be realistic. We will always remain the "little flock." As Christians we belong to a minority that determines the destiny of the world. And we will remain a minority. Only if you have this sober knowledge in your heart will you be a strategic outpost—one that does not fall when disappointments come.

Yet with all this sober realism, you are to be a joyful and hilarious person—one who radiates hopefulness. For the victory is already won. Christ won it once and for all. The battle is decided. Mission work does not stand or fall with its success. The christianization of the world is not promised to us. But what *is* promised is a new world and a new creation. What is promised is that his kingdom shall come.

There is much talk now concerning the indigenous church as the goal of mission work. But the indigenous church is only a milestone on the road. The goal of mission work is not the church or churches. The goal is the kingdom—the lordship of Christ over the world and the whole universe. Missions live between the resurrection and the Second Coming of Christ.

This is the testimony of missions: At Easter the new world of God broke through and made a beginning in our midst.

This is the message of missions: The new world of God will finally win the victory over all evil powers, including death, when Christ comes again.

And when He comes again on the clouds of heaven, with power and great glory, *it will not happen in a corner!*

Notes

Love Is a Feeling to Be Learned

[1]Harper and Row, New York—Lutterworth Press, London E.C. 4.

My Beautiful Feeling

[1]See Schulte/Tölle, *Psychiatrie,* 2nd ed. (New York: Springer-Verlag, 1973), p. 125.

[2]Horst Wrage, *Mann und Frau* (Gütersloh: Gerd Mohn Verlag, 1916), p. 69.

[3]Ibid., p. 159.

[4]Ibid., p. 86.

[5]See Cornelius Trimbos, *Leben mit der Liebe* (Germany: Matthias Grünwald Verlag).

[6]See Seymour Fisher, *The Female Orgasm* (New York: Basic Books, 1972), p. 336.

[7]Ibid., pp. 235 and 278.

[8]See Affemann, *Geschlechtlichkeit und Geschlechtserziehung in der modern Welt* (Gütersloh: Gerd Mohn Verlag, 1970), pp. 87ff.

[9]See "The Tiger Story" from *I Loved a Girl,* pp. 88-90.

[10]Affemann, p. 139.

[11]Walter R. Johnson, *Masturbation, Siecus Study Guide No. 3* (New York: Sex Information and Education Council of the United States, 1968), p. 7.

[12]Ibid., pp. 73 and 88.

[13]Ingrid Trobisch, *The Joy of Being a Woman* (New York: Harper and Row, Jubilee Books, 1975).

[14]Fischer, pp. 334ff.

[15]See H. J. Prill, *Psychosomatische Gynäkologie* (Germany: Verlag Urban and Schwarzenberg), p. 35.

[16]See Walter Trobisch, *Love Yourself: Self-Acceptance and Depression* (Downers Grove, Ill.: InterVarsity Press, 1976).

[17]See *The Joy of Being a Woman.*

[18]Ernst Lange, *Die Zehn grossen Freiheiten* (Gelnhausen: Burckhardthaus Verlag, 1965), p. 7. The translation is Ilona's. This book is also available in English as *Ten Great Freedoms,* trans. David Priestley (Downers Grove, Ill.: InterVarsity Press, 1970).

[19]See Helmut Thielicke, "Anthropologische Grundtatbestände in individuellen Konfliktsituationen," *Zeitschrift für Evang. Ethik* (May 1974), p. 140.

[20]Gini Andrews, *Your Half of the Apple* (Grand Rapids: Zondervan, 1972), pp. 94-95.
[21]See Mary Stewart, *Sexual Freedom* (Downers Grove, Ill.: InterVarsity Press, 1974).

A Baby Just Now

[1]I. P. P. F. Medical Handbook "Contraception," 1967, p. 49, 1810 Tower Regent St., London, S. W. I, England.
[2]See *I Loved a Girl,* letter of August 3rd.
[3]Family Planning in Kenya," p. 3, Report published by the Ministry of Economic Planning end Development, Nairobi.
[4]I. P. P. F. "The Role of Family Planning in African Development," p. 8 and 68.
[5]On masturbation see *My Parents Are Impossible* and *My Beautiful Feeling.*
[6]See also *I Loved a Girl,* letter of Aug. 3rd.

Love Yourself

[1]Dr. Guido Groeger, unpublished letter 1967.
[2]Romano Guardini, *Die Annahme seiner selbst,* 5th ed. (Werkband verlag: Wurzburg, 1969), pp. 14, 16.
[3]Compare the exegesis of Leviticus 19:18 by Martin Noth in *Das Alte Testament Deutsch* (Göttingen: Vandenhoek and Ruprecht, 1962), p. 122.
[4]Hermann Hesse, *Steppenwolf* (New York: Holt, Rinehart and Winston, 1961), p. 10.
[5]Theodor Bovet, *Die Liebe ist in unserer Mitte* (Tübingen: Katzmann Verlag), p. 177.
[6]Paul Tournier, *A Place for You* (New York: Harper and Row, 1968), p. 66.
[7]Ibid., p. 67.
[8]See chapter 3, "Living in Harmony with the Cycle and Fertility," of Ingrid Trobisch, *The Joy of Being a Woman and What a Man Can Do* (New York: Harper and Row, 1975), pp. 33-63.
[9]Walter Uhsadel, "Der depressive Mensch in theologischer Sicht," *Wege zum Menschen* (August 1966), p. 313.
[10]Quoted according to August Hardeland, *Geschichte der Speciellen Seelsorge* (Germany, 1893).
[11]Letter of November 22, 1532, to Johannes von Stockhausen.
[12]See Walter Trobisch, *Spiritual Dryness* (Downers Grove: InterVarsity Press, 1970).
[13]See Klages in *Wege zum Menschen,* op. cit., p. 226.
[14]Rainer Maria Rilke, *Letters to a Young Poet* (New York: W. W. Norton, 1954), p. 53.
[15]Ibid., pp. 69-70.